Working Stiffs,
Union Maids,
Reds, and Riffraff

Working Stiffs, Union Maids, Reds, and Riffraff

An Expanded Guide to Films about Labor

TOM ZANIELLO

ILR PRESS

an imprint of Cornell University Press

Ithaca and London

First published 2003 by Cornell University Press
First printing, Cornell Paperbacks, 2003

Printed in the United States of America

Library of Congress Cataloging-in-Publication Data

Zaniello, Tom, 1943–
    Working stiffs, union maids, reds, and riffraff : an expanded guide to films about labor / Tom Zaniello.
        p.   cm.
Includes bibliographical references and index.
    ISBN 0-8014-4009-2 (cloth : alk. paper)—ISBN 0-8014-8851-6 (pbk. : alk. paper)
    1. Working class in motion pictures.   I. Title.
    PN1995.9.L28 Z36 2003
    791.43′655—dc21   2002154816

Cornell University Press strives to use environmentally responsible suppliers and materials to the fullest extent possible in the publishing of its books. Such materials include vegetable-based, low-VOC inks and acid-free papers that are recycled, totally chlorine-free, or partly composed of nonwood fibers. For further information, visit our website at www.cornellpress.cornell.edu.

Cloth printing   10 9 8 7 6 5 4 3 2 1

Paperback printing   10 9 8 7 6 5 4 3 2 1

For my uncle,
Christopher Morelli,
who took me to
Radio City Music Hall
a long time ago

Contents

Working Stiffs,
Union Maids,
Reds, and Riffraff

Introduction

This guide has been written for viewers looking for films about working people, labor activism, or labor history and related economic, political, and sociological issues. This is the second and expanded edition of the only comprehensive, annotated guide available that includes critical commentary and sources for further reading and research.

Each entry surveys the relevant historical or cultural issues of the film; where appropriate, I also explore issues of cinematic tradition and artistic style. Some films, such as *Matewan*, may gain an audience not only because the subject is compelling but because the material is presented with cinematic verve. In feature films, the quality of the acting sometimes can overshadow other aspects of the production: *On the Waterfront* became a classic in large part because of Marlon Brando's acting style, whereas *The Killing Floor*, which involves even more complex historical, economic, and political issues, remains relatively unknown in part because of the low profile of most of its actors.

Working people, their unions, labor issues in general, and political movements involving the working class have always been a part of Hollywood, independent, and foreign filmmaking. But some of the most popular films about labor have presented their subjects in an unfavorable light, while lesser-known works with more balanced or even positive views go unseen and unnoticed. Yet, because we live in a culture that receives so much of its information and ultimately derives many of its opinions from visual media, it is especially important to see, to understand, and to study more than the usual selection of media images.

The differences between the first and second editions of *Working Stiffs* lie in intention and scale. The first volume surveyed 150 labor films, the majority of which were available on videocassette. This expanded volume of 350 films (including most but not all of the films in the first volume) surveys labor films that were produced and distributed or broadcast, whether or not they are currently available on videocassette or DVD. Furthermore, this volume is global in scope, with examples of labor films from every major country or continent.

Nothing has been lost, I believe, by adding many films not easily available or not currently available at all. Much will be gained, I hope, in providing readers with a sense of how many more labor films have been made than we have been aware of or have access to. Readers will know whether a film that may interest them is available or not, as all films that are available are clearly listed as such.

The selection of films has been based on, first of all, Images of Labor in Film, my labor studies course for the National Labor College at the George Meany Center for Labor Studies. I have also received suggestions over the years as I lectured about labor films in many other venues. Labor educators and trade unionists over the years have also reviewed my proposed lists of films. Many other individuals, both by post and e-mail and on list serves, have been the sources of many other suggestions.

The five criteria for inclusion in the first edition remain operative for the second:

1. Films about unions or labor organizations
2. Films about labor history
3. Films about working-class life in which an economic factor is significant
4. Films about political movements if they are tied closely to organized labor
5. Films that focus on production or the struggle between labor and capital from a top-down perspective, either entrepreneurial or managerial

While police officers, cowboys, and professional athletes are certainly working in virtually every film they appear in, their films are not listed in this guide, with one exception: *Net Worth*, about the unionization of Canadian hockey players.

Entries from the first volume have in some instances been rewritten to correct errors or to reevaluate my assessment if a re-viewing of the film warranted it. I have streamlined the old entries in other small but important ways by reducing cast lists to their essential players, by including the Motion Picture Association rating only (without additional comment), and by suggesting only the most relevant films for additional viewing in the "See also" line.

Both the old entries and the new have some significant new features. I have included relevant Web sites and indicated whether a film is available in DVD format. I have classified each documentary according to the types explained in the section headed "Documentaries," under "Select Labor Film Categories."

I have added more than fifty new publicity stills and frame enlargements, while keeping about fifteen from the first edition.

As in the first volume, the entries are of uneven length. Usually a longer entry and a more substantial "Further reading" section indicates a film of greater importance or controversy (whether because of the subject or of the film itself).

I have greatly expanded the "Thematic Index of Films" at the end of the volume and have added two other sections at the beginning of the book to help the reader discover labor films either over time ("Tracing the History of Labor Films: A Chronology") or by cinematic movement or national cinema ("Select Labor Film Categories").

Because of the obvious limits in scale, I regret that I could not include every labor film whose title crossed my desk. Two areas were of special concern, silent films and left-affiliated films of the 1930s.

A selection of important silent films that are available on videocassette is included, but many intriguing silent films, such as *The Blacklist* (1916), about the Ludlow Massacre of miners in 1914, and the only film version of Upton Sinclair's *The Jungle* (1914), starring Sinclair himself as a radical orator, have not been available, although they are carefully documented in Steven J. Ross's *Working-Class Hollywood: Silent Film and the Shaping of Class in America* (Princeton: Princeton University Press, 1998).

Similarly, I have included documentaries and other films closely allied to the left in the 1930s, but numerous others, carefully analyzed in William Alexander's *Film on the*

Left: American Documentary Film from 1931 to 1942 (Princeton: Princeton University Press, 1981) are available in archives only and are not included in this volume.

Readers are encouraged to send me additional recommendations for films not covered here and to make any suggestions or corrections overall by contacting me at tzaniello@nku.edu.

How to Read the Entries

See also. In this line I point to other films in *Working Stiffs* related to the film of the entry by subject, theme, or style.

Availability. I have rated the ease of access to VHS videocassettes or DVDs at the end of every entry according to the following keywords:

Easy: available at major videocassette rental chains.

Not: not available currently in any format.

Selected collections: available at unusually well-stocked rental stores, public libraries, universities, labor unions, and archives. In addition, most of the films in this category are available for rental or purchase from the following: Eddie Brandt's Saturday Matinee, Evergreen Films, Facets, Movies Unlimited, and Video Library. See the Web sites provided under "Sources for Rental or Purchase" below. This line may also contain three other notations:

DVD: the film is also available in DVD format.

UK (PAL standard only): to view this film in the United States, the videocassette must be translated into NTSC standard.

A specific distributor may be listed: consult "Sources for Rental or Purchase" below for specific Web sites.

Videocassettes and DVDs go in and out of print quite regularly, and even some titles listed as "Not" here may become available in the future.

Further reading. A review or article that appears in the "Further reading" section without a page number may be accessed on the Internet. As a rule, it is simplest to access any article by using the title of the film in a search engine or at any of the following general film review Web sites, where multiple reviews of a film are easy to find:

Internet Movie Database ⟨www.imdb.com⟩

Movie Review Query Engine ⟨www.mrqe.com⟩

Rotten Tomatoes ⟨www.rottentomatoes.com⟩

The IMDb is my first choice for locating detailed production and other information about films.

Alternatively, some of the entries may be found at the Web sites of the following, although in some cases the archives are limited by year or subscription fee and the sites are not as easy to use as the general sites:

Austin Chronicle ⟨www.austinchronicle.com⟩

Boston Globe ⟨www.boston.com/globe⟩

Boston Phoenix ⟨www.bostonphoenix.com⟩

Chicago Sun-Times ⟨www.suntimes.com/ebert/ebert.html⟩

Chicago Tribune ⟨www.chicago.tribune.com⟩

Los Angeles Times ⟨www.calendarlive.com⟩

New York Times ⟨www.nytimes.com/pages/movies⟩

San Francisco Chronicle ⟨www.sfchron.com⟩

San Francisco Examiner ⟨www.examiner.com⟩

TV Guide ⟨www.tvguide.com/movies⟩

Variety ⟨www.variety.com⟩

Washington Post ⟨www.washingtonpost.com/wp-adv/archives⟩

World Socialist Web ⟨www.wsws.org⟩

Despite the occasional disappearance of a Web site, I have included specific Web sites for some citations. If you cannot find the Web site I cite, type some of the key words of the citation into a search engine and perhaps it may be accessed in a different location, or at least similar material may be found.

Many citations may of course be accessed in libraries through hardcopy or microfilm or online (since many libraries subscribe to for-fee services not available on the Web without payment).

Web sites. These are Web sites I have found helpful. Clearly many others would provide important information as well and will be found by using your favorite search engine.

There is a problem with Web sites, however: they are not around forever. As I write this, the Web sites for two documentaries in this edition, *Troublesome Creek* (⟨www.pbs.org/wgbh/pages/amex/trouble⟩) and *The Richest Man in the World* (⟨www.pbs.org/wgbh/pages/amex/carnegie⟩), are still available. Thus you can have access not only to a great deal of information about these films but also to the complete transcripts of the narrative voice-overs and characters' speeches, which you can download, print, and consult at your leisure. These two sites have been up for more than three years, but there is no way of knowing for sure how much longer they will be there.

When these Web sites are gone, the texts will not be as readily available, although one helpful development, the Wayback Machine at ⟨www.archive.org⟩ may serve as a cyberspatial library or archive that would hold on to such documents indefinitely.

Sites that are probably quite stable may not retain material indefinitely. The site of the director Michael Moore's production company, Dog Eat Dog Films (⟨www.dogeatdogfilms.com⟩), for instance, did not retain the information on *The Big One* (clips and transcripts of the 1998 Web site shootout, complete with outtakes, between Moore's Web site and that of Phil Knight, CEO of Nike (⟨www.nikebiz.com⟩) that I discuss in the entry on *The Big One*. On the other hand, such sites are likely to have lots of other interesting tidbits handy.

Sources for Rental or Purchase

For films listed as in "Selected collections" I rely on the following:

Rental and sales

    Facets Video: ⟨www.facets.org⟩ or 800-331-6197.

    Evergreen Video: ⟨www.evergreenvideo.com⟩ or 212-691-7362.

Sales only

    Movies Unlimited: ⟨www.moviesunlimited.com⟩ or 800-4-MOVIES.

Rental only

    Eddie Brandt's Saturday Matinee: 818-506-4242 or fax 818-506-5649. No Web site.

    Video Library: ⟨vlibrary.com⟩

In addition, the following Web sites are for specific distributors cited under "Availability":

A and E (Arts and Entertainment Network) ⟨www.store.aetv.com/html/h01.jhtml⟩

Amber Films ⟨www.amber-online.com⟩

Appalshop ⟨www.appalshop.org⟩

Bullfrog Films ⟨www.bullfrogfilms.com⟩

California Newsreel ⟨www.newsreel.org⟩

Chicago Reader ⟨www.chireader.com⟩

Cinema Guild ⟨www.cinemaguild.com⟩

Criterion Pictures (for DVDs) ⟨www.criterionpic.com⟩

Filmakers Library ⟨www.filmakers.com⟩

Frameline ⟨www.frameline.org⟩

Hollywood's Attic ⟨www.hollywoodsattic.com⟩

Icarus Films ⟨www.frif.com⟩

Icestorm ⟨www.icestorm-video.com⟩

Indiana University ⟨www.indiana.edu/~mediares/catalog.html⟩

Kino International ⟨www.kino.com⟩

National Film Board of Canada ⟨www.nfb.ca⟩

National Labor Committee ⟨www.nlcnet.org⟩

New Day Films ⟨www.newday.com⟩

New Yorker Films ⟨www.newyorkerfilms.com⟩

PBS Video ⟨www.shop.pbs.org⟩

Pyramid Media ⟨www.pyramidmedia.com⟩

Women Make Movies ⟨www.wmm.com⟩

Zeitgeist Films ⟨www.zeitgeistfilm.com⟩

Zipporah Films ⟨www.zipporah.com⟩

Abbreviations

I have used the standard Motion Picture Association codes (R, PG, PG-13, G) as well as the following other abbreviations:

UK = United Kingdom

TVM = TV movie

M = mature audience (a TV movie rating)

B&W = black-and-white film

Alphabetization

Entries are alphabetized letter by letter; thus *Alamo Bay*, for instance, precedes *À l'attaque!*

This guide departs from the usual practice by alphabetizing foreign titles just like English titles, that is, by ignoring the article. Most film guides list *La Promesse*, for instance, among the *L*'s, for *La*, which of course means *The*, although it would never occur to them to list *The Bicycle Thief*, say, among the *T*'s.

Acknowledgments

The students, faculty, and staff of the National Labor College at the George Meany Center for Labor Studies have been important allies in constructing the list of films in this guide and discussing many of them with me. Many thanks for all of their suggestions and ideas. I thank Sue Schurman, president of the National Labor College, and her colleagues for providing an ideal teaching environment for labor studies at the Center in Silver Spring, Maryland.

The following students were especially helpful in locating titles and supplying valuable information: Ed Bernas, Henry "Butch" Carner, Brenda Ching, Carol Dupuis, Greg Fischer, Ellen Garza, Jeff Hughes, Rick Inclima, Connie Johnsey, Michelle Kikta, Rick Moralez, Bill Moyer, Terry Nicoludis, Cosmo Mannella, Robert O'Reilly, and Matt Witt.

Other individuals have also kindly sent me videocassettes or helpful information: Larry Adelman, Steffi Domike, Dan Fitzgerald, Rose Feurer, David Frank, Anne Lewis, Brian McWilliams, Peter Rachleff, Peter Slade, Noah Soudrette, Carolyn Sturgil, Steve Trusdail, and Sarah Zaniello.

The first edition of *Working Stiffs* benefited from the advice of Joseph Agonito, John Alberti, David Alexander, Judy Ancel, Dexter Arnold, Ken Margolies, Robb Mitchell, William J. Puette, Jim Rundle, and Alan Harris Stein.

Administrators and staff at Northern Kentucky University have been extremely supportive of my research interests over the years; this group includes, but is not limited to, Bob Collier, Nancy Hands, Marcia Johnson, Danny Miller, Rogers Redding, Paul Reichardt, Mary Ryan, and Sharon Taylor.

A special note of thanks goes to the other members of the Z-Team, Belle Zembrodt and Aaron Zlatkin, who administer the Honors Program at what we call the Ho Ho (the Honors House) at Northern Kentucky University.

Distributors and organizations have been generous in their loans of videocassettes for my study and in some cases photo stills for reproduction: Appalshop, California Newsreel, Cinema Guild, Filmakers Library, Icestorm, Mintleaf Productions, New York State School of Industrial and Labor Relations at Cornell University, Pyramid Media, and Women Make Movies. Without their help, this volume would be indeed very incomplete.

The first edition was dedicated to the memory of Bill Worley, artist, film fan, and friend. I remember his contagious enthusiasm for films fondly. Since the first edition was published, a wonderful teacher, film fan, and friend has also passed away: I think of Tony Mazzaro often, because of his love of films and his ability to teach students and colleagues alike with every conversation.

A very special "thank you" goes to Frances Benson, publishing manager of ILR Press, whose support of this project through two editions has been so extremely important to me.

Select Labor Film Categories

Although labor films do not themselves constitute a distinct cinematic genre, many viewers perceive documentary as somehow the natural cinematic form for labor issues, as there has been a wide range of successful documentaries with a strong labor focus. Edward R. Murrow's *Harvest of Shame*, on migrant workers, for example, is a classic of investigative journalism, while the Maysle brothers' *Salesman* was a breakthrough cinema verité film. *With Babies and Banners* and *The Life and Times of Rosie the Riveter* offered new strong feminist perspectives on labor history sorely missed in early documentaries. Barbara Kopple won two Academy Awards for her "purely" labor films, *Harlan County, U.S.A.* and *American Dream*, an unprecedented accomplishment, while Michael Moore's postmodern spoof on the chairman of General Motors, *Roger & Me*, was the first major labor-related documentary to make a profit in commercial theaters.

Nonetheless, some cinematic movements focus so strongly on labor that it seems as though they form a virtual genre in themselves. British social realism in both feature and documentary films, for example, seemed to be the model for the American social-realist documentary movement of the 1930s; Italian neorealism of the late 1940s and 1950s and the Cuban cinema of the 1970s and 1980s covered similar ground in quite dissimilar cultures. Films from all of these movements are significantly represented in this volume. Almost all of them, both feature films and documentaries, center on working-class individuals, emphasize the importance of work, and are visually realistic.

But if we consider the variety of national cinemas that use less realistic and more symbolic modes of discourse, such as contemporary African, Latin American, and other Third World (Third Cinema) films, and even postmodern American documentaries, social realism is no longer the point. Films from these cinematic movements and traditions have fewer consistent generic components and in fact may even be defined as consciously undermining social-realist conventions.

In this group of films, the elite (capitalists, managers, politicians) share screen time with workers. The economic situation of an individual is often linked directly to larger forces such as downsizing or globalization. Actions may be presented out of sequence, an approach not consistent with traditional canons of realism. Workers may interact with symbolic forces over which they have little or no control but which they gradually understand as a legacy of capitalism.

Each section that follows begins by highlighting two films of particular note discussed in the volume and concludes with a selection of relevant print materials. These books and articles are not repeated in the entries unless the source has an extensive discussion of a specific film.

Documentaries

> Most influential film: *Harlan County, U.S.A.*
> A neglected film: *Surviving the Good Times*

Documentary is the film form often identified with topics of labor, in part because of the social-realist documentaries of the Depression era, when unemployment, union organizing, revolutionary rhetoric, and natural disasters dominated people's lives, and their representation in documentary films followed a Depression photo-journalistic style.

This expanded edition has almost a hundred documentaries, almost 30 percent of the total (compared to 20 percent of the 150 titles in the first edition).

The documentaries in this edition are classified according to the following six types (and one related type):

1. *Social-realist documentaries*: I have reserved this term for the documentaries of the 1930s, produced primarily in the United States and Great Britain. They were often sponsored by government or quasi-government agencies to illuminate a social problem or argue for a massive change in public priorities. They typically used an authoritative voice-of-God narrator, black-and-white contemporary footage, and informational titles and maps. In Britain, poets and composers sometimes worked on the sound track, while American films used strongly rhetorical prose. British documentaries, such as John Grierson's *Drifters* (1929) and Robert Flaherty's *Industrial Britain* (1933), and New Deal documentaries, such as Pare Lorentz's *The River* (1937) and his *The Plow That Broke the Plains* (1936), epitomize this tradition.

2. *Traditional documentaries*: These films are derived in spirit from the social-realist documentaries of the 1930s in that they favor social problems and historical events for subject matter. They use a mixture of interviews, archival footage, news or newsreel footage, still photos, and informational titles, linked by an obvious chronology or location or by a central theme, carried by a strong, often objective-sounding voice-over narrator and in some cases with either actual or commentative music and sound. Whether in color or in black and white, some of the best documentaries of the 1970s, such as *With Babies and Banners* and *The Wobblies*, helped launch a golden age of labor documentaries that continues to this day.

3. *Cinema verité*: With the introduction in the 1960s of portable and lightweight cameras with synchronized sound, these documentaries relied on extended long takes of actions or conversations or interviews, filmed somewhat spontaneously with minimal or no lighting and with minimal or no presence of the investigative reporter or a voice-over narrator; they tend to have no musical track and no other interpretive or framing devices. Stephen Mamber defined it succinctly as filming "real people in undirected situations."

In part a reaction to the overcontrolling nature of traditional documentaries, cinema verité has such critical successes as the Maysle brothers' *Salesman* and two Academy Award–winning films, *Harlan County, U.S.A.* and *American Dream*, both by Barbara Kopple, to its credit.

4. *TV documentaries*: These films were intended primarily for broadcast TV, although some early ones (Edward R. Murrow's *Harvest of Shame*) and many more recent ones may also be released on videocassette. They may have the strong voice-over narrator and singleness of purpose of a traditional documentary, but they are usually introduced or narrated by a star or celebrity reporter (who may even be in the shots) and can be investigative in purpose. They stress location shooting, as if reporting a news event, and use numerous interviews, either in the field or in the studio. *Harvest of Shame* is the most famous and most influential TV documentary, but it is not typical of TV reporting in a conformist era, because Murrow's work was unusually forthright on political issues. Like traditional documentary, these films were heavily edited: Murrow's juxtaposition of cattle trucks with strict safety rules and mistreated migrant laborers in rickety trucks is a famous example of this style.

5. *Agitprop*: Drawing on the techniques of traditional and TV documentary styles, these films were often sponsored by political groups or unions to convey a strong political message or call to arms. While many labor documentaries endeavor to influence viewers about their subject matter, agitprop films are specifically designed to organize workers or mobilize community support for a boycott or expose an injustice. Agitprop films differ from documentaries in categories 2 and 4 above and 6 below because they do not take the long view of history, they do not deliberately challenge the form of the documentary itself, and they do not offer a balanced journalistic report. California Newsreel produced some outstanding examples of this form in the late 1960s, notably *Black Panther* and *San Francisco State: On Strike*, documenting resistance to the Vietnam War and spreading the news of the university protest movement. One of the most famous agitprop films of the last twenty-five years is *The Wrath of Grapes*, used by the United Farm Workers to persuade consumers to boycott California grapes. More recently, the Association of Flight Attendants released *Chaos*, a film explaining their unique selective strike strategy, and the National Labor Committee made *Mickey Mouse Goes to Haiti* to build awareness of corporate exploitation in Latin America. The last three films were successful in part because of their attention-getting titles.

6. *Postmodern documentaries*: These films were hybrid forms, drawing freely on documentaries of the first five categories and intercutting scripted or fictional scenes as well as sequences from other films (sometimes Hollywood films, sometimes deliberately campy or absurd films) and often starring the filmmaker as an essential part of the action. Michael Moore, following the pioneer efforts by Errol Morris (*The Thin Blue Line*) and Diane Keaton (*Heaven*), made *Roger & Me*, the first feature-length postmodern labor documentary, and has since then adapted the form for network and cable TV in his series *TV Nation* and *The Awful Truth*. Moore's guerrilla TV style is evident, with hit-and-run filmed confrontations and with

creatively staged and semiscripted surprise filming opportunities. The films sometimes were chronological, but their mixed modes of pop and high culture made them seem more like MTV than Pare Lorentz.

A genre related to documentary is the mock-doc, the mock documentary or pseudo-documentary. These films have the form of traditional or other documentaries but use professional and nonprofessional actors in scripted or semiscripted action, with the effect of convincing (or even fooling) viewers into believing that what they are seeing actually happened and was being filmed as it occurred. *Native Land*, a 1940 mixture of staged and actual footage, documented violations of civil liberties as presented in testimony before the La Follette Committee in the Senate. Mock-docs in Hollywood have had two major successes, Rob Reiner's *This Is Spinal Tap* (1984) and Woody Allen's *Zelig* (1983), although few doubted they were watching scripted films. Lower budget and independent classics of the form include the navel-gazing *David Holzman's Diary* (1968) and Michele Citron's feminist classic, *Daughter Rite* (1978). Both of these films were scripted but fooled most viewers into assuming they were documentaries. *Dadetown* is a contemporary example of the form included in this volume.

Further reading

Heider, Karl G. *Ethnographic Film*. Austin: University of Texas Press, 1976. A survey and interpretation of a type of documentary that attempts the realism of observed cultures through long takes and other measures of authenticity ("whole acts, whole bodies, whole peoples"); a precursor of or parallel to cinema verité.

Mamber, Stephen. *Cinema Verité in America: Studies in Uncontrolled Documentary*. Cambridge: MIT Press, 1974. An early but still valuable account of the movement and its history.

Films of Migrant Labor

Most influential film: *Harvest of Shame*

A neglected film: *And the Earth Did Not Swallow Him*

The Thematic Index to this volume lists eleven films about migrant labor, about evenly divided between feature films and documentaries, almost all of which were broadcast on TV.

Given the number of hours available for TV programming even in the early days, the slots devoted to the millions of farm workers were of course remarkably few; nonetheless, documentary programs about migrant farm workers include the first and arguably the best classic of TV investigative journalism, Edward R. Murrow's *Harvest of Shame*. Murrow covered virtually every issue of importance to the migrant worker, including the relatively little known bracero program, whereby the growers could import Mexican workers and pay them even less than the pitiful wages they were paying American workers.

The three follow-up TV programs included in this volume are also excellent but unfortunately are not available on videocassette: *New Harvest, Old Shame; Legacy of Shame;* and *Children of the Harvest*.

The year before Murrow broadcast his film, Ernesto Galarza made *Poverty in the Land of Plenty* to support the AFL-CIO's efforts to organize farm labor (shown briefly at the end of *Harvest of Shame*), but powerful California growers managed to suppress the film with a dubious but successful congressional and legal campaign starring Richard Nixon as the growers' ally.

Three other TV documentaries were broadcast to positive reviews, but they too have never been circulated (and are not covered in this volume):

> *What Harvest for the Reaper?* shown on *NET [National Educational Television] Journal*, 1968: Mort Silverstein focuses on just one of Murrow's targets, a labor camp in Cutchogue, Long Island, that "would make slave life on the old Dixie plantation appear attractive" (*Variety*).
>
> *Hunger in America*, shown on *CBS Reports*, 1968: Martin Carr sends Charles Kuralt and others to focus on poverty among Mexican-Americans, Navajos, southern blacks, and Virginia tenant farmers, the latter occupying the estates of Senator Everett Dirksen and the popular TV entertainer Arthur Godfrey.
>
> *Migrant*, shown on NBC, 1970: Carr (again) sends Chet Huntley and others out in the field to document how Coca-Cola and its subsidiaries (Snowcrop, Hi C, Minute Maid, and Tropicana) exploit Florida farm workers; *Variety* noted that the show's sponsor, Coca-Cola, tried to "kill the exposé," which was shown, in the end, without a single commercial. Solidarity forever!

Migrant laborers have been depicted in at least four feature films, all of them made for TV broadcast. *Migrants*, which focuses on white workers, and *And the Earth Did Not Swallow Him*, which focuses on Mexican workers, are two of the best.

Further reading

Bacon, David. "Labor Fights for Immigrants." *Nation*, 21 May 2001, 15–18. Surveys the changes in the 1990s in attitudes toward immigrants, culminating in the AFL-CIO's adoption of policies favoring undocumented immigrants.

Belluck, Pam. "Mexican Laborers in U.S. during War Sue for Back Pay." *New York Times*, 29 April 2001, I, 18. The braceros may have been disrupting the migrant laborers' wage scale in the United States, but they were also being cheated out of their own wages, part of which they were to have received after they returned to Mexico.

Galarza, Ernesto. *Merchants of Labor: The Mexican Bracero Story*. Charlotte: McNally & Loftin, 1964. Galarza's carefully researched exposé of one of the early missing links of the Mexico-American migrant labor story—the braceros brought in to work the fields and to lower wages for all migrant workers.

——. *Spiders in the House & Workers in the Field*. Notre Dame: University of Notre Dame Press, 1970. Brilliant exposé of the lengths to which the DiGiorgio Fruit Corporation went, with the help of congressional flunkies such as Richard Nixon, to stop union organizing among migrant workers in the 1940s; this business-government combine also stopped distribution of *Land of Poverty*, probably the earliest documentary film exposing the terrible conditions of the workers.

McWilliams, Carey. *Ill Fares the Land: Migrants and Migratory Labor in the United States*. Boston: Little, Brown, 1944. An early and still powerful review of all aspects of migratory labor. California growers called the author, who served as commissioner of the California Department of Agriculture, "the number one agricultural pest" in the state.

"Migrant." *Variety*, 22 July 1970. Review of Martin Carr's NBC-TV film exposing the terrible conditions permitted by Coca-Cola's subsidiaries: "When an old-fashioned (circa 1950–'60) muckraking telementary like this one appears on the home screen it's as though a flock of rare whooping cranes swooped into the living room."

Rosenthal, Alan. *The New Documentary in Action*. Berkeley: University of California Press, 1971. Includes a chapter on *What Harvest for the Reaper?*

Thompson, Ginger, and Stephen Greenhouse. "Mexican 'Guest Workers': A Project Worth a Try?" *New York Times*, 3 April 2001, A4. It's déjà vu all over again, as the once-dubious bracero program comes back in the Bush administration renamed as "guest workers."

Variety Television reviews: *Harvest of Shame*, 30 November 1960; *NET Journal* [*What Harvest for the Reaper?*], 7 February 1968; *Hunger in America*, 29 May 1968; *Migrant*, 22 July 1970. Uniformly positive reviews, almost all of which point out that the shows represent "a reminder to the industry of what it can do when it gets up a little nerve" (29 May 1968).

Peckerwood and White Trash Films

Most influential films: *Tobacco Road* and *God's Little Acre*

A neglected film: *Cabin in the Cotton*

The 1990s saw a rush of documentaries on the uneasy alliance of poor white and black labor in the rural South: *The Uprising of '34, Our Land Too, and Oh Freedom after While*. These films may have begun the process of de-hillbillyizing the South, because until recently the dominant image of southern white labor has been that of shiftless white trash, known in the 1930s as peckerwoods.

Erskine Caldwell has always had the corner on the peckerwood or white trash novel market with *God's Little Acre* and *Tobacco Road*, both of which were made, if not faithfully, into major Hollywood films. On a comic level, Al Capp's *Lil' Abner* may have come close. But the matter is really much more complicated because of the regional and state variations of the hillbilly type; Robert Penn Warren's *All the King's Men*, for example, as well as Robert Rossen's brilliant 1946 adaptation, dramatized the Louisiana up-country variant, based on the real-life career of Huey Long. *A Lion Is in the Streets*, discussed in this volume, is still another variant, perhaps too close to Warren's story to merit distinction, the story of the rise and fall of another backwoods peckerwood, played incongruously by Jimmy Cagney, who becomes governor of Mississippi.

The Hollywood cycle of white trash films began in earnest in the 1930s with *Cabin in the Cotton* and fairly died with Cagney's film and *God's Little Acre* in 1958. The more politicized peckerwood stories are quasi-Marxist, although probably none of their authors or screenplay writers would have accepted the designation. But the poor white trash are actually lumpenproletariat—basically shiftless ne'er-do-wells who don't or won't farm for their living. Potentially they are a populist or anti-elite force for change in favor of tolerating their black brothers in poverty (as the Socialist and Communist labor organizers of the Southern Tenant Farmers' Union in the 1930s hoped); inevitably, however, their champion must seize power from the rich by using questionable allies—organized crime or gun thugs who are on the people's side. Inevitably, even their best friends realize that peckerwood power corrupts, too.

The TVA, with its controversial practice of hiring both blacks and whites, gave rise to one remarkable film, *Wild River*, an adaptation of two novels. Borden Deal, author of one of the novels, also wrote *The Tobacco Men*, on the Kentucky tobacco wars of 1905 between the farmers and the developing tobacco trusts. It was based on a screenplay by the novelist Theodore Dreiser, who wanted *The Tobacco Men* to dramatize "the aggressive and dynamic plans and actions of a certain group of American industrial leaders, practical and of course ruthless in their approach toward the lesser individual and his life." The course of Hollywood's portrayal of poor whites might have been radically different had Dreiser gotten his way, but the film was never made.

Further reading

Deal, Borden. *The Tobacco Men*. New York: Holt, Rinehart & Winston, 1965. With an introduction by Hy Kraft explaining Dreiser's original participation in the project.

Williamson, J. W. *Hillbillyland: What the Movies Did to the Mountains and the Mountains Did to the Movies*. Chapel Hill: University of North Carolina Press, 1995. Unexpectedly light on Hollywood image making, but a good introduction to the subject.

British Social Realism I: Angry Young Men

Most influential film: *Look Back in Anger*

A neglected film: *The Kitchen*

Although it may be too neat a categorization, British labor films follow the long tradition of social realism, pioneered by John Grierson and the British Documentary Movement of the 1930s and continued by the Free Cinema movement of the 1950s and the films of the Angry Young Men (and kitchen sink realism) of the late 1950s and early 1960s.

The Angry Young Men movement of the 1950s and 1960s spawned a remarkable group of working-class plays and fictions. Perhaps only since Italian neorealism of the 1940s and 1950s has there been such a significant and unified body of working-class literature and cinema. British cinema has always had a strong class-conscious spirit, but with such authors as John Osborne and Alan Sillitoe the self-consciousness was usually aggressive and anarchistic, especially when the characters faced a representative of middle-class authority or upper-class pretentiousness.

In less than five years, films made from Osborne's play (*Look Back in Anger*, 1959) and the novels of John Braine (*Room at the Top*, 1959), Alan Sillitoe (*Saturday Night and Sunday Morning*, 1960, and *The Loneliness of the Long-Distance Runner*, 1962), and David Storey (*This Sporting Life*, 1963), not to mention such stage hits as Arnold Wesker's *The Kitchen* in 1961, established the British working-class scene with a visual anthology of petty thievery, social climbing, violence toward women, and drunken escapades. Once in a while the angry young men in these films actually worked for a living, but they complained bitterly when they did. Although many of the women in the films were angry as well, neither their resentments nor those of militant trade unionists were ever a serious part of the movement. The rugby player in This *Sporting Life* keeps his day job at the factory, but the film touches only lightly on a scandal or two involving workman's compensation.

Labor films are also found in two other significant traditions of British filmmaking—the costume and historical film (later the heritage film) and the eccentric comedies, typified by those produced by the Ealing Studio. These films have some of the surface features of social realism, but strike out in various other ways.

Brassed Off and *The Full Monty*, for example, mark a return to the old British comedies that used labor situations for satire and comedy, such as *The Man in the White Suit* and *I'm All Right, Jack*. In all of these films, both old and new, the trials and tribulations of the labor force are as much about the funny bone as they are about the class struggle. This tradition might be epitomized in the 1966 cult favorite, *Morgan, a Suitable Case for Treatment* (not included in this guide), a film that virtually spins out of control around Morgan's antics to retain his upper-class ex-wife, while his mother (played by Irene Handl, a British working-class icon) keeps warning him about being "a traitor to the working class."

Further reading

Ashby, Justin, and Andrew Higson, eds. *British Cinema, Past and Present*. London: Routledge, 2000. Very extensive collection of essays, with two especially relevant to our survey of the social-realist film: John Hill's "From the New Wave to Brit-Grit: Continuity and Difference in Working-Class Realism" and Amy Sargeant's "Making and Selling Heritage Culture: Style and Authenticity in Historical Fictions on Film and Television."

Friedman, Lester. *Fires Were Started: British Cinema and Thatcherism*. Minneapolis: University of Minnesota Press, 1993. An excellent collection of essays, featuring discussions of political issues during the Thatcher era (1979–90) that were important for understanding British films, especially those of Channel 4, the heritage film movement, independent filmmakers, and films about labor, working, class, and multicultural issues.

Hill, John. *Sex, Class, and Realism: British Cinema, 1956–1963*. London: British Film Institute, 1986. Extensive analyses of the Angry Young Man and kitchen sink realism of the class-saturated films in these pivotal years.

Orbanz, Eva, ed. *Journey to a Legend and Back: The British Realistic Film*. Berlin: Volker Spiess, 1977. This volume, in English but not easy to find, has the virtue of surveying all the major figures in British social realism, from the 1930s through Free Cinema to the Ken Loach collaborator Jim Allen in the 1960s and 1970s.

Stead, Peter. *Film and the Working Class*. London: Routledge, 1989. Covers numerous films from the 1930s through the beginning of the Thatcher era (1979).

British Social Realism II: Ken Loach

Most influential film: *Cathy Come Home*

A neglected film: *Days of Hope*

Ken Loach's career may be said to have taken off with *Cathy Come Home*, one of the most influential films in British cinema in the modern era. This film about homelessness is also one of the most seldom seen films of this era, as it has had no circulation on videocassette and only rarely is exhibited. It joins five other Loach films (*The Big Flame, Days of Hope, The Price of Coal, Looks and Smiles*, and *The Flickering Flame*)—out of the eight in this volume—that have virtually no distribution of any kind to this day. Although *Cathy Come Home* is often cited as a documentary, by most definitions it is not, although its screenplay was carefully researched and it distills the actual experiences of real people. In the end, however, we note that it had a script, all of its principal characters were actors, and the scenes were staged.

It established Loach's career as a socially committed filmmaker, usually with a working-class focus that is solidly in the middle of the British social-realism tradition. He adapted two best-selling books at the end of the decade, Nell Dunn's *Poor Cow*, starring Carol White, who had played Cathy, and Barry Hines's *Kestral for a Knave* (film title: *Kes*), both films widely acclaimed for their realism and fresh subject matter. He continued to make feature films throughout his career, but he was also in the news because of his open support of militant trade unionism and socialism, whose issues he developed in documentaries. Ironically, perhaps, his early reputation was based on an unusual film often designated as a documentary.

Loach's last two films, *Bread and Roses* (2000) and *The Navigators* (2001), on the Justice for Janitors campaign in Los Angeles and the privatization of British Rail, respectively, are evidence of his tremendous range and political daring. He is in a class by himself.

Further reading

Loach, Ken. *Loach on Loach*. Ed. Graham Fuller. London: Faber & Faber,1998. Interviews with Loach.
McKnight, George. *Agent of Challenge and Defiance: The Films of Ken Loach*. Westport, Conn.: Greenwood Press, 1997. Comprehensive collection of excellent essays; a guide to Loach's career through the mid-1990s; extensive bibliography and videography.

Italian Neorealism

Most influential film: *The Bicycle Thief*

A neglected film: *La terra trema*

As a result of the devastation of World War II, Italian filmmakers were left with no studios, no sound equipment, and often limited access to professional actors. They were also left with a hollow economy and a country where the black-market law of the streets ensured or denied an individual's survival. And finally they suffered not only the physical destruction of the war but also the psychic wounds associated with their country's Fascist era, its alliance with the Nazis, its subsequent alignment with the Allies, an invasion of German troops, and a fierce partisan struggle directed against both German troops and their Italian collaborators. (A short course in this history—minus the German occupiers—may be achieved by watching Bertolucci's *1900*; to add the German occupiers, see the Taviani brothers' *Night of the Shooting Stars*.)

But a survey of all the neorealist films would reveal, as George A. Huaco's neglected but revealing *Sociology of Film Art* demonstrates, that the explosion of filmmaking in postwar Italy (as well as in the Soviet era and Germany in the 1920s) was the product of a variety of social and economic factors, including a film industry and filmmakers disposed politically toward similar ideals, in this case a Marxist belief in the working class and its allies as the fundamental vehicle for historical change, and dedicated to making films literally in the streets with as much fidelity to the political and economic struggles of the workers as possible.

For our purposes the movement splits in subject matter into two major groups—films focusing on war and occupation (whether by German or Allied troops) and films focusing on the economic survival of workers and other people at the bottom of society. The former group includes such classics as *Germany Year Zero* and *Paisan* and is outside the reach of this guide.

The second group actually contains working-class people, riffraff, and even street children (represented most forcefully by the child partisans of *Open City* and the two teenagers in *Shoeshine*). Thus while the neorealist movement certainly emphasizes the working class, I have included only those films that come closest to emphasizing economic issues or, in the case of *Bitter Rice*, an actual labor dispute.

Further reading

Huaco, George A. *The Sociology of Film Art*. New York: Basic Books, 1965. A neglected but revealing study of Italian neorealism that correlates its ideology with the social conditions of both the film industry and its social context.

African Films

Most influential film: *Xala*

A neglected film: *The Blue Eyes of Yonta*

Unfortunately, many viewers have never seen an African film of any kind: theatrical distribution is virtually unheard of, videocassettes are not easy to come by, and even international film festivals do not always cover all the continents equally. Between 1993 and 2000, however, the distributor California Newsreel released more than fifty videocassettes in its Library of African Cinema, supported financially by the National Endowment for the Arts, the Ford and Rockefeller foundations, and the Film Resource Unit of Johannesburg. Finally access to African cinema was possible through videocassette rental (through participating public libraries), a Web site (⟨www.news-reel.org/topics/acine.htm⟩), and excellent catalogs.

This guide features five of the films in the California Newsreel series and an earlier film of great importance, *Xala*. While virtually every African film emphasizes economic issues of some kind and all portray working-class people, two short films by Djibril Diop Mambéty, *Le Franc* and *The Little Girl Who Sold the Sun*, are both films about street markets—an important urban institution in virtually every African nation—and the workers who must cope with living on the margins.

Most of the African films dramatize the corruption of the black elite as well as the lingering dislocations of the economy caused by the colonial occupier. Films such as *Hyenas* and *The Blue Eyes of Yonta* use symbolic action—magic realism, if you will—to focus on the power of European money and the accommodation of the national leadership in disabling real economic change. The directors of these films, some commentators have argued, are striking out in a different "third" way, attempting to avoid both commercial filmmaking (First Cinema) and the European art film (Second Cinema).

Further reading

Library of African Cinema: 1993–94 and Library of African Cinema: 1995–96. San Francisco: California Newsreel, 1993, 1995. These guidebooks prepared by the distributor are very helpful for tracing themes in the series; the first has a brief "political and economic overview" of "Africa's second independence"—that is, the struggles against reactionary national elites—by Julius O. Ihonvbere.

Wayne, Mike. *Political Film: The Dialectics of Third Cinema*. London: Pluto, 2001. Argues that Third Cinema is not the same as Third World cinema, although it emerged there, but "it is a cinema of social and cultural emancipation."

Tracing the History of Labor Films: A Chronology

American feature (fiction) films are in the first column, all other feature films are in the second column, and all documentaries, regardless of country of origin, are in the third. When a film's production and release dates differ significantly, the film is listed under the date of its first broadcast or production, followed by the date in parentheses when it was actually released.

Year	Feature films made in United States	Non-U.S. features	Documentaries
1909	A Corner in Wheat		
1924		Strike	
1926		Metropolis	
		Mother	
1927		The End of St. Petersburg	
1928		The General Line	
1930		Earth	Enthusiasm
1931	Street Scene	Kameradschaft	
1932	Cabin in the Cotton	Kuhle Wampe	Land without Bread
	I Am a Fugitive from a Chain Gang	¡Que viva México! (1979)	
	Uncle Moses		
1933	Female		
	Gold Diggers of 1933		
	Heroes for Sale		
	Wild Boys of the Road		
1934	Our Daily Bread		
1935	Black Fury		
	Riffraff		
	Sons of Steel		
1936	Black Legion		The Plow That Broke the Plains (*see* New Deal Documentaries)
	Fury		
	Fury Below		
	Modern Times		

Year	Feature films made in United States	Non-U.S. features	Documentaries
1937	Slim	South Riding	The River (see New Deal Documentaries)
1938		The Citadel	
1939	Of Mice and Men I One Third of a Nation	The Stars Look Down	
1940	The Grapes of Wrath The Long Voyage Home They Drive by Night	The Proud Valley	Power and the Land (see New Deal Documentaries)
1941	The Devil and Miss Jones Sullivan's Travels Tobacco Road	How Green Was My Valley Love on the Dole	
1942	Native Land		
1943		Millions Like Us	
1944	An American Romance		
1945	The Corn Is Green The Southerner The Valley of Decision		
1947		The Bicycle Thief Captain Boycott Hungry Hill La terra trema	
1948		Bitter Rice	
1949		Fame Is the Spur	
1950		Chance of a Lifetime Los olvidados	
1951	I Can Get It for You Wholesale The Whistle at Eaton Falls	The Man in the White Suit	
1953	A Lion Is in the Streets	Illusion Travels by Streetcar	
1954	On the Waterfront Salt of the Earth		
1955	Marty		
1956	Inside Detroit The Solid Gold Cadillac	The Roof	
1957	Desk Set Edge of the City The Garment Jungle Island in the Sun The Pajama Game		Automation Every Day Except Christmas (see Free Cinema)

Year	Feature films made in United States	Non-U.S. features	Documentaries
1958	God's Little Acre	Look Back in Anger	We Are the Lambeth Boys (*see* Free Cinema)
		Sun Seekers (1971)	
1959	Never Steal Anything Small	I'm All Right, Jack	
	Tamango	Rocco and His Brothers	
1960	Wild River	The Angry Silence	Harvest of Shame
1961	A Raisin in the Sun I	Flame in the Streets	
		The Kitchen	
		Saturday Night and Sunday Morning	
		The White Rose	
1963		Carbide and Sorrel	
		Ladies Who Do	
		The Organizer	
		This Sporting Life	
1964	Nothing But a Man	I Am Cuba (1995)	The Inheritance
1965			Cathy Come Home
1966			Trace of Stones (1990)
1968		Ramparts of Clay	
1969	The Learning Tree	Ådalen '31	The Big Flame
			British Sounds
			Salesman
1970	Joe	Burn!	Finally Got the News
	The Molly Maguires	Goin' Down the Road	
1971	Brother John	Joe Hill	
		Sacco and Vanzetti	
		The Working Class Goes to Heaven	
1972	Boxcar Bertha	Blow for Blow	
	Sounder	Eight Hours Are Not a Day	
		Tout va bien	
1974	The Migrants	Bread and Chocolate	The Buffalo Creek Flood
1975	Hester Street	Days of Hope	Controlling Interest
		Land of Promise	
		Sunday Too Far Away	
1976	Bound for Glory	The Churning	Union Maids
		The Last Supper	
		1900	
		Xica	
1977		Perfumed Nightmare	Harlan County, U.S.A.
		The Price of Coal	
1978	Bloodbrothers		With Babies and Banners
	Blue Collar		
	Convoy		
	F.I.S.T.		

Year	Feature films made in United States	Non-U.S. features	Documentaries
1979	Freedom Road	Camera Buff	The Wobblies
	Norma Rae	Man of Marble	
	Northern Lights	Portrait of Teresa	
	The Triangle Factory Fire Scandal		
1980	Angel City		Children of Golzow
	Coal Miner's Daughter		The Free Voice of Labor
	The $5.20 an Hour Dream		The Life and Times of Rosie the Riveter
	9 to 5		Taylor Chain I
	Power		The Willmar 8
	Steel		
1981	Of Mice and Men II	Looks and Smiles	Año Nuevo
	Take This Job and Shove It	Man of Iron	Moving Mountains
1982		Boys from the Blackstuff	Coalmining Women
			Trouble on Fashion Avenue
			We Dig Coal
1983	Blood Feud	Educating Rita	The Electric Valley
	Keeping On	Sugar Cane Alley	Miles of Smiles, Years of Struggle
	Nightsongs	Up to a Certain Point	
	El Norte	Waterfront	
	Silkwood		
1984	Burning Rage	Quilombo	America and Lewis Hine
	The Dollmaker	Turumba	Brass Valley
	Half-Slave, Half-Free	Yellow Earth	Buffalo Creek Revisited
	The Killing Floor		Shout Youngstown
	Signal 7		Taylor Chain II
	Swing Shift		
	Wildrose		
1985	Alamo Bay	Seacoal	Final Offer
		Canada's Sweetheart	Voices from a Steeltown
			Women of Steel
1986	Act of Vengeance	Aclà's Descent into Floristella	Down and Out in America
	Gung Ho	Spices	The Women of Summer
		Yellow Earth	The Wrath of Grapes
1987	Born in East L.A.	Business as Usual	Business of America
	Matewan	Comrades	Computers in Context
	Uncle Tom's Cabin	John and the Missus	
	Wall Street	Red Sorghum	
1988	High Hopes	To Kill a Priest	Collision Course
	Tucker		Our Land Too
	Working Girl		The Golden Cage
			Lightning Over Braddock

Year	Feature films made in United States	Non-U.S. features	Documentaries
1989	Last Exit to Brooklyn		Roger & Me
	A Raisin in the Sun II		Who Killed Vincent Chin?
1990	The Raid		American Dream
	Rising Son		New Harvest, Old Shame
	Stanley and Iris		Out of Darkness
	To Sleep with Anger		
1991	Long Road Home	The Efficiency Expert	Chemical Valley
	Other People's Money	Riff-Raff	Roving Pickets
			35 Up
1992	Barbarians at the Gate	The Blue Eyes of Yonta	Fast Food Women
	Hoffa	Hyenas	Harry Bridges
	Newsies	Making Steel	JFK, Hoffa, and the Mob
	Of Mice and Men III		Jimmy Hoffa
	Teamster Boss		On to Ottawa
			These Hands
1993	Mac	Daens	At the River I Stand
		Germinal	The Great Depression
			The River Ran Red
			Sit Down and Fight
1994	And the Earth Did Not Swallow Him	Le Franc	Chaos
	The Burning Season		Goin' to Chicago
			TV Nation
1995	American Job	Net Worth	Deadly Corn
	Picture Bride		Evelyn Williams
			Homecoming
			Justice in the Coalfields
			Legacy of Shame
			Struggle in the Heartland (*see* Deadly Corn)
			The Uprising of '34
1996	Dadetown	Brassed Off	A. Philip Randolph
		Margaret's Museum	The Flickering Flame
		Mother Trucker	Mickey Mouse Goes to Haiti
		La Promesse	Out at Work
		The Worker and the Hairdresser	Struggles in Steel
			Who's Getting Rich and Why Aren't You?
1997		The Full Monty	The Big One
		The Scar	Degrees of Shame
			East Side Story
			The Fight in the Fields
			The Richest Man in the World

Year	Feature films made in United States	Non-U.S. features	Documentaries
			Riding the Rails
			Rough Side of the Mountain
			Troublesome Creek
			Wittstock, Wittstock
1998	Clockwatchers		Children of the Harvest
1999	The City	Human Resources	42 Up
	Cradle Will Rock	The Little Girl Who Sold the Sun	Oh Freedom after While
	October Sky	Ratcatcher	To Save the Land and People
	Office Space		
2000	Bread and Roses	À l'attaque!	The Awful Truth
	Harlan County War		Belfast, Maine
			The Gleaners and I
			One Day Longer
			Surviving the Good Times
2001		The Navigators	A Day's Work, a Day's Pay
			Life and Debt
			The New Rulers of the World
			Secrets of Silicon Valley
			Startup.com
			Taxi Dreams
2002	10,000 Black Men Named George		American Standoff

Aclà's Descent into Floristella

The pits

1986, 86 mins., Italy, in Italian, with English
 subtitles
Director: Aurelio Grimaldi
Screenplay: Aurelio Grimaldi
CAST
Aclà = Francesco Cusimano
Caramazza = Tony Sperandeo

Perhaps it is unfortunate that *Aclà* has been
marketed and distributed mainly as a gay-
interest film, because its realistic portrayal of
virtual child slavery in a Sicilian mine in the
1930s deserves a wider audience. Aclà, an 11-
year-old boy, descends into a hellish sulfur
mine named Floristella as a boy worker, but
it turns out that the boys are "owned" by
adult diggers for eight years.

Aclà hauls sulfur chunks all day and has to
guard them from thieves at night. Naked
during the day belowground and naked
huddled together sleeping in a cave at night,
the boys are routinely subjected to sexual
abuse. Aclà has a dream based on descriptions of the sea written by an aunt who has
emigrated to Australia. When he does finally
try to escape to the sea, he is of course appre-
hended and brutally punished.

Nothing about this film is easy to watch,
although it will certainly match—if not
exceed—some of the horrors of child labor
dramatized in the Belgian film *Daens* and the
work of Lewis Hine, the American photographer of child labor. Some aspects of
Sicilian culture are nonetheless hard to
understand. When some of the children are
taken off to boarding school, their mothers'
grief seems disproportionate. When the
alternative is Floristella, losing a child temporarily to compulsory schooling should be a
blessing.

The film has some of the harsh realism of
the early Italian neorealists. It has, alas, very
little of their occasional heroism.

See also: *America and Lewis Hine*; *Daens*.
Availability: Selected collections.

Further reading

Holden, Stephen. "Aclà." *New York Times*, 3
 December 1993, C12. The reviewer deempha-
 sizes the film as "a brutal exposé" and stresses
 the impossible innocence of the young boy and
 the sordid world of the mines.

Note: Also known as *Aclà*.

Act of Vengeance

Act of viciousness

1986, 96 mins., TVM, M
Director: John MacKenzie
Screenplay: Scott Spenser, from Trevor
 Armbrister's nonfiction book of the same
 title
CAST
Jock Yablonski = Charles Bronson
Margaret Yablonski = Ellen Burstyn
Charlotte Yablonski = Carolyn Kava
Ken Yablonski = Alf Humphreys
Chip Yablonski = Joseph Knell
Paul Gilly = Robert Schenkkan
Annette Gilly = Ellen Barkin
Tony Boyle = Wilford Brimley
Buddy Palmer = Keanu Reeves

On 30 December 1969 Jock Yablonski;
his wife, Margaret; and their daughter,
Charlotte, were murdered by three men
hired by intermediaries for Tony Boyle, the
president of the United Mine Workers
(UMW). Yablonski, after working for Boyle
for years, had decided six months earlier to
challenge him for the presidency.

Trevor Armbrister's book and the film
argue that Yablonski might have had to
tolerate Boyle's lack of identification with
the miners after one mining disaster too
many. In November 1968, seventy-eight
miners were trapped in a Consolidation Coal
Company mine in Farmington, West Virginia,
after a coal gas explosion. Two days after the
blast, Boyle appeared in Farmington and
called it "an unfortunate accident." Although
Consolidation had received numerous

federal safety citations, Boyle announced that it was "one of the better companies to work with as far as cooperation and safety [were] concerned." The company's response was to seal up the mine a week later, after many more explosions. The trapped men were given up for lost.

John L. Lewis, UMW president for many years and a popular and influential leader, had selected Boyle as his assistant in 1948. In 1963, Boyle succeeded Lewis, whose bushy eyebrows and powerful voice made him virtually an icon of tough and dedicated union service. Boyle's dyed reddish-brown hair couldn't compete.

The film opens with three parallel-edited sequences at different locations. It is an obvious but effective way of developing an uneasy triangle: Jock Yablonski's happy home life with his extended family, Tony Boyle's speech following a sexy African American singer at a UMW testimonial dinner, and miners in a pit facing a deadly explosion. In short (and perhaps too obvious): the good, the bad, and the dangerous.

The action hero Charles Bronson, playing Yablonski, seems to have wandered onto the set from another film. He seems uncomfortable as the union gofer for Boyle while married to an intellectual woman. (Unlike Jock, who stopped schooling in the tenth grade, Margaret Yablonski was college-educated and aspired to be a writer.) The film has scenes of union politics, on both local and national levels, but the director was clearly in a hurry to introduce Yablonski's killers and make this more of a TV crime film filled with violence and scuzziness than a film about union politics.

The first two killers are incredibly inept, dangerous, and brutal specimens of riffraff. One of the more repulsive ones at one point brags: "If —— shot my old lady and she didn't press charges!" They are also cowards. After the arrival of a third killer, played brilliantly and diabolically by Keanu Reeves, the film becomes a real Bronson film (like his *Death Wish* series); that is, one filled with senseless shooting and the slaughter of innocents.

See also: *Harlan County, U.S.A.*
Availability: Easy.

Further reading

Armbrister, Trevor. *Act of Vengeance*. New York: Saturday Review Press, 1975. The source book for the film.

Geoghegan, Tom. *Which Side Are You On?* New York: Farrar, Straus & Giroux, 1991. A union lawyer's reminiscences, including some about the Boyle years.

Zieger, Robert H. *John L. Lewis, Labor Leader*. New York: Twayne, 1988. Includes background on the Yablonski–Boyle struggle in the context of Lewis's ailing last years.

Ådalen '31

Romance and the picket line

1969, 115 mins., Swedish, with English subtitles, X
Director: Bo Widerberg
Screenplay: Bo Widerberg
CAST
Kjell = Peter Schildt
Kjell's mother = Kerstin Tidelius
Kjell's father = Roland Hedlund
Åke = Stefan Feierbach
Martin = Martin Widerberg
Anna = Maria De Geer
Anna's father = Olof Bergström
Anna's mother = Anita Björk

The somewhat unusual title of this film refers to the year 1931 (14 May 1931, to be precise), when five sawmill workers were killed during a demonstration in Ådalen, Sweden. A bitter strike had dragged on for months before the authorities called in strikebreakers and eventually the army in an attempt to break the strike.

A sensitive young worker, Kjell, spends a lot of time with the sawmill manager and his family—they wish to cultivate his talents—and he falls in love with their daughter, Anna. Once she becomes pregnant, crossing over class lines is no longer possible. When Kjell's father is then killed during the

March of the sawmill workers in Ådalen, Sweden, 1931. Courtesy British Film Institute Stills, Posters, and Designs.

demonstration, his options have narrowed considerably.

The essence of Widerberg's art seems to be in his portrayal of doomed but heroic lovers, at least two of whom (Kjell in this film and Joe Hill in the film of that title) are no less romantically inclined that the officer in Widerberg's apolitical film of thwarted love, *Elvira Madigan*. The critic Stig Björkman has argued in Widerberg's defense that his heroes are romantics who are rebelling against the domination of the upper classes, so it does not matter whether the struggle is played out on factory floor or army barracks (as in *Elvira Madigan*).

Ådalen '31 has the mixture of politics and poetic imagery characteristic of Widerberg's filmmaking. Children on the roof of a barn jump off, flapping little homemade wings. Fortunately for them, there is a haystack below. With seduction of the local young women in mind, a young man takes a correspondence course in hypnotism. When he finally induces a trance in one young lady, he doesn't really know what to do next. When Kjell's father is killed, however, wearing the clean shirt his wife just readied for him, Kjell tears up the shirt and side by side with his brothers and mother begins to clean some dusty windowpanes. The detail here is still visually strong, but its message has become more charged with significance.

Widerberg's young man (like the director himself, argued Vincent Canby) is slightly schizoid, torn apart by loyalties to two conflicting classes. In a Widerberg film even the conflict is lyrical: at Anna's house Kjell learns to play Chopin; later he will go to the People's House and practice the "Internationale" with the workers' band.

While Widerberg's other films, such as *Raven's End* (1963), acknowledged social inequities—a would-be writer lives in poor working-class housing—*Ådalen '31* dramatizes probably the most important event in modern Swedish history. The titles at the end of the film acknowledge that the events in a sense created Sweden's welfare state, as the Social Democrats came into power after the Ådalen strike.

See also: *Joe Hill.*
Availability: Not.

Further reading

Björkman, Stig. *Film in Sweden: The New Directors.* London: Tantivy Press, 1977. A thorough survey of Widerberg's career and films.

Canby, Vincent. "Adalen '31." *New York Times,* 20 September 1969, 21. Emphasizes the interesting clash between Widerberg's political interests and his "barely controlled passion for visual images so lush they are intoxicating in a numbing way."

Note: Also known as *Adalen 31* (without diacritic or apostrophe) and *The Adalen Riots.*

Alamo Bay

Remember the Alamo (Bay)!

1985, 98 mins., R
Director: Louis Malle
Screenplay: Alice Arlen
CAST
Shang = Ed Harris
Glory = Amy Madigan
Dinh = Ho Nguyen
Wally = Donald Moffat
Honey = Cynthia Carle
Luis = Martino Lasalle

The struggle between "native" Texas fishermen and recent Vietnamese immigrants on the Gulf Coast lasted three years (1978–81), during which the Texans and the Klan attacked the Vietnamese fishermen for taking away their livelihood. Although the Vietnamese were anticommunist Catholics, they were treated as if they were a battalion of the Viet Cong.

The film is a loose interpretation of the shooting of Billy Joe Aplin by Sau Van Nguyen in Seadrift, Texas, in 1978. The Catholic Vietnamese immigrant was acquitted because the jury believed he fired on Aplin after the Texas fisherman repeatedly beat him. (Aplin himself was also a transient, his family having wandered the South in search of work.) The trial was the culmination of a guerrilla war in which Texans and Vietnamese cut each other's crab pot lines, let moored boats go adrift, and fished illegally at night (although both sides said they were only out to protect their lines from the others). The violence, however, was mostly one-sided, as the Vietnamese were often the victims of racist attacks, eventually led by the Klan.

The filmmakers simplified this complex story. Shang, whose behavior and attitudes resemble Aplin's, is at first a fairly passive villain. He clearly reflects the sentiments of most of the Texas fishermen, who taunt the Vietnamese at every opportunity. Only Glory (played by Amy Madigan), the daughter of a waterfront fish wholesaler, and Dinh, a recent Vietnamese immigrant (played by Ho Nguyen), have the nerve to stand up to the Klan. Glory has also been romantically involved with Shang, who becomes an angry leader of a group of Vietnam vets the Klan is recruiting. His jealousy when Glory rejects him and sides with the Vietnamese makes him murderous. When the proceeds from his daily catch cannot support the payments for his new boat, he blames the Vietnamese for stealing his fish and launches a bay lockout against the Vietnamese and Glory's business. The result is a vicious parody of a workers' action to protect their jobs.

The Klan and the fishermen, most of whom are armed American vets, make a frightening combination in the film. When a flotilla of fishing boats, each dotted with a robed Klansman and a vet riding shotgun, sail into the harbor to police and intimidate the Vietnamese, Louis Malle's almost cartoonish vision of American violence seems more than vindicated.

The film's Klan leader is modeled closely on the kind of real-life Klan organizer that Ross Milroy profiled in his article on the incidents on which the film is based. This leader's attempt to organize "his people" would be ludicrous if it were not so homicidal: "We are already aware of Communist agents among the refugee community who are actively stirring up trouble between blacks, Mexicans, and Vietnamese in Houston and elsewhere in the United States. There are a number of Vietnam veterans like myself who might want to do some good old search and destroy right here in Texas. They don't have to ship me 12,000 miles to kill Communists. I can do it right here. They trained me for it, and with sufficient motivation, I'm ready."

Although there is no Alamo Bay in Texas, there certainly was a battle for the Alamo, and Malle captures in his title the siege mentality of the Texas vets when they are faced with another wave of the "Mexicans" they thought they had defeated. Besides the film's title, Malle points to the violent history of Texas in a brief scene featuring a worker named Luis. When Shang asks Luis what he thinks of the "Vietmanese" (sic) taking all the fish, Luis replies, simply enough, "I'm a Mexican," and refuses further comment.

The screenwriter, Alice Arlen, was also the co-author (with Nora Ephron) of *Silkwood*. Both screenplays demonstrate a feel for the frustrations of workers who are being displaced, they think, by the manipulation of a lot of liberal do-gooders.

See also: *Who Killed Vincent Chin?*
Availability: Easy.

Further reading

Canby, Vincent. "Screen: 'Alamo Bay,' Ethnic Strife in Texas." *New York Times*, 3 April 1985, C23. A negative but comprehensive review: "Its mediocrity is especially surprising" in view of the director's previous credits.

Milloy, Ross. "Vietnam Fallout in a Texas Town." *New York Times Magazine*, 6 April 1980, 39–56. A comprehensive article about the original events retold in the film.

New York Times: "Americans and Vietnamese Agree on Fishing Limits," 17 April 1980, 20; "Videotapes of Klan Leader Shown at Shrimper Hearing," 13 May 1981, A18; "750 Attend Klan Rally for Fishermen in Texas," 15 February 1981, I36. Samples of the news coverage of the Seadrift incidents and the Klan's involvement, highlighting (in the second article) "a fishing dinghy labeled 'U.S.S. Viet Cong.' "

À l'attaque!

To the bank!

2000, 90 mins., France, French, with English subtitles
Director: Robert Guédiguian
Screenplay: Robert Guédiguian and Jean-Louis Milesi
CAST
Xavier = Jacques Piellier
Yvan = Denis Podalydès
Lola = Ariane Ascaride
M. Moreau = Pierre Banderet
Marthe = Frédérique Bonnal
Henri = Patrick Bonnel
Neils, the banker = Alain Lenglet
Mouloud = Miloud Nacer
Vanessa = Laetitia Pesenti
Pépé Moliterno = Jacques Boudet
The old man = Francis Caviglia
The baby = Romane Dahan
Jean-Do = Jean-Pierre Darroussin

À l'attaque! is an unusual kind of anti-globalization comedy, featuring a family of immigrant workers and their hangers-on in L'Estaque, a working-class quarter in the French port of Marseilles made famous years ago by paintings by Paul Cézanne. Since these second-generation Italian workers are owner-operators of an auto repair garage, they are not exploited in the most obvious ways, such as police harassment, racism, and unemployment. They are nonetheless caught in a particularly difficult economic squeeze. Their formerly generous bank officer has called in their loan, but the money to pay off the loan does not come in because their biggest client—a container shipping business significantly named Eurocontaineur—is cleverly moving fiscal operations elsewhere and declaring bankruptcy locally.

The director, Robert Guédiguian, son of an Armenian dockworker and a German mother, specializes in working-class comedies with a political edge. He uses virtually the same actors from film to film, such as *Marius and Jeannette* (1997), the love story of a grieving widow and a security guard, set in a neighborhood of socialists similar to L'Estaque, and *À la place du coeur* (1998), an interracial love story whose youngsters must survive a racist policeman's vendetta (adapted from James Baldwin's *If Beale Street Could Talk*).

Unlike these two films, however, *À l'attaque!* is a postmodern film, with its sturdy and comically melodramatic plot interrupted every once in a while by an increasingly absurd conversation between the film's supposed two screenwriters (actors as well, of course). The screenwriters bicker, write, rewrite, introduce new characters at will, and change the plot as they struggle with each other. The older writer is more of a traditional humanist, desiring character development and clear ideas, while the younger one wants sex, more sex, and even gratuitous bonking if necessary. When we first see them "writing the film," the entire cast peers over the fence of the garden of the older screenwriter, who is asleep, demanding that he wake up and give them something to do.

Guédiguian is an eternal optimist, a socialist with deep faith in the survival of ordinary working-class people.

See also: *Human Resources*.
Availability: UK (PAL standard only).

Further reading

French, Philip. "Do the Ends Justify the Means?" *Observer Review* (London), 22 July 2001, 7. Positive review stressing Guédiguian's "warmhearted movies about ordinary working folk."

Romney, Jonathan. "A Fresh, French Marxist Spark." *Independent* (London), 22 July 2001, 10. "The frothiest study of Marxist economics you're ever likely to see."

Note: Also known as *Charge!*

⚉

America and Lewis Hine

Photographing "hell with the lid off"

1984, 60 mins.
Director: Nina Rosenblum
Traditional documentary
PRINCIPAL FIGURES
Lewis Hine, photographer
John Crowley, Jason Robards, and Maureen Stapleton, narrators
Walter Rosenblum, photographer
Anthony "Shorty" Slick, coal miner
Harold McClain, ironworker

The career of Lewis Hine was the result of the remarkable moment in American cultural history when the expanding industrial machine, massive immigration, and the concentration of the urban poor and working classes imploded. "Hell with the lid off" was Pittsburgh, but metaphorically, of course, it was virtually any major industrial city at the beginning of the twentieth century.

Nina Rosenblum documents the career of America's premiere photographer of this immigrant and working-class experience, especially that of child labor. Although most traditional documentaries use a mixture of archival motion picture footage and still photographs, I felt that in this instance the footage upstaged Hine's photos, which should have been the starring exhibits. Some of this archival footage is amazing and rarely seen, while Hine's stills have been exhibited and reproduced many times over as book illustrations and jacket photos.

Hine really began his career in the early 1900s by winning the confidence of some of the 15,000 immigrants from Southern and Eastern Europe who passed through Ellis Island every day. He literally followed these immigrants to the Lower East Side and other tenement areas of New York City, photographing whole families making a dollar a day fashioning artificial flowers or—with three-year-old children helping—shelling a hundred pounds of nuts on a Sunday. The 1907 *Pittsburgh Survey,* with Hine's photographs, scored a double first: it was one of the first statistical studies of an American city and the first to use photography to make such a survey compelling. When one person in Pittsburgh said that he lived *under* America, not *in* it, the direction of Hine's career was set: he would expose such an unjust world.

He worked for ten years for the National Child Labor Committee, photographing children at work in southern textile mills, mines, and tenant farms. In one photo he exhibited a mill run virtually entirely by children—a hundred children in grubby clothes except for one boy in a suit, with a football: the mill superintendent's son. Hine was probably the first guerrilla photographer: when he was refused entry to a factory, he would get in somehow and shoot away. He traveled more than 50,000 miles a year for the committee, making the photographs deemed essential to prove their contentions about the horrors of child labor—working in a river in Texas, rolling cigars in Tampa, picking cranberries in Maryland, harvesting beets in Colorado, and picking cotton in Texas. Some establishment figures called his photos fakes, but he documented how the working class contributed to middle-class Americans' comforts.

Back in the urban jungle, some of his famous photos were of newsies and telegraph boys. One particularly famous photo shows a boy asleep on his stack of papers on a staircase. The committee he worked for was barely out of the Victorian era: for them "the moral dangers [were] more deadly than circular saws."

His photos helped the committee lead President Woodrow Wilson to sign the first child labor law in 1916. With war patriotism in full swing, however, the law was declared invalid so that more and more children could go back into the factories to help with war production. After the war, he turned to the images of workers we now see as heroic: a shot of men high in the air working on the Empire State Building became his signature. He created a genre of romantic industrial images as he tried to portray the workers as athletes and acrobats. He himself would take a daring ride out on the arm of a derrick to get just the right monumental look to his shots. As a photographer for unions and other progressive groups, he created some of the most startling images of the 1920s: one classic, often reprinted, shows a worker framed inside a giant wheel, tightening a nut.

Hine's career virtually collapsed during the Depression. The major photographic survey of this era was conducted by the federal Farm Security Administration, led by Roy Strykker, who simply did not like Hine, perhaps because of his independent spirit. By 1940 he was broke and he died soon after. His photos are, of course, an amazing legacy.

See also: Daens.

Availability: Selected collections; Cinema Guild.

Further reading

Hine, Lewis. *America and Lewis Hine*. New York: Aperture, 1977. The book that formed the inspiration for this documentary.

——. *Men at Work: Photographic Studies of Modern Men and Machines*. New York: Macmillan, 1932. New York: Dover, 1977. The only book of Hine's work published during his lifetime.

——. *Women at Work: 153 Photographs*. Ed. Jonathan L. Doherty. New York: Dover, 1981. The photos in this collection, published after Hine's death, emphasize the "positive documentation" of women workers, to distinguish them from his "reform" photos, which "show the evils of the industrial society—slums, tenements, and tiny children behind giant looms" (from Doherty's Introduction).

Pardi, Robert. "America and Lewis Hine." At ⟨www.tvguide.com⟩. The reviewer is very impressed with the film's success in restoring Hine to his social and cultural context: "This eloquent movie is a somber history of the immigrant experience and America's industrial revolution, as well as a biography of an individualist staunchly dedicated to using his camera as a weapon of enlightenment."

American Dream

Local P-9 vs. everybody

1990, 100 mins., PG-13
Director: Barbara Kopple
Cinema verité documentary

American Dream earned Kopple her second Academy Award for best documentary; her first was for the classic *Harlan County, U.S.A.,* which, like many documentaries that focus on labor conflict, presents the perspectives of two groups: labor and management. In the case of *American Dream,* the conflict was between local union P-9 of the United Food and Commercial Workers and Hormel Meats of Austin, Minnesota, but here there was a third side to present: that of the local's international union. And just in case we want to blame the messenger, Kopple didn't make up the three sides. They were real.

Kopple and her crew worked on this film for five years, first as part of the action in Minnesota soon after the strike began in 1985. When asked how she felt about working on the same project for so long, she replied: "I feel really lucky. I feel lucky because I've been trusted by people. I've been able to go in behind closed doors and have people really trust me. I've had people pour out their hearts and souls to me and not feel awkward about doing it" (quoted in Di Mattia).

The strike began in 1985 when Hormel proposed a cut in pay and other givebacks during contract negotiations. The members of Local P-9 felt betrayed because in 1978, in order to keep Hormel in Austin, they had in a sense subsidized a new $100 million plant by agreeing to put their incentive pay into an escrow account that would float a $20 million loan to Hormel. Now Hormel was violating that settlement by making new demands. Although the local had a militant beginning (a sit-down strike in 1933 created the local), it had not had a strike since then.

Unfortunately, the national leaders of the United Food and Commercial Workers felt that Local P-9's strike was ill timed and did not accord with their national strategy of pattern bargaining, which might involve some concessions. Further disagreements arose when P-9 decided to hire the controversial Ray Rogers, head of Corporate Campaign, Inc., as a consultant.

Kopple's approach in filming a complicated situation also helped to create the controversy over the film. Because she so carefully presents the strengths and weaknesses of all three sides in the conflict and because she profiles three extremely strong participants (P-9 president Jim Guyette, Ray Rogers, and Lewie Anderson of the UFCW), viewers sometimes cannot tell what her position is.

Of course, the simple answer is that she supports no particular group. As a cinema verité filmmaker, she supposedly records; she doesn't judge. In *Harlan County, U.S.A.,* however, she may film "objectively," but she is clearly inside the strikers' camp.

Despite what appears to be Kopple's efforts to let her characters speak for themselves, I have always felt that Ray Rogers comes off much less positively than Guyette or Anderson. (The opening-night crowd at the New York Film Festival, where the film premiered, booed Rogers when he was introduced.) Rogers seems somewhat arrogant, a know-it-all, more than a little disdainful of the gains international unions have made. Both Rogers and Guyette feel that the UFCW is selling them down the river, conceding too much to the company.

By the time the film ends, the gloom is pervasive. Brothers are enemies; a rump caucus, nicknamed "P-10" by the P-9 loyalists, is criticizing Guyette's handling of the strike. Eventually P-10 gains control of the local. Rogers's strategy is shown at least in this instance to be unsuccessful. Anderson is dismissed from the UFCW's packinghouse division unit and eventually organizes a reform movement.

At last count, five books have been written about what may be one of the best-documented strikes of the modern era.

Viewers may have to consult one of them or articles about the strike before they can make a final judgment on the complex struggles Kopple attempts to capture in the film.

See also: *Harlan County, U.S.A.*
Availability: Selected collections; Movies Unlimited.

Further reading

Crowdus, Gary, and Richard Porton. "American Dream: An Interview with Barbara Kopple." *Cineaste* 18 (1991): 37–38, 41. A detailed discussion of her access to participants in all aspects of the conflict.

Di Mattia, Joseph. "Of Politics and Passion." *International Documentary,* Winter 1990–91, 12–16. Another good interview with Kopple.

Green, Hardy. *On Strike at Hormel: The Struggle for a Democratic Labor Movement.* Philadelphia: Temple University Press, 1990. Although the book is solidly anti-UFCW and its subtitle promises more than it can deliver, this is still a very thorough and revealing history of this strike, written by a former Corporate Campaign associate and later a *Business Week* writer.

Hage, Dave, and Paul Klauda. *No Retreat, No Surrender: Labor's War at Hormel.* New York: Morrow, 1989. A detailed, readable, fairly neutral account of the strike by two reporters.

Horowitz, Roger. "American Dream." *American Historical Review,* October 1992, 1170–72. In analyzing Kopple's "brilliant but flawed documentary," the reviewer is bothered that the film "slights the non-wage issues," does not explore the "UFCW's—and Anderson's—significant culpability in the failure of the strike," and does not recognize the "high visibility in the strike" of the strikers' wives.

——. *"Negro and White, Unite and Fight!" A Social History of Industrial Unionism in Meatpacking, 1930–1990.* Urbana: University of Illinois Press, 1997. Analyzes the strategy of P-9, concluding that they created "a movement that combined broad participation of working-class people with a coherent strategy for subduing a multiplant national corporation."

Klawans, Stuart. "Films." *Nation,* 30 March 1992, 425–28. An excellent review: the film is "moving; it's absorbing; it understands everything but is too wise to pardon all."

Main, Jeremy. "The Labor Rebel Leading the Hormel Strike." *Fortune,* 9 June 1986, 105–10. A positive profile of Rogers, the controversial labor consultant, although the article states: "Consultant Ray Rogers looked like an organizing genius after his tactics helped force textile giant J.P. Stevens Co. to sign a union contract. Today he is leading Hormel's strikers to disastrous defeat."

Moody, Kim. *An Injury to All: The Decline of American Unionism.* London: Verso, 1988. Argues that the "elements of the P-9/United Support Group/Corporate Campaign Inc. infrastructure built in Austin and the aggressive solidarity campaign launched from it are a model of what unionism can be," although P-9 lost (presumably and primarily because of the failure of the UFCW); includes an analysis of the UFCW's pattern bargaining during the Hormel strike.

"'More' Is Less and Less: Thirties' Tactics, Unions Learn, Don't Work in the 'Eighties." *Barron's,* 24 February 1986, 11. An early gloating editorial in the business press about P-9's fight with the international.

Rachleff, Peter. *Hard-Pressed in the Heartland: The Hormel Strike and the Future of the Labor Movement.* Boston: South End Press, 1993. A leader of community support groups for the strike offers overall an excellent survey of the issues and criticizes Kopple's film for being too pro-UFCW.

Roberts, Sam. "'American Dream' Charts Labor's Loss." *New York Times,* 24 May 1992, II.16. Reviews the film as "a labor nightmare from real life."

Rule, Sheila. "A Film Maker Balancing the Inequities of Life." *New York Times,* 24 March 1992, B1. Another interview with Kopple and a survey of her career.

Schleuning, Neala J. *Women, Community, and the Hormel Strike of 1985–86.* Westport, Conn.: Greenwood Press, 1994. Extensive interviews with the women of the Austin United Support Group, a key factor in the campaign and one (according to some viewers) undervalued in Kopple's filming.

Slaughter, Jane. "Ray Rogers: 'Workers Don't Have to Keep Losing.'" *Progressive,* June 1988, 26–28. An interview with Rogers: "There have to be reforms in unions like the UFCW. There are some awfully sleazy leaders at the top of the labor movement, and they are the biggest obstacles to workers winning."

Web sites:

⟨www.reapinc.org⟩ Official site of Research-Education-Advocacy-People (REAP), an "organization founded in 1989 by a small

number of UFCW members and union officers," including Lewie Anderson, and presumably reflects his viewpoint: the UFCW's "sabotage of its own Packinghouse Division, mid-term contract concessions, 'sweetheart' deals with employers for union membership numbers and substandard contract settlements drove the wages down in the meat packing industry."
⟨www.gen.umn.edu/faculty_staff/yahnke/filmteach /teach1.htm⟩ Detailed summary of the film.

ᔰ
American Job

American disaster

1995, 90 mins.
Director: Chris Smith
Screenplay: Chris Smith, Randy Russell, Doug Ruschaupt, based on Randy Russell's essays published in his own 'zine, *American Job*
CAST

The American Worker = Randy Russell
Factory Manager = Matt Collier
Telemarketing Manager = Ed English
Tom = Tom Wheeler
Cook = Eric Lezotte
Housekeeper = Dan Layne
Bartender = Mike Hope
Guy = Guy Wagner

Alas for the Clintonian economics of the 1990s, this film is the perfect (and scary) antidote to all the "growing the economy" fixes of his administration. Filmed in what seems to be a mock-doc, cinema verité style, Randy—our antihero, despite his credit title of "The American Worker"—launches himself into the workaday world in a series of what used to be called dead-end jobs, but which now, of course, are called service industry jobs. Virtually all of the jobs represent special niches—cleaning services, central warehousing and distribution centers, entertainment complex staff—which in the 1990s were booming and seemed always to be hiring.

What is not booming is Randy Scott, who is played by Randy Russell with such low energy and attentiveness that it's clear that the interview for any job is not going to end with his employment. Randy drifts from job to job, seven in all: cleaning motel rooms, guessing people's weight at an amusement park, tending a machine that makes a little plastic gizmo (function unknown), cleaning in a fast-food restaurant, taking inventory on the night shift in a warehouse, telemarketing, and, finally, as a convenience store clerk. Randy rarely receives sufficient training for these jobs, management assuming (perhaps rightly) that menial jobs require no explanation.

The slow-paced documentary-style film has set itself a formidable challenge—how to make real-time boring experiences come alive in film time. Randy's employment history—after he was "in housekeeping" at an amusement park hotel in Sandusky, Ohio, he was "promoted" to attendant at a guess-your-weight booth—seemed to promise improvement in his career path. At a plastics factory he works at an injection molding machine where he must push a button once every 45 seconds. Yes, you guessed it, for the other 44 seconds he must be at the ready but is bored out of his skull. As he tries to figure out how to stimulate himself during the wait, he neglects his trainer's absolute rule "never to let the hopper run dry" and his machine crashes. He walks out, only to return the next day to be fired in what should be regarded as one of the classic moments in worker-management absurdity. His boss insists that Randy take his chair and tell him, boss-acting-as-Randy, what he, Randy-acting-as-boss, would do. Randy says quietly, "Fire me?"

The humor of the film is bittersweet, since we know so many people actually stuck at the jobs Randy cannot even begin to handle. The manager of a fast-food chicken shop has him clean both the fryers and the bathrooms: "It's a tough job, but from what I hear, you'll be up to it." After three days Randy hears a fellow worker mocking a warehouse job; Randy feels compelled to take it. At the warehouse job, his fellow workers dream of winning the lottery, but Randy is mostly fascinated by a man who "dries" his luncheon meat in the back window of his car. Some reviewers (such as Marjorie Baumgarten) see Randy's refusal to cope as mildly rebellious; I'm not so sure. His passivity can get on the viewers' nerves, too.

Chris Smith was the director of photography on Michael Moore's *The Big One* and has also done segments of John Pierson's *Split Screen* for cable. *American Job* originated in a magazine by the same title that Smith developed in 1987, "a collection of job stories from low-wage workers around the country" (Web site below). The lead actor, Randy Russell, has a piece on dishwashing on the on-line magazine as well. Some of the contributors to the magazine were the director's friends: "At least 90 percent of our friends are still working these kinds of jobs, for which there is seemingly no way out that I can see" (quoted by Patricia Thomson).

Smith shot *American Job* for only $14,000, using nonprofessionals in the cast. It turns out that these nonprofessionals for the most part were playing workers who, like themselves, will take dead-end jobs while waiting for something better to come along; in their case, they are waiting to act in a film.

Smith's next film was a documentary, *American Movie,* a portrait of an amateur filmmaker that easily convinces viewers that he should never give up his day job. Unfortunately for him, his day job is too typical of underachieving Randy, American Worker.

See also: Fast Food Women.
Availability: Selected collections; Web site below.

Further reading

Baumgarten, Marjorie. "American Job." *Austin Chronicle,* 3 September 1998. Sums up the plight of the workers in this film as suggesting that "playing the lottery is a sound business investment."
Thomson, Patricia. "On 'American Job,' 'Dadetown,' and 'Struggles in Steel.'" *Independent,* June 1996, 33–38. Discusses three very different and important films, all released the same year and all showcased at the Sundance Film Festival.

Web site:
⟨www.americanmovie.com/amjob/index.html⟩ The director's official Web site, which features the filmmaker's various projects, including his (now) on-line magazine, *American Job,* and offers his videos for sale.

An American Romance

Labor and capital make nice

1944, 122 mins.
Director: King Vidor
Screenplay: Herbert Dalmas and William Ludwig
CAST
Steve Dangos = Brian Donlevy
Anna = Ann Richards
Howard Clinton = Walter Abel
Anton Dubechek = John Qualen
Teddy Dangos = Stephen McNally

Having made three successful films with populist themes in the late 1920s and 1930s (*The Crowd, Our Daily Bread,* and *The Citadel*), Vidor saw his predominantly progressive spirit apparently evaporate in the war years. Perhaps it was a mistake to jettison the first script for *American Romance*, by Louis Adamic, the chronicler of American labor violence in *Dynamite* (1934); as Francis R. Walsh has argued, the new scriptwriter gave Vidor a Horatio Alger rags-to-riches story with a bizarre strike as its resolution.

Immigrant Steve Dangos starts out as an ironworker in the Mesabi Range of Minnesota, moves to an Ohio steel mill, and eventually gains control of his own auto company. Because the post-Adamic script eliminated the sit-down strike at his auto factory—in response to the Breen office's censorship of the most important union tactic of the 1930s—Steve's workers miraculously disappear from the factory at one moment only to reappear with Steve's son Teddy as their bargaining representative. (He had been "learning the line" on the factory floor.) In a scene reminiscent of the father-son (brain-heart) unity of Fritz Lang's *Metropolis* and with some new lessons in fascistic collectivism (Teddy: "Why don't we have faith in each other?"), the strike is settled.

Vidor's faith in an open-shop industry is obvious, as is his belief in the intrinsic power and beauty of the American factory: documentary footage, shot by Vidor himself, of an auto assembly line and of an aircraft factory reinforce the view that the unions have a formidable job, especially if they choose the boss's son as their negotiator.

See also: *Our Daily Bread.*
Availability: Not.

Further reading

Dowd, Nancy, and David Shepard. *King Vidor.* Metuchen, N.J.: Scarecrow Press, 1988. Among other things, discusses Vidor's inclusion of documentary-style industrial sequences in the film.

Walsh, Francis R. "The Films We Never Saw: American Movies View Organized Labor, 1934–1954." *Labor History* 27 (1986): 564–80. Contains an excellent short section on the production background of the film.

⤶
American Standoff

Hoffa to the second power

2002, 95 mins.
Director: Kristi Jacobson
Cinema verité documentary
PRINCIPAL FIGURES
James P. Hoffa, president, Teamsters
Jimmy Hoffa, former president, Teamsters
John Murphy, local president
Hope Hampelman, Mike, and Lenny,
   Teamster truckers
Leo Suggs, CEO, Overnite Transportation

There is really more than one standoff in this documentary about the contemporary Teamsters, produced by Barbara Kopple, who helped the director, Kristi Jacobson, with advice and even pitched in on the filming of a significant number of sequences.

The primary standoff is between the Teamsters, led by James P. Hoffa, son of the legendary Jimmy Hoffa, and Overnite Transportation, the vehemently anti-union trucking arm of the Union Pacific (Rail) Corporation. The film documents the first eighteen months of the standoff, which was called off in late 2002.

Another standoff is between James P. Hoffa and his father, or, to put it another way, between a new generation of Teamsters led by one Hoffa and a powerful historical force, the old Teamsters, led by his father. And although this film is cinema verité, with extensive sequences of direct action and interaction, the old ways are represented by archival footage (more typical of traditional documentaries) of Jimmy Hoffa and his past battles. And even viewers sympathetic to the current Teamsters' struggle with a powerful adversary will have to sigh and say, "Those were the days!"

The complications of contemporary Teamster history and its contested leadership also form part of the difficult situation portrayed in the film. James P. Hoffa lost his first close election to Ron Carey of the UPS, only to win a second election when federal overseers accused Carey of cheating on campaign funds. Although Carey was subsequently exonerated, Hoffa nonetheless retained his presidency, albeit of a union divided by allegiance to Carey and what many perceived as the antimobster faction.

Although the situation remains fluid by the end of the film, one cannot help conclude that the legendary Teamster muscle has gone a little flabby in the end.

See also: *Jimmy Hoffa.*
Availability: Selected collections.

Further reading

Hubbell, Anne. "Documentarian Kopple: Creating 'A Sense of Trust.' " *CNN News*, 15 January 2002, at ⟨www.cnn.com/2002/SHOWBIZ/Movies/01/15/sun.barbara.kopple/index.html⟩. Interview with Kopple about the film and her role as active producer.

Web site:
⟨www.teamster.org/overnite⟩ The Teamsters' site
on the strike and its history in the courts and in
front of the National Labor Relations Board
(NLRB).

↩

And the Earth Did Not Swallow Him

The Midwest migrant stream

1994, 99 mins.
Director: Severo Pérez
Screenplay: Severo Pérez, from Tomás
   Rivera's novella *Y no se lo tragó la tierra.*
CAST
Marcos = José Alcalá
Bartolo = Danny Valdez
Florentina = Rose Portillo
Joaquín = Marco Rodríguez
Lupita = Evelyn Guerrero
Doña Rosa = Lupe Ontiveros
El Mojado = Sal López

This film is based on what must be a unique
literary document—a novella written by
Tomás Rivera, a former migrant worker who
became a professor of Spanish and eventually chancellor of the University of
California at Riverside. His experience as a
child of migrant workers is distilled in the
novella, but Rivera wrote other stories,
essays, and poems about the Chicano experience in the Southwest. Rivera was born in
Texas of a migrant family who spent many
months every year working throughout the
Midwest. As he grew older, his parents
allowed him to work with them only three
months of the year, reserving the rest of the
year for his schooling.

   Luis Leal has written that Rivera's novella
"exalts the values of the Chicano family (*la
casa*), the community (*el barrio*), and the
struggle [*la lucha*] to obtain justice." These
three elements are captured in the film adaptation as well. The young boy's slightly older
voice-over recounts a variety of episodes,

some amusing, some very disturbing, that
punctuate the migrant family's year as they
move out from Crystal City, Texas, to the
near and far Midwest. They even journey as
far north as Minnesota, where the boy takes
some solace in the neat, imposing grave-
stones in a garden-like setting for the northern dead, quite unlike the ragtag, scrappy
graveyard where the migrants bury their
dead, a dusty space marked by a gate sign
that begs, "No me olvídes" (Don't forget me).
In fact, the boy can never forget his youth, as
scenes and images tumble out of his mind
and establish the continuities of the family's
and the community's culture.

   This film, like its source novella, is about
migrant labor culture and its hardships.
When an oily salesman of "three-
dimensional" painted wood images comes by
to solicit their business, they reluctantly part
with 25 of their hard-earned dollars and the
only photograph of the boy's brother, who is
missing in action in Korea. Since the army
had represented one of the few ways out of
migrant labor, it is especially sad when we
realize that not only have they been swindled
but they have lost the only image they had of
their loved one.

   The rickety truck that carries the family to
the fields, the backbreaking labor, the
chicken coops they are forced to live in,
the sicknesses that strike in the blazing sun,
the casual viciousness of their supervisors—
all these features of the migrant laborers' lot
are graphically and movingly (but almost too
beautifully) presented. These features are
virtually identical in Tom Gries's 1973 film,
The Migrants, which features a white family,
reminding us that the situation is at its heart
an economic one, not simply an ethnic or
racial one.

   Although *And the Earth Did Not Swallow
Him* was produced for noncommercial television and eventually went straight to video,
it has a more daring cinematic structure than
many such ventures. Like the source novella,
the film fractures a clear narrative line
numerous times, moving us back and forth
from one incident in the past to a contem-

porary moment. The result is occasionally disorienting but visually stimulating. The boy's placidity is sometimes unnerving, as in scene after scene we see him registering with only slight variations in emotion both amusing and horrendous events in the life of his family and community.

But the matter-of-fact attitude of the boy is very close to Rivera's original conception. In the novella he narrates briefly a scene—omitted from the film—reminiscent of *Harvest of Shame:* a truck of packed workers collided with a car and burst into flames. The section concludes with only these four words: "There were sixteen dead."

The film was the feature film debut of Pérez, who had once been a playwright for the Farm Workers' El Teatro Campesino. The *corrida* singer or balladeer was played by Danny Valdez, who starred in *Zoot Suit,* a dramatization from a Chicano point of view of the L.A. zoot suit riots of the 1940s.

See also: *Angel City; The Migrants.*
Availability: Selected collections.

Further reading

James, Caryn. "Going Straight to Video Stores." *New York Times,* 11 April 1997, B19–20. Because the film did not play theatrically, it received only some tiny but positive notices, such as this one: "The film accumulates its power through calm realism and small touches."

Kamiya, Gary. "A Touching Story of Migrant Laborers." *San Francisco Examiner,* 22 September 1995, C3. A "slight but sincere film" that "records the experiences of a dispossessed people."

Leal, Luis. "Tomás Rivera." In *Chicano Writers, First Series,* ed. Francisco A. Lomeli and Carl R. Shirley, vol. 82 of *Dictionary of Literary Biography.* Detroit: Gale, 1989. A biographical and critical survey of Rivera's career.

Rivera, Tomás. *The Complete Works.* Ed. Julián Olivares. Houston: Arte Publico Press, 1991. The definitive collection of the author's work, including the novella on which the film is based, here translated as *And the Earth Did Not Devour Him.*

Angel City

Hell town

1980, 90 mins., TVM
Directors: Philip Leacock and Steve Carver
Screenplay: James Lee Barrett, from
    Patrick Smith's novel of the same title
CAST
Silas Creedy = Mitchell Ryan
Jared Teeter = Ralph Waite
Cloma Teeter = Jennifer Warren
Kristy Teeter = Jennifer Jason Leigh
Bennie Teeter = Robert MacNaughton
Cy = Paul Winfield
Fred = Bob Hannah
Loan Shark = Will Knickerbocker
Jabbo = Bob Minor
Sud = Red West

Although this film focuses on one poor white family who are trapped in a prison-like migrant laborers' camp near Everglades National Park in Florida, the plot has implications for the plight of all migrant workers. Like the earlier *Migrants* in 1974 and the later *Long Road Home* in 1991, *Angel City* uses some of the conventions and stereotypes of the TV movie genre to its advantage: we have a poor white family in the midst of agricultural plenty, taken advantage of by a virtually lawless society controlled by their employers. This startling summary holds true whether the film is set in the Depression or in the contemporary era.

When the Jeeter family falls into the clutches of Silas Creedy and his thugs, we watch in horror as not only their dignity but their daughter is subjected to Creedy's viciousness. When Creedy decides to replace the daughter he's allowed his men to abuse with the Teeters' new baby as a hostage to prevent them from leaving, we realize that even pond scum can sink. Teeter could see trouble coming, but he wanted a job so badly that he went along with Creedy, who, casting a dirty look at the family dog, says: "I wasn't informed about no dogs. Dogs are counterproductive." And when Jeeter balks about the locked gate, Creedy looks him up and down and adds, "I do hope you are not going to be counter-productive."

The abuses in this film are phenomenal and sometime even hard to watch, yet such things have happened in varying degrees to migrant families for generations. What seems a holdover from the awful conditions of *The Grapes of Wrath* continues to happen, sometimes in a way that the law cannot touch, as when crew leaders keep their workers poor by charging them high fees they virtually cannot work off, as in the film *Migrants*, and sometimes illegally, as in the hell that is Angel City or even—to choose another Florida example—the confinement of Mexican-American migrant laborers in *Legacy of Shame*.

See also: *Migrants; Legacy of Shame*.
Availability: Selected collections.

Further reading

Smith, Patrick D. *Angel City*. St. Petersburg: Valkyrie Press, 1978. The source novel.

Note: Also known as *Field of Tears*.

∽
The Angry Silence

Like murderous bees

1960, 95 mins., B&W, UK
Director: Guy Green
Screenplay: Bryan Forbes
CAST
Tom = Richard Attenborough
Anna = Pier Angeli
Joe = Michael Craig
Connolly = Bernard Lee
Travers = Alfred Burke
Davis = Geoffrey Keen
Martindale = Laurence Naismith

Faced with an unsanctioned walkout led by an unscrupulous shop leader who follows the advice of an outsider (no doubt a Communist), family man Tom (played by Richard Attenborough, who also co-produced the film) says no and returns to work. For this act of defiance he is sent "into Coventry" (given the silent treatment) by his mates, bullied by the shop steward, and betrayed by his best friend. Furthermore, his son is injured in a tarring incident and Tom is attacked and loses an eye, all because he has broken the rule of union solidarity. The film ekes out a superficially happy ending, with some of Tom's workmates showing guilt and sorrow.

Because the behavior of the union members in the film was so vicious, several British unions urged a boycott. Attenborough was incensed: "This sort of fascist behavior is just what the film is about. Mob rule by a few scheming communists" (quoted by John Hill). But even the *New York Times* reviewer emphasized that "a particular and arbitrary set of circumstances has been organized in this film," and that even though it is "one of the best" films of the year from Britain, one must be careful "lest one find oneself distrusting the entire working class."

See also: *I'm All Right, Jack*.
Availability: UK (PAL standard only).

Further reading

Crowther, Bosley. "The Angry Silence." *New York Times*, 13 December 1960, 25. An appreciative American review.
Hill, John. *Sex, Class, and Realism: British Cinema, 1956–1963*. London: British Film Institute, 1986. Discusses the film in the context of similar British features.
Stead, Peter. *Film and the Working Class*. London: Routledge, 1989. Discusses the film in the British cultural context and makes some interesting comparisons with *On the Waterfront*.

∽
Año Nuevo

Old ways

1981, 55 mins.
Director: Todd Darling
Mixed traditional and agitprop documentary

Donald Garibalci, owner, Año Nuevo
Flower Ranch

Bonafacio Gómez, Gabriel Salgado, and
other workers

Peter Baird, North American Congress on
Latin America (NACLA)

Richard Fagen, political scientist

Jorge Bustamente, sociologist

The Año Nuevo workers were mostly undocumented Mexican nationals who came to pick flowers in Pescadero, on the San Mateo coast south of San Francisco. Through a connection with a Tijuana coyote, they paid $250 for illegal passage to the United States.

At the Año Nuevo Ranch they lived in substandard housing, for which $45 a month was deducted from their pay. Fear of deportation generally keeps such workers in line. What makes this film so unusual is that it follows a court case brought by the Año Nuevo workers, an unprecedented and successful legal action by noncitizens for back pay and money illegally deducted. It is not likely that such a feat could be repeated today.

See also: *Legacy of Shame.*
Availability: Selected collections; Cinema
Guild.

Further reading

Iovine, Julie V. "Not Just a Roof, But Roots for a Season." *New York Times*, 26 October 2000, B1, 12. Documents a crusading architect's drive to design—and persuade growers to build—low-cost comfortable housing for migrant workers.

⤶

A. Philip Randolph: For Jobs and Freedom

A prime mover

1996, 86 mins.
Director: Dante James
Traditional documentary

A. Philip Randolph, founder and president
of the Brotherhood of Sleeping Car
Porters (BSCP)

Lynne Thigpen, narrator

William Harris, president, Alabama State
University

John Bracey, Nelson Lichtenstein, and John
Hope Franklin, professors

Maida Springer-Kemp, labor organizer

Dr. Dorothy Height, president, National
Council of Negro Women

Paula Pfeffer, author

Leroy Shackleford, former Pullman porter

C. L. Dellums, vice president, BSCP

E. D. Nixon, former Pullman porter and
organizer of Montgomery bus boycott

James Farmer, founder of Congress of
Racial Equality (CORE)

Congressman John Lewis, member of
Student Nonviolent Coordinating
Committee (SNCC)

A. Philip Randolph occupies a prominent niche in labor history as the leader of the black Brotherhood of Sleeping Car Porters, the union that achieved the first national labor agreement for its employees in 1931. Because this important victory was only part of Randolph's history, this film will go a long way to establish the context for understanding him as one of the pivotal leaders in African American history.

The film documents Randolph's rise to prominence as a leader in the Harlem Renaissance of writers and cultural activists, especially with the founding of *The Messenger*, the militant magazine Randolph and Chandler Owen edited so effectively that the attorney general of the United States called them "the most dangerous Negroes in the U.S."

Randolph proved time after time how dangerous he was to the racist status quo in America by challenging the federal government to change its Jim Crow ways or face an embarrassing march on Washington. So effective was the threat that in the first two instances—challenging Franklin D. Roosevelt to end discrimination in federal hiring and calling on Harry Truman to ban segregation in the armed forces—the marches never had to be held. Against John F. Kennedy's administration he helped to organize the March on Washington forever identified with Martin Luther King's mountaintop oratory.

Like a number of documentaries on African American history, this film demonstrates conclusively that labor history and the history of the campaign for civil rights for all Americans are indissolubly joined.

See also: *At the River I Stand; 10,000 Black Men Named George.*
Availability: Selected collections; California Newsreel.

Further reading

Anderson, Jervis. *A. Philip Randolph*. 1972. Berkeley: University of California Press, 1986. A "biographical portrait."

Bates, Beth Tompkins. *Pullman Porters and the Rise of Protest Politics in Black America, 1925–1945*. Chapel Hill: University of North Carolina Press, 2001. Stresses the importance of the union in developing a distinctive black protest movement.

Goodman, Walter. "Civil Rights before the 60's." *New York Times*, 1 February 1996, B2. Mostly positive review of this "dutiful if slow-paced chronicle," which may come as a "revelation" to those who do not already know the history of the civil rights movement before the 1960s.

Harris, William H. *The Harder We Run: Black Workers since the Civil War*. New York: Oxford University Press, 1982. Although only one chapter covers the BSCP, Harris's discussion gains by its placement among other attempts by black workers to gain jobs in a racist workforce.

——. *Keeping the Faith: A. Philip Randolph, Milton P. Webster, and the Brotherhood of Sleeping Car Porters, 1925–1937*. Urbana: University of Illinois Press, 1977. "Even in ruins," the BSCP was "a lasting and important monument to the progress of Afro-Americans."

Pfeffer, Paula. *A. Philip Randolph: Pioneer of the Civil Rights Movement*. Baton Rouge: Louisiana State University Press, 1990. Less a biography than an exploration of "the consequences for the black community of the strategies and movements Randolph devised to help African-Americans attain equality."

Web site:
⟨www.georgemeany.org/archives/apr.html⟩ Extensive on-line exhibit of Randolph's career, with numerous photos and historical documents.

~

At the River I Stand

"One more river to cross before I lay my burden down"

1993, 56 mins.
Directors: David Appleby, Allison Graham, Steven Ross
Traditional documentary
PRINCIPAL FIGURES
Coby Smith, community organizer and leader of the Invaders
Taylor Rogers, Clinton Burrows, sanitation workers
T. O. Jones, local union organizer
Henry Loeb, mayor of Memphis
Jerry Wurf, president, American Federation of State, County, and Municipal Employees (AFSCME)
Rev. Ralph Jackson, leader of boycott
Rev. James Netters, Lewis Donelson, and Bob James, city council members
Martin Luther King Jr., head of the Southern Christian Leadership Council (SCLC)

Martin Luther King Jr.'s famous "I have been to the mountaintop" speech was delivered on 3 April 1968 in Memphis, the day before he was assassinated. *At the River I Stand* reminds us that, although King went to Memphis as part of his Poor People's Campaign, he also went there because 1,300 sanitation workers had been on strike for higher wages and recognition of Local 1733 of AFSCME. The film is a persuasive and moving argument for the position that the Memphis sanitation strike was the culmination of the civil rights struggle in the South. King's assassination changed the strike's status from a local struggle to one of national significance. The assassination also signified the turn in the civil rights movement from

Memphis sanitation workers on strike. Photo by Ernest Withers. Courtesy California Newsreel.

nonviolent to violent protest (although the film suggests that that distinction may itself be problematical).

The film captures the complexity of the civil rights movement, especially in respect to King's sometimes contested leadership. There were at least four contending centers of leadership in Memphis as the struggle evolved: (1) the sanitation workers, strongly united behind the union organizer T. O. Jones; (2) AFSCME's mostly white national leadership, especially Jerry Wurf; (3) the ministerial nonviolent civil rights leaders, including both those on the local scene and Martin Luther King Jr.'s people; and (4) the militant youth of Memphis, including the Invaders, a Black Power group led by Coby Smith. Standing firm against these sometimes united, sometimes quarrelsome allies was the Memphis establishment, led by the city's unyielding mayor, Henry Loeb.

The film carefully traces the various stages of the Memphis struggle, establishing clearly how the sanitation workers, always courted by various leaders, remained steadfast in their determination to prove, as their most famous picket sign indicated, that they were men. Their signs read, "I Am a Man," and they were often photographed by the national media with the tanks of the National Guard rolling down the Memphis streets behind their picket lines.

The impetus for both the film and Joan Turner Beifuss's book *At the River I Stand* was an oral history project involving 364 interviews done by the Memphis Search for Meaning Committee, a group formed by "progressive white Memphians" to try to understand what happened in their city.

See also: *Miles of Smiles, Years of Struggle.*
Availability: Selected collections; California Newsreel.

Further reading

Beifuss, Joan Turner. *At the River I Stand: Memphis, the 1968 Strike, and Martin Luther King*. New York: Carlson, 1989. A very helpful narrative and analysis of the struggle, based on extensive interviews.

Graham, Allison. *Framing the South*. Baltimore: Johns Hopkins University Press, 2001. One of the directors analyzes the images of the civil rights movement and related issues in mainstream films.

Honey, Michael K. *Southern Labor and Black Civil Rights: Organizing Memphis Workers*. Urbana: University of Illinois Press, 1993. Essential historical background to King's visit to Memphis as well as to the film.

⤳

Automation

See it then

1957, 82 mins., B&W
Director: Edward R. Murrow
TV documentary
PRINCIPAL FIGURES
Edward R. Murrow, narrator
Walter Reuther, president, United Auto
  Workers (UAW)
Tom J. Watson Jr., president, IBM
Neville Bean, Ford engineer

This episode of Edward R. Murrow's successful and influential *See It Now* series of feature news stories on CBS came at the dawn of the computer age and its subsequent revolutionizing of American industry through automation. Given his sympathetic view of work and organized labor, Murrow characteristically includes not only industry heavyweights such as Tom J. Watson of IBM and such key union leaders as Walter Reuther but also the men on the front lines of industrial change—workers on the line, local and regional union officers—in order to give a fair view of what was really happening.

The film gives the weight of its argument to the successes of automation in assembly lines, steel production, aircraft, telephone exchanges, frozen food preparation, and even Pap smear analysis. These accomplishments have come at a cost. UAW shop stewards complain about not being notified of changes brought about by automation, but even more worrying, they say, is the unemployment that will result. Similarly union leaders at the Freihofer Bakery in Philadelphia, producing 450,000 loaves a day,

wonder about the need for a shorter workweek.

Murrow would normally cast a cold eye on Cold War hysteria, but at one point an engineer at Ford, having visited an exceptionally "well engineered" and automated ball bearing plant in Russia, says that the Reds may be ahead of us in automation.

The *See It Now* series has become a time machine, but some of its stops in the past may be worth visiting, at least to assess how labor and management coped with rapid technological change.

See also: *Computers in Context.*
Availability: Selected collections.

Further reading

Curtin, Michael. *Redeeming the Wasteland: Television Documentary and Cold War Politics*. New Brunswick: Rutgers University Press, 1995. Traces the explosion of TV documentary from late 1959; includes a section on a later documentary on automation, *The Awesome Servant*, broadcast on ABC by Bell & Howell's *Close Up!* series in October 1961.

Thompson, J. Walter. "Automation—Weal or Woe?" *Variety*, 12 June 1957. For this reviewer it's all weal, as he raves about Murrow's "thoroughly absorbing and sometimes fascinating documentation of automation," although Reuther's warnings about the loss of jobs in the auto industry are duly noted.

⤳

The Awful Truth

"Everything else is pure fiction."—
Advertising slogan

2000, TV (Bravo), first season, 3 cassettes,
  300 mins.; 2001, second season, 3 cassettes,
  300 mins.
Director: Michael Moore
Postmodern TV documentary

Selected Episodes

"Beat the Rich" (working-class Pittsburgh
  vs. Manhattan)

"Crackers vs. Mickey Mouse" (the treatment of employees at Disneyland)

"Sal, the Bill Collector" (longshoreman tries to "collect" 2,000 jobs from UPS)

"The Awful Truth Man of the Year—Ira Rennert" (No. 1 private company polluter)

"150 Feet from NBC" (Ira Rennert's restraining order on Mike)

"Work Care!" (paying health bills by working at a hospital)

"Manpower, Inc."

"Crackers vs. The Egg Farm" (Ohio chicken exploiter criticized)

"NAFTA Mike" (Mike's shadow self from Mexico)

"Strikebreakers" (scabs need health benefits and a living wage)

"The Merger" (a marriage ceremony for Daimler and Chrysler)

The Awful Truth is like *TV Nation*, Moore's first TV (network) series, but on steroids. It is as if the Fourth International of socialists organized a leveraged buyout of the *National Enquirer* and nobody told the staff person who was giving out the new assignments, such as drive a Winnebago stocked with gay men having sex through states with antisodomy laws and see what happens. Or if Swiss banks won't allow descendents of Holocaust victims to claim the assets stolen by the Nazis, then send an Adolf Hitler look-alike to Zurich and fill out some withdrawal slips. Michael Moore does not know the meaning of caution as he bashes his way into capitalist strongholds defending the rights of the underpaid and unemployed.

But is this a series in which labor plays a part? Or is it simply Mondo Capitalismo, with Moore finding the shaggy underbelly of American myths and scratching it silly? The answer to both of these questions is a qualified yes. Nobody else on a national TV program, as far as I know, is publicly calling UPS to account for its contracted promise to offer more jobs as a result of its contract settlement in 2000, or trying to embarrass Disney into treating its workers better, or calling attention to a new trend in management of hospital bills, by having poor patients work in the hospital they were treated in. On the other hand, nobody else is showing close-up shots of a man's neck after a voice box operation or the mock-funeral of a man not yet dead of pancreatic failure.

For Moore, more is always more, never less, never subtle. Bravo's ad campaign was also not subtle: "It's an age of moral outrage and rampant corruption. Relax and enjoy it." The format of *The Awful Truth* is a little off-putting to my eye (and ear), especially since every episode begins with a brilliant credit sequence, featuring heads of the men (such as Bill Gates, Ted Turner, and the UK's Robert Murdock) who virtually control the world's media, after which Moore cuts to the program's tag line, "The People's Democratic Republic of Television," which circles a red star. Moore then takes center stage in front of a live studio audience, talks a little, and runs the tape of an episode. Occasionally he will engage some of the audience in conversations designed to set up the episode. In some ways this follows the format of *TV Nation*, in which Moore often spoke with the people on the streets of New York City, but I find the stand-up routine a little forced and often awkward: usually the tape of the episode speaks for itself. (In the second season of *The Awful Truth*, in 2001, Moore returned to the *TV Nation* format.)

The London *Times* astutely summed up Moore's guerrilla TV approach: "It is the presence of the camera that makes the trap work, because we can enjoy watching Moore's victim feel torn between wanting to punch him for his audacity and knowing that when a camera is pointed at you, the safest thing to do is just smile and squirm." The *Times* concluded that Moore was a "mixture of barking for the underdog and vaudeville" (4 March 1999). Woof.

See also: *The Big One; Roger & Me; TV Nation*.

Availability: Selected collections; Movies Unlimited; DVD.

Further reading

Andrews, Edmund L. "G.M. Opel Unit Say It's Likely to Pay Nazi-Era Slaves." *New York Times*, 14 December 1999. Support for Moore's accusation of G.M.'s profiting from its Nazi subsidiary; also suggests that Ford had "asked Washington for compensation for a [German] factory that Allied forces bombed."

Berger, Warren. "Giving a Guerrilla Journalist the Freedom of Cable." *New York Times*, 4 April 1999, 35. Berger applauds this "labor-loving Everyman, shambling into corporate lobbies and jousting with public relations people," because "Moore's segments touch on serious subjects like race, class, free trade, environmentalism, or health care."

Goodman, Walter. "A One-Man Confrontation Band, Loudly." *New York Times*, 9 April 1999, B28. Sums up Moore as "insistent, persistent and far beyond embarrassment," "satisfyingly outrageous," and a man whose main premise—about Clinton's impeachment manager—is: "Henry Hyde is an adulterer, right?"

Moore, Michael. *Downsize This!* 1996. 2d ed. New York: Crown, 1997. Political satire, with chapters subtly titled "Don't Vote—It Only Encourages Them," "Corporate Crooks Trading Cards," and "Why Are Union Leaders So F#!@ing Stupid?"

Moore, Michael, and Kathleen Glynn. *Adventures in a TV Nation*. New York: HarperPerennial, 1998. A tour through the episodes and characters and issues of the first Moore series on TV.

Web sites:

⟨www.theawfultruth.com⟩ Official program Web site, with certain episodes featured, extensive documentation and links about issues covered, and sometimes clips from the show.

⟨www.michaelmoore.com⟩ His official Web site, which features information about his films.

⟨www.dogeatdogfilms.com⟩ Official Web site of Moore's production company, with numerous discussions of his films, TV shows, and books, including his (sometimes) monthly "Message from Michael Moore" on political and related topics.

⤳

Barbarians at the Gate

Let 'em through

1992, 105 mins., TVM, R
Director: Glenn Jordan

Screenplay: Larry Gelbart, from the book of the same title by Bryan Burrough and John Helyar

CAST

F. Ross Johnson = James Garner
Henry Kravis = Jonathan Pryce
Laurie Johnson = Leilani Sarelle
Peter Cohen = Peter Riegert
Linda Robinson = Joanna Cassidy

As a film about leveraged buyouts, perhaps not quite so effective as its evil twin, *Wall Street,* this HBO film has nonetheless a few moments of enjoyable absurd comedy and numerous sequences based closely on the facts of the eternal battle for the invisible soul of one of American's largest food corporations. Of course, there is always cosmic irony to fall back on: F. Ross Johnson, the CEO of RJR Nabisco, attempts to buy his own company while fending off hostile takeover bids. Complications abound, although everything seems clear when you are watching the film.

James Garner is an acquired taste, but even he sometimes fails to make F. Ross lovable. Johnson is worried about the 140,000 RJR Nabisco employees; what he's not worried about is the effect of his potential $53 million severance package on the company's ledgers. Johnson points out that if anyone at a George Bush Sr./Dan Quayle fund-raiser is worth less than nine figures, you're on food stamps. Such a sensitive guy.

One of the wonderful moments in the film comes when CEO Johnson is checking out one of RJR Nabisco's research breakthroughs—the ill-fated Premiere cigarette venture. The new cigarette did not use tobacco. Unfortunately, those who took the marketing test said that it tasted like excrement. Now that's a marketing challenge.

See also: *Wall Street.*
Availability: Easy; DVD.

Further reading

Burrough, Bryan, and John Helyar. *Barbarians at the Gate*. New York: Harper & Row, 1990. A richly detailed and exhaustive account; the film omitted the Reggie! candy bar promotion, named after the baseball star Reggie Jackson, a friend of Johnson's, who would be showered with the candy bars every time he hit a home run.

Collins, Glenn. "Investors to Say They Won RJR Nabisco Vote." *New York Times,* 20 February 1996, C1. Four years after this film was released and years after the barbarians were at the gate, investors fought about splitting the food operations from the tobacco holdings.

⌒

Belfast, Maine

Fish, Inc.

2000, 240 mins., TVM
Director: Frederick Wiseman
Cinema verité documentary

This is the thirtieth film from America's leading cinema verité documentary filmmaker, who has pioneered the in-depth study of American institutions ever since *Titicut Follies,* a harrowing look at a mental institution, was banned in Massachusetts. Although Wiseman does not like the term "cinema verité," his unnarrated, fairly leisurely long takes of employees and clients of public institutions interacting have become key exemplars of this documentary style. In this instance it works ideally to capture a broad range of representative workers in one coastal town in Maine. Wiseman once described his works as "reality fictions"; he says he did it ironically but the term caught on. Wiseman combines a very high shooting ratio (sometimes the footage shot is a hundred times the footage used in the final film), with an intense concentration on realistic detail in long takes.

Wiseman has acknowledged that to a certain extent *Belfast, Maine* is a kind of retrospective or "cumulative" film: "I thought of looking at Belfast through the institutions that were the subjects of my other films— hospitals, police, welfare, etc., which exist everywhere. In addition to referring to the other films, it helped me to decide what and where to shoot" (quoted in Deirdre Boyle).

Sometimes what to shoot is obvious to Wiseman. One of the key sequences involves a local high school teacher teaching up a storm about *Moby Dick,* relating the region's obsession with fish to Melville's tragic voyage of Ahab and the seamen (workers all) he leads to their doom. As he filmed it, he "knew that it was the key sequence." On the other hand, having selected the sardine factory as an important focus, he ended up with four hours of footage, which he edited into a nine-minute sequence with 270 shots, a shooting ratio of 25 to 1, considerably less than his usual ratio.

Philip Lopate captured this aspect of Wiseman's career when he characterized him as "less an angry prophet than a grateful mystic of the materialist realm." Wiseman's camera begins with cinema verité but moves toward a "personal expressionism." "We know why Wiseman is on this specific location at this specific moment," Lopate argues, "because he has selected out of much footage shot a self-contained sequence which follows location, not character."

Viewers of other Wiseman films—such early classics as *Titicut Follies* and *High School* or the later social-issue films, such as *Hospital, Meat,* and *Welfare*—may find any or all talk about his "mysticism" a bit unnecessary. For years he has established himself as the premier filmmaker of American institutions and some of their inherent flaws and contradictions. No one eats meat, visits an inner-city hospital, or argues about the welfare system in quite the same way after seeing his social-issue films on those topics.

What is more of a surprise in this film is the emphasis on work pure and simple carried out by the people of Belfast. In *Meat* we had a precursor of this concern, as union butchers argued with their boss, but in *Belfast, Maine,* for the most part, work defines its people. There are revealing food production lines—creating potato puffs, canning sardines, slicing salmon—which are marvels of efficiency if not cuisine. They scream New England, but the town's biggest employer turns out to be a credit card company perched on a hill overlooking

Penobscot Bay. For many viewers this will be a typical Wisemaniac vision: fish, fishermen, and cannery workers everywhere, but on the hill stands the virtual dollar.

See also: *Brass Valley*.
Availability: Zipporah.

Further reading

Boyle, Deirdre. "Frederick Wiseman: An American Inspector." *Independent Film and Video Monthly*, May 2000, 36–40. Fascinating interview, with a good overview of Wiseman's career and revealing chat about *Belfast, Maine*.

Holden, Stephen. "Seaside Town under the Microscope." *New York Times*, 28 January 2000, B17. Wiseman offers a "breathtaking landscape with the troubled lives of many of those living there."

Klawans, Stuart. "As Maine Goes, So Goes . . . ," *Nation*, 14 February 2000, 34–37. "An immensely rich and immeasurably valuable microcosm of American life at the end of the twentieth century" and "most unexpected . . . a microcosm of Wiseman's art."

Lopate, Philip. "Composing an American Epic." *New York Times*, 1 January 2000, II.11, 26. In this overview of Wiseman's career, Lopate echoes other critics by arguing that as Wiseman fiercely pursues "life as it is," he nonetheless establishes "a wonderment at reality's surreal forms."

Mamber, Stephen. *Cinema Verité in America: Studies in Uncontrolled Documentary*. Cambridge: MIT Press, 1974. One of the earliest surveys—and still a valuable one—of cinema verité and its leading filmmakers, with a chapter on Wiseman.

Wright, Chris, and Robert David Sullivan. "Belfast, Maine." *Boston Phoenix*, 1 January 2000. Two discussions of Wiseman's film and career, stressing the "sense of mystery that Wiseman adds to several scenes of everyday life" (Sullivan), especially food factory/production line sequences.

Web site:

⟨www.zipporah.com⟩ Official site of Wiseman's film company; provides an overview of his thirty films with some critical/appreciative articles.

✍

The Bicycle Thief

Spoked

1947, 90 mins., B&W, Italian, with English subtitles

Director: Vittorio de Sica
Screenplay: Cesare Zavattini, from Luigi Bartolini's novel *Ladri di biciclette* (*Bicycle Thieves*)

CAST

Antonio = Lamberto Maggiorani
Bruno = Enzo Staiola
Maria = Lianella Carell
The Medium = Elena Altieri
The Thief = Vittorio Antonucci
Baiocco = Gino Saltamerenda

The Bicycle Thief has been for many years *the* world cinema classic that most experienced viewers have identified with the postwar Italian cinematic movement known as neorealism. Vittorio de Sica was one of the leading neorealist filmmakers of the pioneering postwar Italian film industry: *The Bicycle Thief* is his masterpiece. Like other de Sica films—*Shoeshine,* for example, about Italian street kids—*The Bicycle Thief* defines the thin line between poor working-class people and riffraff. Antonio is desperate for a job. When one comes along—as a poster hanger—he needs his bicycle to keep it. But his bike is cleverly ripped off by a thief and his accomplice, and for the rest of the film Antonio and his son, Bruno, travel an almost Dantesque circuit of Rome's streets searching for the bicycle or the thief. Ironically, the lowest circle of this hell is a church mission for the poor: he spots an old man who has had some truck with the thief, but Antonio becomes virtually a prisoner in the locked chapel as the guardians of the poor subjugate their charges and obstruct Antonio's search in exchange—they insist—for his free meal. When Antonio tries to badger his contact, the fury of the righteous workers is directed against him as a disturber of *their* peace and the old man gets away.

De Sica achieved the working-class look of this film in large part by casting nonprofessionals in virtually every role except that of the thief. A bizarre side plot has Antonio's wife seeking access to The Medium, a vaguely Catholic walkup mystic who peremptorily dispenses advice—for a fee, of course. Even Antonio in the end is driven to

Antonio (Lamberto Maggiorani) hangs Rita Hayworth in *The Bicycle Thief*. Courtesy British Film Institute Stills, Posters, and Designs.

see this pathetic woman, who seems to be too authentic for words.

Zavattini diverged so far from Bartolini's novel that the only feature the two have in common is bicycle spokes. Bartolini's first-person novel features an art professor who has more bicycles than he can in conscience keep track of, so when one is stolen we don't have much sympathy. Zavattini's radical reworking of this story brought us to a neorealist hell by making the protagonist working class and his (just one!) bicycle essential for survival.

See also: *The Roof; La terra trema.*
Availability: Easy; DVD.

Further reading

Bartolini, Luigi. *Bicycle Thieves*. Trans. C. J. Richards. New York: Macmillan, 1950. This English translation of the source novel appeared after the film's release. It's a good thing, for it would not have won any friends for the film.

Bazin, André. *What Is Cinema?* Trans. Hugh Gray. Vol. 2. Berkeley: University of California Press, 1971. A detailed, positive discussion of the film:

"Not one frame that is not charged with intense dramatic power, yet there is not one either which we cannot fail to find interesting, its dramatic continuity apart."

Crowther, Bosley. "The Bicycle Thief." *New York Times,* 13 December 1949, 44. "A brilliant and devastating film" about "the irony of a little fellow buffeted by an indifferent world."

Phillips, William H. *Analyzing Films*. New York: Holt, Rinehart & Winston, 1985. Offers a detailed outline of the film's sequences.

Samuels, Charles Thomas. *Encountering Directors*. New York: Putnam, 1972. Includes an interview with de Sica.

Sitney, P. Adams. *Vital Crises in Italian Cinema*. Austin: University of Texas Press, 1995. Extensive discussion of de Sica's films and his collaboration with Zavattini.

Zavattini, Cesare. *The Bicycle Thief*. Trans. Simon Hartog. New York: Simon & Schuster, 1968. The "cutting continuity script without divisions into shots or scenes" (Phillips).

Web site:
⟨www.gen.umn.edu/faculty_staff/yahnke/filmteach /teach.htm⟩ A detailed summary of the film.

Note: Although there is obviously more than one thief, as the Italian title (*Ladri di biciclette*) makes clear, *Bicycle Thieves* as an alternative title has not always caught on. Maurizio Nichetti's *The Icicle Thief* is a detailed and amusing parody of *The Bicycle Thief*.

The Big Flame

Extinguished?

1969, 85 mins., UK, TVM
Director: Ken Loach
Screenplay: Jim Allen
CAST
Jack Regan = Godfrey Quigley
Danny Fowler = Norman Rossington
Peter Conner = Peter Kerrigan
Freddie Grierson = Ken Jones

The Big Flame, one of five films directed by Ken Loach not available (unfortunately), was a television feature film for the BBC's *Wednesday Play* series. The story concerns a dock strike that becomes a sit-down action or occupation. The strike actually happened in Liverpool in 1968, but it was typical of politicized workers' actions throughout Europe at that time.

That the dockers occupy their workplace, as far as the establishment was concerned, is bad enough. That they decide to carry their experiment in workers' control to running all the docks themselves is of course a dock too far. The police, army, courts, and right-wing politicians all attack the strikers, who are also betrayed by their own national trade union leaders and the Labour Party, a recurring theme in Loach's films.

Julian Petley's analysis of the film emphasizes the role of the sitting Labour Party, which the trade union leadership was committed to support. These leaders, Petley concludes, "were certainly not in favor of rank and file demands for more 'workers' power,' since this directly undermined their own position in the political hierarchy."

For Raymond Williams, Loach's film was an experimental breakthrough in social realism, incorporating features of the tradition—nonprofessional actors, actual locations, typical actions—with a movement toward a new film practice: keeping the camera always within the ranks of the workers and establishing that the "particular hypothesis" (workers' control) is "defeated in terms of the local action" but not "defeated as an idea."

Loach returned to this subject in *The Flickering Flame*, whose title indicates metaphorically that the struggle of the dockers is in fact going out. The screenwriter of *The Big Flame*, Jim Allen, a former industrial worker and blacklisted labor organizer, was Loach's constant collaborator, having worked with him on five other projects, including *Days of Hope* (from Allen's novel of the same title) and *Raining Stones*.

See also: *The Flickering Flame*.
Availability: Not.

Further reading

Petley, Julian. "Factual Fictions and Fictional Fallacies: Ken Loach's Documentary Dramas." In *Agent of Challenge and Defiance: The Films of Ken Loach*, ed. George McKnight, 28–59. Westport, Conn.: Greenwood Press, 1997. An excellent essay, placing the film in the context of the debate between so-called objective documentaries and what we call docudramas.

Williams, Raymond. "A Lecture on Realism." *Screen* 18 (1977): 61–74. Discusses the film as originating in traditional social realism but moving toward a new form using a hypothetical future, "a hypothesis which is played out in realistic terms, but within a politically imagined possibility."

The Big One

Phil & Me

1997, 96 mins., PG-13
Director: Michael Moore
Postmodern documentary
PRINCIPAL FIGURES
Michael Moore as himself
Phil Knight, CEO, Nike
Garrison Keillor, writer and radio
  performer
Studs Terkel, author
Rick Nelson, guitarist for Cheap Trick

The Big One, Michael Moore's first feature-length documentary since *Roger & Me*, is on the surface a road movie made about Moore's book tour for his best-seller *Downsize This! Random Threats from an Unarmed American* (1996). It consists of three related story lines. There is of course the book tour itself, perilously close in kind to the satiric footage of a wayward rock band featured in the great mock-rock-doc *This Is Spinal Tap*. But whenever possible Moore sneaks off with his film crew to track down striking and organizing workers. Typical of this second story line is the evening when workers at a Borders bookstore meet him clandestinely in their parking lot at night, since Moore has been supporting such actions at bookstores when he signs books and also documenting union organizing efforts at Borders on his Web sites. And finally Moore constantly develops a third theme featured in *Downsize This!* and also the subject of one of his best *TV Nation* episodes ("Free Trade in Mexico"): the run over the border by corporations that intend to exploit Mexican workers in maquiladoras as they fire ("downsize") American workers.

After the film had generated fairly positive reviews (although not an astounding box office), one sequence began to dominate Moore's interviews whenever he toured with the film: the climactic encounter with Phil Knight of Nike. Perhaps Knight thought—in his arrogance—that he could go where no other CEO would dare go: *mano a mano* against Moore, *the* CEO-baiter of our era. The sequence comes at a point in the film when it is clear that Moore will be allowed to meet only corporate flack-catchers, who appear periodically in the film like two- or three-headed guard dogs from hell. In scene after scene in corporate lobbies across the land, one or two or three PR people try to explain, with a great deal of patience, that the reason they are sending work to Mexico is "to remain competitive." This remark usually causes Moore to whip out a four-foot-long check made out to the corporate entity for 80 cents—the hourly wage of a typical Mexican worker. The absurdity of the PR dilemma is summed up in Moore's question to one of Procter & Gamble's PR people in Cincinnati: was it an average profit of $5 billion over a three-year period or just $5 billion for all three years?

Finally Moore gets a call from Nike's PR man, who says come on up, Phil's ready to talk. In the Portland headquarters everyone is in jeans and is way cool. Phil is smarmy (on my radar) but acts nice. Concedes nothing and contradicts Moore's assertion that Indonesian workers are only 12 years old. Turns out they are really 14. In the meantime Knight repeats his mantra: American workers do not want to make shoes. Moore offers a typical challenge: if he, Moore, can find 500 workers in Flint who are willing to make shoes, will Nike build a plant there? Phil smiles. Later—after we see maybe fifty Flint workers pledging to make shoes— Knight says that unemployed workers would say anything to get a job.

Moore tries another gambit: two free tickets to Indonesia to check on the factory workers. Phil declines. (But read the results of the dueling Web sites below.) Moore challenges him to match Moore's $10,000 gift to Flint. Phil agrees. Round to Knight?

Knight apparently was left gnawing the minimum-age bone. It turns out that Nike also filmed the interview and soon offered its footage on its Web site to prove how wrong Moore was: Knight would have agreed to go to Indonesia to check up on what should have been 16-year-old workers. Before one could say "Shazam," Moore's production

Phil Knight, CEO of Nike, *mano a mano* with Michael Moore in *The Big One*.

company added outtakes not used in the film to *its* Web site. The debate about workers' ages grew more heated, since it included Moore's assertion that Nike had stopped using 8-year-olds to make soccer balls in Pakistan only because of the bad press it received.

Moore also "proved" that the real reason Knight wouldn't go to Indonesia with Moore had to do with Moore's insistence that he bring his camera along: "Your people said that I couldn't bring along a camera, and I said that's like me asking you not to wear your Nikes." Knight replies in Moore's outtake: "Obviously, there's a lot of poverty in Indonesia, and I just was very reluctant to have my picture taken in some type of background where there was poverty. I just thought that was a sound bite that I didn't need."

In an interview with Hubert Herring, a business reporter, Moore suggested that there was another outtake that did not even reach cyberspace. It involved the only CEO Moore has openly praised in his documentaries—Alex Trotman, former CEO of Ford, who accepted the "CEO challenge" in a *TV Nation* episode and changed the oil on a pickup truck, unlike IBM's CEO, who wouldn't format a floppy disk. Herring was told that when Johnson Controls (a villainous company in *The Big One*) fired its strikers and hired replacement workers, "Trotman refused to buy car seats made by replacement workers." This pressure forced Johnson Controls "to settle with the union."

In a very practical (and perhaps rare) consequence of documentary exposure, Phil Knight agreed—after most people recognized that his site lost the duel of the Web sites with Moore's Dog Eat Dog Films—to raise the minimum age for labor in the Third World to 16 or 18 years, depending on local traditions. Knight did admit that the American public has begun to equate "the Nike product" with "slave wages, forced overtime, and arbitrary abuse" (Cushman). The time has come, he said, to end employment of underage workers and meet the "strict" American standards for health and safety. Both Moore's documentary and Gary Trudeau's endless satire of Nike's factories in his cartoon strip, *Doonesbury,* reinforced the already considerable flack Nike was receiving from advocacy groups such as the Transnational Resource and Action Center and Press for Change. Besides, it was mid-1998 but Nike's stock price was falling and sales were weak.

Nike's Web site argued that the company had paid attention for a long time to fair labor policies, although its first director of labor practices, Dusty Kidd, took over those duties only in October 1996. The Nike "Factory Profile" on its Web site in 1998 was the Samho factory in Qingdao, China, which features an "on-site beauty salon: prices lower than those in the surrounding area"; a "monthly birthday party," at which the Korean factory owner, Y. K. Park, "officiates, hands out gifts, and has learned how to sing happy birthday in Chinese"; "weekly movies: free of charge to all workers"; "free karaoke"; and "TVs available for all workers to watch in the evening." It is clear that Mike and Phil need to go to Samho factory for their next meeting, perhaps punch in a cassette (not pirated) of *The Big One,* and wait for the good karaoke times to roll.

Whether *The Big One* was the most Web-linked labor film in recent years remains to be seen, but even before its wide circulation in 1998 Michael Moore was already heavily involved in using and redefining cyberspace as a new form of documentary. The Web sites for *TV Nation,* his book, and his production company all directed those who logged on to pursue the Boycott Borders site and other evidence of union organizing. The Boycott Borders site, for example, posted a "confidential" manual, "Union Awareness Training for Borders Managers," which exhaustively documents what managers need to know about union organizing ("Employees start gathering to talk in areas that are off the beaten path"), their own employees ("Borders is a national corporation with a large pool of full-time employees who generally tend to be a little left of center"), and unions in general ("Unions are businesses which survive solely on the dues of their members"). This remarkable document, I suspect, would obviously not have been so readily available without the Web; furthermore, it becomes part of the documentary network of Moore's film. The United Food & Commercial Workers Union, however, was not able to follow up on its early successes in organizing a number of Borders stores in 1997.

Viewers who have found a comic champion in Moore will be pleased with *The Big One*. A few reviewers have found Moore's ego to be itself "the big one," while others have applauded this jolly not-so-green giant. The trailer for the film has Big Mike kicking in the door at a corporate fat-cat meeting. This moment was also developed in the film's first ad campaign, which portrayed Moore as a Man in Black, "protecting the earth from the scum of corporate America," but the execs for Columbia Pictures did not appreciate Moore's holding a giant microphone in a parody of the guns of *their* Men in Black ("protecting the earth from the scum of the universe"). In the end Moore had to settle for a Superman parody (in one hand he holds a microphone, in the other he holds up a giant foot like the Man of Steel).

See also: *The Awful Truth; TV Nation.*
Availability: Easy.

Further reading

Cushman, John H. "Nike Pledges to End Child Labor and Apply U.S. Rules Abroad." *New York Times*, 13 May 1998, C1, 5. It turns out there really are 14-year-olds making Nikes, but from now on those factories will require workers to be 16, unless of course they are already working there; in that case they can still be 14. But their younger sisters will have to wait until they are 16. (See Knight below.)

DePalma, Anthony. "Company Is Told to Stay and Face New Union." *New York Times*, 23 November 2000, C1. Los Angeles District Court rules that a California corporation (Quadrtech) that announced it was moving to Tijuana on the day after the Communications Workers of America was certified to represent its mostly immigrant workforce had to stay.

Egan, Timothy. "The Swoon of the Swoosh." *New York Times Magazine*, 13 September 1998, 66–70. On the troubles facing Nike because of the critiques typified by Moore's film.

Herring, Hubert B. "Chasing Michael, or, How to Corner a Corporate Nemesis." *New York Times*, 12 April 1998 (available at ⟨www.dogeatdogfilms.com⟩). Interview with Moore by a business reporter, who surveys virtually every major idea in Moore's arsenal, including still another (small) tribute to Alex Trotman, CEO at Ford.

Knight, Phil. Transcript of speech to the National Press Club, 12 May 1998, at ⟨www.nikebiz.com⟩, posted May 1998. The announcement of Nike's new Third World labor policies, discussed in Cushman but worth a look for corroboration of Moore's insight into Knight's character. Sample: "Whenever I'm asked about how we became the biggest sports and fitness company in the world, I'm reminded of John Kennedy's answer on how he became a war hero. 'It was easy,' he said. 'They sank my boat.'"

Maslin, Janet. "A Sly Lens on Corporate America." *New York Times*, 10 April 1998, B1. Reviewer applauds Moore's ability to get "labor issues" to folks who go to the multiplex, although she finds his *Roger & Me* tactic "of ambushing captains of industry" a "novelty [that] has faded."

Moore, Michael. *Downsize This! Random Threats from an Unarmed American*. 1997. Rev. ed. New York: Random House, 1997. An outrageous catalog of Moore's obsessions and corporate America's dirty deals: a must-read.

Turan, Kenneth. "Moore Fun and Commentary in 'Big One.'" *Los Angeles Times*, 10 April 1998 (also available at ⟨www.dogeatdogfilms.com⟩). Positive review typical of the press Moore received: Turan celebrates his "old-fashioned populist zeal that's a throwback to the likes of Mother Jones and Big Bill Hayward."

"Union Awareness Training for Borders Managers." "Prepared" by Anne Kubek, vice president for human resources at Borders in September 1996. Originally at ⟨www.parsons. iww.org/~borders/manual.html⟩ and discussed at ⟨www.motherjones.com/sideshow/borders. html⟩, this fascinating 22-page single-spaced read includes a guide to two attempts by the Industrial Workers of the World (IWW) and the United Food & Commercial Workers (UFCW) to organize the chain. Are these two unions equivalent in corporate Borders Land? A helpful self-test is included: Is it legal or illegal for a Borders manager to say, "Vote against the union and we will match whatever the union promises you"?

Wines, Michael. "An Odd Rift Develops between an Author and a Chain Promoting His Latest Book." *New York Times,* 18 November 1997. The "odd rift" is of course Moore's support for the union drive against Borders.

Web sites:

⟨www.corpwatch.org⟩ Political and economic exposés of Nike and many other corporations.

⟨www.dogeatdogfilms.com⟩ The official site of Moore's production company, with topical comments by Moore, reviews of his films, "People We Like" (list of "groups that are active in social change"), and occasional bonuses such as the Knight-centered outtakes from *The Big One,* which, unfortunately, are no longer available, but here are some sample "titles": "You're the boss—just tell 'em!" (to raise the minimum age); "You should have let me bring the camera" (to Indonesia); "Whiplash of the wrist" (carpal tunnel syndrome).

⟨www.nikebiz.com⟩ Nike's official site, with extensive corporate bulletins and Knight worship.

✍ Bitter Rice

Po Valley tales

1948, 107 mins., Italian, with English subtitles
Director: Giuseppe de Santis
Screenplay: Giuseppe de Santis, Carlo Lizzani, and Gianni Puccini
CAST
Silvana = Silvana Mangano
Francesca = Doris Dowling
Walter = Vittorio Gassman
Marco = Raf Vallone

When earthy Silvana Mangano became internationally known for playing the doomed heroine of this film, her sexy peasant looks forced the *New York Times* reviewer into a fit of comparisons with other actresses: she was like "Ingrid Bergman with a Latin disposition and Rita Hayworth plus twenty-five pounds." The reviewer could tell he was dealing with a very raw tale of migrant rice workers (*mondine*) in the Po Valley, but he missed perhaps the film's placement in the postwar Italian tradition of neorealism, where laboring folk, the criminal riffraff, and untrustworthy crew leaders alike vie for the viewer's attention.

Giuseppe de Santis, like other social-realist filmmakers, often included numerous scenes with nonprofessionals, in this case rice-field workers, whose migrant work camp, filled with women who chose to be on the make as well as the objects of leering men, has a caged-in look. Unity among the contract workers and scabs is achieved only after a spectacular brawl among the women in the rice paddies.

The melodramatic plot involves two couples joined in a lusty dance of death. Francesca and Walter, on the lam from a jewelry theft, travel on the same train as the rice workers. At their destination, Francesca falls in love with Marco, while Walter persuades the Hollywood star-struck Silvana ("Miss Rice Worker, 1948") to steal the harvest. Silvana, with a characteristically tragic and operatic gesture, shoots Walter because he has given her a piece of worthless costume jewelry (it proves he's a liar) and then commits suicide. The climactic sequence is a classic of Italian neorealism: with the rice harvest safe, Silvana's companions in the fields file past her body, tossing handfuls of dry rice on her as the camera carries us away from their scene of tragic unity.

De Santis admired the films of such American directors as King Vidor (*Our Daily Bread*) and John Ford (*The Grapes of Wrath* and *How Green Was My Valley*) for their portrayals of working people. For his film, Peter Bondanella argues, de Santis used Hollywood genres such as the gangster film (the jewel thieves), the musical (the *mondine* sing as they work), and the Western (the shoot-out) as models, but he also wanted to satirize the negative effects of Hollywood star ideology on working-class characters such as Silvana. Film is a fickle medium, however, and Silvana Mangano became the very type of international star de Santis thought he was satirizing. (See Ben Lawton.)

The sequences of work in the fields almost always overshadow the Hollywood dreams in the *True Romance* magazines the rice workers read. Silvana wants to go to North

Silvana (Silvana Mangano), one of the rice workers, in *Bitter Rice*.

America, where everything is electric, but her stolid friend Walter warns her that the electric chair is also American and he holds out the possibility of building a family in South America instead (the other destination of so many Italian emigrants in the twentieth century).

The masses of laboring women, sometimes beautiful but always strong, are the real heroines for de Santis's camera. He almost can't bear to cut away from them to stick to his melodramatic plot.

See also: *The Bicycle Thief; The Organizer.*
Availability: Selected collections.

Further reading

Bondanella, Peter. *Italian Cinema from Neorealism to the Present.* 3d ed. New York: Continuum, 2001. Analyzes the film and its place in Italian film history.

Crowther, Bosley. "Bitter Rice." *New York Times,* 19 September 1950, 39. A very positive review— "hundreds of actual rice-field workers appear in the beautiful and pulsing scenes of camp life and rice-field cultivation."

Lawton, Ben. *Giuseppe de Santis and Postwar Italian Cinema.* Toronto: University of Toronto Press, 1996. An extensive review of de Santis's career and this film; takes up the issue of his exploitation or eroticization of Silvana Mangano.

~

Black Fury

An impossible terrorist

1935, 92 mins., B&W
Director: Michael Curtiz
Screenplay: Abem Finkel and Carl Erickson, from Michael Musmanno and

Paul Muni's screenplay *Jan Volkanik* and Harry R. Irving's play *Bohunk*

CAST

Joe Radek = Paul Muni
Anna Novak = Karen Morley
Mike Shemanski = John Qualen
Slim Johnson = William Gargan

It is hard to believe Curtiz directed *Casablanca* just seven years after this film. The heavy-handed Joe Radek, who embodies the miners' "black fury," will give way to Humphrey Bogart's suave and cynical expatriate Rick. Both men are fighting injustice, of course, but Muni's Joe is as good as he is dull. He has been a loyal union man, more out of friendship than solidarity. Thus when he's drunk and jilted, he too easily disrupts a union meeting by siding with a rebel group led by a company agent provocateur.

Characteristic of Warner Brothers' more socially conscious productions, this was one of the first (if not the first) feature-length labor union film to portray the tough life of the miners sympathetically. The story was based on an incident in 1929 in which a union man was brutally beaten to death by two agents of the Coal and Iron Police in western Pennsylvania. As a result of this murder, Ralph Musmanno, an appeals lawyer for Sacco and Vanzetti and later a crusading congressman, led a successful campaign to abolish the private armies the coal companies had considered their right for fifty years. The murder remains in the film, with its brutality intact. (See *The Molly Maguires* for another portrayal of the Coal and Iron Police.)

Many critics have commented on the unbelievable melodramatic ending. Joe sneaks into one of the main shafts of a mine, distributes dynamite, and phones topside. If the union and management don't stop the strike, he will blow up the mine and himself. He convinces them, the strike is saved (it's back to business as usual, an arrangement that the union wanted in the first place), and the death of one of Joe's friends (like the historical incident) is avenged by the law. He even gets his girl back, by golly.

Musmanno's original script (*Black Hell*) ran into flack from the National Coal Association, whose executive secretary told the Hollywood Production Code Office (the so-called Breen office, named after its chief censor) that Warner Brothers needed to be reminded that (among many other things) "the miners have little to complain" about. The conclusion of Francis Walsh's excellent research on this episode was that "the Breen Office accomplished its goal."

See also: *The Molly Maguires; The Stars Look Down*.
Availability: Selected collections.

Further reading

Maltz, Albert. "Coal Diggers of 1935." *New Theatre*, 8–9 May 1935. Radical novelist criticizes the film's lack of realism and its ending: "a ridiculous, impossible, terroristic solution."

Musmanno, Michael A. *Verdict! The Adventures of the Young Lawyer in the Brown Suit*. New York: Random House, 1958. The autobiography of the state congressman who challenged the Coal and Iron Police.

Sennewald, André. "The Screen." *New York Times*, 11 April 1935, 27. "Warner Brothers exhibited almost a reckless air of courage in producing the picture at all."

"Story behind a Story." *New York Times*, 21 April 1935, X.3. Ralph Musmanno meets Paul Muni and the two collaborate on *Black Fury*.

Walsh, Francis R. "The Films We Never Saw: American Movies View Organized Labor, 1934–1954." *Labor History* 27 (1986): 564–80. An in-depth discussion of the script, with details on behind-the-scenes maneuvering to "eliminate anything unfavorable to the coal mining industry" (Warner Brothers memo).

Black Legion

A legion of racism and murder

1936, 83 mins.
Director: Archie Mayo
Screenplay: Abem Finkel and William Wister Haines

Frank Taylor = Humphrey Bogart
Ed Jackson = Dick Foran
Ruth Taylor = Erin O'Brien-Moore
Betty Grogan = Ann Sheridan
Pearl Danvers = Helen Flint
Prosecuting Attorney = Addison Richards
Joe Dombrowski = Henry Brandon

This topical film was based on a Michigan incident in which a terrorist group called the Black Legion was responsible for the assassination of Charles Poole, a Works Progress Administration (WPA) worker. The assassin, Dayton Dean, turned state's evidence at the trial and implicated the rest of his super-patriotic gang.

Bogart's fictionalized Dean, Frank Taylor, is an auto worker whose family is more than a little put upon by Depression problems, despite his decent wages. To get ahead, Frank wants to be promoted to foreman. His simple-minded anger makes him an easy target for a group of fascists, who recruit him when a "foreigner," Dombrowski, gets promoted instead of Frank. The film historian Peter Stead pointed out that Warner Brothers depoliticized the Black Legion by making them more like racketeers than an overtly political group, although the studio obviously succeeded in giving the film an authentic working-class look.

More disturbing was Warner Brothers' publicity plan (see Stead) to have hooded figures with torches in theater lobbies and even to have someone carried out of the theater to an ambulance by two of the hooded men. Although few theaters actually engaged in this heavy hype, reviewers such as Frank S. Nugent of the *New York Times* certainly wanted the film to succeed: "I hope its message reaches the type of mind to which the Michigan organization's aims appealed." (It may have been getting away with murder for years: Malcolm X, for example, believed that the Black Legion was responsible for his father's murder in Michigan in 1931.)

Warner Brothers in the 1930s was especially tuned to Nugent's desires. One of the screenwriters of *Black Legion*, Abem Finkel,

had just the year before also worked on *Black Fury*, the equally hard-hitting film about miners and the fascistic Coal and Iron Police.

See also: *Fury*.
Availability: Selected collections.

Further reading

"Black Legion." *Newsweek*, 30 May 1936, 9–10; 6 June 1936, 10; 13 June 1936, 10. A series of news articles on the Black Legion murder of Poole, a WPA worker.

Davis, F. "Labor Spies and the Black Legion." *New Republic*, 17 June 1936, 169–71. Interprets the actual events in terms of labor unrest.

Higham, John. *Strangers in the Land: Patterns of American Nativism, 1860–1925*. 1963. New Brunswick: Rutgers University Press, 1988. Places racist, antiforeigner, and anti-immigrant attitudes on the same historical and conceptual map.

Nugent, Frank S. "At the 86th Street Casino." *New York Times*, 18 January 1937, 21. "Editorial cinema at its best—ruthless, direct, uncompromising."

Sklar, Robert. *City Boys: Cagney, Bogart, Garfield*. Princeton: Princeton University Press, 1992. Analyzes the film's use of a new kind of Hollywood hero—urban and tough.

Stead, Peter. *Film and the Working Class*. London: Routledge, 1989. Analyzes the film in the context of what Stead calls the "sociological punch" of the 1930s films.

Ward, Paul W. "Who's behind the Black Legion?" and "Caliban in America." *Nation*, 10 June 1936, 728–29, 731. Contemporary political analysis on the growth of American fascism.

Bloodbrothers

Ties that blind

1978, 116 mins., R
Director: Robert Mulligan
Screenplay: Walter Newman, from Richard Price's novel of the same title
Stony de Coco = Richard Gere
Chubby de Coco = Paul Sorvino

Tommy de Coco = Tony Lo Bianco
Albert de Coco = Michael Hershewe
Marie = Lelia Goldoni
Dr. Harris = Kenneth McMillan
Annette = Marilu Henner
Cheri = Kristine DeBell

Bloodbrothers should have been a 1950s ethnic working-class drama, but it was a couple of decades late. We have two pairs of brothers, old-guard construction electricians and union men: Tommy de Coco and his brother Chubby, and Tommy's two sons, Stony and Albert. We have wives and lovers, too, but they are clearly subsidiary to this male-dominated Italian-American world. Tommy wants his son Stony to follow along in his union footsteps, but Stony's got other ideas. At first he does give it a try, and some of the best scenes involve his initiation into the world of high-rise building construction, where the regulars like to play tricks on the new boys to get them ready to booze and fight like real men.

Unfortunately for his father, Stony really wants to become a nurturer of some kind—a teacher or social worker or some such non-proletarian. Stony has been especially attentive to his brother Albert, who has to be the only male anorexic character in modern film history. The level of tenseness in the de Coco household would make the viewer dysfunctional. On top of the usual macho Italian-American shouting just to make oneself heard, the father's exaggerated sense of importance has brought him into violent conflict with his wife (whom he beats when he hears about a particularly sordid incident involving a neighbor) and his sons (who in his eyes are just a pair of sissies).

The film clearly wants to do in hard-hat family values by showing most of the men as boozy whore-chasers who are clearly disdainful of any kind of justice but a punch in the nose. After a few of these incidents, the viewer will long for some of the Saturday-night boredom the characters of *Marty* complained about. Also targeted—we guess satirically—is the generosity and sentimentality of the men when they are among their own. Thus a party the hard hats throw for a bar owner who was crippled on the job makes sense only if we accept the cliché that soft hearts beat inside hard bodies. The director, Robert Mulligan, who is a seasoned Hollywood veteran (*To Kill a Mockingbird,* for example), probably wanted this scene to be exactly what it seems to be on the surface: a male ritual to prove that men can bond and cry too.

The film's finale, with Stony lighting out for the territories (Queens?) in a taxi with his younger brother, is a little unrealistic. Even Stony suspects "they" will come after them and take Albert away. Before he picks up his brother, however, his father and uncle stand on either side of the taxi and throw money in the windows for Stony's journey while screaming at him not to go. These gestures seem a lot closer to the real world of these impossible men than what Stony thinks he is about to experience, although most viewers will presumably want his escape to be successful.

See also: *Marty.*
Availability: Easy.

Further reading

Price, Richard. *Bloodbrothers*. New York: Penguin, 1976. The source novel.
Schonberg, Harold C. "Bloodbrothers," *New York Times,* 29 September 1978, 52. Finds the film too contrived and sentimental.

Note: Also known as *A Father's Love* in a 98-minute TV version.

Blood Feud

Hoffa vs. Kennedy at Indian hand wrestling

1983, 240 mins., TVM
Director: Mike Newell
Screenplay: Robert Boris, from his and Edward Hannibal's novel of the same title; also based in part on Clark Mollenhoff's *Tentacles of Power*

CAST

Jimmy Hoffa = Robert Blake
Robert F. Kennedy = Cotter Smith
John F. Kennedy = Sam Groom
Lyndon B. Johnson = Forrest Tucker
J. Edgar Hoover = Ernest Borgnine
Edward Bennett Williams = José Ferrer
Hoffa's attorney = Michael C. Gwynne
Randy Powers = Danny Aiello
Johnny Masseta = Michael V. Gazzo
Edward Grady Partin = Brian Dennehy

One has to acknowledge all the fuss paid to the so-called blood feud between Hoffa and Bobby Kennedy, in part because American TV and Hollywood have placed it on the labor history agenda as virtually the only issue of note involving Hoffa (and of course the crime angle) and in part because Hoffa himself admitted in his autobiography that he was obsessed with the feud and said it was one of two "disastrous mistakes" in his life: "The first was coming to grips with Robert F. Kennedy to the point where we became involved in what can only be called a blood feud." (The "second mistake was naming Frank Fitzsimmons" as his successor.)

This film did not deserve all of the critical and public neglect it received, although occasionally it tries to compete with *The Godfather*, using the wonderful Michael V. Gazzo (who played Frankie Pentangeli in *The Godfather*) as a Mob boss. In addition to the primary characters of importance, there are about forty other characters, ranging from a *capo di capi* (Mafia talk for a captain of captains) and a restaurant captain (restaurant talk for a captain of waiters). And Hoffa's attorney is called . . . "Hoffa's attorney"! Is this the feisty Frank Ragano, He Who Must Not Be Named? The subject of his own TV documentary, *JFK, Hoffa, and the Mob*, as well as a book, *Mob Lawyer*, by Himself and Selwyn Raab (New York: Scribner, 1994)?

With a four-hour running time, it seems hardly credible for the filmmakers to expect us to take seriously the opening title, which tells us names have been changed and "other individuals and certain events have been altered or compressed for reasons of dramatic economy." *Variety*'s reviewer concluded that the film had to be a "sure TV attraction," as it had Hoffa, Kennedys, and the Mob. (The fourth sure thing, a disease, was missing.)

Robert Blake would not be many people's idea of a Hoffa stand-in. If you come to this film after seeing Hoffa himself in a documentary like *Jimmy Hoffa* or Jack Nicholson playing him in *Hoffa*, Robert Blake at first seems to have the right intensity. By the end of the film, however, Blake plays Hoffa as an almost deranged obsessive, scared to death of the Mob and of doing prison time.

There is an extraordinary amount of negative information here about Hoffa, presented mostly from the government's (and RFK's) point of view. At the height of the investigation against Hoffa, Bobby Kennedy had almost twenty lawyers working in the "get Hoffa" division of the attorney general's office. That they got Hoffa on only two of the things (jury tampering and pension fraud) they said he masterminded is an enigma this film cannot answer. It certainly demonstrates how Hoffa seemed to crowd so much of the Kennedys' other agendas—civil rights, for example—to the side.

Clearly Bobby Kennedy had the troops and Hoffa had the muscle, which in this film, without a doubt, belongs to the Mafia. So what else is new? Not much. Unless you didn't know that Bobby maintained that Hoffa challenged him to Indian hand wrestling, but the match was aborted by a call from Ethel Kennedy. The film does explicitly endorse the notion that the Mob had both Kennedys assassinated because they were breaking the Mob's long implicit truce with J. Edgar Hoover, who would not pursue a foe he knew he could not defeat.

Without trying to finesse an important issue, do we dare to ask if the "blood feud" might also be traced to the long internal cultural and class struggle between the lace-curtain Irish (the rich upper-class Kennedys) and the shanty Irish (the working-class Hoffas, who were part Dutch)? In the film Hoffa concludes: "I was born to burlap," but "Bobby was born to silk."

See also: *Jimmy Hoffa; JFK, Hoffa, and the Mob.*
Availability: Not.

Further reading

"Blood Feud." *Variety,* 11 May 1983. This snippy review calls the film a "variation of 'The Untouchables' without the quality."

Hannibal, Edward, and Robert Boris. *Blood Feud.* New York: Random House, 1979. Essentially a blueprint for the film: "Although certain scenes, characters, names, and chronological sequences of events have been altered for dramatic impact, the basic facts in this novel are as they happened."

Hoffa, James R. *Hoffa: The Real Story*. New York: Stein & Day, 1975. "The only authorized book of Hoffa's life . . . as told to Oscar Fraly"; also includes the Indian hand-wrestling incident, which Hoffa says was Kennedy's idea but that Hoffa won twice.

Mollenhoff, Clark R. *Tentacles of Power: The Story of Jimmy Hoffa.* Cleveland: World, 1965. Mollenhoff's book—a credited source for the film—says Kennedy had to leave before the hand-wrestling match was consummated and that Hoffa was "a stench in our democratic society."

Blow for Blow

Tit for tat

1972, 90 mins., France
Director: Marin Karmitz
Screenplay: Marin Karmitz
CAST
Marin Karmitz, the director
Women workers at Elboeuf

It is a shame that this film is not generally available, for it is a remarkable cinematic experiment as well as an unusual portrayal of a strike. The central action of the film is a wildcat sit-down strike organized by women textile workers when two of their number, regarded as troublemakers by management, are fired. In addition to the firings are other grievances: speedup, lack of access to the bathroom, low wages. The firings really are the last straw for the women, who have to worry about condescending union leaders *and* their husbands.

The women are quite militant, virtually imprisoning their boss, who tries to sneak out the back door during their occupation of the factory. They up the ante, dabbling in sabotage and calling for more violent actions. The political forces at play during such a volatile situation reflect some of the same situations that led to the demonstrations of 1968, when a general strike persisted for weeks. The police seem to be stuck in a dilemma characteristic of some capitalist countries: they are reluctant to attack the strikers in part because the government is afraid that bad treatment of the strikers will actually be good for their movement.

Karmitz drafted the script with the help of the actual workers who play themselves in the film, while the roles of the various management layers (foremen, forewomen, bosses) as well as some goons are played by professional actors. For the most part this is a convincing exercise of political filmmakers in the Godardian mode of the 1960s, who abandoned traditional mainstream narratives and the trappings of a glamorous industry in pursuit of authenticity and political revolution. Of course even low-paid extras during a strikebreakers' scene would know better than to smile and acknowledge the camera. But that may be a small price to pay for a cinematic revolution (one that Karmitz presumably left long behind when he became the producer of Krzysztof Kieslowski's Three Colors films in the 1990s, among many other successful projects). Jean-Luc Godard's somewhat similar film, *Tout va bien*, may seem overly self-conscious and deconstructed after *Blow for Blow*.

See also: *Tout va bien.*
Availability: Not.

Further reading

"Coup Pour Coup." *Variety*, 1 March 1972. The reviewer praises the film for its honesty and the producer for his frugality: the result is "a truly remarkable attempt to give a worker point of view and be as collective as possible"; of special interest to "women's lib orgs."

Rapin, Anne. "Films Can Change Your Life: Interview with French Producer Marin Karmitz." At ⟨www.arts.uwaterloo.ca/FINE/juhde/karm982. htm⟩. A 1998 interview that stresses Karmitz's radical plans for revitalizing working-class districts of Paris with film theaters.

Note: Also known as *Coup pour coup*.

⤿
Blue Collar

The tight blue collar

1978, 114 mins., R
Director: Paul Schrader
Screenplay: Paul Schrader
CAST
Jerry = Harvey Keitel
Smokey = Yaphet Kotto
Zeke = Richard Pryor

Our three stars play a band of workers who unfortunately decide to rob the office of their own (fictional) American Auto Workers local. They find only $600 and a curious ledger book. When they discover in the book evidence that the local has been loan-sharking, however, they decide to blackmail the local officers. They are surprised when the local first announces that $10,000 was stolen and later raises the figure to $20,600 in an effort to cheat the insurance company. This gang, who couldn't rob straight, has some very dangerous knowledge, and soon our heroes' unity begins to crumble.

There's a combination of brutality and convincing reality in *Blue Collar*, Schrader's first film, that sets it apart from many films in this guide. It's in part the feel for actual work that the film manages to convey: compare its auto assembly lines with those in *Gung Ho*, for example, to see the difference. The film tries to do a lot—explore racism, friendship, union corruption, the crushing of working-class militancy and spirit, and so on. Its scope is ambitious, its presentation often gross (especially a short but unpleasant

sex-and-drugs party and a disturbing murder scene).

Overall, *Blue Collar* is a depressing portrayal of American unionism, although there are flashes of individual integrity. Unionism in this world, however, is an elaborate scam, in which little attention is devoted to looking out for the welfare of the membership.

Smokey at one point makes a brief speech to his buddies, which is repeated as a voice-over at the end of the film after Smokey has been killed and the workers' unity has been destroyed: "Everything they do—the way they put the lifer against the new boy, the old against the young, the black against the white—is meant to keep us in our places."

See also: *Finally Got the News*.
Availability: Easy; DVD.

Further reading

Georgakas, Dan, and Marvin Surkin. *Detroit: I Do Mind Dying*. Rev. ed. Cambridge, Mass.: South End Press, 1998. Insights into the political and nationalist struggles of black auto workers in the late 1960s.

Puette, Wiliam J. *Through Jaundiced Eyes: How the Media View Labor*. Ithaca: ILR Press, 1992. Using this portrayal of the UAW, Puette argues convincingly that Hollywood was attacking one of the three principal and powerful unions then outside the AFL-CIO (the other two being the Longshoremen in *On the Waterfront* and the Teamsters in *F.I.S.T.*).

⤿
The Blue Eyes of Yonta

First revolution, then fashion

1992, 90 mins., Guinea-Bissau, in Criolo, with English subtitles
Director: Flora Gomes
Screenplay: Flora Gomes, Manuel Rambout Barcelos, and Ina Cesaire
CAST
Yonta = Maysa Marta
Vicente = Antonio Simão Mendes
Ze = Pedro Dias
Nando = Adão Malan Nanque
Amilcar = Mohamed Lamine Seidi

Two postrevolutionary generations coexist and eventually clash in this film: that of Vicente, Nando, and the parents of our heroine, Yonta, who fought against the Portuguese in a guerrilla war that created an independent Guinea-Bissau, and that of Yonta and Amilcar, the literal children of revolutionaries who must come to some kind of relationship with an increasingly difficult present and an unknown future.

Yonta has a crush on Vicente, her father's old comrade. Vicente, obsessed with trying to make a fish distribution company flourish (in a country where power blackouts can ruin an entire warehouse of fish), does not notice her attraction. She in turn is pursued by Ze, a student who has cribbed a Swedish love poem and sends it to her, celebrating his beloved's blue eyes (which Yonta, of course, does not have). She is obsessed with material things and what Vicente sees as bourgeois affectations—pretty dresses, dances, flirtations. Amilcar, her brother, named after the great revolutionary leader Amilcar Cabral, who was assassinated at the moment of victory over the colonial Portuguese, has a more symbolic role: he is part of a band of boys who at the beginning of the film roll tires—each marked with a year of their country's independence—down the dusty streets of the capital city, Bissau, and at the end leads them (with his sister) in a dance around the swimming pool while their elders sleep.

Vicente encounters some of his old revolutionary comrades, such as Nando, who still wanders the countryside, unable to find a niche in the new society. Gradually Vicente himself feels out of place in a developing capitalist economy, turning into, he realizes, a vulture. Yet he complains to Yonta that she has "replaced ideals with clothes and night clubs." She very sensibly replies: "It's not my fault if your ideals are spoiled. I want to be free to choose—isn't that what you fought for?"

Flores's first film, *Mortu Nega* (1988), translated as *Those Whom Death Refused*, can be seen as a prequel to *The Blue Eyes of Yonta. Mortu Nega* covers the country's war

Yonta (Maysa Marta) studies a letter at the dock. Courtesy California Newsreel.

against Portugal, when 500 years of colonialism ended. It traces the guerrilla war, the seemingly successful creation of an independent country, and the first arrivals home of the demobilized revolutionaries. Vicente is one of these veterans. Both films end with scenes of magic realism concerning water: in the earlier film an ancient deity of the Balanta people (the country's largest ethnic group) is summoned in a dream sequence to break a drought; in the later film an upper-class swimming pool is the site of an attempted reconciliation of the generations.

Guinea-Bissau has been through terrible times: after Cabral was assassinated in 1973, his Cape Verde Islands home and Guinea-Bissau were united until a military coup in 1980 led by a guerrilla commander (João Bernardo Vieira) broke up the union and formed a virtual dictatorship, which persisted through recent times. The national film industry is tiny, but it has produced at least one outstanding director and in *The Blue Eyes of Yonta* a sleeper of a masterpiece.

See also: *Hyenas*.

Availability: Selected collections; California Newsreel.

Further reading

Dhada, Mustafah. *Warriors at Work: How Guinea Was Really Set Free*. Boulder: University Press of Colorado, 1993. A history of the anticolonial war.

Web site:

⟨www.newsreel.org/topics/acine.htm⟩ Site of the Library of African Film section of California Newsreel's official site, with distribution information, essays on Gomes's films, many other African films, and the culture of African films in general.

Note: Also known as *Udju azul di Yonta*.

⌒

Born in East L.A.

Marginal crossings

1987, 85 mins., R
Director: Cheech Marin

Screenplay: Cheech Marin, from his own MTV video parody of Bruce Springsteen's song "Born in the U.S.A."

CAST

Rudy = Cheech Marin
Jimmy = Daniel Stern
Dolores = Kamala Lopez
Javier = Paul Rodriguez
Rudy's Mother = Lupe Ontiveros
The What's Happening Boys: Jason Scott Lee, Ted Lin, Sal Lopez, Jee Teo, and Del Zamora

Cheech without Chong is like Jerry Lewis without Dean Martin: separately or together, even a little bit goes a long way. But like the French, who apparently love Jerry Lewis films to pieces, fans of Cheech can unslouch a little higher in their seats because *Born in East L.A.* is supposed to have political consciousness and some redeeming social value. It does.

It also has the usual—for Cheech with or without Chong—complement of jokes about breasts, pot-smoking, and hustling of all kinds. It has a spectacular, over-the-top, sexy totemic woman (who speaks only French-accented English) visually identified with the Mexican flag: she has red hair, white skin, and a green dress. It has Chicano low-riders whose cars move in ways unknown to Detroit. It has some stereotypical gay prisoners who "lend" Cheech some money when he ends up behind bars. In short, it has a reasonably high level of offensive, tasteless, politically incorrect humor.

So what is this low-class film doing in a nice book like this? Christine List would say this: "Recent studies . . . have argued that self-derogatory ethnic jokes operate within marginalized cultures as sophisticated means of self-affirmation" (quoted in Chon Noriega). Whoa. Rosa Linda Fregosa would say this: "Marin's representation of the repatriation problem through humor deepens and extends the spatial boundaries for social criticism within commodified popular culture."

I would say this (in large part agreeing with Fregosa): there are many uncouth reasons to watch this comedy, but three really good ones—the film's premise and either one of its two finales. In the first place, Cheech uses virtually every Chicano stereotype to satirize and deconstruct American immigration law: Cheech's Rudy is arrested because he looks like an illegal immigrant, but as a third-generation Mexican-American and acculturated Angeleno he in fact cannot even speak Spanish. When he is deported to Mexico, he has difficulty surviving because of course he cannot speak Spanish there, either. He spends most of the film in various kinds of hustles to earn enough money to pay a coyote to lead him illegally back into his legal homeland.

Two of the best extended jokes embed Cheech's satire on cultural stereotyping. Both of them turn on the perception that white means American, while nonwhite signals illegal and dangerous. In one sequence, Rudy chooses an innocuous older white American couple's RV as the means of smuggling himself across the border from Tijuana. It turns out that they are smugglers of megakilos of dope, which the guards' sniffing dog discovers. Unfortunately, the dog also discovers Rudy. In another recurring sequence, Rudy is hired to teach five Asian men how to behave like Mexican-Americans so that they can pass for brown-skinned locals once they successfully cross the border.

Not everyone will find Cheech's satire successful. I can imagine *someone* not laughing at this exchange, a test of a suspected illegal. Immigration officer to Rudy: "Who's the president of the United States?" Rudy: "That's easy. That guy who used to be on *Death Valley*. John Wayne."

The two finales are by turns spectacular and whimsical. In the first, Cheech leads hundreds of illegals in a human wave across the border in the teeth of two buffoony border guards, in a multileveled parody of a Western land-rush scene. In the second, he and his new Salvadoran girlfriend emerge from a manhole in the middle of a Cinco de Mayo parade. Cheech knows the name of this parade ("We have it every year") but of course does not know it is the celebration of Mexican freedom, the equivalent of the Fourth of July. The Mexican flag in the form of the totemic woman is also involved in this scene: to say more would be to convince the wrong kind of people to watch this film.

See also: *The City*.
Availability: Easy; DVD.

Further reading

Fregosa, Linda Rosa. *The Bronze Cinema: Chicana and Chicano Film Culture*. Minneapolis: University of Minnesota Press, 1992. Although Fregosa misses the fact that every Chicano *and* Chicana in *Born in East L.A.* (not just the men) are mesmerized by the totemic French woman, her essay on the film is generally a must-read.

Harrington, Richard. "Born in East L.A." *Washington Post*, 31 August 1987. The reviewer argues that the film is "so ambiguous about ethnic stereotypes it might just as well have been made by insensitive Anglos."

Noriega, Chon A., ed. *Chicanos and Film: Essays on Chicano Representation and Resistance*. New York: Garland, 1992. Collection of wide-ranging essays, including Christine List's "Self-Directed Stereotyping in the Films of Cheech Marin."

Noriega, Chon A., and Ana M. Lopez, eds. *The Ethnic Eye: Latino Media Arts*. Minneapolis: University of Minnesota Press, 1996. Although there are only passing references to Cheech's film and others in the brief period known as the "Hispanic Hollywood" of the 1980s (*La Bamba*, *Stand and Deliver*, and *The Milagro Beanfield War*), an essay such as Noriega's "Imagined Borders" is an extremely helpful resource.

Bound for Glory

Another guerrilla folksinger

1976, 147 mins., PG
Director: Hal Ashby
Screenplay: Robert Getchell, from Woody Guthrie's autobiography of the same title
CAST
Woody Guthrie = David Carradine
Mary Guthrie and Memphis Sue = Melinda Dillon
Ozark Bule = Ronny Cox

Although this is quite a long film, it covers only a small portion (1936–40) of Woody Guthrie's autobiography (published in 1943). Thus we see the early clairvoyant Woody, the family Woody (when he tried), and the footloose Woody, but only some of Woody the guerrilla folksinger, when he made his reputation. Some of the great songs that have become working-class anthems ("This Land Is Your Land") are included, but we don't see the politicized Woody, whose guitar had a big sticker that read: "This machine kills fascists." The film stops before he wrote the great Dust Bowl Ballads (including "Tom Joad," which he wrote after seeing *The Grapes of Wrath*) and his anti-Hitler songs and before he supported the Communist left (drafted on the day Germany surrendered, he said, "I don't know if it was me or that big Red army or those few million Yanks there acrost his fence that caused [Hitler] to give in").

Woody's autobiography is a big book, and the film does not include the sharper political confrontations. There is thus no room in this somewhat romantic film for a revealing incident when Woody and Cisco Houston (re-named Ozark Bule in the film) took on some anti-Japanese fanatics in Los Angeles after Pearl Harbor. Cisco tried to calm the crowd with such remarks as "Nine-tenths of [the local Japanese] hate their Rising Sun robbers just as much as I do, or you do."

To fill in the missing pieces of Woody's amazing career, the documentary *Woody Guthrie: Hard Travelin'* (directed by his son, Arlo, also a folksinger) is helpful: it combines a view of Woody as a radical and as an inspiring figure for the generation of folk singers who came to prominence in the 1960s (such as Bob Dylan, Joan Baez, and Judy Collins).

But Ashby's film does capture the spirit of Woody's life and his commitment to poor and working people. We see the populist

Woody Guthrie (David Carradine) entertains farm workers' children in *Bound for Glory*.

Woody, less stuck on any political line, an aw-shucks kind of guy who can't stand to see laboring people being pushed around by the big boys. His friendship and work relationship with Ozark is typical of the passive way David Carradine plays Guthrie: as a rule it is Cisco who hits the road while taking a break from their country-western radio show to talk up the union to stoop laborers, but it is typically Woody who is a bit slow on the drawl to clear out when the company goons come rushing in. It is Ozark who wants to paint slogans on a farmer's fence, but it is Woody who wants to take the time to make the lettering look just right. Nonetheless, Ashby's portrait is convincing, if not in its biographical completeness, at least in conveying Woody's spirit. It is Ozark who organizes the radio show, but it is Woody who always dedicates his songs to the workers and whose lyrics irritate the program's sponsors.

Woody's life and songs captured the troubles and high-energy life he lived among the riffraff riding the rails during the Depression: "Men fighting against men. Color against color. Kin against kin. Race pushing against race. And all of us battling against the wind and the rain and that bright crackling lightning that booms and zooms, that bathes his eyes in the white sky, wrestles a river to a standstill, and spends the night drunk in a whorehouse." The young man from Okemah, Oklahoma, knew a lot of hard travelin', riding the rails.

At the age of 55, Woody lay dying of a rare disease, while faithful friends and new apprentices (such as Bob Dylan) paid deathbed visits. The film's title comes from one of his songs, and as usual it's about a train, a train "bound for glory."

See also: Riding the Rails.
Availability: Easy; DVD.

Further reading

Canby, Vincent. "In Films, Acting Is Behavior." *New York Times*, 12 December 1976, II.1. Celebrates Carradine's portrayal of Woody.

Green, Jim. "Bound for Glory." *Cineaste* 8 (1977): 36–37. Sees some positive aspects in the portrayal, but concludes it fails to do justice to Woody's politics or his music.

Guthrie, Woody. *Bound for Glory*. 1943. New York: Dutton, 1976. The Dutton edition has an excellent introduction by Studs Terkel.

Hampton, Wayne. *Guerrilla Minstrels: John Lennon, Joe Hill, Woody Guthrie, Bob Dylan*. Knoxville: University of Tennessee Press, 1986. Discusses the reality and the myths associated with these radicalized folksingers.

Boxcar Bertha

Hoppin' trains to hell

1972, 97 mins., R
Director: Martin Scorsese
Screenplay: Joyce H. and John William Corrington, from Boxcar Bertha's autobiography, *Sister of the Road*, as told to Ben L. Reitman
CAST
Big Bill Shelley = David Carradine
Bertha = Barbara Hershey
Van Morton = Bernie Casey
Rake Brown = Barry Primus
H. Buckram Sartoris = John Carradine

Martin Scorsese's first Hollywood film was this exploitation (read: sexy, violent, and fairly stupid) imitation of the incredibly popular and successful *Bonnie and Clyde*: both films tried to paint a heroic and romantic portrait of Depression-era itinerant riffraff or hobo rebels. Eric Hobsbawm has called such popular heroes "social" or "primitive" rebels, because their banditry has a populist and inevitably antigovernment cast. We see them in many Hollywood films about railroads, such as *End of the Line*, in which the fired worker tries to get even with the company, and *The Wild Bunch*, in which one of the outlaws says you can't pledge your word to a railroad.

Boxcar Bertha's exploits—she and her collaborator, Ben L. Reitman, swear they were real—did not quite capture the popular imagination the way the doings of other populist outlaws did. Bertha was promiscuous and pro-union—a fatal combination in the 1930s South, but unlike the men in her life, she lived to tell the tale. She was a supporter of the Industrial Workers of the World (the IWW), a Wobbly in deed and spirit, as her autobiography makes clear.

Perhaps because this is a proto-Hollywood film (its producer was the speed king of exploitation films, Roger Corman), Scorsese has his male rebel take more of the lead, something readers of Boxcar Bertha's autobiography would find doubtful. This makes Barbara Hersey seem decidedly sluttish and more of a follower than a leader. In any case, she outwits the law most of the time.

We follow Bertha and her gang as they move from supporting railway strikers to robbing the rich "to help the poor." Most of the time they're nonviolent thieves, unlike Bonnie and Clyde, but the law—in the form of two company thugs, the McGivers—just keeps on coming until the bloody end. Bertha's main man is called Big Bill Shelley, presumably a nod to the Wobbly leader, Big Bill Haywood. (In the film the union is called the Brotherhood of Workers.) A black worker from Bertha's past (the mechanic at her dad's crop-dusting business) and an eastern gambler round out this improbable group of primitive rebels.

Only Big Bill is bothered by the gang's criminal exploits: "I ain't no criminal. I'm a union man," he insists, and he decides to bring his share of a railway robbery to the union. Unfortunately for his pride, the union officer will take Big Bill's money but only after complaining that he is running with "whores and niggers"—"some company for a union man."

To salve their consciences, the gang hold up a railroad payroll office and make the cashier slip an extra ten bucks in every worker's envelope. Bill is never comfortable with his role, however, while Bertha likes to wear a lot of rich folks' jewelry on her naked body.

A few scenes of discreet sex hardly prepare the viewer for what has now become a classic sequence in exploitation films: the company thugs crucify Big Bill on the side of a boxcar. If this makes Boxcar Bertha Mary Magdalene, then it's (almost) time to appreciate the virtually apolitical *Bonnie and Clyde*.

See also: *Bound for Glory; Joe Hill*.
Availability: Selected collections; DVD.

Further reading

Boxcar Bertha (Thompson). *Sister of the Road*. 1937. Reprinted as *Box Car Bertha: An Autobiography*. New York: AMOK, 1988. Reads like fiction and folklore, but whether as a character or a real person, Boxcar Bertha got around.
Hobsbawm, Eric. *Bandits*. New York: Dell, 1969. Hobsbawm's cultural studies develop the model of armed riffraff who are social or primitive rebels.
——. *Primitive Rebels*. New York: Norton, 1959.
Scorsese, Martin. *Scorsese on Scorsese*. Ed. David Thompson and Ian Christie. Boston: Faber & Faber, 1990. Interviews include discussion of *Boxcar Bertha*.
Thompson, Howard. "Boxcar Bertha." *New York Times*, 18 August 1972, 19. Celebrates the cast; calls the film "beautifully directed by Martin Scorsese."

Boys from the Blackstuff

"Gizza job"—Yosser

1982, Part I, "Jobs for the Boys"; Part II, "Yosser's Story"; 250 mins., TV series
Director: Philip Saville
Screenplay: Alan Bleasdale, from characters developed from his teleplay *The Blackstuff*
CAST
Chrissie Todd = Michael Angelis
Angie Todd = Julie Walters
George Malone = Peter Kerrigan
Loggo Logmond = Alan Igbor
Yosser Hughes = Bernard Hill
Dixie Dean = Tom Georgeson
Snowy Malone = Chris Darwin

The titles given for the two BBC-marketed videocassettes are actually the titles for the first and fourth episodes of the five-part BBC

TV series: 1, "Jobs for the Boys"; 2, "Moonlighting"; 3, "Shopping Thy Neighbor"; 4, "Yosser's Story"; 5, "George's Last Ride."

Inadequate distribution channels for British videocassettes and the tendency of PBS to show only British heritage films have probably kept this outstanding dramatic investigation into the unemployment woes of a group of Merseyside workers from reaching the wider audience it deserves. (In the United States, as far as I know, only Eddie Brandt carries it.) Even the appreciative critic Peter Stead noted that the series "became something of a seasonal wonder discussed in the pubs and by the television critics but then relegated to the edge of the collective memory." As a portrait of struggling workers and their families it is by turns funny and terrifying.

The five-part format allows the filmmakers the advantage of focusing on a given individual or two in one episode, with families and mates taking turns as major or bit participants, depending on the situation. As a devastating portrait of Thatcher's England in its economic death throes it is probably unsurpassed. There is a sharpness and honesty in virtually every scene as we follow these workers who were once all road-tar workers (the "blackstuff"), the subject of Bleasdale's first TV special, *The Blackstuff* (not available on videocassette). In that program, the "boys" try to "fiddle" a road contactor and get caught.

Stead analyzed the startling characters in Bleasdale's series as a brilliant surrealistic cross between the regional and idiomatic drama of the Merseyside playwright Alun Owen and the absurdist intensity of Harold Pinter. The result was "notoriously funny, deeply moving, profoundly disturbing, and totally anarchic." One of the most appreciative commentaries on the series (by Bob Millington in George Brandt) argued that "a striking feature of the series' appeal was the offsetting of emotional drama with verbal and visual comedy." This "folk-humor," Millington suggests, was pure Liverpool: not only "surprising and extravagant" but also "an instrument of social justice." "Sniffers,"

or social work spies, get a ticket when chasing our heroes, a policeman who uses violence in turn gets shot in the butt with an air rifle, and so forth. It is, in many instances, the comic revenge of the people at the bottom of the social order.

Bernard Hill's Yosser Hughes burns with an intensity that is hard to watch: he doesn't understand why he cannot get a job or why, when he has even just a temporary one, he cannot hold it. His love for his children is fierce, but its ferocity deprives them of any normal human contact. Even his mates groan when he heaves into view: a giant of a man, with deep-set, disturbed eyes, he seems perpetually lost. His approach to all situations and all the people he encounters is breathtakingly simple: "Gizza job" ("Give me a job"). It's so simple that he cannot understand why no one ever gives him one.

Most of "Yosser's Story" involves his struggles with the child welfare branch of his local government. It's clear to him and to us that they will have to take his children away from him. He's crazed with fear at the thought of it, but we begin to realize that the children are pawns even to him. If he can just hold on to them, he seems to believe, all will eventually be right and he will return to (un)happy married life and a job.

When his children are finally removed from his flat—only because the police have beaten him into submission—the next downhill move is eviction. We are prepared of course for another scene of ultraviolence, but Yosser accepts his removal somewhat calmly. In fact, as the workers are boarding up his windows and door, he turns to them and says: "I can do that." Why can't I have that job? We don't know whether to laugh or cry. Yosser is one of the ultimate creations of a downsizing economy, and Bernard Hill's portrayal is so convincing I cannot imagine him playing another role. (He does, however, as Lech Welesa in Tom Stoppard's *Squaring the Circle*, a film about Poland's Solidarity movement.)

Yosser reappears in the last episode of *The Boys from the Blackstuff*, "George's Last Ride." George has been one of the leading

One of the boys (Michael Angelis) running from the dole police in *Boys from the Blackstuff.* Courtesy British Film Institute Stills, Posters, and Designs.

radicals of "the boys"—fighting the bosses, striving for a class-conscious workforce, never divorcing the shop floor from national politics—and the struggle has about worn him to death. His "last ride" is in a wheelchair, as Chrissie takes him round the old shipyard one more time. What could have been a moment of perfect sentimentality turns into a reaffirmation of George's spirit to fight on: he stands up—with Chrissie's help—to look out one more time over the wharves he worked on for so long. In what we think will be the series' last shot, the camera pulls back to a long-distance view of Chrissie rushing to get help, George slumped in his wheelchair, and a mud-silted wharf area where we know no ships will ever come again.

The filmmakers surprise us, however, by turning to another sequence—George's funeral and home visitation party—which (although filled with disturbing moments of its own) really sets up the final scene in the series: the pub near the wharf. Here all the principal "boys" and many of their friends and acquaintances are reassembled. We are treated to one of the silliest pieces of pub frenzy I have ever seen on the screen: pub character after pub character struts his stuff as Chrissie and Loggo try to understand George's death and where they are heading next. Yosser shows up, of course, and in a final bit of comic violence head-butts the character known as Shake Hands, whose schtick is

simple: if you succumb to his mighty hand squeeze, you have to buy him a drink. When a rowdy but friendly group of redundancy boys—they've just received their buyout wad of cash—turn the pub into a free-for-all, Chrissie turns to Loggo and says: "There isn't a man in there who is certified. They are all sane people." These remarks may be taken a number of ways, including the possibility that if that collection of loonies are sane, then the rest of the world is really crazy.

It is the world that's insane, of course: not the most politically astute conclusion but a pretty convincing one after we've viewed all of the episodes. The camera pulls back from Chrissie and Loggo to reveal the empty shell of a Tates & Lyles warehouse—the great sugar company that survived the Thatcher years but of course closed individual factories. (Another British sleeper, *Business as Usual*, profiles the demise of one branch of this company in some detail.)

The other episodes also have an intensity that exists in the background domestic drama of these unemployed workers. In "Moonlighting," Dixie struggles with his sons' apathy as he himself must stand by and watch the stealing that goes on in front of him as he moonlights as a night watchman. In "Shop Thy Neighbor," Chrissie and his wife, Angie (played brilliantly by Julie Walters of *Educating Rita* fame), literally come to blows over the shortage of food in their house.

British television is celebrated for its *Masterpiece Theatre* "heritage" films and other upper-class literary adaptations. But *Boys from the Blackstuff* is a class act from the bottom up, and one of the best pieces dramatizing the "economic terrorism" that Michael Moore speaks of in *Downsize This!* I ever have seen. The five episodes are to my mind endlessly fascinating, a blend of the personal and political rare in any medium. We can regret the unavailability of two of the related TV movies scripted by Bleasdale—*The Blackstuff*, directed by Jim Goddard in 1980, dramatizing the boys *in* the blackstuff, and *The Muscle Market*, directed by Alan Dossor the following year, tracing the fate of the boss of the blackstuff. Even without these additional films, Bleasdale's vision of an era in pain and denial on the personal level, violence and economic manipulation on the public level, remains a working-class and labor cinematic standard rarely equaled.

Philip Saville is still primarily a director of TV films, with numerous credits. Probably his only other strongly political film was his docudrama *Mandela* (1987), with Danny Glover playing the great South African anti-apartheid fighter. His *Metroland* (1997) offered an intriguing social satire of suburban middle-class London commuters.

See also: *The Flickering Flame.*
Availability: Selected collections; Eddie Brandt.

Further reading

Ansorge, Peter. *From Liverpool to Los Angeles.* London: Faber & Faber, 1997. A series of essays on developments in theater and film, stressing the explosion of talent on the British scene, particularly the Liverpool social realists such as Bleasdale, as evidenced by *The Boys* ("the most influential [British] television drama of the 1980's").

Brandt, George W., ed. *British Television Drama in the 1980s.* Cambridge: Cambridge University Press, 1993. Includes an excellent essay on *The Boys* by Bob Millington, who calls it "the TV drama of the eighties" on the basis of its "intervention" into the "burning social problem of the day"—"rocketing unemployment."

Caughie, John. *Television Drama: Realism, Modernism, and British Culture.* Oxford: Oxford University Press, 2000. The series "promises the security of realism and a familiar reality, only to undermine it with something else."

Edelstein, Jillian. "Bleak Scouse." *Sunday Times Magazine* (London), 1 August 1999, 16–20. Portrait of the director, who "may indeed be the most socially aware writer of our day."

Stead, Peter. *Film and the Working Class.* London: Routledge, 1989. A brief but very positive discussion of the series, which went "well beyond the clichés and stereotypes almost to surrealistically expose the social and economic hypocrisies and illogicities of a post-industrial urban world."

∽

Brassed Off

Gloria days

1996, 107 mins., UK/USA, R
Director: Mark Herman
Screenplay: Mark Herman
CAST
Danny = Pete Postlethwaite
Gloria = Tara Fitzgerald
Andy = Ewen McGregor
Ida = Mary Healey
Grimley Colliery Brass Band =
    Grimethorpe Colliery Band

This film has no shame and we probably wouldn't have it any other way. It is such a pleasure to see a class-conscious film with a big dollop of politics that we can put up with almost anything: that Tara Fitzgerald's Gloria, coal-town bred but now college-educated, who would be drop-dead gorgeous on any runway much less on a Yorkshire colliery town lane, would be interested in a local mutt with whom she had ten minutes of interesting hanky-panky when they were both 14, or that Pete Postlethwaite, who plays the leader of the Grimley Colliery Brass Band, would be named Danny so his band can serenade him when he is sick in the hospital with their version of "Danny Boy," or that . . . we could go on and on.

We are in the Thatcherite '80s. The Iron Lady has closed many of the mines, with a semblance of due process: the miners can choose to vote for a review (which will probably do no more than buy a little time) or for redundancy pay, a fairly hefty pile of pounds.

The miners have lost their spirit and the toot has gone out of their band. In fact, some of the band members are no longer responding to Danny's dream of reaching the national finals at the Albert Hall in London and are ready to call it quits. For various personal reasons, most of the leading players are going to be secretly happy if they get their lump of cash. Enter an angel in the form of Tara Fitzgerald's Gloria, the granddaughter of Danny's old pal and a great flugelhorn player from the old days when no one laughed (as they do now) when Grimley took the stand. Gloria, it seems, can play her granddad's flugelhorn. Soon the all-male band is happy to make a gender exception just so they can watch Gloria play.

Complications set in, of course. In a memorable moment (Gloria: "Do you want to come up and have some coffee?" Andy: "I don't drink coffee." Gloria: "I don't have any"), one of our band members gets to revisit his historical moment of hanky-panky, but not just halfway. Soon, however, he realizes that Gloria is management—she works for the coal company as the analyst of the review that almost everyone but Gloria knows is a joke. (It actually proves the mine has plenty of coal and would be profitable.) The grumpier members of the band shun her—they say she's nothing better than a scab. Furthermore, Danny is dying as fast as the colliery.

I'm not sure Marx or Engels ever got to hear a brass band or whether they would have understood how it represents typical British working-class culture—not only in the anthropological sense (the community) but also in the artistic sense (the music). The film neither idealizes nor condescends to this form of popular culture. Play on, but reopen the mines.

See also: *The Full Monty*.
Availability: Easy; DVD.

Further reading

Holden, Stephen. "Sentimental Coal Dust with a Brass Band." *New York Times*, 23 May 199, B21. "Shamelessly manipulative and sentimental, but in an agreeably familiar way." The reviewer is generally impressed by the film's class consciousness.

Lane, Anthony. "Bandstand." *New Yorker*, 26 May 1997, 88–89. Approves of the film mainly as "fun," but is bothered when the film takes on the Tories every once in a while.

Macnab, Geoffrey. "Brassed Off." *Sight and Sound*, November 1996, 44. The reviewer thinks it is "rare for mainstream British filmmakers to tackle class and politics as directly" as this film does.

Wilsher, Peter, Donald Macintyre, and Michael Jones. *Strike: Thatcher, Scargill, and the Miners*. London: André Deutsch, 1985. The real unfunny lowdown on the Thatcherite assault on the mines and the miners' union by a team of London *Times* reporters and editors who (unlike their newspaper's editorials) do not always take an anti-union position.

Brass Valley

Brassed on

1984, 86 mins.
Director: Jerry Lombardi, Jan Stackhouse, and Jeremy Brecher
Traditional documentary
PRINCIPAL FIGURES
Sarah Catella, John Hollingworth, and Rachel Doolady, brass workers
John Galt, mill owner
Bill Moriarty, staff member, United Auto Workers (UAW)
Donald Doyle, spokesperson, Anaconda Copper

Connecticut's Naugatuck Valley *was* Brass Valley: by the end of the nineteenth century 50,000 brass workers had created an industry that manufactured buttons, coffins, and cartridges for bullets. They were divided by ethnicity and skill: the mostly immigrant Irish, Italians, Poles, Lithuanians, and French Canadians had the unskilled jobs, while old

Yankees (Irish, English, and Germans) were skilled mechanics. The model for the factory was paternalistic—picnics and athletic teams, but no unions.

The need for shells during World War I created a boom and signaled the rise of a union movement. The film describes delegates from nineteen ethnic groups at the first union meeting and a successful strike for higher wages. But the Palmer raids, widespread anti-immigrant bias, and the Red Scare of the 1920s struck deep in this valley, as they did in many urban centers in America.

The 1930s saw a complex of maneuvers by both labor and capital: the Big Three copper companies (Scovill, Anaconda, Kennecott) bought up all the local companies while the Mine, Mill, and Smelter Workers of the CIO sent organizers to revive the union movement, relying on its East Coast profits when the unionized western union locals went on strike. (*Salt of the Earth* describes such a strike in the 1950s.)

But even after a successful period in the 1940s, factionalism split Mine-Mill, as it was usually called, when it came under McCarthyite attack for being Red. Its rightwing members joined the UAW, which won successful contracts but with none of the militancy or member activism characteristic of the past. The rest of the story is depressingly familiar: black workers and women remained in lower-paying jobs while the plants—lacking the modernization to remain "competitive"—were closed and the work was sent to Mexico and Brazil.

This is traditional labor history—accurate, thorough, and sad. Probably few of us outside the region know of its strengths and only with this film will most of us learn of its history.

See also: *Salt of the Earth*.
Availability: Selected collections.

Further reading

Brecher, Jeremy, et al., ed. *Brass Valley*. Philadelphia: Temple University Press, 1982. Stories of the workers in the brass industry.

✍

Bread and Chocolate

Yummy

1974, 109 mins., in Italian, with English subtitles
Director: Franco Brusati
Screenplay: Franco Brusati, Nino Manfredi, and Iaia Fiastri
CAST
Nino = Nino Manfredi
Elena = Anna Karina
Italian Millionaire = Johnny Dorelli
Police Inspector = Giorgio Cerioni
The Turk = Gianfranco Barra

This is a comic but revealing look at the European problem of "guest workers." Like many offensive comedies, it is either hilarious or in bad taste or both. Italians love salami sandwiches and the Swiss prefer elegant set lunches. Swiss men always dress in suits, while Italian men will occasionally pee in the street if necessary. And so it goes, all played for laughs and usually succeeding.

Nino is desperate for a job as a waiter, in part to send money back home and in part because it is a "good job"—that is, respectable. Needless to say, his luck as a waiter runs out, and he loses his job to The Turk, another guest worker. When he ends up on a chicken farm, living literally in a coop with other guest workers who are slowly being transformed into chickens themselves, he knows he's been down so long it looks like up to him. Even a brief friendship with an Italian millionaire backfires: the man commits suicide before he can actually give Nino any money.

Part of a series of Italian films using variations of the title *Bread and Love* (*Pane e amore*) made from 1958 to 1968, *Bread and Chocolate* also drew on the cinematic tradition of *commedia all'italiana*, characterized by Mario Monicelli (director of *The Organizer*) as films that mix "laughter with a sense of desperation" (see Bondanella).

The film also stars the iconic actress of the French New Wave, Anna Karina (famous

Nino (Nino Manfredi) tries chicken processing in *Bread and Chocolate*. Courtesy British Film Institute Stills, Posters, and Designs.

from Godard's *Vivre sa vie*), as a Greek immigrant whose solution to the guest worker problem is to marry a Swiss immigration official. Not much irony there.

See also: *The Organizer*.
Availability: Selected collections; DVD.

Further reading

Bondanella, Peter. *Italian Cinema from Neorealism to the Present*. 3d ed. New York: Continuum, 2001. The "most brilliant comedy of the period."

"Pane e Cioccolata." *Variety*, 6 March 1974. A pan by an unhappy reviewer who never really got a handle on the Italian humor and satire in this film.

~~

Bread and Roses

"¡Sí se puede!" (We can do it!)

2000, 110 mins., UK, R
Director: Ken Loach
Screenplay: Paul Laverty
CAST
Maya = Pilar Padilla
Sam = Adrien Brody
Rosa = Elpidia Carrillo
Bert = Jack McGee
Simona = Monica Rivas
Luis = Frank Davila

Ken Loach's career as a director of labor-related films, both documentary and feature, has been so extensive that he has merited a separate section in the introduction to this guide. *Cathy Come Home* is one of the most influential social-realist films made in the United Kingdom; it has never, unfortunately, been released in the United States. Nor have almost all of his labor documentaries, many of which have been timed as cinematic interventions in ongoing political debates. His feature films have fared better: from *Riff-Raff* in 1991 through *My Name Is Joe* in 1998, limited theatrical releases have made him (with Mike Leigh) one of the most highly regarded British directors of working-class, labor, and political cinema.

Although Loach's brand of social-realist drama has played at Cannes before, *Bread and Roses*, set in an organizing drive of janitors—almost all immigrant workers—in Los Angeles, did not seem to be pitched appropriately at this French resort film fest as the British entry for the millennial competition. But wait: who is cleaning all the rooms at Cannes? Algerians? Turks? Maybe this is not such a parochial film after all.

Paul Laverty, Loach's screenwriter on two other fairly different films (*My Name Is Joe*, about a working-class guy trying to cope, and *Carla's Song*, in which a Glaswegian bus driver travels to Nicaragua), combined two constants in the lives of immigrants and laborers in Los Angeles: the flow of illegal immigrants and the thousands of janitors who work every night in office buildings.

Bread and Roses follows somewhat closely the organizing campaign of the Service Employees International Union (SEIU) called Justice for Janitors. Using both comic and scary incidents, Laverty traces the fortunes of two immigrant sisters, Rosa, who is already working as a janitor and is married to an Anglo, and Maya, who has just arrived in L.A. after a harrowing escape from a lascivious coyote. Sam, an Anglo union organizer, literally crashes into Maya's work life and then her love life, as the organizing drive has targeted Maya's building for recruitment.

With Loach's usual care in casting local workers rather than professional actors and realistically conveying the difficulties of the harried lives of these immigrant workers,

Bread and Roses is one of the best labor films of the early twenty-first century.

See also: *El Norte*.
Availability: Easy; DVD.

Further reading

Callis, Stephen, et al. *La Gran Limpieza/The Big Sweep*. Los Angeles: California Classics Books, 1993. A photographic "graphic novel" sponsored by Janitors for Justice, in which a Mexican journalist searches for a union activist, a janitor, who has disappeared during the unionization drive; as in a film noir, the suspect is a corrupt boss in a corrupt industry.

Cleeland, Nancy. "A Fight for Dignity." *Los Angeles Times*, 21 June 2000. Extensive account of the film's production, emphasizing the film's origin in the screenwriter's experience of seeing "poor immigrant women leaving some of the priciest real estate in the world for the long bus ride home" after their night cleaning jobs in Beverly Hills.

David, Mike. *Magical Urbanism: Latins Reinvent the U.S. City*. London: Verso, 2000. Includes a chapter, "Uprising of the Million," on Latino organizing in Los Angeles.

Delgado, Hector. *New Immigrants, Old Unions*. Philadelphia: Temple University Press, 1993. Essential background study about (as the subtitle states) "organizing undocumented workers in Los Angeles."

Greenhouse, Stephen. "Los Angeles Warms to Labor Unions as Immigrants Look to Escape Poverty." *New York Times*, 9 April 2001, A14. Resurgence of organizing among the more than 1.3 million Hispanics who moved to L.A. from 1990 to 2000.

Hohenadel, Kristin. "Championing Those Who Clean the Office Suites." *New York Times*, 27 May 2001, II.9, 12. On Laverty's "research" in Los Angeles and Loach's collaborative style of filmmaking.

"Janitors Relive Story of Their Struggle." *New York Times*, 18 June 2000, I.Y16. Describes probably the first Hollywood premiere given over entirely to the workers who appear in the film, shown at Century City, site of major demonstrations in 1990 and 2000 for the janitors' drive for better wages and health care benefits.

Laverty, Paul. *Bread and Roses*. Eye, Suffolk: ScreenPress Books, 2001. The screenplay, with essays on the film's conception and production.

Malcolm, Derek. "Now We're All Casuals, Hired and Fired at Will." *Guardian Films Unlimited*, 5 May 2000. At ⟨filmunlimited.co.uk/Feature_Story/interview/0,5365,217326,00.html⟩. Interview with Ken Loach on the occasion of the film's competition for the Palme d'Or at Cannes; he made the film to explore the "parallel world of people from Central America who come in illegally, who do the worst jobs and, because they are without papers, are very easy to exploit."

Matthews, Peter. "Beyond Our Ken." *Sight and Sound*, May 2001, 36–37. "The keen sense of moral responsibility informing the production makes most current cinema look fatuously self-absorbed by comparison."

McCarthy, Todd. "Bread and Roses." *Variety*, 11 May 2000. The reviewer calls this "Euro 'art' film" a "minor piece of agitprop drama from Ken Loach that is remarkable only for its timeliness," but has to admit that the "root of the janitors' protest—low pay—is legitimate."

Scott, A. O. "On the Bumpy Road of a Union Drive." *New York Times,* 1 June 2001, B14. "The film makes a powerfully persuasive case" for the organizer's "efforts and for his unorthodox, confrontational tactics."

Waldinger, Roger, et al. "Helots No More: A Case Study of the Justice for Janitors Campaign in Los Angeles." In *Organizing to Win*, ed. Kate Bronfenbrenner, 101–19. Ithaca: ILR Press/Cornell University Press, 2000. Thorough and revealing narrative and analysis of the campaign.

Web sites:

⟨www.geocities.com/SoHo/Exhibit/5693/locatingloach.htm⟩ David Nicholls's "Locating Loach," an extensive discussion of Loach's career and its relation to social realism in film.

⟨www.justiceforjanitors.org⟩ Official site of Justice for Janitors, an organizing campaign for the Service Employees International Union (SEIU).

Note: A New Zealand film with the same title but on a different topic, directed by Gaylene Preston in 1994, is based on the autobiography of Sonja Davies, socialist and labor leader; it is unfortunately not available in any format.

The British Documentary Movement: E.M.B. Classics

Films were started

Drifters, 1929, 49 mins., B&W; director: John Grierson
Industrial Britain, 1933, 21 mins., B&W; director: Robert Flaherty
Song of Ceylon, 1934, 39 mins., B&W; director: Basil Wright
Social-realist documentaries

Although Kino Video released seven volumes in this series, representing a thorough review of the social-realist documentaries that dominated nonfiction filmmaking in the 1930s, at least three films in the first volume meet the criteria of this guide, those sponsored by the E.M.B., or Empire Marketing Board, a quasi-governmental agency whose brief was to promote colonial trade.

The second and third volumes also contain documentaries of interest, however, such as Alberto Cavalcanti's *Coal Face* (1935), John Grierson's *Granton Trawler* (1934), and Basil Wright and Harry Watt's *Night Mail*. The other volumes include three sets of wartime documentaries and a volume of postwar films of a somewhat more experimental direction than the earlier films of the movement.

This entry offers three films that pioneered John Grierson's early definition of documentary as the "creative use of actuality," a phrase open to many interpretations but one that covered the practice characteristic of many films produced or directed by Grierson. These films were characterized for the most part by location shooting and the record of actual work of working-class Britons. In fact, Grierson felt no apology was necessary to use reconstructions or stage the action whenever necessary, since these practices were within his idea of the "creative use of actuality." Thus in Basil Wright's *Night Mail*, location shots of a train were intercut with shots of mail sorters at work inside the train, except that the sorting was done in a constructed mailroom in a studio. For

Drifters, Grierson constructed a trawler cabin on the docks for inside shots.

The lengths to which these documentary filmmakers would go for authenticity ranged from the amusing to the dangerous: Nanook in Robert Flaherty's *Nanook of the North* built an igloo with techniques he hadn't used in years and actual fires were set to recreate the dangerous work of wartime firefighters in Humphrey Jennings's *Fires Were Started*. Perhaps these are only postmodern quibbles today, although cinema verité filmmakers were acutely aware of these reconstructions when they argued for an aesthetic of direct cinema, realizing of course that many of the arrangements in the 1930s were necessitated by bulky cameras.

But the movement celebrated work and castigated social problems, even if their patrons—the General Post Office and the Crown Unit, which, like the Empire Marketing Board, sponsored many of these documentaries—would not have to worry about images or discussions of colonized labor or imperialism in Wright's *Song of Ceylon*, about the tea industry, which was based on colonial exploitation by definition.

Industrial Britain uses traditional British craft industries—glassmaking and pottery—as well as a heavy industry such as steel and workers at the docks to portray "the history of daily work done, of people who kept on through the centuries." *Drifters* is a portrait of the fishing industry, while *Song of Ceylon* traces the tea culture of one of Britain's colonial outposts. They are an excellent introduction to a remarkable tradition of social realism.

See also: *Free Cinema; New Deal Documentaries*.
Availability: Selected collections; Kino International.

Further reading

Macdonald, Kevin, and Mark Cousins, eds. *Imagining Reality*. London: Faber & Faber, 1996. Excellent collection of essays, including both contemporary and modern essays on the British Documentary Movement, with an interview with Basil Wright.

Winston, Brian. *Claiming the Real*. London: British Film Institute, 1995. An extended and brilliant study of the issues of "reconstructing" reality for the documentary lens.
Web site:
⟨www.gen.umn.edu/faculty_staff/yahnke/filmteach /teach1.htm⟩ Detailed summary of *Industrial Britain*.

⤵

British Sounds

French noise

1969, 52 mins.
Director: Jean-Luc Godard
Postmodern documentary
PRINCIPAL FIGURES
Unnamed auto workers and revolutionary students

The alternative title of Godard's documentary, filmed for London Weekend Television, was *See You at Mao*, which probably conveys a little more of the film's political anarchy than *British Sounds*. Nonetheless, it is the significant cacophony of *industrial* British sounds that many viewers will take away with them, such as those that accompany the initial tracking shot (which goes on for more than ten minutes) at Ford's assembly line in Dagenham. Godard said that the whole point of playing the film "very loud" was "for bourgeois people to be uncomfortable with that scene for only eleven [*sic*] minutes [*and*] make them think that those workers must deal with that screeching every day all their lives" (quoted by Carroll in Brown).

The film's TV broadcast was canceled by its own producers. One wonders what they thought they were going to get: did they ever screen any of Godard's films? Perhaps this film may appeal to us now as one of his more successful documentaries. The slogans flashing on the screen, the workers at the British Motor Car factory at Cowley, Oxford, being interviewed, the University of Essex students making revolutionary posters—all these scenes have a loopy 1960s charm and—dare we say it?—a kind of logic often lacking in

Godard's other political films, such as *One Plus One* (a.k.a. *Sympathy for the Devil*), in which the Rolling Stones rehearsed the song that gave the film its alternative title while actress Anne Wiazemsky wandered through an auto graveyard by the Thames with an automatic rifle. Perhaps the London Weekend TV staff were at the 1968 London Film Festival when Godard punched his producer for adding a complete recording of the Stones' song to the end of *One Plus One* without Godard's permission.

Godard was clearly high on the French "revolution" of 1968, the dizzying moment when it seemed that French students, intellectuals, workers, and revolutionaries had finally reached some kind of modus vivendi. He went so far as to announce the formation of the "Dziga-Vertov Group," named after the only genuine (to Godard) Marxist revolutionary filmmaker of the Soviet era, the filmmaker known for his Kino-Eye series of experimental documentaries. The "group" apparently had only one film maker—Jean-Pierre Gorin, who collaborated with Godard on a number of political projects (including the somewhat notorious *Letter to Jane*, deconstructing and mocking Jane Fonda, the Hollywood star who had collaborated with Godard in *Tout va bien*). One of Gorin's best films, *Poto and Cabengo*, about Southern Californian twins who seemed to speak a special language, was made independently of Godard and seemed to represent an end to the political phase of Dziga-Vertov.

Godard's politics always had the air of a man who knew he was right even while he was supposedly waiting for the workers to pick up a camera and join his revolution. When asked, for instance, why *British Sounds* features the nude body of a woman and not a man, he replied: "Because we were actually discussing how to try and build an image for women's liberation" (quoted by Carroll in Brown). With this kind of confidence, the fact that every French film, bourgeois or not, usually features the beautiful nude body of a woman is not going to matter much.

And what are we to say of a filmmaker who—during this period of rebelliousness in his native France and elsewhere—apparently believed that "people like Jerry Lewis or Laurel and Hardy, if they were in the Russian Revolution, could have delivered Marxist movies because they had the biological capacity of doing these things" but that the Marx Brothers could not because they were "more the Jerry Rubin type" (quoted by Carroll in Brown)? Perhaps such fine lines between comic anarchists in American films *could* be drawn, but it also may be true that by the end of the 1960s Godard spent more time explaining than filming.

Only Godard's *Tout va bien* (1972), featuring media workers played by Jane Fonda and Yves Montand held hostage during a factory occupation by its workers, comes close—as a feature film—to the spirit of havoc Godard loved during this period of his filmmaking. It is hard to argue with a New Wave master who said: "Film is truth at 24 frames per second."

See also: *Tout va bien*.
Availability: Not.

Further reading

Brown. Royal S., ed. *Focus on Godard*. Englewood Cliffs, N.J.: Prentice-Hall, 1972. Collection of essays on Godard's career through 1972, including a review of *British Sounds* by Penelope Gilliat for *The New Yorker* (30 May 1970) and an interview with Godard and Gorin by Kent E. Carroll ("Film and Revolution").

Dixon, Wheeler Winston. *The Films of Jean-Luc Godard*. Albany: SUNY Press, 1997. A helpful overview of Godard's career, with a filmography from 1954 to 1995 and a section on *British Sounds*.

Greenspan, Roger. "See You at Mao." *New York Times*, 22 May 1970.

MacBean, James Roy. "'See You at Mao': Godard's Revolutionary 'British Sounds.'" *Film Quarterly* 24 (Winter 1970–71).

Web site:
⟨www.geocities.com/hollywood/cinema/4355⟩ A very complete and useful filmography and some other features.

Note: Also known as *See You at Mao*.

Brother John

Sister Easy

1971, 94 mins., PG
Director: James Goldstone
Screenplay: Ernest Kinoy
CAST
Brother John Kane = Sidney Poitier
Doc Thomas = Will Geer
Lloyd Thomas = Bradford Dillman
Louisa MacGill = Beverly Todd

If *Last Exit to Brooklyn* is one of the strangest and most violent labor films in my experience, then *Brother John* has to rank as one of the strangest nonviolent labor films, period. The character Brother John, played by Sidney Poitier with his most saintly look, is one of the most restrained outside agitators ever to come to a southern town whose principal industry—a sand and gravel company, perhaps, or some other primary materials site, but the film is never precise about it—is involved in what seems to be a hotly contested strike. Hackley is a town crawling with saints, actually, since the formerly blacklisted actor Will Geer (the sheriff in *Salt of the Earth*) plays Dr. Thomas, the genial white G.P. for most of the black population.

Brother John—as almost everyone calls him—has the remarkable habit of appearing as if by magic whenever a member of his family dies or is near death. Otherwise he is always away, on unspecified globe-trotting business, including visits to unlikely tourist sites—Cuba and Albania, among others. Dr. Henry thinks he might be a messenger angel, come to tell us of the impending apocalypse (which may or may not be a racial one). The doctor's son is an ambitious local politician who thinks he can snare a bigger political office if he exposes Brother John as some kind of international traveling Red. (Given the Cuban and Albanian stamps on his passport, I'd say it was a good guess.) The sheriff thinks he is, at the very least, an emissary from unknown radical forces supportive of the strike. The local strike leader simply thinks he's an old friend. The strikers are expecting some out-of-town messenger with some much-needed strike funds, but Brother John doesn't deliver the goods.

If Brother John is a spiritual messenger (John the Baptist?) or an angel, he's got some interesting habits, such as sleeping with an old friend who is a schoolteacher and pounding a deputy sheriff into submission with karate chops because the officer disrespected John's brother-in-law in front of his children. (Here we seem to be straying into the territory of *Bad Day at Black Rock*, where Spencer Tracy played a similar enigmatic outsider who uses a karate blow or two against the bad guys when push comes to chop.)

The film has obviously mystified or frustrated critics ever since its release in 1970, following a string of Poitier triumphs, such as *Guess Who's Coming to Dinner* (1968), and earlier, in 1961, when Poitier recreated his successful Broadway role of the chauffeur Walter Lee for *A Raisin in the Sun*.

Since Poitier's own production committee bankrolled *Brother John*, we can only assume that Poitier wanted his character to be an African American Cheshire Cat—all enigmatic smile and very little substance. The strike leader ends up murdered (offscreen) in the end, but the sheriff is less concerned about catching the killer than preventing some kind of race riot. Although we've been told by this very strike leader earlier that he never thought he'd see the day when these "crackers would be in a coalition with the brothers," how this integrated strike is proceeding—or even got started—will remain a mystery to viewers.

This muddle has a certain charm nonetheless, but in the end will frustrate almost everyone except diehard fans of Poitier's charm. We never find out what happens to the strike or who the hell Brother John is. The awful truth may be that in the end we don't really care. The only other person in serious pain is the schoolteacher Brother John dumps after a one-night stand.

Perhaps Brother John has been sent (or is self-propelled) to monitor the racist quotient of southern cities like Hackley. (What if God is so shocked at what is going on in America that he sends an angel down to investigate … hmmm.) A fair amount of racism is still around, but the second most violent scene is black on black: the schoolteacher has an insistent and jealous beau who challenges Brother John to a fight.

Poitier himself was clear about Brother John's origins: "The picture was about an observer from another world who walks the earth meticulously recording his impressions of the human condition—impressions that will ultimately determine whether mankind is worthy of salvation" (*This Life*). Since the story idea came exclusively from Poitier's imagination and not from professional scriptwriters, this scenario, which would be a cliché for teenage science fiction and fantasy fans and would-be writers, failed to attract an audience. Perhaps Brother John needed to spend less time observing a sexy school-teacher and more time observing (what seem to be) integrated picket lines.

See also: *Edge of the City.*
Availability: Easy; DVD.

Further reading

"Brother John." *Variety*, 24 March 1971. A sharp reviewer spots this as "an obtuse mystical melodrama starring Sidney Poitier as literally a super-hero, Jesus-like figure whose sudden return to a small Dixie town irritates the gentry while puzzling his old friends." Enough said.
Poitier, Sidney. *This Life*. New York: Knopf, 1980. Unfortunately, this is only a fairly standard star autobiog of the breakthrough actor of his generation.

✍

The Buffalo Creek Flood: An Act of Man *and* Buffalo Creek Revisited

"I don't believe it was an act of God. It was an act of man."—Shirley Marcum

[I] 1974, 40 mins., B&W; [II] 1984, 31 mins.
Director: Mimi Pickering
Traditional documentaries

Both of these films chart the history of a flood and its physical and psychological

aftermath. The disaster was not, however, the result of a river gone wild after heavy rains. The dam that collapsed was owned by the Pittston Company to control coal waste. Thus when it collapsed on 26 February 1972, its rushing waters carried coal sludge and other debris as it flooded a populated hollow in southern West Virginia. Within a day 125 people were killed and 4,000 were homeless. The company said it was an "act of God." Viewers of the first film, completed not long after the disaster, will probably agree with the flood survivor Shirley Marcum that it was an "act of man." (A similar "act of man" happened in Kentucky in October 2000: see "Further reading.")

The first film documents, with news and other footage of the flood and its destructive power, the fragile balance that was upset when the Pittston dam gave way. The company, it turns out, was already concerned about the riskiness of the dam and also that it violated state and federal regulations.

The second film explains what it calls the "second disaster," the enormous obstacles placed in the path of the survivors as they attempt to reestablish their communities.

Pickering's films, like most Appalshop documentaries about Appalachia, continue to gather awards and festival screenings not only for the high quality of their filming and editing but also because they document the human side of economic and political forces. Appalachia continues to be America's poor cousin, suffering from both economic disasters and media stereotyping. Company attitudes toward its primary workforce, the coal miners, have been remarkably similar throughout the twentieth century. An elderly miner, during a strike in 1989, recalled: "I worked in water up to my knees for a dollar a day loading coal by hand, and if I said anything about it the boss would tell me, 'If you don't like it, there's a barefoot man waiting outside ready to take your job'" (Couto in Fisher).

See also: *Justice in the Coalfields.*
Availability: Selected collections; Appalshop.

Further reading

"Coal Sludge Spill Fouls Kentucky Rivers." Environmental News Service, 18 October 2000. At ⟨www.ens.appalachianfocus.org/_mine1/0000014a.htm⟩ Latest disaster of coal sludge at Inez, Kentucky.

Erikson, Kai T. *Everything in Its Path: Destruction of Community in the Buffalo Creek Flood*. New York: Simon & Schuster, 1976. The noted Yale sociologist and consultant to the flood victims documents the psychological disaster of the flood.

Fisher, Stephen L. *Fighting Back in Appalachia*. Philadelphia: Temple University Press, 1993. Excellent collection of essays on the "traditions of resistance and change," especially Richard A. Couto's "The Memory of Miners and the Conscience of Capital" (placing the Pittston strike in the context of the miners' collective memory).

"U.S. Study of Coal Waste Ponds Is Criticized in West Virginia." *New York Times*, 3 April 2001, A13. Ongoing investigations and accusations over the coal company tradition of building waste ponds over existing or deserted mines, the kind of situation that caused the Buffalo Creek disaster.

Burn!

Brando lite

1970, 112 mins., PG, Italy, in English
Director: Gillo Pontecorvo

Screenplay: Franco Solinas and Giorgio Arlorio

CAST

Sir William Walker = Marlon Brando
José Dolores = Evaristo Márquez
Teddy Sánchez = Renato Salvatori
Shelton = Norman Hill
General Prada = Tom Lyons
Guarina = Wanani

Pontecorvo's reputation as a radical filmmaker is based on his two well-known 1960s films about revolutions: *The Battle of Algiers* and *Burn!* The latter is included in this guide because it attempts to portray an important complex of actors and issues on the economic stage: sugar-cane workers, their change in status from slaves to wage earners, and the relation of a colonized people to the agricultural monoculture controlled by native (often light-skinned offspring of European liaisons with locals) business interests supported by European military powers. I have not included *The Battle of Algiers* because its drama is almost exclusively the pursuit of Algerian cells of revolutionaries by French paratroopers. In both films the revolutions fail, although clearly the Algerians eventually win their independence from France and by the end of *Burn!* the natives of a fictional Portuguese colony, Queimada (the island of *Burn!*), are no longer slaves.

Both films are linked to the wars in French Indochina, especially in Vietnam. The para-

Walker (Marlon Brando) mediates between the leaders of the newly freed slaves and the new national (mestizo) elite in *Burn!*

troopers succeed in Algeria although the French failed in Vietnam, while the American adventurer William Walker, hired by the British to steal the Portuguese colony for them, mentions at one point a mysterious assignment in Indochina to attend to.

Here the similarities between the films end. *Burn!* has the look of a mismanaged epic film, with flashes of brilliance; *The Battle of Algiers* is so startling a recreated mock-doc that the producers had to append a statement to the effect that no archival footage of any kind was used in the film. The War for Algerian Independence did happen; the story of Queimada is a fictional mélange of the story of William Walker's adventures in Nicaragua, Toussaint l'Ouverture's victory in Haiti, Fidel Castro's guerrilla army in the Sierra Madre, and counter-guerrilla warfare in Vietnam. It is hard to imagine any single film carrying the weight of all those significant moments in revolutionary history. Certainly Pontecorvo tried.

He had to contend with twentieth-century capitalism as well: when he was forced to finish the film in Spain, his producers insisted that he change the European colonial power from Spain to Portugal, which had no Caribbean colonies but was not likely to host as many future film productions.

Pontecorvo went on to make only one more film (*Ogru*, 1979, about Basque terrorism); he spent the rest of his career bemoaning the difficulties of making truly political films. He has been president of the Venice Film Festival, one of the world-class commercial venues for new films. He has reinvigorated his film career (he was 81 in 2001) by coordinating more than fifty Italian film directors in making a documentary film about the antiglobalization protests in Genoa in the summer of 2001.

See also: *The Last Supper*.
Availability: Easy.

Further reading

Calhoun, David. "Lights, Camera, Protest . . . " *Observer Review* (London), 29 July 2001, 8. Discusses Pontecorvo's role in filming the Genoa G8 demonstrations.

Georgakas, Dan, and Lenny Rubenstein, eds. *The Cineaste Interviews on the Art and Politics of the Cinema*. Chicago: Lake View Press, 1983. Two interviews with Pontecorvo with the director's detailed commentary on his own films.

Glass, Charles. "The Hour of the Birth of Death— Pontecorvo's Long Silence and the Demise of Political Film-making." *TLS*, 26 June 1998. Survey of Pontecorvo's career, including discussion of the production of *Burn!*

Rosenstone, Robert. *Visions of the Past*. Cambridge: Harvard University Press, 1995. Includes a chapter on the strategies for portraying such historical and controversial figures as Walker; Cox's film *Walker* is discussed, but not *Burn!*

Shohat, Ella, and Robert Stam. *Unthinking Eurocentrism*. London: Routledge, 1994. Discusses Pontecorvo's *Battle of Algiers* as representative of Third World filmmaking—"cinematic counter-telling of the history of colonialism and neocolonialism"—but unfortunately there is no discussion of *Burn!*

Slotkin, Richard. *The Fatal Environment*. Middletown, Conn.: Wesleyan University Press, 1985. Also no discussion of *Burn!* but an analysis of the fatal mixture of race and economics in Walker's invasion of Nicaragua.

Solinas, Franco. *Gillo Pontecorvo's "The Battle of Algiers."* Ed. PierNico Solinas. New York: Scribner, 1973. Of interest mainly for the screenplay of Pontecorvo's other major film, this edition nonetheless also has a long interview with the director with remarks on both films.

Note: The IMDb Web site lists *Burn!* under the production title, *Queimada!* and also says there is a 132-minute version.

Burning Rage

The Dukes of Vashti

1984, 90 mins., TVM
Director: Gilbert Cates
Screenwriter: Jeff Benjamin
CAST
Kate Bishop = Barbara Mandrell
Tom Silver = Tom Wopat
Will Larson = Eddie Albert
Mary Harwood = Carol Kane
J. D. Moses = Bert Remsen

Burning Rage is a great title for a film about a mining community that has everything bad: an underground coal fire that won't quit, a deep mining vs. strip mining situation, and an unscrupulous rich man who has the police and the town newspaper editor in his pocket. It also has two former country TV personalities as leads—the singer Barbara Mandrell as an inspector for the Bureau of Mines and Tom Wopat (Luke Duke from *The Dukes of Hazzard*) as forest ranger. So how can a film with the working poor and some charming champions not put its good simmering class hatred to good use?

We are in Vashti, Tennessee. The Bureau of Mines wants the locals on the south side of town to move to a neat trailer camp so that they won't fall victim to gases from the out-of-control underground fire. Inspector Bishop says that it is only one of 260 such fires her agency is monitoring. The miners, who are out of work, smell a rat. Why has smiling Will Larson (Eddie Albert) closed his coal mine if there is still coal down there? First they give Inspector Bishop a piece of their mind. "I ain't budging," says one, "tell that to Washington." They can't hear, says another, "cause their jaws are always flapping."

It turns out that the richest man in the community got that way because he is a thief and a murderer. Finally someone has noticed that another town has been abandoned because of an underground fire, and Larson—who owned the mineral rights—strip-mined the town into oblivion. Add that to Larson's list of crimes.

This film's inept pacing and awkward scripting is unfortunate. When one of the locals, who calls himself an "ignorant old coot," gets to spit in the eye of the bad guy when he's hauled off to jail, you may be willing to put up with a lot.

Gilbert Cates has been almost exclusively a director of TV movies, with the exception of a critical and commercial success, I *Never Sang for My Father* (1970), with Gene Hackman. His last film was an adaptation of James Agee's classic, *A Death in the Family* (2001). *Burning Rage* is also about a death in the family, but it is simply not angry enough. Stars Lopat and Mandrell retain their TV iconic status: they smile a lot.

See also: *Chemical Valley*.
Availability: Selected collections.

Further reading

Revkin, Andrew C. "Underground Fires Menace Land and Climate." *New York Times*, 15 January 2002. The number of these fires worldwide is staggering: "Fires are burning in thousands of underground coal seams from Pennsylvania to Mongolia, releasing toxic gases, adding millions of tons of heat-trapping carbon dioxide to the atmosphere and baking the earth until vegetation shrivels and the land sinks."
Web site:
⟨www.offroaders.com/album/centralia/centralia. htm⟩ The coal mines in Centralia, Pennsylvania, have been on fire since 1960; the town is gone, courtesy of a buyout of the residents by the state government.

The Burning Season

The fires are still on

1994, 123 mins., TVM
Director: John Frankenheimer
Screenplay: Ron Hutchinson, from Andrew Revkin's book of the same title
CAST
Chico Mendes = Raul Julia
Regina de Carvalho = Sonia Braga
Wilson Pinheiro = Edward James Olmos
Ilzamar Mendes = Kamala López-Dawson
Estate Boss = Luis Guzmán
Steven Keyes = Nigel Havers
Darly Alves = Thomas Millian
Darci Alves = Gerado Moreno

Chico Mendes, the leader of the rubber tappers' union in the western Amazon state of Acre (*ah*-cray) in Brazil, was murdered in 1988 by a rancher and his son (Darli and Darci Alves), locals who routinely burned the forests for agricultural expansion. Mendes led the *empates* or sit-down strikes of the rubber tappers of the Xapuri (shah-*poo*-ree) Rural Workers' Union as a nonviolent means of protecting their livelihoods and their forest.

Xapuri was a rubber-trading outpost (population: 5,000), where in 1977 Mendes helped found the local union of rubber tappers and other Indian workers who needed to stop the destruction of the forest. After a fairly successful campaign that slowed the chain-saw crews of the ranchers, Mendes was invited to the United States by environmental groups that hoped to persuade international development banks to stop financing the paving of roads into the Amazon rain forest.

Unfortunately, Xapuri was also a very dangerous place for union members. Mendes's mentor and friend, Wilson Pinheiro, president of Acre's first rural workers' union, was murdered in 1980. Darly and Darci Alves, the ranchers who were eventually convicted of killing Mendes, had a 10,000-acre ranch in Acre and a formidable reputation for murdering anyone they chose. Darly's brother also worked in the office of the sheriff of Xapuri. The Alveses were convicted of murder in 1990 and sentenced to nineteen years in prison, but not long afterward reporters observed that the rules of their incarceration were extremely easy; the Alveses escaped.

The film stays close to Revkin's account of Mendes's life and death. It was originally to be a Brazilian film, but the rights were sold to Warner Brothers, which built a set in Ecuador. When this location shoot failed, Warner's subsidiary, HBO, then used Mexico as the new location for the film, with Mexicans playing Brazilians. Only one Brazilian, Sonia Braga, became part of the final cast. Brazilian critics treated the film harshly, arguing that it was not surprising that a North American film with Mexican extras did not convey the Brazilian reality accurately.

Despite these (possible) problems, the film is remarkably sincere in its depiction of the interrelationships of the economic and social forces in the region and the competing demands of the cattle ranchers, rubber tappers, and Indian forest dwellers. Some scenes are also unnerving, deliberately so.

For example, we see a murder Mendes witnessed as a boy, of a man who tried to organize the workers: a foreman poured gasoline on him and burned him to death.

Frankenheimer has been a noteworthy filmmaker for many years. His first major film, *The Manchurian Candidate* (1962), a tale of paranoia and assassination, has rarely been equaled in its genre. In the 1990s, with *The Year of the Gun* (1991), on Italian political assassinations, and *Against the Wall* (1994), on the Attica prison uprising, he returned to more topical and political subjects.

Film buffs will see in Chico's comic verbal duel with his future wife's father echoes of Zapata's courtship of his wife in *Viva Zapata!* and, on a much more disturbing note, they will recognize a quotation from the scene in *The Manchurian Candidate* in which a senator is assassinated holding a milk bottle to his chest. Chico's assistant is murdered while rubber-tapping, and the bullets cause the white sap to spurt from the container he is carrying.

The forest fires Mendes died trying to stop continue unabated to this day, raising concerns not only about local Brazilian workers but the literal survival of the earth's lungs in this crucial greenbelt.

See also: *El Norte*.
Availability: Easy

Further reading

Brooke, James. "Brazil Winces at a Film on its Hero." *New York Times*, 3 September 1994, 9.
——. "Hostility in Amazon Drives Makers of Chico Mendes Movie Out of Brazil." *New York Times*, 27 July 1991, 13. These articles explain the controversy about the film's production and the Alveses' imprisonment.
O'Connor, John J. "The Little Guy as the Big Hero." *New York Times*, 16 September 1994, B4. "The movie makes its points powerfully, although its anger can sometimes be simple-minded."
Revkin, Andrew. *The Burning Season: The Murder of Chico Mendes and the Fight for the Amazon Rain Forest*. Boston: Houghton Mifflin, 1990. This source book provides a thorough review of the case.

Schemo, Diana Jean. "More Fires by Farmers Raise Threat to Amazon." *New York Times*, 2 November 1997, I8. More fires than ever before are being recorded.

~

Business as Usual

Sexual politics in the small shop

1987, 89 mins., UK, PG
Director: Lezli-An Barrett
Screenplay: Lezli-An Barrett
CAST
Babs Flynn = Glenda Jackson
Kieran Flynn = John Thaw
Josie Patterson = Cathy Tyson
Peter Barry = Eamon Boland
Mark = James Hazeldine
Paula Douglas = Buki Armstrong
Terry Flynn = Stephen McGann
Steve Flynn = Mark McGann

Although this film did not find a commercial/theatrical audience in the United States, it is a very careful and entertaining look at a strike in a small dress shop in Liverpool, England. When a new line of clothing and a new hip look are to be introduced to a store in a chain, the regional manager, Peter Barry, uses an excuse—that he has been falsely charged with sexual harassment of one of the "shop girls" who works for the store's manager, Babs Flynn—to fire Flynn and create a new ambience in his store: Babs, it seems, doesn't have the new "Aelita" look.

Neither Babs nor the shop workers belong to the Transit and General Workers Union (TGWU), but British law permits Babs to join and file a grievance. Her husband had belonged to a union-management team that tried to save his factory (a Tates & Lyle sugar refinery) from being eliminated by the demands of the new European Economic Community (EEC), formerly the European Common Market, for limits on an individual country's production. Protracted high-level negotiations did not save his company or his job. We see video interviews with his younger self as he tries to negotiate to save "his" factory.

Although Babs's struggle is on a smaller scale, the younger members of her family, friends, and union mates all talk her into fighting back by striking the shop. Meanwhile her husband is becoming more and more discontented with his househusband role. He is especially irritated by his wife's new militancy and his son's (old) socialist militancy.

Business as Usual seems like a narrowly focused film, but it pays more attention to details of the organization of the picket line, the rallying of unemployed workers and other sympathetic supporters, and the negotiations than most films. Also of interest is the origin of the strike, since sexual harassment issues had only relatively recently entered into workplace discussions in Britain.

The look of contemporary England—its potential for positive interracial relationships, the emergence of small businesses into international corporate sleekness, and the negative feelings toward Prime Minister Thatcher—mark this as an impressive feature film debut for its director, Lezli-An Barrett. Excellent performances by Cathy Tyson, Glenda Jackson, and John Thaw (who played Inspector Morse on the PBS series named after his character) make this film a real sleeper.

The most disturbing scene in the film involves police brutality. After a humorous and energizing moment—Mr. Barry pops open a bottle of champagne and releases the curtains on Aelita's new opening day, only to be faced by a massive picket line from the TGWU—the picket line settles into the usual ups and downs of confronting a public that is not yet aware of the issues involved in the strike. Suddenly a flying squad of police officers pick off most of the leadership—Babs's family and friends—and haul them off to jail. On the pretense that one woman, Paula, is hiding drugs in her dramatic Afro, she is aggressively strip-searched by two women officers (who are pointedly shown putting on rubber gloves).

Eventually this incident works in the strikers' favor as they gain much sympathetic publicity because of the disproportionate force used by the police. The women are acquitted of the obstruction charges and provoke a parliamentary inquiry into the strip-search incident. After three weeks of totally successful picketing, Babs addresses a socialist political rally: "I got sacked," she says, "because I stood up for myself and the girls in the shop." Most British viewers would no doubt recognize this rally as fairly typical of the activities of the Labour Party/socialist left in England, but it would not be clear to most American workers, who might be surprised by the somewhat open alliances that occasionally develop between trade union locals, the Labour Party, and various socialist organizations.

Glenda Jackson has been a Labour Party activist, having been elected a member of Parliament from a North London district in 1992.

See also: *Riff-Raff.*
Availability: Selected collections.

Further reading

Barnes, Julian. "Letter from London," *New Yorker*, 4 May 1992, 78–92. On Jackson's political career.

〜

The Business of America

. . . used to be business

1987, 60 mins.
Directors: Larry Adelman, Lawrence
    Daressa, Bruce Schmlechen
Traditional documentary
PRINCIPAL FIGURES
Paul and Maureen Trout, former
    steelworkers
David Roderick, president of U.S. Steel
Ron Weisen, president, Local 139, United
    Steelworkers (USW)
Jack Bain, grievance man, Local 1397, USW
Marvin Weinstock, USW staff
Mark Green, The Democracy Project
John Naretto, narrator.

Which of these statements about the Reagan era, selected from the film, are true?

1. American corporations spent more money suing one another than doing basic research.
2. U.S. Steel had only 25 percent of its assets in steel—the remainder was in plastics, real estate, and a Disney hotel.
3. The National Association of Manufacturers once predicted the advent of the flying automobile.

All are true, according to this film, despite Calvin Coolidge's oft-quoted observation that "the business of America is business." This film is a chronicle of the collapse of the steelworks of western Pennsylvania; it is also a study in the potential and actual absurdity of these three statements.

The steelworkers by and large were loyalists during the Vietnam War; they also voted for Ronald Reagan. By the 1980s their most famous work site—U.S. Steel's Homestead Works—was closing down and the workers were being laid off in record numbers; they were also literally besieging the corporate headquarters in Pittsburgh to protest. These loyalists began to question the corporation, which seemed to have no loyalty to the region or the people who had worked in its factories for years. Nearby in Youngstown, Ohio, community groups in coalition with workers tried, unsuccessfully, to buy the U.S. Steel plant. A smaller company, Weirton Steel, *was* purchased and became the model for new ways of combating community decline.

The film concludes with a follow-up report on several of the principal figures. Two steelworkers, Paul and Maureen, are now minimum-wage workers, she as a grocery clerk, he as a night watchman. U.S. Steel is importing foreign steel for a local construction project. The only positive note is the creation of the Tri-State Conference on Steel, which brings together forces (labor, academic, community) to prepare a blueprint for regional development using the natural resources and expertise of the region's

U.S. Steel demolishes its steel mill in Youngstown in *The Business of America*. Photo by Paul Schell, Youngstown *Vindicator*. Courtesy California Newsreel.

workers. One plan called for developing new power plants that would utilize the region's resources (coal reserves, steelmaking capacity, skilled workers, and metallurgical research facilities).

See also: *Shout Youngstown*.
Availability: Selected collections; California Newsreel.

Further reading

Juravich, Tom, and Kate Bronfenbrenner. *Ravenswood*. Ithaca: ILR Press/Cornell University Press, 1999. The subtitle, *The Steelworkers' Victory and the Revival of American Labor*, indicates the importance of a successful campaign by the Steelworkers from 1990 to 1992.

Lieber, James B. *Friendly Takeover*. New York: Viking Penguin, 1995. Explains how a non–AFL-CIO union established an employee stock ownership plan (ESOP) to save Weirton Steel.

Lynd, Staughton. *The Fight against Shutdowns*. San Pedro, Calif.: Singlejack Books, 1982. Lynd's strategy for saving jobs.

∽

Cabin in the Cotton

Hanky-panky in the ledgers

1932, 77 mins., B&W
Director: Michael Curtiz
Screenplay: Paul Green, from Henry Harrison Kroll's novel of the same title
CAST
Marvin Blake = Richard Barthelmess
Betty Wright = Dorothy Jordan
Madge Norwood = Bette Davis
Old Eph = Henry B. Walthall
Lane Norwood = Berton Churchill
Lily Blake = Dorothy Peterson
Tom Blake = David Landau

One of seven films Bette Davis made in 1932, *Cabin in the Cotton* adapted a popular novel that dramatized—as Erskine Caldwell was beginning to do as well—the stresses in what seemed to many people (especially in the North) to be the solid alliance of working-class and wealthy whites in the South. Certainly there seemed to be the potential for great conflict throughout the region between landlords and tenant farmers, despite the political compromises that returned the southern blacks to virtual serfdom after Reconstruction was dismantled.

Curtiz used a favorite Hollywood plot for examining the tenant farming system—have the son of one class (the peckerwoods) be caught between a dame of the highfalutin class of richies that pay for his education and a sweet young gal of his own class. Richard Barthelmess plays Marvin, the young man suspended between classes, tempted by Bette Davis on one (high) end ("I'd like to kiss you, but I just washed m' hair") and Dorothy Jordan on the other. In what appear to be pre-Code moments, we get a disturbing lynching of a white tenant farmer who has killed a planter and a not-so-subtle seduction of Marvin: in both situations Barthelmess's character can do little more than wring his hands (so to speak).

Both sides want Marvin to spy or cheat for them: his new boss wants inside information on which peckerwoods are stealing his cotton and of course the peckerwoods want Marvin to fence their stolen cotton. The really big evil, it turns out, is Norwood's usurious interest rate and attendant cooking of the books, which keep the tenant farmers forever in debt. In fact it is clear to Marvin that his own father was virtually cheated to death by this system.

That we end up with what seemed to be in the Hollywood air as a solution to the Depression—cooperative farming à la *Our Daily Bread*—seems to be a desperate solution to a desperate problem: Marvin forms a tactical alliance with a crusading state attorney to work out some fair contracts between planters and tenants. At a dramatic meeting of the two sides Marvin lays out the system that has corrupted both classes and (incidentally) loses out on messing up Bette Davis's hair for the foreseeable future.

It will always be difficult to find a generic name for films like *Cabin in the Cotton*, one of the first of the cycle of "peckerwood" (the somewhat older term used by African Americans as a put-down for whites) or "poor white trash" films. Most of the nonagricultural and nonsouthern viewing public tended to use "hillbilly" and "Appalachian" as synonyms as well.

See also: *God's Little Acre; Tobacco Road.*
Availability: Selected collections.

Further reading

"Cabin in the Cotton." *Variety*, 4 October 1932. "Picture has all the flaws of an adapted book. Incident is blurred and character is foggy." Plus "little hussy" Bette Davis does a "coy strip" that almost went unnoticed by the hero. (Ha!)

A peckerwood (Richard Barthelmess) is seduced by an upper-class dame (Bette Davis) and ignores his gal young-un (Dorothy Jordan) in *Cabin in the Cotton*. Courtesy British Film Institute Stills, Posters, and Designs.

Hall, Mordaunt. "The Screen." *New York Times*, 30 September 1932, 17. An "uneven" and "muddled" film, although the reviewer recognizes the seriousness of the film's issues.
Kroll, Henry Harrison. *The Cabin in the Cotton*. 1931. Various editions available. This novel by a sharecropper-turned-writer portrays Dan as "neither whole peckerwood nor whole planter."

Camera Buff

Camera ready

1979, 112 mins., B&W, Polish, with English subtitles
Screenplay: Krzysztof Kieslowski
CAST
Filip Mosz = Jerzy Stuhr
Filip's Wife = Malgorzata Zabkowska
Anna Wlodarczyk = Ewa Pokas
Company Director = Stefan Czyzewski
TV Producer = Boguslaw Sobczuk
Osuch = Jerzy Nowak
Witek = Tadeusz Bradecki
Krzysztof Zanussi as Himself

Camera Buff is slow to take off: it appears to be a drama of the birth of a couple's first child and its recording on film by the husband, a new amateur cameraman. The film takes a turn, however, when the boss announces that he would like to have Filip film the factory's twenty-fifth anniversary celebration, for, as someone once said, "film is important." "Lenin said it," Filip remarks, and the beginning of the end of his innocence has already started.

Kieslowski's reputation as an auteur of intricate, emotional, and beautiful films is based on his *Double Life of Veronique* (1991) and the *Three Colors* series (1993–94), films that trace the intensity of relationships among mostly urban sophisticates of the new Europe. *Camera Buff* is a much earlier film about the intensity of the relationships among a worker, his family, and his workmates, relationships that he at first treats nonpolitically, to his eventual discomfort. In Poland in the 1970s everything is political.

Camera Buff followed a decade of worker-related films for Kieslowski. Influenced by Ken Loach's *Kes*, he did a series of documentaries such as *Factory* (1970) and *Before the Rally* (1971), the former about a tractor factory lacking proper equipment and the latter about a Polish racing car driver whose car was built poorly. *Workers* (1971), subtitled *Nothing About Us without Us*, featured the December 1970 strike wave and *Bricklayer* (1973) focused on a worker who doubts his contribution to the revolution.

Railway Station (1974), about the frustrations of passengers who await too few trains, prepares the way for *Camera Buff*, because Kieslowski uses surveillance cameras at the station to pinpoint the meaningless but degrading state security apparatus. The theme of the ineptitude of Polish society continues in *Camera Buff*, as the new-minted filmmaker makes the mistake of filming important visitors to his factory who wish to remain anonymous and an abandoned construction site for which the town had already received state funds.

Kieslowski's worker-filmmaker begins to turn his camera everywhere, like a child with a new toy. He reads about some of the masters of social realism—Ken Loach, for example, and Andrzej Wajda, the legendary Polish filmmaker responsible for *Land of Promise*—and even meets Krzysztof Zanussi, another Polish filmmaker, at a screening of his film *Camouflage* (in which keeping to the official political line for students is contested). In another self-reflexive gesture, Kieslowski casts an actual TV producer—Boguslaw Sobczuk, who played the same role in Wajda's *Man of Marble*—as the man who gives Filip film to shoot further exposés of corruption.

Kieslowski himself turned away from purely social-problem filmmaking, but Filip is more or less a self-portrait. Annette Insdorf analyzes Filip as Kieslowski's stand-in, so much so that Filip films subjects that Kieslowski had at one time considered as projects for himself.

See also: *Land of Promise; Man of Iron; Man of Marble.*
Availability: Selected collections.

Further reading

"Amator." *Variety*, 5 September 1979. A rave review, stressing the parody of filmmaking that is certainly part of the film's appeal, but the reviewer ignores for the most part the antibureaucratic and anticommunist (not-so-subtle) subtexts of the film.

Insdorf, Annette. *Double Lives, Second Chances: The Cinema of Krzysztof Kieslowski.* New York: Miramax Books, 1999. An intensive analysis of Kieslowski's career with discussions of *Camera Buff* and the early documentaries of workers.

Note: Also known as *Amator*.

Canada's Sweetheart: The Saga of Hal C. Banks

Strange bedfellows

1985, 115 mins., Canada
Director: Donald Brittain
Screenplay: Donald Brittain and Richard Nielsen

CAST
Harold Chamberlain Banks = Maury Chaykin
Narrator = Donald Brittain

This docudrama of the career of the successful Red-baiting union pseudo-organizer and (apparently) Canadian government-sanctioned thug Hal C. Banks was co-produced by the Canadian Broadcasting Corporation and the National Film Board of Canada. If two such prestigious sponsors are involved in exposing what has to be one of the more despicable moments in Canadian labor history, should we assume we are finally getting the "true story" of the elusive Hal C. Banks?

The opening credits would have us think so, explicitly associating the film's script with "court transcripts, sworn affidavits, minutes of meetings, eyewitness statements, and the verbatim records of the Norris Commission of Inquiry," the latter being the 1962 commission headed by a British Columbia judge, T. J. Norris, to investigate the violent methods used by Banks to maintain control of the

Seafarers' International Union (SIU), an affiliate of the AFL-CIO.

Banks, an American of doubtful reputation with a number of felony convictions, was handpicked by the Canadian government in 1949 to destabilize the Canadian Seamen's Union, led by Communists who were "actively directed by Moscow." Apparently Moscow did not know how to handle gangsters, because within fifteen months the CSU was destroyed, having had one of its potentially successful strikes in the port of Halifax crushed by Banks's men wielding water hoses and shotguns, while the authorities stood by. Viewers from south of the Canadian border will recognize the McCarthyite parallels in the United States: the expulsion of Communist-led unions from the AFL-CIO and the control of waterfront locals by New York gangsters.

The film is one continuous tale of murder and mayhem, as virtually anyone—rank-and-filer, labor leader, shipping line owner, politician—who attempts to exert some democratic control of the Banks machine is beaten or killed or neutralized. The title of the film—*Canada's Sweetheart*—may be too clever by half, since however much the Canadian government accepted this murderous lout, his real damage came in his sweetheart deals with shipping owners, which gave union members no say in joining or running their union. Any shipping line exec who challenged Banks soon found his ships immobilized; furthermore, the Canadian Labour Relations Act, it turned out, did not apply to workers in the shipping industry.

The fact that Banks was an American, with a union whose principal loyalty was to the American Federation of Labor and with the power to force a boycott on any Canadian ship in an American port, eventually raised the patriotic if not the solidarity temperature of other Canadian labor leaders. After an initial coziness with Banks, Claude Jodoin, the strongest labor leader in Canada as head of the Trade and Labour Council, eventually turned on Banks and expelled his SIU from the council. Banks's reign of terror was beginning to crumble when the Norris Commission convened and announced that he was "the stuff of the Capones and the Hoffas."

Banks was convicted of a conspiracy to attack one of his critics and was sentenced to five years' imprisonment. He never served a day; he nipped across the Vermont border, and the offense for which he was convicted proved not to be extraditable. When he was then convicted in absentia of perjury and was finally ordered to be extradited to Canada in 1968, Secretary of State Dean Rusk took time out from his busy efforts to promote the Vietnam War to quash the extradition order at the request of a Canadian cabinet minister, unnamed, alas, in this film.

If only one-tenth of Banks's exploits in this film prove to be true, he is a top candidate for the Labor Miscreant Hall of Fame. The viewer must seethe, seemingly forever, as he watches this film, as Banks beats and murders his way into apparent respectability. And while it took Canadian labor years to undo his mischief, Banks lived out his years in San Francisco, untouched by Canadian justice or even bad American publicity. If this film were better known or as readily available in the United States as it is in Canada, this lack of recognition would at least be remedied.

At moments this docudrama turns into pure documentary, when we are confronted with an actual interview with someone we have just seen in a previous sequence being portrayed by a professional actor. The interviewee, inevitably older than his fictional self, is offered primarily as proof that the fictional sequence is accurate and no doubt to prove that life was possible after Hal C. Banks. The film won in the Best Feature Film category at the Toronto International Film Festival in 1985.

See also: *Mother Trucker.*
Availability: Selected collections.

Further reading

Kaplan, William. *Everything That Floats: Pat Sullivan, Hal Banks, and the Seamen's Unions of Canada.* Toronto: University of Toronto Press, 1987. A detailed history of the two unions featured in the film.

Palmer, Bryan D. *Working-Class Experience: Rethinking the History of Canadian Labour, 1800–1991.* Toronto: McClelland & Stewart, 1992. Includes a short section on the machinations of Banks and other anticommunist efforts: "The Canadian labour movement . . . entered the 1950s largely purged of communist influence."

~

Captain Boycott

Clash of the tenants

1947, 93 mins., B&W
Director: Frank Launder
Screenplay: Frank Launder and Wolfgang Wilhelm, from the novel of the same title by Philip Rooney
CAST
Hugh Davin = Stewart Granger
Anne Killain = Kathleen Ryan
Captain Boycott = Cecil Parker
Charles Stewart Parnell = Robert Donat
Watty Connell = Mervyn Johns
Father McKeogh = Alastair Sim
Daniel McGinty = Noel Purcell

In what seems like occupied territory—Ireland in the nineteenth century—Captain Charles Boycott, the English landlord whose name became synonymous with an organized refusal to have dealings with someone, turns even more tightfisted and obnoxious than usual. His tenants organize against him so doggedly that he cannot get any substitutes for the tenant families he throws off his land. In the meantime, an Irish people's militia is building its forces—drilling with guns in secret—for the time when they can confront the English in a revolutionary move. As this is, after all, a British film, it is probably not surprising that the rebels' leader, a firebrand of a schoolteacher, always turns tail when the fighting gets rough.

While a film that traces the cultural history of the word "boycott" is certainly of interest, this drama of the Irish "troubles" of the 1880s has many other things going for it: a script that tries mightily to make sense of a political movement led by Charles Stewart Parnell, the controversial Irish Republican leader, and a plot that involves Irish tenants in rebellion not only against their landlords but often against Irish who seem willing to accommodate the British.

We hear echoes of the twentieth century when an older Irishman says: "Do you think you and a crowd of young jackanapes can bring down a revolution on those who have been running things for hundreds of years?" And even those who have been running things for hundreds of years are not so sure they want to support Captain Boycott, even if he is one of their own. A joke that ran through the islands when the struggle between Boycott and his tenants reached its height went like this: "What is the difference between Robinson Crusoe and Captain Boycott?" Answer: "Crusoe had a man named Friday but Captain Boycott can't get a man any day of the week."

As many of us are outsiders to this bitter struggle, we should have no illusions about the difficulty of commenting on the age-old clash of Irish and English for the control of Ireland's countryside and its soul. It is obvious from this film, however, that the Irish radicals had two goals that were not always compatible—reducing oppressive rents on the farms and resisting or destroying English control. Equally obvious is that the British have two weapons—the law and the military—and they will use them indiscriminately when pushed to make the simplest reforms.

One moment in the film must seem impossible to any contemporary viewer: some British soldiers at a pub (horrific to contemplate in this era!) resolutely follow their class instincts and urge everyone to drink not to the Queen or to Parnell but just to themselves.

This is a classic costume drama, a British heritage film of the 1940s, with lavish sums spent on sometimes very unconvincing studio tenant farms. This is a much more tender subject than most heritage films, since the film accepts Boycott's defeat but will not allow the revolutionaries to triumph unabashedly.

See also: *Hungry Hill*.
Availability: Selected collections.

Further reading

"Captain Boycott." *Variety*, 10 September 1947. The reviewer either does not see or does not want to comment on the politics of this film, because not enough attention was paid to the lovers.

Crowther, Bosley. "Captain Boycott." *New York Times*, 6 December 1947, 11. The reviewer suggests that the film comes at a time when such American congressmen as J. Parnell Thomas—a namesake of the Irish hero—should be worried about a film that so "hotly and approvingly reveals a case of farmer rebellion against the landed and privileged class."

Rooney, Philip. *Captain Boycott*. New York: D. Appleton–Century, 1946. Subtitled *A Romantic Novel*, because it is, but the historical section is based on tales the author heard as a child.

〜

Carbide and Sorrel

Lunch break

1963, 84 mins., B&W, East Germany, German, with English subtitles
Director: Frank Beyer
Screenplay: Frank Beyer and Hans Oliva
CAST
Kalle = Erwin Geschonneck
Karla = Marita Böhme
Karin = Margot Busse
Giant = Kurt Rackelmann
Opera Singer = Rudolf Asmus
American Officer = Hans-Dieter Schlegel

Although this is a road movie with an East German locale set at a very precise moment in history—1945, when Soviet and America troops had staked out their positions in their respective zones of occupation—its humor and its celebration of life are bigger than politics. In fact, that is one of the satiric points of the film: both sides in the developing Cold

War are infinitely pompous and equally foolish.

Kalle, played by Erwin Geschonneck (who became one of East Germany's most popular actors as a result of this film), has been sent by his Dresden mates to Wittenberg to procure carbide, an essential mineral needed for the destroyed cigarette factory they hope to rebuild. Kalle doesn't smoke but he's a vegetarian (he can eat sorrel, a salad green, on the way), and his brother-in-law works at the Wittenberg carbide factory.

Although he soon has seven large barrels of carbide in hand, he has no way to transport them and no permit to do so. His adventures (with various attractive women and a mined field) and misadventures (he is arrested by Soviet troops for profiteering) make up the core of the film. The point of the film is of course his eternal optimism and his ability to finagle almost every situation to his advantage: when he is stuck on a support of a bombed bridge in a river dividing the Soviet and U.S. zones of occupation, he manages to trick a passing American officer and take off in his speedboat.

As in many comedies, the payoff for the hero or heroine is being reunited with a lover: Kalle delivers one barrel of carbide but turns around and heads back on the road to return to the one women who appreciated him and his vegetarianism. And perhaps while a cigarette factory is not of the highest priority in a struggling economy, nonetheless it is to Kalle's credit that he solved its problem as well.

Director Frank Beyer did not fare so well: years after making this comedy, his much more telling satirical drama, *Trace of Stones*, was banned.

See also: *Trace of Stones*.
Availability: Selected collections; Icestorm.

Further reading

Pflaum, Hans Günther, and Hans Helmut Prinzler. *Cinema in the Federal Republic of Germany*. Bonn: Inter Nationes, 1993. This very thorough reference work includes essays and production data on GDR films and filmmakers, including a section on Beyer and his films.

Web sites:
⟨www.icestorm-video.com⟩ Official site of Icestorm, the international distributor of films released by DEFA (Deutsche Film AG), the state-run film production company; includes numerous commentaries on the films.
⟨www.umass.edu/defa⟩ Sister educational site of the Icestorm DEFA film collection, with rental information, a bibliography, and other helpful information.

Note: Also known as *Karbid und Sauerampfer*.

Cathy Come Home

Homes for the homeless

1966, 78 mins., B&W, UK
Director: Ken Loach
Screenplay: Jeremy Sandford
CAST
Cathy = Carol White
Reg Ward = Ray Brooks
Mrs. Ward = Winifred Dennis
Property Agents = Geoffrey Palmer and Gillian Paterson
Grandad = Wally Patch
Welfare Officer = Gabrielle Hamilton
Housing Officer = John Baddeley

Cathy Come Home was one of the first British TV productions to unflinchingly condemn the policy of separating husbands from families and placing the latter in "apartments" for the homeless. Although it is often cited as an important documentary, its status as a fictional or dramatic film is both more complicated and more interesting: it was virtually entirely scripted with a cast of (mainly) professional actors. Its screenplay was based on Sandford's careful research on contemporary welfare laws and arrangements and in some cases he incorporated actual incidents, dialogue, and courtroom testimony in his script. Through lucky persistence, the film team was able to shoot its actors performing on one of the actual locations that Sandford had researched and visited, Newington

Lodge, "the most infamous of all homes for the homeless" (Rosenthal, 1971).

Ken Loach and his filmmaking team were very conscious of experimenting with a fiction/documentary mix: he stated that the film's "time slot was after the news and we wanted to keep the feeling of the news, to stop it being like, here's the real world, here's the fiction. We wanted to keep the same perception and critical attitude in the audience." Furthermore, Loach concluded, "we were all Brechtians" and "our prime connection was with the news and documentaries, not the cinema" (Smith).

Sandford himself felt that his screenplay was "a new idea, halfway between drama and documentary" (Rosenthal, 1971). Loach's reputation was then not quite so well established as it is today, but the director's fierce political instincts helped make this a moving and disturbing indictment of a system that virtually guaranteed that a family, once fallen through whatever safety nets their own resources or those of early social welfare interventions provided them, would soon be hopelessly adrift.

This fall is precisely what Sandford wrote and Loach filmed: working-class Cathy and new husband Reg begin in a "luxury flat," but when they both lose their jobs, they gradually take less and less pleasant accommodations until, at one point, in a high tenement block, they end up in the kind of flat (in the words of one of the inhabitants, whose voice the filmmakers recorded and used as a voice-over) "where you can sit on the toilet and be cooking the dinner on the kitchen stove at the same time." Unfortunately, their situation deteriorates even further, as they become separated first by choice (the injured Reg is looking for work elsewhere) and then by rules—Reg cannot live with Cathy when she and their children move into a "temporary" homeless shelter. In a situation that calls to mind Ken Loach's more recent feature film *Ladybird, Ladybird*, Cathy's children are taken from her and she is left to fend for herself on the streets.

Cathy Come Home had a significant effect on social work policy and legislation in Britain. At first the authorities tried to deny its typicality, but Sandford's meticulous

On the verge of homelessness in *Cathy Come Home*.

research and the simple facts of the situation soon made this film one of the rare "documentaries" (for so it was often perceived) that generate almost immediate social change.

Despite its hybrid form, *Cathy Come Home* has been one of the most influential social-realist films of all time. It remains a convincing and unusual cinematic intervention in the social and political world. It is a cinematic crime that it remains out of circulation even in its country of origin.

See also: *Down and Out in America.*
Availability: Not.

Further reading

Brandt, George W., ed. *British Television Drama.* Cambridge: Cambridge University Press, 1981. *The* standard collection of essays on TV writers during the '80s; includes an essay on Sandford by Martin Banham, who comments: "The sense of authenticity that is conveyed in [*Cathy Come Home* and *Edna, the Inebriate Woman*] by the reportage style of writing and by the deliberate application of filming techniques patterned on newsreel immediacy caused considerable controversy and unease when first televised."

Caughie, John. *Television Drama: Realism, Modernism, and British Culture.* Oxford: Oxford University Press, 2000. Includes an analysis of *Cathy Come Home* emphasizing its radical and modernist use of "voice as a montage element."

Levoin, G. Roy. *Documentary Explorations.* New York: Anchor/Doubleday, 1971. The interview with Loach is quite good, but one with Richard Cawston, the director of documentary at the BBC, is quite revealing: *Cathy Come Home* "borrowed documentary techniques so much that the audience were slightly misled into believing it was a documentary, that it wasn't acted, and that these were real people." (Carol White, by the way, who played Cathy, was already a well-known actress.)

Loach, Ken. *Loach on Loach.* Ed. Graham Fuller. London: Faber & Faber, 1998. Virtually a complete survey of Loach's films through 1998 with his own comments about them.

McKnight, George, ed. *Agent of Challenge and Defiance: The Films of Ken Loach.* Westport, Conn.: Greenwood Press, 1997. An excellent collection of essays on Loach's films, including discussions of *Cathy Come Home* and an extensive filmography and bibliography.

Rosenthal, Alan. *The Documentary Conscience.* Berkeley: University of California Press, 1980. Another interview with Sandford; also covers his second powerful film, *Edna, the Inebriate Woman.*

———. *The New Documentary in Action.* Berkeley: University of California Press, 1971. Includes an excellent interview with Sandford emphasizing the origins of the screenplay and its relation to the realities of homelessness in the 1960s.

Sandford, Jeremy. *Cathy Come Home.* London: Marion Boyars, 1976. The rewritten screenplay with a record of additional scenes improvised during shooting and some voices "of real people living in the various locations" used in the film.

Smith, Gavin. "Sympathetic Images." *Film Comment*, March–April 1994, 58–67. Revealing interview with Loach up to the release of *Raining Stones* (1993).

⤳

Chance of a Lifetime

Don't miss it!

1950, 89 mins., B&W, UK
Director: Bernard Miles
Screenplay: Walter Greenwood and
　Bernard Miles
CAST
Alice = Hattie Jacques
Baxter = Niall MacGinnis
Stevens = Bernard Miles
Morris = Julien Mitchell
Adam = Kenneth More
Dickinson = Basil Radford
Xenobians = Peter Jones, Eric Pohlmann,
　and Bernard Rebel

Shot in actual factory locations whenever possible with professional actors and workers recruited to play themselves, this engaging and impossible foray into workers' control has a simple premise: when management throws up its collective hands, it's a "chance of a lifetime" for the workers to take over the factory. And so they do.

And everything, of course, goes much better for quite a while. And then they run into trouble with bankers. In fact, bankers turn out to be the main enemy to the

Workers take control in *Chance of a Lifetime.*

progress of workers' control of industry. When the new worker-management team gets a big order for their innovative "one-way" plow from a Marx Brothers country known as Xenobia (with the characters speaking a Baltic comic pidgin language), bankers make their money funny and unacceptable. And when the local banker boasts to the old manager (the wonderful comic actor Basil Radford—see *Millions Like Us*), even he refuses to be a part of their dirty deeds.

By the end of the film we get cooperation between the workers and the old boss: they know how to make a one-way plow and he knows how to get new orders to replace the lost Xenobian business. As Alice, the secretary, concludes, "We found the one way, too, haven't we?" It is the ending of *Metropolis* updated, with worker and capitalist in a new unity. The engineer who was once in charge

of the plant said he didn't want to work with any "half-baked bolshies" (Bolsheviks). Even the workers knew that this was not going to be quite that revolutionary: when they repaint the plant, red is not one of their color choices.

See also: *Ladies Who Do.*
Availability: Selected collections; Eddie Brandt.

Further reading

Miles, Bernard. "Chance of a Lifetime." In *The Cinema 1952*, ed. Roger Manvell. Harmondsworth: Penguin, 1952. Discusses on-location shooting and includes an excerpt from the screenplay about the workers' difficulties.

Stead, Peter. *Film and the Working Class*. London: Routledge, 1989. Argues that the class cooperation offered by the film's plot as its chief virtue was a throwback to World War II conditions and idealism.

T.M.P. "Chance of a Lifetime." *New York Times*, 15 March 1951, 37. "A noble experiment in labor relations ... examined with less than stimulating cinematic effect."

〜

Chaos

... is coming!

1994, 15 mins.
Agitprop documentary
PRINCIPAL FIGURES
Pat Friend, international president,
  Association of Flight Attendants (AFA)
Gail Bigelow, local AFA president for
  Alaska Airlines
Mary Jo Manzanares, AFA representative

A wildcat strike is unauthorized by definition: workers take matters into their own hands, either because conditions are horrendous or because they have no desire to wait until their union takes official action. Most companies would find the threat of a wildcat unnerving—it's unpredictable, uncontrollable, and way too militant for most managers.

What if you ran an airline and a wildcat strike could break out in your flight crew on any flight, on any day, at any hour? Well, that would be chaos, wouldn't it?

Welcome to *Chaos*, an agitprop documentary sponsored by the Association of Flight Attendants, who created this new strategy and made "chaos" a trademark (literally) of their militancy. In view of Alaska Airlines' traditional hostility to the union, when the flight attendants' contract expired in 1993, it was clear that every moment of negotiation was going to be difficult and filled with demands of cuts, give-backs, and benefit reductions, not to mention downsizing. The leadership devised a new strategy. They simply announced that CHAOS (*c*reate *h*avoc *a*round *o*ur *s*ystem) was in play, sat back, and watched management react.

At first not much happened. Alaska Airlines started to advertise for replacement workers and began to train its headquarters staff in the techniques of being a flight attendant. Finally a flight crew that was due to check in suddenly did not appear. And another flight crew plus co-conspirators flying in the cheap seats put on green CHAOS T-shirts (also trademark items) and began distributing leaflets about the union's contract demands during a flight.

It took only one or two more of these work actions to bring Alaska Airlines to a more favorable negotiation strategy, because, as Mary Jo Manzanares says to her union members, "So, where do we strike? When do we strike? What do we strike? I don't know. And none of you know. And none of management knows. And none of the traveling public know."

As an agitprop documentary *Chaos* is not very flashy—talking heads, some job actions, and lots of TV news footage. It relies—like many agitprop documentaries, such as *The Wrath of Grapes*—on its distinctive slogan or gimmick to do its work, in this case its trademark catchy word. In March 2000, as negotiations with US Airways broke down, the AFA announced that it was time for more CHAOS. Like a typical nervous passenger, I switched my reservation to another airline—the kind of public reaction the union wanted. Soon US Airways was inundated by requests for changes and cancellations, which they felt they had to honor (with no penalty). Although they threatened to cancel all flights, they soon went to the bargaining table.

The video performs a clear introduction to this new technique, but does not mention (as the AFA official Web site makes clear) that CHAOS can be used only after the thirty-day cooling-off period if no agreement is reached.

See also: *The Wrath of Grapes*.
Availability: Selected collections; local union offices.

Further reading

Greenhouse, Steven. "Down to the Wire, US Airways and Union Try to Resolve Contract."

New York Times, 24 March 2000, C9. Reviews the chaotic situation in a threatened strike situation without using the word "chaos," but does show a picket line with green-shirted flight attendants.

Web sites:

⟨www.afanet.org⟩ Official site of the AFA, with numerous links to current and past job actions; the union's slogan: "AFA is the world's largest flight attendant union, with 47,000 members at 26 airlines, and is the nation's leading advocate for airline cabin safety."

Numerous articles and bulletins from the AFA about job actions can be found and accessed from its Web index (by entering the search word "chaos").

❦

Chemical Valley

"They killed the Indians, now they're killin' the hillbillies too."—Yolanda Sims

1991, 58 mins.
Directors: Mimi Pickering and Anne Lewis
PRINCIPAL FIGURES
Yolanda Sims, Mildred Holt, and Betty Ray, residents of Institute, West Virginia
Warren Anderson, CEO, Union Carbide
Fred Miller, Friends of the Earth

The epigraph quotes Yolanda Sims, resident of Institute, West Virginia, for whom "they" means Union Carbide, not General Custer's troops, and the Indians they killed lived in Bhopal, India. Institute is a Union Carbide company town populated mostly by African Americans in a region of approximately 250,000 people. Thus when 500 gallons of a toxic chemical leaked at the plant in August 1985, not even a year after a cloud of poisonous gas escaped from the Union Carbide plant in Bhopal and killed 6,400 people, and local residents learned that there had been a twenty-minute delay in notifying the community, they became understandably alarmed.

The Institute plant was the prototype for the Bhopal facility; both plants manufacture pesticides. The company prides itself on saving the cotton crop in Egypt and the wheat crop in India. Local people who support Union Carbide, such as Betty Ray, worry that the company and its jobs may leave the area. Critics argue that the company's safety standards are not always sufficient and that the most dangerous plants are placed in communities that have little or no political clout.

Institute is in Kanawha County, named after its principal river and valley. It had been nicknamed Miracle Valley, because of the success of its plastics industry. This ambitious film tells another story, that of Chemical Valley, with industrial pollution, concern for community safety, and even the possibility of cancer clusters (patterns of cancers among residents).

The film will help you make up your mind about whether, in the words of Fred Miller of the environmental watchdog group Friends of the Earth, "chemical energy" can be made "socially accountable." Certainly when the film closes on the startling orange waters of a river near what you think is Bhopal and that turns out to be in West Virginia, you may become significantly more worried. Probably many of the Union Carbide workers are themselves worried, although the film does not pursue labor issues per se.

See also: Silkwood.
Availability: Selected collections; Appalshop.

Further reading

Lewis, Anne S. "Neighborhood Watch." Interview with Anne Lewis at ⟨www.austinchronicle.com/issues/vol18/issue50/screens-doctour.html⟩.

Scott, Rachel. *Muscle and Blood*. New York: Dutton, 1974. A very readable survey of numerous industries and their health hazards; Union Carbide stars in several chapters.

Waldman, Amy. "Bhopal Seethes, Pained and Poor 18 Years Later." *New York Times*, 21 September 2002, A3. A tale of two Bhopal monuments: a statue of a mother with two children and a sign "Hang Anderson," referring to Union Carbide's former CEO, Warren Anderson.

Web sites:

⟨www.bhopal.com⟩ Union Carbide-sponsored site: "The December 1984 Bhopal, India, tragedy continues to be a source of anguish for Union Carbide employees. It was a tragic incident that killed many innocent people. The legacy of those killed and injured is a chemical industry that adheres voluntarily to strict safety and environmental standards—working diligently to see that an incident of this nature never occurs again."

⟨www.bhopal.org⟩ A site sponsored by supporters of the Bhopal victims, with details about their ongoing efforts to make Union Carbide fully accountable in criminal as well as civil court: "Although the Indian government's civil case against Carbide was settled in 1989 for $470 million, criminal matters against the defendants are still pending in India."

∽

Children of Golzow

Young adults of Germany

1980, 256 mins., B&W and color, East
   Germany, in German, with English
   voice-over
Directors: Barbara and Winfried Junge
Cinema verité documentary
PRINCIPAL FIGURES
Jürgen, painter and wallpaperer
Gudrun, political science student
Bernd, chemical factory worker
Brigitte, poultry farm worker
Dieter, carpenter
Elke, draftsperson
Marieluise, chemical laboratory worker
Winfried, computer science student
Ilona, electronics technician

Most of us have blithely assumed that the longest-running documentary study of youths growing up was Michael Apted's British series that began with *7 Up* in 1965 and continued with *42 Up* in 1999. With the release of more and more East German (GDR) films from DEFA (Deutsche Film AG), the state-run film production company, it turns out that the *Children of Golzow* series is in fact the record holder, having begun in 1961 with *When I Start School*, followed by twelve other films, some of

which concentrate on one or another of the original children. The directors, Barbara and Winfried Junge, began with twenty-six almost exclusively working-class children but soon narrowed the field to nine because of the costs involved in following so many children. Even after the Wall came down, the Junges continued to follow them as they grew up, with films that continue to appear to this day.

This current release surveys the children as they grow up to be 26-year-olds. Golzow is a tiny village on the German–Polish border: its rural character meant that the children would tend to remain in the area; even after the reunification of Germany, only one (Marieluise) has gone west. The village in a sense becomes a test case for the Communist policies of the GDR—how well it educates its children and how they find jobs and prosper. The Junges describe Golzow—heavily bombed during World War II—as "a devastated village now getting back on its feet." Thus GDR agricultural policies—"land reform, modern irrigation, and the introduction of a new high-tech tractor"—are all covered in the film; furthermore, although the prologue and epilogue show "long tracking shots of a country landscape," the epilogue clearly represents a transformed region (Alter).

Because this project straddles the dismantling of the Wall as well as of a culture, the Junges have come to believe that "history exists only in film": obviously, what existed before the camera no longer exists, not only in a material sense but in political and cultural senses: the GDR, with its restraints and advantages (at least for some filmmakers), is gone. In *Screenplay* Winfried Junge says, "We can now talk about what we could and couldn't portray then" (quoted in Alter).

Although there have been thirteen films in the series, none is available in English except the Icestorm release under review here:

1961   *When I Start School* (*Wenn ich erst zur*
       Schule geh)
1962   *After a Year* (*Nach einem Jahr*)
1966   *Eleven Years Old* (*Elf jahre alt*)

1969	When You Are Fourteen (Wenn man vierzehn ist)
1971	The Examination (Die Prufung)
1975	I Talked to a Girl (Ich sprach mit einem Mädchen)
1980	Children of Golzow (Lebenslaufe)
1983	People of Golzow—Description of a Village
1992	Screenplay
1994	Jürgen of Gozlow: His Life (Das Leben des Jürgen von Gozlow)
1995	The Story of Uncle Willy from Golzow (Das Geschichte vom Onkel Willy aus Golzow)
1996	My Life Is My Own Affair—Elke (Was geht euch mein Leben an Elke)
1999	I'll Show You My Life—Marieluise (Da habt ihr mein Leben—Marieluise)

See also: 42 Up; Wittstock, Wittstock.
Availability: Selected collections; Icestorm.

Further reading

Allan, Sean, and John Sandford, eds. *DEFA: East German Cinema, 1946–1992.* New York: Berghahn Books, 1999. Excellent resource book on DEFA generally, with two essays on documentary (but not about the Golzow project).

Alter, Nora M. "History in the Making: The Children of Golzow Project." "Icestorm" (videocassette jacket essay). Northampton, Mass.: Icestorm, 1999. Extensive notes on the film and the series.

Hollywood Behind the Wall: East German Cinema on Video, 1946–1990. Icestorm: Northampton, Mass., 1999. The catalog from the distributor (Icestorm) has helpful mini-essays on the films (as do the videocassette jackets).

Pflaum, Hans Günther, and Hans Helmut Prinzler. *Cinema in the Federal Republic of Germany.* Bonn: Inter Nationes, 1993. This very thorough reference work has essays and production data on GDR films and filmmakers, including a section on the Golzow project and other documentaries from the DEFA period and afterward.

Web sites:

⟨www.german-cinema.de/archive⟩ Offers brief reviews, directors' bios, and production data; "a database offering information on the German films presented in previous issues of KINO-Magazine," including entries in English on the last three films of the series.

⟨www.icestorm-video.com⟩ Official site of Icestorm, the international distributor of the DEFA films; includes numerous commentaries on the films.

⟨www.umass.edu/defa⟩ Sister educational site of the Icestorm DEFA film collection, with rental information, a bibliography, and other helpful information.

Note: Also known as *Lebenslaufe.*

Children of the Harvest

Underage and illegal

1998, 60 mins.
Producers: Andy Court and Victor Arango
TV documentary
PRINCIPAL FIGURES
Jane Pauley and Stone Phillips, *Dateline* hosts
Dennis Murphy, investigative reporter
The Flores and Villanueva families, migrant workers
Mike Yaegel, cucumber farmer
Ron Brooks, vice president for agriculture, Heinz North America

In 1997 an NBC *Dateline* film crew and reporter Dennis Murphy followed two Mexican-American families in the central stream of migrant workers, mainly from Texas northward. What they found, of course, was that children under the legal age of 12 were working alongside their parents and older siblings. The documentary focuses in particular detail on James, a very bright and hardworking 11-year-old who is seen carrying cucumber buckets at least half his size. (He weighs 71 pounds.) He is picking the future Heinz pickles: "from James's hand to our supermarket shelves," Murphy concludes at one point.

Like most TV documentaries about migrant workers, the film shows gross violations of law, not to mention ethics and respect for human dignity. Heinz has a zero tolerance policy for any of their contract growers who employ children illegally, but Mike Yaegel—once the documentary team blows the whistle on him—is only the second farmer they've ever cut off.

The acceptance of child labor is so widespread that the film crew has little difficulty filming children of all ages working in the fields. Some of the footage is heartbreaking: after they film a group of kids in one town smashing their faces happily on blueberry pies in a pie-eating contest, they cut to the children of the Villanueva family picking vats of blueberries in a nearby field. Although we don't see any of the horrors inflicted on children by pesticides, it is clear that they are more vulnerable than adults to the poisons.

Pablo Flores—"the Job of the migrant trail," Murphy calls him—spends almost as much time trying to repair their rickety van with his son James as he does picking. He stops at a junkyard to buy windshield wipers . . . and a door falls off. Among the other surprises of the film is the sincerity of the farmers interviewed, who say—apparently without irony—that they worked with their dads when they were kids, too. A policeman in Ohio stops Pablo and asks to see his green card, but lets him go when he convinces the officer that he is an American citizen and doesn't need one.

Will this ever end? From 1992 to 1996 59 children died and 400–600 were injured working in the fields. The farmer disciplined by Heinz predicts that when children are kept out of the fields, Heinz will go out of the pickle business.

See also: *The Wrath of Grapes.*
Availability: Not.

Further reading

Goodman, Walter. "A Child Too Busy Working to Go to School." *New York Times*, 3 December 1998, B7. "The hour is a painful look at the immigrant worker condition and at an engaging, plucky boy" who is giving up school to help his family.

The Churning

"My village on the riverbank/With its rivers of milk"

1976, 134 mins., India, in Hindi, with English subtitles
Director: Shyam Benegal
Screenplay: Vijay Tendulkar and Kaifi Azmi
CAST
Dr. Rao = Girish Karnad
Sarpanch = Kulbhushan Kharbanda
Bindu = Smita Patil
Mishra = Amrish Puri
Bhola = Naseeruddin Shah

The epigraph quotes the credit sequence song and points to the unusual origin of this film: its financing scheme for production costs will not appeal to all execs, since a half-million farmers of the Gujarat Co-operative Milk Marketing Federation donated two rupees apiece to float this extraordinary project, a feature film that intentionally lifted traditional Indian feature-film making into a more provocative political realm.

Sympathetic but somewhat narrow government officials are sent to a dairy village to help the locals organize a cooperative. They have three "opponents" or difficult "clients" to overcome—the owner of the local private dairy, the *sarpanch* or village headman, and the mass of workers who are Untouchables. Just when the leader of the delegation, Dr. Rao, is on the verge of success, he is falsely charged with the seduction of a local women (played by the activist actress Smita Patel—see *Spices*) and forced to leave. Bhola, the leader of the Untouchables, takes up the crusade, arguing that it is the people themselves who must save the cooperative idea.

Perhaps because of this stress on self-organization, Benegal positioned this film as the final entry of his trilogy of films on castes in rural life, following *The Seedling* (1974) and *Night's End* (1975). Earlier in his career he had made advertising films and documentaries, a training that one critic (Binford in

Downing) said prepared him for the "striving toward visual and aural authenticity" and "strong sympathy for the oppressed of Indian society" evident in this film. The "churning" of people's views and emotions becomes a metaphor in the film for fundamental social change.

See also: *Spices*.
Availability: Indian grocery stores (usually in American NTSC standard).

Further reading

Chakravarty, Sumita S. *National Identity in Indian Popular Cinema, 1947–1987*. Austin: University of Texas Press, 1993. Very thorough history and analysis, with discussions of Benegal, Patel, and the film (briefly).

Downing, John D. H. *Film & Politics in the Third World*. New York: Autonomedia, 1987. Includes an essay by Mira Reym Binford, "The Two Cinemas of India," which stresses *The Churning* as an example of India's New (alternative to strictly commercial) Cinema.

"Manthan." *Variety*, 26 January 1977. Very positive review, stressing the film's insights into the caste system and other Indian issues.

Rai, Saritha. "Battling to Satisfy India's Taste for Ice Cream." *New York Times*, 20 August 2002, W1, W7. Latest news from the Gujarat Cooperative—competitive marketing of ice cream.

Tendulkar, Vijay. *Shyam Benegal's "The Churning."* Trans. Samik Bandyopadhyay. Calcutta: Seagull Books, 1984. A reconstruction of the original screenplay, with a helpful introduction by the translator.

Note: Also known as *Manthan*.

The Citadel

A doctor chooses: sick miners or the idle rich

1938, 112 mins., B&W, US/UK
Director: King Vidor
Screenplay: Frank Wead, from A. J. Cronin's novel of the same title

CAST
Andrew Manson = Robert Donat
Denny = Ralph Richardson
Chris = Rosalind Russell
Dr. Lawford = Rex Harrison
Owen = Emlyn Williams
Toppy LeRoy = Penelope Dudley-Ward

The Citadel depicts an unusual moment in British working-class history when Welsh miners had enough clout to employ (through a voucher system) their own doctors. Andrew Manson works for the miners, but as an intellectual and a scientist he feels his research into lung disease—using the miners as well as animals as guinea pigs—will be more beneficial for them in the long run. In the short run, however, he runs afoul of miners who want quickie excuses not to work and truly sick miners used to a little medicine now and then to ease their pains. Manson's mini–research lab falls victim to one of the malingerers, who—using the cry of "no animal harmful experimentation"—destroys Manson's gradually successful research.

Forced to go to London, he and his wife become estranged as he begins to take on society patients who have minor ailments or none at all but pay big fees. After laboring at the bottom, he is more than ready to be top dog. Even the nurses at his new clinic have svelte outfits and high heels, not to mention the society dames he caters to. (One of them tells him right away that he needs to "get a tailor.") Only the death of his best friend (who fails to sell Manson on a community health clinic scheme) and the love of his ever-patient wife (played with style and a confident air by Rosalind Russell) lead Andrew back to the path of righteousness.

The film mixes what Vidor could do best with some Hollywood imperatives. Since it keeps Manson's wife alive (she dies in the novel), she is by his side after his triumphant speech at his trial for helping an unlicensed practitioner work on a pneumonia case. And when he realizes that the incompetent surgeons of the rich he has been hobnobbing with have failed to save his friend, he roams the city at night and may even consider suicide until he hears the heavenly voice of his friend urging him to stand up straight.

If much of this sounds a bit too sentimental and moralistic, you would not be far wrong. But Robert Donat's ever-chirpy ironic style and the strength of the film's realism keep the viewer going during teary intervals. When Andrew wanders London, he sees people scrounging in garbage cans, the blind begging, and children playing in traffic. In short, he sees the have-nots and he stops wanting to be a have. He returns to the radicalism of his earlier days—when he and his friend dynamited a horribly pestilential sewer to force the government to replace it—and challenges the stodgy medical establishment.

See also: *How Green Was My Valley; The Stars Look Down.*
Availability: Easy

Further reading

Cronin, A. J. *The Citadel*. 1937. Numerous editions of this best-seller are available.

Nugent, Frank S. "The Citadel." *New York Times*, 4 November 1938, 27. "A splendid transcription of a dramatic story, with strong performances to match a sensitive director's design."

Note: A later version of this film, a miniseries directed by Paul Bryant for British TV in 1983, is not currently available in videocassette.

The City

Real Tales of the City

1999, 88 mins., B&W, in Spanish, with English subtitles, and English
Director: David Riker
Screenplay: David Riker
CAST
"The Photo Studio":
The photographer = Antonio Peralta

"Bricks":
The men = Moisés García, Marcos Martínez García, Mateo Gómez, César Monzón, Harsh Nayyar, Fernando Reyes, Víctor Sierra, Carlos Torrentes
The boy = Anthony Rivera
The contractor = Joe Rigano
The organizer = Miguel Maldonado
Voice-over = Maite Bonilla
"Home":
The young man = Cipriano García
The young woman = Leticia Herrera
"The Puppeteer":
The father = José Rabelo
The daughter = Stephanie Viruet
The city worker = Gene Ruffini
The health worker = Eileen Vega
The friend = Denia Brache
The school registrar = Marta de la Cruz
"Seamstress":
The seamstress = Silvia Goiz
Her co-workers and friends = Rosa Caguana, Guillermina de Jesús, Ángeles Rubio, Teresa Yenque, Valentina Zea
The sweatshop managers = Hyoung Taek Limb, Jawon Kim
The designer = María Galante
Workers in hallway = Mónica Cano, Ernesto López
The cousin = Galo Rodin Schneider
The dress store manager = Jaime Sánchez

The City is an unusual experiment in contemporary filmmaking, not only in subject matter but in its overall conception and method of building stories. The director, David Riker, has created four stories of Latino immigrants that typify some of their struggles—homelessness, dangerous day work, difficulties in coping with urban life, and working without immediate pay. His achievement will remind viewers of the approach pioneered by the Italian neorealist filmmakers after World War II—the use of nonprofessionals in acting roles, nitty-gritty street life, and respect for the working poor.

Riker's method of filming, once he decided that he would use nonprofessionals for the key roles, was to recruit workers literally from the streets, work with them in creative and story-building sessions, and write a script out of their experiences. Thus for "Bricks" he combined his research into street-corner labor pools and a story he had read in a newspaper about a homeless man killed while scavenging for bricks in the Bronx: "The idea of brick scavenging," he stated, "struck me as a metaphor not only for the whole transformation of the city that is occurring, but also for the idea of uprootedness, which is the central drama every immigrant experiences." He leafleted labor pools with a Dominican organizer who worked for the Center for Immigrant Rights.

Similarly, for "Seamstress," he handed out 40,000 leaflets during shift changes at the Eighth Avenue garment workshops. Workers curious to see what he was up to watched "Bricks" to understand what they were getting involved with. The story that evolved was a portrait of a worker who badly needs her overdue pay to help a sick relative: her employers treat this "demand" as some kind of rebellion. The drill for "Home" was a little different, in that it came out of an invitation to a young girl's Mexican Sweet 15 party: "Seeing this cultural tradition so firmly transported from Mexico to the Bronx," he asked the girl's father to recreate the party for his camera. The man agreed and invited 200 of his relatives to stage the party again.

The framing story of these four urban tales of Latino immigrants in contemporary New York City is a neighborhood photographer's studio. Here the very poor and the working poor spend their money on photos, perhaps to send back home, perhaps just to memorialize important moments in their lives. For a brief moment they smile or even laugh, as each one of the principal characters in the four tales takes his or her place before the camera. Their friends and neighbors and even strangers are included in these brief connecting moments to give us a sense of a community captured in an instant. But usually only the faces are shown in this fascinating and authentic way of linking the seemingly unrelated characters of the four stories.

A year after completing the film, Riker traced the lives of some of his cast: "Most are still in New York City, but some have unfortunately been deported, including the lead actress in the love story, "Home," who was arrested in an INS sweatshop raid and sent back to her small village in Puebla, Mexico. The lead in "Seamstress" continues to work in the sweatshops of New York. Most of the men in "Bricks" are still on the street corners looking for work, although one of them, the young man who dies, is now working in the agricultural fields of North Carolina. Two of the men have been able to bring their wives to New York City after being separated for as long as ten years. The young girl in "Puppeteer" is now 16 years old, in high school, and working in a variety of jobs."

Day laborers carry the body of an injured worker in *The City*. Photo by Victor Sira. Courtesy Zeitgeist Films.

See also: *Nightsongs*.
Availability: Selected collections; Zeitgeist.

Further reading

Anderson, John. "'The City': American in Any Language." *Newsday*, 22 October 1999, B15. Short but very incisive review stressing (ironically) that the film "meets all the standard requirements for a foreign film—subtitles, spartan aesthetics, black and white photography, foreigners—while actually being the most American movie of this or any other recent year."

Ebert, Roger. "The City." *Chicago Sun-Times*, 1 January 2000. Emphasizes Riker's ability not to close his stories but to keep to the reality of the subjects' lives in that their struggles continue.

Holden, Stephen. "Citizens of Poverty Yearning to Be Free." *New York Times*, 22 October 1999. Call this an "indelible, deeply disquieting film" whose "understatement makes it all the more devastating."

Klawans, Stuart. "The City." *Nation*, 8 November 1999. Another rave review: "Given a magazine to fill and not just a column, I would find words sufficient to praise" this film.

Sklar, Robert. "Rediscovering Radical Film Style: An Interview with David Riker." *Cineaste* 24, no. 2–3 (1999): 6–9. Reviews the film's production history, with emphasis on Riker's attempt to find a third way (Italian neorealism and cinema verité documentary style being the other two ways).

Waldman, Amy. "In Film, Immigrants Bring Real Life to Acting Jobs." *New York Times*, 25 October 1999. Feature article on how the non-professionals were recruited to act for the film, concentrating on César Monzón, one of the "Brick" workers, and Silvia Goiz, the featured seamstress.

Web sites:

⟨www.itvs.org/thecity⟩ Extensive press releases from Public Broadcasting Service (PBS) for the film, including a Postscript in part about the non-professionals in the film: "Certainly they will tell you, if asked," Riker states, "that being in the film was one of the most special experiences they have had since arriving in this country. But it is the simple act of having broken their silence, of expressing in the film feelings which were deeply suppressed, that has given many of them a new sense of confidence living here, without papers."

⟨www.zeitgeistfilm.com/current/the%20city/city.html⟩ The distributor's official Web site, with synopses of the four segments, production details, and helpful information about the process of making this film as well as information about the filmmakers.

↩

Clockwatchers

Waiting for Parker Posey

1998, 110 mins., PG-13
Director: Jill Sprecher
Screenplay: Jill and Karen Sprecher
CAST
Iris = Toni Collette
Margaret = Parker Posey
Paula = Lisa Kudrow
Jane = Alanna Ubach
Cleo = Helen Fitzgerald

If the mere mention of the name Parker Posey is enough to tickle your funny bone, then *Clockwatchers* will be a very good opportunity for more Parker Posey watching. This "queen of the indies" has been in so many small films that often the main reason for watching them is to see this sweetly anarchistic urban gal dish it out. In *The House of Yes*, for example, she dishes it out as Jackie Kennedy. She gets another ideal role in *Clockwatchers*, and although Toni Collette (the Muriel of *Muriel's Wedding*) is the lead with the most screen time and the temp worker whose journey through inane work routines the film has as its focus, when Parker Posey leaves her job (that's an understatement), the film sags.

The "clockwatchers" are four temps who slowly bond as a result of their sorry status as Global Credit Corporation workers at the absolute bottom of the corporate ladder. The mailroom boy is upbeat and seems to have more status than they do: he, after all, is on the regular payroll. We are taken through their mind-numbing day, at first step by step as the new temp, Colette, joins the other three. Not much happens, or, to put it another way, the only things that happen are demeaning and job-threatening. The company hires a new regular secretary, for example, without giving any of the temps a shot at the position, and some minor thievery sweeps through the office suite. Unfortunately, it is the temps who are suspected of the thefts, and for a while Parker Posey looks guilty as hell, since she has a few suspicious objects in her desk drawer.

The fact of the matter is that we are more or less cheering for the thief, not only because the corporation deserves a little bashing but also because theft seems like the only rebellion the temps seem capable of. The friendship of the four temps seems to work: Parker Posey is of course the know-it-all, dismissing any demands on her time unless they satisfy her definition of real work (e.g., a permanent job or a decent recommendation that will get her one); Lisa Kudrow is bimbo-ish, hoping her figure will get her an acting role or at least a boyfriend; Alanna Ubach plays a woman whose only goal is to get married, although we know— and she suspects—her fiancé is a loser; Toni Collette's role is a little more complex—we meet her dad, who wants her to get a real job (a sales position), and she keeps a mildly self-conscious diary.

In the end Parker Posey's little rebellion— she doesn't call in sick one day, assuming her buddy temps are all making a similar statement by not showing up for work—fails. When she is literally dragged from her desk, she screams about the loss of support from her three office mates and friends. But the collective doesn't hold.

It's easy to say that what they really needed to do was organize in some way. But the office suites of the world are filled with unorganized temps, not to mention unorganized regular workers. The ad campaign says that this film is like "Mary Tyler Moore meets Franz Kafka." Maybe. Kafka also knew the mind-numbing bureaucracies and the petty rebellions of the clerks, but he was a satirist and humorist. It's more like Kafka on Prozac here. Nothing much happens in this film: too often feminist rebellion takes the form of women dashing down the hallways when the clock strikes five.

See also: *Office Space*.
Availability: Easy; DVD.

Further reading

Cook, Christopher. "Temps Demand a New Deal." *Nation*, 27 March 2000, 13–19. Argues that the "explosion of temping and the shifting of employment relationships away from traditional jobs poses what may be organized labor's greatest challenge and opportunity since World War II: organizing the swelling ranks of temps, day laborers, and contract and leased workers whose perpetual job insecurity forms the porous foundation of today's economy."

Ebert, Roger. "Clockwatchers." *Chicago Sun-Times*, 5 May 1998. "This is a rare film about the way people actually live"; "a wicked, subversive comedy about the hell on earth occupied by temporary office workers."

Holden, Stephen. "'Clockwatchers': Sedition and Subjugation." *New York Times*, 15 May 1998. Celebrates this "small, gently surreal comedy" in part because of its ability to capture an office's "particular blend of boredom and paranoia" and in part because of Parker Posey's portrayal of a temp worker "whose proud fighting spirit has curdled into a kind of free-floating hysteria."

McDonagh, Maitland. "Clockwatchers." *TV Guide*. Memorable but short review categorizing our antiheroines as "the migrant workers of the desk set," part of the "subtle but rigid caste system of low-level cogs in the corporate machine."

Nichols, Peter. "4 Young Women Watch the Clock." *New York Times*, 16 October 1998, B26. Stresses the difficulties of promoting this "drily funny and disturbing look at four young women squelching their promise and dreams" as temps.

Porton, Richard. "Clockwatchers." *Cineaste* 23, no. 4 (1998): 64. Calls it "the best independent fiction film to explore the world of work since Chris Smith's scandalously overlooked 'American Job.'"

Rogers, Jackie Krasas. *Temps: The Many Faces of the Changing Workplace*. Ithaca: ILR Press/Cornell University Press, 2000. Studies clerical workers, "focusing especially on issues of race, gender, power, and identity," with a somewhat surprising conclusion that temps often work harder than regular employees, even though "they have no established social relations in the workplace."

Web sites:
⟨www.fairjobs.or⟩ and ⟨www.wpusa.org⟩ Helpful official sites for the film with information about temp workers organizing.

Coal Miner's Daughter

More music than coal

1980, 125 mins., PG
Director: Michael Apted
Screenplay: Tom Rickman, from Loretta
  Lynn's autobiography
CAST
Loretta Lynn = Sissy Spacek
Doolittle Lynn = Tommy Lee Jones
Patsy Cline = Beverly D'Angelo
Ted Webb = Levon Helm
Clara Webb = Phyllis Boyens
Moonshiner = William Sanderson

Most of Loretta Lynn's life has become an open book: married at 13, four children by 20, just a country gal from Butcher Holler, Kentucky. It was a long way from the Saturday-night Grange Hall crowd to the Grand Ole Opry, but the film makes it seem like an inevitable if not a risky journey, despite the difficulties of rural poverty.

Making a film set in an Appalachian mining community is not an easy task, since the visual imagination of most Americans is already filled with moonshiners, barefoot children, married teenagers, and miners coughing on coal dust. Michael Apted shows all of these too, but he manages to dispose of the moonshiner in the first five minutes. This is too bad, because he is a lively early chorus on the difficulties of life in this neck of the woods. There are only three things you can do if you are from rural Kentucky, the moonshiner tells Doolittle, Loretta's future husband: moonshining, mining, and "movin' on down the line." Fortunately for Doolittle, he doesn't try the first, because the moonshiner is killed while trying to poach on a rival's still. Loretta's dad tells Doolittle that at least he was smart enough not to get mixed up with him; but it is characteristic of Apted's humor and vision that her dad adds: "But at least if you had, you would've had a job!"

Doolittle ends up trying options two and three. As for coal mining, he tells Loretta that if he stayed down in the mine, he would have a "chest full of coal dust and be an old man at forty." He tries the third and takes Loretta off to Washington, where he gets a logging job and she starts to sing around the house. Doolittle decides to launch her as a professional singer, although she doesn't even know what the expression "pay your dues" means.

She gets more than a few breaks, and "Honky-Tonk Girl" becomes a hit. Soon she is touring with the Patsy Cline Show and we have yet another story of a working-class gal who breaks into show biz. In this way, then, Apted is working within a tradition of music bio-pics: the story of a star's rise from rags to riches, the old ways she leaves behind, the drugs she has to take (in Loretta's case, only headache pills), and the obligatory breakdown on stage when the pressures get to be too much. (*Lady Sings the Blues* and *The Doors*, to name just two, have precisely these generic elements.)

Apted seems to want to do more and succeeds somewhat. Loretta's roots as a coal miner's daughter are shown to be co-opted into her role as "just a country gal": "If you're lookin' at me," she sings, "you're lookin' at country." When Doolittle tells her that coal dust caused her daddy's headaches but that he, Doolittle, caused hers, we are brought up short. Is Apted telling us that Loretta is— without knowing it—exploiting her working-class roots? Acting out a fantasy for her poor and working-class audiences? She's no union maid, that's fer sure. If the UMWA was in Butcher Holler, it kept quiet when Loretta's family was around.

Both Sissy Spacek and Beverly D'Angelo sing Loretta Lynn's and Patsy Cline's songs themselves and do so convincingly. When Spacek finally sings the title song, so much of Loretta's class resentment comes through that the references to washboards and bare feet don't loom as important: "He shoveled coal to make a poor man's dollar," she sings, but her father always tried to find the money to buy them at least one pair of shoes every winter.

See also: *The Dollmaker*.
Availability: Easy.

Further reading

Lynn, Loretta, and George Vecsey. *Loretta Lynn: Coal Miner's Daughter*. New York: Warner, 1976. Lynn's autobiography.

Maslin, Janet. "Coal Miner's Daughter." *New York Times*, 7 March 1980, C8. The reviewer is especially keen on the four leads.

~

Coalmining Women

"If you can't stand by my side, get outta my way."—Hazel Dickens

1982, 40 mins.
Director: Elizabeth Barret
Traditional documentary
PRINCIPAL FIGURES
Coal miners from Kentucky: Mavis Williams, Viola Cleveland, Marilyn Vanderfleet
Coal miners from Colorado: Nan Livermore, Linda Sexton, Pat Farnsworth

Other coal miners: Barbara Angle, Nancy Prater
Al Blankenship, manager, General Mine
Betty Jean Hall, Coal Employment Project, Oak Ridge, Tennessee
Helen Lewis, narrator

One of the historical lessons of this film is that women have worked in mines for decades, especially in Great Britain, where whole families went underground in the early nineteenth century, and in the United States during World War II, when they were employed mainly as surface sorters. (*Germinal* depicts women working underground in France into the mid to late nineteenth century.)

More recently women in the United States have been in support roles, as wives and family members of miners who were men, but also as militants on picket lines and at rallies (such as the Black Lung Rally in Washington, D.C., in 1981), and as grieving witnesses to mine disasters (such as the Scotia

Friends gather after work in *Coalmining Women*. Photo by Earl Dotter, American Labor Educational Center. Courtesy Appalshop.

mine disaster in Letcher County, Kentucky, in 1976). The film documents these events and similar ones with archival footage.

When gender roles were challenged in other areas of society and the superstition that women were bad luck in the mines was defied, women and their supporters used the fact that organizations such as the Tennessee Valley Authority (TVA) had federal contracts and could not discriminate in hiring as a legal wedge to open the mines to women.

Women miners, the majority in Kentucky and Colorado, tell their stories in this film. Not surprisingly, safety issues are among the most important and recurring themes. One woman explains, as we watch her somewhat unconsciously moving her injured right arm with her good left hand, how dangerous operating a shuttle car can be. Another woman carefully tucks her long braid of hair into her jacket as she prepares to go underground.

The women also tell of harassment both petty and grand. Barbara Angle, a coal miner from Maryland, sums it up this way: "It's basically the last locker room in the world. These guys take a lot of pride in what they do, and justifiably so. But it's hard for them to accept the fact that women can do the same work." The film shows women doing the same work: securing the tunnel ceilings, laying bricks for ventilation barriers, and shoveling coal.

See also: *We Dig Coal; Moving Mountains*.
Availability: Selected collections; Appalshop.

Further reading

Moore, Marat. *Women in the Mines*. New York: Twain, 1996. A comprehensive collection of interviews with women who are miners or active in union organizing and support movements.

↩

Collision Course

Even on the ground

1988, 47 mins.
Director: Alex Gibney
Traditional documentary

Frank Borman, chairman, Eastern Airlines
Charles Bryan, president, District 100, International Association of Machinists (IAM)
Robert Cole, professor of business administration, University of Michigan
Leo Romano, chief steward, Logan Airport, IAM
Joe Lapointe, shop mechanic
John "Buddy" Sugg, chairman, Combined Shop, Miami Base
Jeff Callahan, director of labor relations, Eastern Airlines
Frank Lorenzo, president and owner, Texas Air
Peter Coyote, narrator.

Although air passengers never like to think of a "collision course," it is an apt title for the struggle between Frank Lorenzo's Texas Air and the International Association of Machinists after his acquisition of Eastern Airlines in 1986. Two more unsuitable partners could hardly have been found: Texas Air (which owned Continental and New York Air) was traditionally anti-union, while the Machinists had begun a fairly radical restructuring of their relationship with Eastern in 1983, when the company, in very bad shape financially, agreed to a plan that gave the workers a 25 percent share in the company and created "work teams" that seemed to lead the way to a recovery.

The film reviews both the complicated history of airlines in the era of deregulation and the specific history of Eastern. In the wake of deregulation and the subsequent rise of about a hundred nonunion airlines such as People's Express, Eastern posted enormous losses in 1983. Both Braniff and Continental (with Lorenzo at the helm) went bankrupt. Eastern's move to counter the trend was to bring in the former astronaut Frank Borman as chairman.

To some observers, Borman had charisma. (Do astronauts get charisma by being exposed to ultraviolet rays in space?) To others he was an unreconstructed military man used to a strict chain of command. He openly referred to the workers as children and at first reacted to the proposal that management share governance with the workers as equivalent to letting the monkeys run the zoo. Nonetheless, he accepted what appeared to many people as a real alternative to most received traditions of corporate culture.

The deal was that management would get from the workers an 18 to 22 percent wage cut, productivity increases, and a change in the work rules management found too limiting; the workers would receive a 25 percent stock share, four seats on the board of directors, the right to open the company books, the "right to organize work" as they thought best, and pay increases if productivity increased.

By 1984 it looked as if the deal would work: Eastern went into the black and all benefited. But the recovery was short-lived. After a 1985 fare war and the cost of maintaining Eastern's overlarge fleet, management demanded a 20 percent wage cut. Enter Frank Lorenzo, one of the models for Gordon Gekko of *Wall Street*: "We're airline builders, not airline busters." After the sale, Borman resigned, but Eastern did not survive.

Most of the workers and a fair number of the managers at Eastern believed that they had broken through to a new level of labor-management cooperation that could be an industry model if not for corporations in general. They would have us believe that a collision course does not require a collision as its only outcome.

When Secretary of Labor Robert Reich was at Harvard, he was enthusiastic about the film's value (according to California Newsreel): "If up to me, I'd project it on a mountainside and have the audio boom over valley and stream." But don't let it interfere with the radar or the traffic controllers' jobs! Not to mention the flight attendants and the pilots, who are, perhaps unfortunately (given the film's focus inevitably), not really major players in the film.

See also: *Wall Street*.
Availability: Selected collections; California Newsreel.

Further reading
Robinson, Jack E. *Freefall: The Needless Destruction of Eastern Air Lines and the Valiant Struggle to Save It*. New York: Harper Business, 1992. Discusses Lorenzo and the unions that squared off against him (the pilots, the flight attendants, and the machinists).

Computers in Context

Creativity, not redundancy

1987, 33 mins.
Director: Jim Mayer
Traditional documentary
PRINCIPAL FIGURES (VERY SELECTED)
Oslo Savings Bank:
Leif Johansen, president, Sparebanken Buskerud
Knut Koe and Espen Trenoy, Norwegian Bankworkers Union
Oyvinn Ottestad, Ann Sofie, Turid Petterson, and Tom Johnrud, Fellesdata
Tor Andersen, Secretary, Norwegian Labor Organization
Utopia Project:
Malle Ericsson and Walter Carlsson, Swedish Graphic Union
Pelle Ehn and Susanne Bodke, Center for Working Life
Scandinavian Airlines (SAS):
Ulf Lindström, production manager
Torsten Björkman, consultant

Although computerization of industry and business has developed in many ways since this film was produced, it nonetheless raises a fundamental question whose implications remain with us to this day: How do computers become a part of the process of human work and not a substitute for human workers?

The film surveys three Scandinavian companies involved in improving human-computer interaction in the 1980s, and in every instance the watchword was worker participation. The workforce throughout Scandinavia was then 80 percent unionized, and government organizations such as Sweden's Center for Working Life, which fosters "co-determination," existed to facilitate worker-management interaction.

The three case studies share an approach that is referred to during the Oslo Savings Bank section as "treating the moment": studying and facilitating the interaction between the front-line worker and the computer with the customer. In the first case examined, it was important to involve the workers in deciding what computer hardware and programs would do the best job in meeting the customers' needs and deepening the front-line workers' authorization to carry on a fairly complex layer of business at the moment of customer interaction. The result transformed bank tellers into "personal account managers."

In the second case, graphic design workers from the Swedish Graphics Union went to the Center for Working Life for what was called the Utopia Project, which involved the design and implementation of new computer software that would enable designers of daily newspapers to continue to use their creative skills. The third case involves Scandinavian Airlines maintenance shops where an "expert" computer system at first had increased the numerical turnover of items serviced but led to a decline in quality. A new system brought workers in as diagnostic experts and planners for repairs.

The film is somewhat overloaded with interview clips and could have provided a more detailed account of the unions' negotiations to achieve their goals in using computers to develop rather than eliminate jobs. (It does a better job on this point with the third case study.) Nonetheless, the film presents a convincing argument for more widespread "co-determination," avoiding, it is to be hoped, the end game to which such an approach, in general, led during the development of the Eastern Airlines–IAM agreement in the 1980s (see *Collision Course*).

See also: *Collision Course*
Availability: Selected collections; California Newsreel.

~

Comrades

"You pay for the entertainment, the news is free."—The Lanternist

1987, 180 mins., UK
Director: Bill Douglas
Screenplay: Bill Douglas
CAST
Lanternist/Diorama Showman/Laughing
  Cavalier = Alex Norton
George Loveless = Robin Soans
James Loveless = William Gaminara
Old Tom Stanfield = Stephen Bateman
Young John Stanfield = Philip Davis
James Brine = Jeremy Flynn
James Hammett = Keith Allen
Mrs. Carlyle = Vanessa Redgrave
Norfolk = James Fox
Lone Aborigine = Charles Yunipingu

This portrayal of the Tolpuddle Martyrs, early farm labor organizers and virtual martyrs, must be one of the most highly regarded British labor films and the least seen: with the exception of the year of its release and during some festivals (it won the Berlin Festival Golden Bear award in 1987), it has never had widespread circulation in any form even in Britain. A lack of circulation is an obvious problem and a common one for labor films, but with *Comrades* we have a film that is on the edge of the traditional British social-realist mode, closer to the European auteur model of the individualistic art film. It is in part a film about the making of images, how labor history is created or eclipsed, for that matter.

Bill Douglas had always been a personal filmmaker. His autobiographical trilogy of films, *My Childhood, My Ain Folk,* and *My Way Home*, defined his upbringing and eventual escape from his working-class roots in the mining village of Newcraighall, outside of Edinburgh. His fierce attachment to the common folk and an interest in popular entertainments that preceded the cinema were joined in his exploration of the Tolpuddle Martyrs, a group of farmers who tried to form a union in the 1830s when their wages were cut. Repression by governmental agents and landlords was relentless, and six of the leaders were arrested and sentenced to seven years' transportation to Australia. Their militancy may be assessed from these remarks made by George Loveless, their leader, in 1837: "Arise, men of Britain, and take your stand! Rally round the standard of Liberty, or for ever lie prostrate under the iron hand of your land- and money-mongering taskmasters."

Douglas included numerous traveling entertainers, circus acts, diorama producers, and other pre-cinema pieces of apparatus (lantern slides, the heliotrope, still photography) as a way of demonstrating changes in rural life but also to show that popular art and history also create—like film—the very lives they are attempting to interpret. Duncan Petrie's essay on the making of the film concludes that Douglas's film was in the end a "reconciliation of two opposing philosophies of cinema"—on the one hand, the realism (through location shooting and attention to period detail) required to reveal the world to viewers and, on the other, insistence on the medium's artificiality (the art of the "magic lantern" in projecting images) or unreality.

The film has some brilliant moments set in a compelling narrative of oppression and eventual liberation. Payday, for example, when the men gather for their meager wages, is filled with the contradictions the working poor suffered—some could not write or do sums, some could sign their names to their wage receipts, others signed X's, and so forth. The sense of inadequacy not only in wages but in human culture is very moving. Jill Forbes isolated one of the most telling innovations in Douglas's stereophonic sound track: one of the martyrs bolts his Anglican parish church as the priest stresses the rightness of the social order and rushes over to the nonconforming Methodist chapel to hear a simple but cheering sermon. The sound of an elite culture blends into the sound of a populist faith.

Travelers in the Thomas Hardy countryside of Dorset will come across references to the Tolpuddle Martyrs and they can even go to the Tolpuddle Museum. The irony of *Comrades* is that in the end a film that has valiantly attempted to put Tolpuddle on everyone's map has had in a sense no survival in the marketplace itself.

See also: *Hungry Hill.*
Availability: Not.

Further reading

Douglas, Bill. *Comrades*. London/Boston: Faber & Faber, 1987. The screenplay.

Forbes, Jill. "The Lanternist's Tale." *Sight and Sound*, Winter 1986/87, 66–67. Review of the film, recording Forbes's belief that this is less a labor history film than an exploration of the laborers' attempts to understand their class-bound experience.

Petrie, Duncan, ed. *Bill Douglas: A Lanternist's Account*. London: British Film Institute, 1994. Scripts of all of Douglas's films, including *Comrades*, as well as essays on the production of the films and Douglas's career.

Web site:

⟨www.tolpuddlemartyrs.org.uk/mus_frms.html⟩ The Tolpuddle Museum site offers the history of the martyrs, available resources, and visual features.

Controlling Interest: The World of the Multinational Corporation

Don't cry for us, Chile

1975, 46 mins.
Directors: Bruce Schmiechen and Larry Adelman
Traditional documentary
PRINCIPAL FIGURES
Gene Currier, lathe operator, Ingersoll Rand
Anne Giniusz, assembler
Earl Marsh, Don Tormey, and Shirley Gagnon, staff, United Electrical Workers (UE) Local 274
Octavio Cáceres, Workers Administrative Council, Bola Vista Textile Mill

Edward Kerry, U.S. ambassador to Chile
Amador Aquila, former Chilean soldier
Philip Agee, former CIA agent
Raul Sánchez, local president, Copper
    Foundry Union
General Gustavo Leigh, member, Military
    Junta
Charlie Freeman, president, Business
    International, former secretary of
    agriculture
George Ball, former under secretary of
    state
Michael Tanzer, author, former Exxon
    economist

This is a controlled but angry political interpretation of multinational corporations, completed just after one of the more blatant exercises in American imperialism—the military overthrow of the democratically elected government of Chile's Salvador Allende, whose party came to power on the promise of nationalizing the extremely profitable copper mines (among other industries) that had made Chile the personal preserve of the Anaconda and Kennecott copper companies.

Controlling Interest has some of the rawness of the militant 1960s, with interviews of Chileans who have been imprisoned and exiled and in at least one case tortured for their role in defending Allende's vision of Chile. Similarly black-and-white footage of unnamed American officers of multinationals portrays a pasty-faced group of bureaucrats, seemingly interchangeable, who discuss the people of the Third World in ways that still have the power to shock: for various kinds of assembly jobs (electronics) the companies prize such things as the "native ability of the people to work with their hands," the fact that they will work for 30 cents an hour, and how fortunate they are not to have any "social distractions" the way we do here. Even the presumably quite sophisticated George Ball, under secretary of state for President Carter and then a senior partner of the Lehmann Brothers investment firm, does not seem to notice what his remarks reveal. As an example of how a bad thing can turn out OK, he brings up our overpowering of the Dominican Republic: after the invasion, things were fine and the people happy.

We learn the by-now familiar statistics of oligarchic control: 100 companies control half the industrial wealth, while only two companies make 22 percent of the profits. Oil companies control half the coal and uranium deposits as well as the oil. One important section of the film traces the relationship of an Ingersoll Rand welding plant (purchased from a local firm) in Greenfield, Massachusetts, and its corporate parent's multinational maneuvering. One Greenfield union leader concludes: "Freedom is the freedom for multinationals to make profit in any place in the world."

This sobering and revealing documentary about globalization (before we used the term) represents a transitional stage between California Newsreel's immediate political news documentaries of the late 1960s (*The Black Panthers*) and their more traditional and professional films (with higher production values) of the 1980s.

See also: *The New Rulers of the World*.
Availability: Selected collections; California
    Newsreel.

Further reading

Pilger, John. *The New Rulers of the World*. London: Verso, 2002. An update on the powers and the abuses of the leaders of globalization.

Convoy

Truckers ticked off mightily

1978, 110 mins., PG
Director: Sam Peckinpah
Screenplay: B. W. L. Norton, from C. W.
    McCall's pop song of the same title
CAST
Rubber Duck = Kris Kristofferson
Melissa = Ali MacGraw
Lyle Wallace = Ernest Borgnine
Pig Pen = Burt Young
Widow Woman = Madge Sinclair
Governor Haskins = Seymour Cassel

I think we can safely conclude that Bill Clinton's Rhodes Scholarship was more relevant to his career than Kristofferson's was to his. No one should make a film with a character named Rubber Duck, but coming from a director like Sam Peckinpah, whose earlier films were depressing but impressive milestones of cinematic innovation and violence (*The Wild Bunch* and *Straw Dogs*), this film should have been more appealing. The truckers here are independent owner-operators who are wary of The Law and are the closest thing to open-road cowboys American culture is likely to have for a while. But a film as old-fashioned as *They Drive by Night,* which emphasized the risks the drivers face more than their run-ins with the law, was superior to this film based on a one-note hit country song.

The essence of the film is the mighty and only weapon the truckers have—their ability to form a convoy and make access to the nation's interstates hard for almost everyone, especially the bad guys, who in this worldview are, of course, the Smokies, the highway patrol. The leading Smoky is the crooked archvillain of the film, played with a particularly silly scuzziness by Ernest Borgnine. Communicating by CB, the truckers can do almost everything, including pick up an incredible out-of-place middle-class fashion plate (Ali MacGraw), who is out on the road looking in all the wrong places for authentic photographs and maybe a turn or two in the back of Rubber Duck's cab. Breaker one-nine, cut loose this film!

See also: *They Drive by Night.*
Availability: Easy.

Further reading

Canby, Vincent. "Truckers and Women." *New York Times,* 28 June 1978, C17. Assesses Peckinpah as someone who would "sell his grandmother for five percent of the gross."

Ouellet, Lawrence J. *Pedal to the Metal: The Work Lives of Truckers*. Philadelphia: Temple University Press, 1994. A participant-observer sociologist and part-time truck driver reports on the life and work of nonunion truckers.

Sayles, John. "I-80 Nebraska M.990–M.205." In *On the Job,* ed. William O'Rourke, 226–43. New York: Vintage, 1977. An excellent short story on the mythic aspects of truckers on their CB's.

A Corner in Wheat

The labor theory of value dramatized

1909, 12 mins., B&W, silent
Director: D. W. Griffith
Screenplay: D. W. Griffith, from Frank Norris's short story "A Deal in Wheat" and sections of his novel *The Octopus*
CAST
The Wheat King = Frank Powell
His Wife = Grace Henderson
His Assistant = Henry Bualthals
The Farm Family = James Kirkwood, Linda Arvidson, W.
Chrystie Miller, and Gladys Egan

In 1909 D. W. Griffith released two short American Biograph Company films that he labeled "editorials." The first, although sentimental and condescending, was a rarity—*The Redman's View*, the Indian wars as seen from the point of view of a vastly outnumbered and pacifist people. The second "editorial" was *A Corner in Wheat*, a less sentimental, more sharply focused attack on capitalism, in which the rich get richer and the poor pay more for bread.

Griffith's film was his contribution (as Scott Simmon has argued) to the muckraking decade at the turn of the twentieth century. Lincoln Steffens had already blamed big business for most of what he called "the shame of the cities" and Griffith had just finished *The Song of the Shirt* in 1908 (just three years before the Triangle Factory Fire), in which a shirtwaist worker has her home-assembly work rejected and her sister dies in their tenement room because the shirtwaist worker is not paid for her work.

A Corner in Wheat is potentially an even more radical film than *The Song of the Shirt.* It combines a vision of farm labor, a wheat king's monopoly, and the failure of city relief (the breadline is suspended). Griffith, following Norris's original story lines closely, presents a grim class-conscious vision of a system that can benefit only a few. When the relief line is suspended, the city dwellers organize and rush the bread shop. The shop owner calls the police, who deals the leader of the demo several sharp blows to the head and draws his revolver.

The title, however, is a pun: as the Wheat King gains a corner on the market—even ruining some of his fellow capitalists—he accidentally falls into his own grain shaft and is buried in a corner of the cascading wheat.

This death scene, while memorable, is not the only important sequence in the film. In the midst of the Wheat King's triumph, Griffith inserts a freeze frame of a breadline, as if to emphasize the hopelessness of the poor. (They are some of the demonstrators in the earlier sequence.) And in the first and last shots of the film, as a farmer is sowing wheat (he should, as a contemporary reviewer noted, be *planting* the wheat), Griffith deliberately recreates a famous painting of the nineteenth century, Jean-François Millet's *The Sower*. The lingering final shot of the landscape is a futile gesture toward the agrarian source of wealth, ruined (as the film demonstrates) by monopolies and trusts.

Griffith's reputation as a racist and reactionary, based on *Birth of a Nation*, is quite accurate. Scott Simmon has demonstrated, however, that there is a second Griffith, whose urban films and *Intolerance* indicate the complexity of life and urban unrest in New York City after the Panic of 1907.

See also: *Street Scene*.

Availability: Selected collections; Kino International (its 1992 release is titled *A Corner in Wheat and Selected D. W. Griffith Shorts, 1902–1913*).

Further reading

Norris, Frank. *A Corner in Wheat and Other Stories of the New and Old West* (1903) and *The Octopus: A Story of California* (1901). Norris's short story was published posthumously; both story and relevant sections of the novel are available in Pratt and in many other editions of Norris's work.

Petric, Vlada. *D. W. Griffith's "A Corner in Wheat": A Critical Analysis*. Cambridge: University Film Study Center, 1975. A pamphlet with a detailed shot analysis of the film.

Pratt, George C. *Spellbound in Darkness: A History of Silent Film*. New York: New York Graphic Society, 1973. A reprint of the fictional sources for Griffith's film; analyzes many of his films.

Simmon, Scott. *Films of D. W. Griffith*. New York: Cambridge University Press, 1993. An essential discussion for the study of *A Corner in Wheat* and Griffith's other muckraking short films.

Steffens, Lincoln. *The Shame of the Cities*. 1904. An important muckraking classic, available in various editions. "In all cities, the better classes—the business men—are the sources of corruption."

⤷
The Corn Is Green

Educating Morgan

1945, 114 mins., B&W
Director: Irving Rapper
Screenplay: Casey Robinson and Frank Cavett, from Emlyn Williams's play of the same title
CAST
Miss Moffat = Bette Davis
Squire Treverby = Nigel Bruce
Morgan Evans = John Dall
Bessie Watty = Joan Lorring
Mr. Jones = Rhys Williams
Mrs. Watty = Rosalind Ivan
Miss Ronberry = Mildred Dunnock

Bette Davis recreated in this film Ethel Barrymore's role on stage as the mighty Miss Moffat, the reformer of a rural Welsh coal-mining village. What obviously worked well on stage—Miss Moffat's numerous cutting remarks and set speeches as she deflates self-satisfied locals regardless of their class—makes the film look like a set of elocution lessons in front of a cardboard set. Miss Moffat is fortunate enough to have, as she puts it, inherited money and a house, and so she opens a school to keep the local boys from going into the mines at the age of 12. She concentrates on one star pupil, Morgan Evans, whose first composition about the mines knocks her woolen socks off: "When I walk in the dark, I can touch with my hands where the corn is green." (I'm not sure what this means either, but Miss Moffat knows it's poetry.)

But Miss Moffat also has enemies. Particularly Squire Treverby, who "owns the Hall" and a "half share" in the mine and doesn't take kindly to "his" workers' speaking English (instead of Welsh) or even becoming literate, period. Looking and sounding like Sherlock Holmes's Dr. Watson (whom Nigel Bruce played for years), the squire questions everything about Miss Moffat, beginning with her degree, an M.A. "A female M.A.? And how long's that going to last?" Her reply: "Quite a long time, I hope, considering we've been waiting for it for two thousand years."

Miss Moffat is an early feminist and is never shy about her opinions. On why she never married, she says: "I've never talked to a man for more than five minutes without wanting to box his ears." So much of the satisfaction one gets from the old black-and-white British films comes from such exchanges that we almost forget we are in a mining village. Actually, we almost always see the miners returning home—they never seem to go *to* the mines or spend time *in* the mines—and, of course, they are always singing, like their brother Welsh miners in *How Green Was My Valley*. (Barry Fitzgerald visits from that film as an uncredited—surprise!—bartender.) It may be that miners in Wales used to sing on their way home from work, but surely that activity occupied only a small percentage of their waking hours.

We are expected to believe that the squire is so dumb that he would agree to Miss Moffat's scheme to sponsor Morgan for an Oxford exam even after hearing her response to his suggestion that she take up croquet. Her comeback sets out a reasonably witty class analysis of the countryside: "I know I shall be sticking a pin into a whale, but here are just two words about yourself. You are the Squire Bountiful, are you? Adored by his contented subjects, intelligent and benignly understanding, are you? I should just like to point out that there is a considerable amount of dirt, ignorance, misery, and discontent in this world, and that a good deal of it is due to people like you, because you are a stupid, conceited, greedy, good-for-nothing, addle-headed nincompoop, and you can go to blue blazes."

Her assistant teacher says what everyone is thinking: "A miner can't go to Oxford!" But Morgan does, after Miss Moffat deals with a potentially embarrassing subplot in which her star pupil gets a student pregnant.

See also: *Educating Rita; How Green Was My Valley*.
Availability: Selected collections.

Further reading

Crowther, Bosley. "The Corn Is Green." *New York Times*, 30 March 1945, 18. The reviewer applauds Davis but mocks the film's sets.

Williams, Emlyn. *The Corn Is Green*. New York: Random House, 1941. The film is a close adaptation of this playscript.

Note: Another version of *The Corn Is Green*, directed by George Cukor in 1979 with Katharine Hepburn as Miss Moffat, is available on videocassette.

↩

Cradle Will Rock

And down will come . . . capitalism?

1999, 133 mins., R
Director: Tim Robbins
Screenplay: Tim Robbins
CAST
Marc Blitzstein = Hank Azaria
Hallie Flanagan = Cherry Jones
Countess La Grange = Vanessa Redgrave
Margherita Sarfatti = Susan Sarandon
Aldo Silvano = John Turturro
Olive Stanton = Emily Watson
Orson Welles = Angus MacFadyen

John Houseman = Cary Elwes
Nelson Rockefeller = John Cusack
Tommy Crickshaw = Bill Murray
Hazel Huffman = Joan Cusack
William Randolph Hearst = John Carpenter
Diego Rivera = Ruben Blades
Will Geer = Daniel Jenkins

Marc Blitzstein's agitprop operetta *The Cradle Will Rock* was one of the defining moments of New York's left-wing cultural scene in the 1930s; a similarly dramatic one was the staging of Clifford Odets's *Waiting for Lefty*, another agitprop drama, which concludes with taxi drivers on stage calling for a strike and the (then) audience roaring for the same. Add Orson Welles and John Houseman, the leaders of the Federal Theatre Project; lock the doors on the opening night of *The Cradle Will Rock*, courtesy of the right-wing House Un-American Activities Committee's investigation into left-wing theater; and creatively change the date of the destruction of Diego Rivera's anticapitalist mural for Rockefeller Center in 1934, and before you can say "boy wonder" (as Welles was known), you have the three-ring circus written and directed by Tim Robbins called *Cradle Will Rock*. (One measure of the difficulties reviewers have had in categorizing this film is their collective frustration—and annoyance— over Robbins's insistence in dropping the *The* from Blitzstein's original title: see McCarthy and Maslin in "Further reading" below.)

One could watch *Waiting for Lefty* today. I am not so sure about Blitzstein's *The Cradle Will Rock*: I would be driven crazy by characters with names like Moll (a sort of Brechtian *Three-Penny Opera* hooker), Mr. Mister (the top capitalist), Rev. Salvation (the religious leader–toady of the Liberty Committee), President Prexy (another toady) . . . well, you get the idea. Robbins wisely does not restage Blitzstein's work but instead focuses on Blitzstein's search for the right scenes as he wanders through Depression-era New York, with the opulence of the rich among the demonstrations of the poor and working class accompanied by his two private demons or inspirations (Brecht himself, looking like a Berlin cutie from the 'hood, and Mrs. Blitzstein, in a wedding gown, who had committed suicide not long before).

The only scene Robbins stages combines two "Nightcourt" sessions of the original. In what strikes me as a ludicrous premise, the right-wing Liberty Committee has been mistakenly thrown in jail with some of our heroes—Moll, Larry Foreman (a union working stiff who is an ex-foreman), and Harry Druggist (who allowed Mr. Mister's crooks to use his drugstore as a staging area for a bombing). In this part of Robbins's film, what is the most exciting bit of cultural warfare takes place: when Welles discovers his production has been locked out, he leads a march of cast and audience to another theater, puts Blitzstein on the stage with a piano, and (some say this was spontaneous, others say it was planned by the boy wonder himself) has the cast recite and sing their parts from seats in the new audience (Actors Equity having refused them permission to go onstage).

At this point Larry Foreman confronts the Liberty Committee in jail. Larry is played by John Turturro, who explains the title of the show: "Upon the topmost bough of yonder tree now, the lords and their lackeys and wives, a swingin' 'Rockabye Baby' in a nice big cradle." But when the working class gets organized, "the final wind blows, and when the wind blows, the cradle will rock!" And later, when "everybody gets together, like Steel's gettin' together," then "the storm breaks" and "the cradle [capitalism] will fall!"

This is the height—not the average—of political analysis in Blitzstein's play. Well, at another point, he does explain the difference between an open and closed shop to Moll, who is not unionized. Wisely Robbins has lassoed a few other plots, certainly with more political stakes then the original *Cradle*: both government and private censorship of the arts become the real issue of Robbins's world and he wants us to recognize these as issues today.

The 1930s, therefore, have come back: we have right-wing politicians refusing to allow government funding of the arts whenever they are controversial, not to mention the direct censorship of art in various places. Meanwhile the union—Actors Equity—is not allowing its actors to perform for what seems to be a technical reason (the lockout is not by management). Their rep is a cad who has taken advantage of Olive Stanton's naiveté, but since she can't act anyway, we may be immune to her pain. Meanwhile this loser is replaced on opening night by Larry, who in turn has been fighting the pro-Mussolini sentiment in his own extended Italian-American family. So the message here is don't count on your union, but look to the CIO, which is organizing steel. This film has a big heart. What it doesn't have is a lot of sense.

Robbins has got a lot of details just right: in one scene a poster announcing a lecture by V. J. Jerome, the Communist Party's cultural maven, appears. It is easy to see why Robbins revived *The Cradle Will Rock* and not *Waiting for Lefty*: the latter just doesn't have enough pizzazz and celebrities.

OK. Here's the test. Who played Mr. Mister for the first time in 1937? In Robbins's film Daniel Jenkins plays the actor who then plays Mr. Mister. This is the same blacklisted actor who played the sheriff in the banned film *Salt of the Earth*. Need a Playbill?

See also: *One Third of a Nation*.
Availability: Easy; DVD.

Further reading

Bentley, Eric, ed. *Thirty Years of Treason*. New York: Viking, 1973. This stupendous collection of "excerpts from hearings before the House Committee on Un-American Activities, 1938–1968" includes the testimony of Hallie Flanagan, who, in her verbal duel at one point with Chairman Martin Dies, explained that Christopher Marlowe was Shakespeare's predecessor and not a Communist. Robbins, therefore, did not have to exaggerate the absurdities of this committee—just quote them.

Blitzstein, Marc. *The Cradle Will Rock: A Play in Music*. New York: Random House, 1938. The original play, with prefaces by Archibald MacLeish and Orson Welles and dedicated to "Bert Brecht"; it has ten scenes, only two of which (both called "Nightcourt") are staged in the film as the finale.

Klawans, Stuart. "'Rock' in a Hard Place." *Nation*, 27 December 1999, 34–36. Fascinated (but frustrated) by the "caricatures" that Robbins has created to represent Welles, Houseman, and Blitzstein, since they were all very "intelligent and committed" politically active artists.

McCarthy, Todd. "Cradle Will Rock." *Variety*, 19 May 1999. Complains that Blitzstein's original "pageant of a worker rebellion against corporate America is obvious and derivative both politically and musically." (Also: "Film's title [is] curiously minus the initial definite article of its source of inspiration.")

Maslin, Janet. "'Cradle Will Rock': Panoramic Passions on a Playbill." *New York Times*, 8 December 1999. A "big, brave, sometimes maddeningly reductive film that rises through sheer talent and enthusiasm over its own limitations." (Also: "Whether to avoid or create confusion, the 'The' has been dropped from the title of the film.")

Robbins, Tim. "A Look at the 30's." Letter, *New York Times*, 23 January 1999, II.4. Explains that his film was designed to be "a fast-moving ensemble piece in the spirit of screwball comedy to introduce the 1930's to generations of people who have long forgotten or never knew it," and argues that the demonstrations in Seattle against the World Trade Organization in 1999 demonstrated the relevance of the political organizing evoked in Blitzstein's original vision.

Robbins, Tim, and Theresa Burns. *Cradle Will Rock : The Movie and the Moment*. New York: Newmarket Press, 1999. Movie tie-in edition, with shooting script, numerous production notes, and archival photographs of the original Federal Theatre Project and contemporary scenes.

Schiff, David. "The Labor Pains of a Leftist Musical in an Angry Era." *New York Times*, 5 December 1999, IV.17. Detailed and convincing account of the origins of Robbins's approach in the original show and its political context.

Welles, Orson. *The Cradle Will Rock: An Original Screenplay*. Ed. James Pepper. Santa Barbara: Santa Teresa Press, 1994. Welles's own version of the events in a screenplay that (like many of Welles's projects) almost got made; actually quite close to Robbins's, especially the idea of trailing Welles and Houston around as they attempt to stage Blitzstein's opera.

Dadetown

Class struggle at the cappuccino bar

1996, 93 mins.
Director: Russ Hexter
Screenplay: Russ Hexter and John Housley
CAST
Tom Nickenback = Jim Pryor
Dan Barlitz = Stephen Beals
Ed Hubbell = Fred Worrell

This film is so convincing in its imitation of documentary style that it is almost criminal to give its secret away, so I won't. One might argue that for a film to rely on a Big Secret to deliver its Big Bang doesn't speak well for the total viewing experience. I am of two minds on this matter, secret or no. I would not have wanted to know, for example, the secret of Neil Jordan's *Crying Game* before seeing it, but the fact is I simply cannot remember if I knew ahead of time what was going to happen to Janet Leigh in the shower the first time I saw Hitchcock's *Psycho*. Now it no longer matters: both films circulate to those who know and those who don't. *Dadetown* will never have the fame of either of those films and for a little while at least we will pay our respects to its director, who died soon after completing this film, by keeping his cleverness alive a little while longer.

Dadetown is like so many former one-industry towns, in this case in New York state. Its Gorman factory helped win World War II with its airplane fusilages; now it barely survives making paper clips and staples. Its economic come-down is also felt as a blow to the town's self-esteem: the war was bad, sure, one of the townspeople says, but it was good for Dadetown. To complicate matters and to provide the main motor for the film's plot, a high-tech firm, API ("What does it stand for ... Alien People Invade?"), has moved in, replete with tax breaks, upper-middle-class outsiders, and a cappuccino bar. Most of the film's comedy concerns the distance between traditional small-town working-class values and the high-earning, high-spending ways of the cyber-yuppies. The

clash between the two ways of life cannot be avoided: after all, the president of API says, what else is computerization about but the elimination of paper and subsequently paper clips and staples?

Hexter was heavily influenced by both cinema verité political documentaries such as Barbara Kopple's *Harlan County, U.S.A.* and the postmodern films by Errol Morris (*Vernon, Florida* and *Gates of Heaven*), in which documentary style and fictional re-creations are not always distinguished. But audiences were never fooled by either Kopple or Morris—usually they knew what they were going to get (Kopple was real, Morris was weird)—but some viewers complained that Hexter was manipulating them. In fact, Hexter argues, what he did in his casting was to look for actors and nonprofessionals who had "personalities that fit the personalities" he had scripted. In a sense Hexter returned to the pseudo-documentary style of the 1930s and 1940s, when filmmakers recruited actual families to play themselves (*The Plow That Broke the Plains*) or local folk to play people like themselves (*Native Land* and *The Forgotten Village*). In both instances the Marxist approach to cinematic art (pioneered by Sergei Eisenstein) was supposedly vindicated—real people needed to be played by similar types.

See also: *Roger & Me; TV Nation.*
Availability: Not.

Further reading

Arthur, Paul. "Let Us Now Praise Famous Yokels: 'Dadetown' and Other Retreats." *Cineaste*, July 1997, 30–33. Places Hexter's film in the context of a cultural celebration of rural values in the 1990s, and while the reviewer is quite positive about the film's strengths, he argues that it (and other somewhat similar rural-themed documentaries and feature films) comes dangerously close to idealizing rural subjects and making them palatable for urban sophisticates.

Goldberg, Vicki. "Photos That Lie—and Tell the Truth." *New York Times,* 16 March 1997, II.1, 34. An intriguing argument—*Dadetown* is part of the same impulse that has led a number of still photographers to create the photo opportunities they cannot be present at.

McDonald, William. "A Timely Tale, with Endings Unforewarned." *New York Times,* 15 September 1996, II.15, 24. A detailed history of the concept of the film and an overview of its director's short career.

Thomson, Patricia. "Images of Labor." *Independent Film and Video Monthly,* June 1996, 33–38. Includes an interview with Hexter, in which he distinguishes between "parodying" documentaries and "utilizing the powerful form" to tell a story.

∽

Daens

The "cruelty of greedy speculators"—Pope Leo XIII

1993, 134 mins., Belgium, Flemish and French, with English subtitles
Director: Stijn Coninx
Screenplay: François Chevallier and Stijn Coninx, from Louis Paul Boon's novel *Pieter Daens*
CAST
Father Adolph Daens = Jan Decleir
Charles Woeste = Gérard Desarthe
Nette Scholliers = Antje de Boeck
Pieter Daens = Wim Meuwissen
Bishop Stillemans = Julian Schoenaerts
Nuncio = Rik Hancke
Cardinal = Giovanni di Benedetto
King Leopold II = Gerald Marti

Father Adolph Daens was fond of quoting Pope Leo XIII's famous encyclical *Rerum novarum* (Of new things), usually titled *Of the Condition of the Working Classes.* Written as a rebuttal to socialist and Communist agitation among Catholic workers throughout Europe, Leo's statement nonetheless has ample ammunition for a reformer like Daens: "The first concern of all," the pope states, "is to save the poor workers from the cruelty of greedy speculators, who use human beings as mere instruments of moneymaking. It is neither just nor human so to grind men down with their excessive labor as to stupefy their minds and wear out their bodies." It also offered tentative but explicit warnings against exploiting women and children as laborers.

Belgium's industrial economy in the late nineteenth century was as strong as its presence in King Leopold's Belgian Congo, whose Euro-imperialism and exploitation were so brilliantly dissected in Joseph Conrad's *Heart of Darkness*. But there were some big unpleasantnesses in the home country as well: child and female labor was widespread (with sexual abuses as dramatized in the film), safety and hygiene standards were low, and city workers as well as peasants lived on potatoes. Images of the depressed working classes come through in Vincent van Gogh's paintings, in part a reflection of his three years as a lay minister in the Borinage, one of the major mining districts. Karl Marx also knew Belgium well. With or without his help, however, a socialist movement as well as various co-ops, peasant leagues, and trade unions grew.

Conservatives of all stripes, especially Catholic ones, opposed these movements, but programs favoring the working class were supported by the Christian Democrats and working-class Catholics. Only in 1894 did universal male suffrage (all males over the age of 25 were *required* to vote) result in large numbers of socialist and Catholic members of parliament.

Daens's mixture of Flemish roots and Catholicism was a problem for him. As a follower of the spirit of Leo XIII's encyclical, Daens kept close to the Catholic party line, but his nationalistic fervor for Flemish over French, the language of the upper classes and Parliament; his radical temperament; and his direct participation in the workers' movement made him a threat to capitalist and cardinal alike.

The film takes a close look at the women and children working in one textile factory. Even when Daens forces the government to send out a committee to investigate labor abuses, the workers at this factory, who speak only Flemish, cannot communicate with the French-speaking committee members. The factory manager keeps the children hidden from the committee by locking them in the storeroom during their visit.

Eventually one of the children crawls underneath the dangerous semi-automatic looms in the factory and is crushed. His sister takes the body and with her co-workers attempts to march on the committee to report this latest horror. Her march is attacked by the gendarmes and the body literally stolen out of her arms.

Daens and his Christian People's Party are memorialized in Aalst to this day in the Daensmuseum en Archief van de Vlaamse Sociale Strijd in the Schepenhuis, or Old Town Hall. This film will remind viewers of another piece of labor history that needs revisiting.

See also: *America and Lewis Hine*.
Availability: Selected collections.

Further reading

Bright, Martin. "Daens." *Sight and Sound*, April 1994, 41–42. Unnecessarily cranky review, mocking the film's "candyfloss approach to history" because it resembles British TV adaptations of Dickens and Brontë.

Leo XIII. *Rerum novarum* [literally, "Of new things"], in *The Papal Encyclicals in Their Historical Context*, ed. Anne Fremantle, 167–95. New York: NAL, 1956. The classic pro-worker, anti-Marxist encyclical used by Father Daens as a rallying cry; available in many other editions as well.

∽

Days of Hope

"Pit villages nursing a hundred years of grievance"—Jim Allen

1975, UK, 410 minutes, TV series
Director: Ken Loach
Screenplay: Jim Allen, from his novel of the same title
CAST
Ben Matthews = Paul Copley
Sarah Hargreaves = Pamela Brighton
Philip Hargreaves = Nikolas Simmonds
Jenny Barnett = Christine Anderson
Peter = Peter Kerrigan

Another lost, stolen, or strayed Loach film, this time a four-part TV series based on Jim Allen's novel of British working-class life, political activism, and Labour Party politics from World War I through the General Strike of 1926. Each part focuses on one defining moment for the principal characters and British history (the middle two lack subtitles):

Part 1. Days of Hope 1916: Joining Up
Part 2. Days of Hope 1921
Part 3. Days of Hope 1924
Part 4. Days of Hope 1926: The General Strike

The political angle on the Labour Party's seeming abandonment of the radical potential of the General Strike recurs in Loach's overall interpretation of British left history. One of the characters sums up this position as a consequence of Stalin's belief that socialism could be built in one country: "The role of the Party ceased to be revolutionary. For why should [Stalin] be interested in revolution, when it is now possible to live side by side in peaceful coexistence with capitalist states?" By analogy, Labour and Communist parties don't want militant trade unions because the only thing their leaders are "interested in is forming good industrial relations with progressive employers."

The film follows the activities and political commitments of a relatively small number of characters (given its almost seven-hour length). Ben deserts from the army and participates in the great mining lockout of 1921. His militant sister, Sarah, marries a man (Philip) who becomes one of the first Labour MPs and a leader in the Labour Party "sellout" during the General Strike of 1926, the culminating incident of the story.

Loach received some criticism for his decision to build a convincing and "authentic" mise-en-scène through historical location shooting and period costumes, in effect creating an imitation British heritage film about the working classes instead of the upper classes. By avoiding the star system and a conventional ending, he began to forge a style now characteristic of many of his later films, such as a sense of the radical past, a moment of labor history, when for reasons good and bad a great cause ran downhill. In this regard, his film of the failure of the Spanish Revolution, *Land and Freedom,* and his tribute to the Nicaraguan Sandinistas, *Carla's Song,* are remarkably similar in spirit, although they have less of a strictly labor focus than *The Flickering Flame*, a documentary that focuses on a contemporary Labour Party "betrayal."

See also: *The Flickering Flame.*
Availability: Not.

Further reading

Caughie, John. *Television Drama: Realism, Modernism, and British Culture*. Oxford: Oxford University Press, 2000. Argues that the documentary and dramatic impulses of the miniseries resulted in "quality television drama which is beginning to wish it was film"; that is, that it could present working-class issues in a complex and sometimes contradictory way not possible in traditionally realistic TV.

MacCabe, Colin. "Days of Hope—A Response to Colin McArthur." *Screen* 17 (Spring 1976): 98–101. A reply to the article following, stressing that the film is a costume drama whose only (un-self-conscious) message is the betrayal of the working class by its leaders.

McArthur, Colin. "Days of Hope." *Screen* 16 (Winter 1975–76): 139–44. A helpful discussion of the film despite the astonishing remark that "it is reasonable to expect an allegedly radical film to tell us something about the problems of making films for a large broadcasting institution."

Symons, Julian. *The General Strike*. London: Cresset, 1957. Good general history.

⤳

A Day's Work, a Day's Pay

"WEP sucks."—Jackie

2001, 57 mins.
Directors: Kathy Leichter and Jonathan Skurnik
Traditional documentary

PRINCIPAL FINGURES
José Nicolau, Jackie Martie, and Juan Galán, Work Experience Program (WEP) workers
Paul Getsos, director, Community Voices Heard (CVH)
Rudy Giuliani, mayor, New York City

This documentary traces three New York City WEP workers, former welfare recipients who participate in the "workfare" or welfare-to-work initiative so popular in many cities as a quick fix to cutbacks in welfare support and the federal mandate of a five-year limit on further welfare payments (as legislated by the Personal Responsibility and Work Opportunities Act of 1996). It turns out, among other problems, that the city jobs they took paid below minimum wage. The filmmakers follow three individuals as they ally themselves with two community organizations, Association of Community Organizations for Reform Now (ACORN) and Community Voices Heard (CVH), to struggle for workplace protection, the right to unionize, decent wages, and access to college. The film surveys three campaigns: a unionization drive for WEP workers, the establishment of a grievance procedure, and the creation of permanent jobs.

While President Bill Clinton launched the concept of "workfare" to take welfare recipients into the job market, it was Mayor Rudy Giuliani of New York City who made it a reality. His program to stop the "increasing dependency" of people on welfare was designed to end welfare in the city by 2000. Unfortunately, those who ended up in WEP received a quarter of the pay of their counterparts who worked the same jobs at union wages. The scene was ripe for a major confrontation between a group of potentially desperate workers and the mayor, whose spin on charm was meanness.

The filmmakers focus on three WEP workers who move from frustration to political activism. We get a close if not intimate look at their personalities and dreams. José's dad was a custodian and José sees himself in the same role but extremely good at it: "I want to put my signature on my work." Jackie, a welfare mom who was nonetheless one semester away from graduating from college, says that she was "forced" to enter a WEP program rather than complete school. And the formidable Juan channels his anger into organizing and leading demonstrations for two important community initiatives, a grievance procedure for WEP workers and a plan to hire more workers at standard pay scales.

The film alternates between the growing self-consciousness of the three WEP workers as they enter the political realm and the main target of their actions—City Hall. José and Juan become active in ACORN, while Jackie joins CVH. We see them at their own meetings and the meetings of the City Council.

The filmmakers in the end capture two moments that reveal both the politics and the personal drama of this major political and economic movement. Mayor Giuliani finally has to deal with the fact that the City Council has passed the two bills the activists have campaigned for. Before announcing his veto, he snaps at the crowd: "Put your signs down. This is a hearing, not a rally." (They don't.) And Jackie is on the subway when she spots her old caseworker, who she maintains forced her to drop out of college. She speaks sharply to him and announces: "WEP sucks." Of course he doesn't remember her.

Despite the importance of this topic, relatively few filmmakers have turned their attention to it. Michael Moore's *The Awful Truth* has one episode, "Work Care!" with a similar focus (paying health bills by working at a hospital).

See also: *The Awful Truth*.
Availability: Selected collections; New Day Films.

Further reading

Aronowitz, Stanley. *From the Ashes of the Old: American Labor and America's Future*. Boston: Houghton Mifflin, 1998. Includes a section on ACORN's successes in organizing the poor, including WEP workers, and recounts both difficulties and breakthroughs with local unions.

Bernstein, Nina. "As Welfare Comes to an End, So Do the Jobs." *New York Times*, 17 December 2001. A sobering report, confirming the film's main points.
Web sites:
⟨www.cvhaction.org⟩ Site of Community Voices Heard (CVH), "an organization of low-income people, predominantly women on welfare, working together to make improvements in our community, and advance the political, economic and social rights of low-income people on welfare and other low-wage workers."
⟨www.nyc.gov/html/hra/html/abouthra_overview. html⟩ The official New York City site for the Human Resources Administration for WEP, at one time including "Mayor Giuliani's Speeches on Welfare."

Deadly Corn *and* Struggle in the Heartland: Staley Workers Fight Back

Decatur woes

Deadly Corn, 1995, 27 mins.
Struggle in the Heartland, 1995, 18 mins.
Director: Rose Feurer (with David Rathke on first film)
Agitprop documentaries
PRINCIPLE FIGURES (BOTH FILMS)
Dave Watts, president, United Paperworkers International Union (UPIU) Local 7837
Jerry Tucker, New Directions activist, United Auto Workers (UAW)
Ray Rogers, director of Corporate Campaign, Inc.
PRINCIPAL FIGURE (*DEADLY CORN*)
Jeffrey Summers, Staley worker
PRINCIPAL FIGURES (*STRUGGLE IN THE HEARTLAND*)
Jack Spiegel, Chicago Support Committee member, former leader of Amalgamated Clothing Workers
Rev. Darren Cushman-Wood, Methodist minister, Indianapolis
Father Martin Mangan, Catholic priest, Decatur

Gene Vanderport, Indiana Education
   Association leader

These two agitprop films really need each other for best viewing effect. *Deadly Corn* is used as agitprop shorthand for the dangerous conditions under which the locked-out A. E. Staley sugar workers of the United Paperworkers International Union (formerly the Allied Industrial Workers) struggle until the company's dramatic lockout occurred in June 1994. *Struggle in the Heartland* focuses on the attacks by Decatur police on the locked-out strikers and their requests for strike support and boycotts.

Deadly Corn is mainly a talking heads documentary: worker after worker explains the toxic substances he or she had to handle, often without knowing what they were or with any safety precautions or even guidelines. The creators of the first video release, Rose Feurer and Dave Rathke of Labor Vision, a cable-access group dedicated to workers' issues in St. Louis, intended it to be simultaneously a boycott tool of the corporate campaign (boycott Domino Sugar; don't buy State Farm insurance) and as a fundraiser for the union local.

Both films have the strengths of the best agitprop documentaries—strong, memorable titles, the immediacy and excitement of an important story, and the sense that the issues raised by the Staley workers will reverberate not only in their industry but across the board for many workers.

It was two years after Staley workers were locked out that they accepted a contract offered them on 22 December 1995, after a bitter battle that saw widespread union solidarity across the region and the country, unprovoked police attacks on picket lines, various in-plant slowdown strategies suggested by Jerry Tucker (of UAW New Directions), and a corporate campaign led by Ray Rogers, whose leadership in the controversial Hormel P-9 strike of the 1980s was profiled in Barbara Kopple's *American Dream*.

The corporate campaign for the Staley workers was, as a number of commentators

have indicated, a tricky one. Campaigners had to persuade the public to boycott Domino Sugar, plus Miller Beer and Pepsi (both major users of Staley's corn sweetener), and State Farm Mutual Insurance, a major stockholder in ADM (Archer Daniels Midland), a supposed competitor of Staley's also located in Decatur but a company that actually owned a major share of Staley. (In fact, one of the bizarre corporate twists shown in the film is a pipeline between the two companies with which ADM planned to send some sweet stuff to keep its "competitor" going during the lockout.)

The workers in *Deadly Corn* speak particularly of one disturbing death—of a fellow worker caught in a tank when propane oxide came pouring in, apparently a deadly accident but of course two men were working in a tank without protective gear of any kind. Staley was fined by OSHA for this incident and deemed grossly negligent. One of the reasons for the dangerous conditions in the plant was a reflection of a new company shift policy: all workers worked a twelve-hour shift three days a week, then had three days off; those on the 6 P.M.-to-6 A.M. shift were rotated to the 6 A.M.-to-6 P.M. shift every thirty days. This scheme increased the worker-hours per year but at a grave cost. The workers responded with "work to rule" (a strategy they learned from Tucker): slowing down the work as a tool to control conditions within the plant without resorting to a strike.

Like the Hormel P-9 strike, the Staley workers' struggle has generated much controversy. Although John Sweeney, president of the AFL-CIO, invited Dan Lane, a Staley hunger striker, to address the AFL-CIO convention and promised to support the Pepsi boycott, the international president of the Paperworkers apparently wanted to settle the strike, and he urged the local to accept the contract offer in December 1995, supposedly just nine days before the day Pepsi had decided was their deadline to drop Staley as a supplier.

The producer, Labor Vision, followed *Deadly Corn*'s release of 600 copies with

2,000 copies of a follow -up videocassette, *Struggle in the Heartland,* which captures more of the actual strike activities, including the pepper-spraying of demonstrators by Decatur police. Although Staley strikers and their supporters attempted a nonviolent civil disobedience sit-in at the plant gates, the police took an imaginary or inadvertent push by someone as an excuse to aim pepper spray directly into the faces of sitting workers. That no one was blinded is probably a miracle, since the demonstrators were sitting ducks. The film concludes with requests for support: "adopt" a locked-out worker by donating money, join nonviolent civil disobedience at the plant, and boycott Miller Beer, Staley's largest customer.

As if Decatur, Illinois, didn't have enough troubles with its three strikes in 1994—the Bridgestone/Firestone Tire, Staley, and Caterpillar factories—and the price-fixing scandal of Archer Daniels Midland, the flagship company of the Soybean Capital of the World, by the end of the millennium it was blamed for all the many Ford SUV accidents. Some commentators wondered if labor unrest and the poor manufacture of Firestone tires were related: was Bridgestone rushing unskilled replacement workers onto the assembly lines without sufficient training?

Of course these films are not expected to review all of Decatur's labor troubles or subsequent disasters, but one has to wonder if the jinxed-town concept is a way of avoiding the kind of economic, political, and cultural analysis that would situate Decatur's industry at what seems to be the tail end of Reaganite downsizing, a reflection of corporate policy and not a star-crossed inevitability. Certainly Stephen Franklin's book *Three Strikes* begins this process by focusing on the patterns of anti-union activity among the corporate giants in Decatur.

See also: American Dream.

Availability: Selected collections; local union offices.

Further reading

Barboza, David. "Firestone Workers Cite Lax Quality Control." *New York Times,* 15 Septem-

ber 2000, C1; "City Winces in the Glare of the Spotlight on Tires." *New York Times,* 25 September 2000, A14. Journalistic compendia of Decatur woes.

Frank, Tom, and Dave Mulcahey. *Solidarity in the Heartland.* Westfield, N.J.: Open Magazine Pamphlet Series, 1996. A short history and analysis of the Decatur strikes, suggesting that "social unionism" (community support, boycotts, and solidarity campaigns) may be supplanting "business unionism" (unions "partnered" with their corporate bosses).

Franklin, Stephen. *Three Strikes: Labor's Heartland Losses and What They Mean for Working Americans.* New York: Guilford, 2001. A remarkably thorough survey of the three major strikes, the corporate attack on the unions, and the human costs among the workers who took part in these struggles.

Singer, Mark. "Town on a String." *New Yorker,* 30 October 2000, 58–62. Still another reporter's visit to a supposedly jinxed town.

Web sites:

⟨www.irs.princeton.edu/pubs/pdfs/461revised.pdf⟩ Princeton University researchers argue in a report, "Strikes, Scabs, and Tread Separations," that "a long, contentious strike and the hiring of permanent replacement workers by Bridgestone/Firestone in the mid-1990s contributed to the production of an excess number of defective tires."

⟨www.frmartinmangan.com⟩ Source for Father Mangan, "Decatur War Zone" priest.

⤳

Degrees of Shame: Part-Time Faculty—Migrant Workers of the Information Economy

Road scholars

1997, 30 mins.
Director: Barbara Wolf
Traditional documentary
PRINCIPAL FINGURES
Part-time faculty: Charlene Crupi, Sarah Heath, Eric Jackson, Bob Miller, and Thomas Winter.

Anyone familiar with teaching at most public and many private American colleges and universities knows that the books are balanced and the students taught because of the underpaid and underappreciated labor of part-timers (adjuncts) and graduate student teaching assistants. At a typical state university the part-time instructor makes one-tenth to one-third the pay for a course that a full-time tenured or tenure-track professor makes, other issues (nonteaching duties such as advising and research) to the side for a moment.

Pay aside, the "migrant workers of the information economy" do not receive the respect and academic opportunities that their full-time colleagues do. Barbara Wolf's documentary is the first film, I believe, to call attention to their plight. (Yale University's organizing drive for graduate students was documented in Laura L. Dunn's film *The Subtext of a Yale Education* two years later, in 1999.)

Wolf chose a title that calls to mind Edward R. Murrow's classic *Harvest of Shame* deliberately and with care, recognizing that the plight of migrant workers is a genuine horror with which the plight of part-time faculty members cannot be compared. Nonetheless, the part-timers do not have an easy time: their pay is low, they have no health insurance and no job security, and they work in crowded offices. The strength of her film lies in letting the part-timers speak for themselves; she often films them in their cars as these "freeway flyers" or "road scholars" travel from campus to campus, often holding part-time jobs at three institutions. She also includes university administrators, union leaders, and politicians in her mix of interviews.

Wolf's other projects include *This Call Originates,* an exposè of the prison-industrial complex, and *These Old Buildings Raised Our Many Children,* a critical look at the gentrification of a Cincinnati, Ohio, low-income neighborhood. She is currently working on a sequel to *Degrees of Shame.*

See also: *Harvest of Shame.*
Availability: Selected collections.

Further reading

Budd, Mike. "Degrees of Shame': Adjuncts and GAs Organize." *eJumpcut* at ⟨www.ejumpcut. org/Budd/templabor.html⟩. An exhaustive essay reviewing the film and assessing the situation of organizing part-timers and graduate assistants nationally.

Dubson, Michael, ed. *Ghosts in the Classroom.* Dorchester, Mass.: Camel's Back Books, 2001. Twenty-six adjunct faculty members recount their stories.

Martinez, Katherine. " 'Degrees of Shame' Shines Light on PTers." At ⟨www.faccc.org/pubs/ FACCCTS/1998/Wolf.htm⟩. Review of the film and interview with Wolf.

Nelson, Cary, ed. *Will Teach for Food: Academic Labor in Crisis.* Minneapolis: University of Minnesota Press, 1997. Collection of essays on the Yale graduate students' strike and part-time and other academic labor issues.

Web site:
⟨www.members.aol.com/csadjunct/reads.html⟩ A rich source of further reading on the situation, with links to organizations working on the problem.

Full Disclosure Department: My name is on the credit list for this film because I supplied *Harvest of Shame* photo stills; part-timers who have worked at my university (Northern Kentucky) appear in this film.

Desk Set

When Univac was king . . .

1957, 103 mins.
Director: Walter Lang
Screenplay: Phoebe and Henry Ephron, from William Marchant's play of the same title
CAST
Richard Sumner = Spencer Tracy
Bunny Watson = Katharine Hepburn
Peg Costello = Joan Blondell
Mike Cutler = Gig Young
Sylvia = Dina Merrill

Since *Desk Set* was made with the "cooperation and assistance of IBM," one should not expect a sharp satire on the computerization of office life in the 1950s. Potential satire is included, however, in part because the threat of computers' taking away jobs from workers is a theme of the film. Spencer Tracy plays a "methods engineer" ("efficiency expert" sounds too threatening) who is called in to introduce computers to a major broadcasting corporation in general and to Katharine Hepburn's information department—staffed by herself and three women—in particular. Since the women simply deal in facts, they should be easily replaceable by a machine whose specialty is facts. When the computer gets hung up on differentiating "Corfu" from "curfew," the women—who are clearly smarter than both the men and the machines—do their stuff.

Although the satire about computerization is light, the film inadvertently provides a window on office politics and gender roles in the 1950s. Hepburn's Bunny is waiting endlessly for a marriage proposal from her supervisor, played with pleasant smarminess by Gig Young, but in the meantime she ghostwrites his important reports. The other women spend a lot of time worrying about men, marriage, and their jobs, often in that order. Office parties with too much booze, workplace fashion, and witty conversation fill up a good part of their days.

The film has a few giggles, but the real story—automation and layoffs/firings—is not so funny. By now a company on the order of IBM would no longer be so innocent about lending its image to such a story.

See also: *The Efficiency Expert; 9 to 5.*
Availability: Selected collections.

Further reading

Crowther, Bosley. "Desk Set." *New York Times,* 16 May 1957, 28. "The next time they bring up automation, they'll have to pick someone less formidable than Kate [Hepburn]."

Two efficiency experts, led by Richard Sumner (Spencer Tracy), stand with their computer between the workers (the women) and management (the men) in *Desk Set*.

The Devil and Miss Jones

Fantasy on 38th Street

1941, 92 mins.
Director: Sam Wood
Screenplay: Norman Krasna
CAST
Mary Jones = Jean Arthur
John P. Merrick = Charles Coburn
Joe O'Brien = Robert Cummings
Hooper = Edmund Gwenn
Elizabeth Ellis = Spring Byington
George = S. Z. Sakall

This impossible labor union fantasy has a *Miracle on 34th Street* air about it: John P. Merrick, "the richest man in the world," is burned in effigy outside his department store on 38th Street in Manhattan, becomes a humble clerk to catch out the culprits, and ends up on the committee of the local to negotiate with himself. In the meantime, he discovers love and union solidarity and rents an ocean liner to take all his employees on his honeymoon cruise.

What is going on here? With a slickness and collective nose for topicality, Hollywood used real-life situations—an organizer is discharged and blackballed from other department stores, for example—and gave them a comic twist. Robert Cummings plays Joe O'Brien, an all-American union man and organizer, who handcuffs himself to the pipes in Merrick's store in order to make speeches to the employees cowed by Merrick's anti-union tradition. Joe's girlfriend, played by the very popular Jean Arthur, works at the store and is always ready to provide the women's point of view for Joe's organizing campaign: these are "moral issues," she always insists.

Joe is very sincere; he plays the straight man to everyone's jokes. When he is arrested, the police have to decide whether it is worth the trouble to keep him in jail, since he is driving them crazy about his rights. "When they start reciting the Constitution," a police sergeant says, "look out!" It's a great comic scene, because these fantasy officers are of course more concerned about peace and quiet in their station house than in the streets. Joe really doesn't mind being arrested because then he can test the system.

While the audience is no doubt chuckling over the various love affairs and newfound friendship between the (secret) millionaire and the average Joe, a few progressive points develop about the oppressive anti-union atmosphere of the store and the need for improved wages and conditions. This is a comedy, however, so the real issue is how to reunite feuding couples. In the end, the millionaire with the opulent mansion out of *Citizen Kane* (it looks as though the studio recycled the giant fireplace) finds a companion in the sweet staff woman who loves him "for what he really is," a nice guy who happens to be "the richest man in the world." But she didn't know that!

See also: *The Pajama Game*.
Availability: Selected collections.

Further reading

Crowther, Bosley. "The Devil and Miss Jones." *New York Times,* 16 May 1941, 21. The reviewer celebrates this "frothiest" of comedies.
Zinn, Howard, Dana Frank, and Robin D. G. Kelley. *Three Strikes*. Boston: Beacon, 2001. Includes Frank's narrative and analysis of the 1937 Detroit Woolworth's retail clerks' sit-down strike, which the film comically imitates.

The Dollmaker

The great inland Appalachian migration

1984, 150 mins., TVM
Director: Daniel Petrie
Screenplay: Susan Cooper and Hume Cronyn, from Harriet Arnow's novel of the same title
CAST
Gertie = Jane Fonda
Clovis = Levon Helm
Mamie = Amanda Plummer
Mrs. Kendrick = Geraldine Page
Reuben = Jason Yeargood

Enoch = David Brady Wilson
Clytie = Starla Whaley
Sophronie = Susan Kingsley
Taxi Driver = Studs Terkel

The Dollmaker makes a revealing companion piece to *The Killing Floor:* just as rural blacks moved to Chicago in search of jobs during World War I, Appalachian whites moved to Detroit and other midwestern cities during World War II. Fonda plays Gertie, the title character, a rural Kentucky woman with a talent for making wooden dolls and animal figures. She follows her husband north after he moves to take a factory job as a mechanic, although she really wants them to stay in Kentucky and buy a farm. The Detroit housing project they move to is pretty dispiriting, even if a whimsical cab driver (played by Studs Terkel) ferries them over from the railroad station to the unpromised land.

Kentucky begins to look awfully good, despite its poverty and lack of medical facilities. One of the most dramatic scenes, back in Kentucky, involves a medical emergency as Gertie is called upon to give her choking son a tracheotomy by the side of the road. After cutting a passage into his throat, Gertie sticks a hollow reed into his windpipe. A passing army vehicle stops, but the men aren't much help; in fact, the captain faints. So much for menfolk. Gertie, as ever, carries on.

The slummy conditions of Detroit project life do get to her, however, as do her husband's poor pay (when he manages to be working), sneers at her Appalachian traditions, incidents of fascist behavior, and the layoffs as the war work slackens. She really begins to lose her spirit when her daughter, Cassie, is killed by a train.

In both the novel and the film, Gertie's final act of indignation is her destruction of her block of cherry wood, a kind of mystical and artistic talisman, which she breaks to make smaller "whittled" objects for sale. The screenwriters made a major alteration in the novel's ending, in which Gertie must accept staying in depressing Detroit. The film places her in a pickup truck heading joyfully back to Kentucky.

See also: *Coal Miner's Daughter.*
Availability: Easy.

Further reading

Arnow, Harriet. *The Dollmaker.* New York: Macmillan, 1954. The filmmakers significantly whittled Arnow's great novel down to size.
"The Dollmaker." *Variety,* 23 May 1984. "Certainly one of the finest telepics of the season."
Farber Stephen. "'It's as Far from What I Am as Anything I'll Ever Play.'" *New York Times,* 13 May 1984, II.33. Extensive discussion of Fonda's role and details about the production of the film.
O'Connor, John J. "Jane Fonda, Gritty Mountain Woman," *New York Times,* 11 May 1984, C30: Fonda's "performance . . . is nearly always spellbinding, even when the film becomes a bit too reverential about Gertie."

Down and Out in America

"It's a war."—Homeless Korean vet

1986, 57 mins.
Director: Lee Grant
TV documentary
PRINCIPAL FIGURES
Jeff Farmer, Minnesota AFL-CIO
Robert Hayes, national director, Coalition for the Homeless
Bob Killeen, Minnesota UAW
Nancy Minte, attorney, Inner City Law Center, Los Angeles
Tom Styron, volunteer, Coalition for the Homeless
Kenneth Rusk, minister
Anne Kanten, assistant commissioner of agriculture, Minnesota
Norman Larson, Alfred and Bobby Polsean, and Bob Hanson, farmers
Lee Grant, narrator

In the mid-1980s the actress and director Lee Grant filmed this disturbing portrait of poverty and joblessness in America. Grant's is one of the earliest documentaries to deal with a wide spectrum of economic and systemic personal losses. She begins, curiously enough, not with the homeless but with farmers who have lost their farms. The talk among those still standing in the fields is of foreclosures, suicides, and other desperate measures.

The film has five major lines of inquiry: farmers losing their farms; unemployment caused by factory closings; homelessness; renovation of abandoned apartments; and welfare hotels. In all these instances the working poor and homeless struggle to survive. Grant films homeless people who create a shelter, Justiceville, which is bulldozed; a Latino group who do unauthorized renovations of city-owned apartments; and a couple who live in a gross "temporary" hotel.

Grant's film emphasizes two million homeless in 1985, a figure that may seem incredible if you think of it as representing 10,000 people in each of 200 American cities. During this time 140 farms a week were auctioned in Minnesota as well; that's 140 families displaced every week, if not literally made homeless.

Grant's voice-over narration is somewhat unusual. Each of the major episodes has a traditional interpretive voice, but the voice does not link the episodes together. The viewer has the final judgment. According to Carl Plantinga, "the voice-over describes each situation, but draws no comparisons between them." In this regard, then, Grant's documentary is probably closer in form to cinema verité than TV documentary, especially since she does not offer the balanced summing up typical of a network production.

Lee Grant made her reputation mainly as an actress in both Hollywood fluff (*Shampoo*) and some more serious films (*Voyage of the Damned*), but her directing efforts have been, unfortunately, not so well known. She did two films about the strike of bank tellers in Willmar, Minnesota: the documentary *The Willmar 8* (1980) and the perhaps deservedly lesser known feature film based on the same group of women, *A Matter of Sex* (1984).

See also: *Cathy Come Home*.
Availability: Selected collections.

Further reading

Plantinga, Carl. *Rhetoric and Representation in Nonfiction Film*. Cambridge: Cambridge University Press, 1997. Discusses the film as a type of documentary in which the viewer is responsible for the final judgment on the material.

Earth

Earthy

1930, 69 mins., B&W, Soviet Union, silent, with English title cards
Director: Alexander Dovzhenko
Screenplay: Alexander Dovzhenko
CAST
Vasily = Semyon Svashenko
His fiancée = Elena Maksimova
Vasily's father = Stepan Shkurat
Village priest = V. Mikhailov

Film historians have consistently rated this film as one of the classics of world cinema. Set in the director's native Ukraine, the film develops two parallel stories: the personal and familial consequences of the murder of a young man active in the collectivization of agriculture and the struggle between poor and rich peasants [kulaks] over that policy. In the end, the film's visual strategy argues for a unity of the two stories, so that the death of the activist and the success of the new collective farm are inextricably combined.

Three important sequences, remarkable moments in a remarkable film, were censored by Stalinist puritans. They were missing for many years, but the Video Yesterday cassette has all three, even if the overall quality of the reproduction is low. As the eagerly awaited tractor approaches the village, it stops dead. A peasant diagnoses the problem—a dry radiator—and immediately commands a group of men to pee into the radiator. The second censored sequence consists of a series of tableaux of young peasant men each with one hand resting on the clothed breast of a young woman. It is oddly beautiful, as it realizes one of Dovzhenko's themes—that of the love and fecundity of the earthy life. The final sequence is truly disturbing and again oddly moving: Vasily's fiancée, instead of "celebrating" his death as the beginning of the new era of collectivization, is shown, naked, throwing herself about her cottage in a frenzy of mourning. Eventually she will became part of the new order by marrying another man.

Dovzhenko's finale, in which he cross-cuts five sequences, is a triumph of parallel editing that rivals D. W. Griffith at his best. The funeral procession for Vasily, his fiancée's frenzied mourning, the priest's attempt to curse the collective, the birth of Vasily's sibling, and the "confession" of his killer all alternate, in effect each commenting on the other and earlier sequences. Vasily's killer, for example, does a hysterical dance near the funeral gathering, imitating Vasily's final dance before he was killed. Perhaps it was in this kind of moment that Dovzhenko courted danger from his sectarian supervisors—the kulak's motive for the murder is less a matter of economic competition than his jealousy of Vasily's great spirit, manifested in his dancing.

Officially Dovzhenko's filmmaking was criticized in the same absurd ways as Eisenstein's in the 1930s: an excess of "formalism" (too much interest in beautiful com-positions) and an absence of ideological rigor (too little interest in Stalinist slavishness). So many of these films celebrate exactly what the censors argued they did not—an unbounded joy in creating a new society, however impossible it may have seemed to Stalinists and revolutionaries alike at the time.

See also: *Mother*.

Availability: Selected collections; DVD.

Further reading

Dovzhenko, Alexander. *The Poet as Filmmaker*. Trans. and ed. Marco Carynnyk. Cambridge: MIT Press, 1973. A collection of the director's statements and diaries, but the best feature of the book is the editor's introduction.

Hall, Mordaunt. "The Screen." *New York Times*, 21 October 1930, 34. The reviewer finds Eisenstein a much better director, in part because too many sequences seem to him "chaotic" (including the now-classic widow's lament).

Perez, Gilberto. *The Material Ghost: Films and Their Medium*. Baltimore: Johns Hopkins University Press, 1998. Analyzes *Earth* in detail and calls it "one of the last Soviet silent films and perhaps the greatest."

Two Russian Film Classics. New York: Simon & Schuster, 1973. The scenarios of Pudovkin's *Mother* and Dovzhenko's *Earth*; the latter was written twenty years after the film was made and was described by Dovzhenko as "a kind of literary equivalent" of his original ideas for the film.

Youngblood, Denise J. *Soviet Cinema in the Silent Era, 1918–1935*. Austin: University of Texas

Peasants pee in the tractor radiator in *Earth*. Courtesy British Film Institute Stills, Posters, and Designs.

Press, 1991. Especially good on the reception of Dovzhenko's film among the critics and censors.

Note: Some video libraries catalog the film as *Earth—Zemlia* or *Zemlya*.

⌇

East Side Story

Let's put on a show, comrades!

1997, 77 mins., Germany, German, with English subtitles and narration
Director: Dana Ranga and Andrew Horn
Traditional documentary
PRINCIPAL FIGURES
East German filmmakers: Karin Schröder, Brigitte Ulbrich, Helmut Hanke, Hans-Joachim Wallstein, Margarita Andrushkevitch, Chris Doerk, and Frank Schöbel

Communist Party commissars: Barbara Harnisch, Andrea Schmidt, and Brit Kruger.

The two major communisms of our era have had trouble scripting singing and dancing workers on the screen. In China, the route taken by the culture queen Chiang Ching (Madame Mao) was to transform traditional Chinese opera into revolutionary art. On film, dashing ballerinas with gun belts and peasants with attitude in such Cultural Revolution classics as *The East Is Red* and *The White-Haired Girl* seemed curiously stuck in a socialist realist fantasy. The issues were important, the dancing was sprightly, but the totality remained difficult to absorb for many people who would at least be sympathetic with some of the themes—the overthrow of the landlord system or the destruction of feudal values, for example. It was too much like giving Papageno a license to kill.

A member of the proletariat in an arabesque in *East Side Story*.

Soviet and Eastern Bloc communism went another route. They took the American musical as their not-so-secret model and tried to create the equivalent of *Singing in the Rain,* a kind of *Springtime in the Ukraine.* These were not unsophisticated artists: there is even a self-reflexive entry, *Midnight Revue* (1962), in which morose directors and screenwriters are portrayed sitting around (in very comfortable digs, much more comfortable than the average Soviet worker's), trying to solve the problem of creating a Soviet worker's musical film.

Not only the USSR but Poland, East Germany, Romania, and Czechoslovakia are (mis)represented in this survey of the genre of Communist musicals. The East German teen hit of 1968, *Hot Summer,* features relentlessly cheerful boys and girls who look as though they haven't a political bone in their collective body. When it came to nonmusical comedies, East Germany sometimes did better, as *Carbide and Sorrel* was a popular release as well, had some satirical punch, and remains fun.

See also: *Carbide and Sorrel.*
Availability: Selected collections; DVD.

Further reading

LaSalle, Mick. "It Was Springtime for Stalin: 'East Side Story'—A Fascinating Look at Soviet Musicals." *San Francisco Chronicle,* 14 November 1997. Argues that "the clips are a window on the dreams, the desperation and the oppression of whole nations."

⮎
Edge of the City

An interracial contender, also "on the waterfront"

1957, 85 mins., B&W
Director: Martin Ritt
Screenplay: Robert Alan Aurthur, from his own TV play *A Man Is Ten Feet Tall*
CAST
Axel North = John Cassavetes
Tommy Tyler = Sidney Poitier

Charles Malik = Jack Warden
Ellen Wilson = Kathleen Maguire
Lucy Tyler = Ruby Dee

Martin Ritt's career in labor-related feature filmmaking began with this impressive debut. He acquired a ready-made controversial story from TV and kept Sidney Poitier as Tommy Tyler, a black dockworker who befriends Axel North, a fairly unpleasant new white worker, played by the usually semisnarling John Cassavetes. Add Jack Warden as an evil and racist foreman and the mix is clearly explosive. Warden plays Charlie Malik, a foul-mouthed bully who discovers that Axel North has something to hide (his imagined responsibility for a brother's death) and blackmails him. After a friendship develops between Tyler and North, the Tylers invite North to their apartment, where we see a fairly rare moment in contemporary film: social life across racial lines.

Tyler steps in during the inevitable fight between Malik and North. Although Tyler has Malik at a disadvantage, he chooses to turn the other cheek and is stabbed in the back and killed. Tyler's wife has to awaken North's sleeping conscience and persuade him to go to the police so that Malik can be brought to justice. Critics have commented (see Johnson) that too often the price of integrating African Americans into mainstream film in the 1950s was death or the threat of death.

Poitier's sacrificial status was apparent the following year in another unusual interracial friendship drama, *The Defiant Ones* (1958), in which a white convict (played by Tony Curtis) survives being shackled to a black convict (Poitier) for a good part of the picture.

See also: *On the Waterfront.*
Availability: Not.

Further reading

Cripps, Thomas. *Making Movies Black.* New York: Oxford University Press, 1993. Discusses the film's critical reception and its role in Poitier's career.

Crowther, Bosley. "Edge of the City." *New York Times,* 30 January 1957, 33. Applauds a few of the moments of brotherhood in the film but finds it too derivative of *On the Waterfront.*

Johnson, Albert. "Beige, Brown, or Black." *Film Quarterly* 13 (Fall 1959): 39–43. Analyzes roles for African Americans in 1950s films, including this one.

Educating Rita

... to become middle-class

1983, 110 mins., PG-13
Director: Lewis Gilbert
Screenplay: Willy Russell, from his play of the same title
CAST
Rita = Julie Walters
Dr. Frank Bryant = Michael Caine
Brian = Michael Williams
Trish = Maureen Lipman
Julia = Jeananne Crowley
Denny = Malcolm Douglas
Rita's Father = Godfrey Quigley

This is the English version of the story of the working-class kid who makes good by giving up her/his roots and making it into the middle class. When one's accent is such an obvious class marker in England and a college education is limited to only a few percentage points of the population, Rita's heroic attempts to become independent and "intelligent"—just like "real" college students—is full of humor and spunk. The walk she walks, the talk she talks ... all make it clear that in most people's eyes (including hers at first) she's just a good old gal from the corner pub. But Rita wants more, and she forces the system to deliver it.

Fortunately for her, the British university system opened a few more doors to working-class students with its adult education program, the Open University, which combines aspects of our public TV education network with on-campus tutorials. The film celebrates the value of such programs for people with enough energy and self-confidence to try them. The film makes it clear that Rita also educates her alcoholic middle-class tutor, played admirably by Michael Caine, who in real life jumped out of the working class into the acting class, but with his accent more or less intact. Rita's enthusiasm for literary study reignites her tutor's passion for it, although he becomes upset because she's "done" the poet William Blake at a summer session without his help.

Although Rita's class origins are played at first for big laughs—shots of her teeter-tottering in heels and a miniskirt on the stones of Dublin's austerely traditional

Rita (Julie Walters), a student at the Open University, in *Educating Rita.* Courtesy British Film Institute Stills, Posters, and Designs.

TUTORIAL ROO

Trinity College grounds set this tone early on—the film wants us to believe that Rita will be the better for having shared the experiences of two social classes. Like Willy Russell's other comic heroine, Shirley Valentine (filmed in 1989, also by Lewis Gilbert), Rita is a survivor who is not about to be held back by anything as dubious as a thousand-year-old class system.

Rita is hard to classify. She refuses to go off the pill and have a baby. Her alienation from her husband and the rest of her family is inevitable. She is so impressed with Rita Mae Brown's *Rubyfruit Jungle* that she gives up her name of Susan and takes the novelist's first name. No academic jungle would be able to contain her, either.

See also: *The Corn Is Green.*
Availability: Easy.

Further reading

Canby, Vincent. "What Makes Audiences Fond of Rita?" *New York Times,* 13 November 1983, II.17. Mocks the film's spunk but indicates its part in the tradition of "valentines to literacy."

Maslin, Janet. "Learning." *New York Times,* 21 September 1983, C21. The reviewer finds the film "an awkward blend of intellectual pretension and cute obvious humor."

⤶
The Efficiency Expert

"Reduce unnecessary contact among employees."—The First Law of Efficiency

1991, 97 mins., Australia, PG
Director: Mark Joffe
Screenplay: Max Dann and Andrew Knight
CAST
Wallace = Anthony Hopkins
Carey = Ben Mendelsohn
Wendy = Toni Collette
Mr. Ball = Alwyn Kurts
Fletcher = Dan Wyllie
Robert = Bruno Lawrence
Cheryl = Rebecca Rigg
Kim = Russell Crowe

In the last quarter of the twentieth century the New Australian Cinema produced a series of notable films—the metaphysical mystery film *Picnic at Hanging Rock,* the young woman's coming-of-age film *My Brilliant Career,* and the historical drama *Breaker Morant.* Less well known are the films on labor such as *The Efficiency Expert,* directed by Mark Joffe, who made a successful thriller (*Grievous Bodily Harm*) that was not released in the United States.

The opening titles strike a whimsical note that will run throughout this comic look at an efficiency expert, played by Anthony Hopkins in his usual intense and sympathetic style. He doesn't like to be called a "time-and-motion man" because his company surveys a client's "whole corporate picture," including its financial health. When he takes a look at Ball's Moccasins in Spotswood, a "small, shabby industrial suburb of Melbourne," he finds a paternalistic boss and a utopian workplace: the employees work as much as they want, when they want, and have time to gossip, to manage the company's "slot car" racing team, and to dance to "Deep in the Heart of Texas" when the mood strikes them.

And it does, because Ball's Moccasins hasn't made a profit in decades. The owner has been selling off assets (parcels of his real estate, for example) and cooking the books to make it look as if everything is fine. He cannot bear to make his employees unhappy. He ignores the failure of such sales campaigns as "Mocc and Roll" and treats them all as business coups.

In a parallel plot our efficiency expert, Mr. Wallace, has just recommended to an auto parts factory that it cut a quarter of its staff. When a fellow efficiency expert leaks an inflated layoff figure to the unions, all hell breaks loose and the auto workers try to storm their plant. Whimsy wins the day, however, and Mr. Wallace ends up helping Ball's Moccasins survive with its (obviously) impossible work culture. (The auto parts factory ends up cutting "only" 500 jobs.)

In Australian films, the impossible is often celebrated as the most likely outcome, so that we leave the expert in the end with his newfound soul intact and the old cohort of workers streaming back into Ball's Moccasins.

The original screenplay (and perhaps the British Commonwealth videocassette, which I have not seen) ends with these bittersweet end titles: "Ball's Moccasins closed two years later. Arthur Ball died three months after that. The Moccasin factory now houses an arts collective."

Although the film is supposed to be set in the 1960s—Donovan's song "Catch the Wind" is featured over the end credits—the film shows Carey and Wendy happily biking off to work as if time had stopped in 1955. They should fall in love, we know that almost immediately, but Carey has to fall for the boss's beautiful daughter before he comes to his senses and realizes that homespun Wendy (who, like her counterpart in *Peter Pan,* may be able to fly) is the gal for him. Carey also has to realize that being an apprentice to an efficiency expert is a sure way to destroy workplace friendships.

This is a PG film suitable for children. It may help teach about the evils of corporate maneuvering for profits. Mr. Wallace's suggestion that Ball's become a cooperative with workers holding the shares in the company may also teach them about another kind of corporate ownership, however rare. If they ask you for an airplane ticket to Australia so they can get a job at Ball's Moccasins, then Australian whimsy has won again.

See also: *Sunday Too Far Away.*
Availability: Easy.

Further reading

Dann, Max, and Andrew Knight. *Spotswood.* Sydney: Currency Press, 1992. The original screenplay, with brief essays by the director and a critic.

Murray, Scott. *Australian Film, 1978–1992.* New York: Oxford University Press, 1993. A review of the film, emphasizing its utopian attitudes toward the factory.

Note: The original title in British Commonwealth countries was *Spotswood.*

Eight Hours Are Not a Day

Or enough

1972–73, 472 mins., in five parts, West Germany, German, with English subtitles, TV series
Director: Rainer Werner Fassbinder
Screenplay: Rainer Werner Fassbinder
CAST
Jochen = Gottfried John
Marion = Hanna Schygulla
Grandma ("Oma") = Luise Ulrich
Gregor = Werner Finck
Franz = Wolfgang Schenck
Ernst = Peter Gauhe
Harald = Kurt Raab
Monika = Renate Roland
Irmgard Erlkönig = Irm Hermann
Rolf Rudolf = Waldemar Brem

An industrial soap opera might sound like a dismissive description of this West German *Arbeiterfilm* (worker film) from the early 1970s, but with its cast of characters who come and go through the five major parts or episodes, its emphasis on everyday life and love affairs, and the intention of its director to use the popular forms of the media, Rainer Werner Fassbinder's contribution to this short-lived genre of German television films had all the characteristics of a popular "family series" hit (Raynes). (One thinks of the working-class characters in *The East Enders* or *Brookside* in England, but with the factory much more prominent.)

This unusual experiment in mass media was successful, earning a significant share of the viewing audience in 1972. It came about because of the decisions taken by a Cologne television station, Westdeutscher Rundfunk (WDR), which began commissioning documentaries about workers' lives in the late 1960s. *Red Flags Can Be Seen Better* (*Rote Fahne seht man besser*), a documentary about a factory closing from the point of view of the workers effected, was broadcast in 1971.

In *Eight Hours Are Not a Day,* Fassbinder, who had already established himself as a daring experimentalist in theatrical films such as *The Bitter Tears of Petra von Kant,* created a wide range of characters living in Cologne, beginning with Jochen, a skilled factory worker, and Marion, who works in the advertising department of a newspaper. Their families, friends, and lovers move in and out of the five episodes.

These episodes cover a remarkable range of contemporary issues and situations, including housing, public transportation, new participatory management schemes, and immigrant workers. Fassbinder's film, like a number of the *Arbeiterfilme* of the WDR, was an experiment as powerful as it was short-lived. With a shift in political control at the WDR, the last film appeared in 1976. And because of their unavailability in videocassette, there is a little danger that they may be forgotten.

See also: *Wittstock, Wittstock.*
Availability: Not.

Further reading

Collins, Richard, and Vincent Porter. *WDR and the Arbeiterfilm: Fassbinder, Ziewer, and Others.* London: British Film Institute, 1981. The definitive English account of the genre, with details on all of the television films and their origin in German political and media culture.

Iden, Peter, et al. *Fassbinder.* Trans. Ruth McCormick. New York: Tanam Press, 1981. A survey of Fassbinder's career by diverse hands; a section on *Eight Hours* concludes that the "conventional separation in art between private life and the workplace is overcome."

Raynes, Tony, ed. *Fassbinder.* London: British Film Institute, 1980. Manuel Alvarado compares *Eight Hours* with *Coronation Street,* "its closest British counterpart."

⤳
The Electric Valley

Creepy socialism

1983, 90 mins.
Director: Ross Spears
Traditional documentary

PRINCIPAL FIGURES
Wilma Dykeman, narrator
John Siegenthaler, editor, *Nashville Tennessean*
W. A. Dykeman, writer
Barrett Shelton, publisher, *Decatur Daily*
Henry Clark and Beryl Moser, farmers
Albert Gore and George Norris, senators from Tennessee
Louis Lowery and Curt Stiner, TVA dam workers
David Lilienthal, director, TVA (1933–46)
Arthur E. Morgan, chair, TVA
Harry Caudill, author, *Night Comes to the Cumberlands*
David Freeman, director, TVA (1977–1989)
Hank Hill, environmental lawyer

The Tennessee Valley is the "electric valley" charted in this film—the recipient of one of the greatest social, political, and economic experiments of the twentieth century. What began with a daring interstate project to preserve flooded lands and generate electricity ends with the deployment of Big Bertha, Peabody Coal's strip-mining derrick, the world's largest. How did a seemingly progressive showpiece of Roosevelt's New Deal become a force for strip mining and eventually for nuclear power?

The film emphasizes that there were problems from the start, and not only from the representatives of Congress, manufacturers' associations, and power companies who were adamantly opposed to the idea. In 1945, for example, black workers at the Fontana Dam site, with its segregated living and eating facilities, still needed guards because local whites "hated the colored." Beryl Moser, a local white landowner, describes losing her land in a scene right out of *The Grapes of Wrath,* when a front loader wrecked her house and trees because the TVA exercised the right of eminent domain.

And while the TVA could not always be accused of destroying the land in order to protect it, nonetheless there were serious human costs to their plans to control the floodplain over millions of acres. Elia Kazan's *Wild River* (q.v.) dramatizes—

somewhat melodramatically but convincingly—what happens when a family's precious homestead is due to be flooded as a result of a new dam. Spears's film holds on to many of these human stories while it dissects the history of a very intricate government project. He is clearly more skeptical than most about the direction the TVA has taken. We see clips, for example, from a TV film, *Strip Mining Land Can Be Reclaimed,* and we learn that half of the energy generated by the TVA went for atomic weapons and research.

The TVA was created to improve river navigation, create electricity, establish lakes for recreation, and be a model agency for planting trees and using scientific means of farming. It did these things, but it did much more, and when it lost billions of dollars in the phasing out of nuclear plant development, it seemed to be a long way from its roots.

Spears continued his emphasis on southern issues with *To Render a Life* (1992), a cinema verité portrait of a Virginia family's struggle with poverty.

See also: *Wild River.*
Availability: Selected collections.

Further reading

McDonald, Michael J., and John Muldowny. *TVA and the Dispossessed: The Resettlement of Population in the Norris Dam Area.* Knoxville: University of Tennessee Press, 1982. Charts the controversy when local residents were forced to move.

༄

The End of St. Petersburg

Capital of the tsars

1927, 75 mins., Soviet Union, B&W, silent, with English title cards
Director: Vsevolod Pudovkin
Screenplay: Natan Zarkhi
CAST
A Bolshevik Worker = Aleksandr Chistiakov

His Wife = Vera Baranovskaya
Peasant Boy = Ivan Chuvelev
His Employer = Sergei Komarov
Factory Manager Lebedev = V. Obolensky

Like Eisenstein's *October* (also known as *Ten Days That Shook the World*), Vsevolod Pudovkin's film was commissioned by the Central Committee of the Communist Party of the Soviet Union to celebrate the tenth anniversary of the October Revolution in 1917. He chose to dramatize a prerevolutionary strike at a munitions company that has just received a big government contract. The company decides to extend the workday. The workers, under Bolshevik leadership, strike.

Pudovkin uses a naive peasant boy, part of a group of scabs recruited to break the strike, as the catalyst for the second stage of the film. The boy knows the Bolshevik Worker from their old village. When the police search for the worker, the boy tells them where he lives, trying to be of help. When he realizes his horrible mistake, he rushes to the factory and attacks the manager and is arrested as well. Conscripted against his will to fight in World War I, he returns eventually to join the revolutionaries, who, at the very end, cry out in an end title, "Long live the city of Lenin," or Leningrad, as St. Petersburg was renamed.

See also: *Mother.*
Availability: Selected collections; Kino International; DVD.

Further reading

Clark, Katerina. *Petersburg: Crucible of Cultural Revolution.* Cambridge: Harvard University press, 1995. Argues that (and demonstrates how) St. Petersburg developed a rich alternative culture.
"The End of St. Petersburg." *Variety,* 31 May 1928. "Eminently satisfying propaganda," the reviewer asserts, almost "as though this film were a remarkable newsreel of the Russian Revolution."
Pudovkin, V. I. *Film Technique and Film Acting.* 1949. Trans. and ed. Ivor Montague. New York: Grove Press, 1976. The director's classic study of editing, with numerous discussions of his and other Soviet filmmakers' works.

Note: The Kino release translates "Bolshevik" as "Communist," not quite accurately, historically speaking.

⤵ Enthusiasm

. . . for a five-year plan

1930, 75 mins., Soviet Union, B&W, no
  subtitles or title cards
Director: Dziga Vertov
Social-realist documentary

During Soviet debates in the 1920s on the function of cinema in a socialist society, Dziga Vertov valorized documentary film over fictional features. One eventual result of the debate was the so-called Lenin Proportion, Lenin's decree in 1922 that established a higher proportion of documentary to fiction films produced under state auspices (as all films were). Such filmmakers as Sergei Eisenstein took a middle ground, making documentaries with scripted stories and feature films with documentary sequences and ideas.

Vertov pioneered the concept of the "kino-eye" or the camera eye/lens as more successful and revealing than the human eye because of its ability to travel through space and time. Vertov also pioneered the newsreel "magazine" called *Kino-Pravda* (literally Cinema Truth), named after the Communist Party newspaper *Pravda,* but delivering the news in a single reel of two or three episodes.

Vertov's *Man with a Movie Camera* (1929), a dawn-to-evening tour of Moscow, was self-reflexive (people watching the same film we are watching), using split screens, variable film speeds, and experiments in sound. But as with Eisenstein and Lev Kuleshov, the other great experimentalist and—bad word—formalist, Vertov fell afoul of Stalin and was eventually relegated to more routine documentary assignments.

Enthusiasm, a tribute to the Soviet farmers and workers of the Don River Basin who completed their five-year plan, is a strange documentary mix of Soviet antireligious propaganda and a celebration of Soviet industry. It has no narrative line to speak of and is more interested in an experimental sound track of actual sounds and music. In its heavy industrial section it is typical Soviet social realism of the 1930s, with muscular workers, hard work, and big pieces of infrastructure (cranes and trains) in frenzied operation. Every once in a while, Vertov cuts to a split image or a double image, which is more in keeping with the experimental visual style of his *Kino-Pravda*.

The film splits in two or, to phrase it more closely to Vertov's aims in content and sound, into counterpoint, according to Kristin Thompson's convincing argument. We begin with shots of people crossing themselves and kissing the feet of Jesus on a crucifix. These shots are intercut with shots of church steeples and factory smokestacks. Presently workers are sawing off the steeple and carrying icons and religious pictures out of the church. A recurring image of an attractive young woman, listening to a radio headset, seems to stand in for the filmmaker—and sound experimentalist?—himself. In short, industry has trumped religion and cinema has captured the moment.

This is a cinema of image and sound virtually without narrative in any traditional documentary sense. One of the banners in a parade of workers at the end states simply "XII," representing the twelfth year of Soviet rule in 1929, when the film was begun. Simple enough, as Vertov would see it, without much discussion.

See also: *Earth; Mother.*
Availability: Selected collections; Hollywood's Attic.

Further reading

Kataev, Valentin. *Time, Forward!* 1932. Trans. Charles Malamuth. Bloomington: Indiana University Press, 1976. A literary cousin to the film, as the novelist Kataev celebrates the champion concrete-pourers of the Magnitogorsk metallurgical complex in the Ural Mountains.

Thompson, Kristin. "Early Sound Counterpoint." *Yale French Studies,* no. 60 (1980), 115–40. Discussion of a number of Soviet films, including *Enthusiasm,* that use sound counterpoint.

Vertov, Dziga. "Kino-Eye: The Embattled Documentarists." In *Cinema in Revolution: The Heroic Era of the Soviet Film,* ed. Luda and Jean Schnitzler and Marcel Martin, trans. David Robinson. New York: Hill & Wang, 1973. A fragmentary explanation of the director's idea that the "kino-eye" is "what the eye does not see, as the microscope and the telescope of time, as telescopic camera lenses, as the X-ray eye, as 'candid camera'" all do.

Note: Also known as *Donbass Symphony* and *Symphony of the Don Basin.*

Evelyn Williams

"Take care of the land"

1995, 27 mins.
Director: Anne Lewis
Traditional documentary
PRINCIPAL FIGURES
Evelyn Williams and her family
Daymon Morgan, Kentuckians for the
    Commonwealth

This portrait of an African American Appalachian or Afrilachian woman begins and ends with the land, as so many stories of southern Appalachia do. Evelyn Williams was raised in Eastern Kentucky and became a coal miner's wife who cleaned the homes of the mine owners. When her husband was laid off at mid-century, the family moved to New York City, where she attended the New School for Social Research to become a poverty program counselor. When she retired in the 1970s, she came back to the hills of her youth, where she had retained some family property.

In order to protect her property from the strip-mining companies that were about to enforce the broad-form deed provision, which gave them ownership of all minerals below the surface, Evelyn joined Kentuckians for the Commonwealth, an activist organization campaigning against strip mining and other abuses of the environment.

When Anne Lewis catches up with her, Evelyn is sitting down in front of a bulldozer sent to strip her land. When offered a deal to stop her protest, she says: "I'm not interested in money. I'm not a prostitute." In her 80s she is not about to turn her back on the advice given to her by her grandmother, an ex-slave: "Take care of the land. Take care of the land. As long as you have land, you have a belonging."

Lewis documents this remarkable woman's life story as the epitome of what Lewis has said (in her lectures about Appalshop films) about Eastern Kentucky. Three myths persist: that poor whites did not own slaves; that since there were no blacks, there was no racism; and that coal dust made all workers black. Evelyn Williams's life contra-

Evelyn Williams explains her activism against the Appalachian broad-form deed. Photo by Nyoka Hawkins. Courtesy Appalshop.

dicts almost all of these myths. In fact, she vividly remembers Klan cross burnings and the lynching of a black man in the 1920s.

Lewis emphasizes that Williams's activism for the land was part of her abiding concern for social justice throughout her life. One particularly poignant episode involves the death of one of her sons in Vietnam. The military informed her that they had "lost" his body. She and her family waged a campaign to right this wrong and succeeded. Eventually the Kentucky legislature outlawed the broad-form deed. It was another victorious moment for a hardworking activist.

Anne Lewis's film is part of the Headwaters Television series for Appalshop, as is *Fast Food Women* and *Justice in the Coalfields*. Public television stations across the United States have picked up some of the films in the series, validating perhaps the view that these documentaries, although rooted in very specific Appalachian working-class struggles, nonetheless touch issues that cross virtually every regional and economic band.

See also: *Chemical Valley; Fast Food Women; Justice in the Coalfields; To Save the Land and People.*
Availability: Selected collections; Appalshop.
Web site:
⟨www.kftc.org⟩ Official site of Kentuckians for the Commonwealth, who "are working for a day when Kentuckians—and all people—enjoy a better quality of life. When the lives of people and communities matter before profits. When our communities have good jobs that support our families without doing damage to the water, air and land."

≈

Fame Is the Spur

Accommodation is the result

1949, 116 mins., B&W, UK
Director: Roy Boulting
Screenplay: Nigel Balchin, from Howard Spring's novel of the same title

Hamer Radshaw = Michael Redgrave
Ann = Rosamund John
Tom Hannaway = Bernard Miles
Arnold Ryerson = Hugh Burden
Lady Lettie = Carla Lehmann
Young Hamer = Anthony Wager
Young Ryerson = Brian Weske
Young Hannaway = Gerald Fox
Mrs. Radshaw = Jean Shepherd
Grandpa = Guy Verney

This is the story of a Labour Party politician who, after a humble and heroic rise to power as the people's choice, becomes a sellout and a puffy loser. He's so insensitive that he doesn't even support his own wife's suffragette activism. Like its source novel, the film in effect portrays one version of the life of Ramsay MacDonald, the party's first prime minister.

Hamer Radshaw's training to be a leader of his class begins with a curious and compelling flashback. As a young boy, he listens to his granddad's tale of the Peterloo Massacre of 1819, when one of the dragoons who attacked a peaceful demonstration of Chartists murdered his grandfather's girl-friend with a sword. This sword passes to young Hamer as a symbol of the people's resistance to tyranny. He uses the sword symbolically many years later when he rouses a crowd of striking Welsh miners to riot. When he is accused of being responsible for the death of one of the demonstrators, he denies that he "would advocate useless violence."

In fact, he no longer advocates militancy of any kind, and becomes the worst kind of time-serving Labour Party "leader." The filmmakers (director Roy Boulding and his brother, producer John Boulding) made the close of Radshaw's career even more pitiful than Howard Spring's source novel did. As Radshaw approaches his dotage, he attempts to pull the Peterloo sword from its scabbard, hoping to regain his old militancy, but the sword is rusted tight and he cannot budge it. Having avoided militancy for so long, the filmmakers argue, the Labour Party, like Radshaw, has lost its edge, possibly irreversibly.

See also: *Days of Hope.*
Availability: Selected collections.

Further reading

"Accounts from Manchester." *Times* (London), 20–27 August 1819, passim. Under various titles, numerous articles detailing the Peterloo Massacre.

Crowther, Bosley. "Fame Is the Spur." *New York Times,* 8 November 1949, 34. Finds some "vivid authority and fascination" in the film, but worries about its incomplete characterizations.

"Fame Is the Spur." *Variety,* 15 October 1947. For British viewers the film will have "wide appeal" because they are "politically minded"; for American viewers it will explain what the British working class has "suffered since 1870" and "Labour's uncompromising attitude today to many Tory ideas."

Richards, Jeffrey, and Anthony Aldgate. *British Cinema and Society, 1930–1970.* Totowa, N.J.: Barnes & Noble, 1983. Includes an excellent chapter on the film's social and historical context.

Samuel, Raphael. "Fame Is the Spur/The Corn Is Green." In *Raymond Williams: Film TV Culture,* ed. David Lusted. London: National Film Theatre, 1989. A historian praises *Fame Is the Spur* less for its depiction of precise historical fact than for its portrayal of the mythology of the Labour Party.

Spring, Howard. *Fame Is the Spur.* New York: Viking, 1940. Immensely popular, mammoth source novel.

Note: A BBC TV miniseries based on Spring's novel and directed by David Giles in 1982 is not available on videocassette.

Fast Food Women

No fries, no frills, no benefits

1992, 28 mins.
Director: Anne Lewis
Cinema verité documentary
PRINCIPAL FIGURES
Sereda Collier and Angie Hogg, kitchen staff, Druthers Restaurant, Whitesburg, Kentucky
Nellie Kincer, cook, Kentucky Fried Chicken
Marion Clark, co-owner and manager, Druthers Restaurant
Mike Super, human resources manager, Druthers, Inc.
Marcella Fields and Pam Banks, waitresses, Pizza Hut
Zelpha Adams, crew chief, McDonald's
Barbara Garson, author

The "fast food women" interviewed in this brief but excellent film are mostly older women who are the sole support of their families in small Eastern Kentucky coal towns. They are resigned to their fate as low-paid backup workers for their men, who may

Angie Hogg, one of the Druthers kitchen staff in *Fast Food Women*. Courtesy Appalshop.

never get back their well-paying jobs in the coal mines. They speak sincerely and with remarkable good humor of the hard work, the low pay, and the sense that they are serving an indefinite sentence. A few look to the moment when their husbands will go back to work: "Then I'm out of here," says one.

The myth that fast-food workers are teens picking up sneaker money dies hard, especially among corporate executives. Mike Super, Druthers human resources manager, said the teenagers who work at Druthers don't need "frills": "Susie is sixteen years old. Her father works in the coal mine. . . . Susie doesn't need benefits."

"Susie," as Lewis's gentle but probing camerawork reveals, is really 48 years old and has been working for Druthers for years. In fact, Lewis got the idea for her film as she was sitting in her Appalshop media lab across the street from the Whitesburg, Kentucky, Druthers, and noticed how many older women worked there.

On the surface, the most insincere moments occur during the interviews with the top managers of the Druthers chain, headquartered in Louisville. Until the moment of the filming, clearly these two managers have never thought about the implications of the corporate philosophy taught in their equivalent of McDonald's 101 at Hamburger University. When asked whether the restaurant workers need to be creative, one Druthers exec says, "We are not looking for creativity as much . . . ," whereupon his thought is finished by his colleague: ". . . as looking for somebody that would be more content with following procedures and practices and getting their sense of achievement from an area other than being creative about it."

Barbara Garson, who has written extensively on the effects of repetitive work, appears in the film as its only "expert," in one of its moments of traditional documentary. She comments on the decision-making process in such companies as McDonald's, in which people "think creatively about making the other people's jobs uncreative." She ana-lyzes the process by which "the person at the end [cooking the food or serving the public] doesn't have to think at all."

Fast Food Women is simultaneously a front-line political statement about fast-food restaurants everywhere and the exploitation of part-time labor nationally and internationally.

See also: Clockwatchers.
Availability: Selected collections; Appalshop.

Further reading

Beeching, Veronica, and Tessa Perkins. *A Matter of Hours: Women, Part-Time Work, and the Labor Market*. Minneapolis: University of Minnesota Press, 1987. "Part-time work is overwhelmingly women's work"—as of the mid-1980s, 90 percent of these jobs in Britain were held by women.

Ehrenreich, Barbara. *Nickel and Dimed: On (Not) Getting By in America*. New York: Metropolitan Books, 2001. Middle-class author becomes a waitress and takes other low-paying jobs to see if low-wage workers can make it in America. They can't.

Gaines, Jane M. "Appalshop Documentaries: Inventing and Preserving Appalachia." *Jump Cut*, no. 34 (1985), 53–63. A history of Appalshop and a survey of its films; suggests some problems with their somewhat purist "folk" approach to the region.

Garson, Barbara. *The Electronic Sweatshop: How Computers Are Transforming the Office of the Future into the Factory of the Past*. New York: Simon & Schuster, 1988. The title says it all; includes a chapter on MacDonald's "fast food women" (and men).

Howe, Louise Kapp. *Pink Collar Workers: Inside the World of Women's Work*. New York: Putnam, 1977. Documents the ongoing devaluation of women's clerical and restaurant work.

Leidner, Robin. *Fast Food, Fast Talk: Service Work and the Routinization of Everyday Life*. Berkeley: University of California, 1993. The clash of personal autonomy and corporate culture.

Noble, Barbara Presley. "While the Men Wait at Home." *New York Times*, 9 August 1992, II.23. A review of the film with a profile of filmmaker Lewis.

Paules, Greta Foff. *Dishing It Out: Power and Resistance in a New Jersey Restaurant*. Philadelphia: Temple University Press, 1991.

This participant-observation report explains how the "rationalization of service" (teaching workers not to think) is developing in standard family restaurants.

Female

Auto bait

1933, 60 mins., B&W
Director: Michael Curtiz
Screenplay: Gene Markey and Kathryn Scola
CAST
Alison Drake = Ruth Chatterton
Jim Thorne = George Brent
Miss Frothingham = Ruth Donnelly
Harriet Brown = Lois Wilson
Pettigrew = Ferdinand Gottschalk

This oddly titled film is part of Ted Turner's M-G-M/UA collection of "Forbidden Hollywood" releases, all pre-Production Code talkies dating from the three-year period before the Hays office brought the big whiff of Puritanism down Hollywood and Vine. (See *Heroes for Sale,* another film in this series.)

Some of the "Forbidden Hollywood" series were called First National productions, but that studio had already been absorbed by Warner Brothers; in any case, such a producer's label denoted a certain rough-and-tumble kind of film, a little less proletarian than Warner Brothers' products in the 1930s but certainly more provocative than films from other studios.

The "female" of the title is Alison Drake, who, having inherited an auto manufacturing plant from her father, proceeds to run it like a man. That is, she's in charge and everybody knows it. She also treats the young men around her as—well, as a woman would if she were a man and they were women. In any case, she picks out a likely-looking one every once in a while, takes him home, clearly beds him, then sends him on his way the next day and ignores him at work from then on. Some of them become so frustrated that they quit.

Her technique is rather simple, really: if they sip her vodka, she beds them; don't and she doesn't.

She finally meets her comeuppance in an engineer she is trying to recruit to straighten out a design problem. It turns out that he's so handsome and self-confident that the boss's moves don't mean a thing. Of course that makes her want him even more and she does some foolish things to try to get him. Most of these gambits fail and she has to become really a "female" in order to win his love. By then the plot involving designs for new automobile parts has more than gone out the windshield. This is an entertaining and campy look at role reversal at the top.

See also: *Heroes for Sale.*
Availability: Selected collections.

Further reading

"Female." *Variety,* 7 November 1933. Bemoans Ruth Chatterton playing a "female" on a "typical 10th Avenue make" and showing off too much of her executive body.

Hall, Maudaunt. "Female." *New York Times,* 4 November 1933, 18. Other than the fact that the reviewer calls one-night stands "flirtations," a short but positive review.

⌒

The Fight in the Fields: Cesar Chavez and the Farm Workers' Struggle

Reagan eats grapes

1997
Directors: Rick Tejada-Flores and Ray Telles
Traditional documentary
PRINCIPAL FIGURES
Cesar Chavez, United Farm Workers (UFW) organizer
Helen Chavez, his wife
Paul and Richard Chavez, their sons
Dorothy Healy, former Communist organizer
Fred Ross, leader, Community Service Organization (CSO)

Marshall Ganz, Al Rojas, and Ben
Maddock, UFW organizers
Herman Gallego, CSO organizer
Luis Valdez, El Teatro Campesino leader
Bill Kirch, director of organizing, AFL-CIO
Walter Reuther, president, UAW
Robert F. Kennedy, the senator
Ethel Kennedy, his wife and UFW
supporter
Jerry Cohn, UFW general counsel
Cardinal Roger Mahoney
Ronald Reagan, former governor of
California
Lionel Steinberg and John Giumarra Jr.,
growers
Bill Grami, director of organizing, Western
Conference of Teamsters
George Meany, president, AFL-CIO
Jerry Brown, former governor of California
George Deukmejian, governor of California
Arthur Rodrigues, president, UFW

Certainly many Chicano farm workers
believed that Cesar Chavez, their leader,
was a saint: outwardly religious, fasting like
Gandhi, and virtually a martyr to the struggle to bring union recognition and respect
to farm workers, who were excluded from
federal labor-law protection and most union
organizing drives. But what makes this documentary of Chavez's career compelling is
that the makings of a saint are here but so
are the difficulties and triumphs of plain
aggressive organizing, not to mention one
of labor's less wholesome aspects—unions
fighting each other (in this case the
Teamsters, who were signed by some of the
California growers to avoid having "their"
workers organized by the United Farm
Workers).

Most viewers probably already know the
broad outlines of Chavez's story: his early life
as the son of a migrant family, his rise to leadership of the organizing drive using nonvio-
lence as a holy defensive weapon and a
national boycott of grapes as a brilliant
stroke for organizing community support
across the land, his alliance with Bobby
Kennedy, and the successful contracts that

came in the 1970s. These aspects of his career
are carefully documented. But the film does
much more, filling in details, broadening
the scope, revealing that what may have
appeared to be a simple life was really quite
complex. We learn that Chavez's parents
became migrant workers only after losing
their own small farm during the Depression.
And that the Farm Workers' difficulties in
organizing their brothers and sisters at first
had some relation to some families' history
as braceros in the 1940s, imported from
Mexico literally to keep farm wages low and
prevent farm workers from organizing. And
that Chavez's early mentor was Fred Ross,
who had run a model agricultural camp for
the government that John Steinbeck had
known and admired, and who had become
an organizer for the Community Service
Organization.

The film is also adept at establishing
continuities with other pieces of American
history. In this context, for example, Bobby
Kennedy's Century Hotel speech just
seconds before he was assassinated takes on
new meaning: as he spoke to his cheering
campaign supporters of his victory in
California and his support of the Farm
Workers, standing next to him at the podium
was Dolores Huerta. Kennedy had wanted
Cesar Chavez to be there, but Chavez was
delayed in traffic. This sequence is juxtaposed with shots of Ronald Reagan, then
governor of California, fressing on grapes
and announcing, "There is no strike and the
grape boycott is a failure." Later, during the
Salinas lettuce struggle of 1970, we see Ethel
Kennedy virtually being attacked by a pro-
grower crowd shouting, "Ethel, go home!"

The Farm Workers, with or without a
Kennedy, continue their organizing to this
day. They were no match for the strawberry
growers—a major failure in an important
industry—but they have had successes with
the growers of table grapes and wine grapes.

See also: *The Golden Cage.*
Availability: Selected collections; Cinema
Guild.

Cesar Chavez on the United Farm Workers picket line in *The Fight in the Fields.* Photo by Rick Tejada-Flores. Courtesy Cinema Guild.

Further reading

Alinsky, Saul. *Rules for Radicals*. New York: Random House, 1971. "A practical primer for realistic radicals" by one of Chavez's mentors, who introduces his advice in this way: "What follows is for those who want to change the world from what it is to what they believe it should be. *The Prince* was written by Machiavelli for the Haves on how to hold on to power. *Rules for Radicals* is written for the Have-Nots on how to take it away."

Bacon, David. "The U.F.W. Picks Strawberries." *Nation,* 14 April 1997, 18–22. Analysis of a major campaign of the UFW in the 1990s.

Bulosan, Carlos. *America Is in the Heart: A Personal History*. New York: Harcourt, Brace, 1946. This autobiography by the Filipino poet provides a valuable firsthand account of farm and cannery organizing among his fellow immigrants in California.

Ferris, Susan, and Ricardo Sandoval. *The Fight in the Fields: Cesar Chavez and the Farmworkers Movement*. San Diego: Harcourt, Brace, 1997. Companion volume to the film, with numerous additional interviews, photographs, and commentaries.

Greenhouse, Steven. "U.S. Expands Protection for Contract Farm Labor." *New York Times,* 12 March 1997, D22. Report on a major breakthrough for farm workers—regulating the contracting or crew bosses.

——. "U.S. Surveys Find Farm Worker Pay Down for 20 Years." *New York Times,* 31 March 1997, A1, 9. Government, economists, and industry experts all agree that wages have dropped, but they differ on how much.

Matthiessen, Peter. *Sal Si Puedes: Cesar Chavez and the New American Revolution*. New York: Dell, 1973. One of the earliest, and very close, accounts of Chavez as a person and leader during the crucial strike years from 1968 to 1973; includes the memorable meeting of Chavez, Dorothy Day (Catholic labor activist), and Danilo Dolci (organizer of Sicilian peasants).

Scheer, Christopher. "Brave Cesar." *San Francisco Examiner,* 30 October 1996, C1, 3. History of the production of the film and how the directors perceived their subject.

"Union Rallies in California to Get Raise for Strawberry Pickers." *New York Times,* 14 April 1997, A9. Another report on a UFW campaign.

Web sites:

⟨www.paradigmproductions.org⟩ Official site of the film's creators—very thorough, with numerous resources, testimonies, and links with relevant Web sites for a full exploration of Chavez's legacy and farm workers' issues.

⟨www.ufw.org⟩ The official site of the UFW, with current campaigns, white papers (such as "Five Cents for Fairness: The Case for Change in the Strawberry Fields"), links to investigative reports, and historical documents and speeches; a very rich and complete site.

∽

Finally Got the News

Mostly bad

1970

Directors: Stewart Bird, Peter Gessner, René Lichtman, and John Louis Jr.

Agitprop documentary

PRINCIPAL FIGURES

Ron March, chairman, Dodge Revolutionary Union Movement (DRUM)

John Watson and Chuck Wooten, central staff, DRUM

In many ways this film is a time machine transporting us to the revolutionary movements of the late 1960s and early 1970s, at least their Black Power manifestations. Although the documentary begins with a (perhaps overlong) montage of still photos and drawings from the Middle Passage and the days of slavery, we are eventually taken on an imagistic tour of auto struggles in Detroit and Flint, Michigan, including the Great Flint Sit-Down Strike, which many people identify as the key moment in launching the unionization drive that led to a powerful United Auto Workers (UAW). Ironically, of course, this once radical union hardly welcomes such a radical caucus as the Dodge Revolutionary Union Movement (DRUM) in its ranks.

It is also not likely that the Flint sit-down strikers would understand how their movement in just thirty years would be called the "You Ain't White" (UAW) movement, but that is precisely what the League of Revolutionary Black Workers would soon be chanting.

By the close of the 1960s black workers began to organize independently of their UAW locals. They believed that management and their union had practically the same ends, using the same rhetoric of cooperation. Company managers boast that cooperating with the UAW has meant no wildcats and smooth production schedules.

This smoothness meant, the black workers argued, all white supervisors in a plant where 85 percent of the workers were black. Furthermore, the black workers had the most difficult and dangerous jobs, with a speedup on the line to sixty-six cars per hour. Three groups from separate plants eventually formed the League: the Dodge, Ford, and Eldon Revolutionary Union Movements—DRUM, FRUM, and ELRUM. "I don't mind working, but I do mind dying" became their unofficial motto, while "Black Power" soon turned into "Black Worker Power."

The film concludes with an overly intricate speech about the strengths of the League as the revolutionary vanguard of Detroit. It is not a convincing speech for the most part, as it seems to be consumed by its own (limited '60s version of) Marxist-Leninist logic: we must be right because the police are attacking us. But in one especially important way the message rings loud and clear—the need to organize all the black workers in America.

The rhetoric of this speech reflected the only area of agreement between the two groups of the League that formed separate organizations in 1971: the Communist League, which wanted to concentrate on in-plant organizing, and the Black Workers' Congress, which favored auto organizing as only one part of a revolutionary strategy.

See also: *Blue Collar.*

Availability: Selected collections; Cinema Guild.

Further reading

Georgakas, Dan, and Marvin Surkin. *Detroit: I Do Mind Dying.* Rev. ed. Cambridge: South End Press, 1998. This "study in urban revolution" is an expanded edition of the authors' history and analysis of DRUM from its founding in 1967 through its collapse in 1972; its core text remains the same but additional chapters comment on the history of the movement.

Wypijewski, JoAnn. "Pounding Out a DRUM Beat." *New Left Review,* no. 234 (March–April 1999), 141–59. A review of Georgakas and Surkin's reissued book, critiquing the authors' "fear for their own political relevance."

〜

Final Offer

Roger, Bob White, and Me

1985, 78 mins.
Director: Sturla Gunnarsson
Traditional documentary
PRINCIPAL FIGURES
Bob White, president, United Auto Workers (UAW) of Canada
Roger Smith, CEO, General Motors (GM)
Rod Andrew, chief negotiator, GM of Canada
Owen Bieber, president, UAW
Fred Morris, foreman
Danny Johnson, assembly line worker
Brian Blakeney, group leader.

Take the uncomic Roger Smith (General Motors CEO) out of the satiric masterpiece *Roger & Me* and place him in a Canadian variation of Barbara Kopple's controversial *American Dream* and you have this film, a potential Canadian Nightmare. This National Film Board of Canada documentary charts the 1984 contract negotiations between the Canadian section of the UAW and General Motors. The leader of the Canadians is Bob White, an independent and popular figure who soon finds himself caught between Roger Smith of General Motors and Owen Bieber, president of the UAW International union.

Both Smith and Bieber want White to accept an "American" contract, pushed by GM during a flush season, the heart of which is a profit-sharing scheme: workers get bonuses in good years but they take wage cuts in bad. The Canadians have been used to a steady 3 percent hourly wage increase for many years and simply do not trust GM. Bieber, however, wants the Canadians to sign the contract and, more to the point, wants White to accept union "discipline." Encouraged by the Canadian workers' rising militancy and their independent tradition, White digs in and begins to walk a dangerous line, negotiating separately with both the GM leadership in Canada and Bieber himself.

The film begins with an intimate portrait of workers on the line and their immediate supervisors, demonstrating in concrete terms why the tension has been rising. Unlike Kopple's *American Dream,* which moves back and forth between rank and file and their union leadership, Gunnarsson's film soon leaves the assembly line and concentrates on the negotiating team, making only occasional forays out of the hotel where the negotiators are holed up for months at a time.

Perhaps Minnesotans don't curse as much as their Canadian brothers, but *Final Offer* has more f-words than auto workers. At one point, when White's team is on the verge of saving its guaranteed annual hourly wage increase if they can call it something else, White suggests it be called the CFI, in which C and I stand for "Canadian" and "increase."

White knows at the end of the negotiations that he is initiating a divorce: "We are talking about the end of the International." He knows that when you try to fight Owen Bieber and Roger Smith at the same time, you have set yourself up for a big fall. But White's charismatic style and careful maneuvering lead his workers to retain their traditional hourly increase. Roger Smith, who at first seemed to be relying on the fact that Bieber would withdraw the strike authorization given to the Canadians, apparently backs down. As in the struggle between P-9 and the United Food and Commercial

Workers documented in *American Dream,* the casualty may be the principle of international solidarity.

The film presents White as its hero, despite his occasional roughness. It correctly anticipates his becoming the leader of an independent union, the Canadian Auto Workers (CAW), although it does not name the organization. Besides, who can resist a man who, after incredibly strenuous but victorious negotiations, says, "Gotta go call my mother"?

See also: *American Dream; Roger & Me.*

Availability: Selected collections; California Newsreel.

⌇ F.I.S.T.

Looks like Rocky, but still another Hoffa

1978, 145 mins., PG
Director: Norman Jewison
Screenplay: Joe Eszterhas and Sylvester Stallone
CAST
Johnny Kovak = Sylvester Stallone
Senator Andrew Madison = Rod Steiger
Max Graham = Peter Boyle
Anna Zerinkas = Melinda Dillon
Abe Belkin = David Huffman
Babe Milano = Tony Lo Bianco
Vince Doyle = Kevin Conway

F.I.S.T. is another version of the story of Jimmy Hoffa's Teamsters. Joe Eszterhas and Sylvester Stallone's script comes very close to Hoffa's own vision of his career (see *Jimmy Hoffa*): his union had to be in contact with Mob forces, otherwise management would use them.

The acronym for this fictitious union stands for the Federated Interstate Truckers, but of course it refers to the muscle behind the name as well. The film argues that Big Labor is by its nature prone to violence simply because it cannot police itself. None of the establishment policing methods are much better: we meet a crusading but self-

aggrandizing senator who is a satirical portrait of John L. McClellan, chair of the Senate Rackets Committee, also known as the Select Committee on Improper Activities in the Labor or Management Field.

The film is not my first choice for an encounter with Jimmy Hoffa's many fictional selves. It has some exciting moments, mostly when the union is outmaneuvered during some set-piece strikes characteristic of all Teamster epics. In Danny DeVito's *Hoffa,* the camera is so far away from the struggle that it is sometimes impossible to see who is fighting whom. Here the budget is smaller and the camera is closer, but too often all we see is Stallone's blank face.

Jewison has done some important films (*A Soldier's Story* and *In Country*) and some musical epics (*Fiddler on the Roof* and *Jesus Christ Superstar*). This film suggests there is still another Norman Jewison—a director who will let a weak script carry an even weaker star. The result is a cinematic union run by the Godfather.

See also: *Hoffa; Jimmy Hoffa.*
Availability: Easy.

Further reading

Canby, Vincent. "F.I.S.T." *New York Times,* 26 April 1978, C15. Praises the cast and Hollywood's attempt not to "play it safe" with this topic.

——. "F.I.S.T. Delivers." *New York Times,* 14 May 1978, II.17. "A massive, sometimes clumsy and oversimplified but ultimately very moving melodrama."

⌇ The $5.20 an Hour Dream

Not enough

1980, 96 mins., TVM
Director: Russ Mayberry
Screenplay: Robert E. Thompson
CAST
Ellen Lissick = Linda Lavin
Albert Kleinschmidt = Richard Jaeckel
Ginny = Pamela McMyler
Randy = Mayf Nutter

Ed Lissick = Nicholas Pryor
Jive = Taurean Blacque
Checker = Fredric Cook
Bobby Jim = Robert Davi

Like Barbara Kopple's *Keeping On,* this film has been eclipsed in reputation by *Norma Rae,* the gold standard of films about women rising up in male-dominated factories in general and in the labor movement in particular. But it is helpful to know that there have been other films like this one on mainstream TV, in which viewers see feisty working-class women not exactly knowledgeable in the ways of Manolo Blahnik footwear.

Ellen Lissick, divorced mom, needs to make more money at an Oregon engine factory. The dream job is on the assembly line, a male preserve, so watch out, boys, the woman who played the waitress Alice at Mel's Diner in the TV sitcom is coming to take your job. The TV show *Alice* was in turn based on Martin Scorsese's portrayal of a working-class woman in *Alice Doesn't Live Here Anymore.* I'm not sure why this film is out of circulation: it certainly portrays a woman as feisty as the other Alices.

See also: *Harlan County War; Keeping On; Norma Rae.*
Availability: Not.

↩

Flame in the Streets

"There ain't no black in the Union Jack."— British folk saying

1961, 89 mins., UK
Director: Roy Ward Baker
Screenplay: Ted Willis, from his play *Hot Summer Night*
CAST
Jacko Palmer = John Mills
Nell Palmer = Brenda de Banzie
Kathie Palmer = Sylvia Syms

Only rarely have race relations and economic issues been so closely tied in a film

released as early as 1961. *Flame in the Streets* begins with a daring but obvious premise: a white union leader fights hard to maintain and even promote members of the West Indian workforce in London. "When I see this union used," he declares, "to victimize a man because his skin is a different color, I'll get out." Jacko, played by John Mills with his usual intensity and average British bloke style, explains that if the black workers leave, they will become "a pool of cheap nonunion labor." The union banners must stand for something: "United We Stand/Divided We Fall."

His tolerance is tested, however, soon after he brings the union meeting around to his position. His daughter has been dating a West Indian man and his wife chooses the end of the union meeting as the moment to tell him. Furthermore, his wife blames him for daughter Kathie's interest in this man: "You had no time for me or for Kathie," she cries, because he turned their front room into a union office. His task, his wife states, is to bring his daughter home, because the thought of her having sex with a black man makes her "stomach turn."

Meanwhile, all hell is breaking loose in the neighborhood. The local white working-class Teddies use the excuse of the Guy Fawkes fireworks on 5 November to attack blacks. The blacks, not surprisingly, fight back. Jacko and some black co-workers win the day, but it's clearly only a truce for the neighborhood and maybe for the United Kingdom.

See also: *Proud Valley.*
Availability: UK (PAL standard only).

Further reading
Crowther, Bosley. "Flame in the Streets." *New York Times,* 13 September 1962, 32. Film does not have "the material or the punch to project this volatile theme," although Crowther admits that Jacko's contradictory views are common enough.

The Flickering Flame

It might go out

1996, 49 mins., UK/France
Agitprop documentary
PRINCIPAL FIGURES
Brian Cox, narrator
Bill Morris, general secretary, Trades Union
    Council (TUC)
Bob Baerte, International Transport
    Workers' Federation (ITF)
Chris Hain, member of Parliament (Labour
    Party)

An earlier Ken Loach film, *The Big Flame*
(also unavailable), dramatized the 1967
British dockworkers' strike, which lasted six
weeks and involved 9,000 workers. If that
struggle was "big," then the 1995 lockout and
firing of more than 400 workers for demanding an account of overtime pay and then for
refusing to cross a picket line was small and
the flame was in danger of going out. First
80 dockers working for Torside, a private
company, were fired for protests about their
overtime pay. Another group of 329 workers
for the Mersey Docks and Harbour
Company were then fired for refusing to
cross the Torside picket line.

The background struggle of all these
actions turns out to be what the British call
"casualisation," the process whereby permanent workers are replaced by contract
workers who work only when the need arises.

Loach and others (John Pilger) have analyzed what seems to have been a trap set
for the workers: they didn't know about a
company offer to settle, so they walked out,
and thus were branded "illegal" strikers.

Loach's focus in this film is twofold—on
the 300-plus families keeping this struggle
going and on the companies and the national
union leadership and the Labour Party,
which refuse to support the struggle. If this is
an agitprop film, it is one that may discourage activists rather than encourage them to
join the struggle. At every turn the dockers
and their major support group, Women of
the Waterfront, are frustrated and ultimately
defeated. Representatives of all the major
forces of organized labor listen politely,
agree to support the struggle, and then do
nothing.

Actually the recurring theme in Loach's
film is that they do worse than nothing: they
actively support settlements with the owners
or defuse support throughout the rank and
file whenever they can. Loach has returned
to this theme in both feature films (*Days of
Hope*) and documentaries such as this one.
Whatever hope is present in this film, it is
usually seen in groups of rank-and-file
workers in other countries who have supported the Liverpool strikers. In a sense, the
ideal for Loach was the anti-Stalinist (sometimes, but not always, Trotskyist) groups that
fought in the Spanish Civil War against
Franco. Their betrayal is also dramatized in
Loach's *Land and Freedom*.

The dockers have received support from
other influential sources, including the journalist John Pilger, who maintains that the
dockers' struggle is part of the push for
"globalization," which results in unemployment in England and underemployment in
the Third World.

See also: *Days of Hope*.
Availability: Not.

Further reading

Morrow, Fiona. "Modern Times: The Flickering
    Flame." *Time Out* (London), 1 January 1997.
    The film is "a shocking reminder of Thatcher's
    legacy: the struggle continues."
Pilger, John. *Hidden Agendas*. London: Vintage,
    1998. Includes an excellent essay on the dockers'
    struggle.
"Striking Dockers Break Ranks over Pay Deal."
    Independent (London), 29 October 1997, 8. The
    original 1995 group begins to splinter, with
    20 percent of the men taking a lump-sum
    settlement.
Web sites:
⟨www.geocities.com/CapitolHill/3843/dockhome.
    html⟩ Extensive reports by Dave Graham
    on the dockers' struggle, including one on
    "casualisation."
⟨www.labournet.net/docks2⟩ The Liverpool strik-
    ing dockers' site, featuring a complete history
    of the strike, archives of articles, information
    about Women of the Waterfront, and other
    features.

42 Up

Apted upped

1999, 130 mins., UK, PG
Director: Michael Apted
Mixed cinema verité and traditional
  documentary
PRINCIPAL CHARACTERS
Bruce Balden
Jacqueline Bassett
Simon Basterfield
Andrew Brackfield
Nicholas Hitchon
Neil Hughes
Lynn Johnson
Susan Sullivan
Tony Walker

In 1964 Michael Apted was the principal researcher for the Canadian documentary director Paul Almond, who began filming a group of fourteen British schoolchildren, of various classes and backgrounds, when they were 7 years old. The students were selected mainly because they interviewed well; that is, they were willing to talk openly about their lives and aspirations. On assignment for Grenada TV, Apted then returned every seven years as director, at which time he released a filmed report that drew on both old and new footage. The films were *Seven Up* (1964), *Seven Plus Seven* (1970) *21 Up* (1977), *28 Up* (1985), and *35 Up* (1991). The result is a unique sociological and human document of change and aging, a longitudinal record of great interest.

At various stages, some of the participants dropped in or out of the production. Even those who dropped out nevertheless remain in Apted's vision, since each succeeding film draws on footage from the earlier films to show the development of the individuals. In fact, with a shooting ratio of 30:1, Apted in effect had almost sixty hours of unused footage after each round that he could draw on in creating his next film. The result is almost a living psychological museum or personal data bank for each of his subjects, from which Apted can make withdrawals every seven years.

The direction of the *Up* films was set, we now see in retrospect, in the very first sequence of *Seven Up*, repeated in part in *Seven Plus Seven*: the fourteen children are shot as they run about the London Zoo. A voice-over states that these children have been assembled from many different backgrounds to see who will be a shop steward and who will be an executive in the year 2000. The sixth film in the series, *42 Up*, was released in 1998 and the answer to the question, we now realize, had been in front of our eyes the whole time.

The American release in 1999 of two remarkably different films directed by Apted—*The World Is Not Enough*, a James Bond adventure, and *42 Up*—has to be some sort of directorial record. James Bond and British schoolkids (now adults)? How did he do it?

Apted's filmography provides a clue. *42 Up* is the second-longest longitudinal film study in the world (the German *Children of Golzow* is the first). The fourteen British schoolchildren, now all 49 years old, have paralleled the ongoing career of Apted the documentarian: his *Moving the Mountain* (1994), for example, followed the story of the Chinese Tiananmen Square demonstrations of 1989. But in the meantime Apted the feature filmmaker is turning out both big screen and television mainstreamers, such as *Gorillas in the Mist* (1988) and *The Long Way Home* (1989), although in this guide only his *Coal Miner's Daughter* (1980) is featured.

As a cinematic study of class and personality, the *Up* series remains a revelation, not simply because the Jesuit motto that called the first title into being ("Give me a child until he is seven and I will show you the man") seems to be valid, but because of the somewhat eerie simultaneous presence of seven real-life embodiments of the same person. Each time Apted revisits his subjects, the original list of fourteen contracts and expands, as some of his subjects opt to desert the project while others change direction in life or become stronger or more confident individuals.

In *42 Up* the holdouts from *35 Up* continue to absent themselves. One wonders what kind of film could be made from their refusal, which—one speculates on the basis of slender evidence—seems based on class and professional status. They have chosen not to be the subjects of one of the most famous documentary film series in the world.

When Roger Ebert reviewed *35 Up*, he captured the attitude of many appreciative viewers: "I am glad most of the subjects of this project have sacrificed their privacy to us every seven years, because in a sense they speak for us, and help us take our own measure." But another reviewer (Hinson) summed up the opinion of a significant number of others who have watched these films with increasing (and fascinated) alarm—that the Jesuit idea of looking at the child to see the man has turned into a film in which we see a child "as the ghost of what might have been."

I suspect viewers of this latest entry in the series will swing between these poles of opinion. I find it a brilliant if not disturbing revelation of character and class: which of the two is the key determinant remains an open-ended question.

See also: *Children of Golzow; 35 Up*.
Availability: Easy; DVD.

Further reading

Apted, Michael. "Watching While Time the Sculptor Shapes the Self." *New York Times*, 14 November 1999, II.35, 37. The director reviews his own life and admits that one of the film's apparent points—"Maybe it shows that the core character doesn't change—if you're extroverted or timid as a child, then that's how it will always be"—seems not to be supported by his own career.

Ebert, Roger. "42 Up." *Chicago Sun-Times*. 4 April 2000. "This series should be sealed in a time capsule. It is on my list of the 10 greatest films of all time, and is a noble use of the medium."

Hinson, Hal. "35 Up." *Washington Post*, 20 March 1992. The reviewer worries "that simply by their participation" in the series the participants have "somehow been blighted by self-consciousness, turned inward and maimed."

Lyman, Rick. "A Veteran Director, Delighting in Opposites." *New York Times*, 22 November 1999, B1. A review of the career of the director, who was once more interested in European art films by Antonioni and Godard than in the world of James Bond.

Maslin, Janet. " '42 Up': At 42, a Point of Reckoning for Children of 1964." *New York Times*, 17 November 1999. "This haunting group portrait could once be watched for a sense of how its participants were evolving, but by now there is a sense of destiny fulfilled."

Singer, Bennett L., and Michael Apted, eds. *42 Up*. New York: New Press, 1999. Essentially a collection of dialogues from all the characters in the series, organized under each name and by year of film: thus we can read and compare Tony's remarks about himself every seven years.

Le Franc

A colonial lottery

1994, 45 mins., Senegal, in Wolof, with English subtitles
Director: Djibril Diop Mambéty
Screenplay: Djibril Diop Mambéty
CAST
Marigo = Dieye Ma Dieye
Langouste = Demba Ba
Landlady = Aminta Fall

This gem of a film comes from the world-acclaimed director of *Touki Bouki* and *Hyenas*, features that explore the changes in Senegalese society. Like most of the African films in this guide, *Le Franc* combines aspects of traditional African storytelling and symbolic economic discourse about both ends of the spectrum of wealth—street markets and international currency markets.

Marigo is a Chaplinesque figure, a *congoma* street musician who has fallen on hard times. Clearly he loves to play this homemade blend of guitar, drum, and harmonica, but he has not earned enough to pay his rent on a little shack for six months. His landlady has confiscated his instrument and so he is doubly compromised—can't pay her, can't earn any money without his instrument. As luck would have it, he spots a 1,000-franc note dropped by a lottery customer at the market stall of Langouste, a colorfully dressed dwarf. Langouste prevails upon Marigo, by force and then by finesse, to use the note to buy ticket 555, a sure winner, according to Langouste.

The lottery, however, is not just a lottery. Loudspeakers announce that this lottery is called "Devaluation," to protest the French decision in 1994 to devalue the West African franc by 50 percent. Protesting the First World's cheating of its former colonies in the "international swindle of supply and demand," the radio announcer predicts a great contest for the people because Kus, the Dwarf God of Fortune, is embossed on every ticket.

Of course Marigo wins, but his effort to get his ticket redeemed provokes a comic odyssey across the crowded city streets, city dumps, and what looks like a destroyed mosque. To protect his ticket, he has pasted it with a powerful glue to his door, underneath a poster of his hero, Yaadikoone, a Senegalese Robin Hood. The lottery board will redeem his ticket only if they can read the control number on the reverse side, and so it's off to the oceanside to free the ticket from his door. He teeter-totters from street to street, from bus stop to market, carrying his door.

The climax of the story seems to favor the cheering Marigo. He has his ticket in the end. But what has he gained? His pleasure in life had been playing his *congoma* for the children in the streets with great joy (as we see him at one point). What's next?

Mambéty uses flashbacks and flashforwards in intriguing ways throughout this short film. At one point Langouste points to a man who cracked under the strain of winning the lottery and we see a man who looks like (virtually is) Marigo carrying a door. Another time Marigo is crossing a desolate stretch of the city when he turns suddenly to confront himself playing his *congoma*. Is this the Marigo of the future? Or of the past?

Mambéty likes to work in trilogies. *Hyenas* is the second of his feature-length films to trace the fortunes of two characters involved

Marigo (Dieye Ma Dieye) carries his door with the winning lottery ticket in *Le Franc*. Courtesy California Newsreel.

(as Mambéty told Givanni) in dramas about "power and insanity," while *Le Franc* is the first in a proposed trilogy of short films with the series title *Tales of Ordinary People*, all of whom are street people, "people [who] will never have bank accounts; for them, each day presents questions of survival." The second, *The Little Girl Who Sold the Sun*, about a street urchin turned market seller, was released in 1999, just after Mambéty's untimely death the year before.

See also: Hyenas; The Little Girl Who Sold the Sun.

Availability: Selected collections; California Newsreel.

Further reading

Givanni, June. "African Conversations." *Sight and Sound*, September 1995, 30–31. Interview with the filmmaker reviewing his career.

Note: *Le Franc* is the first film in California Newsreel's Library of African Cinema cassette *Three Tales from Senegal*. (The other two are short films by other directors.)

~

Free Cinema

Class tells

Every Day Except Christmas
1957, 40 mins., B&W
Director: Lindsay Anderson
We Are the Lambeth Boys
1958, 20 mins., B&W
Director: Karel Reisz
Social-realist documentaries

The Free Cinema movement began as a series of programs at the National Film Theatre in London and was the project of a constellation of filmmakers with similar aims. They emphasized working-class lives, especially "the importance of people and the significance of the everyday," according to Lindsay Anderson. Anderson's essay about British culture in the 1950s, "Get Out and Push!"—part of *Declaration*, a collection of contradictory but sometimes intriguing statements by the group loosely defined as Angry Young Men—in part defends his cinematic interest (and daring) in taking "a camera and lights into a factory, or a coal mine, or a market."

Anderson's documentary short *Thursday's Child* won an Oscar in 1954. His collaborator in the movement, Karel Reisz (who produced *This Sporting Life*), made the documentary *We Are the Lambeth Boys* under the sponsorship of the Ford Motor Company. Reisz's first feature, *Saturday Night and Sunday Morning*, typical of the Angry Young Men films, was released in 1960.

Although these films have voice-over narrators, a sense of spontaneity in the filmed subjects anticipates some of the more uncontrolled filming experiments of cinema verité. The fruit and vegetable market workers in London's Covent Garden in *Every Day Except Christmas* or even the studied cool young men and women in *We Are the Lambeth Boys* are floating through life unconscious of their roles as film subjects.

The market work portrayed in *Every Day Except Christmas* is really difficult: every crate of fruit or vegetables is hand pushed or pulled, since there are no forklifts available to unload the incoming trucks of any kind. Although clearly somebody is making a profit from this enterprise, the film offers only evidence of tough times, as people scrounge for discarded fruit and a Salvation Army band plays pathetically. By midday, the stall workers are breaking down the market because—except for Christmas—they will be out in the streets working again in the middle of the next night.

The Lambeth boys come from a working-class youth club in South London. The boys are Teds; that is, they are wearing suits and ties, have slicked-back hair (like American "D.A.'s"), and spend an inordinate amount of time dancing. Some of the youths are still in school, others have jobs (dressmaker, butcher, factory worker). If the film has any center—besides chronicling some working-class activities—it must be the cricket match between a public school and our boys, who sing loud and clear, "We Are the Lambeth Boys," as they head out of their neighborhood to venture into the suburb of Mill Hill. There the Lambeth boys' first cricket eleven join their counterparts for tea and a swim in a pond. The second Lambeth cricket eleven seems a decidedly rowdier lot—instead of swimming, they are doing handstands. If there is a point to all this, it must be class distinctions, but the distinctions are as obvious now as they were then.

See also: *Saturday Night and Sunday Morning*.
Availability: UK (PAL standard only).

Further reading

Maschler, Tom, ed. *Declaration*. New York: Dutton, 1958. A collection of essays by those identified with the Angry Young Men movement (including one woman, the novelist Doris Lessing).
Orbanz, Eva, ed. *Journey to a Legend and Back: The British Realistic Film*. Trans. Stuart Hood.

Berlin: Volker Spiess, 1977. Excellent survey of the Free Cinema filmmakers.

~~

Freedom Road

Win the war, lose the peace

1979, 186 mins., TVM
Director: Ján Kádar
Screenplay: David Zelag Goodman, from Howard Fast's novel of the same title
CAST
Gideon Jackson = Muhammad Ali
Abner Lait = Kris Kristofferson
Francis Cardoza = Ron O'Neal
Stephen Holms = Edward Herrmann
Rachel Jackson = Barbara-O Jones
Narrator = Ossie Davis
President Grant = John McLiam
Katie = Alfre Woodard

One of the most controversial periods in American history—the occupation of the South by federal troops during Reconstruction after the Civil War—has never received its due in film. *Beloved* comes close, at least in some of its dramatic implications, but since it is set mainly in postwar Ohio, it is not literally in Reconstruction territory. For years, until W. E. B. Du Bois's *Black Reconstruction* and Howard Fast's novel *Freedom Road* (which uses research by Du Bois and such radical historians as James Allen), the history of this period was told either by the losers (southern historians) or by their sympathizers (so-called objective historians of the war and its aftermath). D. W. Griffith's racist version of the period in *Birth of a Nation* is simply a caricature of what so many other versions shared: a belief that the excesses of Reconstruction—not the racist economic system—was the South's undoing.

It may come as a surprise to some readers, but by the late 1960s *Freedom Road* had sold 25 million copies, through numerous publishers and book clubs (even an Armed Services edition in 1945), went through three editions the first year it was published (1944),

was translated into at least twenty-seven languages, and has virtually never been out of print.

Howard Fast's black hero, Gideon, was a composite character, a model of what Reconstruction was to achieve: he begins as an illiterate ex-slave, having fought with Colonel Robert Shaw's famous black regiment (memorialized in the film *Glory*), he attends the South Carolina convention to rewrite the slaveholders' constitution, and he becomes first a state senator and then one of the first blacks to go to Washington as a congressman.

I don't think this film (even with its movie tie-in edition with Muhammad Ali on the cover) would have turned many viewers into eager readers, but the book is a classic of the idea of a left-organized American popular frontism (radicals, Socialists, Communists, liberals, Democrats, all in one happy coalition) and has a simple social realism that is quite compelling. It features freed slaves, free blacks, poor white trash, and abolitionist types.

Originally a four-hour TV film, as a three-hour videocassette *Freedom Road* still requires a huge cast, only part of which I have listed above. What are we to do, for example, with characters whose names are 1st White Trash Delegate, 2nd White Trash Delegate, and 3rd White Trash Delegate? Well, put out the trash! But even the black characters become stereotypes: Black Delegate, Young Black Man with Scars, Well-Dressed Black Delegate.

The director, Ján Kádar, whose remarkable and moving *Shop on Main Street* won an Oscar in 1965 as best foreign film, died soon after *Freedom Road* was completed. It is hard to disagree with the *Variety* reviewer who felt that *Freedom Road* was not a fitting memorial to the Czech émigré who came to Hollywood in 1969.

Freedom Road is an awkward, only occasionally compelling film. The script is wooden, the chemistry between Ali, a great boxer but no actor, and the stiff Kristofferson fizzles, and important moments in Reconstruction history are mentioned but not explained. The story of the unity of white sharecroppers and former black slaves seems fanciful, but when the Klan and other enemies marshal their forces to destroy their communal experiment, the film briefly catches fire.

The film, like the novel, takes South Carolina as the pivotal state. After the war, the governor appoints the veteran Gideon as senator. He subsequently meets with President Grant, who is worried that the tide of public opinion is turning against the issues the North fought for. Grant is a focus for the main theme—the necessity for federal troops to protect former slaves and their sympathizers. The failure of this protection leads the film inevitably to the Klan. We learn that in Mississippi the election went against Republicans because federal troops failed to protect Negro voters. But the national picture was much more involved.

In 1876, during the reign of Klan terror and the rise of "rifle clubs" for whites, the Democrat William Tilden seemed headed for the presidency over the Republican Rutherford B. Hayes. Both the film and real life asked the key question: Who guarantees the Fourteenth Amendment? Grant, the old warhorse, and Gideon, the freed slave, fear a new South Carolina movement of "red shirts" who openly support Democrats with arms. Grant at first agrees to send troops in, but we see orange (not red?) shirts attack a Hayes rally. By election time in November 1876, Democratic swindlers switch symbols on the ballots so that the mostly illiterate ex-slaves will vote against their own interests. The result in South Carolina and elsewhere—Louisiana and Florida—is a contested outcome that sees two governors and two electoral vote slates for different presidents claiming victory.

In what became the treacherous dismantling of Reconstruction, we cut to February 1877: Hayes seized the presidency by promising former Confederates the governorships of the three key states if their electoral votes were given to him. Hayes completed his smarmy deal by ordering the troops out of the South sixty days after his inauguration.

At this complex historical moment the fictional characters of *Freedom Road* try to negotiate their survival. But the sheriff announces that taxes for the Carwell plantation, which they thought they had bought at auction, had really been paid and the auction that gave the black and white farmers the old plantation was illegal. Gideon suggests they hole up in the plantation house until the governor sends the troops back in.

Soon they are under siege. Gideon's white buddy Abner knows the score: "They are going to burn us to the ground." A remark Gideon made to President Grant becomes prophetic: when the federal government does not act, it is in fact acting . . . for the old ways.

This film can stand alone as neither history nor drama, but the core of its horror signifies the new bondage of the ex-slaves: free in name but not in deed.

See also: *Homecoming*.
Availability: Easy.

Further reading

Allen, James S. *Reconstruction: The Battle for Democracy, 1865–1876*. 1937. New York: International Publishers, 1963. A Marxist interpretation of Reconstruction ("the continuation of the Civil War into a new phase, in which the revolution passed from the stage of armed conflict into primarily a political struggle which sought to consolidate the Northern triumph"), one likely source for Fast's fundamental views in the novel and, unexpectedly enough, supported by the film version.

Bogle, Donald. *Blacks in American Films and Television*. New York: Garland, 1988. Finds the film's "unity of newly freed Negroes and poor Southern whites . . . a fabrication that no one in his right mind can or should believe in."

Fast, Howard. *Freedom Road*. 1944. Various editions available; in part because of the topic and in part because of the author's real-life sympathies with the USSR and Mao's China, the novel has been one of the biggest sellers in virtually all of the world's languages.

"Freedom Road—Part One." *Variety*, 31 October 1979. The reviewer was so hostile to the broadcast of the first part of this "left-wing potboiler" that he clearly had no intention of reviewing the whole thing.

The Free Voice of Labor: The Jewish Anarchists

"If God really existed, it would be necessary to abolish him."—Mikhail Bakunin

1980

Directors: Steven Fischler and Joel Sucher
Traditional documentary

PRINCIPAL FIGURES

Ahrne Thorne, last editor of the *Free Voice of Labor*

Franz Flelgler, secretary of the newspaper's management committee

Paul Avrich, historian

Abe Bluestein, Fanny Breslow, Sonia Farber, Clara Larsen, *Free Voice* management committee

Charles Zimmerman, former vice president, International Ladies' Garment Workers' Union

Irvin Abrams, Chicago activist

Jon Conason, *Village Voice* reporter

This traditional labor history documentary preserves the almost forgotten group of workers and their allies who were both philosophically and politically anarchists and who shared a counterculture of union activism, atheism, and intellectual debate. Most of the Jews in this film came from Eastern European countries in the early twentieth century and almost all of them went to work in New York's needle trades. Most of them firmly believe (to this day) that the Bolsheviks and their American Communist Party counterparts stole their key ideas—factories controlled by the workers, land to the peasants, and power to the soviets—and that Communist bureaucrats anywhere had no intention of following any of those goals. In short, they are militant, convinced, and very feisty.

To organize themselves they founded a newspaper, the Yiddish-language *Freie Arbeiter Stimme* (The free voice of labor), which ran from 1890 to 1977, a remarkable record of independent, crusading, pro-worker journalism. They campaigned for labor unions, working-class culture, and Yiddish literature against the state, capitalists, and the clergy.

The film is a leisurely tour of the aging anarchists at their newspaper office, meeting rooms, and reunion picnics. They look back on their radical youth with pride, as the filmmakers assemble a remarkable collection of archival footage of immigrant life accompanied by period songs in Yiddish with moving lyrics: "Don't look for me where the myrtles grow. . . . I am a slave and where chains ring is my resting place." Another song from Russia asks us to "crush the rule of Uncle Nicky" (Tsar Nicholas II). The film includes two sequences from the wonderful Yiddish-language feature film *Uncle Moses* (without identifying it as such): in one Uncle Moses explains to a union agitator why his patriarchal rule is best for his workers and in another the union meets to decide to strike Uncle Moses' shop.

At one point in the film we see Flelgler in the foreground bemoaning the loss of the great anarchist library assembled by the newspaper staff while Thorne stands on a ladder poking among the bookshelves. No doubt Emma Goldman was on that shelf, along with *God and the State* by Bakunin, whose intriguing remark about God serves as the epigraph to this entry. Labor history would be very much the poorer if these documentary filmmakers had not moved to capture these activists before it was too late.

See also: *Uncle Moses*.

Availability: Selected collections; Filmakers Library.

Further reading

Shepherd, Richard F. "Screen: Jews in Protest." *New York Times*, 3 April 1980, C15. A "wonderful evocation of the radical political past and what has become of its activists."

~

The Full Monty

It worked for Field Marshal Montgomery

1997, 91 mins., UK, R
Director: Peter Cattaneo
Screenplay: Simon Beaufoy
CAST
Gaz = Robert Carlyle
Dave = Mark Addy
Gerald = Tom Wilkinson
Nathan = William Snape
Lomper = Steve Huison
Guy = Hugo Speer
Horse = Paul Barber

It takes nerve to combine a story about unemployed steelworkers and jokes about men's willies, and this film has plenty of nerve. And although we never really get to see them, it has plenty of jokes about what men don't think is funny when they don't work or they aren't up to snuff. We begin with a film within a film, a fake documentary that is a promotional puff piece about industrial Sheffield—the city of the north that is such a success that even industrial smog seems golden. After this cinematic trip to a city that probably never existed, we are taken to contemporary Sheffield, most of whose steel mills have closed. We meet Gaz, a divorced father who cannot keep up his support payments; his good buddy, the overweight Dave; his former foreman, Gerald, also out of work; and assorted other blokes, all of whom are willing to do almost anything to make ends meet.

Gaz is amazed to discover that the local gals will pay a bloody fortune to watch toffs and wankers like the Chippendales strip. He begins to recruit his buddies and others to create a dance routine that will compete with the Chippendales. Like most of Gaz's ideas, such as selling stolen steel I-beams from his deserted factory, this one is ridiculous, but not simply because he and his friends cannot dance worth a wiggle: it turns out that the local gals wouldn't pay tuppence to see this lot. On the other hand, if the boys went the full monty, maybe adoring paying customers would show up to see the spectacle. It is no doubt a tribute to the steelworkers' apprenticeship program that they know what "the full monty" is: full frontal male nudity. (The name is reputed to reflect Field Marshal Montgomery's insistence on a *full* English breakfast every day, even during the war.)

Most of the jokes in the film are at the expense of these six would-be sex symbols: Guy is outrageously built, the black Brit nicknamed Horse is not, and so forth. Unlike *Brassed Off*, the British comedy about a coal town whose mines are threatened with closure, *The Full Monty* lets the economic system that has brought the former steelworkers to this imposture down easy. No speeches about ruinous Thatcherism or the competition of foreign steel. With a self-consciousness that some viewers will find silly and others funny, the film takes out after some less obvious targets—Jennifer Beal's sexy welder, for example, from the 1983 pop hit *Flashdance*: Dave cannot concentrate on the film's dance routines for the tips he should be absorbing because he's too concerned about the bad welds Beal is making in the steelyard scenes.

Gaz and his buddies would do anything just to stay solvent, and if it means going the full monty, so be it. There are sequences that are no doubt right on target for British audiences who have faced unemployment and the dole—"job clubs" for the unemployed, repossession of household goods, couples falling apart under the strain, low-wage service jobs (security guards)—and certainly much of this would have appeal for other national audiences as well.

See also: *Brassed Off*.
Availability: Easy; DVD.

Further reading

Maslin, Janet. "Jobless, Depressed? Men, You Can Always Strip." *New York Times*, 13 August 1997, B2. Observes accurately that "joblessness is a humiliation well beyond nakedness."
Riding, Alan. "A Man Who's True to His Convictions." *New York Times*, 6 August 1997 II.11, 17.

An extensive review of the working-class roles of the lead actor, Robert Carlyle, who has been a regular in Ken Loach films as well (e.g., *Riff-Raff*).
Web site:
⟨www.foxsearchlight.com/fullmonty/index.htm⟩
The official site from the distributors: really only for those who want their foolishness on the Internet rather than from the film; even less political consciousness (if that's possible) than the film itself.

ᔔ
Fury

Depression vigilantism

1936, 94 mins., B&W
Director: Fritz Lang
Screenplay: Bartlett Cormack and Fritz Lang
CAST
Joe Wheeler = Spencer Tracy
Katherine Grant = Sylvia Sidney
District Attorney = Walter Abel
Kirby Dawson = Bruce Cabot
Sheriff = Edward Ellis
Bugs Meyers = Walter Brennan
Tom = George Walcott

Fritz Lang's film (his first American one) is about a lynching or, more precisely, a near-lynching, as an independent gas station owner/operator, played by Spencer Tracy, is mistakenly identified as the kidnapper of a young girl in a California town. The local crowd is incited to vigilante action by a traveling salesman and a visiting scab, who brags that he has just been strikebreaking, where "we know how to take care of guys like this."

Lang based his scenario for the lynching on the Hart kidnapping case in San Jose, which occurred just three years before the film was made: two confessed kidnappers were lynched by a crowd, and their actions were publicly applauded by the governor, James "Sonny" Rolph. Lynchings of African Americans were common in the South; in California in the 1930s, the targets were usually labor organizers and Reds. Lang took pains to emphasize official complicity in the lynching by having an adviser to the governor talk him out of sending the National Guard to protect the jail.

Lang's use of lynching footage shot by a fictional newsreel team is strikingly similar to the videos that are increasingly becoming part of courtroom evidence in controversial trials today. Tracy and his brother only want to make a living from their modest gas station, but Lang's pessimistic view of the Depression suggests that hard work may not be enough. The finale in the courtroom is incredible but fascinating, as Tracy's character comes back from the dead to torment his lynchers.

See also: *They Drive by Night*.
Availability: Selected collections.

Further reading

Bergman, Andrew. *We're in the Money: Depression America and Its Films*. New York: New York University Press, 1971. Describes lynching films in the context of the Depression.
Cormack, Bartlett, and Fritz Lang. "Fury." In *Twenty Best Film Plays*, ed. John Gassner and Dudley Nichols. 1943. New York, Garland, 1977. The screenplay.

ᔔ
Fury Below

And boredom above

1936, 52 mins., B&W
Director: Harry Fraser
Screenplay: Phil Dunham
CAST
Jim Cole III = Russell Gleason
Mary Norsen = Maxine Doyle
Joe Norsen = Rex Lease
Fred Johnson = Leroy Mason
Claire Johnson = Sheila Terry
Emil = John Merton

This is the kind of quickie Hollywood small-studio film in which the screenwriter also doubles as a supporting actor. The title imitates a much better and somewhat similar film, *Black Fury*, a hit the year before. (It is probably of some importance that at least one other producer in Hollywood thought a spin-off film on mining struggles was worth pursuing.) The only fury in this film would presumably have been in the audiences who bought tickets, drawn to the topical issues of mine violence and sabotage coupled with a favorite child actor of the 1920s, Russell Gleason, who plays a recent college grad who don't know nothin' about running a mine but has to do it when his grandfather leaves the screen in the first scene to recover from a bad script.

Unfortunately, Gleason continues to act like a child, while the screenwriter proves that he hasn't studied too many of the articles about mining struggles that appeared throughout the 1930s.

Is there anything that can be recovered from a viewing of this film? Not much, perhaps. That a segment of Hollywood was willing to portray a mining foreman as a leader of a union local who at the same time is in cahoots with the general manager of the mine to sabotage production goes a long way to explain why higher-budget films of the era were easily manipulated by the studio and right-wingers. (See *Black Fury*.) A company president who just happens to attend a union meeting led by the bad foreman; a lovesick and ultimately deranged immigrant miner, Emile (French?!); and a secretary who climbs down a mine shaft in her high heels to interrupt sabotage—these are just a few of the high-camp antics in this film.

The original release ran six minutes longer than the current videocassette version. Would those six minutes have helped? Doubtful.

See also: *Black Fury*.
Availability: Selected collections; Movies Unlimited.

Further reading

"Fury Below." *Variety*, 23 March 1938. A "carelessly slapped together quickie."

The Garment Jungle

Dress shops owned by Murder, Inc.

1957, 88 mins.
Director: Vincent Sherman
Screenplay: Harry Kleiner, from *Reader's Digest* articles by Lester Velie

CAST
Walter Mitchell = Lee J. Cobb
Alan Mitchell = Kerwin Matthews
Theresa = Gia Scala
Artie Ravidge = Richard Boone
Tulio Renata = Robert Loggia
Lee Hackett = Valerie French
Kovan = Joseph Wiseman
Tony = Harold J. Stone.

Like its cinematic cousin, *On the Waterfront*, this film originated in a series of investigative or exposé magazine articles written for the *Reader's Digest* by one of its "roving editors," Lester Velie. *The Garment Jungle* also opens with a murder, but it has three murders to Elia Kazan's two. Lee J. Cobb, who played the vicious union gangster in the earlier film, is here again, but this time he becomes a sympathetic victim: once it is clear that he no longer will pay protection money to thugs, he himself falls victim to them.

Cobb, as Walter Mitchell, owner of a nonunion garment manufacturing plant, has been paying a "protector" $2,000 a week for fifteen years. (That was a lot of money in the 1950s.) When his son rebels against this shakedown and openly allies himself with an organizer for the International Ladies' Garment Workers' Union (ILGWU), Tulio, who is then murdered, father and son resolve their differences so quickly that it makes our heads spin.

The film has some pro-labor moments, surprisingly enough, given the premises of the original story and its source in articles by Lester Velie. As Ken Margolies points out, the union organizer, Tulio, is "portrayed as respectable, reasonable, dedicated, intelligent, firm, and concerned with the wishes of the workers." What would happen to the workers if he were not on the scene is made quite clear when an old Jewish worker complains about a new piece rate: "Mr. Foreman, I don't want to make a big *tsimes* [fuss], but this garment takes too much time for the money." Her foreman replies: "Who don't like, pick up your check and get out of here." Only Tulio's intervention saves the day for the worker who dares to speak up.

When we realize that Hollywood released two films about the garment industry in 1957—this film and *The Pajama Game*—we cannot help wondering who was in charge there. But *The Garment Jungle* opened in eighty-nine neighborhood theaters in New York City, and the producers certainly knew that the issues were hot.

Although *The Garment Jungle* covers ground similar to what we see in *On the Waterfront*, it has never received one-tenth the attention given to Kazan's film. Both films have Lee J. Cobb, of course, but Kazan had Marlon Brando and Eva Marie Saint, while Vincent Sherman had Kerwin Matthews and Gia Scala. (Who?) None of Sherman's actors are household names, although in his day he directed several decent films with top stars (such as *Affair in Trinidad*, with Glenn Ford and Rita Hayworth). But Kazan had the better script and a reputation for realistic drama, which guaranteed that Brando's "I could've been a contenda" speech would come to be associated with one of the most popular labor union films of all time, while Lee J. Cobb's girlfriend must point out—lamely but correctly—that "there's no love in the dress business."

Nevertheless, *The Garment Jungle* is worth a closer look: from its opening moments, when Cobb rips a new dress off one of his bored models and argues with his pro-union partner, who soon plunges to his death in a rigged elevator, to its documentary footage of union demonstrations and funerals, the film rarely lets up. And when was the last time you saw a union organizer in a film holding a baby at the union hall while his wife teaches the rank and file how to dance the mambo?

See also: *Edge of the City; On the Waterfront; The Pajama Game.*
Availability: Selected collections.

Further reading

Margolies, Ken. "Silver Screen Tarnishes Unions." *Screen Actor* 23 (1981): 43–52. Reviews the image of unions in this and other films.

Thompson, Harold. "The Garment Jungle." *New York Times*, 16 May 1957, 28. A positive reaction from a reviewer who wondered out loud why the police and other union officials seem never to show up during violent labor union films.

Velie, Lester. "Gangsters in the Dress Business." *Reader's Digest*, July 1955, 59–64. Surveys the dangers of union organizing in New York's garment district.

The General Line

Marfa and the milk separator

1928, 113 mins., Soviet Union, B&W, silent
Directors: Sergei Eisenstein and Edward Tisse
Screenplay: Sergei Eisenstein
CAST
Marfa Lapkina as herself
Her son = M. Ivanin
Dairy Manager = Vasily Buzenkov
Tractor Mechanic = Kostia Vasiliev

The General Line, also known as *Old and New*, was the first of two attempts by Sergei Eisenstein to film a drama of Soviet agricultural collectivization; the second was *Bezhin Meadow*. Both of these films became controversial and were criticized for their ideological shortcomings and cinematic formalism, so much so that the second was withdrawn, presumably destroyed, and in any case exists today only as a compilation of still images.

Eisenstein and his collaborator Edward Tisse build their story on the shoulders of one "typical" peasant woman, Marfa Lapkina. She was in fact an actual peasant recruited for the filming and fulfilled one of Eisenstein's theoretical programmatic ideas at the time—*typage*, the use of nonprofessionals who matched the profile of the character. Marfa has to combat the lingering legacy of the landlord system and the powerful church; she also has to vanquish various rich peasants or kulaks and even some distant bureaucrats.

A Soviet agronomist visits the village and begins, with Marfa's help, to turn the disorganized poor peasants, into a political force. He presents the new collective with a milk separator for making butter. Marfa wants the profits from this new machine's work for the purchase of a share in a bull, but the peasants still need to be convinced. In the end Marfa and an ally, a tractor mechanic, prove the value of the Soviet "general line," or policy on collectivization.

Although the politics and economic situation (see Bordwell) are quite intriguing, what will stay in the viewer's mind, I predict, are a few of the more fantastic shots—Marfa dreaming of a giant bull that is superimposed on a landscape of cows, orgiastic fountains of milk spurting from the separator, the final parade of hundreds of tractors symbolizing the success of the Soviet "general line." What happened to the kulaks—confiscation of their land, homes, and belongings or worse—is not included.

See also: *¡Que viva México!*
Availability: Not.

Further reading

Bordwell, David. *The Cinema of Eisenstein.* Cambridge: Harvard University Press, 1993. Extensive and incisive analysis of the film.

Eisenstein, Sergei. *The Complete Films of Eisenstein.* Trans. John Hetherington. New York: Dutton, 1974. Abbreviated film scenario with stills.

↬
Germinal

Depardieu underground

1993, 158 mins., French, with English subtitles, R
Director: Claude Berri

Screenplay: Claude Berri and Arlette Langmann, from Émile Zola's novel of the same title

CAST
Maheu = Gérard Depardieu
Maheude = Miou-Miou
Catherine = Judith Henry
Étienne Lantier = Renaud
Chaval = Jean-Roger Milo
M. Hennebeau = Jacques Dacqmine
Mme Hennebeau = Anny Duperey
Deneulin = Bernard Fresson
Bonnemort = Jean Carmet
Souvarine = Laurant Terzieff

Claude Berri's strategy for adapting such a substantial literary classic as *Germinal*—a text thick with sociological and historical detail—was to take the essence of each major scene and carefully reproduce it. Thus Émile Zola's overall vision of a capitalist venture in which both worker and owner are trapped in a system they cannot change is intact in the film. Zola's socialist leanings come through because our sympathy is almost always focused on the miners and their suffering families, but the well-fed and pampered bourgeois have a few problems, too.

The leading character, Étienne Lantier, who is introduced in the thirteenth of Zola's Rougon-Macquart series of twenty novels, comes from a long line of troubled folk in Zola's novels. Étienne is on the lam after a fight with a supervisor on his last job and thus is willing to take a job in what seem to be the murderous conditions of the Voreux mine.

Zola's purpose in his massive series was to examine the effects of heredity and environment on a single multigenerational family. In both the novel and the film, the effects of the mining environment almost always dominate Étienne's life. And so intense is Zola's exposé of the horrors in the mines that it is difficult to imagine any other possibility. Of course Étienne could quit and go elsewhere, and no doubt his somewhat sour personality contributes to his eventual rebelliousness, but these characteristics are hardly exclusively a function of his family. Given some of his notorious blood relatives in Zola's novels—several murderers, suicides, and a famous prostitute, Nana—most commentators (see Tancock below) find Étienne remarkably wholesome.

In both the novel and the film, Étienne boards with the Maheu family and becomes intimately involved with their struggles. Maheu is a gang leader (not a foreman, as some reviewers thought) who is responsible for the production and therefore the income of a handful of miners, including one of his own daughters. We follow this family through a cycle of backbreaking labor, personal scandals, and eventual collapse when Maheu is killed by the military squad guarding the mine during a strike.

The film recreates the miners' life and work in remarkable detail. Berri shot the film in the old mining villages of northern France, specifically the Wallers-Arenberg mine, home of a mining museum, where Zola had witnessed a strike in 1884. The producers recruited 500 extras from among the retired coal miners of the region.

The film ends with an impossibly melodramatic moment underground: a fight between Étienne and another worker named Chaval for Catherine, Maheu's daughter. They have all been imprisoned as a result of the terrorist bombing of one of the mine shafts by the Russian anarchist Souvarine, who has just been moved to do the inevitable since the capitalists won't keep the already-weakened shafts repaired and the union is powerless to compel them to do so. (*The Stars Look Down* has a similar plot development, although a Russian anarchist was not likely to be found in a Welsh coalfield.) Zola's detailed rendition of the death of Chaval—spilling "brains and blood"—may have more in keeping with an Oliver Stone production than a Berri production, where the camera is remarkably discreet.

Several reviewers felt that Berri's adaptation of Zola was over the top—too extreme, too overwrought. But Zola was already way over the top himself: Maheu baring his chest before the troops and asking to be stuck with

a bayonet, Chaval leering grotesquely, a woman gleefully castrating the shopkeeper Maigret after he's dead. All of these "exaggerations" are already in the novel, and Berri actually tones Zola down a bit: the woman uses a knife rather than ripping Maigret's privates off by hand. This is a rich rendition of a rich novel.

Zola's crusade in this novel was to enhance the lives of the miners and reduce the abuses of the owners, but he never flinched from exposing the problems on both sides. The ultimate catastrophe in both the novel and the film—the flooding of the mines by exploding the shaft sunk past underground lakes—is, after all, the result of the anarchist Souvarine's bombs. Souvarine is tolerated by the miners because they seem to like the anarchist's feistiness, but it is clear in both novel and film that he is not a man to be trusted by anybody. In the novel we learn that he is a Russian émigré; in the film we are not told his origins, but the actor bears a remarkable resemblance to Lenin.

The film is dedicated to Berri's father, a politically conscious worker who always voted for the French Communist Party. Publicity for the film also emphasized the working-class roots of the two principal stars: Depardieu's father was a metalworker and Miou-Miou's mother sold vegetables in a market.

Because mining is the occupation most referred to in this guide, it is perhaps appropriate to note that *Germinal* is probably the most ambitious of all the films in its realistic depiction of mining conditions and the politics of both capitalism and labor organizing. Its status as a subtitled foreign film may keep it from as wide an audience as it should receive. That would be unfortunate.

Leonard Tancock's introduction to his translation of the novel argues that Zola's indictment of the French mining situation was already out of date when the novel was published in 1885: the worst abuses of children and women in the mines, for example, had already been remedied. But as a vision of an underground hell, Zola's and now Berri's vision can hardly be faulted.

Zola's funeral cortège in Paris in 1902 was accompanied by coal miners who shouted "*Germinal! Germinal!*" This film makes that spirited send-off understandable.

See also: *Kameradschaft; The Stars Look Down.*
Availability: Easy.

Further reading

Lane, Anthony. "The Shaft." *New Yorker*, 14 March 1994, 90–91. A patronizing review of the film, with some valid criticisms.

Maslin, Janet. "From Claude Berri, a Zola Classic." *New York Times*, 11 March 1994, C1, 14. The film "may be hobbled by obviousness, but it remains a formidable accomplishment."

Perrot, Michelle. *Workers on Strike: France, 1871–1890.* Trans. Chris Turner. New Haven: Yale University Press, 1987. A cultural history of strikes in France, with relevance to Zola.

Riding, Alan. "Does 'Germinal' Speak across a Century?" *New York Times*, 6 March 1994, VIII.31. An overview of the production, its attempt at historical accuracy, and the director.

Traugott, Mark, ed. and trans. *The French Worker: Autobiographies from the Early Industrial Era.* Berkeley: University of California Press, 1993. Seven revealing memoirs of nineteenth-century workers in France (although no miners).

Zola, Emil. *Germinal.* Trans. Leonard Tancock. 1885. New York: Penguin, 1956. Includes an excellent brief introduction by the translator.

〰

The Gleaners and I

How will it be with kingdoms and with kings . . . When this dumb terror shall rise to judge the world . . . ?—Edwin Markham, "The Man with the Hoe"

2000, 82 mins., French, with English subtitles
Director: Agnès Varda
Postmodern documentary
PRINCIPAL FIGURES
Agnès Varda
François Wertheimer
Bodan Litnanski

Agnès Varda has been identified with the French New Wave primarily on the strength of two of her early features, *Cleo from 5 to 7* (1962) and *Le Bonheur* (*Happiness*), both of which share some of the characteristics of the movement pioneered by such directors as François Truffaut and Jean-Luc Godard—a tendency toward improvisational acting, minimal and whimsical narratives and pace, and a healthy disregard of traditional editing conventions (privileging jump cuts, for example, over Hollywood continuity editing).

She also shared with these directors the radical chic of many French antiwar intellectuals, with such openly political documentaries as *Far from Vietnam* (1967), a pro–North Vietnamese Army film, made with other New Wave directors such as Godard, and *Black Panthers*, filmed in the United States. But her subsequent career, alternating and combining somewhat offbeat narratives with a profound sympathy for people at the bottom of the social order, may in the end be seen as closer to her very first film, *La Pointe Courte* (1954), named for the fishing village whose hardworking inhabitants share screen time with a young couple's marital difficulties. In such films as *Murs Murs* (1980), on the Chicano murals in Los Angeles, she started to find her recurring subject: these murals are by "the forgotten people of California" who finally have a voice ("to murmur"), because "mural means I exist" (Forbes).

The French title of this film—*Les Glaneurs et la glaneuse*—points to the fact that Varda regards herself as a kind of gleaner, a film-maker who picks up images wherever she can and then holds on to them to use as she sees fit in her films. She documents her own journey throughout rural France and Parisian suburbs alike, recording (mainly) how poor people everywhere survive by gleaning. Thus we see country people gathering apples, potatoes, and grapes and city people scavenging in markets and dumps.

Most, of course, eat their gleanings, but a few even make art from them. These unexpected variations appeal to Varda, as do the obsessively (to us outlanders) bureaucratic French: people at a bar debate the difference between "gleaning" and "picking" (the latter being a no-no) and a French magistrate standing in a cabbage field quotes from the royal edict of 2 November 1554, which gave people the right to glean, and the contemporary penal code, which regulates the matter. An apple farmer has a system (he explains) for registering gleaners. And so on, through foible and ingenuity. Varda herself reveals that she collects heart-shaped vegetables.

Not too far below the surface of Varda's simple road trip lies an artistic legacy, that of the French nineteenth-century painter Jean-François Millet (1814–75), who celebrated peasant labor in two of the most reproduced paintings in history, *The Sower* and *The Gleaners*. The former celebrates the power of the field laborer, while the latter captures the industry of those who glean to survive. And although she doesn't quote the American Edwin Markham's poem based on another Millet painting, "The Man with the Hoe," published in a San Francisco newspaper in 1899 and reprinted soon after in forty languages and in 10,000 newspapers and magazines, the same regard for "The emptiness of ages in his face, / And on his back the burden of the world" is in Varda's images as well.

See also: *Human Resources*.

Availability: Selected collections; DVD (includes Varda's film, "The Gleaners and I: Two Years Later" from Zeitgeist).

Further reading

Camhi, Leslie. "Lives of Scavengers in a World of Plenty." *New York Times*, 11 March 2001, II.15, 27. Reviews Varda's career and celebrates this "warmly engaging and humorous documentary about people who live off the refuse of our overconsuming society."

Forbes, Jill. "Agnès Varda: The Gaze of the Medusa?" *Sight and Sound*, Spring 1989, 122–24. A review of Varda's career through the 1980s, emphasizing her "aesthetic [as] specifically female" as well as socially responsive.

Scott, A. O. " 'The Gleaners and I': A Reaper of the Castoff, Be It Material or Human." *New York Times*, 30 September 2000. Celebrates "one of the bravest, most idiosyncratic of French filmmakers" and her gleaners, who "retain a resilient, generous humanity that is clearly

brought to the surface by her own tough, open spirit."

~

God's Little Acre

Lintheads and peckerwoods

1958, 118 mins., B&W
Director: Anthony Mann
Screenplay: Philip Yordan, from Erskine Caldwell's novel of the same title
CAST
Ty Ty Walden = Robert Ryan
Will Thompson = Aldo Ray
Griselda = Tina Louise
Pluto = Buddy Hackett
Buck Walden = Vic Morrow
Shaw Walden = Jack Lord
Darlin' Jill = Fay Spain

Erskine Caldwell's reputation as a serious writer has never been high. Because of the controversy generated by two of his most notorious novels—*Tobacco Road* and *God's Little Acre*—and because of the lurid scenes promised by so many of the garish covers of their paperback editions, many readers have never tried to find out what this son of Georgia and chronicler of the riffraff known as "poor white trash" had to say. The same may also be said of the films based on these novels, only one of which is currently available on videocassette.

But avoiding Caldwell's vision of the rural white southerners would be similar to ignoring Steinbeck's vision of the Okies and other California migrant laborers. Caldwell's comic ne'er-do-wells, especially Ty Ty of *God's Little Acre* and Jeeter Lester of *Tobacco Road*, became the representative types of their generation for the entire country. Both of Caldwell's novels were massive best-sellers, and a dramatic version of *Tobacco Road* (adapted by Jack Kirkland) ran for seven successful years on Broadway (1934–41). With Margaret Bourke-White, the Farm Security Administration photographer, Caldwell published four illustrated volumes that supported his contention that his fiction represented the authentic poor white South.

Caldwell's participation in the left-wing literary movements of the 1930s placed his fiction, for a time, in the tradition of the proletarian novel—works that either were written by workers or focused on workers. He published in leading periodicals (an essay about lynching in *The Masses* in 1934, for example) and stories about lynching in anthologies in this tradition. Thus when his novel was transposed to 1950s Georgia and a 1957 Ford Fairlane shares the shot with Ty Ty's immense 1930s touring convertible, the result is incongruous.

The essential dynamic of Caldwell's vision is the white southern farmer's resistance to giving up the land to work in the cotton mills. Ty Ty's son-in-law, Will, has no truck with farming or digging for gold. He's a city man, a factory worker, and he looks down on "lintheads," mill hands with lint in their hair. Unfortunately, the film excised almost all of the interesting stuff about the labor struggle at Will's plant. In the film, Will—who shares with Ty Ty an obsessive drive—wants "to turn the power back on"; that is, to restore to the valley its source of riches—the mill. Although the men on strike duty seem to look up to him, Will—when he is not dilly-dallying with Griselda—is under the illusion that all he has to do to restore the status quo ante is to sneak into the mill and turn the power switches on. Caldwell's novel is much more carefully rooted in the labor politics of his region: Will's plant in the novel is unionized and the workers there are locked out, whereas the rest of the valley is nonunion and working at full capacity. The film portrays what appears to be a lockout but the men seem passive without Will.

Caldwell's status as a best-selling author generated in his publishers and publicists a verbal avalanche that seems hardly credible today. *God's Little Acre* was at one time "the world's most popular novel," by the year of the film's release selling 6 million copies in twenty-one languages in twenty-six countries. All his novels together had sold 60 million copies by the mid-1960s.

While Caldwell's overheated pseudo-poetic white-trash prose ("Griselda has the finest pair of rising beauties a man can ever hope to see") was carefully maintained by Mann's casting of Tina Louise as Griselda and Fay Spain as Darlin' Jill, Caldwell's metaphorical vision of the absurdity of digging for gold instead of crops is only partly maintained. Ryan's Ty Ty is looking for his grandpa's buried treasure; Caldwell's is delving for an impossible vein of gold in Georgia red clay. Either way Ty Ty—the man whose "automobile had been turned down at the junkyard in Augusta"—no longer has the sense to dig holes for planting.

See also: *Tobacco Road; The Uprising of '34.*
Availability: Selected collections.

Further reading

Caldwell, Erskine. *A Day's Wooing and Other Stories*. New York: Grosset & Dunlap, 1944. Contains three of his disturbing and revealing lynching stories.

——. *God's Little Acre*. 1933. Numerous editions available of the source novel, many with covers picturing the trashy women the prose sometimes celebrates; fans of the lurid will prefer the illustrated movie tie-in edition (New York: Signet, 1958), which includes actors' clinches that the film omits.

Caldwell, Erskine, and Margaret Bourke-White. *You Have Seen Their Faces*. 1937. Athens: University of Georgia Press, 1995. This new edition of the book that Caldwell said he compiled "to show that the fiction [he] was writing was authentically based on contemporary life in the South" has a helpful introduction by Alan Tractenberg.

Cook, Sylvia Jenkins. *From Tobacco Road to Route 66: The Southern Poor White in Fiction*. Chapel Hill: University of North Carolina Press, 1976. Places Caldwell clearly in the tradition of such southern writers as Faulkner.

"God's Little Acre." *Variety*, 14 May 1958. Celebrates the film as "adult, sensitive, and intelligent" and argues that the "prime and juicy" sex goes beyond the novel's "peeping-tomism." Is this evidence of a completely different version of the film?

Klevar, Harvey L. *Erskine Caldwell: A Biography*. Knoxville: University of Tennessee Press, 1993. Revealing discussion of the roots of Caldwell's vision in his father's sociological and psychological studies of poor whites.

Weiler, A. H. "God's Little Acre." *New York Times*, 14 August 1958, 23. The filmmakers "have neither kidded nor cheapened" the original story "but have treated it with respect," reports a reviewer who clearly missed most of the show that day.

Goin' Down the Road

"Not bad, eh!"

1970, 88 mins., Canada
Director: Donald Shebib
Screenplay: William Fruet
CAST
Peter = Doug McGrath
Joey = Paul Bradley
Betty = Jayne Eastwood
Selena = Cayle Chernin
Nicole = Nicole Morin
Frenchie = Pierre La Roche

Two young men take off from Nova Scotia to find jobs in the big city—Toronto. They're fairly desperate, although the leader, Peter, is invariably optimistic and totally unrealistic about the job situation. In fact, Peter and Joey do a little bit of everything to stay afloat: warehouse workers, carwash jockeys, pinsetters, and handbill delivery boys.

Whatever the situation—including the pursuit of women, usually unsuccessful—Peter inevitably says, "Not bad, eh!"

In fact, it is almost always bad. In the end, Joey's girlfriend is pregnant, both guys have been laid off, and most of their pathetic possessions have been thrown—with them—out of their apartment. They devise a scheme for stealing food from a supermarket and escape only by braining the clerk who pursues them. All they can really do now is go down the road again.

The handheld camera shots and grainy look give the film an authentic feel. We know these guys are losers but they try to be happy losers. In the face of the relentless pressures of unemployment and potential homelessness, they seem like free spirits. Their bubble will burst again. And again.

See also: *Down and Out in America*.
Availability: Selected collections.

Further reading

Bowie, Douglas, and Tom Shoebridge, eds. *Best Canadian Screenplays*. Kingston, Ont.: Quarry Press, 1992. Includes William Fruet's screenplay for *Goin' Down the Road* and his brief introduction to its origins as a documentary.

Byford, Chris. "Hiway 61 Revisited." *Cineaction* 45 (February 1998): 10–17. Excellent analysis of the film as the epitome of the loser paradigm in Canadian films.

"Goin' Down the Road." *Variety*, 22 July 1970. The reviewer expects that this film will put the

Making plans for jobs over some beers in *Goin' Down the Road*. Courtesy British Film Institute Stills, Posters, and Designs.

Canadian feature film industry on the world map: everything about the film (except some technical difficulties) he finds "a well-deserved success."

Note: Also known as *Le Voyage chimérique*.

∽
Goin' to Chicago

"If you can't make it in Chicago, you can't make it."—folk saying

1994, 71 mins.
Director: George King
Traditional documentary
PRINCIPAL FIGURES
Vernon Jarrett, Chicago TV and print journalist

Those who went to Chicago: Geri Oliver, Frank Lumpkin, Clory Bryant, Christine Houston, Ruth Wells, Viethel Wills, and many others
Unita Blackwell, mayor, Mayersville, Mississippi

The four million African Americans who migrated to northern cities from the rural South after World War II were literally following in the footsteps of the first great migration, which occurred during World War I. The lure of jobs, an escape from racism in the South, the desire to make a new life—all of these factors turned into their opposites for many of these migrants from sharecropping, stoop labor of all kinds, and virtual serfdom in the Mississippi Delta, the origin of many of the people portrayed in this film. And like *The Killing Floor*, which documents

Black migrants and their version of the Joadmobile in *Goin' to Chicago*. Courtesy California Newsreel.

the false promises in the Chicago meatpacking industry, *Goin' to Chicago* documents the barriers so many of the workers faced until some of the victories of the civil rights movement.

The film is also a portrait of the "Bronzeville" or South Side of Chicago that the waves of these black urban migrants created. "If you can't make it in Chicago," so went the contemporary folk wisdom, "you can't make it!" The availability of work, the lack of sustained racial animosity among the average white people encountered, and the liveliness of its musical culture all made Chicago a promised land. Not that some didn't have to work very hard to make it: one man interviewed said that he had worked two jobs for twenty-five years—eight hours at Sears, then eight hours at the post office.

And while the footage of the amazing Klan initiation back home in Mississippi surely makes a convincing case for the migration, Chicago apartments were often not as comfortable as their home places. With the population of the South Side doubling after World War II—from 250,000 to 500,000—footage of the incredibly cramped "kitchenettes"—single rooms in which whole families lived—makes for very disturbing viewing. It also reminds us that the close quarters memorialized in Lorraine Hansberry's *Raisin in the Sun*, with a bathroom down the hall shared with neighbors, was only a decade or so away from the scenes in this film. And the housing discrimination at the heart of that family's decision—and fears—about moving to a white neighborhood is also clearly delineated in this film: "We cater to white clients only" was a common sign in Chicago in the 1940s.

See also: *The Killing Floor; A Raisin in the Sun.*

Availability: Selected collections; California Newsreel.

Further reading

Nesbett, Peter T., and Michelle Dubois, eds. *Over the Line: The Art and Life of Jacob Lawrence*. Seattle: University of Washington Press, 2001.

Catalog of the black artist's works, including his fifty-panel *Migration of the Negro* series done in 1940.

Trotter, Joe William, ed. *The Great Migration in Historical Perspective*. Bloomington: Indiana University Press, 1991. Excellent general collection, including an essay on Chicago by James R. Grossman, "The White Man's Union: The Great Migration and the Resonance of Race and Class in Chicago, 1916–1922."

Web site:

⟨www.pbs.org/gointochicago⟩ Official site for the film, with numerous resources and items of interest, including two black chroniclers of the migration, the poet Langston Hughes and the artist Jacob Lawrence.

Gold Diggers of 1933

"We're in the money!"

1933, 96 mins., B&W
Director: Mervyn LeRoy
Screenplay: Erwin Gelsey and James Seymour, from Avery Hopwood's play of the same title

CAST

Carol = Joan Blondell
Polly Parker = Ruby Keeler
Brad Roberts = Dick Powell
Fay Fortune = Ginger Rogers
Faneuil H. Peabody = Guy Kibbee
Trixie Lorraine = Aline MacMahon
J. Lawrence Bradford = Warren William
Barney Hopkins = Ned Sparks

Gold Diggers of 1933 has the reputation of being fluff—but what beautiful fluff!—because it employed the greatest mass-dance choreographer of all time, Busby Berkeley. But if you have never seen it or remember only the fluff, it deserves another look, for it captures the economic contradictions of the Great Depression in a way rivaled only by Preston Sturges's comedies. The "gold diggers" are of course the chorus girls who want to make it—not by successfully hoofing it in a big Broadway show but by marrying rich guys.

Stanley Solomon characterizes this film as one in which "money looms as an obsession, poverty as an ever-present threat," but Arthur Hove emphasizes that the moral of the story is that "chorus girls really do have hearts of gold." And while we remember the gals costumed as gold coins and dancing a capitalist jig, we forget that the film ends with images of unemployed veterans who have been forced to walk the breadlines. Sound familiar? Styles of filmmaking change, of course, but some problems never go away.

Homeless World War I vets were in the news as part of the threatening Bonus Army that had marched on Washington in 1932 to demand their wartime bonus. Joan Blondell's rendition of her "forgotten man" begins like a wail for a missing lover ("Ever since the world began, / A woman's got to have a man"), but the film's powerful imagery of the homeless vets almost shakes the fluff right out of the film.

Although the film is like a Shakespearean comedy—lovers separated, lovers misidentified, lovers reunited and married—several moments reminded the audience of the troubled world of the Depression outside the theater. Almost immediately one of the unemployed chorus girls serves up their breakfast after casually stealing a quart of milk from a neighbor. The astonishing choreography of Busby Berkeley presents more than fifty chorus girls each playing a violin outlined with neon lights that form one enormous violin, but he also presents a startling final tableau of marching soldiers in a dark parody of a rainbow while homeless vets gather in the foreground. We see shot after shot of the homeless until there is a spectacular marching sequence with men in uniform.

The "gold diggers" reappeared in 1935 and 1937 with new directors but perhaps a little less pizazz; Busby Berkeley himself directed *Gold Diggers of 1935*, which featured the Oscar-winning song "Lullaby of Broadway." But most of the sharp economic analysis (if that's not too strong a term) had by then gone even farther downtown. By 1934, Warner Brothers had secured injunctions against rival companies that tried to cash in on the "gold digger" concept; it was simply worth too much for them to share the wealth. The only coins Warner Brothers ever gave away were the aluminum-covered chocolate tokens used to promote the opening of the 1933 hit.

See also: *The Great Depression; Sullivan's Travels.*
Availability: Selected collections.

Further reading

Bergman, Andrew. *We're in the Money: Depression America and Its Films*. New York: New York University Press, 1971. An excellent film history with a section on the *Gold Diggers* films.

Hall, Mordaunt. "The Screen." *New York Times*, 8 June 1933, 22. Applauds everything about the first *Gold Diggers* film, singling out the "Forgotten Man" number for special praise.

Hove, Arthur, ed. *Gold Diggers of 1933*. Madison: University of Wisconsin Press, 1980. Screenplay and extended commentary on the film.

Solomon, Stanley. *Beyond Formula: American Film Genres*. New York: Harcourt Brace Jovanovich, 1976. A short but excellent analysis of the film.

Sennwald, André. "Gold Diggers of 1935." *New York Times*, 15 March 1935, 25. With jokes about an "all-Eskimo cast" doing Shakespeare, it becomes clear that the series is no longer about the unemployed.

The Golden Cage: A Story of California's Farmworkers

On the road again . . . and again

1989, 29 mins.
Director: Susan Ferris
Traditional documentary
PRINCIPAL FIGURES
Cesar Chavez, United Farm Workers of America (UFW) organizer
Huberto Gomez, UFW organizer
Larry Galper, grape grower
Daniel Haley, Western Growers Association

Enrique Reynosa and Jesús Barajas, former
  migrant farm workers
Lydia Villarreal, attorney
Dr. Marion Moses, UFW physician
B. Haakedael, U.S. Border Patrol agent

This film briefly reviews the origins of the
United Farm Workers in the terrible conditions of these workers in the early 1960s,
covering ground similar to that of Edward R.
Murrow's classic *Harvest of Shame*. They had
little drinking water, no toilets, and no right
to organize, since the farm workers were
excluded from the provisions of the National
Labor Relations Act.

There have always been substantial native-
born migrant workers; but as more and more
Americans, both native-born and naturalized
citizens, left for easier work, illegal
immigrants entered the fields. Despite the
amnesty during the Clinton presidency and
the laws that require employers to obtain
proof of citizenship or legal residency,
growers were willing to hire anybody to do
the work. Illegal aliens, desperate for work,
were literally driven to extremes. Some are
shown living in cardboard-lined miniature
dirt caves; one family took up residence in
the bucket of a giant abandoned construction
vehicle.

The dangers of the workers' lives are
nowhere more persistent than in their exposure to pesticides: one worker, exposed while
pregnant, gives birth to an armless but
otherwise normal child. This is a short but
excellent snapshot of the situation of
migrant labor at the end of the 1980s.

See also: *Harvest of Shame; El Norte.*
Availability: Selected collections; Filmakers
  Library.

Further reading

Levy, Jacques E. *Cesar Chavez: Autobiography of
  La Causa*. New York: Norton, 1975. An early
  biography.
Meister, Dick, and Anne Loftis. *A Long Time
  Coming: The Struggle to Unionize America's
  Farm Workers*. New York: Macmillan, 1977. A
  very thorough history from the mid–nineteenth
  century through the organizing efforts of
  Chavez's UFW in the 1970s.

The Grapes of Wrath

The Depression classic

1940, 129 mins., B&W
Director: John Ford
Screenplay: Nunnally Johnson, from John
  Steinbeck's novel of the same title
CAST
Tom Joad = Henry Fonda
Ma Joad = Jane Darwell
Pa Joad = Russell Simpson
Casey = John Carradine
Muley Graves = John Qualen
Grandpa = Charley Grapewin
Grandma = Zeffie Tilbury
Al = O. Z. Whitehead
Rosasharn = Dorris Bowdon
Connie = Eddie Quillan
Uncle John = Frank Darien
Government Caretaker = Grant Mitchell

Although John Ford has long been identified
with the genre of westerns with such macho
cowboys as John Wayne, all four of his
Academy Awards were for films in other
genres, and two of the four are included in
this guide: *How Green Was My Valley* and
The Grapes of Wrath. Despite Ford's reputation as a bit of a crusty conservative, his films
about workers were fairly progressive. In
taking on John Steinbeck's novel, he was certainly adapting a well-known writer who had
been sympathetic to (but not uncritical of)
radical interests in California for almost a
decade.

Steinbeck's experiences with migrant
laborers, Red organizers, and vigilante committees in California come through in such
novels as *In Dubious Battle* (optioned by the
documentary filmmaker Pare Lorentz but
never filmed) and of course this classic.

Very few people do not know at least one
version of this story of the migration of the
Joad family. Forced out of their homestead,
joined by their son, who has just left the
penitentiary after serving a sentence for
manslaughter, they head west to California,
the promised land, in a rickety truck packed
with their possessions. The visual images of

the Depression, in still photography and film, memorialize their trek and that of many others who were forced by economic and natural disaster to confront an unknown future.

The Joads' drama is hardly over when they get close to California. There are still some cruel twists left for them. In the film, the concluding sequence, featuring a repressive migrant camp with violent gun-toting guards, is brilliantly contrasted (in a New Deal twist) with a federally controlled camp, whose caretaker bears a remarkable resemblance to FDR himself.

The film ends with a conversation between Tom Joad and his mother before he leaves the family again, celebrating the perseverance of the little people. This example of pure Hollywood populism is much less ambiguous than the much more daring ending of Steinbeck's novel. As Joseph R. Millichap points out, the film takes Ma Joad's speech from an earlier chapter when they depart their first Hooverville and moves it to the end of the film, after the dancing to the tune of "Red River Valley," a typically Ford nostalgic moment (a symbol "of an almost mystical harmony," concludes Millichap). The film sends Tom away in a striking composition that echoes his arrival at the beginning, but in the novel the family struggles on to a cotton farm where conditions are terrible. Certainly the final scene, in which Rosasharn shares her milk-swollen breasts with a dying old man, would not have been filmable then (or now), although Steinbeck apparently believed it to be an appropriate life-affirming coda.

Steinbeck's complexity is a little hard to catch the first time through. Certainly the film doesn't do justice to any aspect of his overall vision—either the frustrations of the contest between Red organizers and bread-and-butter unionists in *In Dubious Battle* or the struggle between "bad" capitalists and New Deal capitalists in *The Grapes of Wrath*.

See also: *Fury*.
Availability: Easy.

Further reading

Lorentz, Pare. *FDR's Moviemaker*. Las Vegas: University of Nevada, 1992. Contributes a sense of the narrow line between documentary and feature film during this period and a discussion of his plans to film *In Dubious Battle*.

Margolies, Ken. "Silver Screen Tarnishes Unions." *Screen Actor*, Summer 1981, 43–52. Singles out Ford's film for special praise in a discussion of labor films.

Millichap, Joseph R. *Steinbeck and Film*. New York: Ungar, 1983. An authoritative discussion of Steinbeck's career and excellent comparisons of novel and film: "John Ford's 'The Grapes of Wrath' is a beautiful, moving, and intelligent film, though not the great novel John Steinbeck wrote."

Steinbeck, John. *In Dubious Battle*. 1935. New York: Bantam, 1961. Steinbeck dramatizes the tension between Communist and bread-and-butter trade union organizing among California's agricultural workers.

——. *Working Days: The Journal of "The Grapes of Wrath," 1938–1941*. Ed. Robert DeMott. New York: Viking, 1989. Steinbeck's revealing musings about his work, with excellent annotations situating the novel in contemporary affairs.

Stott, William. *Documentary Expression and Thirties America*. New York: Oxford University Press, 1973. An excellent survey of the documentary impulse in films, still photography, and literature.

✍

The Great Depression

1993, four videocassettes (seven episodes), 420 mins.
Producer: Henry Hampton
Traditional documentary
PRINCIPAL FIGURES (*THE ROAD TO ROCK BOTTOM*)
Mildred Hall Campbell, White House secretary
Joseph C. Harsch, Washington correspondent, *Christian Science Monitor*
Alonzo Fields, White House butler
John Pompanine, Bonus Army marcher from New Jersey
Horace Carmichael, Washington, D.C., police officer

Gore Vidal, grandson of Senator Thomas P. Gore (D-Okla.)
General Douglas MacArthur
20,000 unnamed World War I veterans

While all the episodes in the *Great Depression* series feature well-selected and rarely seen historical footage, the sequences in the second episode, *The Road to Rock Bottom*, are nothing short of amazing: we see the Bonus Army veterans—mostly unemployed workers—gathering across the country to march on Washington, veterans and their families building Hoovervilles on the Anacostia Flats, east of the city, demonstrations at the Capitol, and finally attacks on the veterans and the burning of their shacks by troops led by General Douglas MacArthur. The documentary may be traditional in style (footage, stills, interviewed talking heads, and a magisterial voice-over narrator), but replaying so much footage reminds us of the importance of seeing labor history with a fresh eye.

What was the Bonus Army? Or the Bonus Expeditionary Force (the BEF), as the veterans often called themselves? In 1924 World War I veterans had been awarded monetary compensation for service, a kind of pension that would come due to them in 1945. By the early 1930s it was evident that veterans, like so many other Americans, needed a financial boost sooner rather than later; hence agitation—and some major congressional support—for awarding earlier what became known as the "bonus." With mainstream political allies, left-leaning "councils of the unemployed," and active Communist Party participation, thousands of veterans began to converge on Washington, D.C., for demonstrations in favor of the immediate awarding of the bonus.

On 16 June the House passed the Bonus Bill, but two days later the Senate voted it down. The Senate adjourned, leaving, the film informs us, through basement tunnels rather than face the vets sitting on the Capitol steps. Within a month, because so many veterans refused to leave, military forces under MacArthur attacked—

pointedly ignoring orders from President Herbert Hoover not to do so—and routed the veterans not only on Pennsylvania Avenue (authorized by Hoover) but also on the Anacostia Flats. A few veterans were killed in the attack.

This film does not record the last act: although the veterans tried to repeat their demonstrations the next year, by that time Roosevelt had succeeded Hoover—who had always opposed the bonus—as president, and the vets were invited to join the newly organized Civilian Conservation Corps for work in national forests. Even though Roosevelt also had been opposed to the bonus, an executive order made it possible for 25,000 veterans to go to work for the CCC, New Deal–style.

While the entire *Great Depression* series is of interest, the second episode, which features a contrast between individual appropriation of money—Pretty Boy Floyd robbing banks—and the veterans' Bonus Army, is probably the best. The seven episodes provide a very solid overview of the 1930s, with episodes covering aspects of labor history also visited by a number of other documentaries, especially the fifth, whose events are featured in *The Uprising of '34:*

1. "A Job at Ford's"—the assembly line and the stock market crash.
2. "The Road to Rock Bottom"—Pretty Boy Floyd and the Bonus Army.
3. "New Deal/New York"—new federal agencies and the Triboro Bridge.
4. "We Have a Plan"—EPIC (End Poverty in California) and Social Security.
5. "Mean Things Happening"— organizing in factories and on farms.
6. "To Be Somebody"—lynching, segregation, and anti-Semitism.
7. "Arsenal of Democracy"—the new war economy.

The series producer, Blackside, had already produced the Emmy Award–winning documentary series *Eyes on the Prize*, a history of the American civil rights movement. Broadcast nationally during prime time on PBS, the fourteen-hour series attracted over 40 million viewers. Since making *The Great Depression*, Blackside has also produced *America's War on Poverty*.

See also: *Heroes for Sale; The Uprising of '34*.
Availability: Selected collections; PBS Video.

Further reading

Ballads of the B.E.F. New York: Coventry House, 1932. A collection of poems and songs written by and for the Bonus Expeditionary Force.

Green, James. *Taking History to Heart.* Amherst: University of Massachusetts Press, 2000. A labor historian and consultant to the *Great Depression* series discusses the nuts and bolts plus the politics of organizing the material.

New York Times: Selected articles on the Bonus March, all from 1932, include "Weary Bonus Army Reaches Capital by Truck," 30 May, 1; "Bonus Band Seizes PRR Railroad Yard," 4 June, 1; "Bonus Army Asked to Leave Capital," 9 June, 1; "Bonus Bill Passes in House, 13 June, 1; Senate to Rush Vote," 16 June, 1; "Senate Defeats Bonus, Despite 10,000 Veterans Massed Around Capitol," 18 June, 1; "Reds Urge Mutiny in the Bonus Army," 19 June, 1; "5,000 in Bonus Army Jam Capitol Steps," 3 July, 1; "Bonus Army Boos Hoover at Capitol," 6 July, 1; "Bonus Army Begins an All-Night Siege," 13 July, 1; "Drive Bonus Pickets from White House; Police Isolate Area," 17 July, 1.

Watkins, T. H. *The Great Depression: America in the 1930s.* Boston: Little, Brown, 1993. Companion volume for the series.

Web site:
⟨www.blackside.com⟩ Official site of the films, with an overview of all the episodes in the series.

〰️
Gung Ho

Japanese calisthenics for the UAW

1986, 111 mins., PG-13
Director: Ron Howard
Screenplay: Lowell Ganz and Babaloo Mandell

CAST
Hunt Stevenson = Michael Keaton
Kazihiro = Gedde Watanabe
Audrey = Mimi Rogers
Buster = George Wendt
Sakamoto = Soh Yamamura
Junior = Jihmi Kennedy
Googie = Rick Overton
Willie = John Turturro

Although the United States and Japan have harbored mutual obsessions and suspicions (especially about the surprise attack on Pearl Harbor and the atomic attacks on Hiroshima and Nagasaki) for four decades, only two recent major films besides this one (*Iron Maze* and *Come See the Paradise*) come close to dealing with any economic issues or workers. Indeed, the title of this film is the same as that of a classic anti-Japanese World War II film, in which Randolph Scott and other actors tear up the enemy viciously. Americans, it is true, had already appropriated the phrase "gung ho," often without much consciousness of its Chinese, not Japanese, origins.

In this film, Michael Keaton plays an auto union shop steward named Hunt Stevenson, who confidently journeys to Japan to offer Assan Motors, a corporate giant there, the opportunity to buy out his defunct auto plant. The fact that he comes from Hadleyburg—as in Twain's "The Man Who Corrupted Hadleyburg"—should have warned the Japanese or us that Hunt may have to indulge in a scam to get his way.

His cultural miscommunications and blunderings amuse his Japanese investors enough that they send one of their losers—a disgraced manager—to take charge of their new American branch. Most of the slapstick humor in the film involves the cultural clashes between Japanese managers and American workers. Keaton makes a pact with the devil and keeps it from his membership: if they turn out 15,000 cars in one month, he will guarantee their jobs and their old comfortable wages. Not knowing about Keaton's quota deal, the workers believe that all they have to do is try a little harder and they will be rewarded.

In the end, the film shows us that Americans work as hard as their Japanese counterparts, even if a lot of American cars are defective. Most viewers find this film very funny, even if none of the solutions to the problems of the American auto industry is amusing or even likely to work. Stevenson's local meets once in a while, but basically he is always in charge.

See also: *Tucker*.
Availability: Easy; DVD.

Further reading

Kamata, Satoshi. *Japan in the Passing Lane: An Insider's Account of Life in a Japanese Auto Factory*. Trans. Tatsuru Akimoto. New York: Pantheon, 1982. A critical account of a journalist's six-month job; the last chapter is called "The Dark Side of Toyota."

O'Brien, Tim. *The Screening of America: Movies and Values from "Rocky" to "Rain Man."* New York: Continuum, 1990. Discusses the film in the context of other 1980s films about workers and business (*Tucker*, *Working Girl*, and *Wall Street*).

Note: The World War II film with almost the same title, *Gung Ho!* is most emphatically not about auto workers.

⤿
Half-Slave, Half-Free

"Nothing else is known about him"

1984, 113 mins., TVM
Director: Gordon Parks Sr.
Screenplay: Lou Potts and Samm-Art Williams, from Solomon Northup's autobiography, *Twelve Years a Slave*
CAST
Solomon Northup = Avery Brooks
Anne Northup = Petronia Paley
Henry Northup = Michael Tolan
Jenny = Rhetta Greene
Eliza = Janet League
Epps = John Saxon
Tibeats = J. C. Quinn
Noah = Joe Seneca
Birch = Ralph Pace
Merril Brown = Royce Willman
Bram Hamilton = Thomas Campbell

For twelve years Solomon Northup lived what must have been a common nightmare to free black men and women everywhere in pre–Civil War America: he was stripped of the status of a "free person of color" and became a slave. Northup was a fiddler and a carpenter in Saratoga Springs, New York. In his autobiography he recalls his somewhat naive acceptance of a job in 1841 as a musician in a traveling circus run by two doubtful entrepreneurs, Hamilton and Brown, who convince him that having papers indicating his status as a free man would protect him in slave territory—that is, in Washington, D.C. He accompanies a pathetic set of circus acts to Washington, where he is shanghaied into slavery, most likely with the connivance of his new and very smooth employers. He is then literally beaten into slavery by Birch, a particularly nasty trader who specializes in kidnappings.

The film version of Northup's autobiography makes Hamilton and Brown active and immediate agents in his enslavement. They drug him at the beginning of his trip from New York, and he ends up in the slave owners' pen in D.C. No circus interlude for him.

This costume drama was clearly made on a relatively low budget. The extras and some of the principal characters look like the static performers in a historical theme park. (Their costumes are much too clean.) But the film's portrayal of free black men and women as workers as well as slaves makes it an unusual survey of labor in the mid-1800s. Although the film does not do complete justice to the complexity of Northup's literary rendition of the various jobs both free and slave men and women held in the last decades of American slavery, it certainly helps to highlight slavery as an economic institution. Its board of consultants and labor historians (including Eric Foner, Eugene Genovese, Herbert Gutman, Benjamin Quarles, Willie Lee Rose, and Kenneth Stampp) suggests a commitment to accuracy rare in films about southern history.

Northup's story covers some of the same ground as the salacious and sadistic *Mandingo* (1975), in which interracial sex becomes the only labor on the plantation. In Parks's version of this especially "peculiar institution," interracial sex (never graphically depicted) has economic implications. On the ship that brings him from a Washington, D.C., slave pen to New Orleans, Northup encounters the light-skinned Eliza, who has been the mistress of a Virginia planter. Unfortunately, she and her master's biracial child have been sold away from the homestead by jealous family members (her white half sister in Northup's narrative but a wife in the film). Another young woman, Jenny, purchased in the same "drove" as Northup, falls in love with him in the film but becomes the open mistress of Epps, the last of Northup's slave masters, before he is finally freed by his namesake, the white Henry Northup, whose family had owned Solomon Northup's father.

In the film Northup's considerable talents as a worker become both his protection and a threat to his survival. Because he simply knows so much more than any hereditary slave, he stands out: he can build a bed and household furniture, as well as a raft to float timber downstream. But his intelligence, refined manners, and good speech make him a threat to white trash like Tibeats, who sees him as a challenge to white supremacy.

The film strengthens Northup's view, never made explicit in his narrative, that while a single black person remains a slave, no one can be free. At the time of publication (1853) Northup's book fueled the abolitionists' fires that Harriet Beecher Stowe's novel *Uncle Tom's Cabin* (1851–52) had helped to spread. Gordon Parks's film explores the more philosophical implications of Northup's gruesome adventure: the act of free work (and his music as a fiddler) in a sense creates the idea of a free man. Thus two acts of destruction—a fellow slave takes an ax to Northup's bed and his master, Epps, smashes his fiddle—both dramatize the need of the racist system to destroy the freedom of creative work.

To carry out this vision Parks has to shy away from some of the unpleasantness in which Northup felt compelled to participate. In the film Northup only pretends to whip Jenny at one point, but in his narrative he at first whips her namesake (Patsey) as her hands and feet are tied to four stakes in the ground. Northup delivers almost thirty-five lashes to Patsey's naked body before he finally refuses to continue. Parks suggests that Northup did have a relationship with Jenny and so could hardly whip her almost to death.

The end titles inform us that the New York State trial of the kidnappers (Brown and Hamilton) was inconclusive and that the slave trader Birch was acquitted in his Washington, D.C., trial because Northup as a black man could not testify. Although his book was a best-seller, Northup (like the black packinghouse workers in *The Killing Floor*) has been lost to history: "Nothing else is known about him or where and when he died," reads the film's end title.

Half-Slave, Half-Free joins Parks's other successful film, *The Learning Tree* (based on Parks's autobiography of his boyhood in Kansas), and Martin Ritt's *Sounder* as a film that has successfully developed the rural traditions of life and labor in African American history.

See also: *The Learning Tree; Sounder.*
Availability: Easy.

Further reading

Bennetts, Leslie. "TV Film by Parks Looks at Slavery." *New York Times*, 11 February 1985, C18. Surveys Parks's career and his handling of Northup's story.

Corry, John. "'Solomon Northrup's Odyssey,' Story of a Slave." *New York Times*, 13 February 1985, C25. A review of the film, emphasizing its tendency to be informative about slavery but perhaps a little too benign in its criticism of the institution.

Davis, Charles T., and Henry Louis Gates, eds. *The Slave's Narrative*. New York: Oxford University Press, 1985. A collection of essays on slave narratives, emphasizing the difficulty of accepting such narratives as Northup's as authentic voices since many were edited by white abolitionists.

Douglass, Frederick. *Narrative of the Life of Frederick Douglass, an American Slave*. 1845. New York: Doubleday, 1963. The American classic of slave narrative—Northup's journey in reverse, as it were—as Douglass escapes from Baltimore to New York in 1838.

Guerrero, Ed. *Framing Blackness: The African American Image in Film*. Philadelphia: Temple University Press, 1993. Although there is only a brief discussion of *Half-Slave, Half-Free* and relatively little about Parks's other films, Guerrero's book places the film in the context of other films about slavery.

Osofsky, Gilbert, ed. *Puttin' On Ole Massa: The Slave Narratives of Henry Bibb, William Wells Brown, and Solomon Northup*. New York: Harper & Row, 1969. The autobiographical source of the film, with two other slave narratives and a dated but helpful introduction by the editor.

Stowe, Harriet Beecher. *Key to "Uncle Tom's Cabin."* 1853. Port Washington, N.Y.: Kennikat Press, 1968. In her collection of documents supporting her view of slavery as a vicious institution, Stowe includes and relies on Northup's kidnapping case, "since it is a singular coincidence that this man was carried to . . . that same region where the scene of Uncle Tom's captivity was laid."

Note: *Half-Slave, Half-Free* was originally presented in two parts for PBS/American Playhouse: the first part, the subject of this entry, appears in some video guides as *Solomon Northrup's Legacy* (with an *r* in the second syllable of the hero's last name, as many of his contemporaries and ours spell it); *Half-Slave, Half-Free II*, not included in this book, appears in some video guides as *Charlotte Forten's Mission: Experiment in Freedom*. This film, unrelated to part I except in overall theme, is also based on a true story (an educated free black woman from the North becomes a teacher on a Georgia sea island).

Harlan County, U.S.A.

A never-ending struggle

1977, 103 mins., PG
Director: Barbara Kopple
Cinema verité documentary

PRINCIPAL FIGURES
Lois Scott, leader of women's group
Basil Collins, company gun thug
Lawrence Jones, murdered miner
Tony Boyle, president, United Mine Workers of America (UMW)
Jock Yablonski, challenger for Boyle's presidency
Florence Reese, composer of "Which Side Are You On?"
Norman Yarborough, president, Eastover Mining Company

Harlan County, U.S.A., like Kopple's *American Dream*, demonstrates her knack for finding appropriate and inevitably dramatic labor struggles in which she and her film crew immerse themselves. In this instance they filmed an extended strike at the Brookside Mine of the Eastover Mining Company, a division of Duke Power. Unlike *American Dream*, however, *Harlan County, U.S.A.* leaves you in no doubt as to which side she is on. According to Richard Skorman in *Off-Hollywood Movies* (New York: Harmony Books, 1989), her film was at one time required viewing for all master's degree candidates at the Harvard Business School, although this sounds like a piece of folklore to me.

Harlan County, U.S.A. competes with *Norma Rae* as the most popular labor film. The frustrations of the UMW men when they seem to be losing their strike to court-ordered injunctions, scabs, police officers, and armed company thugs make this a very somber contrast even to *Norma Rae*, in which the heroine at least seems to be on the winning team. But when the miners' wives and other womenfolk join the battle, taking it upon themselves to "woman" the picket lines and plot some strategy and tactics of their own, the mood of the film changes rapidly. (*Salt of the Earth* depicts a similar situation in New Mexico in the 1950s.)

The women's decision to step in also brings problems. First there is the question of violence, since at least one of the women (Lois Scott) makes it clear that she is going to pack her pistol just like many of the men. The women also have to deal with some internal tensions—accusations of stealing a man here and there—but for the most part Kopple captures the newfound heroism that both the men and the women (and even the film crew) share when they go off early in the morning to meet the scabs and their gun thugs.

Kopple includes some early examples of the UMW's use of a "corporate campaign" strategy when she follows a contingent of miners to Wall Street, where they distribute informational leaflets on Duke Power. Furthermore, she covers the murder of Yablonski, Tony Boyle's eventual downfall, and Miller's election as the new president of the union. Viewers who need a good catch-up lesson in UMW and mining history in general will do well to look at both *Harlan County, U.S.A.* and Kopple's related film, *Out of Darkness.*

Kopple celebrates the spirit and courage of the miners and their families in the context of violence that seems never to end, in a class war that seems more appropriate to the 1930s than the 1970s. When a New York City policeman speaks to one of the picketers in the film, it seems to the policeman that the miner has stepped out of a time machine. Indeed he has. For in the Appalachian coalfields the present bleeds into the past—for many people in Harlan County, 1970 *is* 1930. When Florence Reese, the composer of "Which Side Are You On," stands up at a union convention in 1972 and sings her 1930s rallying song, past and present are almost indistinguishable.

See also: *Act of Vengeance; Out of Darkness; Salt of the Earth.*
Availability: Selected collections.

Further reading

Harris, Fred. "Burning Up People to Make Electricity." *Atlantic*, July 1974, 29–36. Senator Harris
from Oklahoma led a blue-ribbon panel to investigate conditions in Harlan County.
Kleinhans, Chuck. "Interview with Barbara Kopple." *Jump Cut* 14 (1987): 4–6. Kopple explains her sympathies with the miners and her film strategies.
Klemesrud, Judy. "Coal Miners Started the Strike—Then Their Women Took Over." *New York Times*, 15 May 1974, 50. Background story on the women's group led by Lois Scott.
Maggard, Sally Ward. "Coalfield Women Making History." In *Back Talk from Appalachia: Confronting Stereotypes*, ed. Dwight B. Billings et al., 228–50. Lexington: University Press of Kentucky, 1999. Traces the women's activism at Brookside Mine, partly in interviews from outtakes of *Harlan County, U.S.A.* archived in the Margaret I. King Library of the University of Kentucky.
Rosenthal, Alan. *The Documentary Conscience.* Berkeley: University of California Press, 1980. Contains a detailed interview with director Kopple.
Web site:
⟨www.gen.umn.edu/faculty-staff/yahnke/filmteach/teach1.htm⟩ Detailed summary of the film.

↩

Harlan County War

Women (agin) to the barricades

2000, 104 mins., TVM
Director: Tony Bill
Screenplay: Peter Silverman
CAST
Ruby Kincaid = Holly Hunter
Warren Jakopovich = Stellan Skarsgård
Silas Kincaid = Ted Levine
Tug Jones = Wayne Robson

Holly Hunter gives a compelling performance as a miner's wife from Brookside, Kentucky, site of a long, violently contested strike in 1973 that revived briefly the old 1930s slogan "Bloody Harlan County." When Brookside Mining gets an injunction to stop the successful picketing and stoppage of scabs, limiting the miners' union to only three men at the gate, Hunter's Ruby Kincaid leads the wives into battle, stopping scabs, fighting the state police, and building public relations against the mine's parent company, Duke Power and Light.

If all of this so far sounds like Barbara Kopple's Academy Award–winning documentary *Harlan County, U.S.A.*, it should, as it is basically the same struggle and to varying degrees the same film. Add, however, the plot and character interaction from *Norma Rae*—outside union organizer becomes very friendly with our heroine and her husband gets jealous—and you have a curious mixture of two labor classics.

Holly Hunter gets to position Ruby in situations (now perhaps too familiar) associated with Appalachian workers. She is stupefied by hotel brass bath fixtures, she makes a heartfelt speech as owner of a single share of Duke Power and Light stock at the company's annual stockholders' meeting, and she has to endure an asinine UMW lawyer at a lobster dinner at some rich supporter's house. "Do you know," the lawyer whispers to her, "that you are the first rank-and-file person I have talked to in my three years with the union?" And then he adds, pompously, that it doesn't much matter that he doesn't know any miners, because "a strike is won inside the [Washington] Beltway, not on the picket line."

But Ruby's struggle is successful, nonetheless: end titles tell us that the Brookside miners won wage increases, safety protections, and increased health benefits. We are also told that less than half the miners in the country are unionized and that 1,500 black lung victims die every year.

With two films like *Norma Rae* and *Harlan County, U.S.A.* in the cinematic background, these filmmakers had a lot of nerve. But they also had Holly Hunter, who is (as she is so often) convincing and charismatic, even when she has to say such things as "Nothing ever bothers me." Less compelling is the United Mine Workers organizer, played by the Swedish Stellan Skarsgård, who tells the Eastern Kentuckians that he comes from two generations of Polish miners. Presumably this ancestry enables him to pass, despite his accent; of course the miners would be too polite to tell him that all outsiders have funny accents anyway.

Skarsgård's Warren Jakopovich has trouble delivering such lines as "The UMW is the first true rank-and-file union in this country." Even for a post–Tony Boyle organizer, that's a mouthful. And not quite true, for one of the telling aspects of Barbara Kopple's rendition of the strike is that it is played out with the collapse of the old UMW and the rise of the miners' reform movement during the Brookside strike.

Skarsgård cannot be blamed for the rush in which the screenwriters got the strike going: at first it seems that Ruby's husband, Silas, is helping to form a union, but the next moment they are at a union meeting where the only item of business is a strike vote. Five minutes later, after promises of weekly strike pay, the meeting is over and the struggle is on.

As perhaps usual with films about poor workers, they seem remarkably tidy and well outfitted, and Holly Hunter resists wearing a form-fitting T-shirt until late in the film (and then only briefly). Despite Showtime's careful warning about V, AL, BN, and AC (violence, adult language, brief nudity, and adult content), this film is remarkably clean-cut, considering that there are a handful of violent actions on the picket line.

This is a very solid film, and it never bothered me for a minute that it was filmed entirely in Toronto. I hope the film crew was unionized. But don't ask Barbara Kopple if she liked it: she would regard it as a discussion of stolen property.

See also: *Harlan County, U.S.A.*
Availability: Easy; DVD.

Further reading

Wertheimer, Ron. "Coal Mine Can't Beat a Strong Woman." *New York Times*, 2 June 2000, B25. The reviewer finds this a "cardboard morality tale"—"more civics lesson than drama"—but he praises Hunter's handling of this somewhat predictable role.
Web site:
⟨www.umwa.org⟩ The official site of the United Mine Workers of America.

Harry Bridges: A Man and His Union

Workers of the docks, unite!

1992, 58 mins.
Director: Berry Minott
Traditional documentary
PRINCIPAL FIGURES
Harry Bridges, founding president,
  International Longshoremen's and
  Warehousemen's Union (ILWU)
James Landis, judge, 1940 deportation trial
Pat Tobin and Bill Bailey, retired
  longshoremen
Tommy Trask, International VP, Hawaii
  ILWU
Sidney Roger, former editor, ILWU
  newspaper
Wayne Horvitz, former VP, Matson
  Navigation Company
Charles Larrowe, Bridges' unauthorized
  biographer
Studs Terkel, narrator

Harry Bridges, the long-standing president and radical voice of the West Coast longshoremen's union, appears at the beginning of this film in an interview late in his life, commenting on the charge that his union was always left-wing. He quotes Marx—"Workers of the world, unite! You have nothing to lose but your chains"—and says, in the Australian accent of his youth, which is barely modified by his fifty years in the United States, "and that's as good as the day it was said."

His trials and tribulations with the U.S. government, which spent millions of dollars and many years trying to prove he was a Communist or "affiliated" with the Communist Party, make up almost half the story of his life. The other half goes a long way in explaining why the government pursued him so relentlessly: he was a tremendously successful radical leader of one of the most powerful unions in the country, and he helped to lead one of the momentous events in labor history—the 1934 San Francisco General Strike.

The film does not hold back on some of the most controversial moments in Bridges' career—his positions in favor of automation (container shipping) and the "steady man" (the company would hire such a man on a continuing basis, thereby taking the process of his hiring away from the union hall), not to mention touches of paranoia in the end. One would have thought that a film that documents forty years of government harassment and persecution would have gone a little easier on a man who thought people were out to get him.

The government could never deport or convict this charismatic leader. Move out of the way, mate!

See also: *Canada's Sweetheart*.
Availability: Selected collections; California
  Newsreel.

Further reading

Bruno, Robert. "Harry Bridges: A Man and His
  Union." *Cineaste* 21 (1995): 48–49. A very posi-
  tive review, with some reservations about the
  film's handling of the end of Bridges's career.
Kimeldorf, Howard. *Reds or Rackets? The Making
  of Radical and Conservative Unions on the
  Waterfront*. Berkeley: University of California
  Press, 1988. A convincing survey of the differ-
  ences between East and West Coast longshoremen's history.
Larrowe, Charles P. *Harry Bridges: The Rise and
  Fall of Radical Labor in the United States*. New
  York: Lawrence Hill, 1972. An unauthorized
  biography made with the cooperation of
  Bridges's union staff (which Bridges did not
  discourage).
Ward, Estolu E. *Harry Bridges on Trial*. New York:
  Modern Age Books, 1940. An extensive account
  of Bridges's first deportation trial, which the
  author argues represented a conspiracy against
  the CIO and the radical labor movement.

Harvest of Shame

A classic of investigative journalism

1960, 53 mins., B&W
Director: Palmer Williams
TV documentary

Edward R. Murrow, correspondent

David Lowe, interviewer

James Mitchell, secretary of labor

Charles Schulman, president, American Farm Bureau

Rev. Michael Cassidy, minister to the migrant workers

Charles Goodlett, chief of police, Belle Glade, Florida

The Parson and Roach families, Irene King, Joseph Woods, and Mrs. Dobie, migrant workers

Norman Hall and Ed King, crew leaders

Howard Jones, farmer

Sen. Harrison Williams, chair, Committee on Migrant Labor

Howard Van Smith, reporter, *Miami News*

Julian Griggs, chaplain to migrant workers

CBS aired this documentary on prime time on the day after Thanksgiving 1960, making it the earliest documentary about the horrible conditions of the American migrant worker to reach a mass audience. Part of Edward R. Murrow and Fred Friendly's justifiably famous TV series *CBS Reports*, which appeared from the mid-1950s through the 1960s, it is Murrow's best work. Its theme music was from Aaron Copeland's *Appalachian Spring*, specifically the motif based on the Shaker hymn "'Tis a gift to be simple, / 'Tis a gift to be free."

This documentary tells a story that is far different from that of the self-sufficient Shaker farmers of the nineteenth century. It is structured as a journey of typical farm workers as they leave their winter shacks in Belle Glade, Florida, and journey north to pick the crops of the "best-fed nation in the world." After a series of interviews with migrant workers, a rarely seen farmer or two, and some public figures, Murrow follows the workers back to Florida.

At various stops in this journey Murrow includes sequences of whole families working in the fields. His voice–over narrative concentrates on a heartbreaking set of statistics, while his crew's cameras offer details of constant privation. So many of his shots recall, certainly deliberately and explicitly, the journey of the Joad family in Steinbeck's *Grapes of Wrath* that we should realize that the Murrow team was following the director John Ford's fictional journey twenty years later.

Murrow's documentary begins with a startling sequence: a town square, Third World in appearance, where numerous black workers and families are milling about. Murrow says: "This scene is not taking place in the Congo. It has nothing to do with Johannesburg or Capetown. It is not Nyasaland [Malawi] or Nigeria. This is Florida. These are citizens of the United States, 1960. This is a shape-up for migrant workers." Murrow also quotes a

Edward R. Murrow reports from a field in *Harvest of Shame*.

farmer: "We used to own our slaves. Now we just rent them."

A mark of Murrow and David Lowe's style is the extended comparison: the legally sanctioned but miserable conditions of the laborers are not as good as those of the fruit and other produce they pick (they must be kept fresh), cattle (they must have fresh water), or thoroughbred horses at a race track (they have more living space).

One of the last interviews is with Julian Griggs, a chaplain to the migrants. He looks like the prototype for the activists in the Poverty Program or Student Nonviolent Coordinating Committee. Griggs asks: "Is it possible to have love without justice?" He recommends not charity but the elimination of poverty as the one goal worth pursuing. With a precision that he would have relished, Murrow's documentary appeared in 1960 at the beginning of a decade that promised but did not always deliver love and justice to the farm workers of America.

Murrow's closing speech just before his signature sign-off was unusual fare for TV watchers: "The people you have seen have the strength to harvest your fruit and vegetables. They do not have the strength to influence legislation. Maybe we do. Good night, and good luck."

A sad footnote to the documentary and Murrow's career came after Murrow had joined Kennedy's New Frontier as head of the U.S. Information Agency. The British Broadcasting Corporation (BBC) had purchased *Harvest of Shame* and planned to run it. Florida politicians leaned on Kennedy's press secretary, Pierre Salinger, who in turn asked Murrow to call his contacts at the BBC to ask if the show that was so embarrassing to the United States—and therefore potentially very useful for the Soviet propaganda machine—would be withheld. Accounts differ about how enthusiastic Murrow was about doing this, but enough of the story leaked that the man who broadcast from London during World War II such stirring and heartfelt radio reports as his description of the dead and dying at Buchenwald was felt to have compromised his legendary integrity.

A CBS producer recalled that it was "sort of like, God had stubbed his toe." Although Murrow tried to resign, Kennedy wouldn't let him, and the show was broadcast as scheduled.

Murrow's views were invariably liberal and almost always progressive, however. He was a rare and major public opponent of McCarthyism as early as 1954, when he broadcast in *See It Now*, his news series, "The Case against Milo Raulovich, A0589839" (about an officer the McCarthyites tried to force out of the Air Force Reserves) as well as another major program that focused on McCarthy's transparent lies. A. M. Sperber reported that someone, before *Harvest of Shame*, had asked Murrow why he was so pro-union. He replied: "Because I hoed corn in a blazing sun." He might have added: Because I worked with the Wobblies in the lumber camps of the Northwest. Both experiences had long-term effects on his attitudes toward the working class.

Murrow's documentary was the standard by which later commentators measured their investigations. Seven years later Mort Silverstein's documentary *What Harvest for the Reaper?* appeared on National Educational Television (NET). The filmmakers visited a Long Island camp where workers were recruited from Arkansas. "I was struck," Silverstein concluded, "by the fact that in spite of the furor over [*Harvest of Shame*], so little had changed in the intervening years" (quoted in Rosenthal).

In 1990, PBS's *Frontline* paid a thirty-year anniversary visit to the same Florida city Murrow had visited. *New Harvest, Old Shame* (directed by Hector Galan) intercuts Murrow's old footage with the contemporary. Unfortunately, the story is the same, except Haitians have gradually replaced African Americans at the bottom of the migrant ladder. "For migrant farm workers," the documentary states, "time has stood still."

See also: *Legacy of Shame; New Harvest, Old Shame*.

Availability: Selected collections; Ambrose Video (videocassette no. 4 of *Good Night and Good Luck: The Edward R. Murrow Television Collection*).

Further reading

Emmet, Herman LeRoy. *Fruit Tramps: A Family of Migrant Farmworkers*. Albuquerque: University of New Mexico Press, 1989. A striking photographic album whose 1980s images eerily recall the great Depression and Dust Bowl photographs.

Persico, Joseph E. *Edward R. Murrow: An American Original*. New York: McGraw-Hill, 1988. A balanced biography, including the transcripts of two of his famous radio broadcasts.

Sonneman, Toby F., and Rick Steigmeyer. *Fruit Fields in My Blood: Oakie Migrants in the West*. Moscow: University of Idaho Press, 1982. The authors were students who became migrant workers (for fifteen years) and organizers (Migrant Workers of America) as they documented this recurring theme: "We're a part of feeding the people who have this contempt for us."

Sperber, A. M. *Edward R. Murrow: His Life and Times*. New York: Freundlich, 1986. A good survey of his career, including the BBC incident.

Heroes for Sale

Reds to bait

1933, 71 mins., B&W
Director: William A. Wellman
Screenplay: Robert Lord and Wilson Mizner
CAST
Tom Holmes = Richard Barthelmess
Ruth Holmes = Loretta Young
Mary Dennis = Aline MacMahon
Max = Robert Barrat
Pa Dennis = Charley Grapewin

Another entry in Ted Turner's M-G-M/UA Forbidden Hollywood series, *Heroes for Sale* deserves all the kudos offered by the film chronicler Leonard Maltin, who brackets the videocassette release with his enthusiastic commentary about the film's daring and other strengths.

Even with an unrealistic nod to Roosevelt's New Deal, the film retains a hard edge of Depression realism and topicality. At least three of the big issues of the 1930s are here—unemployment (especially), lack of respect for veterans, and Red-baiting. First National Pictures was the nominal producer, but by 1933 it was an integral part of Warner Brothers' working-class orientation, including a large serving of Depression fantasy typical of *Gold Diggers of 1933*: at one point a restaurant with a too-friendly owner becomes an endowed soup kitchen for the masses without any public money at all.

The plot is not credible but one might say the same of *I Am a Fugitive from a Chain Gang* (and one would be wrong). Tom Holmes fights for his country but becomes addicted to a painkiller while recovering in a German hospital. When he returns home, his addiction forces him out onto the open road. With luck and some native smarts, he becomes first a laundry truck driver and then a salesman for the company. When one of his ideas for innovation strikes it big, he seems made for life. But his past reputation catches up with him and things get bad again.

Wellman's best-known works are probably *Public Enemy* (1931), which established James Cagney's reputation as one of the tough city guys, and *The Ox-Bow Incident* (1943), an adaptation of Walter Van Tilberg Clark's disturbing tale of lynching. *Heroes for Sale* is more than a little contrived and its hero (antihero, really) more than a little saintly. Wellman was, after all, a studio filmmaker who had to make his films mostly to order: *Heroes for Sale* was one of seven he made in 1933.

See also: *Gold Diggers of 1933*; *I Am a Fugitive from a Chain Gang*.
Availability: Selected collections.

Further reading

"Heroes for Sale." *Variety*, 1 August 1933. Doubts that the film will have much appeal, but admits that "this attempted satire on unemployment conditions just prior to the Roosevelt election" has been "picked for its topical importance."

Nugent, Frank. "Pity the Hero." *New York Times*, 22 July 1933, 14. The two plots don't work well together, but the reviewer likes Max, the Communist turned capitalist.

🔊

Hester Street

"For what purpose are you bringing this woman in?"

1975, 92 mins., B&W, PG
Director: Joan Micklin Silver
Screenplay: Joan Micklin Silver, from Abraham Cahan's novel *Yekl*
CAST
Jake = Steven Keats
Gitl = Carol Kane
Bernstein = Mel Howard
Mamie = Dorrie Kavanaugh
Mrs. Kavarsky = Doris Roberts
Joe Peltner = Stephen Strimpell
Fanny = Lauren Frost
Joey = Paul Freedman
Rabbi = Zvee Scooler
Rabbi's Wife = Eda Reiss Merin

Hester Street provides the dramatic background so sorely missed in a film such as *The Triangle Factory Fire Scandal*; that is, how immigrants adapted—or struggled against adapting—in their new homes and jobs on New York's Lower East Side. Jake has preceded his wife from Russia. He takes a tailoring job, resolves to become an American, and adds a girlfriend. When Gitl, his wife, finally arrives, he realizes that she is so . . . foreign.

At the immigration interview, an officer (with a leer) asks Jake, "For what purpose are you bringing this woman in?" His reply, "For the purpose she's my wife," turns out to be, on his part, a falsehood, since he clearly doesn't want her anymore. She continues to wear the dresses, follow the customs, and use the language of the Old Country, as they resume housekeeping with their child and a lodger, Bernstein, a former rabbinical student. This student, now a tailor, is constantly writing commentaries on the Talmud, except when he's staring at Gitl.

Jake and Gitl cannot become Americans together. But separately, yes. Along the way the work conditions of immigrants are dramatized, sometimes with great irony. When Bernstein can't get the hang of his job at a tailoring shop, the owner says, "The peddler becomes the boss and the Yeshiva student sits by the sewing machine. Some country."

"Some country" is, several reviewers complained, too artfully composed with peddlers' barrows and clothing racks. Take a few carts out here and there and you (unfortunately) have space for all the dancers in *Newsies* (which takes place, in theory, just three years later, in 1899). And without Carol Kane's convincing acting and the tailors hard at work, we might have been stuck with another *Yentl* (directed by and for Barbra Streisand) before its time.

Yekl was published in 1896 with the subtitle *A Tale of the New York Ghetto*. Abraham Cahan's work had been promoted by the mainstream writer William Dean Howells, who praised Cahan as a "new star of realism." Cahan was a socialist who began his career writing a column, "The Proletarian Preacher," a mixture of Old Country folklore and Marxist ideas, for the Yiddish newspaper of the United Hebrew Trades organization of workers. He published his most successful novel, *The Rise of David Levinsky*, in 1917, in which an immigrant worker leaves the ranks of his fellow immigrants to become a dress manufacturer. Cahan was a forerunner of the social-realist writers of the Depression. *Hester Street* is perhaps a too-sanitized introduction to his work.

See also: *The Triangle Factory Fire Scandal; The Inheritance; Newsies.*
Availability: Easy.

Further reading

Eder, Richard. "Hester Street." *New York Times*, 20 October 1975, 44. For this reviewer, the film is a "mostly unconditionally happy achievement."
Goodman, Walter. " 'Hester Street'—Overpraised and Overdone." *New York Times*, 2 November 1975, II.15. A grouchy reviewer accuses the

other reviewers who liked the film of being soft on Jewish women filmmakers.

Howe, Irving. *The World of Our Fathers*. New York: Harcourt Brace Jovanovich, 1976. A detailed re-creation of the Jewish immigrant world.

Gabriel Miller, *Screening the Novel*. New York: Ungar, 1980. Includes a chapter with an extended discussion of both the film and the source novel.

High Hopes

Low expectations

1988, 110 mins., UK
Director: Mike Leigh
Screenplay: Mike Leigh
CAST
Cyril Bender = Philip Davis
Shirley = Ruth Sheen
Mrs. Bender = Edna Doré
Martin Burke = Philip Jackson
Valerie Burke = Heather Tobias
Laetitia Boothe-Braine = Lesley Manville
Rupert Boothe-Braine = David Bamber

Although Mike Leigh and Ken Loach are often linked in discussions of contemporary British cinema, especially when social-realist or political filmmaking is on the agenda, they are nonetheless quite distinct in overall vision. Loach's films tend to be explicitly political, tied to specific political and economic moments in British history and contemporary society, whereas Leigh's films could be characterized as socially obsessed or about class anxiety. His characters tend to be on the cusp of two classes, lower middle or upper working class.

Since eight films by Loach are included in this guide, it would be churlish not to include at least one by Mike Leigh. *High Hopes* is the film that comes closest to an anti-Thatcher economic comedy, with three sets of couples and an aged parent all divided across class lines.

Cyril makes his living as a motorcycle messenger; he and his wife, Shirley, are professed Marxists but are mostly consumed by worries about getting pregnant and taking care of Cyril's mom, Mrs. Bender, who lives in a council house in a terrace rapidly becoming gentrified. Cyril's sister, Valerie, is married to the owner of a used car business and is screechingly nouveau riche, at least at her level of income. The final couple, the Boothe-Braines, are Mrs. Bender's neighbors, an extraordinarily pompous pair who are so broad a caricature of upper-class twitness that one has to hold one's applause for Leigh's audacity.

Cyril and Shirley at one point visit Marx's grave in Highgate Cemetery and contemplate the unlikeliness of change in society. They also visit a friend whose left politics are balmy. Cyril's cynical viewpoint seems to dominate the film: how could we even think of bringing children into this awful world? That Leigh could make the answer to this question a comedy is quite a feat.

See also: *Riff-Raff*.
Availability: Selected collections.

Further reading

Ebert, Roger. "High Hopes." *Chicago Sun-Times*, 18 April 1989. "Leigh is a legendary figure in modern British theater for his plays and television films that mercilessly dissect the British class system, using as their weapon the one emotion the British fear most, embarrassment."

Hill, John. *British Cinema in the 1980s*. New York: Oxford University Press, 1999. Hill's chapter on Leigh's film and Loach's *Riff-Raff* analyzes them as the quintessential anti-Thatcher films of the 1980s.

Quart, Leonard, and Ray Carney. *The Films of Mike Leigh: Embracing the World*. Cambridge: Cambridge University Press, 2000. A very thorough survey of Leigh's career.

Hoffa

The One Big Teamster

1992, 110 mins., R
Director: Danny DeVito
Screenplay: David Mamet

Jimmy Hoffa = Jack Nicholson
Bobby Ciaro = Danny DeVito
Billy Flynn = Robert Prosky
Carol D'Allesandro = Armand Assante
Frank Fitzsimmons = J. T. Walsh
Robert Kennedy = Kevin Anderson

Hoffa was the third in an ambitious series of Hollywood revisionist epics about the 1960s that attempted to do for organized labor what Oliver Stone's *JFK* did for the Kennedy assassination and Spike Lee's *Malcolm X* did for the history of black militancy. All three share the virtue (or the vice) of focusing on a public figure whose biography (or at least some of its major facts) still remains controversial. All three films were greeted with mixed critical and popular receptions, primarily because they could not win a consensus even for the "facts."

But when history deals a complicated hand and then kills off the players one by one, it is hard to believe *everything* the remaining card sharks have to say. The Kennedys are a marking point for the other two films. Malcolm's fall from Muslim grace accelerated when he said that Kennedy's assassination was a case of the "chickens coming home to roost," while Hoffa was hounded unmercifully by the Kennedys in what he regarded as a class war against him and his fellow unionists.

Probably Hoffa's most important contribution to the labor movement, his National Master Freight Agreement of 1964, which resulted in uniform wages and benefits across the country, is unfortunately not considered as important in this film as the visual spectacle—telephoto shots, especially—of clashing armies of workers and thugs. (Or are they workers and scabs? It's impossible to tell.) Danny DeVito's and David Mamet's sympathies are clearly with Hoffa, however: "He did what he had to do," the ad campaign says, and what he had to do, according to the film, was cozy up to some mobsters and ruthlessly fight the aristocratic Kennedys.

In a London interview (Grant), DeVito spelled out his interpretation of Hoffa: "Yes, he was involved with gangsters. Yes, he was a true American hero. Yes, he borrowed from the union pension fund and loaned money to mobsters. . . . He was good with his fists but better with his tongue. There was never a negotiator like him."

The end of Hoffa's career is so well known that DeVito sails through it after borrowing one dramatic sequence from Sam Peckinpah's *Convoy*. As Hoffa is hustled off to prison, his numerous rank-and-file supporters line the road to the prison with their big rigs and give him a salute of their mighty horns.

The frame story for the film is not daring cinematically, but it is valuable in emphasizing the mystery of Hoffa's disappearance from history's stage. We begin and end with—and cut back to a number of times— Hoffa and his long-standing lieutenant, played by DeVito, waiting forever for Hoffa's mob contact to show up. The film— and perhaps real life—makes it reasonably clear how risky this idea of a meeting was, since Hoffa said he would "do what he had to do" to get back the presidency he believed was stolen by Frank Fitzsimmons in collusion with the Nixon administration.

To remind us of one of the real villains of the piece, Hoffa is reading Bobby Kennedy's *The Enemy Within* as he passes the time in his car. Hoffa and Ciaro are assassinated and then taken away, car and all, inside—heavy irony here—a long-haul truck. Hoffa's actual car did surface later. Hoffa never did.

See also: *Bloodfeud; F.I.S.T.; Jimmy Hoffa; Power.*
Availability: Easy.

Further reading

Dowell, Pat. "What Happened to 'Hoffa'?" *In These Times,* 11 January 1993, 30–31. The film "framed Hoffa as the latest Hollywood cliché, as another American dreamer gone astray . . . and . . . depicted his rise and fall without a context to give it meaning."

Franco, Joseph, and Richard Hammer. *Hoffa's Man.* Englewood Cliffs, N.J.: Prentice-Hall, 1987. A good trashy read, this inside-the-world-of-hoodlums book nonetheless gives one of

Hoffa's boys a chance to tell some of the Hoffa legends.

Grant, Steve. "Jimmy Riddle." *Time Out,* 10–17 March 1993, 20–22. An interview with DeVito in London about his views on Hoffa.

Hoffa, Jimmy. *Hoffa: The Real Story.* New York: Stein & Day, 1972. Hoffa's opinions, "as told to" Oscar Fraley.

Kennedy, Robert F. *The Enemy Within.* New York: Harper & Row, 1960. The enemy without is communism, but the enemy within is Hoffa, according to the chief counsel of the Senate Select Committee on Improper Activities in the Labor or Management Field.

Raskin, A. H. "Was Jimmy Hoffa a Hood? Or Was He Robin Hood?" *New York Times,* 20 December 1992, IV.18. A survey of the film's portrayal of Hoffa's career.

Russell, Thaddeus. *Out of the Jungle: Jimmy Hoffa and the Remaking of the American Working Class.* New York: Knopf, 2001. A revisionist and fascinating study of Hoffa, who achieved so much, Russell argues, because of his struggles with other unions.

Sloan, Arthur. *Hoffa.* Cambridge: MIT Press, 1992. The definitive academic biography to date.

⌖

Homecoming

"Grab this land! Take it, hold it . . . and pass it on!"—Toni Morrison, *Song of Solomon*

1995, 56 mins.
Director: Charlene Gilbert
Traditional documentary
PRINCIPAL FIGURES
Charlene Gilbert, filmmaker
Charles S. Dutton, narrator
Toni Morrison, novelist, author of *Song of Solomon*
August Wilson, playwright
Marsha Darling, professor
Lynmore James, farmer

Sometimes I am Haunted by Red Dirt and Clay, the subtitle of this remarkable documentary of the relationship of African Americans and the land, reveals some of the bittersweet memories of many contemporary blacks whose families no longer own the land on which they were raised.

This film will explain the somewhat contradictory and tension-filled relationship between the currently urban-based population of African Americans and their roots in the rural South. The nostalgia for land was real enough for Malcolm X, who argued that "land is the basis of all independence. Land is the basis of freedom, justice, and equality."

Many are the ways black farmers were deprived of the land they held on to despite the failure of the promise of "forty acres and a mule" after the Civil War and the Jim Crow laws enacted after the failure of Reconstruction in 1877. The statistics are startling: between 1910 and 1993 African American landownership fell 96 percent; at the beginning of the century one million black farmers worked the land, but today the figure is close to 18,000.

The establishment and dispossession of black landowners came in waves. The Freedmen's Bureau distributed land to freed slaves during Reconstruction; Jim Crow laws, the Klan, and the return of antebellum owners wiped out a lot of those gains. The Farm Security Administration captured some of the loan money of the New Deal for black farmers, but this success was short-lived. During this period and years later, rural and county political structures favored the legal stripping of land through buyouts of heirs, denial of loans to any farmers active in the civil rights movement, and even discrimination through the U.S. Department of Agriculture.

Legal remedies were few and often too late. A class-action suit filed against the U.S. Department of Agriculture in 1996 was settled three years later, with awards of $50,000 going to black farmers, many of whom had already lost their farms. The Land Loss Prevention Project filed another class-action suit in 1999 for further remedies.

Charlene Gilbert's film records this long and sad history with great clarity, never letting the horror of statistical fact diminish the human story involved. There have been films that look at black tenant farmers (*Roll the Union On* and *Sounder*), but this may be the only film that records the crucial and short-lived phenomenon of black ownership of the land. Gilbert traces her own roots to such a farm in Montezuma, Georgia.

See also: *Freedom Road; Sounder*.
Availability: Selected collections; California Newsreel.

Further reading

Darling, Marsha. "Land Ownership, Black." *Encyclopedia of Southern Culture,* ed. Charles R. Wilson and William Ferris, 168–170. Chapel Hill: University of North Carolina Press, 1989. A short but excellent overview.

Du Bois, W. E. B. *Black Reconstruction in America, 1860–1880*. New York: Atheneum, 1969. The landmark study of the successes and betrayals of Reconstruction in the South.

Schweninger, Loren. *Black Property Owners in the South, 1790–1915*. Urbana: University of Illinois Press, 1990. An extensive study of census records, local tax records, and other manuscripts to determine the ownership of land by free blacks at the beginning of the Civil War and afterward; argues for her approach to measure the "efforts of Negroes to enter the mainstream of America by becoming property owners."

Web sites:

⟨www.coax.net/people/lwf/bfaa.htm⟩ Site of the Black Farmers and Agriculturalists Association, with numerous articles and statements about their activities, including the Land Loss Prevention Project.

⟨www.federationsoutherncoop.com/index.html⟩ A rich and detailed site of the Federation of Southern Cooperatives Land Assistance Fund, "Fighting to Save Black-Owned Land since 1967."

⟨www.itvs.org/homecoming⟩ Official site of the film from one of its producers, Independent Television Service (ITVS). An incredibly rich site, with historical material, video clips from the film, contributions by famous and obscure participants in struggles over the ownership and use of land, and further resources for study.

How Green Was My Valley

Brigadoon for coal miners

1941, 118 mins., B&W
Director: John Ford
Screenplay: Philip Dunne, from Richard Llewellyn's novel of the same title

CAST
Mr. Morgan = Donald Crisp
Mr. Gruffydd = Walter Pidgeon
Huw = Roddy McDowall
Angharad = Maureen O'Hara
Bronwen = Anna Lee
Ianto = John Loder
Mrs. Morgan = Sara Allgood
Cyfartha = Barry Fitzgerald
Ivor = Patric Knowles
Mr. Jonas = Morton Lowry
Mr. Parry = Arthur Shields
Ceinwen = Ann Todd
Singing Welsh miners = Chorus of the Welsh Presbyterian Church of Los Angeles.

John Ford accepted the somewhat sentimental but captivating portrait of a relatively well off Welsh mining family at the end of the nineteenth century provided in Richard Llewellyn's best-seller. Family and community struggle over a variety of issues, especially the decision to form a miners' union (name not specified). The Morgans live well because they have five incomes from the mine (the father and the four sons), but gradually the mine owners cut wages until the sons (all good union men) disagree with their father over the need for a union, since he favors the old way of "speaking to the boss." Look for the startling speech on a snowy hill during a union meeting by Mrs. Morgan, who threatens to kill any miner who messes with her husband.

Numerous subplots involve the youngest son's delicate health and bookishness, Angharad's love life, and the stifling religion of the local chapel. Winner of multiple Academy Awards, this production helped Americans appreciate the eternally folksy Welsh, who usually break into song as they walk home from a hard day's work. Believe it or not, Barry Fitzgerald, Hollywood's favorite Irish drunk, plays a Welshman who loves to drink. Such was multiculturalism in the 1940s.

John Ford had finished *The Grapes of Wrath* the year before he made this film.

Both films celebrate family values in communities under attack by the forces of capitalism (agribusiness in *Grapes*). Ford's instinctive radicalism—the sons are clearly right to resist their father's stubborn acceptance of the paternalistic mine tradition—is constantly at war with his nostalgia—the desire to look back to a time when cooperation (and fathers) ruled the community.

The frame story opens with Huw as a man of 60 packing to leave the valley, which is framed by "stacks, cranes, and towering slag heaps"; this shot dissolves into an edenic view, only lightly scarred by a "small slag heap," with a colliery and a chapel, as Philip Dunne's screenplay closely follows the narrator of Llewellyn's best-selling novel.

The more politically charged material in the novel and the first script about workers seizing control of the mines was dropped in subsequent revisions because Darryl F. Zanuck, the head of the Twentieth Century–Fox studio, said that he'd be "damned . . . to go around making the employer class the out-and-out villains in this day and age" (quoted in Walsh).

See also: *The Corn Is Green; The Stars Look Down.*
Availability: Selected collections; DVD.

Further reading

Crowther, Bosley. "How Green Was My Valley." *New York Times,* 29 October 1941, 27. Crowther calls the film "a stunning masterpiece."

Dunne, Philip. "How Green Was My Valley." In *Twenty Best Film Plays*, ed. John Gassner and Dudley Nichols. 1943. New York: Garland, 1977. The screenplay.

Walsh, Francis R. "The Films We Never Saw: American Movies View Organized Labor, 1934–1954." *Labor History* 27 (1986): 564–80. An excellent discussion of the reduction in the story's militancy during script development.

↶
Human Resources

Inhuman products

1999, 100 mins., France, French, with English subtitles

Director: Laurent Cantet
Screenplay: Laurent Cantet and Gilles Marchand
CAST
Franck = Jalil Lespert
Father = Jean-Claude Vallod
Mother = Chantal Barré
CEO = Lucien Longueville
Mrs. Arnoux = Danielle Mélador
Head of Human Resources = Pascal Sémard

Human Resources focuses on the shifting relationships among workers, their union, and management, a subject that in recent years has dominated mainly British comedies. Viewers who know the popular British film *Brassed Off,* for example, which is in part the story of a working-class woman who becomes part of the managerial staff of the mine where her grandfather used to work, may see *Human Resources* as a French twist on similar material.

Franck has moved—via university—from his working-class roots to a job with the human resources department of the factory in Normandy his father has worked in for thirty years. His father is attached to his stamping-machine work in ways that make him a willing if not timid employee. Because of a mandated 35-hour workweek, his son suggests to his boss that they invite the workers to fill out a questionnaire, in part to make them feel wanted.

The union, led by Mrs. Arnoux, a militant who suspects an end run around its authority, objects, but the rank and file seem taken by the idea. Franck, to his horror, soon realizes that the input gathered will be used to downsize the workforce, including his father. Some of the older workers will get a pension, but not all. Franck's father, it turns out, is not really interested in a pension: it's his relation to a machine—doing, creating, working—that really matters to him.

When Franck finds out that he has been double-crossed by his CEO—or, in managerial terms, has not yet learned his lessons well—he joins the workers in a strike. Unfortunately, at first his father does not. In a horrifying scene at the very end, the son attacks his father verbally, saying that he is ashamed of his father's work, but even more tellingly he concludes that he is "ashamed of being ashamed."

To American eyes a French strike will seem remarkably civilized. Not only are there never any police—maybe the French police only rough up Parisians?—but the strikers set out picnic tables at the factory gates and enjoy the usual enticing al fresco meals.

Whereas *Brassed Off* was a comedy with a bite, most of this film is almost all serious business: Franck obviously feels sorry for his father but regards him nonetheless with some contempt. After all, Franck is no longer a worker: he's a sophisticated university graduate who sees the complexity of things. Laurent Cantet, the director, however, feels that the situation has a telling irony: "On the one hand there's the father, who fights so that his son will become the kind of ambitious go-getter he respectfully imagines executives to be. The wider the gap between him and his son, the happier he is. On the other hand there's Franck, the son upon whom all of the family's hope and pride have crystallized: he fights so that his father gets a hold of himself and conforms to the ideal of a model worker Franck dreams about."

For this factory-centered film that never lacks family and social drama, Cantet cast all nonprofessionals—except for Franck—recruiting them from unemployment lines and jobs that are the same as those they do in the film. Thus Arnoux, the strike leader, played by Danielle Mélador, is a trade union activist in real life, Franck's father is played by a man who has been a factory worker since he was 14, and so on. Cantet and the militant Mélador have used the feature film for agitprop purposes, talking to cinema audiences as a way of fostering the activism represented by the film's striking workers.

The critic Roger Ebert and others have celebrated this French film because "American films are hardly ever about work, especially hard work, factory work." Those viewers who are not intimidated by subtitles will be rewarded with an intense and satisfy-ing film and will agree with the director's desire: "I wanted to film in a factory because you almost never see factories in a movie" (interview with Miller).

Although Cantet's next film, *Time Out* (2001), was not filmed in a factory, its focus on the white-collar world—and its own tensions and shams—is of a piece with the management ethos satirized in *Human Resources*.

See also: *Blow for Blow*.
Availability: Easy.

Further reading

Catalogne, Isabel de. "A Conversation with Laurent Cantet." Shooting Gallery Film Series at ⟨www.film.sgfilmseries.com/press_human_prod.html⟩. An intensive interview, with Cantet's analysis of Franck: "He's a perfect poster boy for the kind of 'humane' capitalism he's been taught in business school, the hypocrisy of which he can't or won't see."

Ebert, Roger. "Human Resources." *Chicago Sun-Times*, 15 September 2000. A "valuable, heartbreaking film about the way [human] resources are plugged into a system, drained of their usefulness and discarded."

Holden, Stephen. "'Human Resources': A White-Collar Innocent in Blue-Collar Territory." *New York Times*, 5 April 2000. "As it burrows into its subject, this smart, coolheaded and ultimately wrenching film, directed by Laurent Cantet, explores class differences, corporate behavior, labor relations and father-son strife with an unusual depth and subtlety."

Hunter, Stephen. "'Human Resources': Pay and Suffering." *Washington Post*, 15 September 2000, C1. The film's "ultimate evocation of very messy labor troubles is particularly pungent."

Lane, Anthony. "Singin' Through the Pain." *New Yorker*, 25 September 2000, 100–101. The "movie has grab as well as grit," mainly because of the nonprofessionals and the location shooting at "a functioning factory."

Miller, Prairie. "Virtual Militancy: A Conversation with 'Human Resources' Filmmaker Laurent Cantet." World Socialist Web at ⟨www.wsws.org/articles/2000/may2000/laur-m05.shtml⟩, 5 May 2000. An excellent interview with the director: "I wanted to film in a factory because you almost never see factories in a movie."

Vincendeau, Ginette. "Human Resources." *Sight and Sound*, December 2000, 50. Applauds the film's social realism and satisfactory experimentation with nonprofessional actors to create "a refreshingly unusual picture of France and of French cinema."

Web site:
<www.afii.fr/France/DoingBusiness/Employment/?p=working_hours&1=en> Official site of Invest in France Agency, with extensive notes on the details of the 35-hour week.

~

Hungry Hill

Eats men

1947, 92 mins., UK, B&W
Director: Brian Desmond Hurst
Screenplay: Terence Young and Daphne Du Maurier, from the latter's novel of the same title
CAST
Fanny Rose Flower = Margaret Lockwood
Copper John Broderick = Cecil Parker
Wild Johnnie Broderick = Dermot Walsh
Henry Broderick = Michael Denison
Lady Broderick = Jean Simmons
Barbara Broderick = Barbara Waring
Hal Broderick = Dan O'Herlihy
Morty Donovan = Arthur Sinclair
Sam Donovan = Michael Golden

Hungry Hill is to labor films as a bodice-ripping romance is to a novel: we know the form is there but the upper-class fabric seems to get in the way. This tale of three generations of feuding upper- and working-class families in nineteenth-century Ireland is the novelist Daphne Du Maurier's Irish version of the Welsh *How Green Was My Valley,* except that the usual class antagonisms are supplemented by ethnic ones. We have British ownership of a mine in Ireland run by Cornish supervisors.

Two films really struggle for ascendancy here: an early heritage or costume drama, replete with love affairs, balls, and beautiful ladies in gowns, and a social-realist story of class and ethnic struggles. In the latter, Copper John Broderick earns his nickname by mining Hungry Hill, once owned a

century ago by the Irish Donovans, who bitterly resent the British occupation of their land.

The film, like its source novel, spans the century from 1820 to 1920, but its tone is set almost immediately by Morty Donovan's curse on Copper John for not asking the hill for "permission" to mine: "Your mine will lie in ruins and your house destroyed, but the hill will be standing to confound you." Donovan organizes a riotous demonstration to attack the mine when Copper John causes the death of a local man who had been stealing his copper.

Raymond Durgnat argues that the viewer inevitably sympathizes with the British upper class, especially since the Brodericks suffer great losses and yet must accept the mob that burns the buildings of the mine and causes the death of a Broderick son. *Captain Boycott,* on the other hand, tends to see the rebellious peasantry in a similar situation much more positively, especially when their leader figures out a better strategy than violence.

See also: *Captain Boycott.*
Availability: Selected collections.

Further reading

Du Maurier, Daphne. *Hungry Hill.* Garden City, N.Y.: Doubleday, Doran, 1944. The mistress of the modern romantic gothic (*Rebecca*) turns to a different scene in the source novel.
Durgnat, Raymond. *A Mirror for England.* New York: Praeger, 1971. Argues that *Hungry Hill* and similar films are a reactionary response to the Labour landslide vote at the end of World War II.

~

Hyenas

Pack of lies

1992, 113 mins., Senegal, in Wolof, with English subtitles
Director: Djibril Diop Mambéty
Screenplay: Djibril Diop Mambéty, from Friedrich Dürrenmatt's play *The Visit*

CAST
Linguere Ramatou = Ami Diakhate
Dramaan Drameh = Mansour Diouf
The Mayor = Mahouredia Gueye
The Teacher = Issa Ramagelissa Samb
Toko = Kaoru Egushi
Gaana = Djibril Diop Mambéty
Mrs. Drameh = Faly Gueye

Afro-pessimism is Mambéty's attitude, magic realism his style: the result has been a remarkable series of films that dramatize an Africa rushing toward Western materialism but destroying its soul in the process. How strange, then, was Mambéty's discovery of "his" story in Friedrich Dürrenmatt's legendary play *The Visit,* or more precisely in the film version with Ingrid Bergman released in 1964.

Adapting Dürrenmatt's play fairly closely has not caused—paradoxically—Mambéty to lose the distinctive Senegalese mood of his story. Dürrenmatt's original tale is remarkably intact: an incredibly rich woman, Linguere Ramatou, returns to the town of her birth—and, we eventually learn, her shame—and in revenge for vicious treatment by her former lover, Draman Drameh (he paid two other men to say they had slept with her), she promises to bankroll her economically depressed hometown if they will do just one little thing for her: kill her former lover. Of course they refuse, with high moral statements about the sanctity of life; of course they gradually give in as they are seduced by the consumer goods the visitor can produce for them.

Mambéty has explained that Ramatou represents a kind of symbolic return of the character Anta from his earlier film, *Touki-Bouki* (*The Hyena's Journey*). Anta and her lover, Mory, yearned to break away from the confines of their culture and escape to Paris, but Anta was forced in the end to make the trip by herself. Their dreams "made them feel like foreigners in their own country . . . so they were marginalized people." Both Draman Drameh and Ramatou, Mambéty asserts, are also marginalized people: in the end, they are of Colobane but not acceptable

to Colobane. The townspeople, dressed in rice bags, literally devour Draman Drameh like the hyenas they represent. After his disappearance the town itself disappears under the blade of the bulldozer: instead of the childhood home of the director, what will rise in its place (Senegalese audiences would know) is "the real-life Colobane, a notorious thieves' market on the edge of Dakar."

Even within the renaissance of African films, Mambéty's approach was unusual. Of course he adapted a modern Swiss play to African conditions. But more than that: "To make *Hyènes* even more continental, we borrowed elephants from the Masai of Kenya, hyenas from Uganda, and people from Senegal. And to make it global, we borrowed someone [Ramatou's bodyguard] from Japan, and carnival scenes from the annual Carnival of Humanity of the French Communist Party in France." Why? "My task was to identify the enemy of humankind: money, the International Monetary Fund, and the World Bank. I think my target is clear."

See also: *Le Franc; The Little Girl Who Sold the Sun.*

Availability: Selected collections; California Newsreel.

Further reading

Dürrenmatt, Friedrich. *The Visit.* 1956. Trans. Patrick Bowles. New York: Grove Press, 1962. The original play, with a helpful afterword by the playwright.

Givanni, June. "African Conversations." *Sight and Sound,* September 1995, 30–31. Good overview of Mambéty's career and his films.

Ousmane, Sembene. *God's Bits of Wood.* 1960. Trans. Francis Price. Oxford: Heinemann, 1970, 1986. This novel about the 1947–48 strike on the Dakar-Niger railway provides excellent background on French colonial control of francophone West Africa.

Pfaff, Françoise. *Twenty-five Black African Filmmakers.* New York: Greenwood Press, 1988. Another overview of Mambéty's career, with emphasis on his first major film, *Touki-Bouki.*

Seymour, Gene. *Newsday,* 3 October 1992, 19. "Funnier and warmer than Dürrenmatt ever dared to be—even with the tale's bleak, ominous edges still in evidence."

Stack, Peter. "African Parable of Greed." *San Francisco Chronicle*, 14 June 1995. Stresses Mambéty's vision of "the destruction of traditional values in Africa" by "European and American capitalism" in a remarkably beautiful and "funny, barbed parable."

Ukadike, N. Frank. *Black African Cinema*. Berkeley: University of California Press, 1994. Thorough survey of African cinema, with a section on Mambéty's career before *Hyenas*.

——. "The Hyena's Last Laugh: A Conversation with Djibril Diop Mambéty," *Transition* 78 (1999): 136–53. Extensive discussions of Mambéty's career and this film.

Web site:

⟨www.newsreel.org/topics/acine.htm⟩. Official site of California Newsreel's Library of African Film, with relevant essays and information.

Note: The film often goes by the French title, *Hyènes*.

I Am a Fugitive from a Chain Gang

"I steal"

1932, 76 or 93 mins., B&W
Director: Mervyn LeRoy
Screenplay: Howard J. Green and Brown Holmes, from Robert E. Burns's autobiography, *I Am a Fugitive from a Georgia Chain Gang*
CAST
James Allen = Paul Muni
Marie Woods = Glenda Farrell
Helen = Helen Vinson
Linda = Noel Francis
Pete = Preston Foster
Barney Sykes = Allen Jenkins
Judge = Berton Churchill
Bomber Wells = Edward Ellis
Warden = David Landau
Rev. Robert Clinton Allen = Hale Hamilton

This extremely popular Depression-era story, in both book and film versions, must have struck a number of people with fear: if a relatively middle-class person could get caught in this nightmare, maybe a lot of others, less fortunate or careful, might easily end up the same way. Jim Allen is framed for a $10 robbery and sent to a prison farm, where he endures the most degrading conditions imaginable. Like Tom Holmes in *Heroes for Sale*, released the following year, Jim is a World War I vet. He finally escapes and creates a new identity in Chicago as a businessman. Unfortunately a double-crossing wife sends him back to the chain gang, where his promised final three-month new sentence is a sham. He escapes again.

When Jim comes out of the shadows at the end of the film to meet his girlfriend, Helen, his startling speech tells the viewers that he is still out there somewhere: "I haven't escaped. They're still after me. They'll always be after me. I hide in rooms all day and travel by night. No friends. No rest. No peace. Keep moving. That's all that's left for me. Forgive me, Helen. I had to take a chance to see you tonight. Just to say good-bye." When Helen asks, "How do you live?" Jim replies, "I steal."

See also: *Heroes for Sale*
Availability: Easy.

Further reading

Burns, Robert E. *I Am a Fugitive from a Georgia Chain Gang!* 1932. Athens: University of Georgia Press, 1997. Reissue of Burns's harrowing story.

"Chain Gangs Are Halted in Alabama." *New York Times*, 21 June 1996, A8. That's 1996, not 1936, as Alabama ends its experiment of shackling inmates together.

O'Connor, John E., ed. *I Was a Fugitive from a Chain Gang*. Madison: University of Wisconsin Press, 1981. Essential companion book to the film: introductory essay, the script, and production memos and debates.

I Am Cuba

"You came to have fun"

1964 (1995), 141 mins., B&W, Soviet Union/Cuba, Russian and Spanish, with English subtitles

Director: Mikhail Kalatozov
Screenplay: Yevgeny Yevtushenko and
  Enrique Pineda Barnet
CAST
María/Betty = Luz María Collazo
Pedro = José Gallardo
Alberto = Sergio Corrieri
Pablo = Mario González Broche
Enrique = Raúl García
Gloria = Celia Rodríguez

Just seven years before *I Am Cuba* was filmed, Kalatozov was deservedly hailed worldwide for *The Cranes Are Flying*, his bittersweet and undoctrinaire mixture of Soviet romance and World War II hardship. Because of Cuban-American politics, however, it is as if *I Am Cuba* never existed, as it was not released in the United States for thirty years. Kalatozov's artistry is obvious: many dizzying shots, seemingly impossible camera angles, fluid long takes—all of these make *I Am Cuba* a tour de force. In fact, the later film is actually much more political than some of Kalatozov's usual Soviet films, alternating (as Ebert suggests) between "lyricism and propaganda." Nonetheless, one culture's propaganda can be another culture's social realism.

I Am Cuba, set in 1956, at the end of the Batista dictatorship, begins with two long takes, the second of which is worthy of comparison with Orson Welles's classic opening shot in *Touch of Evil*. The first has the camera skimming through a river lined with huts, going above and below obstacles seemingly at will. The second begins on one level of the roof of a Havana luxury hotel, ogles some bathing beauties, and then descends to another level with a swimming pool. The camera turns to a bar, follows a waitress serving drinks, and then literally follows a tourist who goes underwater. After surfacing, the camera goes to the edge of the hotel and drops slowly down the side.

The film offers two episodes of prerevolutionary oppression and two of revolutionary activism. In the first, a young woman is ashamed when her Cuban boyfriend discovers she has been a "hostess" to visiting Americans; in the second, a peasant's land is sold to the United Fruit Company. The third dramatizes a university student who resists a bunch of obnoxious American sailors but then sees his friends shot while distributing a pro-Castro leaflet. (This episode is marked by still another brilliant long take: the camera leaves the body of the slain student, climbs three stories, enters a cigar factory whose workers take out a revolutionary flag, and then returns to street level, where it joins the students' demonstration.) In the final episode, as Batista's planes bomb another peasant's family and land, he goes off to join the guerrillas. The film therefore dramatizes the recurring themes of Cuban revolutionary history: economic oppression, cultural degradation, and the city-countryside alliance.

See also: *Portrait of Teresa*.
Availability: Selected collections; DVD.

Further reading

Ebert, Roger. "I Am Cuba." *Chicago Sun-Times*, 8 December 1995. Very impressed by the technical aspects of the film, especially the camerawork, but finds the film's politics unconvincing: "Its depravities and imperialist Yankee misbehavior seem quaint. But as an example of lyrical black and white filmmaking, it is still stunning."

Rosenberg, Scott. "1964 Film 'I Am Cuba' Mixes Art and Propaganda." *San Francisco Examiner*, 14 April 1995. "Kalatozov seems to have invented a new genre: psychedelic socialist realism."

Thomas, Kevin. "'I Am Cuba': Epic of Poetry and Daring." *Los Angeles Times*, 21 July 1995. "A great poetic epic that blends the stirring visual daring of Russia's cinema of revolution with an intoxicating Latin beat."

Note: Also known as *Soy Cuba* and *Ya Kuba*.

I Can Get It for You Wholesale

Sooo?

1951, 90 mins.
Director: Michael Gordon

Screenplay: Abraham Polonsky and Vera Caspary, from Jerome Weidman's novel of the same title

CAST

Harriet = Susan Hayward
Teddy Sherman = Dan Dailey
Cooper = Sam Jaffe
Noble = George Sanders
Marge = Randy Stuart
Four Eyes = Marvin Kaplan

On the way to the film version of Jerome Weidman's novel about New York's garment district, a funny thing happened: his amoral hero became a heroine played by Susan Hayward. Some of the ruthlessness of the original novel is here, but it's tempered with a romance the viewer can spot coming across the runway. Harriet begins as a model but soon opens her own company after stealing two key employees from her former company—star salesman Teddy Sherman and supercompetent supervisor Cooper. Harriet is tough and succeeds in a difficult field. She is tempted to make expensive gowns for a posh store, but her partners disagree. She connives, the partners crumble, and all hell breaks loose.

Paul Buhle has characterized Polonsky's scripts as representing "the clearest concerted attack on the corrupting power of cash ever to come out of Hollywood." But it's not always cash that made Seventh Avenue hum. The film's ad copy read: "She made good—with a plunging neckline, and the morals of a tigress." It's a shame that this campy Hayward vehicle has been out of circulation for so long.

See also: *The Garment Jungle; Trouble on Fashion Avenue.*
Availability: Not.

Further reading

Buhle, Paul. "The Hollywood Left: Aesthetics and Politics." *New Left Review*, no. 212 (July–August 1995), 101–19. Discusses Polonsky's career in the context of other lefties in Hollywood; describes

Ruthless boss (Susan Hayward) in *I Can Get It for You Wholesale.*

Polonsky's film of the garment industry as "never been surpassed," with his "unerring eye for the details of a familiar subject, from the struggling small-time managers to the sexually leering buyers to the factory operatives."

"I Can Get It for You Wholesale." *New York Times*, 5 April 1951, 34. Complains that the major changes in character have reduced the punch of the novel.

"I Can Get It for You Wholesale." *Variety*, 14 March 1951. The reviewer concludes that "it has a soap-opera flavor that should appeal mostly to the femmes."

Weidman, Jerome. *I Can Get It for You Wholesale!* 1937. Numerous editions of this popular novel were published, but at least one of the paperback editions (Avon, 1949) anticipated the film's radical adjustments by cutting a couple of chapters and de-Semiticizing the text; that is, Anglicizing Jewish names (fall guy Meyer Babushkin becomes Michael Babbin), dropping some dirty words ("putz" becomes "dope"), and Americanizing our cad's mom (she makes pancakes instead of blintzes).

∽
Illusion Travels by Streetcar

And Reality pays the fare

1953, 90 mins., B&W, Mexico, in Spanish, with English subtitles
Director: Luis Buñuel
Screenplay: Mauricio de la Serna and José Revueltas
CAST
Lupita = Lilia Prado
Caireles = Carlos Navarro
Tarrajas = Fernando Solo
Pinillos = Agustín Isunza
The Professor = José Pidal

This wonderfully titled farce follows two tram company workers, on the verge of being fired for efficiency, who decide to take their favorite tram—old 333—out for a last spin when it is forced into early retirement. They have embarrassed the front office by repairing this tram ahead of schedule and apparently unnecessarily. The front office manager warns his workers: "Don't forget that excess tends to be prejudicial ... even when it concerns efficiency." Part of the charm of our two Mexican schlemiels is that they think their strategy for service is unique: we don't charge, they say, and we treat passengers with respect. Of course one of them is in love with the other's beauteous sister.

Like the old concept of a ship of fools, the tram gathers up all kinds of flotsam and jetsam from the streets of Mexico City as it runs (paradoxically, of course) freely on its rigid rail system. (Is this an allegory for anarchism?) Slaughterhouse workers, for example, heading home at night, finally get a tram ride; the city has never cared for them before. Everyone rides free, but suspicions abound: an American tourist says it "sounds like communism" to her. The tram passes riotous scenes here and there—one crowd is about to attack a bread store because of rising prices, while another group of locals attack the gangsters who are causing the shortage by hoarding grain in a warehouse.

This is a masterful comic deconstruction of capitalism, exploiting its contradictions and absurdities at every corner. Randall Conrad (in Mellen's *World of Luis Buñuel*) summarizes the implications of Buñuel's subversive plot: "What contradictions and what individual power relationships really make up a public company? Or by what chain of circumstance is there poverty in one part of town and a surplus of products in another?"

The answer, of course, is that capitalism sucks, but what fun, Buñuel knows, to watch it look silly in one absurd incident after another. Our heroes do not get caught, true love blossoms, workers get rides, the exploitive food chain gets briefly disrupted, chaos reigns at night, but the tram stays on its tracks, as a good piece of rolling capitalist infrastructure must. In short, illusion travels by streetcar.

See also: *Los olvidados.*
Availability: Selected collections.

Further reading
Durgnat, Raymond. *Luis Buñuel*. Berkeley: University of California Press, 1970. A survey of

Buñuel's career, with short but helpful entries on all his films included in this guide.

Mellen, Joan, ed. *The World of Luis Buñuel*. New York: Oxford University Press, 1978. An excellent collection of essays about the director's career.

~

I'm All Right, Jack

"Not to worry"

1959, 104 mins., B&W, UK
Director: John Boulting
Screenplay: Frank Harvey, John Boulting, and Alan Hackney, from Hackney's novel *Private Life*

CAST
Fred Kite = Peter Sellers
Stanley Windrush = Ian Carmichael
Major Hitchcock = Terry-Thomas
Aunt Dolly = Margaret Rutherford
Cox = Richard Attenborough
Bertram Tracepurcel = Dennis Price
Malcolm Muggeridge as himself

Since the British are reputed to be more obsessively class-conscious than Americans, this satire on both unions and management was understandably extremely popular in Great Britain when it was released. It had a strong following in the United States as well. Some of its humor remains on target, although the struggle for a factory owner's Oxford-educated nephew to become "one of the lads" on the shop floor seems a little unconvincing and forced. "Work to rule" is one of the satiric targets, as well as the reputed British shop stewards' worshipful attitude toward the Soviet Union, and there is no doubt that unions more than management suffer the more embarrassing jokes.

The British comic Ian Carmichael plays Stanley Windrush, a lovable upper-class twit who, having graduated from Oxford, figures to get a job in management in a factory where he has family connections. He ends up on the shop floor and is astonished to see that no union member actually does any work.

Despite boarding at union leader Fred Kite's apartment, Stanley soon makes it clear that he has no intention of accepting the union's lackadaisical attitude. British audiences would have been familiar with his type, as he and a number of other characters in this film had already appeared in an earlier film, *Private's Progress*, in 1956, the product of the same director, screenwriter, and novelist. Stanley, in the earlier film, had failed to receive an officer's commission and had to go into the army as a private.

After achieving the dubious status of a national hero because he refuses to give in to the union, Stanley ends up on a national TV talk show hosted by the then-popular professional curmudgeon and social critic Malcolm Muggeridge. Having achieved even greater cynicism, Stanley denounces both unions and employers. Muggeridge demands that he "stick to the facts." In response, Stanley throws up a satchel of cash given to him by his family as a bribe, saying that banknotes are the only "facts." He causes a riot in the studio as participants and studio audience alike scramble for the bills. The sound track song sums up the English character quaintly being satirized here: "Wherever you look, it's blow you, Jack, I'm all right."

Stanley's refusal to go along with this universal system of self-serving brings him to the ultimate utopian escape—a nudist colony where the only facts are naked and friendly. At this point we are a long way from industrial strife. The Sunnyglade Nudist Camp is a comic but farcical alternative to the smoky factories Stanley at first thought he was born to manage.

See also: *The Man in the White Suit*.
Availability: Selected collections.

Further reading

Hackney, Alan. *I'm All Right, Jack*. New York: Norton, 1959. The source novel was published in Britain as *Private Life*.

Hill, John. *Sex, Class, and Realism: British Cinema, 1956–1963*. London: British Film Institute, 1986. A thorough survey of Boulting's film and related British films of the period.

Richards, Jeffrey, and Anthony Aldgate. *British Cinema and Society, 1930–1970*. Totowa, N.J.: Barnes & Noble, 1983. Includes an excellent chapter on the film's social and historical context.

〜

The Inheritance

"Golden America, half dream, half nightmare"

1964, 55 mins., B&W
Director: Harold Mayer
Traditional documentary
PRINCIPAL VOICES
Robert Ryan, narrator
Franklin D. Roosevelt, president
Jane Addams, leader of Hull House and settlement house movement
John L. Lewis, president, United Mine Workers of America
Folksingers: Millard Lampell, Pete Seeger, Tom Paxton, Judy Collins, Barry Kornfeld, John R. Winn, and Carlo Totolo

The Inheritance is one of the early work-horses of labor history documentary: not flashy, a little slow, but able to go great distances with good staying power. It surveys the history of numerous immigrant groups as they created multicultural unions at the turn of the twentieth century. Since the film was sponsored by the Amalgamated Clothing Workers of America (ACWA, now part of UNITE!, the Union of Needle Trades, Indus-trial, and Textile Employees), its focus is the garment workers during the first thirty years of the union's struggle to become the chief democratic voice of the exploited ethnic Americans who made up the vast majority of its membership.

Unlike the more specialized and often more radical labor-history documentaries that followed it more than a decade later, *The Inheritance* relies on a combination of labor and standard history to tell its stories: thus a viewer fresh to this film will certainly learn about some of the essential elements of

twentieth-century labor history—sweat-shops, slum housing, child labor, the Bonus Army, the CIO, the Flint sit-down strike of 1937, the Republic Steel massacre of 1937, and labor's involvement in the civil rights movement. To set these important moments in historical context, the film relies on some canned footage about the Roaring Twenties, the Depression, and World War II.

Other perhaps less famous historical moments specific to the labor history of the garment workers also come through loud and clear: the murder of the Chicago garment worker Charles Lazinska by a clothing factory foreman during a 1910 strike; the murder of Ida Brayman, a 17-year-old garment worker, during a strike in Rochester, New York, in 1913; and the pioneering benefits of the ACWA (low-rent co-op housing, a members' bank, unemploy-ment insurance), which were the models for some of the New Deal's legislation.

The ACWA was founded by 75 percent of the delegates who walked out of a United Garment Workers convention in Nashville in 1914 because they regarded it as "fixed" against their interests. Unfortunately, only a little of this history is included in the film. The filmmakers concentrate instead on the feel of being part of the immigrant work-force—through stills, songs, and archival footage—until a composite picture of a union, a labor movement, and a people dedicated to social justice comes through. Millard Lampell's "Pass It On" was written for this film, underscoring the theme that "freedom is a hard-won thing."

The Inheritance was released during the civil rights era in the fiftieth anniversary year of the ACWA, and the film concludes with the sit-in movement in the South and the March on Washington. Regrettably, African Americans are not sufficiently rep-resented in this film until it deals with the 1960s. Individual blacks are in the crowds, but the special exclusions, difficulties, and arrangements of the American labor move-ment and its African American brothers and sisters are scant throughout most of the film.

See also: Hester Street; Norma Rae; The Triangle Factory Fire Scandal; Trouble on Fashion Avenue
Availability: Selected collections.

Further reading

Doherty, Jonathan L. *Women at Work: 153 Photographs by Lewis W. Hine.* New York: Dover, 1981. An excellent collection of vintage photographs of women in the needle trades both north and south.

Ross, Andrew, ed. *No Sweat: Fashion, Free Trade, and the Rights of Garment Workers.* London: Verso, 1997. Both a history of garment labor and an assessment of its contemporary global status.

Web site:

⟨www.uniteunion.org⟩ Official site of UNITE!, with union news, press releases, and sweatshop campaign information.

Note: A revised version, *The Dream Continues*, was released by UNITE! but is generally not represented in selected collections.

Inside Detroit

In need of retooling

1956, 82 mins., B&W
Director: Fred F. Sears
Screenplay: Robert E. Kent and James B. Gordon
CAST
Blair Vickers = Dennis O'Keefe
Gus Linden = Pat O'Brien
Joni Calvin = Tina Carver
Barbara Linden = Margaret Field
Gregg Linden = Mark Damon
Narrator: John Cameron Swayze

Frame stories with a documentary look and high seriousness were popular for serious Hollywood problem films in the 1950s. Nunnally Johnson's *Three Faces of Eve*, for example, has an introduction narrated by none other than Alistair Cooke, who pontificates briefly on matters psychological.

Another veteran TV broadcaster, John Cameron Swayze, takes his turn in *Inside Detroit* as the narrator who introduces the story of a gangster's attempt to take over a United Auto Workers (UAW) local. After a bomb hits the local's headquarters, President Vickers (Dennis O'Keefe, the ubiquitous good guy) begins to pursue gangster Gus Linden (Pat O'Brien, usually a good guy himself). Fortunately for the future of the UAW, Vickers romances the gangster's daughter and puts his moll into neutral.

This unlikely plot comes from the melodramatic film noir tradition, which features—as in better films such as *On the Waterfront*—dark streets, speeding cars, repentant bad guys, seductive gals, and sensitive leads, all filmed with numerous odd angles, shadows, and other cinematic techniques that are used to symbolize a world out of joint.

See also: *On the Waterfront; The Garment Jungle.*
Availability: Not.

Further reading

"Inside Detroit." *New York Times*, 28 January 1956, 10. Finds the film "low on gas."

Island in the Sun

Hot, but not that hot

1957, 119 mins.
Director: Robert Rossen
Screenplay: Alfred Hayes, from Alec Waugh's novel of the same title
CAST
Maxwell Fleury = James Mason
Mavis Norman = Joan Fontaine
Margot Seaton = Dorothy Dandridge
Jocelyn Fleury = Joan Collins
Hilary Carson = Michael Rennie
Mrs. Fleury = Diana Wynyard
David Boyeur = Harry Belafonte
Colonel Whittingham = John Williams
David Archer = John Justin

There seems to be no obvious reason for the fairly limited circulation of the videocassette of this megaproduction of Darryl F. Zanuck's Twentieth Century–Fox: it had Cinemascope, beautiful Barbados, and the popular singer and heartbreaker Harry Belafonte, not to mention the sinsational Joan Collins and Dorothy Dandridge, the "tragic mulatto," as Donald Bogle described her in 1988. The *New York Times* reviewer faulted it for being "dramatically murky and slow" despite the "clear and magnificent" scenery of the islands. The fact that it was about the economic and political consequences of colonialism did not rate a mention in 1957.

Everything about the plot made this a daring film for its day. Black performers were cast as the romantic interests of whites— Harry Belafonte as a labor leader and Joan Fontaine as a wealthy white woman make up one interracial couple, while Dorothy Dandridge as an island woman and John Justin as the governor's assistant make up the other.

A third couple *could* have been an interracial couple, but the fact that they are not provides one of the intriguing moments in the plot, not to mention in the audience's mind as it struggles to work out the fractional genealogy so important to the island's difficulties. (If Jocelyn's grandmother was three-quarters white and her grandfather all white, that makes her father one-sixteenth black and herself only one-thirty-second, assuming her mother is also all white, as she says she is . . . but it turns out her father is not really her mother's husband!)

This third couple finds bliss when it turns out they are free to marry, and since the couple's son was eventually going to sit in the House of Lords, it would hardly do if he were "black." The woman in this couple is played by Joan Collins and it may be the decay of *my* fractional brain but I saw Collins as being cast and made up as a Dorothy Dandridge look-alike who, after all, made a career of playing light-skinned black women. (See *Tamango*.)

Although none of these couples do much more than touch, touch was all that was necessary to make the traditionally southern nightmare of miscegenation seem relevant. A number of politicians in the South

Union leader (Harry Belafonte) and ex-lover (Dorothy Dandridge) in *Island in the Sun*.

threatened a boycott, but Zanuck announced that he would personally pay the fine of any theater operator who ran the film. Probably the successful receipts at all the other box offices made Zanuck feel comfortable enough to make such an offer.

Dandridge, who had received an Oscar nomination as best actress in *Carmen Jones*, her previous film, transforming Bizet's cigarette maker Carmen into a World War II parachute maker (Dorothy the Darner), had been teamed with the popular Harry Belafonte. This exciting but somewhat lurid production had little of the potential seriousness of *Island in the Sun*. The *Carmen* story, although updated and transformed by an all-black cast, nonetheless had none of the signally important issues of miscegenation and colonialism.

Although some critics find it particularly annoying that the interracial couples do no more than touch, the white-on-white hetero couples in 1950s films weren't doing much more than that either. The film signals in an appropriately repressed way that all these couples *are* probably having sex, although characteristically enough, only Joan Collins's character seems to be enjoying it (and combs her perfect hair afterward to show that *something* might have gotten mussed up).

In a strange way the film's reticence about sexuality ends up highlighting the more political aspects of colonialism. Belafonte's character clearly cannot continue his affair mainly for political reasons—his people will get the vote and he needs to be their leader, but not with a white descendant of plantation owners at his side. His gratuitous insult—that someday she'll end up calling him a "nigger"—is used to make them break up, not because it is likely to happen.

Another important subplot—directly and self-consciously lifted from Fedor Dostoevsky's novel *Crime and Punishment*—enables James Mason to suffer and chew a few palm trees along the way: it is usually the reason video guides such as Leonard Maltin's make fun of the film. More to the point might be a criticism of the film's use of plantation labor—picking bananas, cutting sugar cane—as background scenery: we know why this is a racist colonial society but not enough of the nuts and bolts of the economic engine comes through.

Director Rossen's other work has been mixed; some of his films were quite successful and critically acclaimed, such as *All the King's Men* (1949), another peckerwood classic about the rise of a populist/fascist, and *The Hustler* (1961), a very influential low-life epic with Paul Newman, Jackie Gleason, and George C. Scott as pool-hall denizens. He also made some very strange films, such as *Lilith*, with Jean Seberg and Warren Beatty as inmate and guardian, respectively, of a posh insane asylum.

Certainly *Island in the Sun* shares some of the intensity about politics and the passion of committed folk characteristic of some of his other films. Perhaps the film has been unjustly ignored, but not for want of trying: for years only video stores for British expatriates in Los Angeles seemed to have copies available for rental or sale. What did they know that we didn't?

See also: *Burn!*; *Tamango*.
Availability: Easy.

Further reading

Bogle, Donald. *Blacks in American Films and Television: An Encyclopedia*. New York: Garland, 1988. Finds Dorothy Dandridge "a fragile goddess whom the audience cannot help being drawn to," while the rest of the film is "tepid and dull."

———. *Toms, Coons, Mulattoes, Mammies, and Bucks: An Interpretive History of Blacks in American Films*. 3d. ed. New York: Continuum, 1994. Bogle devotes a section of his book to Dandridge, "the tragic mulatto," who (Bogle suggests) was "trapped . . . because of her color."

Crowther, Bosley. "Island in the Sun." *New York Times*, 13 June 1957, 37. Faults both the screenwriter and the director for failing to bring out the complexity of Waugh's novel.

Waugh, Alec. *The Sugar Islands: A Caribbean Travelogue*. New York: Farrar, Straus, 1949. A mixture of gossip and Brit talk about the colonies in a nonfiction book that covers some of the same issues as Waugh's later novel.

——. *Island in the Sun*. New York: Farrar, Straus & Cudahy, 1955. This best-selling novel of the islands offers an obsession not with sun (as one might expect) but with race, more precisely the fractions of race—who is one-quarter black and who is not.

↝

JFK, Hoffa, and the Mob

Jimmy does Dallas

1992, 60 mins.
Directors: Charles C. Stuart and John Baynard
TV documentary
PRINCIPAL FIGURES
Jimmy Hoffa, past president, International Brotherhood of Teamsters
Nick Pileggi, expert and writer on the Mafia
Robert Blakey, staff lawyer
Dan Moldea, author of *The Hoffa Wars*

Jimmy Hoffa both alive and dead has had numerous documentaries devoted to him and "his" Teamsters and quite a few feature films (at least four by my count). In recent years, his bloodfeud with the Kennedys in general and Bobby Kennedy in particular has become the staple of another set of documentaries related to the Kennedys' assassinations and conspiracy theories. This *Frontline* PBS film occasionally surfaces at chain video stores, but if you don't get the conspiracy here, you'll get it elsewhere.

Simply put, it is this: Hoffa exploited his connections with the Mafia (or they exploited their connection with him) and had JFK whacked. And maybe Bobby too, although everyone is less definite about that, since conspiracy is a lot more plausible with Lee Harvey Oswald and Jack Ruby than with Sirhan Sirhan.

Because Bobby forced J. Edgar Hoover to stop wearing tutus and forget about the commies and concentrate on organized crime; because Bobby hired at least twenty prosecutors to get Hoffa; because Hoffa knew Carlos Marcello and Sam Trafficante, two notorious New Orleans Mafiosi; because Jack Ruby met Trafficante in jail; because Hoffa was reported to have said when JFK was killed, "Did you hear the good news? They killed the son of a bitch"; and because Hoffa himself was whacked by the Mob or by rival Teamsters or both, Hoffa was involved in a conspiracy to kill Kennedys, one or more, depending on which version you subscribe to.

Now you know. Or would know if you watched this video or others like it. We have come a long way from labor history here, although Bobby Kennedy would not have thought so: for him, labor history was crime history. Hoffa maintained, for example (in the Hoffa tapes at Cornell University's School of Industrial and Labor Relations), that Bobby would call off his vendetta against Hoffa if Hoffa "allowed" Bobby to pick the next president of the Teamsters.

And one more thing: James P. Hoffa, Jimmy's son (now president of the Teamsters), told Dan Moldea that Jimmy Hoffa knew Jack Ruby. Q.E.D. Case closed.

On a more serious note: all the endless speculation about Jimmy Hoffa may blind some people to the important issues in Teamster leadership today. If crime history becomes labor history, then labor will be in danger of becoming history.

See also: *Jimmy Hoffa*.
Availability: Selected collections.

Further reading
James, Estelle. "Jimmy Hoffa: Labor Hero or Labor's Own Foe?" In *Labor Leaders in America*, ed. Melvyn Dubofsky and Warren van Tine. Carbondale: University of Southern Illinois Press, 1987. A remarkably balanced essay, perhaps in need of a major update, on Hoffa's legacy.
Moldea, Dan. *The Hoffa Wars: Teamsters, Rebels, Politicians, and the Mob*. 1974. Rev ed., New York: Charter, 1978. An exciting conspiracy read; where there's Jimmy, there must be Mafia—that would about sum it up.
Web sites:
⟨www.rust.net/~workers/news/hoffa.htm⟩ The latest on Hoffa, courtesy of the FBI (and the *Detroit Sunday Journal* in 1997).

⟨www.webcom.com/ctka/search_c.html⟩ Web site run by CTKA (Citizens for Truth about the Kennedy Assassination), "a political action group lobbying for full disclosure of all records relating to the assassination of President Kennedy." What could be clearer? They don't like Dan Moldea, either.

⤳

Jimmy Hoffa: The Man behind the Mystery

Pretty close?

1992, 50 mins.
Director: Meg M. Kruizenga
TV documentary
PRINCIPAL FIGURES
James Riddle Hoffa, Teamster leader
James P. Hoffa, his son
Barbara Ann Crater, his daughter
Charles "Chucky" O'Brien, his foster son
John F. Kennedy, as senator and president
Robert F. Kennedy, Senate committee attorney and attorney general
Frank Fitzsimmons, Hoffa's successor as Teamster president
Arthur Sloan, Hoffa's biographer

The ganging up of the two Kennedys on Hoffa is not a pretty sight, and it is at the center of this TV (Arts and Entertainment [A&E] Network) documentary released on video. At one point Jack and Bobby are sitting next to each other at the McClellan Committee's head table, taking turns having a go at Hoffa for his cunning unresponsiveness: "I never took the Fifth," he would later brag.

It is clear that Hoffa saw virtually everything as a class issue, between the working class, which he represented, and the upper class, which had to answer to no one. When, for example, he was told in 1960 that Jack Kennedy had strongly urged him to stay out of the election campaign, Hoffa replied: "Only an arrogant millionaire playboy who does not understand the Constitution of the United States could make such a statement."

Besides the Kennedys as (almost) villains, this documentary, composed of an impressive collection of archival, news, and home-movie footage, points the finger at Mob figures and Hoffa's own foster son, Chuckie O'Brien (never officially adopted), as the culprits in his disappearance and murder. The Teamsters are discussed in a mostly positive way. This film is therefore a must-see to balance some of the more hysterical anti-Hoffa sentiment in American popular culture.

Hoffa was a special target of the Kennedys, who assigned twenty lawyers to investigate him; Hoffa was also a special target of the media, who gave him more coverage than most presidents of the AFL-CIO. He was almost always cast in early TV news shows as the heavy. CBS's 1959 documentary *Hoffa and the Teamsters* was hailed by *Variety* as "a justifiable blow at a rotten phase of the labor movement." *Variety's* reaction to ABC's *Close-up* feature on Hoffa in 1974 (after his release from prison) emphasized the left-wing socialist leanings of one of Hoffa's Minneapolis mentors. The A&E documentary is valuable precisely because so many of these early programs—ignoring the issues of balance for the moment—are simply not available for viewing.

Hollywood, in the form of Budd Schulberg, author of the screenplay for *On the Waterfront*, was next. Schulberg had been personally selected by Bobby Kennedy to make a film of his anti-Hoffa book, *The Enemy Within*. Schulberg took on the project, hoping "to write not merely a sequel to 'Waterfront' but a significant extension of that film on a national scale" (Sheridan). Schulberg reported that Hoffa's allies and hoodlum friends threatened the Hollywood producers until they surrendered and told Schulberg that the project was shelved "indefinitely."

Hoffa's contacts with organized crime have remained one of the major unresolved issues in an assessment of his career. One of his last interviews—in April 1975, just six months before he disappeared—was recorded at Cornell University's School of Industrial and Labor Relations. Hoffa analyzed a typical Teamster local's situation thus: besides the employer, such a local had other "forces" lined up against it; these forces had to be "neutralized" or the employer would employ them as "strike-breakers or supplying muscle." It is clear from the context that Hoffa means the Mafia and other organized crime outfits, but he says he doesn't use such language: the former is a "notorious tagged, titled organization," and the other is a "so-called other element." Are these the Mafia and rival "organized crime" outfits? So it would seem, but Hoffa refuses to identify them as such. The Teamsters had to fight these "forces" but eventually they would make peace with them: "Neither one would get into each other's business . . . but we would help each other." Hoffa saw such groups in a political context, not as a moral or criminal issue: "If they had political trouble . . . we'd help them, and vice versa." This interview therefore offers a remarkably candid look at Hoffa's own involvement in organized crime, a subject—needless to say—he was notoriously touchy about.

The A&E documentary, perhaps appropriately, treats Hoffa's connection with organized crime in a much more balanced way than most Hollywood feature films. It may come as close to Hoffa's own vision as we are likely to get.

See also: *Bloodfeud; F.I.S.T.; Hoffa.*
Availability: Selected collections; A&E Television.

Further reading

Hoffa, Jimmy. *Hoffa: The Real Story*. New York: Stein & Day, 1972. Hoffa's opinions, "as told to" Oscar Fraley.

Jacobs, Paul. *The State of the Unions*. New York: Atheneum, 1963. Essays on Hoffa in the late 1950s and early 1960s—a convincing view of Hoffa in process, working out public and private deals.

Moldea, Dan E. *The Hoffa Wars: The Rise and Fall of Jimmy Hoffa*. 1974. Rev. ed., New York: Charter, 1978. Popular survey by the dean of Hoffa conspiracy theorists (Hoffa conspired to kill Kennedy).

Sheridan, Walter. *The Fall and Rise of Jimmy Hoffa*. New York: Saturday Review Press, 1972. Bobby Kennedy's investigative assistant offers "a chronology of corruption"; its real claim to fame is the introduction by director Budd Schulberg.

Sloan, Arthur. *Hoffa*. Cambridge: MIT Press, 1992. The definitive academic biography to date.

Variety: "Hoffa and the Teamsters," 1 July 1959, and "ABC News Closeup: Hoffa," 30 November 1974. A sample of reviews of other documentaries (none available on videocassette).

Note: Also known as *Hoffa—The True Story*.

Joe

A worker-management alliance against . . . hippies!

1970, 107 mins., R
Director: John G. Avildsen
Screenplay: Norman Wexler
CAST
Joe Curran = Peter Boyle
Mary Lou Curran = K Callan
William Compton = Dennis Patrick
Joan Compton = Audrey Caire
Melissa Compton = Susan Sarandon
Frank Russo = Patrick McDermott

Visiting *Joe* after all these years is definitely a trip to early Archie Bunker Land. Joe works hard, hates hippies and African Americans (they are moving in down the block), drinks beer and burps a lot, and has a wife obsessed with TV soap-opera intrigue. Actually, Dingbat Edith is a lot more progressive than Mrs. Joe. The totally improbable plot has Joe forming an alliance with an advertising executive who is in a rage because his daughter (Susan Sarandon in her first film role) has run off with dope-smoking (and dealing) hippies. The father beats her obnoxious hippie boyfriend to death and escapes detection, but Joe instinctively finds him out and the two form an unholy alliance, with tragic consequences. The film was surprisingly successful, tapping into popular resentment about Vietnam veterans being ignored and the thrill of seeing a genuine hippie orgy.

John Avidsen's broad satiric strokes create a character who is almost unwatchable today. Perhaps *The Quotations of Worker Joe* might have had a chance at best-sellerdom when the film was first released: "Forty-two percent of all liberals are queer," Joe announces at the bar when he first meets advertising exec William Compton. Later he notes that hippies don't respect Easter Sunday: "The day Christ rose they're all screwing."

Joe works hard. Everybody believes that, although only rarely is he seen actually working, grinding a rod or two at some unspecified factory. He has sprung from a screenwriter's anti–hard hat imagination, although some of the construction workers in the early 1970s who rallied behind Nixon's Vietnam War policy might do for the reality.

See also: *Bloodbrothers*.
Availability: Easy; DVD.

Further reading

Canby, Vincent. "Playing on Our Prejudices." *New York Times*, 2 August 1970, II.1. "One of the most outrageously, most wastefully manic-depressive movies ever made, a movie so convincingly schizoid that it has prompted paeans of praise from socially-conscious critics on both the left and the right."

Hamill, Pete. "The Revolt of the White Lower-Middle Class." In Louise Kapp Howe, ed., *The White Majority: Between Poverty and Affluence*. New York: Random House, 1970. A classic analysis of white working Joes, some of whom so resent African Americans that they are more than ready to act out this film's fantasies of revenge.

Thompson, Howard. "Joe." *New York Times*, 16 July 1970, 40. The film has "a devastating, original idea" but "cynically slopes into a melodramatic, surface fiasco," with Peter Boyle as "a dangerous slob come to life."

Joe Hill

" 'I never died,' says he"

1971, 114 mins., Swedish, with English subtitles

Director: Bo Widerberg
Screenplay: Bo Widerberg
CAST
Joe Hill = Thommy Berggren
Lucia = Anja Schmidt
Raven ("The Fox") = Kelvin Malave
Blackie = Evert Andersson
Cathy = Cathy Smith
Paul = Hasse Persson
David = David Moritz
Richard = Richard Weber
Ed Rowen = Joe Miller
George = Robert Faeder
Elizabeth Gurley Flynn = Wendy Geier

Joe Hill was a Swedish immigrant: born as Joel Hagglund, he became Joseph Hillstrom as he worked his way across North America from 1901 until his execution for murder in 1915. He was a worker, organizer, songwriter, and singer for the Industrial Workers of the World (IWW, or the Wobblies), but he was best known as a union songwriter: "There is one thing that is necessary in order to hold the old members and to get the would-be members interested in the class struggle and that is entertainment" (letter, 29 November 1914).

And entertain he did, writing some of the most popular union songs of the twentieth century: "Casey Jones—The Union Scab" virtually changed a folk hero into a folk scab; "The Preacher and the Slave" (stealing the melody from a Salvation Army song) warned of "pie in the sky" from Salvation Army soup kitchens; "The Rebel Girl" celebrated organizer Elizabeth Gurley Flynn and other IWW women; and "There Is Power in a Union" became an unofficial anthem of all unions.

His success in spreading the word may have made him a target for the Salt Lake City police, who arrested him in 1914 for killing a grocery store owner and his son. Joe did have a gunshot wound but he said he received it during a lovers' quarrel; furthermore, he could not produce a witness for his alibi because it would be embarrassing for "her." After a trial with dubious evidence, he was shot by a firing squad on 19 November 1915. The 30,000 mourners at his Chicago funeral began the process of turning Hill into one of the greatest labor heroes of the century. His belief that a song "learned by heart and repeated over and over" is so much more effective than a "pamphlet, no matter how good . . . never read more than once" helped secure his status as a legend. His wish to have his ashes scattered in every continent and all the states of the union (except Utah) and his last will and testament, addressed to IWW leader Big Bill Haywood—"Don't waste any time mourning—organize!"— have made him a symbol of labor union dedication.

The film surveys a remarkable amount of Hill's life and his trial for murder, inventing perhaps only the dialogue nobody could ever known to match the organization Joe gave his life for. When he meets his first organizer for the IWW, for example, the man tells Hill: "The selfish unions are just out to help themselves. Did you ever see a Mexican or Indian with a union card?"

Since Widerberg is clearly sympathetic to Joe Hill, it may not be surprising that he doesn't include the few pieces of information that have convinced writers such as Wallace Stegner that Hill was guilty. (Otto Applequist, Joe's roommate—and for Stegner a partner in crime—disappeared the night of the murders.)

And as much as critic Joan Mellen admires the film, she faults Widerberg for occasional misinterpretations of Hill's beloved IWW. The film ends, for example, with IWW leaders divvying up Hill's ashes to send them to every state. Their task is interrupted by music from a dance in a neighboring room. We then see these men dancing their hearts out with younger lassies. Widerberg's camera brings us back to an abandoned table with Joe's ashes. This scene is a low blow. Joe's last will and testament comes on the sound track as Joan Baez is singing "The Ballad of Joe Hill" ("I dreamed I saw Joe Hill last night"), and so the cynical abandonment of Joe's ashes for a good time seems especially cruel.

See also: *Ådalen '31; The Wobblies.*
Availability: Not.

Further reading

Bjorkman, Stig. *Film in Sweden: The New Directors*. London: Tantivy, 1977. Reviews Widerberg's career.

Dos Passos, John. *1919* and *Midcentury*. New York: Modern Library, 1937. Joe Hill appears in these two novels as an American icon and foil to the run-of-the-mill capitalist heavies and other labor leaders.

Foner, Philip. *The Case of Joe Hill*. New York: International Publishers, 1965. Argues that Hill was framed because he was a Wobbly.

——, ed. *The Letters of Joe Hill*. New York: Oak Publications, 1965. An important collection of letters.

Hampton, Wayne. *Guerrilla Minstrels: John Lennon, Joe Hill, Woody Guthrie, Bob Dylan*. Knoxville: University of Tennessee Press, 1986. Discusses the reality and the myths associated with these radicalized folksingers.

"Hillstrom Is Shot, Denying His Guilt." *New York Times*, 20 November 1915, 4. A detailed account of Hill's execution, including a last-ditch battle in his cell and his own "Fire!" command to his executioners.

Mellen, Joan. "'Sacco and Vanzetti' and 'Joe Hill.'" *Film Quarterly* 25 (spring 1972): 48–53. A critical review; Mellen prefers Widerberg's film, but she faults his version of the Wobblies.

Stegner, Wallace. *Joe Hill* (a.k.a. *The Preacher and the Slave*). New York: Doubleday, 1950. Stegner's "biographical novel" offers Hill as riffraff—a "yegg" (burglar or safecracker)—as well as a Wobbly who *did* commit the murders for which he was executed.

Thompson, Fred. "Letter and Statement." *New Republic*, 9 February and 13 November 1948. Objections to Stegner's novel.

Web site:

⟨www.pbs.org/joehill⟩ An online examination (from a PBS affiliate at the University of Utah) of Joe Hill's career.

Note: Also known as *The Ballad of Joe Hill.*

∾

John and the Missus

No exit. Exit.

1987, 100 mins., Canada
Director: Gordon Pinsent
Screenplay: Gordon Pinsent, from his novel and play of the same title

John Munn = Gordon Pinsent
Missus = Jackie Burroughs
Matt Munn = Randy Follett
Faith = Jessica Steen

Pinsent's story is set in a very specific place, time, and era: Cup Cove (actually filmed in Petty Harbour), a rural copper mining community in Newfoundland, in 1962, when the province began to literally close down rural communities because supplying services to those towns was too expensive and difficult. When Newfoundland joined the Canadian federation in 1949, it had about 1,500 rural communities, each of which averaged fewer than 300 people. After ten years many communities would choose to relocate for a financial consideration if and only if 100 percent of the residents voted to do so (Khouri).

In fictional Cup Cove, John Munn is a holdout. His wife supports him, but his newly returned son and wife urge him to get with the program. The move becomes inevitable when the town's sole means of support—the copper mine—has a terrible accident and is closed. John and the missus are forced to leave, but decide to take their house with them. They float it off the coast to—as the film ends—an unknown location and unknown future.

Although John's decision seems quixotic, the film offers his family's continuities with the past as one valid reason for sticking. Of course militancy at the mine would be a factor too, but the community is torn apart by the accident.

See also: *Margaret's Museum.*
Availability: Selected collections.

Further reading

Khouri, Malek. "'John and the Missus': Progress, Resistance, and 'Common Sense.'" *Cineaction* (Toronto), no. 49 (1999), 2–11. Extremely thorough interpretation of the film and its Newfoundland/Canadian context.

Pinsent, Gordon. *John and the Missus*. Scarborough: McGraw-Hill Ryerson, 1974. In the source novel, John accepts the exit decision but not in such a cinematic way.

↩

Justice in the Coalfields

"If you don't like it, there's a barefoot man waiting outside to take your job"

1995, 57 mins.
Director: Anne Lewis
Traditional documentary

Since Anne Lewis focused with revealing detail on the lives of "fast food women," she has returned to the subject she has filmed at other times: the Appalachian coal miners and their struggles with recalcitrant coal companies. The film traces the development of the United Mine Workers' strike against the Pittston Coal Company. When the company's contract with the UMWA expired in early 1988, Pittston stopped the medical benefits of approximately 1,500 pensioners, widows, and disabled miners. To miners, so often responsible for the welfare of their extended families in traditional Appalachian culture, this was considered a very low and dirty deed.

The film concentrates on struggles in southwestern Virginia, a right-to-work state where the strike was centered. The United Mine Workers and its AFL-CIO and other community allies launched a two-pronged attack on the company: picket lines with mass civil disobedience and a corporate campaign that made "Pittston" a household word of disgust among trade unionists and progressive political forces. At first state and federal judges handed down injunctions and fines of more than $64 million.

The Pittston strike became a model for cross-union solidarity and sustained militancy. The ultimate victory of the UMWA gave analysts such as James R. Green high hopes: "What began as a contract fight became a people's movement against corporate greed and an oppressive legal system, a movement many hoped would provide a model for the revival of organized labor in the United States."

Lewis's title comes in part from the comment of one of the laid-off Pittston miners: "We got plenty of law, plenty of law,

Pittston solidarity march in *Justice in the Coalfields*. Photo by Ron Skeeber. Courtesy Appalshop.

and we didn't have no justice." During the Pittston strike a former miner recalled the company's attitude in his day: "I worked in water up to my knees for a dollar a day loading coal by hand, and if I said anything about it the boss would tell me, "If you don't like it, there's a barefoot man waiting outside ready to take your job'" (quoted in Couto's essay in Fisher's *Fighting Back in Appalachia*).

Depiction of the daily lives of hardworking Appalachian people, whether they are involved in industrial disputes or not, is characteristic of Lewis's style and to a certain extent is almost a house style of Appalshop. Its films are notably personal looks at an often beleaguered people, but they have a directness and insight that come from listening carefully to and filming the people at the bottom. And when the top talks or acts, filmmakers such as Lewis are usually in the middle of the struggle—and the action.

Lewis was the associate director on Kopple's *Harlan County, U.S.A.* and directed the award-winning Appalshop documentaries *On Our Own Land*, about strip mining, and *Chemical Valley*, about a toxic waste spill near Charleston, West Virginia. Her other Appalshop documentaries, *Roving Pickets* and *Mine Wars on Blackberry Creek*, are part of her historical survey of the specific struggles of eastern Kentucky miners. Footage from *Justice in the Coalfields* was included in Kopple's *Out of Darkness*, a historical and contemporary account of coal miners.

See also: *The Buffalo Creek Flood; Roving Pickets*.

Availability: Selected collections; Appalshop.

Further reading

Fisher, Stephen L., ed. *Fighting Back in Appalachia*. Philadelphia: Temple University

Press, 1993. Excellent collection of essays on the "traditions of resistance and change," especially Richard A. Couto's "The Memory of Miners and the Conscience of Capital" (placing the Pittston strike in the context of the miners' collective memory) and Jim Sessions and Fran Ansley's "Singing across Dark Spaces: The Union/ Community Takeover of Pittston's Moss 3 Plant."

Green, James R. "Tying the Knot of Solidarity." In *The United Mine Workers of America: A Model of Industrial Solidarity?* ed. John H. M. Laslett, 513–44. University Park: Pennsylvania State University Press, 1996. Very thorough essay on the Pittston strike.

Oestreicher, Richard. "Justice in the Coalfields." *Labor History*, Fall 1996, 536–38. Reviewer finds the film deficient in "macroeconomic analysis of how national and international economic trends may shape the tactical and strategic options of Pittston miners or working people anywhere else" and wishes the filmmaker had worked harder at exposing the company's apparent lack of interest in its employees.

Web site:

⟨www.appalshop.org⟩ Official site of the film's distributor, with much information about the various programs sponsored by this leading interpreter of Appalachian culture.

✍

Kameradschaft

Solidarity across the border

1931, 93 mins., German and French, with English subtitles, B&W
Director: G. W. Pabst
Screenplay: Karl Otten, Ladislaus Vajda, and Peter Martin Lampel
CAST
Wittkopp, the German miner = Ernst Busch
Frau Wittkopp = Elisabeth Wendt
Kasper = Alexander Granach
Wilderer = Fritz Kampers
Kaplan = Gustav Pütjer
Jean, the French miner = Georges Charlia
Françoise = Andrée Ducret
Emile = Daniel Mandaille
The Grandfather = Alex Bernard
George = Pierre Louis

Kameradschaft celebrates the solidarity that emerges between French and German miners on the border of their two countries when a mining disaster in a French town breaks down mutual distrust and rivalries. The title could be translated as "comradeship" or even by the word we have borrowed from the French, "camaraderie." The dialogue in the film was originally in both German and French to suggest the unity of the miners' struggles, but the current videocassette is subtitled. The film is dedicated to "The Miners of the World," specifically the more than 1,200 miners killed by mine gas in the French mine at Courrières ("Courbière" in the film) in 1906.

G. W. Pabst changed the setting to a mine in Lorraine on the French border in 1919; underground, the mine is actually segregated by country: a wall has been erected like the border aboveground. Actual mining towns on both sides of the border were used for location shooting, although the convincing underground scenes were filmed on carefully constructed studio sets in Berlin.

The film opens with a symbolic visual overture: a German boy and a French boy are happily playing marbles. German miners nearby apply at the border for work, but are turned back by the French. The little boys begin to argue. Pabst then cuts to an interior shot of the German section of the mine, from which a fire on the French side can clearly be seen. The film then alternates between social scenes (a French beer hall) and personal life (the family of Jean, a French miner) and an explosion that spreads the fire throughout the mine.

On the German side of the border, the German miners debate helping the French. Wittkopp begins the discussion by asking if the French have rescue equipment. One of his mates says: "Who cares? They are richer than we are." But Wittkopp leads a rescue party, which the French greet with amazement: "Les allemands! Ce n'est pas possible!" (The Germans! It's impossible!). Three miners who had earlier been treated in an unfriendly way at a French dance hall open up another rescue route by tearing down the fence erected as part of the frontier established by the Treaty of Versailles.

All of these impressive cooperative gestures are temporarily shattered by a brilliant and terrifyingly classic scene: a dazed French miner sees and hears a German man in a gas mask approaching him and hallucinates, thinking the approaching figure is a German soldier. Pabst intercuts shots of a battle during World War I as the French miner attacks his rescuer.

Nonetheless, the daring rescue and cooperation seem to be pointing toward a future of international cooperation. A Frenchman says: "It is because we are *all* miners that you have saved us. We have only two common enemies—gas and war!" The epilogue, showing a new iron fence underground separating the two mine sections, provides the ironic reversal of the new *Kameradschaft*.

This cynical epilogue was offered in the German release of the film but eliminated when it was booed in Berlin, but it was retained in the French version; the 1932 American premiere and the version in most collections offer the cynical German version. An additional terrible irony of the miners' solidarity is that less than a decade after the film's release, the old hatreds boiled over in a new war between the French and the Germans.

Pabst had an unusual if not opportunistic career. *Kameradschaft* followed a similar antiwar film, *Westfront 1918* (1930), which ends with dying French and German soldiers trying to reconcile. In 1933, when the Nazis came to power, he emigrated to Hollywood; later he returned to France. He said he was "trapped" in Austria when the war broke out. Nevertheless, Joseph Goebbels welcomed him back to the German film industry, for which he made a number of films. After the defeat of the Nazis, Pabst made anti-Nazi films through the 1950s.

See also: *Germinal*.
Availability: Selected collections.

Further reading

Atwell, Lee. *G. W. Pabst*. New York: Twayne, 1977. A good survey of the director's career and achievements.

Hall, Mordaunt. "The Screen." *New York Times*, 9 November 1932, 28. A very positive contemporary American review.
Kracauer, Siegfried. *From Caligari to Hitler*. Princeton: Princeton University Press, 1947. Places Pabst's career in the context of "a psychological history of the German film," emphasizing its authoritarian tendencies.

Keeping On

Mill girls and mill rats

1983, 72 mins., TVM
Director: Barbara Kopple
Screenplay: Horton Foote and Leslie Lee
CAST
Luke Rankovich = James Broderick
Gaynor = Guy Boyd
Anne Traylor = Rosalind Cash
Lester Traylor = Danny Glover
Lavania = Carol Kane
Davis = Carl Lee
Mary Goodwin = Marcia Rodd
Anthony Traylor = Dick Anthony
   Williams

In a sense *Keeping On* is Barbara Kopple's variation on *Norma Rae*, a film about southern textile mill organizing. Kopple had finished her Eastern Kentucky documentary classic, *Harlan County, U.S.A.*, and won an Academy Award for it in 1977. Her next major project was to be a feature film based on the life of Crystal Lee Jordan, the model for *Norma Rae*. But Martin Ritt beat her to that story and she turned instead to an original screenplay by Horton Foote (Academy Award winner for *To Kill a Mockingbird* and the author of many other screenplays). Completed in 1981, *Keeping On* premiered in 1983 on *American Playhouse* for PBS.

Kopple dramatizes an inside-outside approach to organizing. Her inside man is Sam, an African American part-time minister who "preaches union." Her outside man is Luke, a white organizer who comes to town on assignment from his union. The mill and the community go on heightened alert as people choose sides.

Kopple's background research for the film was remarkable. She used available oral histories and the archives of the textile mill owners, the union, and the National Labor Relations Board. She also worked two weeks as a creeler in a mill, replacing threads on the machines and doing similar tasks. Even though she worked ten-hour shifts, she realized that "it's much different from knowing that's what you do every single day your whole life" (Padroff).

The film has very solid moments that reflect Kopple's ability, so obvious from her documentaries *Harlan County, U.S.A.* and *American Dream*, to understand her subjects: "I try not to stand apart from people. For as long as possible, I live with them, eat and work with them, and to try to get some first-hand sense of who they really are" (Padroff).

Keeping On received some strong reviews but was never released widely. Kopple went on to other projects, most notably *American Dream*, her second Academy Award–winning documentary, on the extended strike of the meatpackers' union against Hormel.

See also: *Harlan County, U.S.A.; Norma Rae.*
Availability: Not.

Further reading

Kernan, Michael. "Stark 'Keeping On.'" *Washington Post*, 11 February 1983, B2. Commends the film for its documentary strengths but worries about its tendency to be "too low-key, too gray and subdued."

Padroff, Jay. "'Keeping On' Tells of Courage, Dignity." *Boston Globe*, 8 February 1983. Extensive quotes from Kopple on her cinematic and political goals for the film.

The Killing Floor

. . . of both man and beast

1984, 117 mins., PG
Director: William Duke
Screenplay: Leslie Lee
CAST
Frank Custer = Damien Leake
Mattie Custer = Alfre Woodard
Thomas Joshua = Ernest Rayford
Austin "Heavy" Williams = Moses Gunn
Robert Bedford = Wally Taylor
Harry Brenn = Dennis Farna
Dan Michora = Miklos Simon
Bill Bremer = Clarence Felder
Judge Alschuler = Nathan Davis
John Kikulski = Henryk Derewenda
John Fitzpatrick = James O'Reilly
Eliza (the letter writer) = Mary Alice

Leslie Lee's screenplay for *The Killing Floor* was based on a story idea by Elsa Rassbach, one of the founders of the *Nova* series on PBS, who envisioned *The Killing Floor* as a pilot for a proposed series of ten films about the history of the American worker. Unfortunately, the series was never made. Rassbach charged the Corporation for Public Broadcasting with having a bad case of nerves—fear of the corporate contributors, who do not like labor films. The second and third films proposed would survey nineteenth-century labor history: one was to be on the origins of industrial labor in the textile mills of Lowell, Massachusetts, while the other would focus on the lockout at the steel mill in Homestead, Pennsylvania.

Instead of a series, however, we have to date only this portrayal of a dark and relatively little known episode in the history of labor and race relations. William Duke, who later did the remake of *A Raisin in the Sun*, directed this excellent TV movie.

At the outbreak of World War I, two young African Americans, Frank and Thomas, leave the South in what has become known as the Great Inland Migration, they hope, for jobs in Chicago. Because of the war, blacks are being hired in the traditionally Eastern European immigrant job market—the Chicago stockyards. Frank survives because he learns his trade with a knife on "the killing floor" and is befriended by union men, but his friend Thomas is racially harassed and joins the army.

The union—the Amalgamated Meatcutters and Butcher Workmen of North America—is attempting a mass recruitment of all workers, regardless of race. At one glorious moment at a union hall meeting,

Tensions on the killing floor.

speeches are delivered in English and Polish, as Frank and others are urged to join the union.

Other African Americans in the shop, most notably "Heavy" Williams, are more suspicious of the union and argue for all-black unity in the sea of untrustworthy white faces. Heavy is also a front man for the bosses, because at one point he clearly instigates a riot by throwing a brick at a speaker. The film dramatizes a series of complicated episodes in union–management negotiations, including a lockout that tests the resolve of most of the African Americans to remain a part of the union. Management wants to break the union and determines that race rivalry is the best way.

The Big Five meatpackers had reached an agreement with the federal government in 1918 for the duration of the war. The union would guarantee not to strike and the companies, in return, would give the union limited recognition, but with no binding contract. A federal judge would referee any contentious issues that might arise.

Unfortunately for the union, a notorious episode in Chicago history occurred in July 1919: a black youth, swimming in Lake Michigan, crossed the imaginary line (39th Street extended eastward into the water) that separated "colored" from "white" bathing areas. Although eyewitness testimony differed, it seems in retrospect to matter little: the African Americans believed that the young man had been stoned and subsequently drowned, but the police did not arrest anyone. The Chicago race riot of 1919 was under way.

Since Frank and the other black workers had to cross a white zone (Canaryville) filled with Irish gangs to get to their jobs, race rioting and union integration would soon be incompatible. In fact, blacks and whites were in fact ambushed by rioters on both sides and killed. A Lithuanian (Polish in the film) section of town was set on fire; again eyewitness testimony varied, but several historians agree that whites in blackface carried out the deed.

The filmmakers developed this historical moment in several ways. They decided to use the actual names of the union recruits and officers and they integrated documentary footage and historical titles into the film. To solidify the film's objectivity, all the newsreel footage of the Chicago riot, with one or two exceptions, is authentic.

In the end, when it seems that no more conflicts can possibly arise, Frank decides to cross his own union's picket line and go back to work. He has already had to face the double humiliation of ducking bullets from white rioters and receiving charity from the company, courtesy of his old nemesis, Heavy.

The militia, sent out to escort Frank and the other black workers into the meatpacking plant to scab, suddenly leave the area when they receive a signal from one of the Big Five packing company bosses. Instead of confronting the black workers at the company gates, the white union leave, singing "Solidarity Forever," a tribute to their own discipline. But the black workers go to work.

Inside, Frank keeps his union button hidden, but some hope is held out in the form of a young black worker who accepts Frank's closing speech warning the blacks about the company's intention to reduce them to another form of slavery. The closing credits of the film include end titles that trace the subsequent career of the union activists and officials in the film. Ironically, the Frank Custers and the Heavy Williamses literally disappeared into unrecorded history, their only legacy contained in their interviews with the Chicago Commission on Race Relations in the early 1920s. The end titles also indicate that the United Food and Commercial Workers (UFCW) are the inheritors of the union tradition in the film.

See also: *Matewan*.
Availability: Easy.

Further reading

Asher, Robert. "Union Nativism and the Immigrant Response." *Labor History*, Summer 1982, 325–48. Places the Chicago struggle in the context of similar union organizing of (or refusal to organize) immigrants.

Barrett, James R. *Work and Community in the Jungle: Class, Race, and Ethnicity*. Urbana: University of Illinois Press, 1987. Good analyses of the forces that drove such men as Frank Custer and Heavy Williams.

Brody, David. *The Butcher Workmen: A Study in Unionization*. Cambridge: Harvard University Press, 1964. A history of the Chicago unions, including material on some of the film's real-life characters.

Chicago Commission on Race Relations. *The Negro in Chicago: A Study of Race Relations and a Race Riot*. 1922. New York: Arno, 1968. Detailed account by the official investigating commission.

Cohn, Lawrence. "Duke's 'Killing Floor,' amid Brouhaha, to Be Released." *Variety*, 24 February 1992, 40. On the failure to develop the pilot film into a series.

Grossman, James R. *Land of Hope: Chicago, Black Southerners, and the Great Migration*. Chicago: University of Chicago Press, 1989. Authoritative study of the main issues.

Horowitz, Roger. *"Negro and White, Unite and Fight!" A Social History of Industrial Unionism in Meatpacking, 1930–1990*. Urbana: University of Illinois Press, 1997. Traces the origins of the big meatpackers' control of the industry, but its main concern is the period after the events covered in the film.

Klawans, Stuart. "Films." *Nation*, 30 March 1992, 425–28. Reviews the film and surveys Rassbach's controversy with the CPB.

O'Connor, John J. " 'Killing Floor,' American Workers." *New York Times*, 10 April 1984, III.22. One of the few reviews; very positive.

Sandburg, Carl. *The Chicago Race Riots, July 1919*. 1919. New York: Harcourt, Brace, 1969. News articles with excellent brief overview by the young poet.

Sinclair, Upton. *The Jungle*. 1905. New York: NAL, 1960. The first major novelistic exposé of Chicago's meatpacking industry.

Stromquist, Sheldon, and Marvin Bergman, eds. *Unionizing the Jungle*. Iowa City: University of Iowa Press, 1997. A collection of essays on the meatpacking industry, including studies of the role of African Americans.

Tuttle, William M. *Race Riot: Chicago in the Red Summer of 1919*. New York: Atheneum, 1970. The best overall account of the riot by the "historical consultant" to the film.

The Kitchen

Slice and dice

1961, 76 mins., B&W, UK
Director: James H. Hill
Screenplay: Sidney Cole, from Arthur
  Wesker's play of the same title
CAST
Paul = Tom Bell
Max = Martin Boddey
Raymond = Howard Greene
Peter = Carl Mohner
Chef = Charles Lloyd Pack
Kevin = Brian Phelan
Mr. Marango = Eric Pohlmann
Monica = Mary Yeomans

In the notes for the stage production of *The Kitchen* in 1959, Arthur Wesker stated that "all kitchens, especially during service, go insane." Paul, one of the pastry cooks, announces during the film adaptation that "the world is filled with kitchens—only they call some offices, call some factories."

The mise-en-scène of the film fulfills these metaphorical expectations more than adequately. A London restaurant, Wesker knew from personal experience, is a class society in miniature, with the owner on top, the chefs next, followed by various cooks, and finally the porters (kitchen help and busboys). The waitresses, who dominate the dining room, are somewhat parallel in authority and status to the cooks.

In Wesker's vision of a typical 1950s large restaurant, the staff is split between native English workers and immigrants. Since some of the latter are Germans and Jews, the natural tendency for chaos is exacerbated by the burdens of World War II.

The Kitchen combines the realism—in this case, literally—of the kitchen sink plays of the 1950s, with a number of active and failing romantic relationships. Although Wesker insisted that in the stage production

Overwrought chef in *The Kitchen*.

"at no time is food ever used" and that "the waitresses will carry empty dishes and the cooks will mime the cooking," the film uses a conventional realistic approach. Furthermore, as John Hill argues, "the impulse of the movie is to reveal the shared, collective experience of work, its mechanical routine and enervating pace."

The climax of the film comes when Peter, a young German whose parents were killed in World War II, has realized that Monica, a married waitress, will not leave her husband for him. He goes berserk with a meat cleaver, cutting a gas line in the kitchen and then rushing into the dining room before he is subdued.

The Kitchen, like *Cathy Come Home*, is an unseen classic of British social realism, as it has never been available on videocassette, but unlike Loach's film about Cathy's plunge into homelessness, Wesker's kitchen receives scant coverage in labor film history. It is as if Wesker's failed Centre 42 project, designed to bring trade unions, workers, and theatrical productions together, had been a jinx and his other successes as a playwright (such as *Chicken Soup with Barley*) were unimportant.

See also: *Look Back in Anger*.
Availability: Not.

Further reading

Hayman, Ronald. *Arnold Wesker*. New York: Ungar, 1973. A short but very helpful bio-critical study, with a section on *The Kitchen* and interviews with the playwright.

Hill, John. *Sex, Class, and Realism: British Cinema, 1956–1963*. London: British Film Institute, 1986. Short but incisive analysis of the film: "The one film of the period to make the organization and experience of work its central concern."

"The Kitchen." *New York Times*, 2 November 1961, 42. Praises this "polyglot drama rich with the impatient opinions of militant youth striking out against a world in turmoil" and states that Wesker (among "the angry young man school of letters") is "a talent to watch."

Wesker, Arthur. *The Kitchen*. 1960. Various editions available. Wesker's playscript, with substantial production notes.

ᔐ

Kuhle Wampe

Communist calisthenics

1932, 73 mins., B&W, Germany, German, with English subtitles
Director: Slatan Dudow
Screenplay: Bertolt Brecht and Ernst Ottwald
CAST
Annie = Hertha Thiele
Fritz = Ernst Busch
Gerda = Martha Wolter
Karl = Adolf Fischer

Kuhle Wampe, or, to give its full title, *Kuhle Wampe, or To Whom Does the World Belong?* was, according to Siegfried Kracauer (1947), "the first, and last, German film which overtly expressed a communist viewpoint." Certainly the Nazis agreed, since they banned the film as soon as they consolidated their takeover, the same year as the film's release.

To our eyes today, perhaps, the film seems deceptively simple and not very communistic. A family feels the pressure of unemployment and blames the son for not trying hard enough to get a job; he commits suicide ("one unemployed less"). The family follow their daughter to Kuhle Wampe, a kind of Hooverville on the outskirts of Berlin. Critics differ on Brecht's attitude toward this camp or village of the unemployed. Do their neat little houses and gardens simply reproduce the bourgeois world they are excluded from, or does their alternative lifestyle in effect criticize the failure of the state? Certainly the engagement party, with its slobbering drunks, does little to inspire confidence in these workers.

In the late 1920s, with the rise of a significant workers' movement in Germany, Brecht joined with the composer Hanns Eisler and many others in the creation of a short-lived revolutionary culture, at first in opposition to capitalist ideas and then to Nazi ideology. Brecht's play *Die Massnahme* (*The Measures Taken*) was performed with Eisler's music— an experimental drama with Brecht's characters and Eisler's music synthesizing some fairly complicated ideas about revolutionary ethics. The following year Eisler composed the music for *Kuhle Wampe*, where the synthesis was not quite so successful perhaps: the nature song, sung over shots of natural beauty while our hero and heroine frolic discreetly offscreen, is perhaps hard for us to view with the right combination of revolutionary admiration and satisfaction. Another song, "The Solidaritatslied" ("Solidarity Song"), became part of Eisler's Symphony no. 3. Brecht collaborated with Eisler on one more play (*The Mother*), but both artists were soon forced to emigrate when Hitler took absolute power in 1933.

Berlin in the 1920s also provided Brecht with potential breakthroughs in his approach to theater: not only did he work with such actors as Peter Lorre, but his collective began to develop what Brecht called his *Lehrstücke*, or "teaching plays." By the end of the decade German Communists and socialists were at each other's throats and Brecht moved most decisively into the communist movement. Of course the real enemy was the Nazis, but the German left did not always manage the unity that might have hindered Hitler's rise.

This political background helps explain some of the odd moments in this film about the state of the working class in 1932. Why, for example, are there no fascists or even an implied fascist threat? The only difficulties are unemployment, of course (and the state's refusal to keep up welfare benefits), and whether withdrawing into an alternative village (Kuhle Wampe) is a politically smart move. The film suggests that building a physical education movement is probably the best that the workers can hope to do at this juncture—to make themselves physically

Agitprop entertainment in *Kuhle Wampe*.

fit for the moment when they have to fight for their politics, which, by the way, are never explained in the film.

Variety knew it was "Russian communistic propaganda in the German tongue," but found almost everything about the film "garbled and choppy," without revealing what was actually "communistic" about it. (*Variety* also bemoaned a missing sequence involving nudity; it's still missing.) The *New York Times* found the film more effective, especially the lead actress, Hertha Thiele (who starred in the somewhat sultry role of the repressed teen in *Mädchen in Uniform*). Apparently this reviewer knew it was a "Red Sport Festival" laid on by the Labor Sports Union. Maybe you had to be there. In any case, the New York screening was accompanied by a filmed introduction with speeches by active lefties, such as the Socialist leader Norman Thomas, the novelist Henrik Willem van Loon, and the activist spouse "Mrs. Lincoln Stephens," who denounced "Hitlerism and the persecution of the Jews."

The montage of natural loving, done in the Soviet Eisensteinian style, which Brecht was justly proud of, actually did him in—ironically—among his Communist allies (among the leadership, at least). As John Fuga explains it, bringing an Eisensteinian film to Moscow in 1932, just when the Stalinists were criticizing Eisenstein for being too concerned about montage and cinematic theory and not enough about the masses, was a mistake. Furthermore (a final irony, according to Fuga), Moscow workers at the screening became hostile when they saw unemployed German workers with bicycles and watches, unheard-of luxuries among working people in the Soviet Union. (German workers objected to nudity, Russian workers to watches: go figure.)

Brecht was also involved in other notable film projects, with the composer Kurt Weil in Germany (*The Threepenny Opera*, directed by G. W. Pabst) and with Eisler and the German emigrant director Fritz Lang in Hollywood (*Hangmen Also Die*, a chilling but static drama of the anti-Nazi underground). The high point of Eisler's career in the United States was his Oscar for best musical score for *Hangmen Also Die*, but both Eisler and Brecht, having been summoned before the House Committee on Un-American Activities and accused of being Communists—an investigator called Eisler the "Karl Marx of Communism in the musical field"—left the United States and eventually settled in East Germany, where they established themselves as virtually the leading artists in their respective fields through the 1950s and 1960s.

See also: *Metropolis*.
Availability: Selected collections.

Further reading

Brecht, Bertolt. *Bertolt Brecht on Film and Radio*. Ed. and trans. Marc Silberman. London: Methuen, 2001. Brecht's essays on film and a complete shot analysis of *Kuhle Wampe*.

——. "Kuhle Wampe." *Screen* 15 (Summer 1974): 41–48. Various statements by Brecht and other members of the filmmaking team about the film, including the remark that "proletarian athletes" criticized the now-missing sequence of nudity during the lovers' "nature walk."

——. *Letters, 1913–1956* (1981). Ed. John Willett. Trans. Ralph Mannheim. New York: Routledge, 1990. Willett's commentaries throughout the volume provide very helpful guidance to Brecht's career.

Eisler, Hanns. *A Rebel in Music: Selected Writings*. Ed. Manfred Grabs. New York: International Publishers, 1976. Although occasionally the writing or the translation seems daft ("In the classical period pleasure was derived from a music which was based on a philosophy"), this collection serves not only as an analysis of but also a history of many working-class and revolutionary movements and moments in twentieth-century music.

Fuga, John. *Brecht & Co*. New York: Grove, 1964. Covers Brecht's difficulties in the Communist camp and the hostile reaction to his film in the Soviet Union.

Furhammar, Leif, and Folke Isaksson. *Politics and Film*. Trans. Kersti French. New York: Praeger, 1971. Perhaps because it is from a Swedish perspective, this book surveys many films out of our usual Anglo-American rut, including such 1930s German "communist" films as *Kule Wampe* and *Revolt of the Fishermen*.

"German Unemployed." *New York Times*, 24 April 1933, 11. Mostly very positive review, with strong praise for "the chanting of fighting slogans by the young workers" (which, I confess, I did not witness in the British Film Institute's 35mm print or videocassette I have seen).

Kemp, Philip. "Mud in Your Eye." *Sight and Sound*, October 1998, 26–29. Argues that Brecht's annoyance at P. W. Pabst's film adaptation of Brecht's *Threepenny Opera* led Brecht into the more radical aesthetics of *Kuhle Wampe*, but not (ironically) into a different closing mood (one of melancholic resignation).

Mueller, Roswitha. *Bertold Brecht and the Theory of Media*. Lincoln: University of Nebraska Press, 1989. Extensive analysis of the film, with selected sequences illustrated with frames/images.

Pettifer, James. "Against the Stream—'Kuhle Wampe.'" *Screen* 15 (Summer 1974): 48–64. A very helpful review of the economic and cultural context of Germany during the film's production.

"Whither Germany?" *Variety*, 25 April 1933. Finds the dramatic story of the family not up to the political context outlined "imaginatively"; especially annoyed with the bitter irony of the refrain, "One unemployed less."

Note: Also known as *Whither Germany?*

Ladies Who Do

"Money isn't everything"

1963, 85 mins., UK
Director: C. M. Pennington-Richards
Screenplay: Michael Pertwee
CAST
Mrs. Cragg = Peggy Mount
Colonel Whitforth = Robert Morley
James Ryder = Harry H. Corbett

The leader of the charwomen lectures her supporters in *Ladies Who Do*.

Mrs. Higgins = Miriam Karlin
Mrs. Merryweather = Dandy Nichols
Mrs. Parish = Margaret Boyd

The "ladies who do" are charwomen or office cleaners who stumble on an axiom of advanced capitalism (or "capitualism," as one of them calls it): information is wealth. And when that information turns out to be literally picked up from the floors and wastebaskets of business tycoons and financial wheeler-dealers, it soon makes the women and their insider middleman rich indeed. But, of course, "money isn't everything."

What really matters to them is that their London neighborhood is slated for urban removal by one of the tycoons for whom Mrs. Cragg, their leader (played by the formidable and very funny working-class dame Peggy Mount), works. When he suggests that Mrs. Cragg and her neighbors be relocated to a "new town," the battle is on.

This unjustly neglected film is a hoot. The working-class heroines are perhaps British cinematic stereotypes, but they are lovable each and every one. At a meeting to rally her troops, Mrs. Cragg explains how they are going to work the financial markets in their favor. Her friend replies: "The stock exchange is a cancerous growth on the dying body of capitalism. A slave market for the buying and selling of the workers. After the revolution there won't be no stock exchange." This stirring speech is dismissed by Mrs. Cragg, who intends to manipulate that "capitalist" institution: "Now do leave off about the perishing revolution!"

I regard this as one of the great sleepers of comic British working-class cinema. Resist if you can. As one of the defenders of the condemned slums says of her home: "The blood of the bourgeoisie and the proletariat will mingle in the gutters of the Charing Cross Road before we get chucked out of here." Robert Morley, in a star turn as their financial adviser, who has clearly come down in the world, represents the familiar upper-class twit we expect in a film of this type.

See also: *I'm All Right, Jack; The Man in the White Suit.*
Availability: Selected collections.

Land of Promise

The Polish Manchester

1975, 161 mins., Poland, in Polish, German, and Yiddish, all subtitled in English
Director: Andrzej Wajda
Screenplay: Andrzej Wajda, from the novel of the same title by Wladyslaw Reymont
CAST
Karol Borowiecki = Daniel Olbrychski
Moryc Welt = Wojciech Pszoniak
Maks Baum = Andrzej Seweryn

By turns fascinating and disturbing, Wajda's mostly top-down portrayal of three would-be capitalists in turn-of-the-century Lodz is as much an urban panorama of the city nicknamed the Polish Manchester as it is of three friends of different faiths and cultures. We meet an aristocratic Polish factory manager, a Jewish speculator, and the son of a German factory owner who cannot adapt to the mechanization of the textile industry. Lodz epitomizes that industry: with the coming of the textile industry early in the nineteenth century, Lodz developed as a city at the crossroads of Eastern European and Slavic commerce. By the end of the century it had become the most important producer of textiles in the world. Even today, as the second largest city in Poland, it has 50 percent of the country's textile industry.

As the pre–World War II home of over a quarter of a million Jews, virtually all of whom were exterminated by the Nazis and their Polish allies, Lodz has been a capital of another, more horrible sort. And while the city was a melting pot of numerous nationalities before the war, it was also an equally horrific site of numerous concentration camps—for Jews, gypsies, Polish prisoners of war, Polish children, and even Russian airmen.

Lodz's polyglot history is really the inspiration for both the novel by Nobel Prize–winning Wladyslaw Reymont and Wajda's film. Indeed, there is a thin line between the portrayal of the Jewish culture that financed many of the city's factories at the end of the nineteenth century and the anti-Semitic implications of many scenes. Reymont, according to Boleslaw Michalek and Frank Turaj, had written his novel in part to warn the Polish people of the danger in allowing Russian, German, and Jewish capitalists to control their country's financial and industrial destiny.

Wajda was apparently surprised and shocked by the reaction of festival audiences and later reviewers who found the scenes in which the Jews dominated particularly disturbing. Wajda believed that the Jewish speculator was in fact the most sympathetic character of the three friends. But Wajda missed what I think will be obvious to any viewer now: if Polish aristocrats are shown lolling about a country estate oblivious of the disappearance of their class and the German factory-owning family is portrayed watching its tiny and vanishing factory staff twiddle their spindles manually, neither has anywhere near the satirical weight of a room—it looks like a private club or restaurant—literally packed with hundreds of Jews, all counting out stacks of money and shouting wildly at one another about deals they are frenetically pursuing.

Wajda and Roman Polanski are probably the best-known members of the great film school that flourished, not coincidentally, in Lodz itself, in part because the capital, Warsaw, was virtually destroyed by Allied bombing. What began as a necessity ended as a virtue: the Lodz or Polish school of filmmaking had a number of international hits to its credit, perhaps because it operated at a relatively safe distance from the political censors, who would normally be trying to impose a Stalinist purity if not monotony on its work.

Be that as it may, Wajda also gained a sense of Lodz as the perfect setting for the film he was making of Reymont's novel. The great mansions and many of the original factories of the turn-of-the-century financiers, even the Jewish ones, were still intact when he made this film in the 1970s. (The Lodz film school was even housed in one such mansion.)

While Wajda may have expected his Polish audiences to know the unique geographical and political position of Lodz in the nineteenth century, many of us would be a little lost without a key. The Congress Kingdom of Poland, as it was known in the early part of the century, was ruled by Russia, which selected Lodz as an official industrial center where foreign investors and industrialists were welcome. Thus German Protestants made fortunes with their textile mills, Jews developed as merchants and bankers and even as industrialists, while the native Catholic Poles were divided among peasants leaving the countryside for jobs in the mills and aristocrats who—Reymont argued with his novel—did not have the gumption to seize the leadership of their own land. The discontinuation of tariff barriers between Poland and Russia made Lodz the principal supplier of textiles to Russia and (some historians argue) to the world.

Wajda's film *Holy Week* (1995) is a bitter examination of Polish anti-Semitism, contrasting the Warsaw Ghetto uprising with the placidity and unconcern of Polish Christians as they prepare for Easter Sunday. Some of the same criticism leveled at Wajda's approach to Jewish characters in *Land without Bread* arose about this film as well.

See also: *Man of Iron; Man of Marble.*
Availability: Selected collections.

Further reading

Michalek, Boleslaw, and Frank Turaj. *The Modern Cinema of Poland.* Bloomington: Indiana University Press, 1988. A thorough survey of the subject with a good section on the film.

Reymont, Ladislas. *The Promised Land.* 2 vols. Trans. M. H. Dziewicki. New York: Knopf, 1927. The source novel is a baggy monster of a book;

Wajda has politicized the original ending, since in the novel the fire is an accident, not arson, and there is no demonstration of workers to be attacked by the police.

~

Land without Bread

"It is no longer possible to scandalize anybody."—André Breton

1932, 27 mins., B&W, Spanish, with voice-over narration in English
Director: Luis Buñuel
Mock-traditional documentary based on the field research of Maurice Legendre
PRINCIPAL FIGURES
Unnamed peasants, villagers, dwarfs, cretins, a teacher, students, and pathetic children of all ages

When André Breton, one of Buñuel's partners in surrealistic highjinks, made the lament quoted above about the loss of targets, Buñuel agreed: gone were the days when artists could attack capitalism, religion, and private property so easily. Those great days of the 1920s and 1930s were past, Buñuel told Carlos Fuentes, the Mexican novelist, when his goal was "to undermine bourgeois optimism" and force "the public to doubt the tenets of the established order." In all of his films included in this guide, Buñuel certainly strove toward that goal.

The Spanish region in this film is so pathetic that even the honey is bitter. It was an unpromised land camera-ready for urban sophisticates (and leftists) who made what could be called the first tabloid film about peasants who have virtually no land to farm.

If you see *Land without Bread* without some understanding or even a viewing of Buñuel's surrealistic masterpieces such as *The Andalusian Dog* (1928) and *The Age of Gold* (1930), the strangeness of this documentary classic will come through but not much of its rationale. A cultural leftist,

Buñuel made films with some of the most noteworthy, unusual, and unnerving shots in late silent cinema: a razor cutting an eye in close-up, a dead horse draped across a piano, a woman sucking the marble toes of a statue. Obsessively using the Freudian legacy of the libidinal powers of the unconscious, the surrealists sought primarily to shock the audience and if possible to disturb its sense of a rational world. Many but not all of the artistic rebels in Paris, London, and Berlin in the 1920s were politically on the left.

Land without Bread is a surrealist's travelogue to a land that is potentially so absurd that it seems invented for the filmmaker: Las Hurdes, in the northwestern corner of Spain, only sixty miles from Salamanca, one of Spain's cultural centers, where the people have rarely tasted bread. They have an inordinate number of cretins living among them, but they seem to take such facts of life for granted, so that when bees sting both a mule and its master to death on a local mountain trail, it is considered inevitable. To make the point that the *hurdanos* never have meat unless a mountain goat missteps and tumbles to its death in a ravine, Buñuel obligingly shows us such an event. But as he explained to his interviewer in *Objects of Desire:* "Since we couldn't wait for the event to happen, I provoked it by firing a revolver. Later, we saw that the smoke from the gunshot appeared in the frame, but we couldn't repeat the scene because it would have angered the Hurdanos and they would have attacked us. They don't kill goats. They only eat those that fall by accident." A few critics, viewing the film in a print from New York's Museum of Modern Art, didn't see the smoke and thought the whole episode was still another surrealist's joke. But the smoke is clearly there on contemporary videocassette releases.

Because the film makes some unexpected leaps in logic and location, many viewers need a viewing guide. Tom Conley's careful shot analysis (included in Mellen's book), dividing Buñuel's film into fifteen sequences, is such a guide, which I have lightly annotated in parentheses:

1. Credits (human geography)
2. La Alberca (cocks decapitated)
3. The Countryside and Abandoned Churches (toads and snakes)
4. Approaching the Hurdano Region (ruins of eighteen chapels)
5. The First Hurdano Village Scenes (pigs and people in a stream)
6. School and Writing (children learn to obey the state)
7. The Lower Depths: Extreme Hurdano Town and Country (a dying child)
8. Scaped Goats (film crew as hunters)
9. Daily Economy and Tribulation: Beehives (mule stung to death)
10. Cultivation and Gathering of Food (attempting to create arable land)
11. Mosquitoes and Death (malarial diseases)
12. Dwarfs and Cretins (too many of them to be a coincidence)
13. Death: A Child's Funeral (coffin floating in the river)
14. Home Life: Interior Scenes and the Death Knell
15. The End

Even the populist (and popular front) Republican government, with which Buñuel was briefly allied, banned the film because it seemed to be such a gross insult to the nation to have such poverty memorialized. The government even suggested that the region had beautiful peasant dancers and more than enough wheat for bread. But all Buñuel apparently wanted to film, his former allies complained, was "a horrible and cruel party where they rip the heads off of live chickens." (We see only the result of such an event.) The Republicans eventually lifted the ban and provided financing to enable Buñuel to add the sound track (Brahms's Fourth Symphony, a romantic piece of music that ironically floats successfully through some of the horrors of the documentary).

Unfortunately for Buñuel and for the distribution of his surrealistic travelogue, Franco's fascists agreed with the Republicans they had defeated. By the time Franco came to power, however, Buñuel was in Hollywood. After a few disappointing years there and in New York, he moved on to Mexico, where he made many films, two of which are included in this guide.

Raymond Durgnat's enthusiastic response to the film typifies its strongest supporters' assessment: "This morbid fantasy was created, not by a surrealist unconscious, but by dear old Mother Nature, with the willing cooperation of a Christian tradition and the laws of supply and demand." Two of Durgnat's key examples—on the mountain track to Las Hurdes, the film crew stops first to observe a wedding celebrated by horsemen pulling the heads off suspended cocks and then at a monastery inhabited no longer by Carmelites but by snakes—reinforce Buñuel's notion that the spiritual foundations of *this* Spain are constantly being violated.

See also: *Los olvidados.*
Availability: Selected collections.

Further reading

Buñuel, Luis. *Objects of Desire: Conversations with Luis Buñuel.* Ed. and trans. Paul Lenti. 1986. New York: Marsilio, 1992. Good firsthand detail on Buñuel's anarchistic travels in the "land without bread."

Durgnat, Raymond. *Luis Buñuel.* Berkeley: University of California Press, 1968. Survey of Buñuel's career, including a short but excellent chapter on *Land without Bread.*

Fuentes, Carlos. "The Discrete Charm of Luis Buñuel." *New York Times Magazine,* 11 March 1973. Part interview, part commentary, and all Buñuelian irony in this survey of the director's career.

Mellen, Joan, ed. *The World of Luis Buñuel.* New York: Oxford University Press, 1978. Extensive collection of essays on all of Buñuel's films, including one by Tom Conley on *Land without Bread.*

Rothman, William. *Documentary Film Classics.* Cambridge: Cambridge University Press, 1997. Close reading of a twenty-two-minute version of the film, arguing that it is not a "social problem" documentary at all but a philosophical meditation on "our horror of nature, which is also our horror of our own nature, our horror of our own horror"; for his solution of the falling-goat sequence Rothman categorically announces that Buñuel "hurled" it off the cliff himself. Horrors!

Note: The film is also known as *Las Hurdes* and *Unpromised Land*.

Last Exit to Brooklyn

A film with something to offend everyone

1989, 102 mins., R
Director: Uli Edel
Screenplay: Desmond Nakano, from Hubert Selby's novel of the same title
CAST
Harry Black = Stephen Lang
Tralala = Jennifer Jason Leigh
Big Joe = Burt Young
Boyce = Jerry Orbach
Vinnie = Peter Dobson
Donna = Ricki Lake
Georgette = Alexis Arquette

When a German director adapted *Last Exit to Brooklyn,* a maverick and uncouth semi-underground American novel, the result was the most exploitative film in this guide, edging out *Boxcar Bertha.* The central action of the film, a 1952 strike out of the cinematic Teamster tradition, has much in common with such films as *F.I.S.T.* and *Hoffa* with its violent action and very little nuts-and-bolts organizing.

The tough life in the Brooklyn factories and streets is vividly recreated here, with more than a few touches of the grotesque characters from Hubert Selby's novel. In short, it presents a worldview that would disturb many viewers. Harry Black, shop steward and strike captain of the fictional Federated Metal Workers union, rejects his wife for a man and neglects his strike duties; Tralala, a hooker, played with an over-the-top trashy style by Jennifer Jason Leigh, is gang-raped. Eventually the union president has to come in and straighten out the mess, and he kicks the pathetic shop steward out of the strike office. Not a very pretty sight. And

not a film to inspire confidence in any union, or human beings, for that matter.

See also: *Boxcar Bertha.*
Availability: Easy.

Further reading

Canby, Vincent. "Last Exit to Brooklyn." *New York Times,* 2 May 1990, C15. Although viewers may find it hard to believe, Canby wrote that the film "never appears to exploit its sensational subject matter."

Selby, Herbert, Jr. *Last Exit to Brooklyn.* New York: Grove, 1964. No one can argue that the film is any more or less exploitative than the novel by an ex-sailor who wallows in street talk.

The Last Supper

Slave owner as Christ, slaves as the Apostles

1976, 120 mins., Cuba, Spanish, with English subtitles
Director: Tomás Gutiérrez Alea
Screenplay: Tomás González, María Eugenia Haya, and Constante Diego
CAST
The Count = Nelson Villagra
Sebastián = Silvano Rey

The strength of this film is perhaps its ultimate undoing. Virtually no film on slavery has ever scrutinized at such dramatic length the intensity of the relationship between slavery and its Christian apologetics. The film is on one hand a brilliant satire of the traditional and historic role the Catholic Church played in supporting the ultimate illusion: that a slave has an even better chance of eternal bliss in heaven than his cruel overseer or harried master. On the other hand, the centerpiece of the film—the Count's re-creation of Christ's Last Supper with himself as Christ and twelve randomly selected slaves as apostles—is a striking but static and endless scene. Although the "last supper" is literally that for all but one of the "apostles," halfway through the meal we know more than we need to know.

The Last Supper **221**

During this last supper, two slaves tell stories to make sense of their bizarre experience and to interpret Christian and colonial slavery in African terms. One tale is a slave's attempt to understand the distinction between transubstantiation and cannibalism. In order to pay for food, a father is about to sell his son into slavery; when the son sells the father instead, the family in turn sells the son and earns twice as much on the deal. The moral: you can have your family and eat it too.

The other tale is about the creation of Truth and Lie by the African god Olofi. Lie cuts off Truth's head with a machete and puts Lie's head on Truth's body. The moral: "Now truth goes around with the body of Truth and the head of Lie."

The final tableau is reminiscent of the endless line of crucified slaves in *Spartacus*. As a view of slave labor and its consequences, it is equally hard to surpass. The "apostles" have led a slave revolt and are made to pay the consequences, although one, the leader Sebastián, appears to have escaped.

See also: *Burn!*
Availability: Selected collections.

Further reading

Burton, Julianne. *Cinema and Social Change in Latin America.* Austin: University of Texas Press, 1986. Includes an interview with the director.

Chanan, Michael. *The Cuban Image.* London: BFI, 1985. A thorough history of film in Cuba (which the author worships beyond critique), with a short section on *The Last Supper*.

Downing, John D. H., ed. *Film & Politics in the Third World.* New York: Autonomedia, 1987. Detailed analysis of the film's issues in the editor's essay "Four Films of Tomás Gutiérrez Alea": "As a dissection of the class relations in slavery, as a critique of the use of religion to justify oppression, as an analysis of slavery as the historic crucible of white racism, and finally as a superbly crafted work of film art, 'The Last Supper' stands in the van of twentieth-century film."

"La Ultima Cena." *Variety,* 3 May 1978. "Though finely acted and streaked with moments of wry perception, the pic doesn't know when its cards are fully stacked and overemphasizes its politi-

cal barbs to an ultimate point of redundancy and long-windedness." Fair enough.

Note: Also known as *La última cena*.

The Learning Tree

Branches of knowledge

1969, 107 mins., PG
Director: Gordon Parks Sr.
Screenplay: Gordon Parks Sr., from his own novel of the same title
CAST
Newt Winger = Kyle Johnson
Sarah Winger = Estelle Evans
Kirky = Dana Eclar
Marcus Savage = Alex Clarke
Arcella = Mira Waters
Uncle Rob = Joel Fluellen
Silas Newhall = Malcolm Atterbury
Booker Savage = Richard Ward

The Learning Tree was a historical first—the first major Hollywood film directed by an African American and one of the first to feature relatively successful black farmers and ranchers. Trained as a still photographer, Parks developed a distinctive style in his films: "I want a continuity of beautiful pictures and beautiful movement. I try to start each scene with a beautiful still photo," Parks said of his films (Bogle).

The film traces the education young Newt receives in his gentle and accommodationist family, despite the occasional racist flare-up (his teacher doesn't think he's college material). The town itself has a canker in the form of the sheriff, Kirky, who is too quick to shoot any African American in trouble with the law. Newt's shadow self is the abused and angry Marcus, who gets deeper and deeper into trouble and who refuses to accommodate with the white or black community.

After the positive critical reception of *The Learning Tree,* Parks turned to much more commercial properties, perhaps with some reluctance: "You see 'Jaws' and 'The Deep' and all the rest of them making millions of dollars, and you soon begin to realize that if you're going to stay in the business, you'd better begin to do something with a touch of sensationalism to it. Otherwise you just won't be working—and that's tragic" (Georgakis). The films he turned to were the immensely popular *Shaft* films. Always aware of his status as a black director in a mostly white Hollywood world, Parks noted the difficulty of focusing on black subjects: "If you do a film on George Washington Carver, you better have him make a peanut sauce that introduces sex" (Georgakis).

It seems reasonable to see Parks's split sympathies in his overall film output: the heroes of *The Learning Tree* (Newt), *Half-Slave, Half-Free* (Solomon Northup), and the blues singer in *Leadbelly* are for the most part gentle accommodationist types, although they can occasionally flare into anger and violence when pushed; his *Shaft* heroes, on the other hand, are more like the doomed Marcus in *The Learning Tree*—quick to anger, always prone to violence, and trying to survive in a hostile white environment.

As he approaches his ninetieth year, Parks is still going strong, active in a number of projects (even a book on the British painter J. M. W. Turner) and still documenting his world in still photographs in a traveling exhibition called *Half Past Autumn* (the title as well of an HBO documentary in 2000 on his life directed by Craig Rice and written by Lou Potter).

See also: *Sounder*.
Availability: Easy.

Further reading

Bogle, Donald. *Blacks in American Films and Television: An Encyclopedia*. New York: Garland, 1988. Overview of Parks's career.

Bohlen, Celestine. "Portrayer of the Black Experience Reflects on His Own." *New York Times,* 26 November 2000, II.36. A compact but comprehensive survey of Parks's career.

Georgakas, Dan, and Lenny Rubenstein, eds. *The Cineaste Interviews on the Art and Politics of the Cinema*. Chicago: Lake View Press, 1983. Brief interview with Parks on *The Learning Tree* and his career.

"The Learning Tree." *Variety,* 25 June 1969. Very positive review, although the lack of "militancy" in the film ("some are going to accuse Parks of pandering to white liberal attitudes") worries the reviewer endlessly.

Murray, James P. "Now, a Boom in Black Directors." *New York Times,* 4 June 1972, X.1. Surveys Hollywood's courtship of black directors once Parks's film was made.

Parks, Gordon. *The Learning Tree*. 1963. Various editions available. The novel stresses more clearly the work life of Newt's extended family.

Web site:
⟨www.artarchives.si.edu/oralhist/parks64.htm⟩ An interview site exploring Parks's accomplishments in various media.

↝

Legacy of Shame

Another never-ending wrong

1995, 60 mins.
Director: Maurice Murad
TV documentary
PRINCIPAL FIGURES
Dan Rather, host and correspondent
Randall Pinkston, interviewer
Farmers: Dino Cervantes, Jay Yates, Don Hackney, B. J. Floyd, David Healand, Vernon Boolootian
Migrant laborers: Antonia Beltrán and others, unidentified or with pseudonyms
Carlos Marentes, Farm Labor Organizing Committee (FLOC)
Crew leaders: Miguel Flores, Reynaldo Deras, and Nicholas Leon
Wayne Rowlee, attorney for Miguel Flores
Greg Schell, attorney, Florida Rural Legal Services
Robert Reich, Secretary Of Labor
Edward D. Duda, CEO, A. Duda & Sons
Israel Baez, personnel supervisor, A. Duda & Sons

CBS Reports, Edward R. Murrow and David Lowe's famous investigative series, was revived in 1993. Two years later, the series revisited the subject of Murrow and Lowe's most famous broadcast, *Harvest of Shame*. Beginning with a reprise of Murrow's characteristic voice-over from the 1960 program, Dan Rather focuses on California, Arizona, South Carolina, and Florida as sites of migrant labor abuses. With little irony, Rather states: "Thirty-five years ago there were virtually no laws protecting migrant workers; not so anymore. Now the problem isn't the laws; it's their enforcement."

Although some viewers may criticize Rather's concentration on Mexican-American crew leaders instead of farm owners, his program at least covers that aspect of the problem well. We are given specific instances of semilegal and illegal hiring practices, activities that lead, as Greg Schell, an attorney for the Florida Rural Legal Services, concludes, to peonage: "Even if they [the workers] chose to leave, even if there wasn't violence, they don't have any money. They're in the middle of nowhere. They have no choice but to continue to work because that's their only ticket out."

Miguel Flores, the crew leader who seems to be clearly in violation of the law, eventually (eighteen months after the program was first broadcast) pleaded guilty, according to Stephen Greenhouse, *New York Times* reporter, "to enslaving migrant workers in South Carolina as part of a scheme in which the workers were threatened with violence if they sought to escape." Most of these workers were illegal immigrants from Mexico and Guatemala whom Flores and two others picked up at the Mexican border of Arizona and drove to South Carolina for two days "without stopping to let them eat or use bathrooms." The pursuit of Flores and other lawbreakers seemed to be part of the Clinton administration's crackdown on the crew bosses or middlemen who control the supply of labor to the farms, although the Labor Department said it had been investigating Flores as early as 1987 and had already revoked his license as a labor contractor (Greenhouse, 8 May 1997).

The program concludes with a visit to A. Duda & Sons, farmers "just a few miles and thirty-five years down the road" from the sites of the worst abuses, "a farming operation that views decency to its workers as a function of good business." Given the U.S. government initiatives in regulating the crew leader system in 1997 (see Greenhouse, 12 March 1997), it is interesting to note that what the Dudas decided to do about crew leaders is the key, they believe, to overcoming their and the industry's violations: "We have taken those crew leaders," Israel Baez, supervisor of personnel, states, "and put them in-house. Now we call them crew foremen. And their primary responsibility is to, you know, assist with the recruiting and oversee the quality of work that his crew or her crew is performing. We do the paying."

See also: *Angel City*.
Availability: Not.

Further reading

"CBS Reports: Legacy of Shame." 20 July 1995. Transcript/script of the program (for sale from Burrelle's Information Service at ⟨www.burrelles.com⟩).

Goodman, Walter. "CBS News Revisits Migrants 35 Years Later." *New York Times*, 20 July 1995, B3. Generally positive review of the program.

Greenhouse, Steven. "3 Plead Guilty to Enslaving Migrant Workers." *New York Times*, 8 May 1997, A18. Report on Flores's case with a review of current Labor Department strategy on crew bosses or labor contractors.

——. "U.S. Expands Protection for Contract Farm Labor." *New York Times*, 12 March 1997, C22. Report on a major breakthrough for farm workers—regulating the contracting or crew bosses.

——. "U.S. Surveys Find Farm Worker Pay Down for 20 Years." *New York Times*, 31 March 1997, A1, A9. "Wages for the more than two million farm laborers have trailed stubbornly behind inflation for the past 20 years, making it hard for many of them to afford adequate housing and other necessities."

Life and Debt

"How can the machete compete with the machine?"—Jamaican farmer

2001, 86 mins.
Director: Stephanie Black
Traditional documentary
PRINCIPAL FIGURES
Belinda Becker, narrator
Michael Manley, former president of
Jamaica
Jean-Bertrand Aristide, former president of
Haiti
Jerry Rawlings, former president of
Ghana
Stanley Fischer, deputy director of
International Monetary Fund (IMF)
Numerous unnamed farmers and factory
workers

Two stories alternate in *Life and Debt*: in one, American tourists come to Jamaica to play, drink, swim, and sightsee; in the other, Jamaica as an independent economic entity dies. The two stories are related, of course, but the mechanism of the relationship has been obscured by glossy photographs of beaches and bikinis. This "island in the sun" (to use its 1950s nickname as well as the title of a Hollywood melodrama included in this guide) lost its economic self-sufficiency because the main forces in globalization—the World Trade Organization (WTO) and the World Bank—made it an offer it could not refuse.

The film traces, in virtually a case-by-case basis, how two staples of the Jamaican economy—milk for internal consumption, bananas for export—are gradually being destroyed. Part of the deal with the WTO and the World Bank required Jamaica to abandon local subsidies to its milk industry, and with trade barriers no longer in place, cheap imported milk powder undercut domestic milk production.

Similarly the Jamaican banana industry—only 5 percent of the world's market compared to Chiquita and Dole's 95 percent—was hauled before the WTO because it had an exclusive contract, tariff free, with the European Community, mainly the United Kingdom. When the WTO ruled in favor of the United States, acting mainly in the interests of Chiquita Bananas,

Jamaica's locally owned plantations were no longer viable. Soon banana workers' wages plunged to $1 a day and the model imposed on the country was the Chiquita plantations of Honduras (where workers were routinely brutalized and in many cases killed by their own military).

What did Jamaica gain by accepting loans from the World Bank? The right to have the Kingston Free Zone, another name for maquiladoras, identical gray factories that assemble materials carted a short distance from containerized boats and reloaded when the garments are finished. In short, another global sweatshop, where workers earn $30 every two weeks. At one point, in a remarkable sequence, we see Asian workers—imported from where?—being bused in when Jamaican workers refuse to work.

In a culture known for its cuisine—we see tourists munching away from time to time—the irony of globalization is acute: McDonald's imports beef, undercutting the Jamaican beef industry, and even Jamaican chickens are not safe. The growth industries turn out to be tourism, of course, security guards, and coffins.

In some kind of stealth maneuver, a secret report of the World Bank about Jamaica is highlighted: "They have achieved neither growth nor poverty reduction." This is a timely and very disturbing documentary. The fact that Jamaica Kincaid's narrative text was originally about Antigua, not Jamaica, just underlines the horrors facing an entire region.

See also: *Island in the Sun; Mickey Mouse
   Goes to Haiti; The New Rulers of the
   World*.
Availability: Selected   collections;   New
   Yorker Films.

Further reading
Gallagher, Mike, and Cameron McWhirter. "Chiquita Secrets Revealed." *Cincinnati Enquirer*, 3 May 1998, C1–18. This is the notorious "Section C" exposé of Cincinnati-based Chiquita Brands' ruthless and duplicitous control of banana production in Honduras; the

Enquirer was forced (in court) to retract these stories and expunge them from its Web site, because the information, seemingly perfectly valid, was obtained by breaking into Chiquita's e-mail system.

Holden, Stephen. "One Love, One Heart, or a Sweatshop Economy?" *New York Times*, 15 June 2001, B18. "The movie offers the clearest analysis of globalization and its negative effects that I've ever seen on a movie or television screen."

Kincaid, Jamaica. *A Small Place.* New York: Farrar Straus Giroux, 1987. Although Kincaid's scathing essay is about the ruination of Antigua, her island home, many of her targets are similar in Jamaica and other Caribbean islands.

Rapley, John. "Debating 'Life and Debt.'" *Jamaican Gleaner* at ⟨www.jamaica-gleaner.com/gleaner/20010823/cleisure/cleisure3.html⟩. One Jamaican's view from the island's only morning newspaper: the film is a successful polemic but there is irony in relying on Manley as a spokesman for antiglobalization, since "many argue that it was the policies of Michael Manley's government in the 1970s which first led Jamaica into the hands of the IMF."

Tate, Greg. "Journey through Debtor's Prison." *Village Voice*, 13 June 2001, at ⟨www.villagevoice.com⟩. The film exposes "globalization as genocide by calculator."

Web sites:

⟨www.lifeanddebt.org⟩ Official site, with discussion of the film, interview with the filmmaker (both text and audio), Web sites and other information about globalization, and reviews of the film.

⟨www.pbs.org/pov/lifeanddebt/index.html⟩ Official site of the film on PBS, with profiles of the filmmaker, further resources for reading and research, and other information.

〜

The Life and Times of Rosie the Riveter

War of the Rosies

1980, 60 mins., color and B&W
Director: Connie Field
Traditional documentary
PRINCIPAL ROSIES
Wanita Allen, Gladys Belcher, Lyn Childs, Lola Weixel, and Margaret Wright

This film tracks five women who left traditional roles and jobs in the 1940s to become part of the army of millions of women who worked in the factories while the men were at war. Combining archival black-and-white footage, old photographs of the women, and contemporary interviews (most of them set on the locations of the women's early working lives), Connie Field offers us a captivating (and ultimately bittersweet) portrait of women who not only rose to the occasion but exulted in it: the money was good, for the most part they liked their challenging jobs, and they experienced an independence denied to them before the war and unavailable to them afterward.

Before the war, the five women had other jobs: two as domestics (the two black women, Wright and Allen), one as a farm worker (Belcher), and two as housewives (Weixel and Childs); after the war, they returned to the same or similar jobs. In between, they riveted and fabricated planes and ships. Field has a great eye for the telling propaganda film or newsreel. At the beginning of the war American women were told they could operate a lathe just like the juice extractors in their kitchens. Their femininity would be intact: "They come out from work looking like business girls on vacation," reports one cheery voice-over as we see women streaming out of the factory gates. The sound track of contemporary songs backs up the visual messages: we have not only the then-famous "Rosie the Riveter" but also "Minnie's in the money . . . she's a welder," and "If you want your country free, don't be an absentee!"

When the war was over, the government propaganda machine went into reverse: the women's postwar plans had to include going home and giving up their jobs to returning vets. One authoritative documentary voice from the 1940s announces, "The family was founded on the father as patriarch and breadwinner, and the mother as cook, housekeeper, and nurse to the children." The working women, the story went, were also leaving children at home "without adequate supervision or restraint"; one public service ad with a crying baby makes it clear: it's "your baby" or "your job."

Ultimately, gender politics prevailed: Field has unearthed a wonderful clip of Dr. Marynia F. Farnham, co-author of *Modern Woman: The Lost Sex*, in which the author attributes the postwar anxiety the men felt to the fact that "their wives have become rivals."

Field's film was part of the wave of 1970s documentaries that reexamined women and labor history from a feminist point of view. Despite Hollywood's attempt to cash in on this revisionist history (Goldie Hawn in *Swing Shift*, for example), Field's documentary remains remarkably fresh and convincing. Perhaps more on how the women interacted with organized labor would have provided some important background; for this, however, the viewer will have to look at *Union Maids*.

Lola Weixel, formerly of Kaufsky's Welding Shop in New York City, almost steals the film from the other Rosies with her humor. "We were really a smart-looking group of ladies," she reminisces, but in the end "we gave up everything" to raise babies. In the companion book (see Frank et al.), Lola's testimony ends with the difficulties of a woman in the union environment of this era, but her film testimony has her wistfully (and only a little angrily) commenting about her work as a welder: "All I really wanted was to make a very beautiful ornamental gate." She still thinks about it to this day whenever she passes such a gate: "Was that so much to want?"

In both the film and the companion book, the women emphasize the sense of betrayal the owner of the small welding shop in Brooklyn felt when the women began to organize: "We were no longer 'his girls.' " In both, the union's struggle with a lockout is emphasized, and in both the double trouble of being a woman worker becomes increasingly apparent: while Lola and the women of her family worked nights to keep everyone fed and her crowded apartment clean, her brother-in-law, who worked at the Brooklyn Navy Yard, would lie on the couch and listen to jazz records.

See also: *Swing Shift; Union Maids*.
Availability: Selected collections.

Further reading

Frank, Miriam, Marilyn Ziebarth, and Connie Field. *The Life and Times of Rosie the Riveter: The Story of Three Million Working Women during World War II*. Emeryville, Calif.: Clarity Educational Productions, 1982. An essential companion book to the film, tracing and expanding on the role of the women interviewed in the film.

Galerstein, Carolyn. "Hollywood's Rosie the Riveter." *Jump Cut* 32 (1987): 20–24. An excellent survey of films other than *Swing Shift* made about the Rosies (unfortunately not available on videocassette).

Goldfarb, Lynn. *Separate and Unequal: Discrimination against Women Workers after World War II*. New York: Union of Radical Political Economists, 1976. A detailed critique of UAW policies.

Honey, Maureen. *Creating Rosie the Riveter: Class, Gender, and Propaganda during World War II*. Amherst: University of Massachusetts Press, 1984. An excellent analysis of how the media made and remade images of women workers.

Kessler-Harris, Alice. "Rosie the Riveter: Who Was She?" *Labor History* 24 (1983): 249–53. Questions the director's choice of these Rosies as representative of "women in the prewar labor force"—"they were lucky, perhaps they were special; but they were not typical."

Lundberg, Ferdinand, and Marynia F. Farnham. *Modern Women: The Lost Sex*. New York: Harper, 1947. Freudian advice from Dr. Farnham to Rosie and her sisters: stay home, raise babies, and be happy.

Tobias, Sheila, and Lisa Anderson. *What Really Happened to Rosie the Riveter: Demobilization and the Female Labor Force, 1944–47*. New York: Pantheon, 1977. Especially good on examining the role of the UAW.

Zheutlin, Barbara, ed. "The Art and Politics of the Documentary: A Symposium," *Cineaste* 11, no. 3 (1981): 12–21. Field explains her strategy for the film: "not scripted," but "carefully planned before shooting," including extensive interviews with the five Rosies before shooting.

Note: Also known as *Rosie the Riveter*.

Lightning over Braddock: A Rustbowl Fantasy

Anarchy in Steeltown

1988, 80 mins., B&W
Director: Tony Buba
Postmodern documentary
PRINCIPAL FIGURES AND ROLES
Sal Caru as himself and Gandhi
Tony Buba as himself
Steve Pelligrino as himself and Gandhi's
   assassin
Jimmy Roy, singer
Jesse Jackson as himself
Tony Buba's mother as herself

If you substitute Sal Caru, a Braddock, Pennsylvania, street hustler and would-be actor, for Roger Smith, former president of General Motors, and Tony Buba, Braddock's number-one native son and documentary filmmaker, for Michael Moore, you get *Lightning over Braddock*, or more imprecisely, something like *Sal & Me*, Buba's variation on Michael Moore's *Roger & Me,* since both films are extended comic takes on unemployment. In this instance, however, it is Sal who is looking for Tony rather than Michael looking for Roger, which is the motor of this film, since Sweet Sal is pissed that Tony has been getting so famous making films about Braddock, sometimes starring Sal, and Sal ain't gettin' no respect or—much more important—enough cash.

Buba's portrait of Braddock is subtitled *A Rustbowl Fantasy*, since he mixes both documentary footage and fiction sequences in an outrageous collage of images of a dying city, despite Buba's ever-chirpy attempt at shooting sequences of his family members in this wholesome city of parades. In 1995, Braddock, only six miles southeast of Pittsburgh on the Monongahela River, boasted a 30 percent unemployment rate and per capita income of $5,000 in a valley that had lost 20,000 jobs since 1980.

Having made too many serious documentaries about Braddock and the collapsing steel industry of the region and having became known as Pittsburgh's "other" director (the first being George Romero, pioneer of the undead saga begun with *Night of the Living Dead*), Buba was ready to try something new. Perhaps Buba's brief role as an EMT worker with a blood pressure gauge in Romero's *Dawn of the Dead* convinced him that—like Michael Moore—he could be on both sides of the camera at once. Some of the scripted sequences in *Lightning over Braddock* are funny and uncouth simultaneously: Buba films Sweet Sal in an outrageous imaginary film, *Gandhi's Return to Braddock*, has him ride into town with a floozy in a pillbox hat, and then has him assassinated by Steve Pelligrino, a rival actor, à la JFK.

Pelligrino has some wonderful sequences of his own, most notably as an accordion player trying to make it as a serious singer. Unfortunately, his rendition of the Stones' "Jumpin' Jack Flash" is filmed silently because Buba could not come up with the $15,000 for permission to use the song. Thus a joyful crowd at a bar dances to Pelligrino's delirious mute accompaniment. It was just as well, Buba's voice-over announces: what if he had died and found Sacco and Vanzetti, the anarchist martyrs, at the gate of Heaven instead of St. Peter? They would say to him, "No way you are getting in here after spending three times the per capita income of Braddock on *one song*."

Some serious footage intrudes on Buba's farces every once in a while, such as the fight to keep Dorothy 6, an impressive hearth furnace, functioning, a sequence that includes the ubiquitous Jesse Jackson rallying the workers. "I mixed fiction and documentary," Buba has said, "because I wanted the viewers to be in doubt about what was real and what wasn't, instead of just sitting there and being a good consumer" (Aufderheide).

Buba himself was an assembly-line worker before he went to college and eventually to graduate school in filmmaking. He maintains that he learned his sick brand of humor while coping with the monotony of the assembly line. Sputtering obscenities, Sweet Sal quits the film three-quarters of the way through. Like so much of Braddock, Sal is angry at being such a loser. He died just before the film was finally completed. Braddock, at least, is still alive.

See also: *Struggles in Steel; Voices from a Steeltown.*
Availability: Selected collections.

Further reading

"Artists Record the Death of the Mill's Way of Life." *New York Times,* 1 July 1985, D12. Discussion of Buba's serious, pre-*Lightning* work.

Aufderheide, Pat. "Lightning over Braddock." *Washington Post,* 27 March 1989. Overall a very perceptive review, analyzing Buba's mix of documentary and feature film traditions; concludes that it is "both unsettling and entertaining."

Wilmington, Michael. "Calendar." *Los Angeles Times,* 7 October 1989, 8. The reviewer from Los Angeles, for gosh sakes, finds Buba's "fantasy sequences too tacky for the overall vision." "Tacky is as tacky does" would be Buba's reply.

Web site:

⟨www.braddockfilms.com/page1.html⟩ Official site of Buba's films, with background essay and critics' comments.

~

A Lion Is in the Streets

Meow

1953, 88 mins.
Director: Raoul Walsh
Screenplay: Luther Davis, from Adria Locke Langley's novel of the same title
CAST
Hank Martin = James Cagney
Verity Wade = Barbara Hale
Flamingo = Anne Francis
Jules Bolduc = Warner Anderson
Robert Castleberry = Larry Keating
Guy Polli = Onslow Stevens

Because this film about peckerwood politics never found its audience upon its release or even in our videocassette years, many viewers have been deprived of one of the more outrageous Technicolor moments in cinematic history: behind the opening credits a male lion prows at the base of the Lincoln statue in Washington, D.C., growling and leaping at the Great Emancipator. For a moment we think the M-G-M lion has slipped his handlers, wandered down the block to Warner Brothers, and is pissed that he has gone from the studio of heavenly stars to the proletarian lot.

Not to worry: it's only the titular metaphor for the film's political lion, Hank Martin, played by James Cagney in the over-the-top style reserved for southern populist demagogues—even Broderick Crawford, portraying a Huey Long figure in *All the King's Men*, couldn't resist this style. In a fit of spending, Cagney had purchased the rights to Langley's novel soon after it appeared for the then-impressive sum of a quarter of a million dollars. But he sat on the project for eight years, and Robert Rossen's *All the King's Men* came, was seen, and won all the prizes.

In Langley's novel, Hank Martin gained national attention when he—among other exploits—began referring to himself as the Big Lion: "'Cause the lion's king a' beasts, n' I'm king a' this here jungle." The jungle turns out to be backwoods Mississippi, and in keeping with the rural religious folkways Langley tried to capture in her novel, her title actually comes from Proverbs 26:13–14: "The slothful man saith, there is a lion in the way; a lion is in the streets. As the door turneth upon his hinges, so doth the slothful upon his bed." Part of Hank Martin's appeal to the peckerwoods, according to Langley, is that he will not take the domination of the men who control their lives by fixing, for example, illegal weights at the sharecropping station.

This Raoul Walsh film remains intriguing nonetheless, if only to see how a film of the McCarthy era handles the issue of an aroused populace that might follow a right-wing leader. It also provides us with the opportunity to see Anne Francis play a swamp siren who could charm the skin off an alligator. And finally it provides us with a double vision (novel and film) of further examples of the white-trash stereotype, which this film amusingly reduces to the expression (never used by any real person?) of the "folkses."

There may be some truth in Langley's stereotypes, although this film is fairly swamped with them—the cotton mogul, Robert Castleberry, whom Hank calls the Black Skimmer—the bird who steals everything in sight; Jules Bolduc, the indolent representative of old money; Guy Polli, gangster and vote-fixer; and finally the Swamp Thang herself, the Little Flamingo (Anne Francis), whom Hank makes the mistake of saying he'll marry someday (when she grows up). Throw in Hank's virtuous schoolteacher wife; his upper-class nemesis, a cynical newspaperman; and even a mammy, and you have a cast of characters probably more fit for vaudeville than a serious cinematic examination of populist demagoguery. And where *are* the working folkses when you need 'em?

See also: *God's Little Acre; Tobacco Road*.
Availability: Selected collections.

Further reading

Crowther, Bosley. "A Lion Is in the Streets." *New York Times*, 24 September 1953, 39. Praises this "headlong and dynamic drama about a backcountry champion of the poor who permits his political ambitions to pull him down a perilously crooked road" and adds (ominously) that "the theme of public weakness to rabble-rousers is as timely as it was" when the novel was written.

Langley, Adria Locke. *A Lion Is in the Streets*. Philadelphia: Blakiston, 1945. Popular source novel of the film, with enough folksy dialect (both black and white) to irritate but also with enough energy to convince.

"A Lion Is in the Streets." *Variety*, 9 September 1953. Dismisses the film's parallel with Huey Long, in part because of the departure of the script from the novel and in part because of "ludicrously folksy" scenes.

The Little Girl Who Sold the Sun

Market forces

1999, 45 mins., Senegal/Switzerland/France, in Wolof, with English subtitles
Director: Djibril Diop Mambéty
Screenplay: Djibril Diop Mambéty
CAST
Sili Laam = Lisa Balera
Babou Seck = Tayerou M'Baye

This film was released after Mambéty's death in 1998 at age 53. It was to be the second in a trilogy of short films called *Tales of Little People*. The first of these films about "ordinary people" was *Le Franc*, completed and released in 1994, but the third, *The Woman Who Chipped Stones* (*La Tailleuse de pierre*), was probably not finished. (Its topic, laborers breaking up large stones by hand for later use in construction, is remarkably similar to Flora M'mbugu-Schelling's *These Hands*.)

Mambéty begins his tale of the "global economy" (as a title calls it) by tracking a diverse lot of Senegalese as they approach a central market: our little heroine is on crutches, a legless boy is in a wheelchair, and countless others use everything from horse carts to Mercedes Benzes to make their way. In the background of a shot of a man splitting rocks with a hammer (a moment that points to the third film in the trilogy), a jumbo jet takes off. The street market in Mambéty's world becomes metaphoric for the world market—free, seemingly uncontrolled, but at the mercy of ruthless competitors, whether they are teenage gangs or the World Bank. Indeed, in all three of the Mambéty films included in this book, it is France's collusion with the World Bank that keeps former French colonies at the mercy of economic forces they cannot control. French devaluation of the West African franc is literally the name of the lottery the street musician wins in *Le Franc*; in *Hyenas* a billionaire somehow related to the World Bank buys a town's acquiescence in her vigilante justice; and in this film we see a headline that predicts an event that has yet to happen: "Africa Leaves the Franc Zone."

We don't meet the little girl Sili at first; instead we witness a disturbing incident: a woman is arrested as a shoplifter, abused as she resists arrest, and taken off to the nearby jail. She insists that she is a princess, not a thief, but the crowd mocks her. When Sili herself is dragged off to the same police station because an officer thinks she has too much cash in hand, she bravely denounces him for, in effect, asking for a bribe, and wins not only her freedom but that of the poor woman arrested earlier. In short, she is a brave girl attempting to break through the forces that control the market, both literally (the police and gangs of rival salesboys) and metaphorically (the Western countries).

Sili, with the help of one sympathetic boy, Babou, struggles to make a success of her newspaper sales. Her friend sells *The Nation*, which she considers the establishment paper, but she sells *The Sun*, because the people read it. If anyone could sell the sun, this street child could. In Mambéty's poetic vision, you may be poor, handicapped, and a girl, but you persevere. When the gang of rival street vendors steal her crutches, Sili's friend asks: "What can we do?" She replies: "We continue."

See also: *Le Franc; Hyenas; These Hands.*
Availability: Selected collections; California Newsreel.

Further reading

Lu, Alvin. "Djibril Diop Mambety." *San Francisco Bay Guardian*, 21 April 1999. Contrasts the "socially committed and socially realist" cinema of Ousmane Sembene (see *Xala*) with Mambéty's cinema of "dreams and parable."
Ukadike, N. Frank. "The Hyena's Last Laugh." *Transition* 78 (1999): 136–53. Extensive interview with Mambéty, including a discussion of his use of nonprofessionals as his leading actors.
Verniere, James. "Girl and 'Sun' Are Glorious." *Boston Herald*, 31 December 1999, S21. Calls the film "proof [that] neo-realism is as viable and useful a style today as it was in postwar Italy."
Web site:
⟨www.newsreel.org/topics/acine.htm⟩ California Newsreel's Library of African Cinema has a

number of entries on films and related essays by and about Mambéty as well as other African directors.

Note: Also known as *La Petite Vendeuse de soleil*.

Long Road Home

But they get there

1991, 78 mins., TVM
Director: John Korty
Screenplay: Jane-Howard Hammerstein, from Ronald B. Taylor's novel of the same title
CAST
Ertie Robertson = Mark Harmon
Bessie Robertson = Lee Purcell
Jake Robertson = Morgan Weisser
Titus Wardlow = Leon Russom

Unlike migrant families in virtually every documentary and feature film about their plight, the Robertsons in *Long Road Home* do finally get a home of their own. The road there was nonetheless very dangerous and violent. Set in the California agricultural valleys in 1937, when organizing and vigilante reprisals went hand in hand, this film—and Ronald B. Taylor's novel from which it was adapted—recreates many of the incidents in John Steinbeck's unfilmed *In Dubious Battle*. In fact, the final battle between strikers and Titus Wardlow, a particularly nasty grower, differs from Steinbeck's story only in that young Jake Robertson kills Wardlow to protect his father. Wardlow and the vigilantes tried to use the same ruse that Steinbeck witnessed in the 1930s and used in his novels: the strikers manage to camp on a piece of property donated by a sympathizer but the vigilantes create an incident that draws the sheriff and his men into the camp.

In his novel Taylor also drew on other atrocities reported in the 1930s. A "labor agitator" is denounced as a commie and shot in the back. Wardlow calls in some strikebreak-

A migrant worker's accident in the apple orchard in *The Long Road Home*.

ers and labor "experts" who had broken the Salinas lettuce strike.

One of Wardlow's buddies early on suggests to the landowner that he might consider that paying the workers an extra "dime might short-circuit union trouble." But Wardlow is king of El Adobe, his spread, and "no commie's going to pick my crops." He becomes a hero to the local Growers Association, the sponsor of the vigilantes, who parade around with a miniature lynched figure labeled "Union Organizer."

Ertie Robinson gets fired from El Adobe early on because he won't "work for brass"—that is, the company-issued coinage accepted at all the local stores. It takes him a while to come around on the organizing issue, but in the end the film rewards his family's perseverance by having them gain a house. Few migratory workers are ever that lucky.

See also: *The Grapes of Wrath; The Migrants*.
Availability: Selected collections.

Further reading

Taylor, Ronald B. *Long Road Home*. New York: Henry Holt, 1988. The source novel by a former reporter whose beat included migrant labor.

The Long Voyage Home

O'Neilled

1940, 105 mins., B&W
Director: John Ford
Screenplay: Dudley Nichols, from four one-act plays by Eugene O'Neill: *Bound East for Cardiff; The Moon of the Caribbees; In the Zone*; and *The Long Voyage Home*

Ole Olson = John Wayne
Driscoll = Thomas Mitchell
Smitty = Ian Hunter
Cocky = Barry Fitzgerald
Captain = Wilfrid Lawson
Freda = Mildred Natwick
Axel = John Qualen
Yank = Ward Bond

The screenplay for *The Long Voyage Home* was based on four Eugene O'Neill plays. The first, *Bound East for Cardiff*, was a featured production of the famous Provincetown Players, whose identification with O'Neill and his new American drama had intensified when this, his first play, was produced in 1916. All four plays, under the umbrella title of *S.S. Glencairn*, were integrated into a single screenplay by Dudley Nichols and directed by John Ford with his usual crowd of tough and sentimental men.

In John Ford's career, *The Long Voyage Home* is sandwiched between *The Grapes of Wrath* and *How Green Was My Valley*. These dramas of the migrating Okies and the locked-out Welsh miners are stiff competition for this portrayal of the sailors of a British freighter, the S.S. *Glencairn*, as it makes an ammunition run from the West Indies to London. But the film remains compelling, in part because of the understanding we gain of the tough lot of merchant seamen and in part because Ford used his own "family" of actors—John Wayne as a quiet Swede, Ward Bond as a land lover, and Thomas Mitchell as a feisty Irishman, among others.

Dramatic incidents from the various plays rise and fall during the film. Smitty, who is dreaming of land, dies during an air raid. Ole, played by Wayne with a strange Scandinavian accent, is shanghaied during a drunken celebration. He is rescued by his friends, who don't realize that another one of their group has been left behind. By the next day all of the hung-over crew are back on the *Glencairn*, ready for another risky voyage. An end title sums up their story: "The Long Voyage never ends."

Two other film adaptations of O'Neill plays, not in this guide, are worth seeing: *The Hairy Ape* (also set for the most part at sea) retains much of the original stage punch and still holds up as a film; and *The Emperor Jones* is worth a look for Paul Robeson's portrayal of a Pullman porter gone bad. *The Long Voyage Home* is a little creakier, like the freighter these hapless sailors have signed on. Gregg Toland, the cinematographer of *Citizen Kane*, is also a star here, with his deep-focus photography, placing the dark ship in the background on a forbidding sea or, when the men are on shore, capturing their long shadows on wet paving stones.

See also: *How Green Was My Valley*.
Availability: Selected collections.

Further reading

Crowther, Bosley. "The Long Voyage Home." *New York Times*, 9 October 1940, 30. Rave review, emphasizing the dangers (both personal and professional) the sailors face as they remain bound to their ship.

Look Back in Anger

Look back in amazement

1958, 99 mins., B&W, UK
Director: Tony Richardson
Screenplay: Nigel Kneale and John Osborne, from the latter's play of the same title
CAST
Jimmy Porter = Richard Burton
Alison Porter = Mary Ure
Helena Charles = Claire Bloom
Cliff Lewis = Gary Raymond
Inspector Hurst = Donald Pleasence
Colonel Redfern = Glen Byam Shaw
Mrs. Tanner = Dame Edith Evans
Kapoor = S. P. Kapoor

We look back with some amazement on the idea that Jimmy Porter, a British market-stall worker played by Richard Burton, would have been seen in the 1950s as a rebellious character instead of the complaining, unpleasantly violent, and horny—the British would say "randy"—character he now appears to be. His rebellion seems to be mainly against his upper-middle-class wife and her colonial-administrator father, both of whom he constantly berates for not being working class, although he himself moved closer to his wife's class by attending university.

At the same time, he defends an Indian stall worker against racist pressure to abandon his pitch, and he seems to represent an almost trade union solidarity of the stall workers against an obnoxious city inspector (played brilliantly by Donald Pleasence). At one point, he and his wife's best friend watch a film about British colonial troops massacring the local natives.

And, speaking of his wife's best friend, he of course sleeps with her. His love affairs are by turns tender and cruel, extremes that may sum up the film's message about British nonunionized working-class life in the 1950s. Publicity for the play emphasized Jimmy Porter's sexy charm: "You are asked to believe that two women love this volcano of ceaseless, sputtering venom [and] you believe it. . . . The truth about this conscienceless sadist is that he is absolutely alive."

As a hit in London in 1956, John Osborne's play helped to bring a generation of working-class playwrights to center stage. The play's title was adopted to describe this generation.

It is reasonably clear in retrospect that the "anger" in Osborne's play and the other films and novels of the 1950s was mainly class resentment in a society traditionally committed to keeping working-class people in their place. Occasionally, as in Jimmy Porter's struggle against Inspector Hurst (not a trace of which is in the original play), the anger becomes more politicized, but too often the struggle ends up being like that of male deer at rutting time.

Two other versions of the play are available on videocassette in selected collections. Lindsay Anderson directed Malcolm McDowell and Lisa Barnes as Jimmy and Alison Porter in 1980, while a Thames Television production, directed by David Jones (from the stage production directed in turn by Judi Dench) and starring Kenneth Branagh and Emma Thompson as the Porters, appeared in 1989. Although both have very strong casts, neither has the audacity and rebellious potential of the original. Both follow the original stage play more slavishly than Richardson's film does, thus eliminating the subplot with the Indian stall worker, for example, and reinstating Jimmy Porter's very literate references to such writers as Emily Brontë. (Do Angry Young Men read *Wuthering Heights*? Richard Burton's Jimmy Porter didn't.) Both seem more like filmed plays (which they are) than cinematic adaptations of a play. Viewers familiar with British television—especially the productions of *Masterpiece Theatre*—will find these closer to that standard than to the rough-and-tumble world of the original Jimmy Porter of the 1950s.

See also: *This Sporting Life.*
Availability: Selected collections; DVD.

Further reading

Crowther, Bosley. "Look Back in Anger." *New York Times*, 16 September 1959, 45. More cynical than other reviewers about this so-called angry young man, whom Crowther considers "a conventional weakling, a routine crybaby."

Hill, John. *Sex, Class, and Realism: British Cinema, 1956–1963*. London: British Film Institute, 1986. Sets the film among numerous other important working-class films during this period.

Mortimer, John. "The Angry Young Man Who Stayed That Way." *New York Times*, 8 January 1995, II.5. A fellow playwright reviews Osborne's career on the occasion of his death.

Looks and Smiles

But no jobs

1981, 104 mins., B&W, UK
Director: Ken Loach
Screenplay: Barry Hines, from his novel of the same title

CAST
Mick Walsh = Graham Green
Karen Lodge = Carolyn Nicholson
Alan Wright = Tony Pitts

The title of the novel and film comes from a quotation from Anton Chekhov. A young girl asks an older relative, "How did girls attract boys when you were young?" and she replies, "In the usual way—with looks and smiles" (Fuller). This film, like most of Loach's work, however, is very light with looks and smiles à la Chekhov. We follow the at first diverging paths of three English youngsters in Sheffield—two lads, Mick and Alan, desperately searching for apprenticeships that will lead to jobs, and Karen, Mick's girlfriend.

Alan solves the unemployment problem by joining the army. He is sent to Northern Ireland to police the Troubles. Karen leaves her job and a contentious family life to look, with Mick's help, for her dad in Bristol. In the end, nothing comes out right. Karen returns to her job, and Mick, who is tempted to join the army, returns to the dole office. The film keeps to the spirit of the last lines of Barry Hines's source novel: Mick "knew he would have to arrive early to reach the counter.... The queues were longer every time he went."

See also: *Boys From the Blackstuff.*
Availability: Not.

Further reading

Loach, Ken. *Loach on Loach*. Ed. Graham Fuller. London: Faber & Faber, 1998. Interview with Loach discussing *Looks and Smiles*.
Hines, Barry. *Looks and Smiles*. London: Michael Joseph, 1983. The source novel.

Love on the Dole

Cheap

1941 (1945), 89 mins., UK, B&W
Director: John Baxter
Screenplay: Walter Greenwood, from his play and novel of the same title
CAST
Sally Hardcastle = Deborah Kerr
Larry Meath = Clifford Evans
Mrs. Hardcastle = Mary Merrall
Mr. Hardcastle = George Carney
Harry Hardcastle = Geoffrey Hibbert
Sam Grundy = Frank Cellier
Ned Narkey = Martin Walker

Love on the Dole was adapted from Walter Greenwood's successful British play of 1936, which in turn was based on his remarkable novel, a best-seller in 1933. The Hardcastles, a working-class family from Salford (in the Midlands), at first survive as factory jobs are

Two unemployed friends in *Looks and Smiles.*

lost all around them. They get tipped over the poverty line, however, by a new wave of massive unemployment and a controversial governmental means test that whittles away at many people's eligibility for benefits, or "the dole."

The streets fill with angry men and despairing women. The crowd scenes are stirring as Labour Party representatives contest the more radical and revolutionary elements who wish to launch an all-out assault on the authorities. On the street level, only the institutions of poverty such as the pawnshop prosper.

Deborah Kerr delivers a remarkable portrayal of Sally, the good Hardcastle daughter, who becomes the mistress of a sleazy gambling czar as a way of securing jobs for her brother and father. She is the center of the film, but the edges are pretty good too. Sally's great love, Larry Meath, a Labour Party activist, is killed trying to keep an unemployment march from turning violent. He is trampled by a policeman's horse, as demonstrators carrying banners ("Work Not the Dole") attempt to rush the city center.

The *New York Times* reviewer noted that there were rumors about the four-year delay in the American release of the film. The unrelentingly grim portrait of unemployment in the film may have made little sense with war production in high gear. Who wanted to be told how terrible the 1930s were? It is also possible, the reviewer suggested, that Americans would learn to their horror what real labor–management unrest could be like.

The film ends, as does *The Grapes of Wrath*, with a sorrowful mother. Mrs. Hardcastle wonders if change is possible when there are "men who have forgotten

Unemployment demonstration in the Depression in *Love on the Dole*. Courtesy British Film Institute Stills, Posters, and Designs.

how to work and the young who have never learned how."

See also: *Fame Is the Spur*.
Availability: Selected collections.

Further reading

"At the Palace." *New York Times*, 13 October 1945, 11. Intriguing review, as the writer places the film in the context of both the Labour Party's rise to power in England and current American conditions.

Greenwood, Walter. *Love on the Dole*. 1933. Harmondsworth: Penguin, 1969. The source novel covers a wider range of political and economic issues than the film, with graphic descriptions of an unemployed person as "a living corpse; a unit of the spectral army of three million lost men."

Orwell, George. *The Road to Wigan Pier*. 1937. Various editions available. An essential nonfiction companion to the film and Greenwood's novel: Orwell goes semi-underground to experience and record at firsthand the appalling conditions among out-of-work miners.

Mac

Made in Queens

1993, 118 mins., R
Director: John Turturro
Screenplay: John Turturro and Brandon Cole

CAST

Mac Vitelli = John Turturro
Vico Vitelli = Michael Badalucco
Bruno Vitelli = Carl Capotorto
Alice = Katherine Borowitz
Nat = John Amos
Polowski = Olek Krupa
Oona = Ellen Barkin
Papa = Joe Paparone

As a portrait of an Italian-American immigrant carpenter and his three sons in Queens in the 1950s, John Turturro's film is a tribute to his own father, nicknamed Mac for the film. Mac is an ethnic blue-collar craftsman who tries to make it as a skilled worker for an independent contractor building private houses.

When that arrangement falls apart, Mac and his brothers form a construction business of their own. The tensions and triumphs of this self-obsessed family provide us with a comic but convincing Italian-American working-class life (seen in the old days in *Marty* and somewhat updated in *Moonstruck*). To my untrained eye, the brothers, especially Mac, seem to spend an inordinate amount of time having temper tantrums and knocking down the studs and scaffolding of the houses that they presumably built offscreen.

The film concerns the passion of these craftsmen to do a job well and how difficult it is to sustain that passion in capitalist America. The construction businesses in this film are small—a mega-enterprise like Levittown is mentioned only briefly—and so the real competition for Turturro's Vitelli Brothers is another (Eastern European) immigrant's small business. There is also disharmony among the brothers themselves, since Mac's younger brothers simply cannot stand Mac's insatiable appetite for work.

Unionism among construction workers surfaces only briefly, when Mac demands that one of his workers redo a cement floor because of the flotsam and jetsam (pants, a boot, a toilet seat) that the worker has sloppily left in the soup. The worker refuses, threatening to get his "union rep" to back him up. Mac prevails here, as he does so often in his quest to make it as an independent contractor, but the film criticizes his unyielding personality. Quoting his father (who has the best scene when he pops up from the dead at his own funeral to attack the workmanship of his coffin), Mac says there are only two ways to do a job—"the right way and my way," and "both ways are the same." (Papa's remark parodies a moment in *The Caine Mutiny*, when Captain Queeg maintains that there are *four* ways: the right way, the wrong way, the Navy way, and his way.)

There's an amusing subplot with Ellen Barkin as a Jewish beatnik model and poet who fascinates and is in turn fascinated by two of the three brothers. Perhaps inevitably, given this culture, women are subsidiary but interesting, and how Mac finds one as good as his mama (always heard but never seen) is amusing. But it's craft, not union work, that ultimately matters.

See also: *Marty*.
Availability: Easy.

Further reading

Canby, Vincent. "Pride and Craftsmanship in a Blue-Collar Family." *New York Times*, 19 February 1993, C17. Compares the film—"a very good movie with a mind"—to Loach's British film about construction, *Riff-Raff*.

∽ Making Steel

The Canadian way

1992, 60 mins., Canada
Director: Elizabeth Beaton
Traditional documentary
PRINCIPAL FIGURES
Barbara Carver, narrator
Steelworkers: Clarence Butler, Benny Delorenzo, Kay Heinrich, Paul Hallohan, Joe Keller, Mike Lahey, John Lucas, John Miles, Frank Murphy, Sam Murphy, Winston Ruck, Steve Sokol, George Tomie, Harold Whelan, and Dan Yakimchuk

The film is presented in three segments of approximately equal length: "Technology," how steel is made; "History," how the Canadian industry came to be centered in the Cape Breton region of Nova Scotia; and "Culture of Work," how the steelworkers and their families organized their work lives around ethnicity and religion. All three segments use the Sydney steel plant, or SYSCO, as their focal point. Overall, in tracing the ninety-year history of the plant, the film shows us the too familiar pattern seen in other North American films about steel and related metal industries, from boom at the turn of the century to bust in 1989.

The director, the folklorist and historian Elizabeth Beaton, develops at some length parts of the story that she feels even Canadians may not know well, as David Frank has argued, such as the thousand women who were recruited to the plant during World War II, no doubt Rosies all. This recovery of local steelmaking history is part of a major focus of the University College of Cape Breton, but the film was sponsored by the ubiquitous National Film Board of Canada.

See also: *Brass Valley; Shout Youngstown*.
Availability: Selected collections; National Film Board of Canada.

Further reading

Frank, David. "One Hundred Years After: Film and History in Atlantic Canada." *Acadiensis* 26 (Spring 1997): 112–36. Includes a discussion of *Making Steel*, emphasizing the film's achievement in presenting the culture of the steel industry and also asking difficult questions about "the ultimate failure of the plant."
Heron, Craig. *Working in Steel: The Early Years in Canada, 1883–1935*. Toronto: McClelland & Stewart, 1988. A standard history of the industry.

∽ The Man in the White Suit

. . . is a labor–management problem

1951, 84 mins., B&W, UK
Director: Alexander Mackendrick
Screenplay: Roger Macdougall, John Dighton, and Alexander Mackendrick, from Mackendrick's play of the same title
CAST
Sidney Stratton = Alec Guinness
Daphne Birnley = Joan Greenwood
Alan Birnley = Cecil Parker
Sir John Kierlaw = Ernest Thesiger
Bertha = Vida Hope

When Sidney, a lowly lab dishwasher at a textile mill who secretly works on his own experiments, invents a new miracle fabric, his dreams of becoming a research chemist finally seem to be coming true. His fabric will create clothing that will never wear out or become dirty. The mill owner's daughter—for reasons of her own—supports his research, but eventually the implications of his invention strike horror in both management and labor. If clothes never need to be replaced, textile mill managers and workers will soon be unnecessary.

In a fit of capitalist pique, one company decides to monopolize Sidney's invention. But the collective industrial geniuses point out that eventually there will be no profits for anyone. Both managers and trade union leaders want him stopped, by any means necessary. Sidney becomes a hunted man. In a classic scene of Ealing Studio comedy, Sidney is chased up and down the streets at night, literally glowing white in his radioactive-fiber suit, his only supporter a waifish girl who tries to misdirect his pursuers, who consist of both managers and trade unionists. When he is finally cornered, to their great delight and his mortification, Sidney's white suit gradually disintegrates, leaving him standing in his shirt and boxer shorts: it turns out that his miracle fabric has only a very short life.

Although Sidney is virtually silent, somewhere along the way he admits that as a misunderstood Cambridge first-class graduate he has always been a maverick worker and never been appreciated. When we see him in the end, he is clearly ready to go incognito at another factory, where he will disrupt the orderly compromise there that labor and management have so far maintained.

The film ends with the sweet (to Sidney) music of the bubbling flasks of his favorite experiment. In an Ealing Studio comedy like this, a plot is often not resolved but simply waited out. Unlike the central characters of most traditional comedies, Sidney apparently loses both his girlfriends—the fellow trade unionist Bertha and the industrialist's daughter, Daphne: the ways of class conciliation are not always smooth in an Ealing Studio film, either.

See also: *I'm All Right, Jack.*
Availability: Easy; DVD.

Further reading

Crowther, Bosley. "Man in the White Suit." *New York Times*, 1 April 1952, 35. A "deft and sardonic little satire on the workings of modern industry."

Stead, Peter. *Film and the Working Class*. London: Routledge, 1989. Includes a discussion of the Ealing comedies.

⌐∽

Man of Iron

Stalinism vs. Solidarity

1981, 153 mins., Polish, with English subtitles, PG
Director: Andrzej Wajda
Screenplay: Aleksander Scibor-Rylski
CAST
Tomczyk = Jerzy Radziwilowicz
Agnieszka = Krystyna Janda
Winkiel = Marian Opania
Anna = Wieslawa Kosmalska
Captain Wirski = Andrzej Seweryn
TV Editor = Boguslaw Sobczuk
Solidarity leaders Lech Walesa and Anna
Walentynowicz as themselves

According to Gary Mead, Polish cinema of the 1980s was deeply divided between the filmmakers of international reputation and those with national followings. Before Poland shed its Communist leadership, Wajda was an "officially semitolerated" presence rather than an "officially loved" figure. Like his protégé, Agnieszka Holland (*To Kill a Priest*), and the late Krzysztof Kieslowski (*Camera Buff* and *Three Colors: Blue/Red/White*), he eventually consolidated a strong Polish as well as international reputation.

In this sequel to Wajda's *Man of Marble*, Krystyna Janda and Jerzy Radziwilowicz reprise their roles (after a fashion). Janda plays the filmmaker Agnieszka once again, but this time she is searching for the son of Mateusz—the "man of marble." The man of marble in the earlier film and his son, the man of iron, are both played by Radziwilowicz.

The son, however, does not want to be found. His activism with Solidarity has made him a marked man to the Polish authorities. Although no less intense in its celebration of the Polish drive for independence, *Man of Iron* is a little less sharp than the earlier film. Now Agnieszka is given to making remarks like this one to Tomczyk: "You're not afraid of jail if you're already there."

Nevertheless, the film retains its interest, which is due not least to the documentary presence of the Solidarity leaders Lech Walesa and Anna Walentynowicz, who play themselves.

See also: *Man of Marble; To Kill a Priest*.
Availability: Selected collections.

Further reading

Andrews, Edmund L. "Mapping a Glossy Future for a Has-Been Shipyard." *New York Times*, 1 October 2001, A4. The current state of the famous Gdansk shipyards, hovering between privatized capitalist enterprise and industrial heritage theme park.

Canby, Vincent. "Act of Bravery." *New York Times*, 12 October 1981, C14. Sees the film "as more notable as a political than an artistic achievement," given the daringness of making a film about the radical Solidarity strikes, but the reviewer worries about a "cult of personality" growing around Lech Walesa.

Mead, Gary. "Volksfilm for the 1980s." *Sight and Sound*, Autumn 1983, 230–31. Critical analysis of the state of the Polish cinema under military dictatorship soon after *Man of Iron* was released.

Moszcz, Gustaw. "Wajda August '81." *Sign and Sound*, Winter 1981/82, 31–33. Interview with the director, emphasizing the difficulties of making critical films in a "totalitarian society"; even Lech Walesa, according to Moszcz, thought it was "too radical."

Paul, David W., ed. *Politics, Art, and Commitment in East European Cinema*. New York: St. Martin's Press, 1983. Extensive discussion of Wajda's films, with two fascinating appendices: a speech by Wajda and reports on two film festivals held in Gdansk "between the formation of Solidarity and the imposition of martial law" in 1981.

Perlez, Jane. "Ship of Dreams Goes Under in Poland." *New York Times*, 29 March 1997, 4. The giant shipyard and revolutionary home of Solidarity fails to survive in free-market Poland.

Man of Marble

Feet of clay

1979, 160 mins., Polish, with English subtitles
Director: Andrzej Wajda
Screenplay: Aleksander Scibor-Rylski
CAST
Agnieszka Hulewicz = Krystyna Janda
Mateusz Birkut = Jerzy Radziwilowicz
Hanka Tomczyk = Krystyna Zachwatowicz
Witek = Michel Tarkowski
Michalek = Piotr Cleslak
Film Editor = Wieslaw Wojcik
Television Producer = Boguslaw Sobczuk
Cameraman = Leonard Zajaczkowski
Sound engineer = Jacek Domanski
Agnieszka's father = Zdzislaw Kozien

Andrzej Wajda's film dissects a particular type of Communist hero of the Stalin era in the Soviet Union and its Eastern European satellites: the stakhanovite, or superhero worker, the man who in his selfless drive to establish a Communist utopia works harder and longer than everyone else for the collective good. Money, vacations, fame—none of these mattered. The Soviet model was Aleksei Stakhanov, the working stiff as overachieving superstar. Wajda's film is about a Polish bricklayer, Mateusz Birkut, who, selected for his already considerable accomplishments as a worker and his boyish good looks, becomes a national hero when he strives to break a record by laying 30,000 bricks in one eight-hour shift.

The form of the film follows the model of Orson Welles's classic *Citizen Kane*. We learn of Mateusz's life, heroic rise, and tragic fall through films within films, secret archival footage, and interviews—with flashbacks— with his friends, loved ones, and "guardian angels" (those who spied on him). The frame story for the film is the quest by Agnieszka, a film student, to make a film about Mateusz for her graduate diploma. She uses her ambition, her sneakiness, and her attractiveness (she is a tall blonde who towers over most of her subjects in part because she wears enormous platform sandals under her bell bottoms) to get her interviewees to tell "the truth" about Mateusz. The truth, however, is very elusive, although by film's end it is clear that Mateusz was a victim of Communist overachieving, cheating, and bureaucratic evil.

Wajda, Poland's greatest living filmmaker, intercuts the contemporary story of Agnieszka's quest and Mateusz's story by creating an entire set of fictional short films. Thus Agnieszka first screens inflated state-sponsored films about Mateusz, films with such titles as *Birth of a City* and *Architects of Happiness*, which survey Mateusz's superskills and how they were put to service building a new workers' city and steel plant at the "socialist" city of Nowa Huta. She then interviews the celebrated filmmaker of these puff pieces, who gives his own version (in flashbacks) of the time he spent filming Mateusz in the 1950s. The technique—repeated with other characters and other film footage—results in a remarkable series of multiple viewpoints on the same characters and their actions.

Mateusz's honeymoon with the socialist state comes to a crashing halt one sunny day when he is out at a new site "teaching" the local workers how to overachieve and work themselves to death for the common good. He is with his trusted friend and assistant, Witek. The two employ a team approach to bricklaying, which is Mateusz's special contribution to socialism. Thus Mateusz and four assistants lay bricks incredibly quickly: two men prepare the cement base, two others place the bricks, and Mateusz makes the final alignment. As yet another bricklaying feat is about to be staged, Mateusz is handed a burning-hot brick, which cripples his hands. The government spy suspects Witek, who says he's innocent because he was wearing gloves and did not know the brick was booby-trapped.

In continuing scenes of chilling Communist justice, Witek literally disappears from a room at the Public Security Office to which he has been summoned and later reappears in a kangaroo court, where Mateusz is supposed to testify against him. We never know if he is really guilty, but Wajda's point is that it doesn't make any difference; the state is simply looking for scapegoats. First Mateusz and then Witek recant their testimony in front of newsreel cameras, but that footage is repressed and comes to light only years later when Agnieszka is making her film.

The Man of Marble (Jerzy Radziwilowicz) at work. Courtesy British Film Institute Stills, Posters, and Designs.

Wajda's satiric approach is relentless. Witek, it turns out, is rehabilitated after his release from prison and becomes the director of a major steel plant. Mateusz is convicted of leading the "Gypsy Band," a group of "imperialist spies," but in fact they are a hired band of gypsy musicians who were with him when he threw a brick through the window of the Public Security Office.

By the time Wajda was completing his film, the Solidarity movement had been launched from the Gdansk shipyards with Lech Walesa as one of its leaders. In Agnieszka's search for Mateusz—he has literally disappeared since his release from prison in 1956, the year of the Khrushchev "thaw"—she finds his son at the shipyards, who tells her his father is dead.

This section of the film was censored by the Polish authorities in 1977, when the film was finished. In the current videocassette release, Gdansk is just a name—no organized activity is portrayed—and a graveside scene specifying where Mateusz was killed—at the 1970 Gdansk workers' protests—is omitted. Wajda includes this information in the sequel, *Man of Iron* (1980).

Agnieszka, like Wajda, is kept from finishing her film by officials at the TV station and the essential footage she needs is no longer available to her. She does make a comeback, however, in Wajda's sequel, *Man of Iron*.

Wajda rarely overburdens his strong political subject matter. Our first glimpse of Mateusz is actually of a literal "man of marble," a socialist-realist statue of him as a greater-than-life-size worker with a determined jaw and a serious set of muscles. Using this statue as the first step into Mateusz's life, Wajda has challenged a glorified view of art in this remarkable deconstruction of the concept of a socialist hero. A resolute modern artist, he loves the self-reflexiveness of the medium: at one point the "man of marble" statue is presented as a sharp contrast to the "degeneracy" of Western art, represented by Henry Moore's abstract figures with holes in their torsos.

A viewer who needs a crash course in Polish history from World War II to the relatively recent past could rent this film, its sequel, *Man of Iron*, and Agnieszka Holland's *To Kill a Priest* (1992), which dramatizes the very strong Catholic side of the Polish resistance to communism. Holland, now a successful filmmaker in exile, was Wajda's assistant for several years and is the possible source of his heroine's name— if not her radical persistence—in *Man of Marble*.

See also: *Man of Iron; To Kill a Priest.*
Availability: Selected collections.

Further reading

Canby, Vincent. "Man of Marble." *New York Times*, 17 March 1979, 10. A positive review of this "big, fascinating, risky film that testifies not only to Mr. Wajda's remarkable vision, but also to the vitality of contemporary Polish life."

Goodwyn, Lawrence. *Breaking the Barrier: The Rise of Solidarity*. Oxford: Oxford University Press, 1991. A very thorough history of the Solidarity movement.

Moszcz, Gustav. "Frozen Assets: Interviews on Polish Cinema." *Sight and Sound* 50 (Spring 1981): 86–91. Filmmakers, including the actress Krystyna Janda, discuss their participation in Solidarity and that movement's effect on the Polish film industry.

Paul, David W., ed. *Politics, Art, and Commitment in the Eastern European Cinema*. New York: St. Martin's Press, 1983. A detailed survey of the film and Wajda's career.

⤸

Margaret's Museum

Shocks above and below ground

1996, Canada, 118 mins., R
Director: Mort Ransen
Screenplay: Mort Ransen and Gerald Wexler, from Sheldon Currie's short stories, *The Glace Bay Miner's Museum*
CAST
Margaret = Helena Bonham Carter
Catherine = Kate Nelligan
Neil = Clive Russell
Angus = Kenneth Walsh
Jimmy = Craig Olejnik

Set in Glace Bay, an actual Nova Scotia mining town, this film tries mightily to be a story of romantic love and loss rather than coal and hardship. Of course it doesn't happen quite that way, even though Margaret falls in love with a poet and singer who vows never to go down in the mines. Margaret's older bother and father have lost their lives belowground and her granddad is hacking himself to death with black lung: we know it's only a matter of time before her husband and younger brother go underground as well. Because the film has the lovely cinematography of coastal vistas and a script that favors local eccentrics, the horrors, when they come, seem even more shocking.

In one sense Ransen's Canadian film follows where France's *Germinal* has led: a mining feature dwelling on accidents and hardship, miners' lives distorted by same, class conflicts and foolishnesses, and a few big-name actors to carry the weight of an almost labor-intensive story. So far, so good, since we probably haven't had enough of this phenomenon since the good old days of John Ford's *How Green Was My Valley* (1941).

The choice of Helena Bonham Carter as a miner's daughter may rank up there with Ford's Maureen O'Hara: we haven't had so much glamour and refinement smudged up in a long time. Janet Maslin commented that Bonham Carter "shakes off her usual refinement" by playing her "first scene in a flour sack looking like Little Orphan Annie." And not all viewers will be happy with a few pouty scenes as Helena acts the lovesick cow to the bagpipe-playing poet played by Clive Russell. Arrgh! Economics rule their lives, but they can still make love.

The film has a secret, fairly cleverly hidden in the title, and as in the case of *Dadetown*, it is probably better for a viewer to be a clean slate the first time through. I will give the reader no less of a hint than the filmmakers themselves do in the very first scene. A touristy couple stop at what looks like a small provincial museum on the coast; the attendant, dressed like Little Orphan Annie with braids in paper twists, cheerfully admits the

woman into the museum, from which, within seconds, she runs screaming as if she has seen . . . a ghost? Something worse? "Three years earlier," a screen title then announces, and we begin again at the beginning.

David Frank has pointed out some of the historical discrepancies in the film, which he characterizes as confusing the "sensibilities of the 1990s with the social conditions of the 1890s and the historical setting of the 1940s." After viewing the film, one might be left, I think, with no improvement in precise historical understanding but perhaps (instead) a shock of recognition that usually no one in a mining community is left unscarred.

See also: *Germinal*.
Availability: Easy.

Further reading

Atkinson, Michael. "No Wave. Wave." *Village Voice*, 11 February 1997, 74. Accepts the film's strengths almost against his better judgment: "if you can wait out its tiresome offbeatness and affect," the film with its "haunting Canadian emptiness" will "pay off."

Currie, Sheldon. *Glace Bay Miners' Museum*. Montreal, Deluge Press, 1979. *Glace Bay Miners' Museum: The Novel*. Wreck Cove: Breton Books, 1995. The film is still another variant of these two books, the short story collection and the novel, respectively, but its screenplay (as Frank and Urquhart, below, argue) dramatized the less overtly political and labor themes.

Frank, David. "One Hundred Years After: Film and History in Atlantic Canada." *Acadiensis* 26 (Spring 1997): 112–36. Includes a discussion of *Margaret's Museum* as a film that "lacks a sense of history and subscribes instead to the essentialist idea that mining towns are unchanging places exempt from the forces of history."

Maslin, Janet. "Finding Signs of Hardy Life in Tough Surroundings." *New York Times*, 7 February 1997, B18. Very positive review, emphasizing how the film uses the personal and communal life of the villagers to react to the horrors of miners' accidents.

Urquhart, Peter. "'The Glace Bay Miners' Museum'/'Margaret's Museum': Adaptation and Resistance." *Cineaction* (Toronto) 49 (1999): 12–18. Traces the unusual number of literary stages of this story, emphasizing how the film stresses some aspects of the originals (Margaret's role) and avoids others (in the literary versions her brother was not a lovesick youngster but a union organizer).

⌒

Marty

"What do you want to do, Marty?"

1955, 91 mins., B&W
Director: Delbert Mann
Screenplay: Paddy Chayefsky, from his TV play of the same title
CAST
Marty = Ernest Borgnine
Clara = Betsy Blair
Marty's mama (Mrs. Pilletti) = Esther Minciotti
Catherine = Augusta Ciolli
Angie = Joe Mantell

Famous for the question in the epigraph that Marty's bored—and boring—friend Angie asks, the film features a Bronx Italian-American butcher, played wonderfully by Ernest Borgnine, who wants to find "a nice girl to marry," avoid his boring friends at the bar, and perhaps—hard for him to admit—stop listening to his mother. Part of the 1950s ethnic working-class cycle of films, *Marty* also acts out the American myth of "making it on your own"—that is, breaking out of the working class by having his "own little business." Marty has to decide whether to buy out his boss and own the butcher shop himself. Whether it's a union shop or not is never an issue in the film. The threat of supermarkets eating up the small shops, the breakup of the extended ethnic family, and the difficulties two shy people have while falling in love are just some of the problems Marty faces. His new girlfriend is trying to break free of some family ties as well. Despite some 1950s creakiness in the characterizations, most viewers not made entirely of gristle like this film.

Originally a television play, *Marty* became Delbert Mann's first feature film and a classic of 1950s working-stiff social realism. When Marty tells Clara, an equally lonely heart he meets at the Stardust Dance Hall one Saturday night, that she is "not really as much of a dog" as she thinks she is, we are supposed to see that this is the highest compliment a working stiff like Marty can muster.

Marty's mother is pure Italian-American working class, Marty a little less so. Chayefsky (as some critics have been saying for some time) confirmed in Shaun Considine's biography that he always used autobiographical materials in his TV and film work, but because of an implicit ban on Jewish subjects, he was forced to use other ethnic families to tell his stories. If this is true, he became the expert on the Universal Ethnic in New York City in the 1950s, because so much of his work captured the problems and aspirations—in social-realist style—of these working-class people.

Against stiff competition, *Marty* was the first American film to take the top award at the international film festival at Cannes. Such an award and the positive reviews that greeted the newly energized American release of *Marty* virtually guaranteed Chayefsky's continuing string of hits, which lasted through *Network*, the satire on his own original medium, TV.

When another of his TV plays from the 1950s (*The Mother*) was remade for TV in 1994, the leading character was an Irish woman who was trying to get her old job back in the garment district. Although there were certainly Irish-Americans working in the needle trades, Chayefsky had a Jewish working woman foremost in his mind—his own mother.

See also: *Mac*.
Availability: Easy; DVD.

Further reading

Considine, Shaun. *The Life and Work of Paddy Chayefsky*. New York: Random House, 1994. An excellent survey of Chayefsky's career, stressing his innovative TV and film portrayals of working-class ethnic characters and his autobiographical scripts.

Crowther, Bosley. "Marty." *New York Times*, 12
April 1955, 25. A positive review that emphasizes the film's portrayal of the "socially
awkward folkways of the great urban middle
[*sic*] class."

John J. O'Connor. "Nostalgia for Drama of TV
Past." *New York Times*, 24 October 1994, B3. An
interpretation of Chayefsky's ethnic maneuvers.

⤳

Matewan

One big union in one small town

1987, 130 mins., PG-13
Director: John Sayles
Screenplay: John Sayles
CAST
Joe Kenehan = Chris Cooper
Elma = Mary McDonnell
Few Clothes = James Earl Jones
Danny = Will Oldham
Sid Hatfield = David Strathairn
Sephus = Ken Jenkins
Griggs = Gordon Clapp
Hickey = Kevin Tighe
C. E. Lively = Bob Gunton
Mayor Cabell = Josh Mostel
Bridey Mae = Nancy Mette
Rosaria = Maggie Renzi
Fausto = Joe Grifasi
Hillard Jenkins = Jace Alexander
Mrs. Elkins = Jo Henderson
The Singer = Hazel Dickens
Hardshell Preacher = John Sayles

John Sayles's popular film takes a classic
Hollywood western shootout as its climax
but frames it in a traditional Appalachian
story, in which an old man as a voice-over
narrator barely distinguishes between past
and present.

The film's plot sticks reasonably close to a
situation in Mingo County in West Virginia,
at the eastern Kentucky border, after World
War I, when the United Mine Workers
organized a coal mine protected by Baldwin-
Felts agents. The central character, Joe, is a
pacifist union organizer; he had been one of
the Wobblies (who, despite their bad press as

violent types, were sometimes pacifists). The
initial unfriendly reception Joe receives in
the town (except from one young miner,
Danny), Sheriff Sid Hatfield's siding with the
miners against the Baldwin-Felts private
police force, an informer's plots against Joe
and the strike, and the need for an alliance
among white, black, and Italian immigrant miners are portrayed with verve and
conviction.

Joe has to hold together a fragile unity of
Appalachian whites, African Americans, and
Italian immigrants, two-thirds of whom have
been brought to the West Virginia hills to
scab. The suspicions of the locals are not surprising: they need to survive in a company
town, are being harassed by company cops,
and are almost destroyed by a company spy
in their own local.

The film is unified by Danny, a young
miner in the midst of the struggle, and by his
voice-over as an older miner looking back on
the events that brought the union to his
valley. The Matewan Massacre was followed
by the Battle of Blair Mountain (also known
as the Miners' March on Logan), when thousands of miners, many of them World War I
veterans, marched to Logan County in sometimes loosely, sometimes quite sharply organized formations to protest against the Logan
County authorities, who, many miners
believed, let the informer C. E. Lively and
the others get away with the murder of Sid
Hatfield. They were met by an army of
deputies and the U.S. Army as well, including
bomber planes. But that's another story, on
film as rare archival clips only in Barbara
Kopple's documentary *Out of Darkness*. It
was omitted from Sayles's film for obvious
reasons, although the intensity of the reaction in support of and against Sid was also
omitted. He was not simply just a good-guy
sheriff, as the film has it; he also actively supported and helped the union organizing.

The music for the film provides a unity
among the ethnic groups. African American
blues, Italian mandolin music, other songs
(the Communist song of the "red flag,"
"Avanti, populo"), and traditional Appalachian a capella tunes provide the same

fragile unity as the miners' struggle. Hazel Dickens, a contemporary mountain singer, opens the film with "Fire in the Hole," a song celebrating the miners' resistance; later she sings "The Gathering Storm" at the funeral for a friend of Danny who was murdered by Baldwin-Felts agents. Her final song, "Beautiful Hills of Galilee," is a traditional ballad she had already recorded.

Sayles, a political writer and director, wrote some excellent short stories and a novel, *Union Dues* (which has a few pieces of the *Matewan* screenplay embedded in it), before he began to write and direct films. His film *Brother from Another Planet* (1981) portrayed working-class blacks in Harlem sympathetic to an escaped alien slave who looked like them, while *City of Hope* (1991) is an ambitious dramatic survey of the ethnic and racial tensions in urban life. *Men with Guns* (1997) explores right-wing official terrorism in an unnamed Latin American country.

Matewan is certainly one of Sayles's best films and perhaps one of the best features about labor history in years. Carefully researched, it reminds us what so many other labor films sometimes have lacked—a literate and artistic script, evident in the scene when Sid rejects a notice from Baldwin-Felts agents to evict a mining family; he tells the agents: "I know Mr. Felts. I wouldn't piss on him if his heart was on fire."

See also: *Harlan County, U.S.A.; Out of Darkness*.

Availability: Easy; DVD.

Further reading

Corbin, David Alan, ed. *The West Virginia Mine Wars.* Charleston, W. Va.: Appalachian Editions, 1990. Excellent collection of news articles, essays, and court testimonies from sources during the Matewan years.

Jones, Virgil Carrington. *The Hatfields and the McCoys.* Chapel Hill: University of North Carolina Press, 1948. A good, popular account of the West Virginia background of the film's events.

Savage, Lon. *Thunder in the Mountains.* Pittsburgh: University of Pittsburgh Press, 1990. The story line Sayles generally follows in *Matewan*.

Sayles, John. *Thinking in Pictures: The Making of the Movie "Matewan."* Boston: Houghton Mifflin, 1987. An excellent background study about film in general and *Matewan* in particular.

Waller, Altina L. *Feud: Hatfields, McCoys, and Social Change in Appalachia, 1860–1900.* Chapel Hill: University of North Carolina Press, 1988. A definitive background study of the Matewan Massacre.

⟿

Metropolis

"The City of Dreadful Night"—James Thompson

(I) 1926, 120 or 94 or 90 mins., B&W
(II) 1984, 87 mins., B&W and color-tinted
(III) 2002, 120 mins.
Director: (I) Fritz Lang; (II) Fritz Lang and Giorgio Moroder (as editor); (III) Fritz Lang and Martin Koerber (as restorer)
Screenplay: Fritz Lang and Thea von Harbou from the latter's novel of the same title and (II) with revisions by Giorgio Moroder
CAST (ALL VERSIONS)
Maria and The Robot = Brigitte Helm
John Frederson (The Master of Metropolis) = Alfred Abel
Freder = Gustav Fröhlich
Rotwang = Rudolf Klein-Rogge
Slim = Fritz Rasp
Josaphat = Theodor Loos
No. 11811 = Erwin Binswanger
Foreman = Heinrich George

In 1984 Giorgio Moroder, the successful pop composer of film scores (such as *Flashdance*, for which he won an Oscar the year before), created a new version of Fritz Lang's classic futuristic film of the clash between labor and capital. Moroder tinted the film and added his own score plus new songs (by such recording stars as Pat Benatar, Adam Ant, and Freddie Mercury of the group Queen); as a result of extensive archival research, he also reconstituted missing scenes by adding rediscovered footage and stills. He even recreated a key prop (a statue of Freder's mother). He argued that all his efforts were attempts to get closer to Lang's original vision, which was (and still is) in circulation in different lengths with different sequences.

In all versions, the power of Lang's vision of workers oppressed by mighty machines comes through. Moroder's may strike us as being an MTV version of a classic, but there is no doubt that his tinting and reassembled sequences add a glow and pulse that are hard to overlook. In this sense Moroder has achieved on a much more modest scale what he set out to do: to imitate *Napoleon*, the 1927 tinted, triple-image, long-lost silent masterpiece by Abel Gance, restored and re-released by Kevin Brownlow in 1981 with a new score by Carmine Coppola.

The plots of all versions of Lang's film are essentially the same. Freder, at first the care-free son of the Master of Metropolis, learns from the angelic Maria the sufferings of the working-class people who create the wealth of the city. His father, ever watchful for signs of revolt among his workers, spies on an underground meeting of the workers in which Maria offers the startling suggestion that there can never be happiness in Metropolis unless the heart mediates between the hands (the workers) and the mind (the capitalists). She suggests that if they just hang on, a great mediator (a messiah?) will come. The Master hatches a plot in which Rotwang, a mad-scientist type (and his former rival for Freder's mother's love), invents a robot who is given Maria's features and sends her to lead the workers in an ill-fated revolt. If they follow her—and she is so sexy they cannot resist—they will destroy the machines and flood the working-class districts where their children live.

Although this plot has some interest (despite its manifest absurdity), it is the individual shots and sequences of labor that hold the eye. At one point Freder takes the place of a worker who is manipulating the hands of what looks like a giant clock—each time a bulb on the periphery flashes, the worker must move the hand to it. Freder realizes to his horror that he must do this for a ten-hour shift.

Pauline Kael, perhaps unfortunately, made the pre-Moroder version of Lang's film into an object of camp, to be viewed as interesting bad art (especially the hero's knicker-bockers and Maria-Robot's lascivious wink), but she also praised some of the visual successes of the film, such as the way "human beings are used architecturally" and the Tower of Babel sequence. If she had commented on Moroder's version, she might have been impressed by the upper-class "Olympics," set in a surrealistic stadium, or the impressively decadent Yoshivara (Temple of Sin) sequences.

Critics have taken Moroder to task for "interfering" with Lang's vision. But Lang's *Metropolis* is essentially all special effects, odd-angled buildings, and choreographed crowd scenes. Moroder has simply accentuated Lang's pseudo-Marxist film of class struggle, really a successful imitation of H. G. Wells's *Time Machine* (with the laboring class below ground and the leisure class above). Hitler and Goebbels, Lang always reminded interviewers, loved the film too and wanted him to work for the Nazis. They too had a class struggle in mind, but not the heart Lang aimed for.

Ten years after *Metropolis*, Lang was making his first American film, *Fury* (1936), the story of the attempted lynching of a garage owner. In between he made the startling German film *M* (1931), the story of the hunt for a child murderer. Lang was rarely predictable and usually daring.

In 2002 Kino Films released the definitive German archive version digitally restored, with its original sound track re-recorded and numerous lost scenes restored.

See also: *Fury*.

Availability: Easy (all versions); I and III (Kino): DVD.

Further reading

Insdorf, Annette. "A Silent Classic Gets Some 80's Music." *New York Times*, 5 August 1984, II.15, 29. Extensive discussion of Moroder's version.

Jensen, Paul M. *The Cinema of Fritz Lang*. New York: Barnes, 1969. Discusses the original production, changes made, and its critical reception in Europe and the United States.

Kael, Pauline. *Kiss Kiss Bang Bang*. New York: Atlantic Monthly Press, 1968. "One of the last examples of the imaginative—but often monstrous—grandeur of the Golden Period of the German film."

Kracauer, Siegfried. *From Caligari to Hitler: A Psychological History of the German Film*. Princeton: Princeton University, 1947. Outrageous but intriguing interpretation of Lang's version of the film as a concession to authoritarian tendencies in the collective German mind.

Maslin, Janet. "Hey, Don't Forget the Audience." *New York Times*, 19 August 1984, II.15. A very negative review of Moroder's version, mainly because his music becomes "both tiresome and irrelevant."

༄

Mickey Mouse Goes to Haiti

"Hi ho, hi ho, it's off to work we go"

1996, 17 mins., English and Spanish, with English subtitles
Rooster Crow Productions
Agitprop documentary
PRINCIPAL FIGURES
Charles Kernaghan and Barbara Briggs, National Labor Committee
Numerous unnamed Haitian workers

Subtitled *Walt Disney and the Science of Exploitation*, this agitprop documentary about the globalization of garment work was produced by the National Labor Committee, an "Education Fund in Support of Worker and Human Rights in Central America." By using the craze for Disney's Pocahontas designs for children's clothes, the documentary makes a strong case for the level of exploitation involved: for every pair of Pocahontas pajamas a Haitian worker sews, she receives approximately 7 cents. That item at the time sold at Wal-Mart for $11.97. Since the average worker makes about four of these garments an hour, the average pay is something close to $3 a day.

Charles Kernaghan, the leader of the National Labor Committee, with a very

small film crew interviews workers as they commute to the Disney plant. Over and over we hear the workers express amazement at what Disney charges for the clothing they are creating for 7 cents. One of the most visually arresting images is a shot of Haitian workers in a tenement wearing Mickey Mouse T-shirts and silly masks to protect their identity from company spies and others who might get them fired for talking to this film crew.

The committee has been very successful in exposing the carefully hidden facts about government-business collaboration. They pursued, for example, the group that ran the following ad, complete with a picture of a Salvadoran worker, in an American trade journal, which was paid for by the Salvadoran Foundation for Economic and Social Development (FUSADES), which in turn has received millions in U.S. aid: "Rosa Martínez produces apparel for U.S. markets on her sewing machine in El Salvador. You can hire her for 33 cents an hour. Rosa is more than just colorful. She and her co-workers are known for their industriousness, reliability and quick learning. They make El Salvador one of the best buys."

"The Science of Starvation Wages," another piece of analysis done by the committee (but no longer distributed), explains how one set of workers' wages are calculated: "[Bar-code] tickets . . . are attached to each 100-piece bundle that the worker must assemble. This ticket (copy available upon request) shows that a woman worker sewing jeans in Nicaragua will be paid 9.1666 córdobas to close the inside seams on 100 pairs of pants. There are 9.8 córdobas to a dollar. So, for closing 100 seams the worker would earn $.93536—or 93 and 536/1000ths cents."

See also: *Life and Debt; The New Rulers of the World.*
Availability: Selected collections; National Labor Committee.

Further reading

Kaufman, Leslie, and David Gonzalez. "Labor Progress Clashes with Global Reality." *New York Times*, 24 April 2001, A1, 10. Reviews what progress there has been in monitoring labor conditions: "Competing interests among factory owners, government officials, American managers, and middle-class consumers—all with their eyes on the lowest possible cost—make it difficult to achieve even basic standards, and even harder to maintain them."

Klein, Naomi. *No Logo: Taking Aim at the Brand Bullies*. New York: Picador USA, 1999. Devastating critique of global corporations such as Nike and Disney, with some discussion of films such as the National Labor Committee's *Mickey Mouse Goes to Haiti* and Michael Moore's *The Big One*.

Ross, Andrew, ed. *No Sweat*. London: Verso, 1997. A collection of revealing articles on "fashion, free trade, and the rights of garment workers."

The U.S. in Haiti. New York: National Labor Committee, 1995. This pamphlet, subtitled *How to Get Rich on 11 Cents an Hour*, documents in detail which American companies are part of this assertion: "Approximately 50 assembly firms now operating in Haiti are violating the [Haitian] minimum wage law."

Web site:

⟨www.nlcnet.org⟩ The National Labor Committee's official site, with numerous reports (such as *The U.S. in Haiti*) and videos, some available by links, some for sale or suggested donation, surveying the exploitation of Third World workers.

⤸

The Migrants

Back to the present

1974, 78 mins., TVM
Director: Tom Gries
Screenplay: Lanford Wilson, from Tennessee Williams's unpublished story idea

CAST

Viola Barlow = Cloris Leachman
Mr. Barlow = Ed Lauter
Mills Watson = Heck Campbell
Lyle Barlow = Ron Howard
Betty = Cindy Williams
Black Migrant Worker = Claudia McNeil
Molly Barlow = Lisa Lucas
Wanda (Barlow) Trimpin = Sissy Spacek

When David Lowe interviewed migrant workers in Edward R. Murrow's documentary *Harvest of Shame*, he came back repeatedly to the same question: "Do you think you'll ever break out of the cycle of low wages and unpredictable work?" Most of the families expressed a desire to settle down, buy a house, have a regular job, send their kids to school. But uniformly, when Lowe pressed them tactfully, they all replied the same: No, it would probably never happen.

Tom Gries's *The Migrants* dramatizes that question in the figure of Lyle Barlow (played by Ron Howard), the young man of a roughly contemporary (1970s) white migrant family. Can Lyle pay off his family's debt to the crew leader in order to buy his freedom, defined as going off to Pittsburgh or Cincinnati to get a regular job?

Given its lineage, this film should be better known, since it comes from a story idea by Tennessee Williams. Most films of this class (*And the Earth Did Not Swallow Him* or *The Long Road Home*), however, have had TV time and then disappeared, not even appearing in video stores.

Probably only Tennessee Williams and his friend the playwright Lanford Wilson would have the nerve to write still another realistic drama about the plight of the American (white) migrant workers, given such a distinguished nonfictional forerunner as Edward R. Murrow's *Harvest of Shame*.

But Gries's film does more than a creditable job, updating the shame and degradation suffered by migrant workers even to this day. By making the workers more or less part of the 1970s, the writers and filmmakers have achieved an odd time-machine effect: we keep thinking we must be back in the old days but then some glimpse of an automobile or ordinary citizen makes us realize that these workers are among us, however invisible they may seem.

See also: *And the Earth Did Not Swallow Him*; *The Long Road Home*.
Availability: Selected collections.

Further reading

"Tele Follow-up Comment." *Variety*, 13 February 1974. Short but generally positive review situating the film in TV's history of documentaries on migrant workers.

Miles of Smiles, Years of Struggle: The Untold Story of the Black Pullman Porter

Black working-class mobility

1983, 58 mins.
Directors: Jack Santino and Paul R. Wagner
Traditional documentary
PRINCIPAL FIGURES
A. Philip Randolph, founder, Brotherhood of Sleeping Car Porters (BSCP)
E. D. Nixon, former porter
C. L. Dellums, founding officer, BSCP
Rosina Caruthers Tucker, former president of the BSCP's Ladies' Auxiliary

By the 1920s, the Pullman Company employed more black workers than any other company in the United States. But too often these jobs furthered black stereotypes, especially that of the happy servant, the updated version of the happy slave. Not surprisingly, the Pullman logo was a round, fairly abstract black face. But when jobs were scarce and racist hiring policies were in effect in many major corporations, Pullman's were also very good jobs for African Americans. We see footage from a Paul Robeson classic, *The Emperor Jones* (1933), in which Robeson as a newly hired Pullman porter—local man made good—is given a dramatic farewell from his church. The farewell was appropriate, for the porters would be away from home for long periods of time, living in company hostels.

The filmmakers have assembled a small but important group of people associated with the original union drive. Rosina Tucker, 100 years old, was a widow of a Pullman porter and an activist in the Ladies' Auxiliary. C. L. Dellums is the only living member of the BSCP's original founding group.

Some of the other porters return to their old trains to show off their skills, such as getting the beds ready at night for their passengers. Another veteran demonstrates how the segregated dining cars were set up, with a partition across the back of the car. The old men debate the issue of their servant status, a question they cannot totally resolve, in part because they clearly *were* servants and in part because they were proud of their jobs and their skills.

See also: *10,000 Black Men Named George*.
Availability: Selected collections.

Further reading

Harris, William. *Keeping the Faith: A. Philip Randolph, Milton P. Webster, and the Brotherhood of Sleeping Car Porters, 1925–1937*. Urbana: University of Illinois Press, 1977. A history of the union.
Levine, Lawrence. *Black Culture and Black Consciousness: Afro-American Folk Thought from Slavery to Freedom*. New York: Oxford University Press, 1977. Explores porters as middlemen between urban and rural lifestyles (e.g., bringing jazz records to the countryside).
Mergen, Bernard. "The Pullman Porter: From 'George' to Brotherhood." *South Atlantic Quarterly* 73 (1974): 224–50. Examines the porters' nickname, "George," and its implications.
Santino, Jack. *Miles of Smiles, Years of Struggle: Stories of Black Pullman Porters*. Urbana: University of Illinois Press, 1989. Includes and expands upon the interviews in the film.
Terkel, Studs. *Hard Times*. New York: Pantheon, 1970. Another interview with the porter E. D. Nixon, this one about the Montgomery, Alabama, bus boycott in 1955.

Millions Like Us

But only two cricket fans

1943, 103 mins., B&W, UK
Directors: Frank Launder and Sidney Gilliat
Screenplay: Frank Launder and Sidney Gilliat

Charlie Forbes = Eric Portman
Celia Crowson = Patricia Roc
Fred Blake = Gordon Jackson
Jennifer Knowles = Anne Crawford
Gwen Price = Megs Jenkins
Annie Earnshaw = Terry Randal
Charters = Basil Redford
Caldicott = Naunton Wayne

Millions Like Us brought back to the screen two characters who many Americans believe are found in their millions in the British Isles—the cricket-obsessed chums Charters and Caldicott, who almost always steal a film from the leads, a feat they achieved in both Hitchcock's *The Lady Vanishes* and Carroll Reed's *Night Train to Munich*, both spy thrillers written by the same team that scripted *Millions Like Us*.

How do Charters and Caldicott fare in this British class-obsessed view of the home-front workers during World War II? As send-ups of British upper-class twits they can hardly fail; Peter Stead rightly celebrates one of the high points of the film when Charters and Caldicott are laying mines on a beach. Caldicott mentions somewhat casually that they "must remember not to bathe here after the war."

The real energy of the film is in the celebration of women working in arms factories and how they cope with love and life, especially the more middle-class women who must mingle with their working-class co-workers. Many commentators have argued that an implicit belief in wartime class consensus is the real topic of concern in this and other films of the period.

See also: Chance of a Lifetime.

Celia (Patricia Roc) at her lathe in *Millions Like Us.* Courtesy British Film Institute Stills, Posters, and Designs.

Further reading

"Millions Like Us." *Variety*, 17 November 1943. The reviewer finds the film, curiously, too realistic; it "may even prove more interesting" to Americans than to Brits because "in this country it is too close to the 'life' of the proletariat"!

Stead, Peter. *Film and the Working Class*. London: Routledge, 1989. Enthusiastic but brief section on the film in the context of other examples of British social realism during the war.

Modern Times

Never speed up a worker with a bowler hat!

1936, 89 mins., B&W, silent
Director: Charlie Chaplin
Screenplay: Charlie Chaplin
CAST
The Little Tramp = Charlie Chaplin
A gamin = Paulette Goddard
President of a steel corporation = Allen Garcia

This is probably the last great silent film, despite a few moments when unusual bits of sound—Charlie singing what the *New York Times* reviewer called "some jabberwocky to the tune of a Spanish fandango"—seem to leap from this comic/slapstick exploration of the world of factories under the command of the New Efficiency—a 1930s term, of course, for the classic speedup. But Charlie has a hard time being sped up, and in his most famous sequence the Little Tramp becomes the world's unlikeliest assembly-line worker and is fed into—and ground by—the massive gears of a giant factory machine.

The film has a startlingly modern look to this day: the factory boss communicates with his speedup foremen by video screens (that is, when he's not doing jigsaw puzzles or reading comics). Charlie's attempt to turn two nuts on parts riding an ever-faster conveyor belt soon becomes a sequence with wonderful visual puns (the buttons on a woman's outfit, for example, resemble those on Charlie's assigned task and his arms automatically want to twist them).

When the New Efficiency brings in a "feeding machine" for workers to keep them from taking lunch breaks, Charlie (abused by this ridiculous machine) cracks. Chaplin's reputation for being a lefty was probably aided by this satire, although it is in the end a very gentle satire, like the Little Tramp himself. When Charlie accidentally leads a demo with a red flag from a construction vehicle, the satire is distinctly his.

The Little Tramp manages to reverse some of his earlier indignities by the end of the film: after his release from prison, he becomes a helper to a maintenance man who is himself caught in the gears of still another monster machine. This time, Charlie, combining his lessons from earlier disasters, feeds the trapped man carefully through a funnel in his mouth.

In the end, however, Charlie takes to the open road with the gamin and, like so many of his unemployed countrymen during the Depression, becomes the Little Tramp outdoors again, one of the best loved of all the cinematic riffraff.

See also: *Gold Diggers of 1933*.
Availability: Easy; DVD.

Further reading

Nugent, Frank S. "The Screen." *New York Times*, 6 February 1936, 23. Sums up Charlie's career and the tension between his left politics and his comic self.

Wiegand, Charmion von. "Little Charlie, What Now?" In *New Theatre and Film, 1934 to 1937*, ed. Herbert Kline, 245–54. New York: Harcourt, Brace, 1985. A contemporary (1936) political (left) interpretation.

The Molly Maguires

"See you in hell."—James McKenna

1970, 123 mins., PG
Director: Martin Ritt

Screenplay: Walter Bernstein, adapted from Arthur H. Lewis's *Lament for the Molly Maguires* (uncredited)

CAST

Jack Kehoe = Sean Connery
James McKenna/McParlan = Richard Harris
Mary Raines = Samantha Eggar
Captain = Frank Finlay

Although the Molly Maguires have now become virtual legends, no one can say with authority if they even existed or—if they existed—whether they were a self-conscious organization of Irish-American miners. Director Martin Ritt accepted one traditional interpretation of the Mollies and dramatized it in this film: the Pennsylvania Mollies were a secret cell or cadre of terrorist dynamiters, who used the Ancient Order of Hibernians, an Irish benevolent society, as a cover. Individuals became Mollies because they were frustrated by the failure of the strikes led by their union (the Workingmen's Benevolent Association) and decided to blow up the mining companies instead.

To make a film about one of the most controversial episodes in American labor history was a daring move on Ritt's part. As in the case of *Matewan*, which John Sayles said was in part about whether Joe the union organizer could get justice for the miners without using a gun, any discussion of the Mollies raises the question of company and union violence.

Ritt's film in effect rejects an alternative view of the Mollies, first set out back in 1932 by Anthony Bimba, that they were primarily trade union organizers, secretive as a means of self-protection, who were framed and executed for deeds that they did not commit or that were committed by the mining companies and their agents. In Ritt's film, they are guilty as hell, despite the presence in their midst of James McKenna/McParlan (played by Richard Harris), a Pinkerton agent. The agent testified at the trials of the men actually hanged for their crimes as Mollies, as he does in the film. Bimba and others believed that he made up most of his testimony, but Ritt portrays him as a compassionate man who sometimes tried to talk his new friends out of some dangerous deeds. In the end, however, both the real-life and fictional agent betrayed twenty men, who were hanged in 1877.

Ritt builds on McKenna's friendship, hinted at in Arthur H. Lewis's book, with Mary, the housekeeper at his lodgings, and turns it into a somewhat stereotypical romance. The film ends with an extremely unlikely jail-cell confrontation when McKenna/McParlan visits Black Jack Kehoe. McParlan praises Jack for not taking the miners' lot passively: "You made your sound. You used your powder." But Jack resists the spy's flattery and attacks him. "No punishment short of hell will set you free," Jack tells him. "See you in hell," the rising Pinkerton star replies. In a chilling final shot, McParlan strides toward the camera as the gallows has a practice drop with dummies in the background. It repeats one of the opening shots of the film, when Jack walks toward the camera as the mines explode behind him. From terrorism to the gallows is the film's message.

Because the film comes from a respected pro-labor director and because so much of it seems authoritative, it is important to realize that its historical accuracy is open to question. New research on the Mollies raises three distinct but related interpretations of their role in labor history.

First, the region of the Mollies, east-central Pennsylvania, had a contentious political history even outside the mines: some of the men later named as Mollies, specifically Black Jack Kehoe (played in the film by Sean Connery), had been active during the Civil War as draft resisters. (This background information is never offered in the film.) The most active resisters, organized or not, were called Buckshots as well as Mollies; thus various terms for "troublemaker" had already been established. Active trade unionism was often equated with draft resistance, although the draft resisters tended more often to be farmers, who were Democrats and therefore not of Lincoln's Republican Party, rather than miners. It may be that local draft officials (called "provost marshals") used the army to get rid of union trouble-makers by drafting them. Kehoe was accused of killing one of these provost marshals. In this view the Mollies were simply any men standing in the way of two major Republican Party goals—winning the war and extending the centralization of capitalism.

Second, mid-nineteenth-century Americans joined fraternal and secret organizations in extraordinary numbers. Everyone talked about the Irish Mollies, but the Welsh Protestant miners supposedly had the more rarely mentioned Modocs, who may have in fact been company agents as well (see Boyer and Morais below). The Knights of Labor, founded in 1869, the major forerunner of American unionism, was such a secret fraternal organization. Other organizations founded during this period included the Know-Nothings (the anti-immigration party) in 1849, the Copperheads (anti-Republican or pro-southern groups) in 1861, the Ku Klux Klan in 1866, and the Grangers in 1866, for farmers. Many labor unions used the mumbo-jumbo of fraternal rituals for their organizations.

Third, the attack on the Mollies by McKenna and the Pinkertons was part of the nationwide reaction to union and working-class struggles all over America in 1877. The Mollies were executed at the height of the militancy among railroad workers, for example. The *New York Times*, in an editorial of 3 May 1877, complained about a prolonged strike by iron foundry workers in upstate New York and suggested that "it is possible that there is in our State a field for the exercise of a little Pennsylvania justice."

The man who hired McKenna, Alan Pinkerton, published what is virtually a novel about the Mollies, *The Mollie Maguires and the Detectives* (1877), replete with bar scenes and Irish weddings. His more substantial *Strikers, Communists, Tramps, and Detectives* (1878) covered the great strike wave of 1877, emphasizing the involvement of secret organizations such as trade unions and the Mollies, and especially calling attention to the communist and internationalist ideas of Karl Marx and the French Commune of 1871. Here is a sample of the high level of Pinkerton's analysis: "An organization, called the Knights of Labor, has recently attracted some attention in the coal regions of Pennsylvania. It is probably an amalgamation of the Mollie Maguires and the [Paris] Commune. In the vicinity of Scranton and Wilkes-Barre two-thirds of the workingmen belong to it."

"Mollies" may therefore have been a convenient label for individuals caught in an extraordinary mixture of fraternal, national, and political trends. Whether real, legendary, or film characters, however, the Mollies always met the same end—hanging after a kangaroo court. The film does not emphasize the bizarrely unfair proceedings, as when Franklin B. Gowen, president of the railroad, dressed in his U.S. officer's uniform, helped with the prosecution. Nor does it mention (given its time frame, not surprisingly) that McParlan's next major assignment was to arrange the perjured testimony that almost got Wobbly Big Bill Haywood executed for arranging the bomb that wounded Governor Steubenberg of Idaho in 1902.

Ritt's other politically progressive films, *Edge of the City*, a drama about waterfront workers; *Sounder*, about a black share-cropper's family during the Depression; and *Norma Rae*, his most famous film, about textile organizing, are all featured in this guide. He was blacklisted during the McCarthy era but got even in 1976 with his film *The Front* (starring Woody Allen).

See also: *Matewan*.
Availability: Easy.

Further reading

Aurand, Howard W. *From the Molly Maguires to the United Mine Workers*. Philadelphia: Temple University Press, 1971. A good general history.

Aurand, Howard W., and William Gudelunas. "The Mythical Qualities of Molly Maguire." *Pennsylvania History* 49 (1982): 91–105. Argues that the Molly Maguire episode has "the potential . . . to lend credence to any interpretative position."

Bimba, Anthony. *The Molly Maguires*. 1932. New York: International Publishers, 1970. A well-researched left/communist interpretation.

Boyer, Richard O., and Herbert M. Morais. *Labor's Untold Story*. 1965. New York: United Electrical, Radio, and Machine Workers of America, 1976. Includes a substantial section on the Mollies.

Broehl, Wayne G. *The Molly Maguires*. Cambridge: Harvard University Press, 1964. A solid history that assumes the Mollies were an "ancient order" within the Hibernians.

Carnes, Mark C. *Secret Ritual and Manhood in Victorian America*. New Haven: Yale University Press, 1989. Background on contemporary secret societies, including the Knights of Labor.

Dorson, Richard M. *America in Legend*. New York: Pantheon, 1973. Includes a chapter on the legends (folklore) of the Mollies, some persisting to this day.

Goldfarb, Lyn, and Anatoli Ilyashov. "Working-Class Hero: An Interview with Martin Ritt." *Cineaste* 18, no. 4 (1991): 20–23. Ritt on his approach to the Mollies and his other films.

Kenny, Kevin. *Making Sense of the Molly Maguires*. New York: Oxford University Press, 1998. Offers an updated version of Bimba's thesis: "The Molly Maguires may not have existed in terms of the gigantic conspiracy depicted by contemporaries; but as a pattern of violence engaged in by a certain type of Irishman under specific historical conditions, they emphatically did exist."

Lewis, Arthur H. *Lament for the Molly Maguires*. New York: Harcourt, Brace & World, 1964. Despite the title, this source novel for the film more or less accepts the Mollies' guilt uncritically.

"The Mollie Maguires." *New York Times*, 23 December 1875, 2. The Catholic Church announces that "Mollie Maguires, Hibernians, Buckshots or whatever else they may choose to call themselves . . . are excommunicated."

Palladino, Grace. *Another Civil War: Labor, Capital, and the State in the Anthracite Regions of Pennsylvania, 1840–1868*. Urbana: University of Illinois Press, 1990. The political context of the Mollies.

Pinkerton, Allan. *Strikers, Communists, Tramps, and Detectives*. 1878. New York: Arno Press, 1969. The boss of the private police offers his theories and practical advice.

Mother

Red moms

1926, 90 mins., B&W, Soviet Union, silent, with musical score added in 1935 and with English intertitles
Director: V. I. Pudovkin
Screenplay: Nathan Zarkhy, based on Maxim Gorky's novel of the same title
CAST
The Mother = Vera Baranovskaya
Vlasov = A. Chistyakov
Pavel (Pashka) = Nikolai Batalov
Isaika Gorbov = Alexander Savitsky
Vesovshchikov = Ivan Koval-Samborsky
Anna = Anna Zemtsova
Police Officer = V. I. Pudovkin
Misha = N. Vidonov

When this Soviet silent (now classic) film reached the United States in the Depression year of 1934, the *New York Times* reviewer noted, apparently without irony, that "many of the scenes of violence growing out of the struggle between capital and labor are far from being peculiarly Russian or outdated."

Screenwriter Zarkhy kept the central theme of Gorky's novel—a generic mother joins a revolutionary movement—and set it with embellishments in the era of the failed revolution of 1905, which most Russians saw as a dress rehearsal for the October and February revolutions of 1917, which deposed the tsar. The family at the center of this film is divided personally and politically. The father is a drunkard and supporter of the right-wing vigilante group in his factory called the Black Hundreds; the son is in the revolutionary "solidarity" group. The mother of the title is at first apathetic and mindful of authority. Her decision to turn her son in to the police for secreting arms is the turning point of the film. (This incident should have been impossible, given the novel's plot and most citizens' awareness of tsarist oppression.) She eventually realizes that the authorities will not be lenient to her son.

In the course of a major demonstration designed to free political prisoners, the mother sees her son shot. She too joins the struggle by seizing the demonstrator's flag, but she is trampled to death by mounted police. The authoritarian grip of the government is gradually loosening, the film's images argue, with Pudovkin intercutting shots of the winter ice breaking up in the river. The inexorable movement of the ice floes down the river are visually rhymed with the flow of the demonstrators in the city streets.

Pudovkin has often been placed in the company of Eisenstein and Alexander Dovzhenko as one of the great Soviet silent-film directors. Even to come in third in that company is no dishonor. Pudovkin's *Storm over Asia* is a more complex film set in Mongolia, the story of a fur trapper who at first becomes a Soviet partisan but then allows himself to be set up as a puppet ruler by the occupying British.

Maxim Gorky, author of the source novel, was a Bolshevik writer who fictionalized an actual strike in 1902 in a factory town near his birthplace (Nizhny Novgorod, renamed for him during the Soviet era), which included the demonstration with the red flag and a mother-son team from a revolutionary cell. Gorky followed these events closely—Yarmolinsky in the Collier Books edition of the novel states that Gorky actually knew the mother and her son—and after the failed revolution of 1905 came to the United States to raise money for the Bolsheviks and speak against American loans to the tsar. He actually wrote parts of *Mother* in New York; soon after (1906) an American magazine began carrying a translation of the novel.

See also: *Earth; The End of St. Petersburg; Strike.*
Availability: Selected collections; DVD.

Further reading

Gorky, Maxim. *Mother*. 1907. Various translations of the source novel are available; the Collier Books (New York, 1962) translation by Margaret Wettlin has a brief but helpful introduction by Avraham Yarmolinsky.

"Gorky's Mother." *New York Times*, 30 May 1934, 14. A brief but very positive review that notes that the U.S. release was augmented by footage from the 1917 Revolution, the building of the Dnieprostroy Dam, and the 1933 Moscow May Day parade. (These sequences are not in current videocassettes.)

Pudovkin, V. I. *Film Technique and Film Acting*. 1949. Trans. and ed. Ivor Montague. New York: Grove Press, 1976. The director's classic study of editing, with numerous discussions of his and other Soviet filmmakers' works.

"Soviet Film 'Mother' Acclaimed in Vienna." *Variety*, 8 January 1928. Quotes a Viennese critic's rave review of the film.

Two Russian Film Classics. New York: Simon & Schuster, 1973. Zarkhy's screenplay for *Mother*; the second "classic" is Dovzhenko's *Earth*.

∽

Mother Trucker: The Diana Kilmury Story

That's no lady

1996, 92 mins., TVM
Director: Sturla Gunnarsson
Screenplay: Anne Wheeler and J. W. Meadowfield
CAST
Diana Kilmury = Barbara Williams
Sean Kilmury = Blair Slater
Jack Vlahovic = Nicolas Campbell
Ken Paff = Robert Wisden
Pete = Wayne Robson
John = Stuart Margolin

This unfortunately named film about the highest-ranking female Teamster officer, an activist in Teamsters for a Democratic Union (TDU), and a brave Canadian mammoth-truck and long-haul driver, was originally titled, modestly enough, *Diana Kilmury, Teamster*. (It now has more titles than wheels.) In using what was apparently one of the nicknames she acquired in disparagement but eventually could wear proudly, HBO decided to go for an exploitation title for the rougher trade. Maybe packaging doesn't matter. Nonetheless, labor film fans might miss this attempt at docudrama based on actual incidents in Kilmury's life if they don't spot the original Canadian title.

Anyone who thinks Teamster history is not controversial hasn't been at a labor or union meeting when the TDU was discussed. Or paid any attention to the 1996 Teamsters presidential race when the incumbent, Ron Carey—not a member of TDU but supported by the group—was first challenged by Jimmy Hoffa's son, who won after Carey was barred by the Feds from his subsequent election. Or traveled during the election on a main truckers' interstate route such as I-75, which sprouted hand-lettered signs reading "Hoffa Lives." In short, nothing about the Teamsters is going to be easy. *Mother Trucker* dramatizes Kilmury's fight simply to be a woman who drives in this world; her support and disenchantment with her local president, who is in the TDU; her fractured and tragic family life (her son is horribly injured in a car crash); and her dangerous run for the vice presidency of the Teamsters.

Kilmury is portrayed as a reluctant activist at first, increasing her commitment to the TDU when her benefits (related to her car crash) are not forthcoming from the established union slugs, who resent her for being a TDU-er and a woman too. She helps plot the TDU's key strategy to overthrow the big boys by suggesting to prosecutors—who have crusaded to indict both Mafia and Teamster leaders—to insist that the settlement include not only a trusteeship for the leaderless union but also secret and direct election of officers.

Makers of Teamster films (*F.I.S.T., Teamster Boss*) love to stage a raucous and grossly unfair union convention. And Sturla Gunnarsson does it as well as any other, as the tiny TDU contingent is forced to play David to the thick-necked Goliaths (Roy Williams and his crew) who control the microphones. Or Davida, because Kilmury is right up there fighting away for their rights.

Site One, a massive open-pit mining operation in British Columbia, is the opening venue for Kilmury's crusade for justice in 1978. Ten years later the TDU is in high gear and in 1992 Kilmury is sworn in as a Teamster vice president (which she still is). The hour and a half devoted to this packed

history makes it seem a little too fast and a little too easy, although at one point her campaign vehicle (a mobile home) is sandwiched between two mean-looking road hogs at high speed. Of course there would not have been a movie if she hadn't survived that brush with death. But it wouldn't have had such a neat ending, either.

From a review (Wilson) we learn that Kilmury was paid $75,000 for her life story but turned the entire check over to Teamsters for a Democratic Union, hoping that the film would help these reformers defeat James P. Hoffa for the Teamsters' presidency. (He lost in the first go-round to Ron Carey, the latter taking 52 percent of the vote, but the election was thrown out because of accusations of illegal financing in Carey's campaign; although Carey himself was cleared of these allegations in 2001, Hoffa went on to win the next election.) Kilmury's dedication to reform is tempered by her belief that "people make a good living because of the Teamsters. Even at its worst, it was a very good union." Putting such matters in perspective, Kilmury argued, is essential, since so much bad movie time is given to the Hoffas and the Pressers: in such movies, "there are never any members shown. And you never get a sense that the union movement actually improves people's lives" (Wilson).

See also: *American Standoff; Final Offer; Teamster Boss.*
Availability: Not.

Further reading

Swoboda, Frank, and Sharon Walsh. "A Son Also Rises: James P. Hoffa Has Own Clouds to Contend With." *Washington Post*, 19 November 1997, A1. On the state of the TDU and its difficulties in mounting a candidate to replace Ron Carey.

Wilson, Peter. "Divided, She Never Fell" and "Opposites Attract When Teamster Meets the Lady." *Vancouver Sun*, 1 November 1995, C4, 6. Compares the film's details with Kilmury's real life, emphasizing how the film has captured the dangers of this teamster's life, plus an interview with Kilmury.

Web site:
⟨www.tdu.org⟩ The official Web site of the TDU movement.

Note: Also known as *The Lady Is a Teamster: The Diana Kilmury Story; The Diana Kilmury Story; Diana Kilmury: Teamster;* and *Teamster*.

〜

Moving Mountains

"Women hold up half the sky."—
Chinese proverb

1981, 30 mins.
Director: Laura Sky
Agitprop documentary
PRINCIPAL FIGURES
Dave Carroll, president, Local 7884, United Steelworkers of America (USWA)
Local members: Ina Hees, Brenda Forrister, Lon Dansberg, and Anna Bonnell

Moving Mountains makes a good nonfiction companion to *Wildrose:* both are stories of women who rig explosives in open-pit coal mines or drive trucks five times the size of the workers' shuttle bus. When one woman in this documentary is interviewed beside her truck, the wheel is more than twice her height. The work of open-pit hauling is dangerous, the women emphasize: their loads are incredibly heavy, and the roads in British Columbia, where the film was shot, can be slippery.

The documentary was produced by the United Steelworkers to showcase one local's fight to include women in these traditionally male-only jobs. Eventually the local had to take legal steps to force the mines to hire women. The women, interviewed (in voiceovers) as they do their work, explain how the men reacted to their being hired and why they like these jobs. The local union president also comments on his role in supporting the women's cause. At the time of the filming, this local of 1,121 workers in Elkford, British Columbia, had 80 women working in the mines.

See also: *Wildrose*.
Availability: Selected collections.

〜

Native Land

Whose land, whose liberties?

1942, 88 mins., B&W
Director: Leo Hurwitz and Paul Strand
Screenplay: Leo Hurwitz, Ben Maddow, and Paul Strand
CAST
The Farmer = Fred Johnson
His Wife = Mary George
His Son = John Rennick
Sharecroppers = Housely Stevens and Louis Grant
Union President = James Hanney
Stool Pigeon = Howard da Silva
Vice President = Art Smith
Spy Executive = Richard Bishop
Grocer = Robert Strauss
Little Girl = Dolores Cornell
Thug = John Marlieb
Narrator = Paul Robeson

Although the *New York Times* reviewer called this a "feature-length documentary film," we would now call it a mock-doc or possibly a docudrama, as it consists of numerous dramatized incidents in the life and death of civil liberties in America and very little traditional (unstaged) documentary footage. Paul Robeson, whose magnificent voice gives the whole proceeding an air of significance, provides the voice-over narration with both details of individual incidents and a framework for interpreting these fascist-like assaults on Americans, especially those involved with labor and other progressive causes.

Thus we move through or hear about various incidents, some famous, some not, in which right-wing forces have attempted to crush dissent or attack left-wingers. A Michigan farmer spoke out against vigilantes and was attacked. Black and white sharecroppers are chased by thugs. A Cleveland union organizer is found murdered in his

Rural fascists hunt for black and white sharecroppers in *Native Land*. Courtesy British Film Institute Stills, Posters, and Designs.

bedroom. Strikers are massacred at Republic Steel outside of Chicago on Memorial Day, 1937.

By far the longest dramatization concerns a labor spy in the ranks of a union local. Howard da Silva plays the Stool Pigeon, who by a clever dodge manages to come up with the local's secret membership list. The company execs and labor spy honchos are beside themselves with glee at this successful exploit.

The *New York Times* reviewer certainly understood that these mostly pro–Communist Party filmmakers had decided that American unity was the word of the day, because no actual oppressors are named and Robeson's postscript carefully enlists the labor movement in the united front against fascism. In fact, the whole venture is 100-percent Americanism, since the incidents dramatized in the film all come from testimonies given before the Senate Civil Liberties Committee in 1936, distilled in part through Leo Huberman's *The Labor Spy Racket* (1937).

See also: *New Deal Documentaries*.
Availability: Selected collections.

Further Reading

Alexander, William. *Film on the Left*. Princeton: Princeton University Press, 1981. This thorough survey of "American documentary film from 1931 to 1942" includes a very helpful section on the film.

Crowther, Bosley. *New York Times,* 12 May 1942, 16. A very positive review: "one of the most powerful and disturbing documentary films ever made."

Huberman, Leo. *The Labor Sky Racket.* New York: Modern Age Books, 1937. Likely source for the film, based in turn on the La Follette Civil Liberties Committee hearings; the author explains the expensive inner world of industrial spying.

Levinson, Edward. *I Break Strikes! The Technique of Pearl L. Bergoff*. New York: Robert M. McBride, 1936. Another relevant book about strikebreaking supported by tear gas and munitions purchases, also based on the La Follette hearings.

"Native Land." *Variety,* 13 May 1942. Very enthusiastic review ("technically . . . refreshing on many angles, often almost brilliant"), while acknowledging the purpose of the film in fighting fascism and encouraging unions; notes that its premiere was a benefit for the New York Newspaper Guild.

U.S. Senate, Committee on Education and Labor. *Violations of Free Speech and the Rights of Labor.* Pts. 1–75. Washington, D.C.: Government Printing Office, 1936–44. The complete published record of the hearings of the La Follette Civil Liberties Committee.

The Navigators

Off the rails

2001, 92 mins., UK/Germany/Spain
Director: Ken Loach
Screenplay: Rob Dawber
CAST
John = Dean Andrews
Mick = Thomas Craig
Paul = Joe Duttine
Jim = Steve Huison
Gerry = Venn Tracey
Len = Andy Swallow
Harpic = Sean Glenn

In the light of the privatization of the British rail system and its subsequent deterioration in service and safety record, the London *Guardian* columnist Ian Jack recounted a chilling story he heard from "a senior figure in the railways" about foreign visitors to the United Kingdom: "The ones from Europe come because they want to discover how not to privatise a railway. The ones from the Third World come to see how it might be done because the IMF [International Monetary Fund] has sent them. Poor mugs."

Whether this story is true or not matters little: leave it to Ken Loach to make a film about it! In October 2000 a high-speed Virgin train derailed at Hatfield, killing four people. It was the fourth fatal train wreck since the privatization of British Rail in the early 1990s. What made it a greater scandal was that Railtrack, the authority of the system in charge of rail maintenance, knew that the rails were damaged in this locale two years before the accident. Jack cites the sobering statistics that are the essential background to the film: between 1992 and 1997 the number of workers assigned to maintain the infrastructure of the rails fell from 31,000 to fewer than 19,000.

Loach dramatizes the deteriorating relationships among five Yorkshire railway workers who have been friends for years. In 1995 the men are told that British Rail, the nationalized system they have worked for, has been replaced by a private company. At first they are casual, assuming their jobs will last. A strange note is struck, however, when they are told that safety is a priority and that "death has got to be kept to a minimum"— only "two a year." One of the men accepts a buyout and works for a contract agency making twice as much as hour but with no vacation, no sick pay, and no union. The film has a tragic and disturbing twist I will allow viewers to discover for themselves.

Rob Dawber, the screenwriter, was a railway worker, union activist, and columnist for almost twenty years; after losing his job because of the privatization, he continued his writing career but turned to the courts when he discovered that he had been exposed to asbestos while working in a British Rail shed. He won a settlement, but he died of a tumor caused by exposure to asbestos.

See also: *The Price of Coal*.
Availability: Selected collections.

Further reading

Jack, Ian. "Breaking Point." *Guardian Unlimited,* 3 April 2001, at ⟨www.guardian.co.uk/hatfieldtraincrash/story/0,7369,467590,00.html⟩. Uses the Hatfield Crash as a taking-off point for a deep attack on the "disastrous privatisation of Britain's railways."

Murray, Andrews. *Off the Rails.* London: Verso, 2001. A chilling account of the dangerous dismantling of a once great rail system.

Olmstead, Kathleen. *Exclaim!* 10 September 2001, at ⟨www.exclaim.ca/common/display.php3?articleid=812⟩. Loach's "depiction of the effects of privatization and destruction of the permanent workforce is both brutal and honest," according to the reviewer, who confesses: "I'm a sucker for a good Marxist kitchen sink drama."

Wainwright, Martin. "Grim Topicality of Loach's Latest Film." *Guardian Unlimited,* 21 October 2000, at ⟨www.guardian.co.uk/hatfieldtraincrash/0,7368,383867,00.html⟩. Loach attacks "the destruction of the culture of the railway" in this article, comparing the staged crash in his film with the Hatfield crash.

Net Worth

1995, 92 mins., Canada, G
Director: Jerry Ciccoritti
Screenplay: Phil Savath and Don Truckey, from David Cruise and Alison Griffiths's book of the same title

CAST
Ted Lindsay = Aidan Devine
Gordie Howe = Kevin Conway
Marty Pavelich = Carl Marotte
Jimmy Norris = Richard Donat
Larry Suharchuk = Roman Podhora
Les, the Trainer = Billy Van
Milton Mound = R. H. Thomson

I will break my rule on no sports films in this guide for a Canadian docudrama of the campaign, led by the all-star Detroit Red Wings player Ted Lindsay, to form a hockey players' union. Many of the rules and regulations inflicted on the players, some of the best hockey players of all time, were quite similar to those used by many employers in industry. The players were never allowed to discuss salaries with one another, had no control over their own pension plan, and were subject to capricious and demeaning rules of work. The owners would cry wolf whenever they were criticized, saying that players' salaries already had them in the red.

Lindsay has substantial motivation to get the men organized. We witness a former star selling the players' broken hockey sticks to fans for 50 cents to make ends meet. Another player, Larry Suharchuk, Lindsay's former teammate, desperately in need of money but unable to tap into his pension, lives in a car. It is his tragic death that ultimately gives Lindsay the resolve to persevere, after the owners try everything—including Red-baiting and transferring player-organizers to other teams—to break up the players' "association" that Lindsay organizes with the help of fellow all-stars and friends, such as Gordie Howe, and the lawyer Milton Mound, who had successfully represented American baseball players.

Mound helps the players to see that the club owners are making lots of money and even have gangster connections in at least one case. Mound wants the players to form a union, but they resist the word, afraid of its militant sound. The lawyer's irony is heavy: "We freed the slaves a hundred years ago," he tells Lindsay, "but then again they wanted to be free."

Even viewers who never watch hockey will enjoy a number of startling sequences in the film, including some shots from the point of view of the hockey puck. Hockey fans, if they are still interested in a few fistfights, will be happy too.

See also: Final Offer.
Availability: Selected collections.

Further reading

Anderson, Dave. "From Colonel, to Boss, to Good, Old Gehrig." *New York Times*, 13 September 1998, V.47. Even Joe DiMaggio had to put up with secret nonnegotiating sessions for his salary.

Cruise, David, and Alison Griffiths. *Net Worth.* New York: Viking, 1991. The source book that explodes "the myths of pro hockey."

Never Steal Anything Small

Especially this videocassette

1959, 94 mins.
Director: Charles Lederer
Screenplay: Maxwell Anderson, from his
    and Rouben Mamoulian's play *The
    Devil's Hornpipe*
CAST
Jake MacIllaney = James Cagney
Linda Cabot = Shirley Jones
Dan Cabot = Roger Smith
Winnipeg = Cara Williams
Words Cannon = Royal Dano
Pinelli = Nehemiah Persoff

Today this would be called a "high-concept" film in Hollywood: James Cagney as a crooked waterfront union leader who will do anything to become president of his local—including sing a few of the terrible songs that make this film (almost) a musical. Cagney, with deceptions most city cats could spot a mile off, does win his election and spends the rest of the film trying to make some money and steal his naive lawyer's pretty wife. As long as you "never steal anything small," he sings, you can get away with it: steal small and you end up in jail. This backhanded compliment to white-collar crime does not, however, carry the day for Cagney's fighting Irishman, because the film has a few peculiar moral lessons to draw before it mercifully closes.

This film must have been predicated on the success of *The Pajama Game,* another high-concept musical that was extremely popular just two years before and that took up the issue of labor–management relations in a similarly jaunty way. Both films were throwbacks to the old union comedy model of the 1940s, typified by *The Devil and Miss Jones,* in which genuine grievances are resolved in a fantasy land projection of bosses who turn out to have hearts of gold and are really, well, just human.

Never Steal Anything Small had been a successful Broadway play. A film that opens with a jokey scene with an iron lung had a lot

of nerve, given the prevalence of polio in the 1950s. Why the iron lung? Jake needs money to throw a party where he'll fix his election as local president. The money comes from a loan shark whom Jake shakes down, then dopes and stuffs in the iron lung. When the loan shark wakes up, Jake hustles him off to Yuma to recuperate. Equally dubious is the high-class madam Jake hires to turn his lawyer's head while he enjoys the wife's company. Winnipeg (the madam) requires a stiff payment: "I'm sorry, I want a Ferrari," she sings at a car dealer's showroom.

All of this would be so much Hollywood kitsch and beyond retrieval if it did not also contain large dollops of strange anti- and pro-union messages. Although Shirley Jones, in a bare-midriff outfit, sings "I haven't got a thing to wear," she also tells Jake that she doesn't want her husband to be his lawyer because she has researched his strike violence, bribery, and prison sentences. Jake's defense is that in a vicious world unions have to be "fighting fire with fire." In fact, he adds confidently, if he weren't in charge, "the union would be in the hands of crooks even bigger than me." Later, when Jake begins to make a positive impression on her, she responds, "Considering you're a crook and a horror, you're a pretty nice guy." After narrowly escaping an acid attack—à la the notorious blinding of the labor columnist Victor Riesel in 1956—Jake begins to think of himself as the little guy's candidate to unseat the big Mafia types running the international. Here he delves into labor history, making a speech about the "outstanding men" such as Gompers, Lewis, Dubinsky, Meany, and Reuther. How does he compare with them? "They're 100 percent and I'm only 15 percent."

Even that estimate seems high until the film contrives to make Jake into a rebel. Jake's local is ruled with a Mafia fist by Mr. Pinelli of the United Stevedores—and "he doesn't like wildcat strikes." Although Jake has framed his own lawyer for a theft of cargo Jake personally rescued (Cagney in a wet suit!) from the not totally polluted Hudson, Jake eventually takes the rap because he realizes that his defense—that he really stole the money "for the men"—will help his election bid against Mr. Pinelli. Even when you hear something silly about this film, it is still hard not to watch it to see if your expectations come true. They will.

See also: *The Devil and Miss Jones; The Pajama Game.*
Availability: Selected collections.

Further reading
Weiler, A. H. "Never Steal Anything Small." *New York Times,* 12 February 1959, 23. An overly enthusiastic review.

New Deal Documentaries

National recovery cinema

The Plow That Broke the Plains
1936, 26 mins., B&W
Director: Pare Lorentz
The River
1937, 30 mins., B&W
Director: Pare Lorentz
Power and the Land
1940, B&W, 38 mins.
Director: Joris Ivens
Social-realist documentaries

This videocassette offers the work of two of the outstanding social-realist documentary filmmakers of the 1930s, the American Pare Lorentz and the Dutch Joris Ivens. Although Ivens had made remarkable left-leaning films, most notably *Borinage* (1933), an inside look at miners' lives and organizing in Belgium, and *Spanish Earth* (1937), an antifascist account of the Spanish Civil War, he found a niche within the U.S. government–sponsored documentary film unit run by Pare Lorentz.

Ivens took the lead in defending the position that documentary filmmakers could recreate scenes instead of following what he characterized as the "camera-eye school of [Dziga] Vertov," in which a "documentary may only film events that are actually happening before the witnessing camera."

His documentary approach was actually quite similar to that of John Grierson in England during this same period. (See the British Documentary Movement entry.) Within ten years Ivens's approach would be taken over resolutely by such scripted semi- or pseudo-documentaries of the 1940s as *Native Land*. Those films used nonprofessional actors as well as professionals but were photographed and narrated as if they were documentaries. Ivens himself worried (in *The Camera and I*) about the issues that led inevitably to these 1940s documentaries: "If you go deeply into personalization and dramatization of the leading characters in a documentary you inevitably need trained actors to give satisfactory expression to this treatment and you land in the field of fiction film."

Paradoxically, a realistic documentary needs professional acting, Ivens argued: "It is only rarely that you can find natural, untrained acting talents to portray such complicated psychological roles; and in over-training a non-professional actor or actress you get an amateur quality that destroys the force of conviction which is one of the documentary's greatest assets."

This, in brief, is the argument for having professionals play real people—because real people don't look and act like real people.

Lorentz's *The River* celebrates the power of the TVA to transform the South. "We built a hundred cities and a thousand towns," the voice-over announces, as if to say there was nothing here before the dams. Of course there were cities and towns and farms, too, many of which were lost to the new floodwaters, but the film is about destruction and control, not about how many families coped with yearly floods. If this sounds like an advertisement for the New Deal, so be it: "We had the power to take the valley apart. We have the power to put it together again."

The narrator for *The Plow That Broke the Plains* defends Manifest Destiny, although he doesn't call it that: "By 1880 we had cleared the Indian, and with him, the buffalo." The justification for the widespread replacement of the buffalo by cattle is relatively simple: the Great Plains were "a cattleman's paradise."

The social-realist documentaries set a progressive standard that matched the New Deal ideology of FDR and his supporters of many left persuasions. When FDR died, traditional documentary filmmaking persisted, but it had lost its progressive edge.

See also: *Native Land*.
Availability: Selected collections; *Our Daily Bread* DVD.

Further reading

Georgakas, Dan. "Cinema of the New Deal." *Cineaste* 21, no. 4 (1995): 47–49.
Ivens, Joris. *The Camera and I*. New York: New World Paperbacks, 1969. Reflections on his own history as a filmmaker and the documentary movement he helped create.
Lorentz, Pare. *FDR's Moviemaker: Memoirs and Scripts*. Reno: University of Nevada Press, 1992. Scripts for his documentaries and his autobiographical commentary.
Rabinowitz, Paula. *They Must Be Represented: The Politics of Documentary*. London: Verso, 1994. Quixotic but intriguing interpretations of 1930s documentaries, with a fairly full discussion of *The River* and *The Plow That Broke the Plains*, following her reasonable premises that "documentary rhetoric [is] central, not marginal, to popular forms of twentieth-century American culture," and that during and after the 1930s it becomes "difficult to distinguish documentary from fictional modes of address."
Snyder, Robert L. *Pare Lorentz and the Documentary Film*. Reno: University of Nevada Press, 1994. The author's critical analyses of Lorentz's films as well as reactions from Lorentz's critics in the 1930s.
Web site:
⟨www.gen.umn.edu/faculty_staff/yahnke/filmteach/teach.htm⟩ Detailed summary of *The Plow That Broke the Plains*.

Note: A Critics' Choice Video collection of classic New Deal documentaries was also available from Kino as one of its series called Cinema of the New Deal, which also includes King Vidor's *Our Daily Bread* and *Native Land*.

New Harvest, Old Shame

Time has stood still

1990, 59 mins.
Producer: Héctor Galan of Frontline
TV documentary
PRINCIPAL FIGURES
Héctor Galan and Dave Maris, production team
The Flores family

In 1990, thirty years after Edward R. Murrow followed migrant workers from Belle Glade, Florida, to New Jersey in *Harvest of Shame,* the producer Héctor Galan and the correspondent Dave Maris followed in his—and their—trail. Galan focuses on a single extended family, the Floreses, who are Guatemalan immigrants.

The Floreses valiantly follow the harvests northward, but their ancient vehicles break down so often that we see them at numerous rest stops on the interstate (where they sometimes spend the night) trying to repair this or that ruptured part.

The film concludes that "little has changed" in the thirty years since Murrow broke this story. Time has stood still for the migrants, who work for months barely breaking even. One of the few major changes has been in the composition of the workforce. In Belle Glade, Murrow focused on African Americans; now the town has immigrants mainly from Central America and Caribbean countries. Housing in the home cities of the migrants as well as on the road remains substandard in every way.

The film also features the positive union organizing being done by the AFL-CIO's Farm Labor Organizing Committee (FLOC), which is following the model of the United Farm Workers.

See also: *Children of the Harvest; Harvest of Shame; Legacy of Shame*.
Availability: Not.

Further reading

Longman, Jere. "A Town Where Football Is the Glue and the Hope." *New York Times,* 23

November 2001, A27–28. A contemporary look at Belle Glade, as poor and depressed as ever, where Murrow and Galan both begin their journeys with the migrants.

Sengupta, Somini. "Farm Union Takes Aim at a Big Pickle Maker." *New York Times,* 26 October 2000, A18. Surveys FLOC's latest campaign and the status of pickle pickers.

Web site:

⟨www.floc.com⟩ The official site of the Farm Labor Organizing Committee of the AFL-CIO, with information about consumer campaigns (e.g., boycott of Mt. Olive pickles in 1999–2000) and a history of FLOC.

⤶

The New Rulers of the World

World bankers

2001, UK, 53 mins.
Director: Alan Lowery
TV documentary
PRINCIPAL FIGURES
John Pilger, investigative reporter
Stanley Fischer, deputy director of the
  International Monetary Fund (IMF)

John Pilger occupies a special niche in the United Kingdom in print journalism, TV documentary film, and political exposés of all kinds. He has consistently championed the poor and working classes of Ireland, England, and the Third World, exposing both neocolonial violence and governmental schemes and lies in some of Britain's own sore spots, such as Northern Ireland and the recurring labor struggles on the Liverpool docks. It is a pity that he is not better known in the United States, because his politics and crusading spirit are remarkable.

Pilger's access to mainstream media in the U.K. and Australia is also noteworthy, since not a single one of his remarkable documentary films has been distributed widely in the United States. This latest one is a harrowing review of the human costs of globalization, focusing mainly on Indonesia.

Although he does not share Michael Moore's gift for postmodern larks, Pilger's interests have a lot in common with Moore's exasperated attempts to connect with such global exploiters as Nike's Phil Knight. For Pilger the principal target is the World Bank and similar agencies; at one point he successfully corners a World Bank bureaucrat, who loses his cool under Pilger's close questioning. (The same exec, Stanley Fischer, also appears in *Life and Debt*.)

Released in July 2001, the same month that a Group of Eight (G8) demonstrator against globalization was killed in Genoa, and not long after significant protests against the World Trade Organization and the International Monetary Fund in Göteborg, Sweden, and Seattle, Pilger's film borders on agitprop, a remarkable achievement for mainstream TV. Perhaps Pilger's unique role reflects one of his models, the journalism of George Orwell. Orwell "dispenses," Pilger wrote in *Hidden Agendas,* with the "illusion of objectivity": "The more one is aware of political bias, the more one can be independent of it, and the more one claims to be impartial, the more one is biased."

Pilger's producer, Charlton Television, released a booklet in connection with the premiere of the film, stressing the importance of activism in the light of the revelations the films offers about the role of the World Bank in Indonesia. Some of the same material is covered in the official Web site.

See also: *The Big One; Life and Debt.*
Availability: Selected collections; Bulldog Films.

Further reading

Hayward, Anthony. *In the Name of Justice: The Television Reporting of John Pilger.* London: Bloomsbury, 2001. An extensive record and analysis of Pilger's career and all of his film work through 2000 (it therefore does not discuss *The New Rulers of the World*).

Klein, Naomi. *No Logo: Taking Aim at the Brand Bullies.* New York: Picador USA, 1999. Devastating critique of such global corporations as Nike and Disney.

——. "Reclaiming the Commons." *New Left Review,* May–June 2001, 81–89. A survey of the antiglobalization movement.

La Botz, Dan. *Made in Indonesia: Indonesian Workers since Suharto*. Boston: South End Press, 2001. An essential study of the role of the Indonesian workers who helped overthrow President Suharto in 1998 and their ongoing struggle with globalization and issues of human rights.

The New Rulers of the World. Ed. Jane Kahlins. Birmingham: Carlton Television, 2001. The booklet released with the film has extensive analysis of globalization and the role of the World Bank, the IMF, and the WTO, as well as suggestions for political action, a bibliography, and Web sites for further information.

Pilger, John. *Hidden Agendas*. London: Vintage, 1998. Essays on global issues with Pilger's own assessment of his approach to investigative reporting.

——. *The New Rulers of the World*. London: Verso, 2002. Essays on Indonesia and other victims of globalization.

Web site:

⟨www.pilger.carlton.com⟩ Carlton Television's thorough official site for information about Pilger's film, his books, and his political targets; includes an extensive bibliography, filmography, interviews, and other relevant information.

⌒

Newsies

No newsies are good newsies?

1992, 125 mins., PG
Director: Kenny Ortega
Screenplay: Bob Tzudiker and Noni White
CAST
Jack Kelly = Christian Bale
David Jacobs = David Moscow
Les Jacobs = Luke Edwards
Bryan Denton = Bill Pullman
Medda Larson = Ann-Margret
Joseph Pulitzer = Robert Duvall
Racetrack = Max Casella
Crutchy = Marty Belafsky

Now that there are virtually no newsboys anymore, even in the suburbs, it must have seemed safe for Hollywood to make a film about how they became unionized. Safely removed in time as well, the filmmakers' newsboys live in a never-never land of New York street talk. If a real street urchin sang about "mudduh, dawtuh, fadduh" (from newsboy Jack's song "So That's What a Family Is"), no newsboy would ever have been safe. But even contemporary news accounts captured these accents—"Dere's t'ree t'ousand of us, and we'll win sure"—so maybe people really did tawk that way.

This exercise in historical kitsch about the once numerous youthful riffraff who roamed every big city in America only touches on the real problems these youngsters faced. An early muckraking piece by William Hart in 1908 exposed the unpretty side of the daily grind of selling the news on street corners, plus other things some of the night boys sold, such as drugs. The newsies in this film are of course too old, too clean, too well fed, and too happy to be real. Even the boy quaintly called Crutchy gets along fine. And there are even singing nuns in the streets!

Disney, alas, is about pretty, and the newsboys (there are no newsgirls, but fortunately there are sisters of newsboys) in this film have a well-fed wholesomeness that usually works for Disneyland. Since there has been an occasional uproar about violence and strange moral lessons in Disney films (from *Bambi* to *The Lion King*) in the past, it should have occurred to Disney execs when *Newsies* was (mis)conceived that it is not wholesomeness that captures attention and word of mouth, but the Dark Side.

The only Dark Side in *Newsies* consists of newspaper magnates such as Joseph Pulitzer (the *New York World*) and William Randolph Hearst (the *Journal*), who are interested in money and yellow journalism ("Nude Corpse on Rails Not Connected with Trolley Strike"), respectively. The strike portrayed was actually a selective strike, which the film does not make clear: only boys who sold the *World* and the *Journal* struck, and in fact a few women who sold the two scab papers were permitted to carry on as well. "We ain't fightin' women," one of the newsboys told a *New York Times* reporter, who tipped him a dime for his chivalry.

One can only imagine Disney executives screening *Dirty Dancing*—the last successful job for the choreographer and director Kenny Ortega—and deciding that without any of the sexy gals they could have a great children's dance film that could rival *Oliver!* or *Annie*. Instead of the 1950s cultural rebelliousness of *Dirty Dancing, Newsies* subverts the revolutionary rhetoric of the 1960s. At one point, in an unconscious parody of Black Panther and SDS Weatherman sloganmongers, the newsies sing, "Arise and Seize the Day." When the newsies really get ticked off, they sing, "Nothing can break us/No one can make us give up our rights."

Having been somewhat unfair to this film, I should say that Disney does not pull many punches when it comes to the trolleymen's strike of 1899, the model for the newsies' organizing drive. The trolleymen fight back against the police escorts of the scab drivers, burn the trolleys, and generally carry on fairly violently. Labor militancy in the summer of 1899 in New York City was quite extensive, as a reporter for the *New York Times*—not a scab newspaper that year— explained: "The strike fever, after extending from the street car employees and freight handlers on the railroad piers to the newsboys, has now spread to the telegraph messenger boys" (22 July 1899).

The newsboys were able to win their strike in part because they numbered 3,000 in Manhattan alone and in part because their militancy—beating up scab newsboys and ripping up their newspapers—usually went unchecked, since the police were called away to trolley strike duty. For the most part, the police should have been happy that children had their own strike to pursue, since some 10-year-olds had been helping the trolleymen by throwing bricks at scab-driven cars.

The film makes only partial use of this militancy, although the union lessons strike home. One of the newsies says of his father, who has lost his job after being injured at a factory: "He's got no union to protect him." The newsboys had a simple demand: the wholesale cost of each newspaper had to remain at a half-cent per copy. (They sold them for a penny.) It is perhaps a pity that this film was almost thrown away on a fasci-

nating moment in labor history. The film does have one other thing right: there really was a newsboy called Racetrack who was in charge of (unsuccessful) negotiations with the chief of police for parade rights. The chief said no to this leader of the real Newsboys' Union, which clearly didn't always get what it wanted.

Eventually Governor Teddy Roosevelt comes down on the side of the boys, conveniently enough, just when they are about to launch a citywide "child labor" strike, called by what looks like a junior version of the Wobblies—One Big Union of children from the garment sweatshops, the stables, and, of course, the messenger boys, who, in the final demonstration, lead the masses of child laborers against Pulitzer's newspaper citadel. It is (almost) enough to soften the hardest heart. Since this guide lists so few films especially for children, *Newsies* may be helpful in raising some potential young militants.

See also: *Street Scene*.
Availability: Easy; DVD.

Further reading

Burroughs, Harry. *Boys in Men's Shoes: A World of Working Children*. New York: Macmillan, 1944. An immigrant arrives in Boston in 1903, rises from newsboy to lawyer, and establishes a foundation to provide welfare and career services for other newsies.

Hart, William. "De Kid Wot Works at Night." *Everybody's Magazine,* January 1908. In *Popular Writing in America*, 5th ed., ed. Donald McQuade and Robert Atwan, 257–63. New York: Oxford University Press, 1993. Despite the jokey title, Hart's article about the exploitation of newsies led to child labor reform in Chicago.

Maslin, Janet. "They Sing, They Dance, They Go on Strike." *New York Times,* 8 April 1992, C17. A heartless attack on the film's virtues.

New York Times. "Newsboys Go On Strike," 21 July 1899, 2; "The Strike of the Newsboys," 22 July 1899, 4; "Newsboys Act and Talk," 25 July 1899, 3. Sample articles on the newsboys' strike.

——. "Strikers [Trolleymen] Return to Work," 21 July 1899, 2; "Messenger Boys May Strike," 22 July 1899, 4; "The Messenger Boys Strike," 25 July 1899, 3. Sample articles on the other strikes.

~

Nightsongs

"I am bound on a journey without end"

1983, 107 mins., in English, Mandarin, and
  Cantonese, with English subtitles
Director: Marva Nabili
Screenplay: Marva Nabili
CAST
Cousin (Chinese/Viet Woman) = Mabel
  Kwong
Fung Lai Ping = Ida F. O. Chung
Fung Leung = Victor Wong
Fung Tak Men = David Lee
Fung Mei Fun = Rose Lee
Fung Tak Sing = Roger Chang
Gang Recruiter = Geoff Lee
Murray = George LaPorte
ILGWU Teacher = Connie Hsu
Narrator = Lois Taylor

In some obvious ways, an Iranian expatriate
and former actress would not seem to be
the most likely director of an insiders' look
at immigrant work life in an American
Chinatown. But Nabili spent five years
making the film, including a four-month job
in a Chinatown garment factory in New York
City.

A garment sweatshop is in fact the principal location for most of the labor-centered
activities in *Nightsongs*, with Chinatown
streets and a tiny apartment serving as the
only other major locations. The Fung family,
first-generation Chinese immigrants, are
serving as hosts for a Chinese "cousin" who
has been sent to the United States to escape
a refugee camp. As "aristocratic" Chinese
living in Vietnam, her family no longer fits
into the new Communist ways. But she has
as much difficulty in New York, trying to
succeed at her sewing job in an immigrant
sweatshop.

In the meantime her host's teenage son
has been caught up in the world of Chinese
teenage gangs, potentially a fatal risk,
although in the end he avoids death in a
nonetheless tragic incident. The Cousin,
never given a name, writes in a journal and
composes poetry, most of which is read in a

voice-over. We learn from the credits that
Nabili based her screenplay in part on the
actual journal entries of Fae Myenne Ng and
poems from an anthology, *Women Poets of
China*.

There is therefore a sharp contrast
between the nitty-gritty of surviving in
Chinatown and the soft and sad prose and
verses we hear. The film begins with this line:
"My journal begins with remnants of journeys," and when tragedy strikes and Cousin
must leave, we see her departing bus and the
empty streets:

The sky is bright again.
The gates of heaven are near.
I am bound on a journey without end.

See also: *The City*.
Availability: Selected collections.

Further reading

Louie, Miriam Ching Yoon. *Sweatshop Warriors*.
  Boston: South End Press, 2001. The subtitle,
  Immigrant Workers Take on the Global Factory,
  indicates the scope of this polemic that argues
  for the organizing efforts of the Chinese,
  Korean, Thai, and Mexican women in New
  York, Los Angeles, El Paso, San Antonio, and
  Oakland.
"Nightsongs." *Variety*, 25 April 1984. The reviewer
  worries about the film finding its audience,
  which would probably "find it informative and
  often compelling in its tale of labor, education,
  and culture-generation gaps."
Rexroth, Kenneth, and Ling Chung, eds. *Women
  Poets of China*. New York: New Directions, 1972.
  The source book of poems—some rearranged—
  for a number of Cousin's journal entries.

~

1900

Italian workers and bosses at the turn of
the century

1976, 243 mins.; 1991 version, 311 mins.;
  Italy/France/USA, in English, NC-17
Director: Bernardo Bertolucci
Screenplay: Franco Arcalli, Giuseppe
  Bertolucci, and Bernardo Bertolucci

CAST
Alfredo Berlinghieri = Robert De Niro
Anita = Stefania Sandrelli
Ada = Dominique Sanda
Olmo Dalco = Gérard Depardieu
Leo Dalco = Sterling Hayden
Attilo = Donald Sutherland
Alfredo Berlinghieri = Burt Lancaster
Regina = Laura Betti
Signora Pioppi = Alida Valli

The opening credits of *1900* show a famous Italian painting of a militant march of striking workers—Pelizza da Volpedo's *Fourth Estate* (on exhibit in Milan's Metropolitan Gallery of Modern Art). In this freeze frame, determined workers stride toward the viewer, while a woman with a baby is seen ambiguously gesturing toward her husband. Does she want him to stop? Fight on? This painting, both labor-centered and very personal, sets the visual and emotional tone of Bernardo Bertolucci's masterpiece to come.

When an American film depicts the relationship between political or working-class movements and communism, the American Communists are usually portrayed as dangerous criminals, inhuman zombies, slaves of Soviet Russia, and sometimes all three. In a European film such as *1900*, however, Communists are portrayed as another political force in the demographic mix.

The film begins with a dramatization of the peasant and landowning classes on one estate in 1900. The rise of fascism in the 1920s and the surrender of the old landowning class to Mussolini's vision spell hard times for the workers, who begin to return to some strength only with the Communist-led resistance during World War II.

But these political issues are primarily the backdrop for an engrossing story of numerous individuals and the lives of three couples: the *padrone* (landowner) Berlinghieri and his decadent wife, Ada; the revolutionary couple, Olmo and Anita; and the Fascists Attilo and Regina. More narrowly, the film follows the fate of two men born on the same day at the turn of the century: the *padrone*,

Alfredo, and his virtual serf Olmo. They begin as an odd couple of friends, then gradually become separated by class and politics as the film moves through three major acts or periods: pre–World War I, the Fascist era of the 1920s and 1930s, and then the overthrow of Mussolini in 1945.

The narrative structure is actually a little more complicated and visually stunning: the film opens and ends with a frame story—Olmo and Anita's daughter and the peasant women attacking the fleeing Fascists at the end of the war—before beginning the narrative proper in 1900.

Outstanding character portrayals dominate the film's historical scope: Donald Sutherland as the viciously corrupt Fascist Attilo, Stefania Sandrelli as the charismatic leader of the women's movement, and Gérard Depardieu as the stolid and handsome hero of the resistance. Their lives crisscross during these catastrophic years.

Some of the Marxist politics behind Bertolucci's vision need some explaining for viewers new to his films. A recurring red-flag-bedecked train, for example, carries evacuated children away from their starving villages during a strike: in itself, it recalls the evacuation of the children during the IWW-led strike of mill workers in Lawrence, Massachusetts (the *Bread and Roses* strike of 1912). But the train reappears at the end of the film in a dreamlike sequence, signifying the Marxist maxim that "revolution is the locomotive of history." In a similar way, a shot of a burrowing mole during this sequence is a visual pun or joke for a quotation (famous among European Marxists such as Bertolucci) from Marx's *Eighteenth Brumaire of Louis Bonaparte* when Europe "speaks" to Revolution, "Well-grubbed, old mole!"

These bits of Marxist insider jokes should not persuade the viewer to avoid this film as too difficult or intellectual. It is a visual and emotional roller-coaster ride and more than worth the rental price. Its director, cast, award-winning composer (Enrico Morricone), and cinematographer (Vittorio Storaro) joined in an ambitious attempt to

Women blockade the police in *1900*. Courtesy British Film Institute Stills, Posters, and Designs.

present half a century of working-class history in Italy.

See also: *Bitter Rice*; *The Organizer*.
Availability: Selected collections.

Further reading

Bondanella, Peter. *Italian Cinema from Neorealism to the Present*. 3d ed. New York: Continuum, 2001. Sets Bertolucci's films in their Italian political context.

"Red Flags and American Dollars." *Cineaste* 7, no. 4 (1977): 2–9, 50. Interviews with Bernardo Bertolucci, in which he develops extensively his (and his films') politics.

~

9 to 5

No business as usual

1980, 110 mins., PG
Director: Colin Higgins

Screenplay: Colin Higgins and Patricia Resnick

CAST

Judy Bernly = Jane Fonda
Doralee Rhodes = Dolly Parton
Violet Newstead = Lily Tomlin
Franklin Hart Jr. = Dabney Coleman
Tinsworthy = Sterling Hayden
Roz = Elizabeth Wilson

Despite their widely differing acting styles and character types, the three female leads of *9 to 5* seem to mesh amazingly well as they play out a fantasy of revenge on a loutish sexist boss. The film takes advantage of Dolly Parton's film debut by having her sing the title song, a hit with a life of its own ("You're just a step on the boss man's ladder"). And any film that uses her legendary figure to trap her lecherous boss has a lot of nerve.

Although some of the film will seem out of date—the women's pot party (on *one* joint) goes on forever—other jokes still seem to work: Violet mistaking rat poison for her boss's coffee creamer, for example, or Judy Bernly confessing to her ex-husband that she has been playing "M and M" games while her boss has been kidnapped (her husband doesn't know that) and bound in a leather and chain outfit.

The political heart of the film, however, is the rebellion against the petty and grand exploitation of the women office workers. Especially sharp is Violet, the efficient and creative administrative assistant who trains the new men and watches in frustration as they get promoted over her.

The women's revenge is sweet and they make a number of economic points as well. After they kidnap their boss, they simply take over the department in his name: they get to institute equal pay for equal work and flextime, set up a day-care center, and create a humane office environment. Not only are these changes good for them, but they turn out to be good for business.

The film's realistic side is briefly interrupted by its broad comedy and by several fantasy sequences based on film and other popular culture traditions. All three women get to dream about what they would do with their boss: Dolly Parton dreams of hogtying him, Jane Fonda dreams of leading the office workers on a safari against him, and Lily Tomlin as Snow White gets to off him as cute Disney animals cheer.

There's more than a sitcom to this film, but inevitably it is the one-liners that remain memorable: "I killed the boss," Violet says at one point. "Do you think they're not going to fire me for that?!" Or Dora Lee when she tires of her boss's manhandling: "I've got a gun in my purse. I'm going to change you from a rooster to a hen with one shot."

Despite the occasional satire against corporate defensiveness—we hear of the company's need to "clamp down on any sign of unionization"—the film provides only dream solutions to real problems. Nevertheless, the popularity of the film certainly indicated that for a fair number of viewers, that was at least something. It wasn't enough for the *Times* reviewer, however. He felt that the film ignored "the energy crisis, inflation,

recession, job shortages, the disappointing sales of the Chrysler 'K,' urban blight, and the price of gold" (Canby). Too bad there wasn't a sequel.

See also: *Business as Usual*.
Availability: Easy; DVD.

Further reading

Bravo, Ellen, and Ellen Cassedy. *The 9 to 5 Guide to Combating Sexual Harassment*. New York: Wiley, 1992. A popular and informative handbook with revealing analyses and strategies for change.

Canby, Vincent. "Revolt of the Women." *New York Times*, 19 December 1980, C20. A little snippy about the film's "waving of the flag of feminism."

Farley, Lyn. *Sexual Shakedown: The Sexual Harassment of Women on the Job*. New York: McGraw-Hill, 1978. An early but thorough report.

Garson, Barbara. *All the Livelong Day: The Meaning and Demeaning of Routine Work*. 2d ed. New York: Penguin, 1994. Interviews and commentary on many kinds of jobs, including office work.

Howe, Louise Kapp. *Pink Collar Workers: Inside the World of Women's Work*. New York: Putnam, 1977. À la Studs Terkel, interviews and commentary on office workers and other "traditional low-paying female occupations."

Norma Rae

Pure union

1979, 113 mins., PG
Director: Martin Ritt
Screenplay: Irving Ravetch, based on the life of Crystal Lee (Jordan)
CAST
Norma Rae = Sally Field
Reuben Warshawsky = Ron Leibman
Sonny = Beau Bridges
Vernon = Pat Hingle
Leona = Barbara Baxley

Martin Ritt's film version of Crystal Lee's life sticks remarkably close to the story of how her personality developed and the incidents that led to her union activism. The seemingly impossible relationship between Norma and Reuben parallels Crystal's with Eli Zivkovitch, who, while not a New Yorker like Reuben, still found it tough to feel at home in Roanoke Rapids, the North Carolina cotton mill town that was the preserve of J. P. Stevens & Company. Many of Reuben's struggles in the film were also Eli's, as the Amalgamated Clothing and Textile Workers' Union strove to gain a presence in a company traditionally very hostile to unions. The importance of meeting in black churches, of an integrated labor movement, and of Crystal's private and domestic demons are all captured here.

The film dramatizes the frustrations and difficulties of Norma's life and family in a mill-dominated town where everybody knows your business. Norma's mom and dad also work at the (fictional) O. P. Henry Textile Mill: her mom is losing her hearing, while her dad—in a horrifying sequence—literally keels over after Norma (temporarily pro-

moted to a timing supervisor) has clocked his slow rate of work. Norma is constantly involved with men who are up to no good, but eventually she finds her calling in the union as Reuben recruits her to help organize for a certifying election. The company tries to split the workers along racial lines, her new husband doesn't like her staying out all the time, and, in a now-classic scene after she is fired and stands up on a machine with her hand-lettered UNION sign, she is hauled off to jail.

The union wins the election by a close margin—427 to 373—and the film ends wistfully: the never-to-be romance between Reuben and Norma has changed to a friendship, and Reuben's organizing job takes him on the road again.

One of the most popular pro-union films of our era, *Norma Rae* never makes the organizing drive look too easy. It balances the eventual selflessness of Norma with the stubbornness of her father, who mistrusts the

Norma Rae (Sally Fields) being thrown out of work at the mill.

union. It also confronts with some honesty the mixture of personal and altruistic motives that an organizing drive sometimes satisfies: Norma Rae *needs* this union, not only to help protect her job but to maintain her self-respect.

See also: *Keeping On*.
Availability: Easy; DVD.

Further reading

Canby, Vincent. "Unionism in the South." *New York Times*, 2 March 1979, C10; "Sally Field's 'Norma Rae' is a Triumph." *New York Times*, 11 March 1979, II.19. Two rave reviews of the film and Field's acting.

Conway, Mimi. *Rise Gonna Rise: A Portrait of Southern Textile Workers*. New York: Anchor/Doubleday, 1979. Oral histories, à la Studs Terkel, concentrating on workers engaged in union struggles with J. P. Stevens.

Goldfarb, Lynn, and Anatoli Ilyashov. "Working Class Hero: An Interview with Martin Ritt." *Cineaste* 18, no. 4 (1991): 20–23. Ritt on *Norma Rae*: "I was trying to make a labor film with teeth."

Leifermann, Henry P. *Crystal Lee: A Woman of Inheritance*. New York: Macmillan, 1975. A non-fiction book that recounts the origins of many of the incidents in the film.

Toplin, Robert Brent. *History by Hollywood*. Urbana: University of Illinois Press, 1996. Subtitled *The Use and Abuse of the American Past*, this volume documents the uneasy relationship between the filmmakers and Crystal Lee, who for a while tried to have her life filmed by Barbara Kopple instead of Martin Ritt.

Wolf, Jackie. "Filmmakers Take on J. P. Stevens." *Jump Cut* 22 (1980): 8, 24, 37. A review of documentary films (unfortunately not available on videocassette) about Crystal Lee and organizing J. P. Stevens.

El Norte

No pasar

1983, 139 mins., USA/UK, in English and Spanish, with English subtitles, R
Director: Gregory Nava
Screenplay: Gregory Nava and Anne Thomas

CAST
Rosa Xuncax = Zide Sylvia Gutiérrez
Enrique Xuncax = David Villalpando
Arturo Xuncax = Ernesto Gómez Cruz
Lupe Xuncax = Alicia del Lago
Pedro = Heraclio Zepeda
Josefita = Stella Quan
Raimundo = Abel Franco
Nacha = Lupe Ontiveros

"The North" is the promised land of the poor and oppressed children of Guatemalan Indian coffee workers who dare to organize to improve their conditions. When a young man, Enrique, discovers that his father has been decapitated for his union activities, he kills a government soldier. When his mother is disappeared as well, he and his sister, Rosa, escape on a trek to *el Norte*.

The film is divided into three acts: (1) life and death in Guatemala, (2) travel in Mexico from Oaxaca to Tijuana, and finally (3) life as illegal "Mexican" immigrants in Los Angeles. Each stage is filled with horrors and difficulties. To leave Mexico, for example, Enrique and Rosa must find a coyote to lead them across the border. The first one attacks them for their money, but the second one—a "friend of a friend"—sends them successfully through an old sewer tunnel, but it is overrun with rats.

Some moments of sick comedy enliven the siblings' difficult lives. To pass as Mexicans, they are told to add an extremely vulgar Mexican phrase to their oral vocabulary. When they are detained by the *migra* (immigration agents) after their first failed attempt to cross the border, Enrique fools the interviewer by casually cursing every third word. At the overly high-tech home of her new employer, Rosa cannot operate the washing machine. Her employer discovers her washing clothing by hand near the fancy swimming pool and tells her to stop: "I couldn't stand the thought of her . . . *scrubbing*."

The end of the film suggests the difficulty of separating the personal frustrations of the siblings from the economic system, from which there is no exit. Enrique must choose between caring for his sister (who becomes very sick, presumably from a rat bite) and working a good job. In the end he loses both, and must return to the seemingly endless cycle of waiting for a day job at the local pickup stop for illegal immigrant labor. Even the exploitative contract work with a labor gang would seem superior to this dead end.

Most viewers find the scenes in rural Guatemala so vivid and attractive that its horrors seem like hallucinations or a nightmare. Indeed, Nava uses the magic realism of dreams and nightmares to great effect. We see Enrique attacked by a Guatemalan soldier in a foggy Tijuana street before we realize it is simply a nightmare. But Tijuana's shantytown is so ugly that it seems the siblings have simply run from one hell to another. Los Angeles does give them a piece of the Dream—the TV sets, flush toilets, and electricity their old copies of *Good Housekeeping* promised them when they were still in Guatemala. But the *migra* is ever present, waiting to snatch *el Norte* away from them.

Only Ken Loach's film *Bread and Roses* and David Riker's *The City* have successfully dramatized the current immigrant situation *El Norte* once portrayed.

See also: *Bread and Roses; The City.*
Availability: Easy.

Further reading

Canby, Vincent. "'El Norte': A Fine Movie Fueled by Injustice." *New York Times*, 22 January 1984, II.17. "One of the most boldly original and satirical social-political statements ever to be found in a film about the United States as a land of power as well as opportunity."

Maslin, Janet. "A Better Life." *New York Times*, 11 January 1984, C15. Reviewer calls the film "a remarkable accomplishment," with "solid, sympathetic performances by unknown actors and a visual style of astonishing vibrancy."

Northern Lights

Pure prairie mischief

1979, 90 mins., B&W
Directors: John Hanson and Rob Nilsson
Screenplay: John Hanson and Rob Nilsson

CAST
Ray Sorensen = Robert Behling
John Sorensen = Joe Spano
Uncle Thor = Thorbjörn Rue
Sven = Nick Eldridge
Inga Olsness = Susan Lynch
Murphy = Harold Aleshire
Henrik Sorensen = Ray Hess
Henry Martinson as himself

This independent feature dramatizes the plight of Norwegian-American farmers in North Dakota during the period of World War I. The personal story of an engaged couple (Ray and Inga) becomes part of the larger social and economic struggle that their people must wage to survive. Ray reluctantly at first and then more enthusiastically agrees to help organize for the Nonpartisan League. Its politics are more than a little obscure in the film, but it is crystal-clear what the farmers are up against, according to Ray: "Low grain prices, short weights, dockage fees, phony grading [of their crops], land speculation, mortgage fees." Although it is hard to imagine anyone not supporting a group fighting these abuses, the film dramatizes the individualist philosophy that has brought so many of these sturdy hard workers to this spot in time. "The small farmer is better off by himself," one old farmer tells Ray.

The grainy black-and-white footage does give this film a nostalgic look, making it seem as if we are looking at a grandparent's musty photo album of the old country. Ray's father dies at the foot of the wooden frame of an old scarecrow, an upright that looks more like a crucifix than a deterrent to birds. Banker Forsythe, who dispossesses Inga's family when they fail to pay the mortgage, is snug in the only fur coat we see in this chilly countryside. The filmmakers are able to capture the threat and promise of a threshing crew rushing to get in a crop as the first blizzard arrives.

At some points, however, one is tempted to say, "Well, it must be a Norwegian thing," as when we witness Uncle Thor telling an enthralling story of how he once heard "the grass grow." Later, a potential recruit to the

League challenges Ray to a wrestling match. If Ray wins, the man will join. When Ray is pinned, he tells the victor that without the League he'll be a loser.

Ray does succeed as an organizer but at a high personal cost. He must delay his wedding to Inga, and they always live apart. Inga provides the viewpoint of those women who always stay at home: "The people you're fighting," she tells Ray, "won't give up. If we win, we'll be fighting them off the rest of our lives. If we lose, we'll have each other." Ray disagrees: togetherness isn't enough. Some critics of the film found its portrayal of women incomplete: the League supported full suffrage for women, for example, and it had women activists as well (see Markusen or the introduction to Morlan).

Eventually Ray and his brother lose their farm: as League sympathizers, they cannot sell their wheat at a decent price. They rally behind the League candidate in the primary for governor, Lynn J. Frazer, who does carry enough of the rural districts to be a contender for governor. The film's historical survey, however, breaks off at this point; it doesn't cover the actual elections of 1916, which Frazer won.

The film may be an acquired taste. A few speeches in Norwegian (subtitled in English) and a methodical pace based on the voice-over narrator's use of Ray's diary will not satisfy everyone's curiosity about this, a perhaps very unfortunately out-of-the-way episode in labor history. The directors make a virtue of their low budget by filming their characters in impressive close-ups. Divide County and its people make a good showing as well, as nonprofessionals join professionals in the cast. The film's topic *is* important, however, and its message will win over most of those who watch the film.

Ray's story is somewhat ingeniously framed by an introduction and conclusion by a surviving member of the Nonpartisan League, the 94-year-old Henry Martinson, who is filmed looking at Ray's diary and typing *his* version of Ray's life, the version, presumably, that we get in this film. As the film closes, we return to Martinson, whose voice-over strikes a note of optimism not always present in the film: "I'm an optimist. Good comes out of bad. Things are going to change. I'm sure of it. I got time. I can wait."

See also: *Wildrose*.
Availability: Selected collections.

Further reading

Canby, Vincent. "A Look at Long Ago." *New York Times*, 26 September 1979, C19. "When the film's focus is on labor history, remembered or recreated, it is extremely moving."

Garland, Hamlin. *Main-Travelled Roads. 1891–1922*. New York: NAL, 1960. Classic short stories of the hard life of farmers in North Dakota and other Midwest settings.

Gaston, Herbert Earle. *The Nonpartisan League*. New York: Harcourt, Brace & Howe, 1920. An insider's view.

Markusen, Ann. "Who Were Your Grandmothers, John Hansen? A Review of 'Northern Lights.'" *Quest: A Feminist Quarterly* 5 (Summer 1980): 25–35. Argues that the film ignores the political role of women in the League.

Morlen, Robert L. *Political Prairie Fire: The Nonpartisan League, 1915–1922*. 1955. Minneapolis: Minnesota Historical Society, 1985. An excellent history of the movement.

Russell, Charles Edward. *The Story of the Nonpartisan League: A Chapter in American Evolution*. New York: Harper, 1920. An early history of the movement.

~

Nothing But a Man

But nothing less either

1964, 95 mins., B&W
Director: Michael Roemer
Screenplay: Michael Roemer and Robert M. Young
CAST
Duff Anderson = Ivan Dixon
Josie Dawson = Abbey Lincoln
Lee = Gloria Foster
Will = Julius Harris
Driver = Martin Priest
Frankie = Leonard Parker
Jocko = Yaphet Kotto
Pop = Milton Williams

This remarkable independent film, virtually forgotten in the years since it was a minor but solid hit at the 1964 Venice Film Festival, develops two stories, one private, one sociological. In the first, a young black man tries to come to terms with fatherhood: he has virtually abandoned his son (at least he thinks he may be his son) to a friend of his former wife, and he has been cruelly dismissed by his alcoholic father. In the second story, he moves from job to job, experiencing the discrimination and difficulty of holding regular employment in Alabama at the beginning of the civil rights era.

The two stories are closely connected. Duff's father's problem is exacerbated by an injury in a sawmill, which left him with one useless arm. Duff has been reluctant to trace his son because he doubts his paternity, while his stints as a railroad laborer on section gangs repairing tracks have sent him to locations where the men of the gang are holed up in abandoned railway cars for weeks at a time.

When *Variety* reviewed the film, it noted that its chances of playing in the South were "problematical." This understatement reminds us that the film was made and released on the cusp of a heroic and violent era. Children had been killed in a church bombing in Birmingham, where the film is set. Duff's been a union man, but only on the railroad, he tells his white foreman, who has heard (from a fellow black worker who snitched) that Duff believes that the men ought to "stick together." This is enough to get Duff into big trouble. The foreman expects Duff to back down in front of all his fellow workers and say that they shouldn't stick together. When Duff refuses, he's out of the job and blacklisted. And he never tried to organize anything! He simply stopped being (in his words) "a white man's nigger" and stopped saying "Yassuh, boss" over and over.

Although there are a few bluesy and jazz club tunes and some spirituals (by The Gospel Stars)—all in their proper place, of course—the real hits of the film are from the Motown groups that dominate the sound track: Mary Wells, Martha and the Vandellas, The Miracles, Stevie Wonder, and The Marvelettes. (Duff's wife, played by the jazz singer Abbey Lincoln, does not sing.)

By allowing Duff to cross a thin but significant class line—he's a laborer but he falls for the educated schoolteacher daughter of a prominent black minister—the filmmakers set up numerous dramatic opportunities to explore the tensions in the southern black community of the 1950s and 1960s. The white community clearly depends on Reverend Dawson to be an accommodationist of the old school. If the members of his community "behave," some jobs will be available for them. When one of them steps over the line—a lynching happened just eight years before—it's back to the past again. When the minister sizes up Duff as liable to marry his daughter, it becomes clear within seconds that Duff will be found wanting. Not surprisingly, Duff feels that the Reverend is an Uncle Tom; his daughter tells Duff that her father knew who the lynchers were but said and did nothing about it.

The production values of this independent film are quite high: even when Robert M. Young (who wrote and photographed the film) shoots his reluctant hero in black cities in New Jersey, with the backdrop of obviously ordinary (and real) citizens going about their daily lives, the film, oddly enough, only gains in authenticity.

Donald Bogle has argued that some of the scenes, such as Duff's post-wedding dinner party with his old workmates, suffered because a black director would have understood the men's behavior more clearly. But he concluded (in 1988) that "no other American film has yet treated a black male/female relationship with as much sensitivity." High praise indeed.

Although Robert M. Young was credited with the scriptwriting and cinematography of *Nothing But a Man*, his work with Michael Roemer, the director, was consistent with his own directorial efforts during his quiet but very solid career. His documentary work, such as *The Eskimo: Fight for Life* (which won an Emmy in 1971), *Sit In* (an NBC White

Paper), and *Cortile Cascino* (a suppressed white paper about a Sicilian slum), preceded his successes in full-length features such as *Short Eyes* (a prison drama) and *The Ballad of Gregorio Cortez* (about a Chicano folk hero and rebel).

See also: *A Raisin in the Sun.*
Availability: Easy.

Further reading

Bogle, Donald. *Blacks in American Film and Television: An Encyclopedia.* New York: Garland, 1988. Includes entries on the film and Ivan Dixon.

——. *Toms, Coons, Mulattoes, Mammies, and Bucks.* New York: Continuum, 1994. A brief but helpful discussion of the film in the context of other black films of the decade.

Crowther, Bosley. "Nothing But a Man." *New York Times*, 21 September 1964, 37. "An offbeat venture of which this country can be proud."

"Nothing But a Man." *Variety*, 9 September 1964. A very positive review of the film.

Peary, Gerald. "Robert M. Young's Ordinary People." *American Film*, July–August 1982, 67–71. A thorough survey of the director's career.

"Venice Films." *Variety*, 2 September 1964. "One of those rare films delivering an insight into Southern life and the place of the Negro without patronizing or using fake histrionics."

⟋

October Sky

The sky above, the mine below

1999, 108 mins., PG
Director: Joe Johnston
Screenplay: Lewis Colick, from Homer Hickham's autobiography *Rocket Boys*
CAST
Homer Hickham = Jake Gyllenhaal
John Hickham = Chris Cooper
Roy Lee Cook = William Lee Scott
Quentin Wilson = Chris Owen
Sherman O'Dell = Chad Lindberg
Elsie Hickham = Natalie Canerday
Miss Frieda Riley = Laura Dern
Jim Hickham = Scott Thomas

This is a sunny, mostly happy film about the son of a miner and a mining community that become obsessed with rockets. As in a number of American and British films of the 1990s in this guide, the labor issues and economic circumstances are part of the background of the film, while the foreground is filled with what is called—perhaps too condescendingly—a human interest or feel-good story.

By going so mainstream with this topic, the director has trouble holding back on the sentimental formulas of the genre. When Homer Hickham loses a friend (an older man who helped to machine a part for his rocket) in a mining accident, we see it coming and understand his anguish. But when his schoolteacher, the saintly Frieda Riley, played by Laura Dern, who makes Calista Flockhart look like an overeater, contracts Hodgkin's disease and provides still another tearful exit, our patience is stretched.

When a film deals with a coal town—here Coalwood, West Virginia—union and economic issues can rarely be offscreen. But the theme of this film is in part how to escape the coal town by becoming a rocket scientist, a feat I imagine represents a virtually statistical zero in likelihood among the youth in such towns. Of course in this instance it really happened. Homer, son of a working-class man who became a mine supervisor, was an amateur scientist—a "rocket boy"—who grew up to become a NASA scientist.

Director Joe Johnston's previous work includes *Jumanji,* a film about a fantastic and frightening board game that brings extraordinarily dangerous creatures to life; afterward he directed *Jurassic Park III*. Some of the same inventiveness and fantasy characteristic of these films comes through in *October Sky* as the boys try to convert their hard formulas, odd pieces of metal, and naiveté into a rocket-launching moment.

Despite the film's charm, I worry that it is still another example of how the most important issue in a mining community is how to avoid being a miner. A strike that happens during the film is only sketched out, and part of the situation you are supposed to be cheering is that to get an essential piece of Homer's rocket ready somebody has to scab to get entry into the metal workshop.

See also: *Harlan County War.*
Availability: Easy; DVD.

Further reading

Ebert, Roger. "October Sky." *Chicago Sun-Times*, 2 February 1999. "The tension in the movie is not between the boys and their rocket, but between the boys and those who think that miners' sons belong down in the mines and not up in the sky."

Hickham, Homer. *Rocket Boys*. New York: Delacorte, 1998. Retitled as *October Sky* for a movie tie-in, Hickham's autobiography has returned to the title that really captures the spirit of the book and film. He has also published two other memoirs of his experiences, *The Coalwood Way* (2000) and *Sky of Stone* (2001).

Maslin, Janet. "Eyes Toward the Stars, True to His Dream." *New York Times*, 19 February 1999, B14. Since it has a "gung-ho wholesomeness of a Horatio Alger story by way of Norman Rockwell," the reviewer concludes that it is an "earnest, nostalgic film" almost "too good to be true."

Stack, Peter. "Reaching for the Sky: 'October Sky' Tells Poignant, Powerful Tale of a Coal Miner's Son." *San Francisco Chronicle*. The reviewer compliments the film, which has "no villain, really, just a series of bad circumstances: mine cave-ins, union turmoil, economic depression." That's all?!

Office Space

Revenge of the computer nerds

1999, 90 mins., R
Director: Mike Judge
Screenplay: Mike Judge, based on his "Milton" animated short films
CAST
Peter = Ron Livingston
Joanna = Jennifer Aniston
Milton = Stephen Root
Bill Lumbergh = Gary Cole
Michael Bolton = David Herman
Samir = Ajay Naidu

Yes, it's by *Beavis and Butthead*'s creator, Mike Judge, but no, it's not an animated cartoon and it's not simply the character Milton (invented by Judge for a series of animated shorts) going crazy on *Saturday Night Live*, but a convincing and funny "evil twin" (says Ebert) of the office world already satirized by *Clockwatchers*. Actually they are both evil twins, *Clockwatchers* driving its temps to desperation, *Office Space* doing the same to its white-collar computer nerds.

Despite the rise of software and dot.com workers across the land, there have been surprisingly few films about the work of these companies, serious or otherwise. *Office Space* captures some of the frustrations and absurdities of the white-collar computer workers known generically as developers, those who write and maintain software, as well as their co-workers and supervisors. When Peter begins to crack—petty rules and personal angst mounting every day—he at first is persuaded to attend a session with a hypnotherapist, who dies during his session. Apparently the effects of the hypnosis—he was told not to worry about anything—sticks.

Blissed out and filled with insight about the transitoriness of life, Peter follows two options at work: he begins to insult everyone and blows off his job, whereupon management and their consultants are convinced he is finally ready for promotion, and he hits upon a scheme to get rich. The scheme involves enlisting co-workers to withdraw zillions of fractional cents—which would get "dropped in the rounding-off process anyway"—into his personal bank account. Being computer experts, however, they don't get the fractional cents deposited at an undetectably leisurely pace but do it all at once. Peter and his friends are now in big trouble for stealing.

Another comic subplot has a few moments almost as good as Peter's dilemma. Peter's new girlfriend, Joanna, works at a chain restaurant where workers are expected to demonstrate "flair," which is measured by the number of personally selected buttons on their uniforms. "Flair" reflects their individuality and customer appeal. Joanna wears only the minimal number of fifteen, thereby proving she doesn't have enough flair to be successful at her job; other waitpersons have forty-five pieces and look like living billboards for souvenir shops.

The ending of all these shenanigans I will leave to your viewing, except to note that unlike his girlfriend, Peter—his bosses now agree—has more than enough flair.

See also: *Clockwatchers*.
Availability: Easy; DVD.

Further reading

Ebert, Roger. "Office Space." *Chicago Sun-Times*, 2 February 1999. An appreciation of the anarchic comedy of the film, such as scenes like the one in which the "captives" of the office "stagger forth like grotesques" and "take a baseball bat to a malfunctioning copier."

Holden, Stephen. "One Big Happy Family? No. Not at This Company." *New York Times*, 19 February 1999, B14. The reviewer is dismissive, except for Milton, "the movie's only inspired creation."

Marine, Craig. "Lots of Room for Laughs in 'Office Space.'" *San Francisco Examiner*, 19 February 1999. Applauds Judge, who "nails the job angst so prevalent in this beautiful country of ours."

Of Mice and Men

"Nobody gets to heaven, and nobody gets no land."—Crooks

I: 1939, 107 mins., B&W
Director: Lewis Milestone
Screenplay: Eugene Solow, from John Steinbeck's play of the same title (based in turn on his novel of the same title)
CAST
George = Burgess Meredith
Lennie = Lon Chaney Jr.
Mae = Betty Field
Slim = Charles Bickford
Candy = Roman Bohnen
Curly = Bob Steele
Whit = Noah Beery Jr.

Jackson = Oscar O'Shea
Carlson = Granville Bates
Crooks = Leigh Whipper
II: 1981, 150 mins.
Director: Reza S. Badiyi
Screenplay: E. Nick Alexander, based on the 1939 screenplay
CAST
George = Robert Blake
Lennie = Randy Quaid
Mae = Cassie Yates
Slim = Mitchell Ryan
Candy = Lew Ayres
Curly = Ted Neely
Whit = Dennis Fimple
Jackson = Pat Hingle
Carlson = Pat Corley
Crooks = Whitman Mayo
III: 1992, 110 mins., PG-13
Director: Gary Sinise
Screenplay: Horton Foote from John Steinbeck's novel of the same title
CAST
George = Gary Sinise
Lennie = John Malkovich
Mae = Sherilyn Fenn
Slim = John Terry
Candy = Ray Walston
Curly = Casey Siemaszko
Whit = Alexis Arquette
The Boss = Noble Willingham
Carlson = Richard Riehe
Crooks = Joe Morton

Steinbeck's adaptation of his best-selling novel for Broadway won the New York Drama Critics Circle award for the best play of the 1937–38 season. Unfortunately, he did not write the screenplay for the 1939 version of his tale of California hoboes ("bindle stiffs" in the novel). This box-office dud, directed by the then-popular Lewis Milestone, preceded a more successful film version of a Steinbeck novel, John Ford's Academy Award–winning adaptation of *The Grapes of Wrath*. By then Steinbeck was financially stoked. No one could touch him. He complained long and loud about Hollywood nonetheless, essentially always unhappy that the process of film production changed his dramatic vision. Eventually he was involved in two somewhat independent films, certainly not, strictly speaking, Hollywood productions: *The Pearl* and *The Forgotten Village,* both featuring Mexican peasants.

Of Mice and Men, part of Steinbeck's agricultural trilogy (the other two are *The Grapes of Wrath* and *In Dubious Battle*), is the most personal book of the three. It focuses on the recurring working-class dream of just setting up a little business for oneself, opting out of both capitalist exploitation and mass organizing. The story of Lenny and George is familiar to most literate readers, but some of the other aspects of the story probably have received less attention than they should. The crippled stable hand Crooks, for example, like the one-armed Candy, are both potential allies for George's scheme to get a little spread of one's own. The problem, Crooks reminds them, is simply this: "Nobody gets to heaven, and nobody gets no land. It's just in their head. They're all the time talkin' about it, but it's just in their head."

Granted that this was never a really dirty story, but why a PG-13 for the latest film adaptation (III)? The obvious flashpoint was Curley's Wife (whose own name is as invisible in this filmed version as it is in the novel), whom Steinbeck described as having "full, rouged lips and wide-spaced eyes, heavily made up." With Sherilyn Fenn from *Twin Peaks* as Curley's Wife, one would have thought that at least one stretch of the film would be hotted up. Fenn, however, is almost too nice, despite her Steinbeckian "cotton house dress and red mules." But no. And it may be because the screenwriter is Mr. Safe Americana himself, Horton Foote, or it may simply be that we have gone so far from the daringness of Steinbeck circa 1937, when the novel first appeared, that nothing in the film was going to rate an R. In any case, not one of these three versions would touch Curley's gloved hand ("That glove's fulla Vaseline. . . . Curley says he's keeping that hand soft for his wife"), surely the most disturbing of images in the book.

In fact, the story is really suitable for all ages, because its central premise—cynical guy with a good heart takes care of a powerful but mentally retarded giant—is not so far from a fair amount of TV fare. Or mainstream Broadway, for that matter, because Sinise and Malkovich played George and Lennie in the 1990 revival of Steinbeck's play. (The film is not the record of the play but an independently developed production.)

Sinise's version is at least the fourth major film production, if we count a version starring George Segal and Nicol Williamson as George and Lennie. Of the three listed in this entry, each has virtues that would attract viewers, presumably for different reasons. Quaid in II is the goofiest Lennie, while Chaney and Malkovich in I and III seem equally powerful. Sinise is too clean and buffed for my taste and Blake too much, well, like Blake. Fenn is probably the sexiest Wife of Curley, although Betty Field cradling one of the pups in her bosom must have raised a few thermostats in her day.

There are relatively few divergences in plot in all three versions, although II seems to suggest that Slim turns George over to the sheriff at the very end in a gesture not supported by the logic of the story or (certainly) Steinbeck's novel. None of the three even touches what I feel is the elegant conclusion of the novel, in which George and Slim go off for a drink while Whit grumbles about their seeming touchiness. (In a sense their pairing off caps their developing friendship in the novel and in all three filmed versions.)

Unfortunately, this novel and any one of the filmed versions have been assigned to death in American high schools. It has become a dreaded classic, not too far on the shelf from *The Scarlet Letter* (although a scarlet *A* on Demi Moore may be a stretch). This is sad: when *Of Mice and Men* is read with the other two books in Steinbeck's agricultural trilogy, the power of Steinbeck's radical vision of exploited labor comes through loud and clear on the page and equally so in John Ford's film of *The Grapes of Wrath.*

Each film is very much part of a specific era: Milestone's Depression grays dominate the 1939 version, while Sinise's frame story (we see George in the opening and closing shots alone in a boxcar, presumably remembering the story we are about to see) focuses more on the lone hero; Badiyi's 1981 version relies on the telegenic charm of Blake, then a TV regular, to carry the film. The latest version probably fits current audiences better. The Girl in the Red Dress, for example, whom Lennie messed with in such a way that the pair had to flee their previous job in Weed, actually dashes across the screen in desperate disarray, leaving us no doubt as to Lennie's potential for unpleasant violence. (In the other versions, as in the novel, we only hear about the Girl in the Red Dress.)

See also: *The Grapes of Wrath*.
Availability: I and II: selected collections; III: Easy; I and III: DVD.

Further reading

Canby, Vincent. "Of Mice and Men." *New York Times*, 2 October 1992, C5. Very positive review—the film (III) "remains faithful in almost every way to the stark Steinbeck tale."

Macnab, Geoffrey. "Of Mice and Men." *Sight and Sound*, January 1993, 50. Sinise's version (III) tends to a *Masterpiece Theatre* earnestness.

Millichap, Joseph R. *Steinbeck and Film*. New York: Frederick Ungar, 1983. Extensive discussion of the 1939 (I) adaptation.

Nugent, Frank S. "Of Mice and Men." *New York Times*, 17 February 1940, 9. Rave review of first version: "book and play have been followed as literally as the screen demands and the Hays office permits."

Steinbeck. John. *Of Mice and Men*. 1937. New York: Penguin, 1994. Excellent introduction by Susan Shillinglaw, with a discussion of Steinbeck's intention to develop the novel simultaneously as a play.

Note: A fourth version, not currently available, directed by Ted Kotcheff (the Canadian/British filmmaker loosely associated with the Angry Young Men in the 1950s), with George Segal as George, Nicol Williamson as Lennie, Moses Gunn as Crooks, Will Geer as Candy, and Joey

Heatherton as Curley's Wife, was produced by David Susskind for ABC-TV in 1968 but never released in videocassette; *Variety* [TV], 7 February 1968, judged it a "combination of fine drama and fine performances."

↰

Oh Freedom after While

"Take your eyes out of the sky, because someone is stealing your bread."—Owen Whitfield

1999, 56 mins.
Director: Steve Ross
Traditional documentary
PRINCIPAL FIGURES
Owen Whitfield, vice president, Southern Tenant Farmers' Union (SFTU)
Barbara Whitfield Fleming, his daughter
Thad Snow, plantation owner
Lorenzo Green, professor, Lincoln University
Cynthia Bolt Bonner, former Lincoln University student
Julian Bond, narrator

This is another angle on the history of the Southern Tenant Farmers' Union (SFTU), an organizing force that was intensely political and ultimately dangerous, as any organizing of black and white tenant farmers in the South in the 1930s had to be, and utopian, as the SFTU actually set up an integrated community of its own, Cropperville, which lasted ten years.

The film focuses on an extraordinary demonstration organized by the SFTU in 1939 against the implementation of the Triple A, or Agricultural Adjustment Act, whose funds were supposed to go to both farm owner and tenant in the form of relief for the bad years of the Depression. This New Deal legislation was all virtue but lacked common sense: the owners controlled the county and state boards and other instruments for the distribution of funds, so no sharecroppers would receive a fair share.

The SFTU, led by Owen Whitfield, a minister and socialist, sent about a thousand mostly (but not all) black sharecroppers literally overnight to camp along routes 61 and 60 in the boot heel of Missouri. Hungry and freezing—it was January—the sharecroppers soon roused the nation to their plight because the national newsreel teams found them photogenic. A white plantation owner, Thad Snow, had invited the union to use his land, an act virtually unprecedented for his class. Nearby Lincoln University students followed the advice of their professor Lorenzo Green and brought money slated for their prom to the sharecroppers.

When the forces of the state began to mobilize against the sharecroppers, their demo ended. But Whitfield had another vision, called Cropperville, where eighty black and white families, including Whitfield's own, moved in. The film has recovered, like the best labor history documentaries, a time the reactionaries wanted to bury and managed to do so for more than sixty years.

See also: *Our Land Too; The Uprising of '34.*
Availability: Selected collections; California Newsreel.

Further reading

Robinson, Ken. "Oh Freedom after While." California Newsreel. August 1999. At ⟨www.newsreel.org/guides/ohfreedom/review. htm⟩. Develops the political and economic background of the film.

〜

Los olvidados

"This film, based on fact, is not optimistic."—Luis Buñuel

1950, 81 mins., Mexico, in Spanish, with English subtitles
Director: Luis Buñuel
Screenplay: Luis Buñuel and Luis Alcoriza
CAST
The Mother (Marta) = Estela Inda
Pedro = Alfonsa Mejía

El Jaibo = Roberto Cobo
Lost Peasant Boy (Ojitos) = Mario Ramírez
The Blind Man (Don Carmelo) = Miguel Inclán
Meche = Alma Delia Fuentes
Julián = Javier Amézcua
Pockface = Efraín Arauz
The Principal = Francisco Jambrina

Buñuel's surrealistic view of the youthful riffraff of a Mexican slum was strange enough to be considered a "semidocumentary" (which it was not) in its American release in 1950 as *The Young and the Damned*. It had much more in common with Italian neorealist portrayals of underclass life in which a certain number of authentic-looking nonprofessionals were joined by professional actors. Even the Buñuelian irony of the opening sequence, with titles that suggest that the worldwide problem of poverty and delinquency can be solved only by the "progressive forces" of society, was misunderstood when the film was released. Like the contemporary Spanish director Pedro Almodóvar, Buñuel did not set out to improve society, although his prefatory text is loaded with pseudo-sociological factoids: "Concealed behind the magnificent buildings of our great modern cities, New York, Paris, London, are homes of misery that house children who are badly nourished, dirty, and uneducated, a breeding ground for future delinquents. Society tries to correct this evil, but the success of its efforts is very limited. Only in some near future can the rights of children and adolescents be revindicated so that they can be useful to society. Mexico City, a large modern metropolis, is no exception to this universal rule, and for that reason this film, based on fact, is not optimistic and leaves the solution of the problem to the progressive forces of society."

Like Vittorio de Sica's *Shoeshine* (1946), Hector Babenco's *Pixote* (1980), and Mira Nair's *Salaam Bombay!* (1988), *Los olvidados* takes as its subject the poverty and hopelessness of a large Third World city as a group of "street urchins" tries to survive, sometimes on adult terms (crime) and sometimes on their own (child prostitution).

In *Los olvidados* (sometimes translated as *The Lost Ones*) we are taken through the alternative economy that is at the heart of a metropolis such as Mexico City: street market sellers, beggars, thieves, prostitutes, and even occasionally a person with a regular job (other than policeman).

See also: *Land without Bread*.
Availability: Selected collections.

Further reading

Aranda, Francisco. *Luis Buñuel: A Critical Biography*. Trans. David Robinson. New York: Da Capo, 1976. Surveys Buñuel's career and all his major films.

Buñuel, Luis. *Objects of Desire: Conversations with Luis Buñuel*. Ed. and trans. Paul Lenti. New York: Marsilio, 1992. Excellent interviews in general, including one on Buñuel's amusement at efforts to "reform" this depressing film.

——. *Two Films*. New York: Lorrimer, 1984. Includes the screenplay and an essay on the film by the French critic André Bazin.

Crowther, Bosley. "The Young and the Damned." *New York Times*, 25 March 1952, 23. The reviewer is prostrate with frustration: there is "no focus or point of reference for the squalid, depressing tale."

Fuentes, Carlos. "The Discreet Charm of Luis Buñuel." *New York Times Magazine*, 11 March 1973. The Mexican novelist Fuentes interviews Buñuel and surveys his career.

Johnson, Randal, and Robert Stam, eds. *Brazilian Cinema*. New York: Columbia University Press, 1995. Includes an essay that discusses "street urchin" films.

Note: The title of the American release was *The Young and the Damned,* and it is still occasionally referred to as such.

⤳
One Day Longer

War on the Strip

2000, 45 mins.
Director: Amie Williams
Agitprop documentary

PRINCIPAL FIGURES
Tom and Margaret Elardi, Frontier Hotel and Casino owners
John Wilhelm, president, Hotel Employees and Restaurant Employees (HERE)
Heidi Hughes, HERE organizer and picket captain
Cesar Chavez, former president, United Farm Workers (UFW)
Artie Rodriguez, president, UFW
John Sweeney, president, AFL-CIO
Stephen Yokich, president, UAW
Richard Trumka, secretary-treasurer, AFL-CIO

This is a fine documentary that blurs the distinction between a traditional documentary and an agitprop piece. Sure, it was commissioned by the union it features—the Hotel Employees and Restaurant Employees International Union—but its rendition of a six-year strike in Las Vegas against particularly stubborn casino owners has an authentic feel that makes it as much a traditional doc as agit or prop.

Many of us probably did not pay enough attention to one of the longest strikes in American history. Despite the strong support of the local unions of the bartenders, carpenters, teamsters, culinary workers, and operating engineers, the strike confronted a seemingly immovable object—the Elardis.

The Elardi family—Margaret Elardi and her two sons—purchased the Frontier Hotel and Casino from the estate of Howard Hughes in 1988 with money from their sale of the Pioneer Casino in Laughlin, Nevada. They had an agenda: eliminate the union health, welfare, and pension plans, the grievance system, and the guaranteed workweek, and continue to pay below Las Vegas union scale. When the Hotel Employees and Restaurant Employees Union felt they had no choice but to strike, the Elardis' press release set the tone for the battle to come: "If the union wants to start a war in the state of Nevada, the Elardis will make them wish they never started it."

In an unusual twist, the strike was settled only when the Elardis sold the casino for almost $200 million in cash to Ken Ruffin, a

Kansas businessman who owned Marriott hotels, a casino in Bermuda, and the country's premiere truck-dolly manufacturing plant. Ruffin immediately reinstated all of the striking workers and agreed to a five-year contract that restored virtually all that the Elardis has taken away. Clearly the Elardis were way out of their league, since Bill Bennett, owner of the nearby Sahara Hotel and Casino, sent truckloads of hot meals every day to the strike line and had some box lunches prepared in the kitchen of the hotel when necessary.

Even the governor of Nevada made it clear that the Elardis ought to try another job: "Unfortunately, we do have one employer on the Las Vegas Strip who doesn't understand how important our partnership has been to Nevada's economic growth—one employer who doesn't play by the rules. . . . The strike at the Frontier is the longest running AFL-CIO-sanctioned strike in the country. It's a blight on the image of Nevada."

This is an inspiring film, filled with images of union solidarity as well as difficult picket duty. It is also a tribute to a multicultural workforce that marched as many as 10,000 strong during the strike.

See also: *Chaos*.
Availability: Selected collections; union locals.

Further reading

Berns, Dave. "Frontier Strike Sign of Times for Labor." *Las Vegas Review-Journal,* 3 November 1997, at ⟨www.lvrj.com/lvrj_home/1997/Nov-03-Mon-1997/business/6342139.html⟩. Commentary on the importance of this strike, which involved the growing sector of service workers.
Miller, Kit. *Inside the Glitter: Lives of Casino Workers*. Carson City: Great Basin Publishing, 2000. A photographer and journalist documents the workers who keep the casino industry humming.
Web sites:
⟨www.homepages.skylink.net/~boscoe⟩ Official site of the "Frontier Strike Page," with a complete history of the strike, supporting unions, and detailed lists of issues and abuse from the (now former) owners, the Elardis.

⟨www.search.vegas.com/sun⟩ A complete set of news articles on the Frontier strike is available at this archive of the *Las Vegas Sun*.

↜

One Third of a Nation

Waiting for the landlord

1939, 75 mins., B&W
Director: Dudley Murphy
Screenplay: Oliver H. P. Garrett, from Arthur Arent's play of the same title.
CAST
Mary Rogers = Sylvia Sidney
Peter Cortlant = Leif Erickson
Sam Moon = Myron McCormick
Donald Hinchley = Hiram Sherman
Joey Rogers = Sidney Lumet
Ethel Cortlant = Muriel Hutchison
Arthur Mather = Percy Waram
Assistant D.A. = Otto Hulitt

One Third of a Nation was first of all a play, part of the Living Newspaper series of agit-prop performances sponsored by the Federal Theatre Project of the Works Progress Administration, the New Deal agency that put so many Americans, including intellectuals and artists, on the government payroll during the Depression. The Federal Theatre Project, like many similar New Deal programs, was led by various left and progressive forces; it was also for the most part successful box office: *One Third of a Nation* and two other Federal Theatre plays were hits on Broadway simultaneously in 1938. Among other achievements, it staged "twenty-one simultaneous openings" of *It Can't Happen Here,* a dramatic version of Sinclair Lewis's novel by the same name, which demonstrates exactly how fascism could happen in the United States.

The Project did both rural and urban outreach, employing not only new talent but already rising stars. Orson Welles and John Houseman were both leaders in the Negro theater branch, for example, staging plays by both black and white playwrights, such as

Eugene O'Neill's *Emperor Jones,* Welles's staging of *Othello* with an all-black cast, and the original *The Cradle Will Rock.*

The original play of *One Third of a Nation* was much closer to the style and intentions of the Living Newspaper series: the history of unfit urban housing was presented in a series of sometime related vignettes, with real and imagined characters literally quoting lines from either historical commissions or *New York Times* articles. The point, in the end, was to show how the housing crisis could be solved only by the U.S. government, not by private enterprise. Some of the distinctive features of the play were incorporated into the film, such as the talking tenement building, the cross-class mixture of characters, and the tragic fires.

The play ends in fact with a fire, highlighting a man cowering on the fire escape as flames, smoke, screams, and sirens fill the stage. A loudspeaker announces: "Ladies and gentlemen, this might be Boston, New York, St. Louis, Chicago, Philadelphia—but let's just call it 'one third of a nation!'" This is a rousing close to a rousing agitprop piece of theater rivaling but not outdoing the famous close to Clifford Odets's *Waiting for Lefty,* when both workers on stage and audience members simultaneously began to shout "Strike!" Clearly in this film, FDR is the answer, not union organizing.

The film tells a story of cross-class romance, with Sylvia Sydney's Mary, a tenement beauty, falling for the son of a rich landlord's family. The slightly melodramatic plot may seem awkward, but as an exposé of the housing shortage and tenement conditions, it is crystal-clear.

See also: *Cradle Will Rock; Street Scene.*
Availability: Selected collections.

Further reading

Arent, Arthur. *One Third of a Nation*. In *Federal Theatre Plays*. New York: Random House, 1938. Arent's original playscript; this volume's preface by Hallie Flanagan, the director of the Federal Theatre, is a brief but helpful history of the project.

Nugent, Frank S. "One Third of a Nation." *New York Times,* 11 February 1939, 13. "An interestingly presented editorial for slum clearance."

"One Third of a Nation." *Variety,* 15 February 1935. Worries about this first cinematic adaptation of a WPA production "ditching" the "'living newspaper' purpose of the stage version, emphasizing the boy-meets-girl premise, against the shocking slum background."

On the Waterfront

A classic fight, but labor takes the dive

1954, 108 mins., B&W
Director: Elia Kazan
Screenplay: Budd Schulberg, from Malcolm Johnson's *Crime on the Labor Front*
CAST
Terry Malloy = Marlon Brando
Edie Doyle = Eva Marie Saint
Father Barry = Karl Malden
Johnny Friendly = Lee J. Cobb
Charley Malloy = Rod Steiger
"Kayo" Dugan = Pat Henning
Pop Doyle = John Hamilton

This is another film that popularized (eight Academy Awards!) a particularly unsavory stereotype of the American worker and trade unionism. Based on what we would call today investigative journalism and later a nonfiction book, titled *Crime on the Labor Front,* written by the newspaper reporter Malcolm Johnson, the film preceded Budd Schulberg's novel *Waterfront*. Schulberg wrote his screenplay from Johnson's book and his own research. He later turned the same material into a novel that does not end quite so optimistically as the film.

The film's story is so familiar that it is probably necessary to give only a summary here. Marlon Brando, as Terry Malloy, unknowingly sets up one of the neighborhood boys, Joey Doyle, for a rooftop murder because he has been talking to the Crime Commission ("I only thought they was goin' to lean on him," Terry says later). Edie Doyle (Joey's sister), Father Barry, and Terry's conscience all work on him until the hold of the Mob (including that of his own brother, Charley the Gent) has been loosened. Johnny Friendly has Charley killed because he can no longer control Terry.

The scene in the back of the cab when Charley and Terry talk about Terry's lack of allegiance to Johnny Friendly has become one of the classic sequences in twentieth-century film. Terry realizes that Charley in a sense had already betrayed him by getting him to take a dive in the ring for the Mob years before: "You don't understand! I could've had class. I could've been a contenda. I could have been somebody. Instead of a bum, which is what I am, let's face it. It was you, Charley."

After Charley's death, Terry agrees to testify against the Mob. In the final scene, he is beaten by Johnny Friendly's gang but still manages to lead the men into the warehouse, despite Johnny Friendly's threats. In Schulberg's novel, Johnny Friendly is put in jail briefly but still runs the local. Terry disappears, only to turn up in a barrel of lime in a New Jersey swamp. Hollywood, it seems, needed its hero to get up from the count.

When Johnson, Schulberg, and Kazan worked on the material that became this film, the East Coast longshoremen were clearly not doing as well under the current International Longshoremen's Association leadership as their West Coast brothers under the leadership of the controversial Harry Bridges. Most observers noted that the shape-up method (the selection of workers for the day by the dock boss or foreman) led to kickbacks, patronage, and gang control of access to work. This practice in turn led some local unions into loan sharking, accepting kickbacks from the shipping companies, and cozy relationships with management. When rank-and-file leaders developed, they were dealt with violently by union leaders who were thugs. One of the models for Terry Malloy (especially for the Terry of Schulberg's novel), Peter Panto, was found dead in a New Jersey lime pit two years after he began to campaign against Mob control.

Into this volatile situation stepped several activist Catholic priests, especially Father John Corridan, the model for Father Barry in the film. Corridan, a veteran activist with the anticommunist Xavier Labor School in New York, campaigned against the "triple alliance of business, politics, and union racketeering" (see Raymond).

Obviously, the extent of corrupt or mob control of certain unions is an important and ongoing issue. But even assuming that mob control in the 1950s or now is a reality, why was Hollywood so attracted to this particular aspect of the labor movement?

Schulberg and Kazan, at least, had reasons to pursue this story. They were both called stool pigeons because they had named names before the House Un-American Activities Committee. *On the Waterfront* may be seen as a long apology for testifying before a government committee, but it is certainly more than that.

Elia Kazan had already directed Marlon Brando successfully in *A Streetcar Named Desire* and *Viva Zapata!* in 1952. Brando was a natural choice for the slightly punchy but ultimately goodhearted Terry Malloy. His Method acting style was appropriate to the portrayal of still another alienated proletarian: watching Brando, the audience could easily accept one of the Method's ruling ideas—the actor had to believe that his imagined truth was as real as the actual truth.

See also: *Hoffa; Waterfront.*
Availability: Easy; DVD.

Further reading

Basinger, Jeanine, John Frazer, and Joseph W. Reed Jr., eds. *Working with Kazan*. Middletown, Conn.: Wesleyan University Press, 1973. A compilation of comments by numerous film pros who have worked with Kazan.

Bell, Daniel. *The End of Ideology: On the Exhaustion of Political Ideas in the Fifties*. New York: Free Press, 1962. Discusses corruption among the longshoremen in a classic chapter, "The Racket-Ridden Longshoremen: The Web of Economics and Politics."

Burks, Edward C. " 'On the Waterfront' Returns to

Hoboken." *New York Times,* 24 May 1973, 49. Still another model for Terry Malloy (Anthony de Vincenzo) returns to Hoboken with the filmmakers.

Georgakas, Dan. "The Screen Playwright as Author." *Cineaste* 11, no. 4 (1982): 7–15, 39. An extensive interview with Schulberg.

Johnson, Malcolm. *Crime on the Labor Front.* New York: McGraw-Hill, 1950. Investigative journalism, based on the author's Pulitzer Prize–winning newspaper articles.

Kimeldorf, Howard. *Reds or Rackets? The Making of Radical and Conservative Unions on the Waterfront.* Berkeley: University of California Press, 1988. A convincing survey of the differences in the labor history of the East and West Coast longshoremen.

McGrath, Tom. *This Coffin Has No Handles.* New York: Thunder's Mouth, 1988. A more political novel, written in 1947, with the same setting as *On the Waterfront.*

Miller, Arthur. *A View from the Bridge.* New York: Viking, 1955. Another play about waterfront workers, one of whom also rats on his friends.

Neve, Brian. "The 1950s: The Case of Elia Kazan and 'On the Waterfront.'" In *Cinema, Politics, and Society in America,* ed. Philip Davies and Brian Neve. New York: St. Martin's Press, 1981. An excellent detailed article on the film.

Raymond, Allen. *Waterfront Priest.* New York: Henry Holt, 1955. Includes extensive details about the model for Father Barry.

Sayre, Nora. *Running Time: Films of the Cold War.* New York: Dial, 1982. Contains a good chapter on the film in the context of McCarthyism and "friendly" witnesses (like Schulberg) before the House Un-American Activities Committee.

Schulberg, Budd. "Joe Docks, Forgotten Man of the Waterfront." *New York Times Magazine,* 28 December 1952, 3, 28–30. The first version of the film's material, a nonfiction piece emphasizing the ethnic makeup of the docks.

——. *On the Waterfront.* Carbondale: Southern Illinois University Press, 1980. Screenplay with an afterword explaining how the film was produced; a less political version of this essay was published in the *New York Times Magazine,* 6 January 1980.

——. *Waterfront.* 1955. New York: Donald S. Fine, 1987. The novel stresses the Irish-American culture and Catholicism more than the film, but has essentially the same plot.

On to Ottawa

Halfway to victory

1992, 54 mins., Canada
Director: Sara Diamond
Mixed traditional documentary and docudrama of the Tom Hawken play of the same title
PRINCIPAL FIGURES
Trekkers: Robert Jackson, Jean Sheils, and Ray Wainwright

This film of mixed modes documents the Canadian version of the American Bonus March. It consists of archival footage, a stage play or reenactment, and interviews with trekkers, all focusing on the events of a legendary protest movement in the Depression. Hundreds of unemployed men in 1935 intended to march on Ottawa demanding jobs, decent wages, and the closing of relief camps. The trek originated in Vancouver, where single unemployed men, based in relief camps, had been working seven days a week for 20 cents a day. Their plan was to ride the rails to demonstrate at the capital, 3,000 miles to the east. They got halfway, to Regina, where they were attacked by the Royal Canadian Mounted Police.

Although the trek itself was shut down and the men dispersed, the political fallout from the event was significant. Some commentators attribute the fall of the Conservative government of Prime Minister R. B. "Iron Heel" Bennett to the negative publicity associated with the repression of the march and the support given the trekkers. The relief camps, however, were closed by the new incoming Liberal government, and even though the official report blamed radicals among the ranks for the violence, reforms such as unemployment insurance marked the beginnings of the Canadian equivalent of the American New Deal.

See also: *The Great Depression.*
Availability: Selected collections.

Further reading

Brown, Lorne. *When Freedom Was Lost.* Toronto: University of Toronto Press, 1987. History of the On to Ottawa campaign.

Howard, Victor. *We Were the Salt of the Earth: The On-to-Ottawa Trek and the Regina Riot.* Regina: Canadian Plains Research Center, 1985. Another introductory history.

Liversedge, Ronald. *Recollections of the On to Ottawa Trek.* 1961. Toronto: McClelland & Stewart, 1973. Includes Liversedge's original memoir of his experience of the camps and the trek, plus the official report on the Regina "police riot."

Web sites:

⟨www.ontoottawa.ca⟩ Official site of the On to Ottawa Historical Society, which sponsored the film; includes photos, interviews, bibliography, and excerpts from the video.

⟨www.workingtv.com/oto/otohome.html⟩ Another excellent site, with photos and a narrative essay on every phase of the march.

৩

The Organizer

Struggling against the twelve-hour day

1963, 126 mins., Italian, with English subtitles
Director: Mario Monicelli
Screenplay: Furio Scarpelli and Mario Monicelli

CAST

Professor Sinigaglia = Marcello Mastroianni
Niobe = Annie Girardet
Raoul = Renato Salvatori
Pautasso = Folco Lulli

The Professor is the organizer; he is also a socialist, a wanted man, a poor but middle-class man, a man who loves pastries but knows that hunger is often the more likely alternative. Very few actors could carry such a character, but Marcello Mastroianni, a star of Italian films for many years, convinced viewers that he was such a sincere but somewhat inept hero. Coming from the tradition *commedia all'italiana* that usually stressed the foolish side of social and political life (see Bondanella), this film nonetheless offers more of a tragicomic look at the tremendous difficulties that Turin textile workers had in mounting a strike in 1890.

Monicelli had made *Big Deal on Madonna Street* in 1958, a film about criminal riffraff (also starring Mastroianni) who were hopelessly inept. Applying his satiric style to a Turin strike was fairly daring, because "Red" Turin was known for its left labor movement and its pre-Mussolini factory councils.

The Professor arrives in Turin by train, hopping down from a free ride in a cab in the background of a remarkable shot in which the workers are having a half-mean, half-silly snowball fight with one of the comic louts, Pautasso, who has been disciplined for being caught sounding the company's whistle at the wrong time. The naiveté of the Professor's followers is usually assumed by the filmmakers, but not always in a patronizing manner. At one point, to push the people toward collective action, the Professor even resorts to a parody of Marc Antony's funeral oration from Shakespeare's *Julius Caesar*. Since they are about to end their strike, extreme irony is justified: "The majority are wise," he says of those who vote to go back to work. "They find their salary sufficient. . . . No one has actually *died* of starvation yet."

The film is filled with remarkable insights into the poverty of the workers. But none are as poor as the man they call the Sicilian—others call him the Ethiopian, the Bedouin, or the Arab, all terms expressing the casual racism of the North toward the South. The workers assess him as being so poor that he is beneath their notice and they let him scab, grudgingly accepting his desperate situation.

Given their conditions, anything the workers demand would be reasonable. At the opening of the film, they have fourteen-hour days, no accident insurance, no vacations— the list could be endless. Although viewers want them to win, they clearly cannot. The Professor is, after all, only a schoolteacher with a little more experience than they have, and the owners have power—the police and the army.

Although the personality of the Professor dominates virtually every scene he is in, we

Workers' demo in *The Organizer*: "Too Much Work and Too Little Bread." Courtesy British Film Institute Stills, Posters, and Designs.

are always aware that the nastier world he longs to defeat is always nearby. After sneezing into the coffee cup of a new friend (a prostitute with a heart of gold), he explains his separation from his wife in this way: "It's my fault. I've been leading a rather disorganized life." Later this cheery hooker says that she heard that part of his disorganization was wounding an official in Genoa during a demonstration. "Self-defense," he says with a sheepish grin.

See also: *Bitter Rice*.
Availability: Selected collections.

Further reading

Bernardo, Giovanna di, et al. "Red Flags and American Dollars." *Cineaste* 7 (1977): 3–9, 50. Extensive interviews with the director, focusing on his politics.

Bondanella, Peter. *Italian Cinema from Neorealism to the Present.* 3d ed. New York: Continuum, 2001. Brief but helpful discussion.

Crowther, Bosley. "The Organizer." *New York Times*, 7 May 1964, 31. The reviewer celebrates this "simple social drama," which "turns out to be engrossingly human, compassionate, and humorous."

Macdonald, Dwight. *On Movies.* Englewood Cliffs, N.J.: Prentice-Hall, 1969. Includes a short but very appreciative review of the film, stressing the director's use of the anticlimax—deliberately undercutting the operatic style of staging scenes usual in Italian films.

Other People's Money

Use it or lose it

1991, 106 mins., PG-13
Director: Norman Jewison
Screenplay: Alvin Sargent, from Jerry Sterner's play of the same title

CAST

Lawrence Garfield = Danny DeVito
Andrew Jorgenson = Gregory Peck
Kate Sullivan = Penelope Ann Miller
Bea Sullivan = Piper Laurie
Bill Coles = Dean Jones
Arthur = R. D. Call

It's hard to hate Danny DeVito when he plays Larry the Liquidator, a Wall Street lizard reminiscent of Gordon Gekko in *Wall Street*. Larry is a comic villain in this light but engrossing top-down story of what happens to the fictional New England Wire and Cable Company, a Rhode Island firm basically breaking even (with no debt and lots of cash in the bank), while some of its sister divisions are doing much better. Larry's position is clear: dump the loser division, grab the cash, sell the land to a golf course or condo developer, and return a better profit to the shareholders.

Since Jorgenson, the CEO of the company in question, is played by the virtuous Gregory Peck, Larry's scheme is going to take more effort. Peck plays an aging benevolent boss, whose workers are all "family," ever since the days of his own father's paternalistic rule. When we do see workers, sometimes they are working, but their longest exposure comes in the company photo, in which everyone—whether manager or worker—poses for a benign image of all-class unity.

Enter a high-powered lawyer who is going to save the company, first because her mom is now Jorgenson's companion, and second because she loves a good fight. Penelope Ann Miller plays the lawyer as such a chic knock-out that the Liquidator knows that if he wins, he loses her. Fact is, Larry is rich and pathetic without a woman to love. Larry has already made it clear that he loves only doughnuts and money (especially other people's money), but we know—since we've seen many other Hollywood movies—that what he really needs is love.

Of course if that were the only issue, it wouldn't be a particularly interesting film. But when Jorgenson and Larry face each other at the stockholders' meeting that will determine the company's future, it's paternalistic capitalism versus "greed is good." The stockholders go along with greed—although Larry has essentially bought the vote from the cache of stock held by a defecting company officer—even if they seem initially warm to the idea that they really own the company.

The ending is unlikely, even if possible. The Lawyer calms the Liquidator by promising a Japanese company's contract of airbags (made with wire mesh) if he doesn't sell it; he also gets to eat lunch with her and make another try at romance.

Norman Jewison has had a remarkable directorial career, ranging from such blockbusters as *Jesus Christ Superstar* (1973) and *Fiddler on the Roof* (1971) to serious class-conscious drama such as *In Country* (1989), *A Soldier's Story* (1984), *And Justice for All* (1979), adaptations of stage plays (*Agnes of God*, 1985), and even the Hoffa-esque *F.I.S.T.* (1978). Unfortunately, this film is closer to his silly *Moonstruck* (1987), in which the hero, like Larry, pants like a puppy dog.

See also: *Barbarians at the Gate; Wall Street*.
Availability: Easy.

Further reading

Ebert, Roger. "Other People's Money." *Chicago Sun-Times*, 18 October 1991. Ebert cannot help himself: DeVito's comic and other maneuvers impress him, but he hates the ending.
Kempley, Rita. "Other People's Money." *Washington Post*, 18 October 1991. Finds the film as wholesome as a Frank Capra Hollywood fantasy, "full of hokum and homilies" about economics, and fears that Larry and the Lawyer, once joined, will "give birth to little cartoon product spokesmen."

Our Daily Bread

Rural socialism

1934, 74 mins., B&W
Director: King Vidor

Screenplay: King Vidor and Elizabeth Hill, based on one or more uncredited *Reader's Digest* articles

CAST

John Sims = Tom Keene
Mary Sims = Karen Morley
Chris = John T. Qualen
Sally = Barbara Pepper
Louie = Addison Richards

King Vidor's film suggests that creating socialist farming co-ops was the only way out for the unemployed in the early Depression years. Although there is a fairly unnecessary romantic subplot and even a blonde femme fatale, the heart of the film is the movement of numerous unemployed and underemployed workers (plumbers, carpenters, and blacksmiths) out of the city and into the countryside, where they accept the unlikely leadership of a city dweller, John Sims. Many of the extras in the film were actual unemployed and other riffraff who were recruited from the streets of Los Angeles, giving the film an authentic look.

Vidor wanted to counterbalance Hollywood's glamour cycle, but he could not get financing for the film until he borrowed the money on his own stock and real estate. This solution was inevitable, Vidor realized, when bankers he approached read the part of his script in which a bank sends out a sheriff to run a foreclosure sale on a home. Vidor wanted very badly to make the film, since he had witnessed the Hoovervilles springing up all over, while milk trucks were spilling their milk to keep prices high.

The direct inspiration for the film was an article or two in the *Reader's Digest* that profiled cooperatives all over the country that were relying on barter to survive. The most likely article, Scott Simmon and Raymond Durgnat argue, was "An Agricultural Army," which emphasized the need to bring together "*unemployed men* and *unemployed acres.*"

To gain continuity with his earlier film *The Crowd*, which featured a couple going through hard times, Vidor used that couple's names—John and Mary Sims—again: "The same people," Vidor said, "under different economic conditions. It was the 'average man' idea." The couple, and America by extension, could make a comeback if they went co-op.

The co-op must withstand two major attacks, the first simultaneously economic and political, the second natural. In the first attack, the sheriff tries to sell the land at a public auction. The co-op members use the radical technique pioneered in North Dakota and Iowa and celebrated in Josephine Herbst's series of proletarian novels in the 1930s: the farmers control the bidding by keeping (by threats of force if necessary) anyone but themselves from bidding.

The second struggle is resolved in the final sequence of the film as the men cut a long and complicated two-mile irrigation canal to bring water to their parched corn. It celebrates the teamwork of labor rarely seen in films except the innovative Soviet films of the 1920s. Matching the editing rhythms of the film to the muscular rhythm of a gang of pick-and-shovel men imitated the style of the great Soviet films such as Sergei Eisenstein's *Strike* and V. I. Pudovkin's *Mother*.

Vidor also experimented with sound editing for the final sequence of ditch cutting. He used a metronome on a tripod and a bass drum offscreen so that each shot of the men digging would have a controlled but gradually increasing rhythm. By adding an under-cranked camera (making the final film action appear faster) and an inspiring musical score, he created an emotional celebration of pure labor.

The film develops a fairly strong set of internal political themes that mirror, Simmon and Durgnat argue, national political developments. At a political meeting in the film, three major viewpoints are argued: those of a self-important defender of democracy, a socialist (formerly an undertaker before joining the co-op), and an advocate (Chris, the only actual farmer) for a form of dictatorship—a "big boss" for a "big job." Perhaps inevitably this debate is resolved only by work, the digging of the irrigation ditch, when all must pull together to save the crops.

Although the film had good box office, the variety of viewpoints on the co-ops satisfied no particular political camp. Thus the Los Angeles Hearst papers labeled it "pinko," whereas some of the Russian exhibitors found it too capitalistic. Vidor's defense often came down to the film's source: how could it be un-American if its ideas originated in the *Reader's Digest*? In the end the League of Nations gave it an award "for its contribution to humanity," and the 1935 Soviet International Exposition of Film gave it a certificate of merit. The *New York Times* reviewer judged the film as many film historians now do, as "a brilliant declaration of faith in the importance of the cinema as a social instrument."

See also: *Oh Freedom after While*.
Availability: Selected collections; DVD.

Further reading

Dowd, Nancy, and David Shepherd. *King Vidor*. New York: Scarecrow Press, 1988. Interviews with Vidor on the making of the film.

Herbst, Josephine. *The Executioner Waits*. New York: Harcourt, Brace, 1934. One of the proletarian novels of the 1930s whose themes come close to those of Vidor's films.

Reader's Digest. Alexander Legge and Neil M. Clark, "Back to the Land?" 22 November 1932, 45–47, and Malcolm McDermott, "An Agricultural Arm," 21 June 1932, 95–97. Vidor never specified the articles, but these are two likely candidates (according to Simmon and Durgnat).

Sennwald, André. "Our Daily Bread." *New York Times*, 3 October 1934, 25. A rave review, including Vidor's placement in contemporary "socially minded art."

Simmon, Scott, and Raymond Durgnat. *King Vidor, American*. Berkeley: University of California Press, 1988. A thorough analysis of the film and Vidor's career.

Vidor, King. *A Tree Is a Tree*. New York: Harcourt, Brace, 1953. The director's autobiography, with his comments on the ideas behind his film.

↫

Our Land Too

Roll the SFTU on!

1988, 57 mins.
Kudzu Productions
Traditional documentary
PRINCIPAL FIGURES
Eddie Albert, narrator
John Kenneth Galbraith, Harvard economist
H. L. Mitchell, dry-cleaning store owner, later secretary, Southern Tenant Farmers' Union (STFU)
Clay East, manager, gas station
D. C. Clark, Arkansas sharecropper and union worker
George Stiff, organizer

The radical idea of having black and white sharecroppers in a single union originated in 1934 at an organizing meeting near the small Arkansas town of Tyronza. The twenty original founders were both black and white, an astounding fact in itself. They met to discuss how they might get their fair share of benefits as a result of the new Agricultural Adjustment Act (the Triple A). One old black sharecropper proposed that they remain together in an integrated union: "We colored people can't organize without you and you white folks can't organize without us." He argued for the unity necessary to resist the landlord, who "is always betwixt us, beatin' us and starvin' us and makin' us fight each other." After electing an integrated group of officers, they later recruited two known local "radicals," H. L. Mitchell and Clay East, from Tyronza. They were Norman Thomas Socialists and eventually became secretary and president of the new union, which was to be open to all tenant farmers, sharecroppers, and day laborers.

The film makes a persuasive case for the Southern Tenant Farmers' Union's pioneer status in both labor and civil rights history since it was organized in Arkansas, a state not known for its hospitality to labor unions or to interracial organizations. The sharecroppers were, as John Kenneth Galbraith, one of the film's commentators, emphasizes, only one step away from slavery. Even a film clip from a 1936 *March of Time* newsreel points to "the economic bondage of Cotton in the South." Sharecropping was an ideal solution to the post–Civil War planters: they had no money to pay their freed slaves, and the slaves—as well as poor whites—of course had no jobs.

Eventually the modern counterparts of the planters figured out how to take advantage of the New Deal: when the Agricultural Adjustment Act put the subsidy system into place, the farm owners kept the whole cash subsidy even though they were entitled to only two-thirds. A third was to go to their sharecroppers, who in a sense were also supposed to be paid for not working under this system.

Rather than pay the sharecroppers, the farm owners threw them off the land to join the nation's ever-increasing numbers of the homeless. The dangers faced by this curiously political and daring union were real. Norman Thomas, Socialist candidate for president, often spoke at their meetings. A woman who worked for the Department of Agriculture to secure a share of the subsidies for the sharecroppers commented on some of the powers that be lined up against the sharecroppers: "Al Capone's men were pantywaists compared to the boys in Crittenden County [Arkansas]." Meetings were raided, organizers beaten, and union members and other leaders arrested; the film also offers the too-familiar horror stories of lynching and other violence typical of the South in this era.

The close of the film emphasizes some of the political twists and turns of the union's history. In the late 1930s, it became part of the CIO, and several members remember being pressured to join the Communist Party. One of the chief organizers, the Socialist H. L. Mitchell, would emphatically not join. Mitchell's loyalty was always with Norman Thomas, who became a kind of guardian angel to the union. The film appropriately emphasizes Thomas's patronage of the union but does not quote a famous message he broadcast over NBC: "There is a reign of terror in the cotton country of eastern Arkansas. It will end either in the establishment of complete and slavish submission to the vilest exploitation in America or in bloodshed, or in both. For the sake of peace, liberty, and common human decency, I appeal to you who listen to my voice to bring immediate pressure upon the Federal government to act" (quoted in Kester).

The film is appropriately bracketed by the music of Woody Guthrie—"This Land Is Your Land"—and by the folksong that the union pioneered and contributed to the civil rights movement: "We Shall Not Be Moved." Another union classic, "Roll the Union On," was written by an STFU organizer, John Handcox, who recalls some of the southern hospitality that was manifested when he had to run from lynchers. His remarks are typical of the appreciation expressed by everyone in the film for the courage and legacy of a remarkable union.

See also: *The Uprising of '34.*
Availability: Selected collections.

Further reading

Edid, Marilyn. *Farm Labor Organizing: Trends and Prospects*. Ithaca: ILR Press/Cornell University Press, 1994. A history and survey of farm workers' unions.
Kester, Howard. *Revolt among the Sharecroppers*. 1936. New York: Arno Press, 1969. An early and enthusiastic history of the STFU.

Out at Work

Out of luck

1996, 55 mins.; 1999, 58 mins.
Directors: Kelly Anderson and Tami Gold
Traditional documentary
PRINCIPAL FIGURES, 1999 VERSION
Grethe Cammermeyer, narrator
Cheryl Summerville, cook, Cracker Barrel Restaurant, Atlanta
Sandy, Cheryl's partner
Larry Pellegrini, Queer Nation

Lyn Cochran, Martin Luther King Center
for Nonviolent Social Change
Regina Stavers, co-director, Coalition of
Gay and Lesbian City Workers
Ron Woods, auto worker and delegate to
United Auto Workers (UAW)
convention
Don Lingar, president, Local 372, UAW
Mike Harrald, chairman, Local 372, UAW
Big Bill Whitmer, Chrysler Technology
worker
Terry Kremkow, Chrysler electrician
Mark Anderson, securities trainee at
Cantor Fitzgerald
PRINCIPAL FIGURES, 1996 VERSION ONLY
Nat Keitt, New York Public Library clerk,
Bronx
David Sanabria, Nat's partner
Ray Markey, president, Local 1930, District
37, AFSCME

Ron Woods protests at the Cracker Barrel restaurant in *Out at Work*. Photo by Bob McKeown. Courtesy AndersonGold Films.

Probably the first documentary that charts both legal and illegal discrimination against gay workers, *Out at Work* (in its two versions) traces the lives and struggles of four individuals who (with one exception) were met with distressing but perfectly legal hostility in the workplace in response to their sexual orientation. The 1996 or first version of the film reviewed the careers of Cheryl Summerville (a Cracker Barrel cook), Ron Woods (a Chrysler worker), and Nat Keitt (a New York City library clerk); the 1999 version, for the HBO series *America Undercover*, substitutes Mark Anderson (a securities trainee) for Nat Keitt, because HBO wanted to include another example of legal discrimination.

The first two struggles were related because it was on a protest demonstration in Michigan in 1991 against Cracker Barrel, the restaurant chain that fired Cheryl Summerville, that Ron Woods was outed when the media photographed the event. After his photo appeared on the front page of the *Detroit News and Free Press*, virtually all 3,000 of his fellow workers knew he was gay. Some reacted rabidly. "Every bathroom wall had my name on it," Woods reported, "and there was a bull's-eye that was posted with a reward for my assassination." He was later assaulted by both co-workers and a supervisor.

Fortunately, when Woods finally turned to his UAW local for support, his shop steward, Mike Harrald, the first African American skilled worker at the plant, backed him. Harrald's own history of fighting harassment and discrimination proved invaluable, but Woods eventually transferred from Trenton Engine to another facility, the Chrysler Technology Center, where at first the same old gay-baiting began. Eventually a number of co-workers began to resist some of the abusive types, until quite a few, with varying degrees of friendliness, began to accept Woods and even elected him as a delegate—partly because of his pro-union stand—to the UAW convention, which unanimously passed a resolution requiring all future UAW contracts to include a clause prohibiting discrimination on the basis of sexual orientation.

Keitt's situation in the Bronx was quite different: he was openly gay on the job and was a member of the executive board of Local 1930 of AFSCME (American Federation of State, County, and Municipal Employees), District 37. When Keitt's partner lost his health benefits after a diagnosis of AIDS, Keitt began organizing other gay city workers to campaign for health benefits for domestic partners. The campaign was successful and New York City joined more than 35 other municipalities and over 500 other employers who provide such benefits.

When *Out at Work* was acquired for broadcast by Home Box Office in 1999, the filmmakers used an even more outrageous example of gay-baiting for their third story, in effect removing Keitt's story—one in which a gay worker is shown in relatively calm circumstances at work and in his union context—and developing instead the story of Mark Anderson's short tenure at Cantor Fitzgerald in Los Angeles, an extremely successful securities trading firm. Anderson's attackers were at the highest level of the firm: a video that circulated throughout the company showed Mark's supervisors and bosses dancing (badly) around his car, decorated with antigay slogans and curses. He was eventually forced out of his job and offered a settlement. The offensive video, included in the film, is so stupid and vicious and unfunny that it must be seen to be believed.

Although the first version of *Out at Work* received major national exposure at the Sundance Film Festival in 1997, both Anderson and Gold were veteran filmmakers with a number of labor-related titles to their credit. Gold collaborated with Lyn Goldfarb on *From Bedside to Bargaining Table* (organizing health care professionals) and *Signed, Sealed, and Delivered*. Anderson also produced and directed *Labor at the Crossroads*, a monthly New York City television series that ran from 1992 to 1994. Both filmmakers also have a considerable number of films about gender and gay issues and people to their credit.

Unfortunately, in 1997 PBS denied the documentary air time on what many observers considered very flimsy and indefensible grounds—that a lesbian foundation (Astraea) and a few unions had contributed to the production of the film, thereby violating PBS's policy not to air programs underwritten by interested parties. If this were really the case, defenders of the film argued, then PBS should not have carried the *New York Times*–funded documentary on one of its famous writers (James Reston) or such shows as *Wall Street Week* and *Adam Smith's Money World*, both funded by such investment and insurance companies as Prudential Securities and Met Life. (A similar controversy erupted around *The Killing Floor*.) *Out at Work* would have appeared on the series of independent documentaries called *Point of View* (*P.O.V.*), which had already carried other important labor documentaries, such as Anne Lewis's *Fast Food Women*.

Like most documentaries of living people, what happens after may sometimes remain a mystery, unless the subjects have a filmmaker such as Michael Moore who can do a sequel (like *Pets or Meat* for *Roger & Me*). For Ron Woods, at least, the story is dispiriting, since (as James Stewart explains in his *New Yorker* article), Woods's "continuing complaints of gay bias have cost him the support even of his most loyal friends at work, who charge that Woods is using his sexual orientation to demand, and get, preferential treatment." In fact, Woods and his former friend and ally Terry Kremkow traded serious charges at union proceedings and Woods lost. Stewart concludes that Chrysler, although dinosaur-like, has finally caught up with some of the more enlightened corporations in their antidiscrimination efforts. Woods, however, did not survive the peace.

See also: *Evelyn Williams*.

Availability: Selected collections; 1996 version, Frameline; 1999 version, Filmakers Library.

Further reading

Harvey, Dennis. "Out at Work." *Variety*, 3 February 1997. Appreciates the directors, who "cannily focus on three subjects whose lives upend any . . . glib categorizing" of gay lives; a documentary with "an inspiring human dimension beyond blunt agitprop."

Krupat, Kitty, and Patrick McCreery, eds. *Out at Work*. Minneapolis: University of Minnesota Press, 2000. Subtitled *Building a Gay-Labor Alliance*, this volume of essays includes one by Tami Gold about the film, with an excellent discussion of its issues and versions.

Stewart, James B. "Coming Out at Chrysler." *New Yorker*, 21 July 1997, 38–49. A recapping of Woods's career at Chrysler with further developments, mostly emphasizing the serious decline after his initial success at "coming out at Chrysler."

Web site:

⟨www.prideatwork.org⟩ The official site of the AFL-CIO's Pride at Work office, whose slogan is "out and organizing" and whose banner heralds "lesbian, gay, bisexual, and transgender labor"; includes news articles, "tools for organizing," and other information.

⤳

Out of Darkness: The Mine Workers' Story

Into the light, dimly

1990, 100 mins.
Directors: Barbara Kopple and Bill Davis
Traditional documentary
PRINCIPAL FIGURES
Richard L. Trumka, president, United Mine Workers of America (UMWA)
Cecil E. Roberts, vice president, UMWA
John L. Lewis, president, UMWA, 1920–60
Mike Odom, president, Pittston Coal Group, Inc.
Tony Boyle, president, UMWA, 1963–72
Jock Yablonski, candidate for presidency, UMWA
Lane Kirkland, president, AFL-CIO
Arthur Miller, president, UMWA, 1972
Elizabeth Dole, secretary of labor
Sid Hatfield, sheriff of Matewan
Marty Hudson, Pittston strike coordinator
UMWA organizers: Mike Livoda, Don Barnett

Daughters of Mother Jones: Deborah Herd, Edna Sails
Ludlow Massacre survivors: Emma Zanatell, Alex Bisulco, Donald Mitchell, Steve Surisky
Retired miners: John Monroe Smith, Cory Lee Harris, Harry Whitaker, Frank Jackson, Joe Doers, Earl Stuckert, John Valdez, Jack and Shine Miller, Claude and Lawrence Amiacarella, Nimrod Workman

Barbara Kopple and Bill Davis's strategy for this documentary was to combine a history of the United Mine Workers and a chronicle of the Pittston strike of 1990. The former is accomplished through numerous interviews with retired miners and selections from archival and feature films, while the latter offers interviews with current officials and activists and footage of the imaginatively contested Pittston strike.

In ways perhaps not intended by the filmmakers, the earlier struggles are highlighted by death, while the Pittston struggle celebrates collective action, labor solidarity, and community spirit. The history of the mineworkers is punctuated by fatal explosions, assassinations of miners and activists, and countless funerals after disasters in mine shafts. The retired miners tell—and the film demonstrates—the dirty, dangerous business they are in until, too often, early and sudden death hits them belowground or slow terrible death from black lung disease takes them aboveground.

And if these horrors are not enough, miners and their families have too often been attacked by company gun thugs and even by the forces of law and order. The film includes extensive discussion and selected footage of the mining history of Eastern Kentucky and West Virginia, using two classics of labor history, John Sayles's *Matewan* and Kopple's own *Harlan County, U.S.A.*

These classics are supplemented by footage from archival films about other historical incidents, especially the Ludlow Massacre of 1914. Still photos and archival footage are supplemented by tales from survivors of the massacre, who tell story after story of the murderous attacks on the family encampment in Colorado by the state militia.

The footage of the Pittston strike, by contrast, shows the contemporary UMWA using a range of traditional union maneuvers and new organizing strategies. The campaign proceeded on several fronts. Besides traditional roadside picketing, the UMWA orchestrated sit-ins at Pittston headquarters by miners' wives and other women supporters, who nicknamed themselves the Daughters of Mother Jones, in honor of the great leader of miners' struggles. Lane Kirkland, AFL-CIO president, and nineteen other national union presidents were arrested in a solidarity sit-in. In a daring imitation of the great Flint sit-down strike of 1937, UMWA members and supporters occupied the Pittston's Moss 3 Preparation building.

The other footage assembled for this documentary is also impressive. Ann Lewis, director of *Fast Food Women*, contributed footage from her earlier Appalshop film, *Moss 3*. Rarely seen footage of the March on Blair Mountain, for example, carefully documents this Logan County, West Virginia, incident of 1921, which followed the Matewan Massacre of Baldwin-Felts agents and eventually the agency's retaliatory assassination of Sheriff Sid Hatfield. After an excerpt from Sayles's *Matewan*, which dramatizes the killing of the Baldwin-Felts security police, Kopple and Davis show Sid, the World War I vets of the minefields who organized the paramilitary march against the Logan Country sheriff they felt allowed Sid's murder, and the counterforce of federal troops and bomber planes (yes, bomber planes), including one flown by Charles Lindbergh.

See also: *Harlan County, U.S.A.; Justice in the Coalfields; Matewan.*
Availability: Selected collections.

Further reading

Aurand, Howard W. *From the Molly Maguires to the United Mine Workers*. Philadelphia: Temple University Press, 1971. A little dated, but a good general history.

Labor in America—"We Won't go Back": UMWA/Pittston Strike, 1989–90. Clinchco, Va.: Dickinson Star, 1990. A compilation of news stories and photos from the Clinchco, Virginia, newspaper that covered the strike closely.

Zieger, Robert H. *John L. Lewis, Labor Leader.* New York: Twayne, 1988. Biography of the famous founding president of the UMW.

The Pajama Game

One size fits all

1957, 101 mins.
Directors: George Abbott and Stanley Donen
Screenplay: George Abbott and Richard Bissell, from the latter's novel, *7½ Cents*
CAST
Babe = Doris Day
Sid = John Raitt
Gladys = Carol Haney
Hines = Eddie Foy Jr.
Poopsie = Barbara Nichols
Mae = Thelma Pelish
Prez = Jack Straw

Every once in a while a musical about labor unions comes along. Viewers usually ask: Was this funny? Entertaining? The 1930s had *Pins and Needles* (never filmed), the 1990s have *Newsies*, and the 1950s—era of such great musicals as *On the Town* and *Singin' in the Rain*—had *Never Steal Anything Small* and *The Pajama Game.*

If you were lucky enough to be a member of Local 343 of the Amalgamated Shirt and Pajama Workers of America and could have the fabulous picnic featured in this film, complete with choreographer Bob Fosse's great dance team, you might not have worried about the 7½-cents-an-hour raise you didn't get for cutting pajama bottoms.

Stanley Donen's magic clearly worked with Gene Kelly in *On the Town* and *Singin' in the Rain,* but for this labor-management adventure he must have left his lantern home. The leading man and new superintendent of the Sleeptite Pajama Factory, Sid

Sorokin, played by John Raitt (Bonnie Raitt's father), is a stick with a lovely voice. At one point he sings a duet with himself after he has recorded "Hey There, You with the Stars in Your Eyes" on his Dictaphone after giving a memo to his secretary: "The last six lots went over the estimate. Better check your product!" Doris Day, in a remarkable ducktail hairdo, plays Babe Williams, chair of Sleeptite's grievance committee, who at first is at odds with her new boss, then falls in love with him, and finally has a falling out when the local threatens to strike for their $7\frac{1}{2}$-cent raise (because "everyone else in the city is getting it").

We know we are in a fantasy world almost immediately, despite the interior shots of the factory, which look genuine enough (although too clean and neat). The "girls" on the shop floor—some of these union maids are working in high heels—sing a happy song of speedup, "Hurry up! Can't waste time!" with their supervisor. The speedup becomes comic, conveyed by fast-action filming. Later they dance a parody of their speedup as a tactic, singing "Hurry up!" as they slow down.

When Babe realizes a strike is likely, she warns her boss: "That contract, lover, that's important." With his love life in the balance, not to mention his career (he confesses that he's just "a cutting room foreman who bluffed" himself into his new job), Sorokin has the incentive to find a way to come up with the $7\frac{1}{2}$-cent raise. How he does so is too complicated and silly to summarize here, although the bottom line is that *his* boss has been cooking the books and adding the $7\frac{1}{2}$ cents to the cost of their product for the last six months. Sorokin allows the boss to announce the settlement at a union rally as long as the union agrees not to ask for the $7\frac{1}{2}$ cents retroactively.

Since most of the union members are more interested in dancing and modeling pajamas, they easily accept the settlement, despite a rousing trio of workers singing "Steam Heat," which most of us no doubt have long forgotten was a pro-union number: "Come on, union, get hot!" is one of its lines. Other famous tunes, such as "Hernando's Hideaway," are also in this film, but few of them have any union relevance. One of them almost mocks the $7\frac{1}{2}$-cent raise, up to the end the only bit of serious business of the film, or so it seemed. At the rally the grievance committee sings to its members, "I Figured It Out," which means that if they just wait five years, their raise will get them a washing machine or a 40-inch TV set, ten years will get them a trip to France or a foreign car, and twenty years will enable Babe to buy the factory and have its former owner work for *her*. It is clear at this point that all the singing has gone to their heads, and they end up with a real pajama party to celebrate their contract and the marriage of Babe and Sorokin.

Richard Bissell's original novel was only marginally more complicated and certainly not any funnier. It doesn't end with Babe and Sid sharing a set of pajamas (as the film does), but they plan to take their honeymoon "through the steel mills in Gary, Indiana." So much for romance. Bissell's other books, such as *A Stretch on the River* (New York: NAL, 1951), on his life as a deckhand on Mississippi tugboats, have a lot more grit, but they have never been filmed.

See also: *Never Steal Anything Small; Newsies*.
Availability: Easy; DVD.

Further reading

Bissell, Richard. *7½ Cents*. Boston: Little, Brown, 1953. Almost makes you wish for the complexity of the film.
Crowther, Bosley. "The Pajama Game." *New York Times,* 30 August 1957, 12. The reviewer likes the music but ignores the 7½ cents.

∽

Perfumed Nightmare

The last onion dome

1977, 93 mins., Philippines, in Tagalog, with English dialogue and subtitles
Director: Kidlat Tahimik
Screenplay: Kidlat Tahimik

Kidlat Tahimik as himself
Mutter = Katarina Muller
Kaya = Mang Fely
Nanay = Dolores Santamaria
Lola = Georgette Baudry
Big Boss = Hartmut Lerch

Before there was Michael Moore and *Roger & Me,* there was Kidlat Tahimik and *Perfumed Nightmare.* Like Moore's comic creation of himself as a sincere bumbling giant, an amateur filmmaker in search of the soul of General Motors, Kidlat's film is part meditation on the First and Third Worlds, part comic odyssey of a young Filipino who goes in search of the real meaning of progress in Paris (and briefly Bavaria), and part a celebration of the simple but eroding values of people who do things with their hands.

The film gathered a pan or two in the commercial press but was well received in its early festival appearances, winning awards at both the Berlin Film Festival and the American Film Festival. Celebrated by such diverse talents as the German filmmaker Werner Herzog ("one of the most original and poetic works of cinema made anywhere"), the cultural critic Susan Sontag ("makes one forget months of dreary moviegoing, for it reminds one that invention, enchantment, even innocence are still available to film"), and the *Village Voice* film critic J. Hoberman ("one of the year's ten best films"), and distributed in the United States by Francis Ford Coppola's Zoetrope Studios and the maverick independent filmmaker Les Blank's Flower Films, the film comes with the very best postmodern credentials.

The level of these responses is, I believe, generally pitched at the right volume. This is an original and charming film that shares the spirit that animates some of the best and silliest of postmodern documentaries by Errol Morris (*Gates of Heaven*), Diane Keaton (*Heaven*), and of course Michael Moore.

For Tahimik plays a holy fool, a babe in the Filipino backwoods. He is the president and founder of the local Werner von Braun Rocket Fan Club, and he eagerly awaits the arrival of the *Voyager* rocket to Mars as if it were an event that would somehow immediately transform his village, where bamboo hut construction is considered advanced.

And in a way he is right about the power of American and other technology to change his world of handicrafts and markets forever. When he journeys to Paris, he befriends Lola, who appears to be the last street-market saleswoman of free-range eggs. With some of her neighbors, such as the Cherry Man, she holds out for nonindustrial foodstuffs in the face of a mega-supermarket opening on their street.

When Tahimik travels to Bavaria to pay homage to his rocket scientist hero, he discovers a town that is a curious throwback to Third World methodology: workmen are carefully and laboriously fashioning what will be the last of the handmade copper onion church domes so characteristic of the German countryside. In the future, he was warned, the domes will be prefabricated and, worse yet, made of plastic. His visual puns are incessant and usually charming: the Bavarian village onion dome is followed by a giant plastic onion-shaped chimney, designed to be part of one of twenty megaincinerators to process Parisian garbage. He himself lives for a while in a rocket-shaped conical stone barn.

The title refers to the temptations of American technological promise, supported in a sense by the final credit sequence, a finale to Tahimik's witty visual style: the credits are typed on postcards, each one of which has the canceled stamp of a Third World country that has featured the (mostly) American space triumphs.

Tahimik's other major film, *Turumba,* is similarly tongue in cheek, but its mock-Marxism is also right on target: an entire village begins to create papier-mâché animals, previously only the quaint but remunerative folk art of a single family.

See also: Roger & Me; Turumba.
Availability: Selected collections.

Further reading

Aufderheide, Pat. "The Perfumed Nightmare." *Magill's Cinema Annual*, 1981, 2414–17. "This is the kind of Third World film to grind a dogmatist's teeth," but it is "a statement of hope, not a political program."

"Mababangong Bangungot." *Variety*, 10 December 1980. "Tahimik's rejection of American technology and influence is a banal theme familiar from many Third World filmmakers," argues the reviewer, who hated this "painfully naive" film; he especially disliked the stamp end credits.

Note: Also known as *Mababangong bangungot*, the title in Tagalog.

⤙

Picture Bride

Sugar (cane) and spice

1995, 95 mins., PG-13
Director: Kayo Hatta
Screenplay: Kayo Hatta
CAST
Riyo = Youki Kudoh
Matsuji = Akira Takayama
Kana = Tamlyn Tomita
The Benshi = Toshirō Mifune

The "picture" in the title of this drama of Japanese immigration to Hawaii in 1918 is not that of the bride, Riyo, but that of the bridegroom, Matsuji. Or, more precisely, a younger version of him, since Matsuji feels that a picture of him at his current age will not win the heart of a young Japanese woman seeking a husband and security in a new land.

And he is right. Riyo is tricked. She finds her new husband old, repulsive, and addicted to the hard work of cutting sugar cane. She has a lot to get used to as part of the latest wave of brides for the Japanese men who began coming to Hawaii in 1885. By 1918, the year in which the film is set, the Japanese constituted nearly 40 percent of the population of Hawaii, its largest ethnic group. Many of them had the illusion that they would earn enough money to return to Japan someday, but the wages were low and most stayed.

The sugar plantations were sophisticated machines for raising cane and keeping workers segregated by ethnicity. In fact, different ethnic groups were paid different wages. Ironically, the strike that does develop comes about because of the Filipino leadership.

Although this is a beautiful independently made film, it shares with Hollywood one inevitable development in plot: Riyo eventually falls for the gentle man who tricked her and learns to love him. She is helped by a new loyal friend who teaches her how to survive, and even to enjoy what aspects of life in this alien world she can—the traveling silent film cart, for example, staffed by the great samurai actor, Toshirō Mifune, in his

The picture bride (Youki Kudoh) and the experienced worker (Tamlyn Tomita).

last screen appearance as the Benshi, or narrator of silent films.

The filmmakers realized early on that the world they were portraying was about to disappear forever: the remaining picture brides were in their 80s and 90s, most sugar plantations were closing, and many historical sites in Hawaii were becoming shopping malls. *Picture Bride* captures the receding past brilliantly.

See also: *Perfumed Nightmare*.
Availability: Selected collections.

Further reading

Beechert, Edward. *Working in Hawai'i: A Labor History*. Honolulu: University of Hawai'i Press, 1985. Provides background for the labor dispute in the film.

Mark, Diane Mei Lin. *Picture Bride: A Viewer's Guide*. Honolulu: Thousand Cranes Filmworks, 1995. Essays on the background and production of the film, e.g., "The Japanese in Hawai'i: 1885–1920" and "Field Work and Family Work: Picture Brides on Hawai'i's Sugar Plantations, 1910–1920," and an extensive bibliography of resources.

Takaki, Ronald. *Pau Hana: Plantation Life and Labor in Hawai'i*. Honolulu: University of Hawai'i Press, 1983. Provides background on daily life and work.

Portrait of Teresa

"Polish the floor, Teresa"

1979, 90 mins., Cuba, in Spanish, with English subtitles
Director: Pastor Vega
Screenwriter: Pastor Vega and Ambrosio Fornet
CAST
Teresa = Daysi Granados
Adolfo Llaurado = Ramón

In this film we are given great close-ups of Cuban work life, home life, and culture in both cinematic and personal senses. Vega may have been influenced by the documentary filmmaker Robert Flaherty and Italian neorealists in his desire "to reveal the simplicity and the drama of daily life" (according to Aufderheide), but the bright colors of the Cuban mise-en-scène and the vibrant dance routines of the troupe at Teresa's textile factory raise one's spirits even during the difficult times.

Right away we learn Teresa's problem: she's committed to hard work at her factory, making costumes after hours for the workers' dance troupe; she has to raise her children, satisfy her husband's desire for an intimate relationship, and be nice to neighbors and family. Even a superwoman might crack under these pressures. And Teresa more or less does crack, especially when her husband, a TV repairman, leaves after a horrendous argument. While he does not come across as particularly macho, clearly he is not ready for the new Cuba or even the new Cuban woman.

The film also dramatizes the political life of Teresa and her comrades. It turns out her husband is not alone in his male chauvinist attitudes. At her union meeting, Teresa and the women have to put up with a man who says women last only three years at a factory because they fall in love, get married, have a kid, bye-bye. He says he tells the truth because he's ugly and honest. A woman comes back with this remark: "If the two are related, you must be very honest." Teresa shifts the discussion to the women's need for husbands to work more at domestic chores and also the need for a nursery at the factory.

A light but ironic song, mocking the liberated ideas Teresa expresses, is on the sound track:

You reap what you sow,
You sow what you reap.
In love a woman is just like a hen,
When her rooster dies she runs after men.
Teresa, Teresa,
Polish the floor, Teresa.

By the close of the film it is very unlikely that Teresa will accept polishing the floor.

See also: *Up to a Certain Point*.
Availability: Selected collections.

Further reading

Brenner, Philip, ed. *The Cuba Reader*. New York: Grove Press, 1989. Helpful essay collection, with Pat Aufderheide's "Cuba Vision: Three Decades of Cuban Film."

Aufderheide, Patricia. "Portrait of Teresa" at ⟨www.american.edu/subject/media/aufderheide/portrait.html⟩. Discussion of the film, based on an interview with Vega, and a short but helpful bibliography.

〜

Power

Still another fictional Hoffa

1980, 200 mins., TVM
Director: Barry Shear and Virgil Vogel
Screenplay: Ernest Tidyman
CAST
Tommy Vanda = Joe Don Baker
Rose = Karen Black
Eisenstadt = Howard da Silva
Frelinghuysen = Ralph Bellamy
Solly = Red Buttons
Armstrong = Scott Brady
Tony = David Groh

Although this is a Chicago dockland story, the real power behind the lead organizer of the truckers is a Jimmy Hoffa clone. This time the hero also fights for better treatment for his men, despite clashing mobs and truck arson (inevitable for a Teamster film). The Mob also plays its usual role, although the representation of its various Italian types comes too close to *The Godfather* for comfort.

The screenplay was the work of Ernest Tidyman, whose earlier credits had been the remarkable *French Connection* and *Shaft*, both in 1971. He also did *Guyana Tragedy*: *The Story of Jim Jones*, another story of power out of control, the same year as this film. *Power* has never been released in video and rarely (if at all) gets revived on TV. Only if you are interested in collecting a complete set of Hoffa-type films is this a problem.

See also: *Blood Feud; F.I.S.T.; Hoffa*.
Availability: Not.

Further reading

Shepard, Richard F. "TV: 'Power,' a Film about Union Leader." *New York Times*, 14 January 1980, C14. A lukewarm review, stressing that a Hoffa-type story is desperately in need of "new perspectives."

〜

The Price of Coal

. . . is always high

1977, 160 mins.
Director: Ken Loach
Screenplay: Barry Hines, from his own pair of plays of the same title
CAST
Sid Storey = Bobby Knutt
Kath Storey = Rita May
Mr. Forbes = Jackie Shinn
Harry = Ted Beyer

Ken Loach adapted Barry Hines's two related plays, *Meet the People* and *Back to Reality*, with the same cast of characters (more or less) as a TV film under the title *The Price of Coal*. Like several of Ken Loach's films, especially those with strong labor and political topics, they were broadcast, but they were never released on videocassette. The film emphasizes the human as well as the economic cost of mining coal, as both Hines and Loach emphasize the struggles of the miners in the 1970s as the center of a class war between Margaret Thatcher's Conservatives and working families.

The film is set at Milton Colliery in Yorkshire in 1976. The first part sees management preparing for a visit from Prince Charles. The humor of this section is set off by the rush to clean up the pit, whitewash a few walls, and do some plantings around the perimeter of the colliery. The second part involves a mine explosion with subsequent flooding and loss of life. Obviously opposite in tone from the first part, the second is largely taken up with the heroic efforts to rescue several of the trapped miners and the anguish of the waiting families.

The inspiration for Hines's play is discussed in the TV script. King George V and Queen Mary visited a nearby pit, Silverwood, in 1912; at Cadeby Main, the same day, an explosion killed eighty-six men and boys. The royal couple then visited the site of the disaster. Why Hines separated the two events in his script is not obvious; perhaps viewers would find the coincidence of real life not convincing enough.

See also: *Looks and Smiles*.
Availability: Not.

Further reading

Hines, Barry. *The Price of Coal*. London: Hutchinson, 1979. The TV scripts, with a short introduction about the production.

∽

La Promesse

Hard to keep

1996, Belgium, French, with English
  subtitles
Directors: Luc and Jean-Pierre Dardenne
Screenplay: Luc and Jean-Pierre Dardenne
CAST
Igor = Jérémie Rénier
Roger = Olivier Gourmet
Amidou = Rasmane Ouedraogo
Assita = Assita Ouedraogo

Teenager Igor is kept busy at the family "business," helping his father, Roger, with various scams in a grubby district of Liège, such as renting tiny rooms to immigrants, employing them illegally on construction projects, and fixing their papers. As these immigrants are at their mercy, father and son seem admirably matched in opportunism and greed. But things turn rather strange when Amidou, one of their workers from Burkina Faso, falls off a high scaffold and makes Igor promise to take care of his wife and child when he dies. Roger's response is considerably less wholesome: he hides the body in a new cement floor.

No longer comfortable with aiding and abetting the illegal underground economy, Igor has to choose between the promise he has made to Amidou and loyalty to the family firm. Although he at first keeps his father's secret, he begins to help Amidou's wife and child until he can no longer stifle his conscience.

With the Dardenne brothers' close-ups, hand-held camera, and street-level photography, moving about Liège seems claustrophobic and no doubt like other documentaries they had filmed. As Jonathan Rosenblum points out, the Dardenne brothers began their career making documentary films on urban, labor, and other topical political issues such as anti-Nazism and immigration.

This is a remarkably intense drama of the immigrant experience, filtered through Igor's relatively innocent and (at first) racist consciousness. As Igor becomes obsessed with his duty to Assita, Amidou's wife, he moves (as we do as well) closer and closer to her perceptions and understands her oppression. We see louts peeing on her as she waits under a bridge and learn that her husband's "identifying features" are three missing toes, lost in a quarry accident. Whether Igor is attracted to her because his mother has died (Rosenbaum's suggestion) or for some other reason, it is evident by film's end that he has also become an outsider in his own culture. *La Promesse* is a tragic drama that manages to combine many of the Dardenne brothers' earlier interests in a compelling and disturbing film.

See also: *À l'attaque!*
Availability: Selected collections; DVD.

Further reading

Holden, Stephen. *New York Times*, 7 October 1996. Successfully "casts a critical journalistic eye on European multiculturalism and the escalating hostility toward immigrants, especially Africans. What it sees is a Darwinian survival struggle. The movie's portrayal of racist xenophobia is all the more disturbing for its matter-of-factness."
Rosenbaum, Jonathan. *Chicago Reader*. August 1997. The directors "seem to know and under-

stand...the world [Igor and Assita] live in, including the factors that force them together and ultimately make them both pariahs."

~

The Proud Valley

Singing valley

1940, 77 mins., B&W
Director: Pen Tennyson
Screenplay: Louis Golding and Jack Jones
CAST
David Goliath = Paul Robeson
Dick Parry = Edward Chapman
Emlyn Parry = Simon Lack
Mrs. Permys = Rachel Thomas
Bert = Edward Rigby
Gwen Owen = Janet Johnson
Seth Jones = Clifford Evans
Mrs. Owen = Dilys Davies
Singing Welsh Miners = Eisteddfod Chorus
    of Blaendy

The great singing traditions of the Welsh in general and their miners in particular are combined with the powerful voice of Paul Robeson in his prime. The *New York Times* reviewer may not have meant to be ironic when he noted that the film "makes clear two things about the Welsh, that they sing and dig coal exceeding well." *The Proud Valley* had a B budget, used many semiprofessional actors, and came perhaps too soon after the big-budget films about Wales—*The Citadel, The Stars Look Down, How Green Was My Valley*, and *The Corn Is Green*—to compete at the box office or even among the critics.

Peter Stead's analysis of the film includes some important background information: Robeson was cast in part because of his radical politics. He had already appeared in the mining districts of Wales to raise money for the Republican side in the Spanish Civil War, and the script was based on a play written for a British left-wing theater. The Ealing Studio and its producers were com-

David Goliath (Paul Robeson) in a Welsh mine in *The Proud Valley*. Courtesy British Film Institute Stills, Posters, and Designs.

mitted to low-budget filmmaking, but in the end were a little skittish about the film's original politics. It was to have ended with miners taking over a struck pit, reopening it, and running it themselves. This daring exercise in workers' control became instead a patriotic finale in which the miners send representatives to London to persuade the company to aid in the war effort by reopening the mines. Unfortunately, David Goliath dies a hero's death in the mines, saving his co-workers in a collapse.

The film's director, Pen Tennyson, was a descendant of the poet Alfred, Lord Tennyson. He directed only two other films (*There Ain't No Justice* and *Convoy*) before he was killed in World War II. Casting a great singer in a valley filled with song was an inspiration worth having.

See also: *The Citadel*; *The Corn Is Green*; *How Green Was My Valley*; *The Stars Look Down*.
Availability: Selected collections; Movies Unlimited.

Further reading

Crowther, Bosley. "Proud Valley." *New York Times*, 17 May 1941, 19. Short, a little condescending, but generally a positive review.
Greene, Graham. *Pleasure-Dome: The Collected Film Criticism, 1935–1940*. Ed. John Russell Taylor. Oxford: Oxford University Press, 1980. Argues that its reasonably decent scale has been overshadowed by the more successful film set in Wales, *The Stars Look Down*.
Stead, Peter. *Film and the Working Class*. London: Routledge, 1989. Short but detailed account of the political context of the film.

〰

¡Que viva México!

¡Que viva Eisenstein!

1932 (1979), 68 mins., B&W, Soviet Union
Directors: Sergei Eisenstein and Grigory Aleksandrov
Screenplay: Sergei Eisenstein

CAST
Sebastián = Martín Hernández
Sebastián's Brother = Félix Balderas
Matador = David Liceaga
Hacendado = Julio Saldívar
María = Isabel Villaseñor

Not many films have as complicated a production history or as many cinematic spin-offs (illicit and otherwise) as *¡Que viva México!* Originally directed (for the most part) by the great Soviet filmmaker Sergei Eisenstein in the 1930s as part of the romance with Mexican peasant life that spread through not only political lefties of all countries but Hollywood types as well, the film began as a collaborative effort with the muckraker and social-realist novelist Upton Sinclair (author of *The Jungle*), but ended with pieces of the film literally flying in many directions.

Grigory Aleksandrov, Eisenstein's assistant director, transformed one of the larger chunks of the original footage shot in 1931–32 into what he regarded as his mentor's film, based on Eisenstein's script, notes, and sketches. It is Aleksandrov's version, in the end, released forty-five years after Eisenstein left Mexico (never to return), that goes by the original name, *¡Que viva México!* Two Hollywood feature films using footage supplied by Upton Sinclair, *Thunder over Mexico* (directed by Sol Lesser) and *Viva Villa!* (directed by Jack Conroy and Howard Hawks), and two independently produced films by Eisenstein's biographers (Marie Seaton's *Time in the Sun* and Oleg Kovalov's *Sergei Eisenstein's Mexican Fantasy*), using footage from the Aleksandrov pool, have been made.

Of the making of books about this film there seems to be no end in sight. The very first book, by Harry Geduld and Ronald Gottesman, quoted Paul Rotha's review of Lesser's *Thunder over Mexico* in 1934: "Probably more ink has been spilt and more reputations soiled over this picture than any other since cinema began." Geduld and Gottesman echoed his remark nearly forty years later: "The episode of 'Que viva Mexico' remains the cinema's greatest artistic misfortune and its most celebrated scandal." The truth is that we have had more artistic misfortunes and celebrated scandals since the days of these dramatic remarks, but the film's history captures its share of headlines to this day.

The debate was pretty much front-page news. Even the *Variety* reviewer, upon the release of the first unauthorized cut (*Thunder over Mexico*), felt compelled to say that it may not be possible to determine the absolute truth of the debacle. Sinclair, the reviewer noted, "lost some of his literary Red and went a completely physical red" when he began to lose more and more of his money on the venture. In cinematic terms, however, the reviewer concluded, Eisenstein could do virtually nothing wrong: "From a trade standpoint, it ought to be seen by everyone connected with film biz just as an example of what can be done with a camera."

Eisenstein recovered from this Mexican fiasco by making the anti-German *Alexander Nevsky* in 1938. He did less well with his two *Ivan the Terrible* films, in which, curiously enough, Stalin found some objection to portraits of a monomaniacally powerful leader who does good things for his people while killing only the bad ones. The truth of the matter is—despite the successes of such silent films as *Strike* and *The General Line*—Eisenstein was never happy with the principal dictum of Stalinist aesthetics based on the oft-quoted "analysis" formulated fifty years earlier by Friedrich Engels, the father of Soviet socialist realism: "Realism presupposes, in addition to truthfulness of details, truthfulness in the reproduction of typical characters in typical circumstances" ("Letter to Margaret Harkness"). With few exceptions, Eisenstein was obsessed in *¡Que viva México!* with the atypicalness of Mexico, how incredible it was that contemporary Indians resembled their thousand-year-old ancestors.

Essentially a portrait in vignettes of a peasant people, *¡Que viva México!* has Eisenstein's characteristic epic filming style with peasants juxtaposed against ancient Mayan ruins as one recurring motif. The film was to be divided into six sections, some of which were correlated with works done by Mexican artists on visual themes of the project:

1. Prologue (muralist David Siqueiros).
2. *Sandunga*: tropical wedding and celebration of the female body.
3. Maguey (muralist Diego Rivera): young peasant is executed for trying to avenge his wife's rape.
4. Fiesta: the corrida or bullfight amidst religious processions.
5. *Soldadera* (muralist and printmaker José Clemente Orozco): peasant woman as soldiers' wives and revolutionaries.

The Day of the Dead procession in *¡Que viva México!*

6. Epilogue (printmaker José Guadalupe Posada): peasants dress as skeletons to celebrate the Day of the Dead.

Unfortunately, to date, only parts of the footage for all of these episodes has been utilized.

See also: *The General Line.*
Availability: Selected collections; DVD.

Further reading

Azuela, Mariano. *The Underdogs*. 1924. New York: Signet/New American Library, 1963. This "novel of the Mexican Revolution," as it was subtitled, influenced Eisenstein's view of the *soldadera*, especially as the novel was wonderfully illustrated by Orozco.

Bordwell, David. *The Cinema of Eisenstein*. Cambridge: Harvard University Press, 1993. Although the section on *¡Que viva México!* is relatively brief, it is quite helpful, as is this generally excellent overview of the director's career.

Claypole, Jonty. "A Promise to Eisenstein." *Vertigo*, Summer 1999, 49–52. On the filmmaker Lutz Becker's proposal for a new version of the film; also argues that Stalin prevented Sinclair from sending Eisenstein's footage to the Soviet Union.

Eisenstein, Sergei. *The Complete Films of Eisenstein*. Trans. John Hetherington. New York: Dutton, 1974. Includes an abbreviated scenario and stills of the film.

——. *Selected Works*. Vol. 2, *Towards a Theory of Montage*. Ed. Michael Glenny and Richard Taylor. Trans. Michael Glenny. London: British Film Institute, 1991. Eisenstein's essay "Montage 1937" explains his own view of the film, stressing "the idea of the social conquest of death as the continuation of the struggle by a *whole* class after the death of one of its individual members."

Geduld, Harry M., and Ronald Gottesman, eds. *Sergei Eisenstein and Upton Sinclair: The Making and Unmaking of "Que viva Mexico!"* Bloomington: Indiana University Press, 1970. Thorough history of the tragic farce, mostly told through the correspondence of the principal filmmakers and producers.

Goodwin, James. *Eisenstein, Cinema, and History*. Urbana: University of Illinois Press, 1993. Places the film in the context of revolutionary Mexico and its artists.

Karetnikova, Inga. *Mexico According to Eisenstein*. Albuquerque: University of New Mexico Press, 1991. Includes Eisenstein's film treatment and his other essays about Mexico, as well as Karetnikova's extended (and helpful) essay about the film.

King, John, Ana M. Lopez, and Manuel Alvarado, eds. *Mediating Two Worlds: Cinematic Encounters in the Americas*. London: British Film Institute, 1993. Includes Laura Podalsky's essay "Patterns of the Primitive," which situates the film in Eisenstein's readings in "primitive" cultures (e.g., Lucien Lévy-Bruhl's *Primitive Mentality*, 1922, and James Frazier's *Golden Bough*, 1915).

Leyda, Jay. *Kino*. 1960. New York: Collier, 1970. This was for some time the standard "history of the Russian and Soviet film," as it is aptly subtitled; places Eisenstein in a prominent position in that history.

"Moscow Film Fest." *Variety*, 5 October 1979. A brief survey of the issues of the film's problems and a cautious assessment of its value in introducing the viewer to Eisenstein's vision for a film he never made.

"Que Viva Mexico." *Variety*, 5 September 1979. Despite the efforts of Eisenstein's assistant (Aleksandrov), the reviewer concludes that "the dream about its power, brilliance and greatness, offered in part by the films made from it and the rushes, remained only conjecture," whose promise is only somewhat answered by the film.

Ramsey, Nancy. "Eisenstein's Unfinished Ode to an Idealized Mexico." *New York Times*, 19 August 2001, II.18. Review of the Kino International DVD release that contains Aleksandrov's version plus two other shorts done by Eisenstein in the 1930s.

"Thunder over Mexico." *Variety*, 26 September 1933. A fairly thorough review of the crisis over the film; relatively positive about its strengths but does not think it can "stand on its own as a film."

Traven, B. *General from the Jungle*. 1940. Various editions translated by Desmond Vesey available. The closest literary equivalent to the rape/execution section of the film, although the novel is even more graphic.

Quilombo

The slaves' utopia

1984, 114 mins., Brazil, Portuguese, with
English subtitles
Director: Carlos Diegues
Screenplay: Carlos Diegues
CAST
Ganga Zumba = Tony Tornado
Dandara = Zezé Motta
Zumbi = Antônio Pompêo
Ana de Ferro = Vera Fischer

A *quilombo* is literally a forest camp or village in Brazil, but as it is a word derived from West African dialects, here it denotes a colony of escaped slaves. In some cases, these settlements, some of which began in the seventeenth century, became virtually independent regions, with a political structure imitating the West African kingdoms of the slaves. In contemporary Brazil, the descendants of more than 700 *quilombos* still occupy their ancestral lands, in some cases so far from mainstream life in Brazil that they still act as pockets of resistance if not mainstream indifference (see Rohter).

Palmares, the *quilombo* at the heart of Diegues's third film about Afro-Brazilian history and the mythology of slavery, set the record for the longest resistance to the slave-owning Portuguese colony of Brazil, until it was destroyed in 1694.

Quilombo is a fascinating mixture of the brutal depiction of the horrors of slavery and a magical realist celebration of the utopian life of Palmares. It is as if a samba school, that urban institution of Brazilians who reenact glorious moments of history, were to take to the jungles and stage an extended tableau of liberated slaves, all set to the contemporary and popular beat of Gilberto Gil, the Brazilian singer.

The film traces, almost in shorthand, the story of the legendary hero Ganga Zumba, from his initial leadership of a small slave revolt to the kingship of Palmares. The escaped slaves under his leadership practice guerrilla warfare against the Portuguese

slave owners and the army, but Ganga Zumba becomes magically anointed by the previous leader of Palmares, the old wise woman Acarene. Ganga Zumba is able to transform himself, literally becoming the white parrot that perched above—and symbolized—Acarene's throne.

Although Palmares is geographically isolated, its utopian bounty and success story of freed slaves tempts freelance slave catchers and then the colonial administration to destroy it. The defense of the kingdom is protracted, although the outcome seems to be in little doubt, despite the new leadership provided by Zumbi. Palmares is doomed, although remnants of the original colony live on.

The historical development of Palmares may not have been quite as Diegues imagined it. Zumbi, or Zambi as some sources spell it, may have actually rebelled against Ganga Zumba and seized control. He was, as an essay in Richard Price's book suggests, captured and executed by the Portuguese, his head exhibited "to kill the legend of his immortality." In the film, Zumbi is loyal and when seemingly destroyed by the enemy is transformed into a burst of flame.

See also: *Burn!*; *Xica*.
Availability: Selected collections.

Further reading

Canby, Vincent. "Brave New World." *New York Times*, 28 March 1986, C10. Praises the director's attempts to "create a distinctively Brazilian cinema that defines the national character and its heritage" but finds the film somewhat cold.

Johnson, Randal, and Robert Stam, eds. *Brazilian Cinema*. Expanded ed. New York: Columbia University Press, 1995. Extensive discussions of Cinema Novo and the films of Diegues.

Pick, Zuzana M. *The New Latin American Cinema*. Austin: University of Texas Press, 1993. Excellent section on the film.

Price, Richard, ed. *Maroon Societies: Rebel Slave Communities in the Americas*. 2d ed. Baltimore: Johns Hopkins University Press, 1979. Excellent historical essays on four centuries of *quilombos*.

Rohter, Larry. "Former Slave Havens in Brazil Gaining Rights." *New York Times*, 23 January 2001, A1, 4. A remarkable contemporary account of the *quilombo* descendants: "We have been here for 300 years, resisting as best we can, but until recently no one paid us any heed, because we were black and poor and didn't even know we had any rights."

Welch, Cliff. "Quilombo." *American Historical Review*, October 1992, 1162–64. "*Quilombo* stretches thin evidence to portray Palmares as 'a land without wrongs.'"

∽

The Raid

Labor martyrs

1990, 23 mins.
Directors: Steve Rosen and Terri De Bona
Screenplay: Steve Rosen and Terri De Bona, from John Steinbeck's short story of the same title
CAST
Dick = John Rousseau
Root = Matthew Flint
Man = Kerry Hartjen

John Steinbeck published the short story "The Raid" in 1934, two years before *In Dubious Battle*, the most political novel of his agricultural trilogy, completed by the more famous *Of Mice and Men* and *The Grapes of Wrath*. "The Raid" might be said to be a kind of trial run for *In Dubious Battle*, since both fictions involve the relationship between a seasoned older Communist and a new recruit to the Red cause. Both fictions involve the initiation of the younger man into the ways of vigilante justice, for anyone who was an activist in organizing California's farm labor knew that the growers and their right-wing allies would usually stop at nothing to defeat a strike.

The film version of the story follows Steinbeck's text faithfully. Two men, the veteran organizer, Dick, and the new guy, Root, are trudging a little way out of a town that resembles those of Steinbeck's youth—Salinas, perhaps, or Castroville or Watsonville, all towns in the heart of the "long valley" of Salinas. They have been instructed to hold a Communist organizing meeting and

resolve to do so even after a sympathetic local tips them off that vigilantes, not fellow workers, are coming. Dick says they have to stay and take a beating—"that's orders"—because "the men of little spirit must have an example of steadfastness. The people at large must have an example of injustice."

What this order comes down to is basically that the Reds must be stomped by the vigilantes and not fight back. It's a curious message—and lesson—to workers you want to organize. *In Dubious Battle* improves on this kind of situation as the Reds get lots of licks in and are nowhere seen as passive. A curious idea of martyrdom does run through both works, however, and Steinbeck questions this idea—dramatically—in the novel because it seems as if the Reds almost want to be punished or, at the very least, believe that their sacrifice will spur the masses on to a general revolt.

See also: *Long Road Home; Of Mice and Men.*
Availability: Selected collections; Pyramid.

Further reading

Steinbeck, John. *The Long Valley*. New York: Viking, 1964. A collection of California stories (originally published in the 1930s), including "The Raid" and other disturbing minor classics ("The Flight" and "The Vigilante," both about lynchings).

∽

A Raisin in the Sun

"What happens to a dream deferred?"

[I] 1961, 128 mins., B&W
Director: Daniel Petrie
Screenplay: Lorraine Hansberry, from her play of the same title
CAST
Walter Lee Younger = Sidney Poitier
Lena Younger = Claudia McNeil
Ruth Younger = Ruby Dee
Beneatha Younger = Diana Sands
Travis Younger = Stephen Perry

Joseph Asagai = Ivan Dixon
George Murchison = Louis Gossett
Mr. Lindner = John Fiedler
Bobo = Joel Fluellen
Willie Harris = Roy Glenn
[II] 1989, 171 mins., TVM
Director: Bill Duke
Filmed from the stage production directed
  by Harold Scott
CAST
Walter Lee Younger = Danny Glover
Lena Younger = Esther Rolle
Ruth Younger = Starletta DuPois
Beneatha Younger = Kim Yancey
Travis Younger = Kimble Joyner
Joseph Asagai = Lou Ferguson
George Murchison = Joseph C. Phillips
Mr. Lindner = John Fiedler
Bobo = Stephen Henderson
Mrs. Johnson = Helen Martin

Lorraine Hansberry's *Raisin in the Sun* was
voted the best American play in 1958; it was
also a major breakthrough for an African
American woman to have a major Broadway
production. Hansberry took her title from a
Langston Hughes poem, in which a "dream
deferred," if frustrated, may "explode" like
"a raisin in the sun."

The "dream deferred" in both film versions
has an ironic edge. Mrs. Younger's dream is
to have a house and a garden—to escape her
ghetto flat with a shared bathroom in the
hallway. Her son's dream is to quit his job as
a chauffeur and open a liquor store—in
short, the recurring working-class dream of
being self-employed. These dreams are not
compatible, especially when sister Beneatha
also needs money to go to medical school.
The subsequent clash of these competing
dreams propels the action toward a form of
reconciliation. In the meantime, the films
have explored the role of the matriarch and
the extended black family, the rise in consciousness of the African roots of black
culture, abortion, the generation gap, and
the integration ("assimilation") versus sepa-
ratism debates of the 1950s.

Although early reviewers (for example,
Bosley Crowther in the *New York Times*)

assumed Daniel Petrie intended to emphasize the single room of the original script,
the first film certainly accepted it as a way
of emphasizing that "its drama takes place
mainly in the hearts of its people." We now
know from the publication of Hansberry's
original screenplay that she wanted a more
opened-out version of her play. The few
scenes that do leave the Younger flat—
Walter as chauffeur, Walter at the bar with
his mother, the family's arrival at their new
house—do get the film outside. Ironically the
1989 remake, staying closest to the original
intentions for the Broadway staging, seems
nonetheless much more claustrophobic.

The relationship between the hit play and
the first film version is complicated. The play
omitted a few key moments from Hansberry's playscript; Petrie's film followed that
pattern, but also added some additional
scenes, to open up the play somewhat. In a
sense, Petrie used the playscript almost more
than the actual screenplay Hansberry had
written, since about one-third of her screenplay does not show up in the final film. There
are thus *three* literary texts, all with the same
title: the 1959 playscript, the 1988 playscript
(which became the *American Playhouse* TV
film, or *Raisin* II), and the 1992 "unfilmed
original screenplay." These bibliographical
matters are of some importance, because
exactly what has been filmed (or not) reflects
the images of African American working-
class people over three decades.

Raisin II restores three scenes omitted
from both the 1958 Broadway and the 1961
filmed versions of the play: young Travis
chases a rat with his friends in the street,
Beneatha sports an (early) Afro, and the
friendly Mrs. Johnson arrives with the news
of the fire-bombing of the home of a black
family who dared to move into a white
neighborhood. Numerous other scenes that
had been filmed in the first version also
ended up on the cutting-room floor, as
the 1992 edition of Hansberry's screenplay
documents.

The second version therefore develops
a fuller context for the visitor from the
Park Improvement Association—played

both times by John Fiedler—by emphasizing how dangerous it could be for blacks to move into a white neighborhood. And, of course, the rat scene emphasizes how dangerous it was for them to stay behind.

It is sometimes difficult for the new version to compete with the old, especially when the old is a classic with an outstanding cast. Esther Rolle seems too young for the matriarchal role, while Danny Glover seems too old to be her son. Nevertheless, it may be worthwhile to look at the more recent version to see how a contemporary black director such as Bill Duke interprets this material. Duke's *Killing Floor* preceded this film, and that was clearly a fresh look at southern blacks emigrating for jobs in the North. Sidney Poitier's hold as the leading black actor of his generation will remain clearly secure, but we should note with some irony that although Poitier now has on the record books five of the thirty most successful films directed by African Americans, they are all crime caper films (such as *Uptown Saturday Night*).

The first filmed production of Hansberry's portrayal of black working-class life in Chicago reminds us that two great talents associated with it died young: the playwright herself died in 1965 at 35 and Diana Sands, who played the rebellious and early Afrocentric Beneatha, died in 1973 at 39.

See also: *Goin' to Chicago.*
Availability: I and II: Easy; I: DVD.

Further reading

Bogle, Donald. *Toms, Coons, Mulattoes, Mammies, and Bucks: An Interpretative History of Blacks in American Film*. 2d ed. New York: Continuum, 1989. A thorough coverage of Poitier and the rest of the talented cast of the first version.

Cripps, Thomas. *Making Movies Black*. New York: Oxford University Press, 1993. Situates the film in the era of "Hollywood timidity and the resulting wish to launder the more strident aspects of black culture as a device for assuring broader appeal to whites."

Crowther, Bosley. "Raisin in the Sun." *New York Times*, 30 March 1961, 24. A very positive review of the first version, but doubts the effectiveness of John Fiedler's role as the white visitor.

Farber, Stephen. "New 'Raisin in the Sun' for TV Restores Scenes." *New York Times*, 31 August 1988, 18. Argues that this new version "should lay to rest once and for all the misconception that this is a play about a middle-class black family."

Goodman, Walter. " 'Raisin in the Sun' through '89 Eyes," *New York Times*, 1 February 1989, C24. The new version "has lost some of [the original play's] urgency but none of its awkwardness."

Hansberry, Lorraine. *A Raisin in the Sun*. New York: NAL, 1988. This Signet paperback is the "most complete edition" (of the stage version), according to Robert Nemiroff, the playwright's husband and literary executor, in his excellent introduction.

——. *A Raisin in the Sun*. Ed. Robert Nemiroff. New York: Plume, 1992. The original screenplay, with a much longer and more cinematic (less indoorsy) vision than Petrie's film.

——. *To Be Young, Gifted, and Black*. Englewood Cliffs, N.J.: Prentice-Hall, 1969. "An informal autobiography" adapted as a play by Hansberry's husband, Robert Nemiroff.

"Make New Sounds: Studs Terkel Interviews Lorraine Hansberry." *American Theatre*, November 1984, 5–8, 41. A revealing 1959 interview with the author.

"Playwright." *New Yorker*, 9 May 1959, 33–35. Hansberry on her theatrical influences and other aspects of her life.

⤳

Ramparts of Clay

Stony silence

1968, 84 mins., Italy, in Arabic, with English subtitles, PG
Director: Jean-Louis Bertucelli
Screenplay: Jean Duvignaud, from his own *Change at Shebika*
CAST
The Girl = Leila Schenna
The Villagers = The villagers of Tehouda, Algeria

The French colonial empire in Northern Africa does not collapse in this film as it does in Pontecorvo's revolutionary *Battle of Algiers*. It just comes to a dead standstill. Viewers will have to be fortified by the fact that this slow film is worth the effort because of its authenticity, despite the fact that it uses the Algerian landscape and nonprofessional actors to stand in for the village of Tunisian rock salt cutters. For almost forty minutes not much happens, except the daily survival of a people who define stoic endurance. One local girl, played by a professional actress, Leila Schenna, has, however, learned how to read and watches her village with an equally unnerving stillness.

The patience of most viewers is somewhat rewarded when the army arrives, but the men's sit-down strike is deliberately anticlimactic. In a similar way we grasp at the presence of The Girl when she is onscreen, but unfortunately for the politics of the film, many viewers will wonder (as one visitor to the town does) why she isn't married in this very restricted society. She does refuse in the end to draw water from the well, an act we see her (and others) do numerous times. For her trouble she gets chicken blood splashed in her face by the old women of the village, who (we can only guess) are doing some kind of exorcism. (Is it my corrupted eye or do I see the type-casting of an Algerian actress who looks incredibly like the dark-haired beauties of Italian neorealist cinema?)

But our ignorance of this culture in general is a weak but reasonable defense: we simply are told virtually nothing about these villagers—why the 50 percent pay cut, for example—and so it becomes difficult to judge the political currents the filmmakers wanted us to see, and too often we're left wondering about the poor men's forty-eight-hour sit-down strike—without water, food, or obvious sanitary relief. When one man is discovered dead when the strike ends, we do not even have the comfort of the villagers' discussion, inevitably fatalistic, as Duvignaud records it.

The opening titles of the film quote Frantz Fanon's *Wretched of the Earth*: the action of the film is set *after* Tunisia's independence in 1962, but "the bourgeois phase in the history of underdeveloped countries [is] completely useless. Everything since independence must be started again from scratch." Presumably the man in a suit who provokes the strike against a 50 percent cut in wages represents the new bourgeois government of Tunisia.

The filmmakers, by adding The Girl as a central narrative point of reference, opened up Duvignaud's clearly male-centered story. In the quarry episode, which becomes the primary action in the film (rather than just one major incident in the book), women are for the most part passive observers of the men's sit-down strike. The older women do sacrifice a goat, however, calling on God to protect their men. (A man actually cuts the goat's throat.)

See also: *The Blue Eyes of Yonta*.
Availability: Selected collections.

Further reading

Duvignaud, Jean. *Change at Shebika: A Report from a North African Village*. Trans. Frances Frenaye. Austin: University of Texas Press, 1970. The sociologist Jean Duvignaud observed life in Shebika from 1960 to 1965.

Fanon, Frantz. *The Wretched of the Earth*. New York: Grove Press, 1966. The classic statement of North African resistance to French colonialism.

Thompson, Howard. "Ramparts of Clay." *New York Times*, 8 February 1971, 40. Celebrates this "striking, often hypnotic film," but worries about its lack of "cumulative power."

Ratcatcher

1999, 93 mins., UK
Director: Lynne Ramsay
Screenplay: Lynne Ramsay
CAST
James = William Eadie
Da = Tommy Flanagan
Ma = Mandy Matthews
Ellen = Michelle Stewart
Anne Marie = Lynne Ramsay Jr.
Margaret Anne = Leanne Mullen
Kenny = John Miller
Mrs. Quinn = Jackie Quinn

The great Glasgow sanitation strike of 1973 is the background of *Ratcatcher*. The "dustmen" never appear in this film, partly because the director, Lynn Ramsay, wanted the film to be mainly about a boy whose world was falling apart around him. The uncollected refuse bags and the ever-growing population of rats form a memorable cityscape. Scabs in the form of army men eventually—at the end of the film—try to remove the mountains of waste that have been accumulating in the Glasgow public housing estate of tenements on Kintra Street, which, with a bordering canal now no longer used or even usable, is the primary location of the film.

The bleak mise-en-scène of an industrial past in the form of a dirty, treacherous canal and a strike that pollutes a neighborhood with no end in sight nevertheless dominates this debut feature film by the young Scottish director who was trained first as a still photographer and then as a cinematographer. Even though a couple of sequences are set at the construction site of a new housing estate in the countryside, Ramsay's cinematic eye finds interest if not a kind of beauty in all this grit and all this grime.

The story is disarmingly simple. Young James Gillespie's friend drowns in the canal after the two boys wrestle in the disgusting water. James could have gone for help, but he didn't. How he handles this guilt in a family and world of "ratcatchers" of all kinds moves in an inevitable arc of self-destruction. He has to survive among neighborhood toughs, the teenage girl they abuse, a not-quite-all-there friend who loves all kinds of animals including rats, and a family desperate to leave this public housing slum.

The film offers a social realism usually seen only in British films by Mike Leigh (*High Hopes*) and Ken Loach (*Bread and Roses*), who have the ability to portray characters talking about their situations as a partial way out of the impasse of their class society.

With Ramsay's film the realism is tempered by some cinematic flights of fancy: James at one point ends up in a country estate bordering a wheat field through which he bounds ecstatically: a moment so different from his everyday life as to appear surreal. (Indeed, it returns at the end of the film in an equally surreal way.) In another sequence his friend's white mouse escapes in a balloon to the surface of the moon, where fellow mice cavort. And in the most ambiguous sequence of all—is it fantasy?—James's family finally gets to move to that house in the countryside.

See also: *High Hopes*.
Availability: Selected collections; DVD.

Further reading

Bradshaw, Peter. "Poetry from the Rubbish Tip." *Guardian*, 12 November 1999. At ⟨www.filmunlimited.co.uk/News_Story/Critic_Review/Guardian_Film_of_the_week/0,,4267,102485,00.html⟩. A "wonderful film from a brilliant director."

Pendreigh, Brian. "The Catcher with an Eye." At ⟨www.filmunlimited.co.uk/Feature_Story/feature_story/0,4120,73834,00.html⟩. Interview with director Lynn Ramsay.

Ramsay, Lynne. *Ratcatcher*. London: Faber & Faber, 1999. The screenplay includes material that was not included in the final film as well as an interview with the director.

"'Ratcatcher': For a Glasgow Boy, Rats Are Just the Beginning." *New York Times*, 13 October 2000. A "gorgeous blend of beauty and squalor."

Roddick, Nick. "The Roddick Profile." At ⟨www.filmfestivals.com/htmlus/intro8us.htm⟩. Interview with director Lynn Ramsay.

⤺
Red Sorghum

Red heroine

1987, 91 mins., China, in Mandarin, with English subtitles
Director: Yimou Zhang
Screenplay: Jianyu Chen and Wei Zhu, from Mo Yan's novel of the same title
CAST
Grandma (Nine) = Gong Li
Grandpa = Jiang Wen
Uncle Luohan = Ten Rujun
Bandit = Ji Cunhua

Director Yimou Zhang is a member of the so-called Fifth Generation of Chinese film-makers, who were the first graduates of the Beijing Film Academy since its closure during the Cultural Revolution. Zhang's remarkable string of beautiful films—including *Raise the Red Lantern* and *Ju Dou*—starred Gong Li, a Chinese actress of luminous beauty and grace. As Nine in *Red Sorghum*, she is the spare ninth child of a farmer, who sends her off to wed a leper who owns a winery. From this dubious beginning she eventually becomes mistress of the winery, turns it into a virtual commune, and dies heroically fighting the Japanese invaders during the 1930s.

Her grandson, in a voice-over as if in a fairy tale, tells how she came to follow this momentous path. During a rollicking sedan-chair ride to her new husband (one of the many wonderful sequences in the film), Nine is about to be abducted by a bandit. One of the bearers, who turns out to be the narrator's grandfather, intervenes and leads the crew to kill the bandit. Grandpa *is* destined to be Nine's husband, although the path to true love is blocked inconveniently by another husband. Once he is eliminated—who knows how?—the couple run a successful winery until the Japanese come. After some horrendous scenes of torture, the peasants stand up to fight the Japanese, but Nine is killed.

A bare summary of the plot disguises some spectacular cinematic moments throughout the film. Grandpa makes a major impression at the winery, for example, when he pees in a wine vat and turns the vintage into a success. The numerous scenes shot in the red sorghum field—the ultimate source of the wine—are so beautiful that the horror that comes with the Japanese occupation is that much more shocking.

See also: *Yellow Earth*.
Availability: Selected collections.

Further reading

Canby, Vincent. "Orient Expression." *New York Times*, 9 October 1988, 74. Sees Nine as "an idealization of the progressive woman of our time" and therefore a form of "social realist cinema."

Ebert, Roger. "Red Sorghum." *Chicago Sun-Times*, 28 February 1989. "It is some kind of irony that when Hollywood switched over to cheaper and faster forms of making color films, classic Technicolor equipment was dismantled and sold to China—which now makes some of the best-looking color films in the world."

Mo Yan. *Red Sorghum*. Trans. Howard Goldblatt. New York: Penguin, 1994. The source novel, of which only the first two parts were adapted (see Silbergeld).

Silbergeld, Jerome. *China into Film*. London: Reaktion Books, 1999. An excellent survey of contemporary Chinese cinema in general and *Red Sorghum* in particular.

Yuejin, Wang. "Red Sorghum: Mixing Memory and Desire." In *Perspectives in Chinese Cinema*, ed. Chris Berry. London: British Film Institute, 1991. Very helpful essay.

∽

The Richest Man in the World

"Tell Mr. Carnegie I'll meet him in hell."—
Henry Clay Frick

1997, 60 mins.
Director: Austin Hoyt
Traditional documentary
PRINCIPAL FIGURES
Andrew Carnegie, financier
Margaret Carnegie, his mother
John Ingham, Paul Krause, Owen Dudley
    Edwards, and Harold Livesay, historians
Joseph Frazier Wall, biographer
Louise Whitfield, Carnegie's wife
Henry Clay Frick, coal baron and manager
    of the Homestead Steelworks
J. P. Morgan, financier

It came as a surprise to me that Andrew Carnegie, the steel-manufacturing "richest man in the world," was a devoted follower of Herbert Spencer, the social Darwinist. For Carnegie, Spencer's ideas meant primarily the survival of the fittest capitalist in the capitalist world. He rationalized his entire industrial empire, guided by the idea that one needed to "watch the costs and the profits will take care of themselves." Not included in this scheme were unions, which he fought with Pinkertons and scabs from other ethnic groups. When Spencer came to see this marvelous disciple, he nevertheless concluded that "six months in Pittsburgh would be justification for suicide."

This documentary is primarily, perhaps inevitably, top down in its approach. We learn of Carnegie's business methods (spread a rumor that a rival mill is making defective steel, then buy them out), his corporate maneuvering (relying on the coal tycoon Henry Clay Frick to manage his flagship factory at Homestead), and his union-busting (use inter-ethnic rivalry first, then crush all opposition). We also learn of his eventual break with Frick, who Carnegie believed had handled the Homestead strike poorly, allowing the Pinkertons to face off against armed workers.

At the end of his life, Carnegie continued to give away the money he had squeezed out of every industry and factory he controlled by endowing numerous libraries that bear his name to this day (and my pension plan, TIAA-CREF). He also tried to make up with Frick, but Frick would have none of it, no doubt agreeing with an Ohio congressman who called Carnegie "the arch sneak of his age."

See also: *The River Ran Red.*
Availability: Selected collections; PBS.

Further reading

Cohen, Richard. "Reflections on a 19th-Century Downsizer." *Washington Post,* 30 January 1997, A19. Compares Carnegie's Homestead policies with those of contemporary industry downsizers.

Wolff, Leon. *Lockout: A Study of Violence, Unionism, and the Carnegie Steel Empire.* New York: Harper & Row, 1965. A narrative of the Homestead strike.

Web site:
⟨www.pbs.org/wgbh/amex/carnegie⟩ Official site; includes a transcript of the film, a time line, teacher's guide, bibliography. and other helpful information.

Note: Also known as *Andrew Carnegie.*

Riding the Rails

"I rode those freight cars/Just a little too long"—Guitar Whitey

1997, 72 mins.
Directors: Michael Uys and Lexy Lovell
Traditional documentary
PRINCIPAL FIGURES
Teenagers Who Rode the Rails: C. R. "Tiny" Boland, Charley Bull, René Champion, Peggy De Hart, John Fawcett, Clarence Lee, Jim Mitchell, Arvel "Sunshine" Pearson, James San Jule, and Bob "Guitar Whitey" Symmonds

The filmmakers created this film in part from research into the historical archives, films, and popular music of the Depression, but their biggest payoff came from the more than 3,000 letters they received from people who told them stories of their youth. They were among the 250,000 youngsters who left home voluntarily when their fathers were thrown out of work or were forced out when the family could no longer afford to keep them or ran away for reasons of their own—to escape parental abuse, for example.

Whatever the reason, they made up an army of young people on the move, drifting from town to town, sometimes looking for work but mostly just trying to survive by begging or stealing. Their status became so obvious that Warner Brothers sensationalized their story in the film *Wild Boys of the Road*, and in the process made the prospect of hitting the rails attractive to still more moviegoing teens.

The film includes archival footage of officials interviewing the young people, who offer their various reasons for leaving home. One was frustrated because his girlfriend chose a guy who had a steady job; another just went out looking for "adventure."

One of the interviewees for the film, the African American Clarence Lee, told tales of great hardship, but on one occasion he was saved from a lynching when train officials put him off in advance of vigilantes hunting for an alleged rapist. Another youth, "Guitar

Whitey" Symmonds, never got over the thrill of riding the rails and continued to do so through his 70s.

Some of the excitement, verve, and even homesickness comes through on the sound track as well, with country and folk songs from Jimmie Rodgers and Woody Guthrie, among others, and even the "Hoboes' Lullaby" sung by Guitar Whitey:

Go to sleep, you weary hoboes,
Let the towns drift slowly by.
Can't you hear the steel wheels humming?
That's a hoboes' lullaby.

See also: *Wild Boys of the Road*.
Availability: Selected collections; PBS.

Further reading

Minehan, Thomas. *Boy and Girl Tramps of America*. New York: Farrar & Rinehart, 1934. In disguise, Minehan sought out and interviewed teenagers riding the rails.

O'Connell, Kathy. "Riding Out the Depression." *Hartford Courant*, 11 December 1997. Compares the documentary favorably with the Warner Brothers Depression feature *Wild Boys of the Road*.

Uys, Lincoln. *Riding the Rails: Teenagers on the Move during the Great Depression*. New York: TV Books, 1999. Companion book to the film.

Web site:

⟨www.pbs.org/wgbh/amex/rails⟩ Official site for the film, with transcript, interviews, Depression time line, railroad map, "Tales from the Rails," bibliography, and other features.

Riffraff

Not if they have steady jobs . . .

1935, 89 mins., B&W
Director: J. Walter Ruben
Screenplay: Frances Marion, H. W. Haneman, and Anita Loos
CAST
Dutch = Spencer Tracy
Hattie = Jean Harlow
Lil = Una Merkel
Jimmy = Mickey Rooney
Nick = Joseph Calleia
Flytrap = Victor Kilian
Brains = J. Farrell MacDonald
Pops = Roger Imhoff

Despite the "riffraff" tag, almost everyone in this film has a job, either in the fishing industry or in a diner on the wharves. They are more like raffish characters in a Disneyland of Labor than real riffraff. The plot is melodramatic and complicated, but Dutch is a cocksure natural leader of the fishermen, who—despite extensive mentoring by the union leader called Brains—keeps to himself and his girlfriends most of the time. Since one of his girlfriends is played by Jean Harlow, none of his friends and few of his viewers are surprised by this decision.

When agitators of some kind—it's never clear who they are, but we suspect they're Reds—try to push the men into a wildcat strike against the wishes of the union leadership, Dutch comes through and keeps things on an even keel. The somewhat farcical handling of these events turns decidedly nasty and the film becomes less about unions on the wharf than about how working people during the Depression could easily become riffraff or even criminals.

Although the focus shifts away from the union, the film reminds us that with labor unrest and economic instability a part of so many people's lives in the mid-1930s, we should not be surprised that Hollywood, especially Warner Brothers, made more and more of these pictures about tough guys and gals.

See also: *Fury; Harry Bridges; They Drive by Night*.
Availability: Selected collections.

Further reading

Nugent, Frank. "Riffraff." *New York Times*, 13 January 1936, 14. The reviewer finds Harlow's presence so unlikely in a labor film that he can't make any sense of what he has seen.

Roffman, Peter, and Jim Purdy. "The Worker and Hollywood." *Cineaste* 9, no. 1 (1978): 8–13. Discusses the film in the context of other Depression "social problem" films and suggests the San Francisco General Strike of 1934 as a factor in the film's portrayal of the longshoremen.

Riff-Raff

Homeless workers building homes for other people

1991, 96 mins., UK, R
Director: Ken Loach
Screenplay: Bill Jesse
CAST
Stevie = Robert Carlyle
Susan = Emer McCourt
Shem = Jimmy Coleman
Mo = George Moss
Larry = Ricky Tomlinson
Kevin = David Finch

The riffraff represent the lowest class in the scheme developed by the Victorian sociologist Charles Booth, consisting of "occasional laborers, street sellers, loafers, criminals, and semi-criminals"; Marx called this class the "lumpenproletariat." (See *Strike*.) During the Depression the term became popular in the United States for all sorts of people, from homeless migrants to street-wise laborers.

In this tragicomic film, the riffraff are homeless people hired to reconstruct a place that, of course, they could never afford to live in. But since they cannot afford to live *any-where*, they efficiently and knowingly hook up an abandoned apartment as a squat for one of their number. They also strike out at the rich by burning down the very site they've been working on, because, Loach said in 1994, "they've got nothing to lose and it's a gut response" (quoted in Smith).

Loach wanted to confront the effects of "the early Eighties and Thatcherism" in England, but he didn't want to create "a political lecture." His screenwriter had been working on a building site in Glasgow and their resultant conversations about the life and liveliness of the building crews helped to create the "warmth and humor" of the film.

Aside from the dirty hard work and constant bickering over job assignments and money flimflams, the site is dominated by rats. When asked if the rats were metaphorical, Loach agreed, and said he hoped the image wasn't too "pretentious." In fact, the screenwriter had given up his job at a Glasgow building site because the rats had been eating his sandwiches.

When there is some on-the-job agitation about safety, Larry (played by a former plasterer and union activist) threatens to call in an organizer from the Union of Construction and Technical Trades. He is fired immediately.

Loach's film follows a minor but distinctive tradition of contemporary British films about construction sites, squatters, and related political matters: Jerzy Skomolinski's *Moonlighting*, for example, about Polish workers trapped in London when martial law is imposed back home, and a gradually increasing flood of films satirizing Thatcherism in general, such as Mike Leigh's *High Hopes*. In an interview in 1994, Loach emphasized that his view of history was that it was "a class struggle." When people see his films, however, he wants them to think that the situations they see need to be changed.

See also: *Cathy Come Home; High Hopes.*
Availability: Selected collections.

Further reading

Canby, Vincent. "A Blue-Collar Comedy in English, Subtitled." *New York Times*, 12 February 1993, C10. A positive review and background story about the actors and screenwriter.

Malcolm, Derek. "Straight Out of Britain, Tales of Working-Class Life." *New York Times*, 31 January 1993, II.20. A survey of the director's career.

Smith, Gavin. "Sympathetic Images." *Film Comment*, March–April 1994, 58–67. Interview with Loach.

Rising Son

Falling father

1990, 92 mins., TVM, M
Director: John David Coles
Screenplay: Bill Phillips
CAST
Gus Robins = Brian Dennehy
Martha Robins = Piper Laurie

Charley Robins = Matt Damon
Des Robins = Tate Donovan
Carol = Emily Langstreth
Meg Bradley = Jane Adams
Ed = Ving Rhames

Filmed at the Rayloc factory in Georgia, *Rising Son* is a drama of a long-term factory worker and then general production supervisor whose company collapses partly because of Japanese competition in the auto industry and partly because of the leveraged-buyout fever of the Reagan years. The fictional Jillis Company in Travers, Pennsylvania, has been manufacturing starter motors for years, but the family-run company has been sold to a conglomerate whose owners don't care whether its subsidiaries manufacture motors or widgets.

Gus, played as a feisty and domineering family man by the ubiquitous Brian Dennehy (who must average five films a year), is a fictional cousin to Willy Loman in *Death of a Salesman*. Like Loman, Gus has a lot of stories about his brilliant and successful sons, who turn out to be not successful and mighty miserable. And like Loman, Gus tries being a salesman and is suicidal. The title refers to the rebelliousness of Gus's second son and is also a pun on the rising sun, the symbol of Japan.

Although the Japanese material is not always central to the plot, it forms nonetheless an intriguing counterpoint to Gus's life. During a work stoppage, Gus makes a speech to his workers about Americans who—compared with the Japanese—have lost their work ethic. Later he tells his son about a World War II incident in which he interfered when a Japanese soldier tried to commit "honorable" suicide. Both speeches, one public and one private, point to the Japanese as Gus's personal demons. At first he is hostile to the idea of relocating at a new Japanese-American factory, even when his union man from the old plant proudly demonstrates the efficiency of its robots.

TV producers often waste five or six hours of screen time on movies about Long Island tabloid scandals. *Rising Son* is a relatively short film that would have benefited from being longer. The integration of workers and management in such small-town activities as the volunteer fire department is a touch that many films ignore and that we could have had more of. Such details bring to life the complexity of a company town.

See also: *Human Resources*.
Availability: Easy.

Further reading

Miller, Arthur. *Death of a Salesman*. 1949. Numerous editions available. The tragedy Gus manages to avoid.
O'Connor, John J. "Pride in His Sons and His Country." *New York Times*, 23 July 1990, 16. A very positive review.

Note: This film is not to be confused with *Rising Sun*, made from Michael Crichton's novel about a U.S.-Japanese economic war.

The River Ran Red

Epic union-busting

1993, 58 mins.
Directors: Steffi Domike and Nicole Fauteux
Traditional documentary
PRINCIPAL FIGURES
Blair Brown, narrator
Andrew Carnegie, owner, Homestead Steel
Henry Clay Frick, manager, Homestead Steel
Hugh O'Donnell, Amalgamated Association of Iron and Steel Workers
"Honest" John McLuckie, mayor of Homestead
Alexander Berkman, anarchist

The great Homestead strike of 1892 was a landmark in the capitalists' struggle against organized labor. In June 1892 the Carnegie works in Homestead, Pennsylvania, locked out its workers, who were represented then by the Amalgamated Association of Iron and

Steel Workers. Andrew Carnegie, reputed to be the "richest man in the world," allowed Henry Clay Frick a free hand in breaking the union. Frick erected a ten-foot fence around the plant and brought in strikebreakers protected by 300 armed Pinkerton guards. The battle between the Pinkertons and the workers resulted in at least ten deaths (seven were workers), and the union could not regroup.

The film emphasizes that it would be forty-four years before the union, as a result of the Steel Workers Organizing Committee of the CIO, returned to the steel industry.

The film was funded in part by the United Steelworkers of America, the Service Employees International Union, and members of numerous local unions. This is another in a series of films that Steffi Domike has directed on the steel industry: *Women of Steel*, in part the story of her own experience when she and her co-workers were laid off from their jobs at the Clairton Works of U.S. Steel, and *Out of This Furnace*, the story of an immigrant family in Braddock (not included in this guide).

See also: *Women of Steel*.
Availability: Selected collections; University of Pittsburgh Press.

Further reading

Demarest, David P., Jr., and Fannia Weingartner, eds. *The River Ran Red: Homestead 1892*. Pittsburgh: University of Pittsburgh Press, 1992. An outstanding collection of verbal and visual material from the strike era as well as analytical commentary by writers today; an essential text for understanding the Homestead events.
Krause, Paul. *The Battle for Homestead, 1880–1892: Politics, Culture, and Steel*. Pittsburgh: University of Pittsburgh Press, 1992. Definitive study of the factory, the town, and the lockout/strike.
"The River Ran Red." *Labor Studies Journal*, Summer 1994, 46–47. Very positive review: "The visuals benefit from the survival of many of the original locations, shots of which are superbly edited into a seamless flow with the archival photos."
Wolff, Leon. *Lockout: A Study of Violence, Unionism, and the Carnegie Steel Empire*. New York: Harper & Row, 1965. A narrative of the Homestead Strike.

~

Rocco and His Brothers

Rocco alla Milanese

1959, 180 mins. (1991 re-release), B&W, Italian, with English subtitles
Director: Luchino Visconti
Screenplay: Luchino Visconti, Suso Cecchi d'Amico, Pasquale Festa Campanile, Massimo Franciosa, and Enrico Medioli, partly based on Giovanni Testori's novel *I segreti di Milano: Il ponte della Ghisolfa*
CAST
Rocco = Alain Delon
Simone = Renato Salvatori
Vincenzo = Spiros Focas
Ciro = Max Cartier
Luca = Rocco Vidolazzi
Rosaria = Katina Paxinou
Nadia = Annie Girardot
Ginetta = Claudia Cardinale
Cecchi = Paola Stoppa
Luisa = Suzy Delair
Ciro's Fiancée = Alessandra Panaro

Luchino Visconti's range as a director has been impressive, from the neorealist *La terra trema* to the historical costume drama *The Leopard* and such intricate art-house dramas as *The Damned* and *Death in Venice*. With *Rocco and His Brothers* he has created the tragic story of the Parondis, a southern Italian family who have moved to Milan, thereby tackling one of the defining problems of contemporary Italian society: the relationship of the peasant South and the industrialized North.

Sam Rohdie writes that the film was conceived as a sequel to *La terra trema*. In the latter, one of the Silician brothers somewhat mysteriously departs for the "North" (presumably Naples), having been recruited, presumably, for an industrial job. In *Rocco and His Brothers* everyone in the South has headed north, driven by economic hardship to find a job in the expanding economy that has prospered while the South remains backward. Rocco and his brothers have made it to Milan, but the migration will soon destroy their family.

The Parondi family have joined almost nine million of their regional brothers and sisters who have headed north from 1955 to 1971. Rocco and his brother Simone are both boxers, another brother is working at the Alfa-Romeo factory, and still another has married a local woman. Rocco and Simone are at odds because they are both in love with Nadia, a prostitute. Their competition is played out in the end with a vicious and depressing intensity.

The Marxist Antonio Gramsci's essay "The Southern Question" details the economic differences between the southern and northern regions of Italy, stressing the industrial/rural differences and advocating an alliance between northern workers and southern peasants. *Rocco and His Brothers* plays out these tensions within one family, but the result is its tragic self-destruction.

See also: *The Roof; La terra trema.*
Availability: Easy; DVD.

Further reading

Crowther, Bosley. "Rocco and His Brothers." *New York Times,* 28 June 1961, 40. Rave review, comparing the film to both *The Grapes of Wrath* and Greek tragedy because of its ability to deliver scenes of "emotional fullness and revelation."

Lopate, Philip. "A Master Who Confounded the Categories." *New York Times*, 16 November 1997, II.19, 48. A review of Visconti's career, which concludes that *Rocco* was "as close as I could imagine to a novel on film."

Nowell-Smith, Geoffrey. *Visconti.* Garden City, N.Y.: Doubleday, 1968. The first study of Visconti in English; still good on *Rocco and His Brothers.*

Rohdie, Sam. *Rocco and His Brothers.* London: British Film Institute, 1993. A detailed analysis of the film, with emphasis on Visconti's career, the operatic aspects of his style, and the political context of the film, especially Gramsci's essay "The Southern Question."

Roger & Me

Roger Smith can run, but he can't hide

1989, 87 mins., R
Director: Michael Moore
Postmodern documentary
PRINCIPAL FIGURES
Michael Moore, director
Roger Smith, chairman, General Motors
Fred Ross, deputy sheriff in charge of evictions
Rhoda Britton, the bunny lady
Pat Boone, entertainer
Kay Lani Rae Rafko, Miss Michigan (later Miss America)
Bob Eubanks, game show host
Ben Hamper, auto worker and author

Michael Moore's 1989 documentary about the closing of auto plants in Flint was a first for a lot of reasons. It was one of the first documentaries with a labor focus to gain an even wider national audience than Barbara Kopple's Academy Award–winning *Harlan County, U.S.A.* It was the first comic documentary in which the filmmaker, like Woody Allen, basically played himself like a bumbling fool. It was also the first film to be denounced by both General Motors and the United Auto Workers (UAW) for being unfair to them: both organizations mailed out the same critical film review by Pauline Kael, the *New Yorker's* film critic, to counter the film's success. The UAW did not like the way the film portrayed its friendly relationship with management or its inability to celebrate the Great Flint Sit-Down Strike.

The film also aroused forty-five filmmakers to petition the Academy Award nominating committee when the film was denied a nomination, possibly because of a conflict of interest with an official on the committee, who was a distributor for other nominated documentaries.

Why all this fuss? Roger Smith is a perfect comic villain: he's extremely powerful and unattractive, and represents a class of individuals so out of touch with the common person that he cries out for embarrassment. Two of Moore's other subjects—Deputy Sheriff Fred Ross and the bunny lady, Rhoda Britton—are survivors. And, finally, we have Moore himself, a bumbling giant who just wants to talk to Roger Smith. So what's the big deal?

There are no heroes in this story besides Moore, who grins endlessly into his own camera lens. Deputy Fred is an ex-autoworker, but he makes his living by evicting people who don't keep up on their apartment or house payments. The bunny lady attracted Moore's attention because of the sign outside her house: "Rabbits—Pets or Meat." Her breezy self-confidence as she killed and skinned a rabbit in front of Moore's cameras clearly reflected still another kind of survival skill.

Transforming the traditional documentary mix of archival footage, media footage, stills, interviews, and clips from feature films, Moore followed the successful strategy of *The Atomic Café* (1982), a satiric documentary about the obsession with The Bomb in the 1950s. He improved on this strategy of ironic juxtaposition of materials by using as a unifying thread his comic pursuit of Roger Smith. Moore tries to crash the GM boardroom or one of Smith's exclusive clubs, while mocking both the stalwarts of American popular culture (Miss Michigan) and its outsiders (Fred and Rhoda).

Moore's 1992 short follow-up film, *Pets or Meat: The Return to Flint* (released in a trilogy of films, *Two Mikes Don't Make a Wright*), updates the earlier film. Fred Ross has branched out into auto repossessions and auction sales, Rhoda is raising other animals for meat (but saves a bunny for a snake), and Roger Smith's pension is in such danger that Moore thinks about sending him some money.

Roger & Me may come close to the postmodern documentaries of Errol Morris (*The Thin Blue Line*) and Diane Keaton (*Heaven*), but its focus on the auto industry and corporate negligence, not to mention the presence of the filmmaker himself, makes it a must-see.

See also: *The Awful Truth; The Big One; TV Nation.*
Availability: Easy.

Further reading

Bernstein, Richard. "'Roger and Me': Documentary? Satire? Or Both?" *New York Times,* 1 February 1990, B20. A review of the film's controversy.

Cohan, Carley, and Gary Crowdus. "Reflections on 'Roger & Me,' Michael Moore, and His Critics." *Cineaste* 17, no. 4 (1990): 25–30. Another review of the controversy about the film.

Hamper, Ben. *Rivethead*. New York: Warner, 1991. The autobiography of a Flint auto worker and bit-part player in the film.

Harkness, John. "Roger & Me." *Sight and Sound*, Spring 1990, 130–31. A British reviewer argues that Warner Brothers ("part of the largest entertainment conglomerate in the world") released the film because its critique of capitalism is ultimately "harmless."

Jacobson, H. "Michael & Me." *Film Comment*, November–December 1989, 16–26. An interview with Moore that challenges the chronology and facts presented in the film.

Kael, Pauline. "Current Cinema." *New Yorker*, 8 January 1990, 91–92. The negative review circulated by GM and the UAW; the film "uses its leftism as a superior attitude. Members of the audience can laugh at ordinary working people and still feel they're taking a politically correct position."

Marchese, John. "American Scene." *Esquire*, January 1993, 44–47. The continuing misadventures of filmmaker Moore on his first film project (the feature *Canadian Bacon*) after *Roger & Me*.

Moore, Michael. "A Message from Michael Moore." At ⟨www.michaelmoore.com⟩, 1 December 1999. For the first time, Moore's own version of the events that almost doomed *Roger & Me*: he insulted Pauline Kael, the most influential film critic of her day, and she led the movement, Moore argues, to pan the film and cost him an Academy Award nomination.

The Roof

Squatting in the "open city"

1956, 91 mins., B&W, Italy, Italian, with
English subtitles
Director: Vittorio de Sica
Screenplay: Cesare Zavattini
CAST
Natale = Giorgio Listuzzi
Luisa = Gabriella Pallotta
Cesare = Gastone Renzelli

Street life has always been important for
Italian neorealist films. *Shoeshine* and *Open
City*, for example, are about workers and the
dispossessed surviving the postwar period in
Italy literally on the streets. *The Bicycle Thief*
is, after all, about a man who was going to be
a poster hanger! *The Roof* follows a recently
married young couple, Natale and Luisa,
who, because of the terrible housing shortage in Rome, begin housekeeping in their
relatives' apartments. Of course that doesn't
work out, and since Natale and his friends
are construction workers, they decide to take
advantage of a remarkable Roman law that
permits squatting in an abandoned or new
structure if a roof is in place by sundown.

In keeping with the gritty aesthetic of
neorealism, the couple's homestead ends up
being next to a railroad line that separates an
industrial complex from a new high-rise
housing project (which obviously doesn't
have room for them). Natale's family and
friends build frantically all day and finish,
they think, just before the *polizia* visit. One
of the policemen peers in at the young couple
and at first seems threatening as he notices
that they are one plank shy of a completed

The squatters' house is almost finished in *The Roof*. Courtesy British Film Institute Stills, Posters,
and Designs.

roof. But he relents and only fines them; their home is safe in the Ditch of St. Agnes, their new address.

De Sica pulls back and surely undercuts some of their joy as we see this very small shack with a few others amidst a stark landscape of factories and high-rise buildings.

See also: *The Bicycle Thief*.
Availability: Selected collections.

Further reading

Hughes, Robert, ed. *Film Book 1*. New York: Grove Press, 1959. Includes an essay by the screenwriter Cesare Zavattini on the genesis of the ideas behind *The Roof*.

Sitney, P. Adams. *Vital Crises in Italian Cinema: Iconography, Stylistics, Politics*. Austin: University of Texas Press, 1995. Extensive discussion of neorealism, but *The Roof* does not take place "on a roof in Rome."

"Il Tetto." *Variety*, 13 February 1957. Applauds the neorealist elements and its art-house appeal.

∽
Rough Side of the Mountain

Company towns for sale

1997, 57 mins.
Director: Anne Lewis
Traditional documentary
PRINCIPAL FIGURES
Maxine and M. H. Waller, Catherine Grubb, and other residents of Ivanhoe, Virginia
Norma Jean and Dallas "Duck" Powers, Clady Johnson, and other residents of Trammel, Virginia
Helen Lewis, author and community educator

The usual story of a rural community tied to a single industry or mining company tells of company shutdown or closure, unemployment, local economic collapse, and the creation of a virtual ghost town or a population steeped in welfare and poverty. Anne Lewis decided to make a film about two company towns whose residents decided to create an economic alternative. Trammel and Ivanhoe are company towns in southwestern Virginia.

Trammel's "privately owned" town of fifty homes, the company store, and even its post office all went up for auction in 1986. Ivanhoe, faced with the loss of its two major employers, a zinc mine and a carbide factory, hit rock bottom in the early 1980s when its school and virtually every store closed as well.

Legends and folkways are sprinkled through this oral history of the two towns. Local residents use them to explain what has happened to make the two communities come very close to being ghost towns. Maxine Waller of Ivanhoe tells of a preacher who long ago cursed her town for its loose living and predicted it would fall into hell. Sure enough, it (almost) did when the mines collapsed in 1985. Ivanhoe at the turn of the century had a sizable Afrilachian population; after a lynching, the young men began to leave the town forever. Trammel was owned by a rich family whose matriarch would poke around the yards of "her" houses to make sure the residents kept them neat, while on payday the men were told there wasn't enough cash on hand to pay them fully but they'd be taken care of later.

The film is as much about attempts at a comeback as it is about past injustices. Ivanhoe goes after new business as part of the Virginia Southwest Promise enterprise zone, promoting itself as part of a "right-to-work state." Trammel residents organize a homeowners' association and bid successfully for their own homes when the town goes on the auction block. Lewis has captured some of the essential truths of Appalachian towns that are too often invisible from the interstate.

See also: *Evelyn Williams; Fast Food Women*.
Availability: Selected collections; Appalshop.

Further reading

Hinsdale, Mary Ann, Helen M. Lewis, and S. Maxine Waller. *It Comes from the People: Community Development and Local Theology*. Philadelphia: Temple University Press, 1995. Includes Lewis's study of the Ivanhoe Civic League.

Roving Pickets

Breaking contracts

1991, 28 mins.
Director: Anne Lewis
Traditional documentary

This film will help to explain why Eastern Kentucky coal has always been a national issue despite its intensely regional character: one might even say that the difference between Eastern Kentucky and Kentucky is no less important than the difference between West Virginia and Virginia. Certainly in the 1930s the militant union activities and coal operators' thuggery made "Bloody Harlan" a headline throughout a nation that barely knew what Eastern Kentucky was really like. In any case, *Roving Pickets* documents another moment when the regional battles between the coal companies and the miners moved onto the national agenda and helped influence President Johnson's decision to declare a "war on poverty."

Anne Lewis, one of the award-winning documentary filmmakers from Appalshop, surveys the 1950s, when coal operators began breaking their union contracts to save money. Such a decision, of course, was disastrous for a region dependent on coal mining, because of the obvious ripple effect: reduced wages and unemployment also broke up families, many of whom were divided, as they were in the war years when individuals migrated to the "Little Appalachias" of Cincinnati, Chicago, and Detroit in search of work. The final blow came with the cancellation of the United Mine Workers of America's unemployment and health care benefits in 1961–62.

See also: *Justice in the Coalfields*.
Availability: Selected collections; Appalshop.

Further reading

Laslett, John H. M., ed. *The United Mine Workers of America*. University Park: Pennsylvania State University Press, 1996. Very helpful collection of essays.

Sacco and Vanzetti

"The never-ending wrong"—Katherine Anne Porter

1971, 120 mins., Italy/France, dubbed in English, PG
Director: Giuliano Montaldo
Screenplay: Fabrizio Onofri, Giuliano Montaldo, and Mino Roli
CAST
Nicola Sacco = Riccardo Cucciolla
Bartolomeo Vanzetti = Gian Maria Volonté
Katzman = Cyril Cusack
Fred Moore = Milo O'Shea
William Thompson = William Prince
Judge Thayer = Geoffrey Keen
Rosa Sacco = Rosanna Fratello
Newspaperman = Claude Mann

The prosecution and execution of two anarchists for murder in Massachusetts in the 1920s is one of those cases that will not go away: the fiction writer Katherine Anne Porter, for example, who demonstrated for their reprieve in Boston in 1927, called it a "never-ending wrong." Supreme Court Justice Felix Frankfurter, while a professor of law at Harvard, joined the chorus of supporters who demonstrated for their release. Francis Russell wrote two books asserting Sacco's guilt and Vanzetti's probable complicity and his own growing disenchantment with the men's supporters, who he believed were befuddled and blind. And in between there were at least a dozen other books about the case and five volumes of court transcripts and associated legal documents.

Is it likely, then, that a film produced in the wake of the strenuous 1960s by a production company, mostly Italian, whose country had recently been racked by terrorist bombs and show trials could approach some even-handedness or a degree of neutrality in retelling the story? And what of the issue of neutrality in the first place? A film about the Rosenberg spy case, the Lindbergh kidnapping, the assassination of Malcolm X—the list could go on—such a film simply cannot be neutral. In fact, the filmmakers have really only three choices when they engage a polit-ically charged topic of the past: make it from the point of view of what contemporaries actually knew (i.e., the trial transcript and the newspapers), make it from the perspective of newly discovered evidence or facts, or just make up an interesting and cinematically consistent version of the story.

The story of Sacco and Vanzetti really begins with the notorious post–World War I Palmer Raids: at the instigation of John Palmer, attorney general of the United States, local and federal police of various stripes raided radical and immigrant groups all over the country. In part a fearful reaction to the Bolshevik Revolution, in part a racist reaction to immigrants of all kinds, and in part an obsession with the Wobblies (see *The Wobblies*), these raids netted numerous radical and innocent people, many of whom were deported or jailed.

Sacco and Vanzetti were anarchists, and that was enough to get them in big trouble when anarchists and bomb-throwing terror-ists were synonymous in law enforcement circles as well as the yellow press. Their anarchism was in the syndicalist tradition common to many groups in Spain and Italy as well as in immigrant clubs in the United States. It involved the local control of the fields and factories by unions (*syndicale* in Italian), not through a central Bolshevik-like party or other socialist (electoral) efforts. But the authorities relied on the American public not to see that anarchism was a *polit-ical* position.

Sacco and Vanzetti were arrested for a holdup and murder of payroll couriers in South Braintree, Massachusetts. They were supposed to be part of a gang of five who pulled off the job. They themselves were arrested on a streetcar after an apparently strange visit to a friend's boardinghouse, where the landlord called the police. Sacco and Vanzetti were carrying guns, mainly, they argued, because these were dangerous times

The two anarchists outside the courtroom in *Sacco and Vanzetti.*

and recently one of their comrades had been thrown from the window of a police station in New York City.

Every alibi they presented then and later about being elsewhere on the day of the robbery-murder, April 15, simply "proved" to the investigators and eventually the prosecutor that they were guilty. Of course Italians would say they saw Sacco and Vanzetti elsewhere on April 15: they were all Italians, weren't they?!

The film is framed by "The Ballad of Sacco and Vanzetti," written by Ennio Morricone and Joan Baez and performed by the latter. The film recreates numerous moments in the campaign to stay the execution of the two men, but nowhere but in this film (I think) will one see placards crying out for justice for "Bart and Nick," since the men became legends by their last names. This detail is a little off, like the impossible courtroom sequences in which the defense attorney and the prosecutor are simultaneously yelling at each other, haranguing both judge and jury and questioning witnesses, a scene really more reminiscent of the Italian parliament than of an American courtroom.

If this really was (at one time) the most controversial trial in American history, a film will hardly do justice to its complexities. Director Giuliano Montaldo's view is simple and straightforward, an Italian's view of an Italian-American tragedy. For him the law is a political institution likely to be bent by cultural and historical contexts. Should we, as we view this film these many years later, be so surprised?

See also: *Joe Hill.*
Availability: Selected collections; DVD.

Further reading

Anreus, Alejandro, ed. *Ben Shahn and the Passion of Sacco and Vanzetti.* Jersey City, N.J.: Jersey City Museum, 2001. This exhibition catalog reprints Shahn's powerful woodcuts of the case done in 1931–32 with additional commentary by the artist.

Avrich, Paul. *Sacco and Vanzetti: The Anarchist Background.* Princeton: Princeton University Pres, 1991. Documents the "Galleanist" or individual revolutionary violence perspective of Sacco and Vanzetti.

Bondanella, Peter. *Italian Cinema from Neorealism to the Present.* 3d ed. New York: Continuum, 2001. Brief discussion of the film, emphasizing parallels between the Red Scare in the United States and problems in the contemporary Italian judicial system.

Canby, Vincent. "Film: A Moving 'Sacco and Vanzetti.'" *New York Times*, 7 October 1971, 58. The reviewer finds the film a weak representation of an important issue—demonstrating the innocence of the two men; it is clear that it is Joan Baez's sound-track ballad that irritates him the most.

Dickinson, Alice. *The Sacco-Vanzetti Case 1920–27.* New York: Franklin Watts, 1972. An admirably clear and thorough book, with excellent diagrams, encouraging young readers to develop their own ideas about the case.

Ehrmann, Herbert B. *The Case That Will Not Die: Commonwealth vs. Sacco and Vanzetti.* Boston: Little, Brown, 1969. Offers a detailed argument that the robbery and murder in Braintree were the work of the Morelli gang.

Fast, Howard. *The Passion of Sacco and Vanzetti.* London: Bodley Head, 1954. A quirky but fascinating book on the case by a radical novelist (*Freedom Road, Spartacus*) and lefty; reads like a view from the inside of Sacco and Vanzetti's defense movement (e.g., as if from Felix Frankfurter's personal point of view).

Frankfurter, Felix. *The Case of Sacco and Vanzetti.* 1927. Boston: Little, Brown, 1955. This Harvard law professor and future Supreme Court justice's "critical analysis for lawyers and laymen," outlining the likelihood of the men's innocence and attacking Judge Thayer's prejudicial courtroom, was a sensation when first published in the *Atlantic Monthly* five months before their execution.

Porter, Katherine Anne. *The Never-Ending Wrong.* Boston: Little, Brown, 1977. Less a defense of Sacco and Vanzetti's innocence than a gifted writer's reminiscence of her days on the picket line in 1927 to protest their impending execution and her arrest.

Porton, Richard. *Film and the Anarchist Imagination.* London: Verso, 1999. The film "suffers from an ill-conceived effort to find parallels between the frenzied anti-radicalism . . . in the 1920s and analogous examples of contemporary Italian malfeasance" (such as the "suicide" of Giuseppe

Pinelli, an anarchist in the custody of Italian police in 1969).

Russell, Francis. *Sacco & Vanzetti: The Case Resolved*. New York: Harper & Row, 1986. Relies on reminiscences of aged Italians to renew his conclusion that Sacco was certainly guilty of murder and Vanzetti probably a conspirator; reinforces his earlier *Tragedy in Dedham* (New York: McGraw-Hill, 1971).

"Sacco and Vanzetti." *Variety*, 31 March 1971. Loves the Baez song, hates the repetitive scenes and stock footage of demos, and applauds the actors.

The Sacco-Vanzetti Case. New York: Henry Holt, 1929. 6 vols. The first two volumes contain the "stenographic record" of the trial, while volumes 3 through 5 contain the appeals, the report of the advisory committee (headed by President Lowell of Harvard) on the fairness of the trial, the governor's decision not to pardon the men, and the separate "Bridgewater conviction" of Vanzetti.

Sharrett, Christopher. "Sacco and Vanzetti." *Cineaste*, March 2001, 51–52. Reviews the film generally and the reissue in DVD.

Young, William, and David E. Kaiser. *Postmortem: New Evidence in the Case of Sacco and Vanzetti*. Amherst: University of Massachusetts Press, 1985. A short but thorough review, concluding that Sacco and Vanzetti, "two innocent men, most probably were framed for a murder they did not commit."

Note: The director Sidney Lumet did a two-hour *Sacco and Vanzetti Story* (never released on videocassette) for CBS-TV in June 1960, from a Reginald Rose script. *Variety* gave it mixed reviews (13 and 15 June 1960) and duly noted that many Bostonians wanted it banned there because it cast New England justice in a bad light (8 June 1960). Unfortunately, Lumet never made it into a theatrical release, as he did so successfully three years before with Reginald Rose's earlier TV drama *Twelve Angry Men*: the result might have been fascinating. Of additional interest (more for the psychology of a falsely accused immigrant than for the politics) is the film *Winterset*, directed by Alfred Santell in 1936 from Maxwell Anderson's play of the same title.

Salesman

Selling tickets to heaven

1969, 90 mins., B&W
Directors: David and Albert Maysles
Cinema verité documentary
PRINCIPAL FIGURES
Paul Brennan, the Badger
Charles McDevit, the Gipper
James Baker, the Rabbit
Raymond Martos, the Bull
Ken Turner, sales manager, Mid-American Bible Company

The disturbing focus of this film is four high-pressure salesmen working for the Mid-American Bible Company, selling an illustrated Catholic Bible to poor and working-class Catholics. The film traces their successes and failures, but at what a price! Fifty dollars for a red or white simulated-leather-covered Bible, illustrated with the "Old Masters," is clearly a lot of money for the people these men badger and bully into buying books "that no Catholic home should be without." Because most of the salesmen are so pathetic, it is difficult for us to decide whether we want them to make their sales or not. Do we want them to earn their commission or do we hope that their potential customers will hold on to their $1-a-week payment?

They are a curiously compulsive lot, these salesmen. They drive expensive-looking convertibles, seem to believe that selling Bibles is being "about my Father's business," and get in a little moderately high stakes poker game after a company rally. The men get their collective feet in the door by introducing themselves with such remarks as "I'm Mr. Brennan from the Church," or telling their customers that their Bible is "recommended by Pope Paul" or "approved by the Monsignor." They ask their customers if they want to pay cash or go on the "Catholic honor plan" (weekly or monthly payments). They drop bits of inside gossip to win their customers' confidence: Do you know why, one asks, the pope's guards are Swiss? Answer: Because the Swiss are taller than the Italians.

This is, of course, an Irish-Catholic joke. Most of these salesmen tell such jokes endlessly and are constantly sucking up to their customers' ethnic pride, although Brennan the Badger at one point mistakes a Polish customer for an Italian. Their supervisor selects a territory for them to handle after sizing up the local priest to see if "there's a good church in the neighborhood," or, in a loose translation, whether the local parish will let them set up an exhibit of their wares in a church building to gain the aura of sanctity and endorsement.

Although the film has the reputation for being classic cinema verité, the Maysles brothers paid the salesmen $100 each and contributed toward the cost of the company's sales meeting. They then had to accept the company's decision not to let them use footage of the four salesmen handing out calling cards at a Sunday-morning church service. How these matters affect the unmediated action typical of cinema verité must be left to the viewer's judgment, but certainly the filmmakers' attitude came through clearly in the ad campaign, which featured a robed Jesus carrying a salesman's sample case in each hand.

The film is of a piece with Arthur Miller's *Death of a Salesman*, where falling sales and castle-building create a combination most nonsalespeople find overwhelming. But selling is what capitalism is about, and the Maysles brothers clearly consider this disturbing team of door-to-door salesmen typical of the American character. "Get it blessed" is one piece of advice their customers are given; one woman, a reluctant purchaser, says, "I just hope I get around to reading it."

See also: *Rising Son*.
Availability: Selected collections; DVD.

Further reading

Barsam, Richard Meran. *Nonfiction Film: A Critical History*. Bloomington: Indiana University Press, 1982. Sets the film in the context of contemporary documentaries.

Levin, G. Roy. *Documentary Explorations*. New York: Doubleday, 1971. Interview with the filmmakers.

Miller, Arthur. *Death of a Salesman*. 1949. Numerous editions available; the classic American play on the subject.

Rosenthal, Alan. *The New Documentary in Action*. Berkeley: University of California Press, 1971. Another interview with the filmmakers: "[The Bible Company] thought it was bad that Paul, the star of the film, wasn't a very good salesmen. But the other three were, so they were happy."

Salesman. New York: NAL, 1969. A record of all of the scenes and the dialogue, with an introduction by Harold Clurman and production notes by Howard Junker.

$\backsim$
Salt of the Earth

A film ahead of its time

1954, 94 mins., B&W
Director: Herbert Biberman
Screenplay: Michael Wilson
CAST
Ramón Quintero = Juan Chacón
Esperanza = Rosaura Revueltas
The Sheriff = Will Geer
Frank Barnes = Clinton Jencks
Ruth Barnes = Virginia Jencks
Luis Quintero = Frank Talevera

In 1950 the International Union of Mine, Mill, and Smelter Workers, known as Mine-Mill, was expelled from the CIO because its officers would not sign anti- or noncommunist pledges. The same year, its local 890 was involved in a long strike against Empire Zinc in Hanover, New Mexico, in part because Empire would not sign the contract that other companies had already agreed to. With an injunction to bar the miners from picketing, it looked like the strike was broken. But 890's Ladies' Auxiliary decided that the injunction didn't apply to them and that the scabs—and their own men, too—had better watch out. Ultimately, as the women became more public figures, many of their men were forced not only to do "women's chores" but to understand why fresh water and sanitation were union demands too.

This was a very controversial film. In the 1950s, it was the answer to the prayers of the McCarthyites and the members of the House Un-American Activities Committee, who believed that the film industry was chock-ablock with Communists secretly slipping their anti-American and pro-Soviet messages into every film. When there was finally *one* film—this one—that did have fairly active Communist participation, the anti-communist forces, including the AFL-CIO, went bonkers.

Because of the difficulties placed in front of the filmmakers, the production quality of the film is low. The Mexican star Rosaura Revueltas was deported before the shooting was over. A number of her shots, filmed in Mexico, show her against the sky with no other background.

Director Herbert Biberman, screenwriter Michael Wilson, producer Paul Jarrico, and actor Will Geer were all blacklisted by the time they made this film. Jarrico had made the World War II pro-Soviet *Song of Russia*. Wilson was an Academy Award–winning screenwriter. Biberman, who did not direct another film until *Slaves* in 1969, had already served six months in federal prison for refusing to cooperate with the House Un-American Activities Committee after he was named as a Communist by Budd Schulberg, who wrote the screenplay for *On the Waterfront*.

Made and repressed in the 1950s, it was shown sporadically. Even the *New York Times* (15 March 1954) acknowledged the "sub rosa difficulties of the film's producers in getting a theatre in which to show" the film in New York. It was revived in the 1960s by both radical and feminist groups as an alternative to conservative American trade unionism and male-dominated left/liberal politics.

The screenplay was discussed with the local union members, who made suggestions. The local union activist Juan Chacón played Ramón, and many of the union members played themselves. Three other main roles—the sheriff, the Anglo union leader, and Esperanza—went to professional actors.

During production the *Hollywood Reporter* stated that "Hollywood Reds are shooting a feature-length anti-American racial issue propaganda movie." Victor Riesel, syndicated labor columnist, asserted: "Not too far from the Los Alamos Atomic Proving Ground . . . Tovarisch [comrade] Paul Jarrico brought two carloads of Negroes into the mining town" for a scene of mob violence against them. No such scene, however, is in the film. As a result of such reports, virtually the entire network of Hollywood production and distribution systems turned against the film and it was rarely shown in the 1950s. Most prints and cassettes are acceptable, but the fine production values we associate with Hollywood feature films were simply not attainable in this shoestring production. The new DVD release, which includes *The Hollywood Ten*, a documentary about the blacklisting directed by John Berry, is, of course, an improvement.

Some viewers have been puzzled by what appears to be almost a documentary look of the film. The filmmakers followed some of the radical ideas of the Soviet filmmaker Sergei Eisenstein (and other Soviets), who believed in using nonprofessionals, real workers or peasants, wherever possible, for the purpose of authenticity. In *Salt of the Earth*, the five professional actors were supplemented by numerous people recruited locally.

See also: *Harlan County, U.S.A.*
Availability: Selected collections; DVD.

Further reading

Biberman, Herbert. *Salt of the Earth*. Boston: Beacon, 1965. The director's history of the film, with Wilson's screenplay.

Cargill, Jack. "Empire and Opposition: The 'Salt of the Earth' Strike." In *Labor in New Mexico*, ed. Robert Kern, 183–267. Albuquerque: University of New Mexico Press, 1983. Thorough survey of the issues in the original strike.

Crowther, Bosley. "Salt of the Earth." *New York Times*, 15 March 1954, 20. The "real dramatic crux of the picture is the stern and bitter conflict within the membership of the union."

Kingsolver, Barbara. *Holding the Line: Women in the Great Arizona Mine Strike of 1983*. Ithaca: ILR Press, 1989. Kingsolver, a novelist, tells the story of a contemporary mining struggle in which the women played major roles.

Lorence, James J. *The Suppression of "Salt of the Earth": How Hollywood, Big Labor, and Politicians Blacklisted a Movie in Cold War America*. Albuquerque: University of New Mexico Press, 1999. The definitive study of the film.

Miller, Tom. "'Salt of the Earth' Revisited." *Cineaste* 13 (1984): 31–36. How the main figures in the strike and film had spent the thirty years since the filming.

Rosenfelt, Deborah Silverton. *Salt of the Earth*. New York: Feminist Press, 1978. A very detailed, excellent essay on the film, plus Wilson's screenplay.

Note: Karl Francis directed *One of the Hollywood Ten* (2002), a dramatization of the making of *Salt of the Earth*.

~

Saturday Night and Sunday Morning

More Teddy boys at work

1961, 90 mins., UK
Director: Karel Reisz
Screenplay: Alan Sillitoe, from his novel of the same title

CAST
Arthur = Albert Finney
Doreen = Shirley Anne Field
Brenda = Rachel Roberts
Aunt Ada = Hylda Baker
Bert = Norman Rossington
Jack = Brian Pringle
Robbie = Robert Cawdron
Mrs. Bull = Edna Morris
Mrs. Seaton = Elsie Wagstaffe
Mr. Steaton = Frank Pettit

Alan Sillitoe's portrait of still another working-class angry young man, subset Teddy boy, was successfully realized in Karel Reisz's adaptation. In this case it is a young Nottinghamshire man, obsessed with turning out just enough pieces at his bicycle factory lathe to ensure a wage packet of 14 quid a week and making it with as many compliant women, married or otherwise, as he can charm. As a Teddy, he affects the pseudo-Edwardian garb of anarchistic '50s British working-class youth. Sometimes the anarchism is directed against the "system" but most often it is directed simply against other youths spoiling for a fight.

The politics of Sillitoe's novel is more explicit than the film's, possibly because the novel was directed primarily at a British readership while most British filmmakers have to worry about the transatlantic "muney" (as Arthur would call it). Thus there are not as many references to being a Red, voting Labour, and anarchism in the film. But Finney's Arthur captures the spirit if not the letter of the rebelliousness Sillitoe described through Arthur's voice: "Factories sweat you to death, labour exchanges talk you to death, insurance and income-tax offices milk money from your wage packets and rob you to death. . . . Ay, by God, it's a hard life if you don't weaken, if you don't stop that bastard government from grinding your face in the muck, though there ain't much you can do about it unless you start making dynamite to blow their four-eyed clocks to bits."

See also: *This Sporting Life*.
Availability: Selected collections; DVD.

Further reading

Crowther, Bosley. "Saturday Night and Sunday Morning." *New York Times*, 4 April 1961, 44. Praises the film's "documentary" style and finds Finney's Arthur "a happy, comforting relief from the devious, self-pitying rogues and weaklings we have seen in a lot of modern-day films."

Richards, Jeffrey, and Anthony Aldgate. *British Cinema and Society, 1930–1970*. Totowa, N.J.: Barnes & Noble, 1983. Includes an excellent chapter on the film's social and historical context.

~

The Scar

In the pit

1997, 95 mins., UK
Amber Films Production

Roy Cotton = Bill Speed
May Murton = Charlie Hardwick
Tony Murton = Brian Hogg
Becky Murton = Katja Roberts
Dale Murton = Darren Bell

The Scar dramatizes what is rarely seen in commercial filmmaking: what happens to the workers and their families when a major strike is lost. In the aftermath of the miners' strike of 1984–85, May Murton's family is also failing. Her husband has left, literally heading for the hills above Easington on the East Durham coast, where he lives a drunken, ramshackle life; her son is out of work and her daughter blames her for the family's breakup and hates the idea that she seems to have a new beau. Unfortunately, the new beau turns out to be the supervisor of an abomination on the land—an open pit ("open cast" in the UK) mine, which has replaced the traditional deep pit mining that has structured the community life for generations. When May's son gets a job at this site, all hell breaks loose.

Much of the action of the film is triggered at two emotional moments for May and her family—a reunion of the women activists (probably Women against Pit Closures) from the miners' support struggle and the next day's annual Miners' Gala, a festival of community bands, speeches, and a carnival-like celebration that rings hollow because the miners and their families have lost so much.

Rooted in the northeast, like other Amber productions, this film has the solid values of contemporary British social realism: a strong sense of local character, made authentic by nonprofessional as well as professional actors in the cast, location shooting, and an intensity of working-class spirit. (May's family name is, in fact, the name of one of the major pits, established in 1838 and closed in 1992.) When the camera pans the contours of the strip mine and we see located somewhere halfway between the bottom of the pit and the surface strange doorway-like openings, we suddenly realize that they are deep mine passageways, sliced opened as if they were cut pipes. What is usually so familiar in a realistic mining film suddenly becomes bizarre.

What also makes an Amber production unusual is what could only be called a decentered narrative. Sure, May Murton is the focus, but everyone else in her family and a few others occupy screen time even when May is not around. Easington was also the locale of *Billy Elliott*, about the boy who danced his way out of the pit life into the world of London ballet: even though we see a repressive police force in that film and not in *The Scar*, there is little doubt who had the bigger wound.

See also: *Seacoal*.
Availability: UK (PAL standard only); Amber Films.

Further reading

Holden, Stephen. "Air of Change, Not Despair, in New Films from Britain." *New York Times*, 16 April 2001.

Moore, Marat. *Women in the Mines*. New York: Twain, 1996. Includes an interview with a leader of Women against Pit Closures.

Pilger, John. "The Pit and the Pendulum" (30 January 1993). In *Hidden Agendas: The Films and Writings of John Pilger*, at ⟨www.pilger.carlton.com/print/48736⟩. Pilger's report on a visit to the Durham mines and a review of their history. Political and labor reportage at its best: "An insidious violence was directed at miners' families through an increasingly politicised bureaucracy" in the 1980s.

Seacoal

Shore misery

1985, 82 mins., UK
Amber Films Production
CAST (PLAYING THEMSELVES)
The Laidler Family
Critch
Val Waciak
Gordon Tait
John Cook
Stan Robinson

Amber Films, the collective of filmmakers and photographers established in 1969 to create "a film and photographic practice in relation to the working-class communities of the North East of England," created this starkly realistic view of life on a Lynemouth beach.

On one hand, the Amber filmmakers are inheritors of the long British cinematic history of social realism; on the other, they have experimented with their film form so that a film such as *Seacoal*, typical of their output, consists of (according to their own description) "straight documentary, improvised sketches, or fully dramatised reconstructions."

What hits the eye at once in *Seacoal* is the beach, which is black with pieces of coal and coal dye, lying before an industrial landscape one part power station and one part coal pit. The work at the beach is early Industrial Revolution: with the help of horse carts, locals gather waste coal washed ashore from seacoaling barges. The coal gatherers themselves often work for a local entrepreneur, and they have "dole snoops" (welfare cops) and truant officers to cope with. Into this community comes Betty and her daughter, Corinna, who take up with Ray, a local who has taken up seacoaling again after a number of years away at a "regular" job.

The collective was honored in spring 2000 with a retrospective of seven of their films at the National Film Theatre in London. Unfortunately, there has been no major overseas distribution of their films. Only *Eden Valley*, which does not have a labor focus, is available in the United States. The collective consists of Richard Grassick, Ellen Hare, Sirkka Liisa Konttinen, Murray Martin, Pat McCarthy, Lorna Powell, and Pete Roberts.

See also: *The Scar*.

Availability: UK (PAL standard only); Amber Films.

Further reading

Petley, Julian, and John Pym. "Film Cities UK." *Sight and Sound*, Winter 1989/90, 8–12. Documents Amber's film practice, which earned it a

Woman loading seacoal. Courtesy British Film Institute Stills, Posters, and Designs.

British Film Institute award after twenty years; brief discussion of *Seacoal* and other current projects.
Web site:
⟨www.amber-online.com⟩ The official Web site of the filmmakers, with an overview of their approach and discussions of their work and their films and books for sale.

~~

Secrets of Silicon Valley

High tech, low pay

2001, 60 mins.
Directors: Alan Snitow and Deborah Kaufman
Traditional documentary
PRINCIPAL FIGURES
Magda Escobar, director of Plugged In, East Palo Alto
Raj Jayadev, high-tech temp worker, organizer, writer

The main secret of Silicon Valley is that it is an industrial complex with hundreds of thousands of high-tech assembly-line workers, most of whom are immigrants from the Indian subcontinent, Southeast Asia, and Latin America. Many of these workers, however, are actually working for temporary agencies such as Manpower Services, Inc., not for the corporations whose products they make.

This exposé focuses on two very different approaches to the problems of the Valley. Magda Escobar provides a training center for many of the area's African Americans who need computer skills to compete for jobs; Raj Jayadev goes to work for a temp agency that supplies workers for Hewlett-Packard's printer assembly line and tries to organize the workers.

Both approaches have limited success. Escobar manages to get funding and major support from such corporations as Hewlett-Packard, while Jayadev's fellow workers are able to win back pay they were owed. The film also charts their setbacks: Escobar's first building is swallowed up by the Valley's gentrification push, which is nibbling away at East Palo Alto, the traditionally very poor and marginal neighbor of affluent Palo Alto, home of Stanford University. Jayadev is eventually "let go," although the company says it is not because he's organizing a union.

Partly because of Escobar's grasp of public relations and partly because she does not represent the threat of unionization, her screen time is more spectacular than Jayadev's. At one point, her Plugged In team competes with the Valley's corporate giants in the annual Sand Hill Road soapbox derby and her team wins, although competitors have spent as much as $100,000 to win this race. That the race represents the conspicuous consumption of the Valley's moguls is captured by the arrival of one of the CEOs

A workforce of recent immigrants dominates Silicon Valley assembly lines. Courtesy Snitow-Kaufman Productions.

on a camel. The ghost of the economist Thorstein Veblen (who coined the expression "conspicuous consumption"), fired from nearby Stanford University about a century ago, would understand this excess.

Escobar also manages to get President Clinton to come by for the opening of her interim training center. Now that's pulling some Internet strings. And because all of the principals concerned with this film are computer industry veterans, the film is remarkably well documented both in print and on the Internet.

See also: *Office Space*.
Availability: Selected collections; Bullfrog Films.

Further reading

Bacon, David. "Organizing Silicon Valley's High Tech Workers," at ⟨www.igc.org/dbacon/Unions/04hitec1.htm⟩. A leading journalist and photographer of migratory labor and immigrant workers analyzes the recent history and exploitation of the workers on the Valley's assembly lines.

Bernstein, Aaron. "Down and Out in Silicon Valley." *Business Week*, 27 March 2000. Corroboration of the film's muckraking: "Plenty are left behind by the greatest wealth machine in history."

Benner, Chris, Bob Brownstein, and Amy Dean. "Walking the Lifelong Tightrope: Negotiating Work in the New Economy of California." Working Partnerships USA and Economic Policy Institute, 1999. Online at ⟨www.wpusa.org⟩. This groundbreaking study reveals the realities behind the hype, focusing particularly on temp workers at all levels of California's new economy.

Greenhouse, Steven. "The Most Innovative Figure in Silicon Valley? Maybe This Labor Organizer." *New York Times,* 14 November 1999, 26. A profile of Amy Dean, head of the AFL-CIO's Silicon Valley office and a strong advocate of organizing temporary workers.

Harvey, Dennis. "Secrets of Silicon Valley." *Variety*, 9–15 April 2001. "Nicely paced and vid-shot, 'Secrets' takes the high road, finding considerable inspiration from its protags' thumping for equal opportunity advancement, rather than emphasizing the 'cyber selfishness' they struggle to overcome."

Jayadev, Raj. "The Depths of Silicon Valley." *To Do List Magazine*, 2000, at ⟨www.todolistmagazine.com/depths1.html⟩. An extensive analysis of the Valley, including Jayadev's experiences sampled by the film.

Mieszkowski, Katharine. "Can My Mommy Have Her Paycheck?" *Salon*, 1 May 2001, at ⟨salon.com/tech/feature/2001/05/01/secrets_q_a/index.html⟩. Interview with the directors: "[Silicon Valley] is a rich multicultural community, immigrants, all kinds of people living in San Jose and Santa Clara, but you never hear about them."

——. "Take That, Silicon Valley!" *Salon*, 1 May 2001, at ⟨www.salon.com/tech/review/2001/05/01/secrets_of_silicon_valley/index.html⟩. Although the reviewer is bothered by the identification of Jayadev as only a temp worker, she sees the film working best when it "juxtaposes words and images that show Silicon Valley's conflicting ideas about itself."

Nieves, Evelyn. "Filming Another Side of Silicon Valley." *New York Times*, 7 May 2001, A10. Detailed account of the film's production and its successful reception in Silicon Valley theaters.

Web sites:

⟨www.wpusa.org⟩ Working Partnerships, affiliated with the South Bay Labor Council of the AFL-CIO, is "a research center and community resource for temporary workers in Silicon Valley."

⟨www.pluggedin.org⟩ Plugged In is "a community technology center with a mission to ensure that everyone in East Palo Alto, California, has the opportunity to fully benefit from all that the information revolution has to offer."

⟨www.secretsofsiliconvalley.org⟩ Official Web site of the film, with bios of filmmakers, film synopsis, and links to relevant Web sites.

⟨www.svtc.org⟩ Silicon Valley Toxics Coalition: "The most comprehensive site on high-tech impacts on community, worker, and environmental health."

↩

Shout Youngstown

Praise steel

1984, 45 mins.
Directors: Carol Greenwald and Dorie Krauss
Traditional documentary

PRINCIPAL FIGURES
Narrator, John Brouder
Jack Hunter, mayor of Youngstown
Diane Kenney, chaplain, Youngstown State
  University
Staughton Lynd, attorney for local unions
Ron Daniels, community activist
Jim Davis, Joe Gavini, and George Denny,
  steelworkers
Bob Vasquez, president, United Steel
  Workers of America, Local 1330
Arleen Denny, Save Jobs Committee

The film begins with justly famous footage of the demolition of the stacks of Youngstown Steel and Tube. Its title comes from the Armenian-American writer William Saroyan, who recalls what the Armenians vowed when they were forced out of their homeland—that they would always "Shout Armenia!"

Si Kahn composed a song, "Shout Youngstown," that runs throughout the film as a kind of leitmotiv to the fight the workers and community activists in Youngstown fought to save their mills from destruction by three steel companies (Jones & Laughlin, Youngstown Steel and Tube, and U.S. Steel), which had virtually created Youngstown's prosperity over the last hundred years, before they announced at the end of the 1970s that their Youngstown days were over.

The film documents a mildly anti-union "workers' control" movement, as a coalition of workers, religious, and other community leaders plan to buy and modernize the U.S. Steel plant. They failed to secure a federal loan to support the buyout and initiate a series of actions—demonstrations at corporate headquarters and even a factory occupation—to press their case.

But to no avail. One after another, the great steel factories close in the Youngstown area, leaving its streets empty of virtually all previously thriving businesses and massive unemployment. Old documentary footage from a film called *Steel Town*—"We make steel and we talk steel"—looks forever quaint.

See also: *The Business of America.*
Availability: Selected collections; Cinema Guild.

Further reading

Bruno, Robert. *Steelworker Alley: How Class Works in Youngstown*. Ithaca: Cornell University Press, 1999. In his study of retired steelworkers, Bruno questions "the widely held view that laborers in postwar America have adopted middle-class values."
Lynd, Staughton. *The Fight against Shutdowns*. San Pedro: Singlejack Books, 1982. Lynd's strategy for saving jobs.

Signal 7

Try signal 9 or signal 11; see what happens

1984, 92 mins.
Director: Rob Nilsson
Screenplay: Rob Nilsson
CAST
Speed = Bill Ackridge
Marty = Dan Leegant
Johnny = John Tidwell

Although *Variety* does not usually publish raves about low-budget, improvisational independent films, its reviewer loved *Signal 7*, a film about cab drivers that virtually never found its audience. Like Nilsson's other labor history film, *Northern Lights, Signal 7* grows on you and makes you enjoy it despite its occasional cute self-consciousness: the two cabbies, for example, want badly to be professional actors. But we can put up with this successful imitation of John Cassavetes's improvisational filming style because it touches on many important problems in urban work life—the murder of a cabbie, union struggles, and family squabbles.

And there is certainly nothing wrong with the wonderful joke at the beginning of the film when our two would-be actors participate in a long audition for roles in a revival of Clifford Odets's *Waiting for Lefty*, the great radical drama of the 1930s in which cabbies fight the Mob, labor finks, and their own union leadership as they wait in vain for their radical leader. Michael Moore and other postmodern directors (fairly rare in labor film circles) would love what Nilsson has done here: cast actors playing actors who work as cabbies as they audition for parts in a play where they can play cabbies.

The film was shot in less than a week in San Francisco. The actors, accepting Nilsson's homage to John Cassavetes, the director who pioneered this kind of film, may not have had to act all that insincerely, since many of them no doubt have had cabbie jobs or the equivalent in their years of trying to break into show business.

Unfortunately, the film's improvisation seems to be virtually unchecked. Although the incident that comes out of the title— "signal 7" is a cabbie's radio call for help—is very disturbing, the death of a fellow cabbie mostly causes the gang of workmates to cry and promise to bond more. Since their bonding takes the form of telling folkloric tales of seduction (beautiful and sexy women apparently carry off cabbies all the time), one may be forgiven if more time and space on the cabbies' union would have seemed like blessed relief, even if the union was in trouble (as it seems to be).

See also: *Taxi Dreams*.
Availability: Selected collections.

Further reading

"Signal 7." *Variety*, 25 April 1984. Rave review— "the yarn is rife with originality and humanity"—but the reviewer worries about the film's survival in the Hollywood marketplace: he or she was right to be worried.

෴

Silkwood

Mysterious death of a union activist

1983, 128 mins., R
Director: Mike Nichols
Screenplay: Nora Ephron and Alice Arlen

CAST
Karen Silkwood = Meryl Streep
Drew Stephens = Kurt Russell
Dolly Pelliker = Cher
Angela = Diana Scarwid
Winston = Craig T. Nelson
Morgan = Fred Ward
Paul Stone = Ron Silver

When Karen Silkwood was killed in a car crash at the age of 28, she may have been the nation's first nuclear martyr. She was a union activist for the Oil, Chemical, and Atomic Workers (OCAW) in a Kerr-McGee plutonium-processing plant in Oklahoma. Her particular concern as executive officer of her local union was health and safety issues; the company regarded her as a trouble-maker. Because of the nature of the work at this plant—plutonium is made into pellets, then welded into the rods that become the integral part of breeder reactors—the danger of worker contamination was very high. Even the smallest contamination may cause cancer.

Most of this background information is uncontested. The difficulty in understanding Silkwood's short and tragic life lies in determining what Silkwood knew about Kerr-McKee that might be damaging to its reputation and who was responsible for her contamination. In her opinion, the company's lax safety rules and deliberate sabotage led to the contamination of her urine samples with plutonium. The company said she contaminated herself to embarrass the company and put the union in a stronger bargaining position.

As if these issues aren't complex enough, we have the matter of her lifestyle. She was a mercurial individual, given to decisions that sometimes were hard to defend, such as letting her ex-husband have custody of her three children, and in her last years she lived with a boyfriend and a woman, causing not a few people to gossip about her.

Richard Rashke's book *The Killing of Karen Silkwood* established most of the facts of her life. Director Mike Nichols and a strong pair of Hollywood insiders as screenwriters end up emphasizing her relationships and the love life of the three housemates, making Silkwood and Drew lovers and Dolly a lesbian. Cher plays Dolly with the inevitable gallows humor that comes from having as a girlfriend a beautician from a morgue.

The film also expands on the issue of Silkwood's continuing bouts of contamination and that of one of her co-workers, Thelma, taking the position that company sabotage was responsible for at least some of it. In the film, Silkwood believes that her urine kit had been sabotaged, even if the spilling of her urine sample jar itself was obviously an accident.

In the film, Silkwood forms a romantic attachment with a national union officer who helps her out and shows her the scene in Washington when she comes to a hearing held by the Atomic Energy Commission (AEC). Much of what she wants to tell the AEC is important, such as her observation of a "hot" or radioactive truck being dismantled and buried by the company. The national union leadership clearly gets more excited when she mentions that she knows that film negatives showing cracks in control welds have been doctored to disguise the cracks. This potential horror—it could lead to a failure of a major breeder reactor à la *The China Syndrome*—is really a scandal. If she can produce documentation of this skulduggery, the *New York Times* would be very interested.

When her car crashed, she was on her way to a nighttime meeting with a *New York Times* reporter. No such documentation was found in her wrecked car. In the film, she has tried a number of times to get her hands on those negatives, but she has had no luck. Either she cannot find the right ones or they are simply not there in the vast file folders in the room she has been assigned to with just one other worker, a man who is more than a bit of a sleaze and who she has seen, in the past, actually doctoring negatives. (In the film, he admits that is what he is doing.)

The film thus remains more open-ended than Rashke's book on the subject of

Karen Silkwood (Meryl Streep) with her "family," Dolly (Cher) and Drew (Kurt Russell).

Silkwood's final mission. Nichols's direction is lackadaisical. Not until the very end of the film does Nichols's camera come alive, when metal-wire scrub brushes and water hoses virtually assault contaminated workers.

The final sequence delivers what Nichols's other films (*The Graduate* and *Catch-22*, to name two of his best) have delivered in the past—a visually arresting sequence that merges image and idea. In what will be Silkwood's last trip we see her staring apprehensively at her rear-view mirror as the bright lights of a car come much too close. The very next shot shows her crashed vehicle, followed by a pan of the car being towed from the point of view of her friends and union buddies inside a café. The next shot shows her gravestone, but the lively Silkwood is captured by the next slow-motion long take, which turns out to be a flashback to her last farewell to Drew as she drives off to grab the documentation she wants to hand over to the *New York Times* reporter.

In real life, Silkwood's crusade was vindicated by a lawsuit, but Nichols's film touches on none of that. For him she is a will-o'-the-wisp, a passionate, headstrong woman who may have been right about nuclear contamination—who really knows?—but who had a heck of a lot of interesting relationships. Most viewers will not be satisfied with that.

Nichols does include important details on Silkwood's union career: the decertification election in which she helps to maintain the union's contract (but just barely, by a vote of 80 to 61), and a couple of local meetings and a few national meetings that take seriously the importance of the union's monitoring of its members' working conditions. Karen Silkwood's death helped the passage of OSHA's "Right to Know" legislation. It was the final national victory for an activist who started locally.

See also: *Chemical Valley*.
Availability: Easy; DVD.

Further reading

Canby, Vincent. "Accident or Murder?" *New York Times,* 14 December 1983, C27. An overall very positive review, but "the muddle of fact, fiction, and speculation almost, though not quite, denies the artistry of all that's gone before."

Ephron, Nora. "The Tie That Binds." *Nation,* 6 April 1992, 453–55. The author of the screenplay discusses the difficulty of writing a film based on fact.

Kael, Pauline. "Busybody." In *State of the Art.* New York: Dutton, 1985. Criticizes the director's "passive advocacy" and worries about Streep's miscasting as Silkwood.

Kohn, Howard. *Who Killed Karen Silkwood?* New York: Summit Books, 1981. Another exhaustive account.

Rashke, Richard. *The Killing of Karen Silkwood.* 2d ed. Ithaca: Cornell University Press, 2001. The title makes it clear that the author believes Silkwood was murdered by those who were threatened by her disclosures. Kate Bronfenbrenner's foreword is helpful.

Scott, Rachel. *Muscle and Blood.* New York: Dutton, 1974. Muckraking essays on related dangers faced by the OCAW, such as beryllium (used in atomic reactors) and chemical poisoning.

〰

Sit Down and Fight: Walter Reuther and the Rise of the Auto Workers' Union

Of tactics and the man

1993, 60 mins.
Director: Charlotte Mitchell Zwerin
Traditional documentary
PRINCIPAL FIGURES
Walter Reuther, president, UAW, 1946–1970
Victor Reuther, former assistant to the president, UAW
Homer Martin, first UAW president
Harry Bennett, personal director and head of the Service [security] Department of Ford Motor Company
Richard Frankensteen, organizer, Automotive Industrial Workers Association; vice president, UAW
Leonard Woodcock, president emeritus, UAW

Gordon Bellaire, participant, Kelsey Hayes sit-down strike

Kenneth Malone, participant, Flint sit-down strike

Dorothy Kraus, organizer, Women's Emergency Brigade, Flint sit-down strike

This documentary combines the history of auto manufacturing in America with the story of its most famous union organizer. The film chronicles the atrocious working conditions of the 1920s and 1930s through the organizing drives of the CIO, the great sit-down strikes, and finally the recognition of the UAW as the principal bargaining agent with the Big Three automakers. Walter Reuther is an important part of this survey but not the only part. As the film makes clear, the history of organizing the auto industry and Reuther's personal history are popularly assumed to be inseparable, but there were more than a few moments of difficult courtship.

The film includes a reunion of the sit-down workers and their militant right arm, the Women's Emergency Brigade, in Flint, Michigan, in 1990. Their story makes up one of the most familiar and dramatic tales of the UAW's history, but the film's use of interviews counterpointed with remarkable archival footage manages to tell the story in fresh and convincing ways. Without the sit-down strikes, it is hard to imagine that the UAW would have emerged victorious. The film details the tactical maneuvers of the sit-down strikers, their steadfast discipline, and the dangers they faced: security guards' clubs, police tear gas, National Guard machine guns.

The film develops Reuther's history with admiration but notes his ability to compromise and constantly move to the centrist position on ideological and theoretical questions. When it was clear that the first UAW president, Homer Martin, did not have the right stuff (he continued his earlier calling as an erratic preacher and eventually formed a rival union with Henry Ford as his ally), the importance of the Communist Party members within the CIO and Reuther's

eventual handling of them became more and more important. Eventually Reuther went his own way, but the Communists did not persevere as an independent force.

A revealing incident in the history of the UAW was the handling of black workers, then working the hardest jobs in the foundry. Henry Ford had tried to position himself as a friend to black Americans, cultivating the friendship of George Washington Carver, for example. When the UAW launched black organizers to try to bring the black workers into the union, Harry Bennett, the security chief, ordered the black workers to attack the mainly white picketers. This last-ditch race riot strategy failed, and with the slogan "Fordism Is Racism," the UAW succeeded in bringing many of the black workers into the union.

The film recounts the career of Reuther and the UAW in the post–World War II period in more abbreviated fashion. Harry Truman is quoted as opposing the Taft-Hartley Bill as "a shocking piece of legislation," but the bill passed nonetheless. The film closes with Reuther's close contact with JFK, LBJ, Martin Luther King, and Cesar Chavez of the United Farm Workers before his death in 1970.

See also: *Finally Got the News; With Babies and Banners.*
Availability: Selected collections.

Further reading

Cormier, Frank, and William J. Eaton. *Reuther*. Englewood Cliffs, N.J.: Prentice-Hall, 1970. A massive but readable biography.

Keeran, Roger. *The Communist Party and the Auto Workers' Union*. 1980. New York: International Publishers, 1986. A provocative study, calling Reuther "one of the most powerful anti-communists in the CIO."

Pflug, Warner. *The UAW in Pictures*. Detroit: Wayne State University Press, 1971. A photographic history drawn from the Archives of Labor History and Urban Affairs at Wayne State University.

Reuther, Victor G. *The Brothers Reuther and the Story of the UAW*. Boston: Houghton Mifflin, 1976. Memoir by Reuther's brother.

Slim

"Aw shucks"

1937, 80 mins., B&W
Director: Ray Enright
Screenplay: William Wister Haines, from his novel of the same title
CAST
Slim = Henry Fonda
Red Blayd = Pat O'Brien
Cally = Margaret Lindsay
Stumpy = Stuart Erwin
Pop = J. Farrell MacDonald
Wilcox = Joseph Sawyer

Henry Fonda plays Slim, a farm boy who knows excitement when he sees it: being a high-wire lineman. His career, from apprenticeship to mastery, is by turns melodramatic and sentimental, but usually engrossing. The era of the TVA and the drama of rural electrification are the necessary imaginative leaps to prepare for this film: linemen were dedicated public servants who took chances in this landscape, and to some extent they still do. Try fixing your outside electric line yourself in a storm some day.

Slim celebrates the nobility of labor. Our hero, however, has romantic problems. His girlfriend is also the woman who has been waiting for years for Red, Slim's mentor, to settle down. When it becomes clear that Slim has to choose between dangerous construction high-wire jobs and the safer maintenance stay-at-home work, he chooses Red and the open road rather than his girl. (The same safe stay-at-home choice is offered to the Fabrini brothers in *They Drive by Night*, but they eventually take it.)

But life in some 1930s movies has a way of upsetting such decisions. Red and Slim are called out on an extremely dangerous job— fixing "hot" high wires during a blizzard. Red is killed and Slim is temporarily knocked out. He straps on his utility belt and starts to climb the tower again. His girl is at the base of the tower cheering him on. Fade to black. We never learn for sure if Slim will settle

down. There's TVA work to be done and the country to wire.

The *New York Times* reviewer was enthusiastic about the film's "groping" toward "the major truth that there is a nobility inherent in labor from which sparks may be struck and take lodging in the soul of even an ordinary little man." But don't ask Slim to be a maintenance man.

See also: *They Drive by Night*.
Availability: Not.

Further reading

Nugent, Frank S. "Slim." *New York Times*, 24 June 1937, 30. A very positive but balanced review.

The Solid Gold Cadillac

Never give a stockholder Judy Holliday

1956, 99 mins., color and B&W
Director: Richard Quine
Screenplay: Abe Burrows, from the play of the same title by George S. Kaufman and Howard Teichmann
CAST
Laura Partridge = Judy Holliday
Edward L. McKeever = Paul Douglas
Clifford Snell = Fred Clark
John T. Blessington = John Williams
Harry Harkness = Hiram Sherman
Amelia Shotgraven = Neva Patterson
Alfred Metcalfe = Ray Collins
Narrator = George Burns

Every time I watch *The Solid Gold Cadillac* my false consciousness of capitalism creeps up (down?) another notch. I can't help it. It's Judy Holliday's fault. As Laura Partridge she supports the absurd idea of the "little stockholder" gaining control of a billion-dollar corporation with such good humor and sexy pizzazz that it makes me want to buy shares in almost anything she might be involved with.

Of course it's a satire on capitalism. We

shouldn't take it too seriously, but the opening sequence always seduces me: avuncular George Burns, as voice-over narrator, introduces the board of directors one by one as they file into a stockholders' meeting. Each one is frozen briefly on the screen with an appropriately damning comment—"He's a crook." Or: "I wouldn't trust him with a nickel."

Of course this is a prime example of a major capitalists' myth—that the little stockholders really own the company. In this case they eventually do, but along the line we are reminded that the CEO and his cronies usually control the proxy vote and do what they think is best for the company—or for themselves. And there is a silly little subplot about the big-fish company swallowing a little fish only to find out that it had already swallowed the same fish once before. The bad CEO also tries to bribe and seduce the old CEO—now working for the government in a federal contracts office—so that some contracts can be fixed. All these fishy lessons about how capitalism really works makes for amusing viewing and might open the eyes of somebody new to the wonders of free enterprise.

If you are worried about your own impulse to buy shares in a company like the one in this film, or a tendency to believe in too many of Hollywood's myths, try another satirical hit made in Technicolor the following year, *Will Success Spoil Rock Hunter?* and you'll soon be back for some more Judy Holliday in glorious black and white. The spoof on advertising man Rock Hunter and his advertising campaign for Stay Put Lipstick (with Jayne Mansfield and an even more curvaceous standard poodle) will seem ludicrous and trivial. When Hollywood makes fun of itself successfully, wild poodles will roam the earth. In the meantime, it manages with this film to hit capitalism with a well-placed dartlet.

See also: Desk Set; The Devil and Miss Jones. Availability: Selected collections.

Stockholder (Judy Holliday) and CEO (Paul Douglas) celebrate in *The Solid Gold Cadillac*.

Further reading

Brode, Douglas. *Lost Films of the Fifties*. New York: Citadel, 1991. Here "lost" really means "neglected," as Brode celebrates Holliday's "street smarts and common sense," which "stun the more sophisticated men around her."

~

Sons of Steel

Fathers of dumb

1935, 65 mins., B&W
Director: Charles Lamont
Screenplay: Charles Belden
CAST
Philip Mason = Charles Starret
Rose Mason = Polly Ann Young
Tom Mason = Richard Carlyle
Sarah Mason = Florence Roberts
Ronald Chadburne = William Bakewell
John Chadburne = Walter Walker
Enid Chadburne = Aileen Pringle
Curtis Chadburne = Holmes Herbert

This is a steel industry variation of the old chestnut of a story in which twins are separated at birth and grow up in radically different social and economic circumstances. In this version the Chadburne brothers separate their sons from birth: one is reared in Chadburne affluence, the other farmed out to a working-class family. Both boys go on to college, but the working-class lad is much more motivated and successful as a student. When the boys become young college grads, they are misplaced by the expectations of their respective social classes. Affluent Ronald Chadburne makes a mess of his management job because he really wants to do things with his hands, while Philip (Chadburne) Mason can't keep his mind on his milling machine because what he really wants to do is design. The situation is complicated by young Mason's anger and his eventual leadership of the union's wildcat efforts to keep wages fair.

To understand this film in terms of auto union organizing, picture the famous moment in 1937—two years after this film was released—when Walter Reuther and members of the CIO Organizing Committee for the auto industry were confronted by a pack of Ford's hired thugs at the Battle of the Overpass. Instead of bashing Reuther in the head, security head Harry Bennett embraces Reuther and announces that he is Henry Ford's brother's long-lost son. Wouldn't this have changed labor history somewhat?

See also: *Female*.
Availability: Selected collections.

Further reading

Nugent, Frank S. "The Screen." *New York Times*, 15 April 1935, 16. Very brief negative review: "about as unexciting and meaningless a drama of industry as the Chesterfield studios could have produced."
"Sons of Steel." *Variety*, 17 April 1935. Calls the film a "better than average" independent production.

~

Sounder

Sons and daughters of the dust

1972, 105 mins., G
Director: Martin Ritt
Screenplay: Lonne Elder III, from William
    H. Armstrong's novel of the same title
CAST
Rebecca Morgan = Cicely Tyson
Nathan Lee Morgan = Paul Winfield
David Lee Morgan = Kevin Hooks
Mrs. Boatwright = Carmen Mathews
Ike = Taj Mahal
Sheriff Young = James Best
Camille Johnson = Janet MacLachlan

This story of a rural black sharecropping family in 1933 was filmed in rural Louisiana. By Hollywood standards, it is a "small" film. Barely a year in the life of the Morgan family passes, but we see Nathan's arrest for stealing food, the rest of his family keeping up their end of the tough sharecropping bargain, and young David's quest for his father, who is held at a prison labor camp about a day's walk away.

The reason the father steals from a white neighbor's smokehouse is that his family is hungry. Having failed to bring home a raccoon from a hunt, Nathan justifies his stealing to his wife: "I did what I had to do." His sentence seems severe—a year at hard labor—but the greater pain is that suffered by his family. Quaint Louisiana parish rules exclude women from visiting the jail at any time, while men can visit only on Sundays and holidays. Visits soon matter little, since the sheriff announces that another rule is that the family will not be told what labor camp he has been sent to. In the meantime, the difficult job of tending to the farm is left to Rebecca and her three children.

When the only sympathetic white character—a woman for whom Rebecca does laundry—ignores the sheriff's threats to embarrass her in front of the whole community and tells the Morgans where Nathan is being held, David Lee goes off on a journey to visit his father. He never finds him, but he is taken in by a kindly black schoolteacher, who raises the first sparks of black consciousness in the boy by telling him about Harriet Tubman and Crispus Attucks and reciting a passage from W. E. B. Du Bois.

This film will appeal to children as well as adults, although the original novel is now marketed primarily to "young readers." Two incidents of violence would disturb children: the family dog, Sounder, is shot in the face and David Lee's hand receives a vicious swipe of a switch from a prison guard. The physical wounds heal. The psychological violence of the 1930s South is also painful to watch, but the stoical Rebecca manages to get in a rejoinder or two: "That is some low-down job you got," she tells the sheriff.

The details of the sharecroppers' poverty and frustrations are central to the film, so that the actual farm labor is presented in a sketchy though convincing way. We also see the operation of a cane press with an endlessly circling mule as the driving force. (The same apparatus is used in a scene set in the 1850s in *Half-Slave, Half-Free*.) The issue of labor is presented here in human terms, however.

Cicely Tyson's portrayal of the hardworking wife was one of the breakthrough roles for black actresses, who too often had been relegated to the position of Shaft's latest big score in the wave of black exploitation movies of the 1970s. (Tyson followed this film with the even more challenging lead role in *The Autobiography of Miss Jane Pittman*, which has a much wider historical and political sweep than *Sounder* but less immediate labor relevance.)

In the end, *Sounder* is a coming-of-age film. Upon his father's return from prison, David Lee will leave the farm and live with the schoolteacher he admires. His father warns him, "Don't get used to this place," and clearly hopes that his son will break out of the sharecropping cycle. From what we have seen of sharecropping, David Lee's decision seems like an easy one, but clearly the filmmakers' intention was also to show what he would be missing, too.

See also: *Our Land Too.*
Availability: Easy; DVD.

Further reading

Canby. "All But 'Super Fly' Fall Down." *New York Times,* 12 November 1972, B1. Compares Ritt's film—not too favorably—with many of the twenty black (mostly exploitation) films that opened in 1972.

Greenspun, Roger. "Sounder." *New York Times,* 25 September 1972, 49. A mixed review, stressing the film's strong performances.

Holly, Ellen. "At Long Last, the Super Sound of 'Sounder.' " *New York Times,* 15 October 1972, B15. A rave review: "It constantly discovers an excruciating beauty in the unremitting toil and materially barren lives of the working poor."

Kael, Pauline. *Reeling.* New York: Atlantic Monthly Press, 1976. Calls Tyson "the first great black heroine on the screen."

Thomas, Sam, ed. *Best American Screenplays.* New York: Crown, 1986. The screenplay with a brief bio of its author.

Note: *Sounder, Part 2* (1976), the sequel, with a completely different production team and cast, is not available on videocassette, and, according to Donald Bogle in *Blacks in American Films and TV* (New York: Garland, 1988), it is just as well.

~

The Southerner

Frenchified peckerwoods

1945, 91 mins., B&W
Director: Jean Renoir
Screenplay: Jean Renoir, from George Session Perry's novel *Hold Autumn in Your Hand*

CAST
Sam Tucker = Zachary Scott
Nona = Betty Field
Devers = J. Carroll Naish
The Grandmother = Beulah Bondi
Harmie = Percy Kilbride
The Mother = Blanche Yurka
Tim = Charles Kemper
Finley = Norman Lloyd

The fluid camerawork and revealing compositions that signify the mature style of Renoir's masterpieces (*Rules of the Game* and *The Crime of Monsieur Lange*) are for the most part missing from this foray into Texas sharecropping. Oh, there is the occasional cloudscape passing over the grumpy grandmother's head when she refuses to leave the truck and settle in on the new piece of land the Tucker family is renting, but as a rule Renoir seems so smitten by the portrayal of this pathetic couple that he allows them to coo without much going on. Renoir's five American films were all made with major casts and produced for the most part in the American way, as if moving to Hollywood and becoming an American citizen could make an American director out of a French legend.

Some details Renoir got right. Tucker's city friend tries to talk Tucker into giving up this farming foolishness and work in a factory for $7 a day—that is, stop being a peckerwood and become a linthead (See *God's Little Acre*). Since Tucker and his wife have just a little more than $3 to purchase milk and vegetables for their pellegra-stricken child, this idea has got to be tempting.

At other times Renoir succumbs to mythologizing his Texas crackers: Tucker explains his bad luck at hunting as caused by the fact that the moon has been moving toward the North Star: "Animals don't like that." And at other times he directs as if he is making a popular front film in France in the 1930s: our hero's friend, who has become a linthead with a decent salary in a town job, observes that "without us workers," farmers wouldn't have plows, guns, or tractors. "It takes all kinds," the men solemnly agree.

Tucker is not a man easily deterred: despite a flood, harassment by his grumpy jealous neighbor (Tucker caught the ferocious beast of a catfish named Lead Pencil before him), and singularly dubious financial terms (only marginally better than sharecropping but not as good as working as a day laborer), Tucker perseveres. Much banter is expended on propositions like these: "It's wrong for a man to get too big for his britches" (that is, stay a sharecropper); "If you don't have money, you work for others" (e.g., stay a sharecropper).

We are only five years after John Ford's classic adaptation of Steinbeck's *Grapes of Wrath*: Renoir loads up an auto that is a dead ringer for the Joadmobile. Even his grandmother (Beulah Bondi) seems to have escaped from Ford's film, although Renoir's is definitely grumpier and at times much more irritating to watch. Tucker's wife apparently agrees: she takes a switch and flails Grandma's butt for one of the more amazing moments in peckerwood film history.

See also: *God's Little Acre*.
Availability: Selected collections; DVD.

Further reading

Agee, James. *Agee on Film*. Vol. 1. New York: Grosset & Dunlop, 1958. Reprints a mixed review from *The Nation* (9 June 1945) in which Agee complains that Renoir hasn't gotten the work done by his characters accurately.

Leprohon, Pierre. *Jean Renoir* (1967). Trans. Brigid Elson. New York: Crown, 1971. A survey of the director's career with a section on the film.

"The Southerner." *Variety,* 2 May 1945. Reviewer whines that the film "creates too little hope for a solution to the difficulties of farm workers," during a time when the appropriate Hollywood response should be "escapism."

Weiler, A. "At the Globe." *New York Times,* 27 August 1945, 22. Finds the film an honest and convincing portrait of the sharecroppers' plight: "as unfashionable a subject for screen treatment as could be contemplated."

South Riding

Yorkshire deals

1937, UK, 91 mins., B&W
Director: Victor Saville
Screenplay: Donald Bull and Ian Dalrymple, from Winifred Holtby's novel of the same title

CAST

Sarah Burton = Edna Best
Robert Carne = Ralph Richardson
Madge Carne = Ann Todd
Joe Astell = John Clements
Huggins = Edmund Gwenn
Midge Carne = Glynis Johns

Apparently the source novel of this strange but intriguing dramatic venture into the local politics governing the deserving poor and the avaricious rich in the Yorkshire countryside had something of a reputation as a "socialist" (pro–Labour Party) novel, at least among the Reds writing for the British Communist Party newspaper in 1938, because their reviewer felt its radical politics were betrayed by the film's "national government propaganda" (see Stead). Even assuming the reviewer—or even a modern reader—could plow through the first five pages of lists of characters (twenty-five characters to a page), much less the interminable discussions by upper-middle-class schoolgirls and their headmistresses, one could hardly sustain the notion that this is a radical novel. It does have a Councilor Astell, who is called a socialist and who calls himself and others "comrade" on occasion, but his politics can only be described as pro–working class. So much for this novel, the last written by Winifred Holtby, whose early death may have inadvertently contributed to making this 600-page novel about the duties of a county council a brief best-seller.

But in this case, blessed are the filmmakers who reduced the 125 characters to a manageable 7 or 8 major ones. Compression of plot and reduction of complexity has made the film in the end quite telegraphic in its message and left its plot lines swinging in the Yorkshire breeze. We can nonetheless enjoy a vision of country politics as it is filtered through an early British heritage film.

There is in actuality no *South* Riding county council; Yorkshire was in fact administratively divided into North, East, and West sections. This little fiction preserves some of the pretense that the film treats county politics generically. In fact we might more precisely say it treats matters stereotypically. We have as councilors a big landowner on the skids, a religious zealot who is secretly a sinner, a conniving businessman, the aforementioned socialist, and the kind of woman who was always described as a formidable dame. To this cast of politicos add the heroine, Sarah Burton, the new headmistress of the county boarding school, who must reconcile the working class (Lydia Holly, Shakespearian scholar in the making, saddled with a motherless family) and the upper middle class (Midge Carne, the landowner's daughter, as broke as a landowner's daughter can be in these fantasies). Needless to say, she does it, managing to get a new school for herself and her charges and new housing for the district's working poor. *How* she does it will make your head spin, but suffice it to say no real damage is done to the British class system, the economics of a region, or even respectability; only the religious hypocrite is shown the door.

See also: *Hungry Hill.*
Availability: Selected collections.

Further reading

Bostridge, Mark. *The Clear Stream: A Life of Winifred Holtby*. London: Virago, 1999. A biography of the talented and politically courageous woman who died shortly before her novel and the subsequent film became popular classics in Great Britain.

Holtby, Winifred. *South Riding*. New York: Macmillan, 1936. The source novel; my rating: one and a half field hockey sticks out of ten.

Richards, Jeffrey, and Anthony Aldgate. *British Cinema and Society, 1930–1970*. Totowa. N.J.: Barnes & Noble, 1983. Includes an excellent chapter on the film's social and historical contexts.

Stead, Peter. *Film and the Working Class*. London: Routledge, 1989. Perhaps a bit too enthusiastic about the film's "realistic treatment of social problems, especially inadequate housing," but notes the film's imitation of Hollywood's "technical excellence."

Note: Another version, a TV series with thirteen episodes, directed by James Ormerod, was broadcast in 1974, but is not available on videocassette.

〜

Spices

Ah-choo

1986, 98 mins., India, in Hindi, with English subtitles
Director: Ketan Mehta
Screenplay: Shafi Hakim and Ketan Mehta
CAST
Sonbai = Smita Patil
Abu Miya = Om Puri
The Subidar = Naseeruddin Shah
Mukhi = Suresh Oberoi
Mukhi's Wife = Deepti Naval

Ketan Mehta's recurring emphasis on exploited women and village laborers made him one of the leading directors of the New (or Parallel) Indian Cinema, a self-consciously political cinema, in contrast to the overwhelming majority of popular or commercial Bombay films (usually nick-named "Bollywood"). India has the largest film industry in the world, but the split in recent decades between popular and New Indian cinema is similar to that between Hollywood and independent productions. In 1980 there were 65 million paid admissions every week in a country of almost 700 million people using sixteen official Indian languages.

Mehta's training and career is typical of the New Cinema advocates. As a theater enthusiast he followed the Marxist ideas of Brecht and believed in street theater: "From college, we would go out on the road, into 'jhuggies' (slums), and put up one-act plays against imperialism." Later at India's Film Institute he decided that "all cinema is political—it either wants change or cunningly maintains the status quo. Every film reflects the ideology of its director, whether he supports justice or evil" (Cunha).

The Indian title of *Spices* is *Mirch Masala,* translated in early releases as *Chili Bouquet,* a phrase that captures literally if not intelligently the term *masala,* which is used for both a mixture of spices and contemporary popular Indian films that mix genres. The opening song points to the idea of the film's colorful variety in a lighthearted way: "After creating matter, man, and mind, God was bored. So he sprinkled some chilies and spices, and made the world more colorful."

The lead character, Sonbai, was played by Smita Patil, a pioneering Indian actress in the New Cinema who pushed the range of available roles to encompass more freedom for women, although she herself at one stage in her career accepted mainstream roles "because," according to Rosie Thomas (in Kuhn and Radstone), "she recognized that her self-imposed marginality was helping no one—without a name and market potential in mainstream cinema, she could have little effect on public consciousness or on the development of a more popular alternative cinema practice." Typical of her overtly feminist roles was *Threshold* (1981), in which she leaves her husband, a lawyer who attacks a rape victim's credibility to benefit his client, the accused rapist.

This remarkable film picks its ideological

targets carefully. Certainly the primary focus is the subjugation of women in many ways: the village head, the Mukhi, will not permit his wife to send his daughter to the local school, which is "for boys only." Opening titles situate the Subidar's power as derived from the British—the taxes he squeezes from the villagers in large part go to the British (although he certainly cheats them as well). The future is suggested by the role of the schoolteacher, one of only two men in the village who want to protect Sonbai: he is called "a follower of Gandhi" and beaten for his opinions.

Spices in one sense is the epitome of Smita Patil's career, as she plays the ultimate rebel—the one who will not give in to local authority, "federal" (military) power, or even the cultural and immediate pressure of her sisters in the pepper factory, where she hides to escape her would-be rapist, the Subidar.

Spices closes with one of the most glorious moments of revenge in modern world cinema. While we have been prepared for this moment in many ways and it has in a sense been in our faces throughout the film, it still comes as a surprise on first viewing. Abu Miya, the guard who is responsible for security at the pepper factory, has been killed and the gate destroyed. Our heroine (armed with a short scimitar-like tool) faces the Subidar. Since he is backed up by armed soldiers and her only armed male defender is dead, we are caught up short wondering how the filmmakers will resolve the moment. Out of nowhere rush the other women in waves of two carrying blankets loaded with red pepper powder, which they shower on the Subidar, choking and blinding him. He has truly collected his tax.

See also: *Hyenas*.
Availability: Selected collections; Movies Unlimited.

Sonbai (Smita Patel) at the chili factory in *Spices*. Courtesy British Film Institute Stills, Posters, and Designs.

Further reading

Cunha, Uma da, ed. *Film India: The New Genera-tion, 1960–1980.* New Delhi: Directorate of Film Festivals, 1981. Extensive guidebook to the New Indian Cinema, with an entry on the director, Ketan Mehta, highlighting his radical career.

Dissanayake, Wimal, ed. *Cinema and Cultural Identity: Reflections on Films from Japan, India, and China.* Lanham, Md.: University Press of America, 1988. Includes several essays on Indian cinema. Mira Reym Binford's "Innovation and Imitation in the Contemporary Indian Cinema" is an especially helpful overview with a section on *Spices* and other films by Ketan Mehta.

———, ed. *Melodrama and Asian Drama.* Cam-bridge: Cambridge University Press, 1993. Although the entire volume is of interest, the editor has an essay on the relationship of evil and social relationships in Indian film melo-drama that is relevant to *Spices*.

Gupta, Udayan. "New Visions in Indian Cinema." *Cineaste* 11, no. 2 (1982): 18–24. Includes an interview with Mehta, who discusses his desire to make films about such subjects as "landless laborers, untouchability, and the lower castes."

Kempley, Rita. "Spices." *Washington Post,* 18 November 1989. "There is a grunting ruthless-ness to the drama, a vibrancy of character and moral obstinacy that compare favorably with Akira Kurosawa's admittedly more elegant samurai movies."

Kuhn, Annette, and Susannah Radstone, eds. *Women in Film: An International Guide.* New York: Fawcett Columbine, 1990. The entry on Smita Patil stresses the tensions in a career that swung between mainstream roles and alterna-tive (even feminist) cinema; she died (of com-plications after childbirth) at age 31.

~

Stanley and Iris

An odd (working) couple

1990, 107 mins., PG-13
Director: Martin Ritt
Screenplay: Harriet Frank Jr. and Irving Ravetch, very loosely adapted from Pat Barker's novel *Union Street*

CAST
Stanley = Robert De Niro
Iris = Jane Fonda

Only one chapter or "story" in Pat Barker's best-selling novel became the direct inspira-tion (I guess) for *Stanley and Iris*: a working-class woman has worked in a bakery, has a daughter who becomes pregnant, and is a more than competent survivor: other than those plot details, Frank and Ravetch's screenplay goes in its own direction in so many ways that one might call Barker's work only a distant kin.

This is an actorly film, with Fonda and De Niro taking on—seemingly effortlessly—the roles of the two blue-collar workers. De Niro's performance as an illiterate adult, coping as best he can in the workaday world without being able to read, is convincing and moving. Fonda's role of a widow not quite ready to reattach herself to a man comple-ments De Niro's style well. The economics of these two struggling at unskilled labor some-times takes one's breath away: they try so hard and still they often fall behind.

There are really two stories here: the tutoring of Stanley by Iris and Iris's survival as a working mom. The stories don't always work well together but they are both worth watching.

See also: *Marty.*
Availability: Easy.

Further Reading

Barker, Pat. *Union Street.* 1982. Various editions available. This is a fascinating and disturbing col-lection of stories about working-class women in northern England, but it has virtually nothing to do with the film.

Canby, Vincent. "In Movies, Working Stiffs Have Become Nearly Extinct." *New York Times,* 18 March 1990, II.1. Reviewer complains that American movies about working-class charac-ters, unlike those made in England, don't con-stitute a strong genre of their own, but he does link this film, *Roger & Me,* and Spike Lee's *Do the Right Thing* for their portrayal of "the quality of life of the endangered species that used to be called the working stiff."

Howe, Desson. "Stanley & Iris." *Washington Post,* 9 February 1990. "No one seems to have taught this 'Norma Rae' reunion team (director Martin Ritt, writers Irving Ravetch and Frank) how to spell 'screenplay' or 'credibility.' " Ouch!

The Stars Look Down

. . . on miners in the dark

1939, 110 mins., B & W, UK
Director: Carol Reed
Screenplay: A. J. Cronin, from his novel of
   the same title
CAST
David Fenwick = Michael Redgrave
Robert Fenwick = Edward Rigby
Martha Fenwick = Nancy Price
Jennie Sunley = Margaret Lockwood
Joe Gowlan = Emlyn Williams
Mr. Barras = Allan Jeayes

Carol Reed's adaptation of A. J. Cronin's *The Stars Look Down* is more resolutely a mining film than Reed's adaptation of *The Citadel*, made the year before. Both feature idealistic heroes whose lives are dedicated to helping those left behind in the mines. In *The Stars Look Down* Reed simplified a novel complex in both plot and British mining history. By narrowing the focus to one main subplot—the safety of the Scupper Flats section of the Sleescale mines—we are prepared for the disaster that occurs, but we know less about the culture and conditions of the miners.

David Fenwick and his family are the central characters. His father, Robert, leads an extended wildcat strike against both the union (unnamed) and the mine owner, Barras, because of the danger of flooding in the notorious Scupper Flats. Robert Fenwick maintains that there are old plans that indicate the thinness of the wall separating the current shafts from the flooded ones, but Barras denies their existence. We know he is lying.

When the locals revolt against a particularly obnoxious butcher, Robert is arrested for looting the shop, a scene similar in all but the women's ferocity to one in *Germinal*. In the meantime, David wins a scholarship to university and raises the issue of the private ownership of the mines at debates. Peter Stead has called this debate sequence, in which images of his old mining buddies are superimposed on David as he speaks, "one of the most stunning and effective sequences in the history of British cinema." David falls in love, however, and allows his wife to talk him out of completing his degree.

When Scupper Flats finally does get flooded, the shots of men running through the mines to escape the flood and the townspeople aboveground rushing through the streets when they hear the distress whistle are unnerving. David helps in the rescue, but he loses his father and brother. The novel is clearer about a moment at the end of the film when we know the elder Fenwick is going to die: he is writing something we don't see, but it turns out that it is a note about the owner's knowledge of the thin walls of Scupper Flats.

The rescue sequences look remarkably similar to those in *Kameradschaft*, filmed just seven years earlier. The shots of the trapped miners drifting into death are horrifying. Reed's realistic and moral vision persisted, culminating in his classic black-and-white thriller *The Third Man*. For *The Stars Look Down* he reassembled some of the cast (especially Redgrave and Lockwood for David and Jenny) of Hitchcock's successful thriller of the year before, *The Lady Vanishes,* although there are very few comic flourishes in his mining film.

Although the owner clearly comes into sharp disfavor in this film, a disturbing antiunion sequence occurs before Scupper Flats has blown, when David tries to persuade the national union executive board to authorize a strike. After an impassioned speech, his argument is punctured by a member who mocks his concern as self-serving revenge for a personal problem, since David's wife has run off with the man making a deal for Scupper Flats coal. Not only do they reject his proposal, but the next order of business they take up is a paint job for a local's headquarters. David will eventually be proved right and the union executive wrong, of course, but it is at a terrible cost.

See also: *The Citadel; Germinal; Kameradschaft.*
Availability: Selected collections.

Further reading

"The Stars Look Down." *New York Times,* 24 July 1941, 15. A very positive review—the film "says what it has to say with complete and undeviating honesty."

Stead, Peter. *Film and the Working Class*. London: Routledge, 1989. Sets the film in the context of other British mining films; this one "depicted the miner more fully than in any previous film."

Note: Clearly a slightly different UK version of this film is in circulation, since an opening and closing voice-over (according to Peter Stead) stating, among other things, that the miners are "often without a spokesman" is missing in the version available in the United States.

⤚

Startup.com

This end up

2001, 100 mins.
Directors: Chris Hegedus and Jehane Noujaim
Cinema verité documentary
PRINCIPAL FIGURES
Kaleil Isaza Tuzman, Tom Herman, Chieh Cheung, and George Fatheree, founders, GovWorks.com

This film joins the relatively thin ranks of cinematic investigations of the computer industry. We get a look at the top—how dot.coms get started, how their investors find them, and how they can implode. And while there were four founders of GovWorks.com, a site that was designed to facilitate the interaction of the public and government agencies, only two bear the microscopic scrutiny of the filmmakers' relentless camerawork. Isaza Tuzman and Tom Herman were high school buddies whose friendship is tested as they fight to create a company that starts with an idea (helping people pay parking tickets!), becomes a business plan, attracts millions in venture capital, and struggles to survive in an economy that once seemed so hospitable to startups.

From parking tickets, Tuzman and Herman's idea evolved into a grander scheme. GovWorks.com would facilitate all of the average person's contact with local, state, and federal government agencies, and take advantage of literally trillions of dollars in transactions. Their advertising slogans parodied Americans' "inalienable rights": "You have the right to attend a town meeting in your underwear"—in other words, whenever you want—via GovWorks.com's portal.

At first the company seemed destined to succeed. It opened branch offices, hired workers (up to 250 at its height), and continued to attract investors. The partners eventually had a falling out. After losing millions of dollars, they sold the GovPay software they developed to eOne Global LP and Management Systems, where it is still in use in Boston, Memphis, and New York (according to the *New York Times*).

In retrospect, the rhythm of their roller-coaster ride to dot.com loop-the-loops is set in one of the opening sequences when the two primary partners are in the offices of Highland Capital, a venture capital firm that has just offered as much as $17 million if they agree to their terms within an hour or so. Unfortunately, they cannot get their lawyer on the phone to review the deal and they sit in Highland's office being abused (to my eye) by one of the Highland execs, who mocks their contact (when it is eventually established) with their lawyer.

The filmmakers had the kind of intimate access to their subjects needed to convince viewers that they are getting an unprecedented insider's view of daily life at the top. Filmmaker Chris Hegedus had worked on numerous projects, including *The War Room*, about Bill Clinton's 1992 presidential campaign, which she co-directed with the pioneer cinema verité director D. A. Pennebacker; her co-director on *Startup.com*, Jehane Noujaim, was Tuzman's roommate and had begun her acquaintance with him just as he left his investment banking job with Goldman Sachs to pursue a dot.com dream.

Depending on your taste in youthful

moguls and maybe even your own age, you may find the two whiz kids in this film appealing. I didn't. I found them at worst crass and pompous, at best single-minded and untiring. Eventually even they couldn't stand each other, although the film fails to mention that they reunited to form a new company, The Recognition Group, which specializes in (according to Schwartz) helping other failed dot.comers "work through the legal and emotional maze of bankruptcy and near-bankruptcy" or (according to their Web site) help "clients realize maximized financial value from troubled companies, avoid potential legal and reputational liability arising from mishandled insolvencies, and economize on time and effort required in restructurings." That's called learning your lesson.

See also: *Secrets of Silicon Valley.*
Availability: Easy; DVD.

Further reading

Dillullo, Tara. "Startup.com." *@n-zone* at ⟨www.atnzone.com/moviezone⟩ Extensive interview with the directors.

Ebert, Roger. "Startup.com." *Chicago Sun-Times*, 25 May 2001. "As an inside view of the bursting of the Internet bubble, 'Startup.com' is definitive."

Kuo, J. David. *Dot.Bomb*. Boston: Little, Brown, 2001. An account of a startup, Value America (consumers order directly from manufacturers), that also becomes a dot.flop.

Paternot, Stephan, and Andrew Essex. *A Very Public Offering*. New York: Wiley, 2001. Another dot.flop—Theglobe.com—that makes it clear that much of the creative energy went into raising venture capital and making the stock at initial public offering seem more valuable than the company could ever be.

Schwartz, John. "The Internet Bubble Bursts on the Screen." *New York Times*, 30 April 2001, C1, 4. An extensive analysis and history of the production of the film.

Stark, Jeff. "Startup.com." *Salon.com*, 11 May 2001, at ⟨www.salon.com/ent/movies/review/2001/05/11/startup⟩. Sees the lack of focus on the actual work of the company as "a fault of the film, but one that works to its advantage. You can read it as a minor misstep or a winking joke on the company and the Internet boom itself. We know

all this money is flying around . . . but we have only a vague idea of what it's all about."
Web sites:
⟨www.recognitiongroup.net⟩ Site of Tuzman and Herman's new venture.
⟨www.startupthefilm.com⟩ The official dot.com of the film, with production details, profiles of the filmmakers, and reviews.

Steel

Ain't nothing higher than a skyscraper in Lexington, Kentucky

1980, 99 mins., PG
Director: Steve Carver
Screenplay: Leigh Chapman
CAST
Mike Catton = Lee Majors
Pignose Moran = Art Carney
Lew Cassidy = George Kennedy
Cass Cassidy = Jennifer O'Neill
Eddie Cassidy = Harris Yulin
Harry = Redmond Gleason
Valentino = Terry Kiser
Cherokee = Robert Tessler
Surfer = Hunter Von Laer

Like many TV movies, *Steel* has a disease (or at least almost a disease) to motivate the plot: one of the top-flight hard hats, played by Lee Majors, once froze on the job zillions of feet in the air. Will he still be able to walk a girder thirty stories aboveground? The cast even includes a model, Jennifer O'Neill, who plays the hotel owner's daughter who vows to finish her father's building after he is killed in an accident. She put the *New York Times* reviewer in mind of a "fashion model who is being photographed against an industrial background."

Since this film is very rarely available anywhere, no one has to worry about its unrealistic portrayal of how skyscrapers get built. The first ten minutes with George Kennedy playing a tough-talking roughneck of a builder are at least exciting: "Tall buildings give me a hard-on still," he tells his chauffeur, who is riding in the backseat while Big Lew drives recklessly to his final job. Black-and-white stills and archival 1930s footage of ironworkers heroically climbing higher and higher prepare us in the credits sequence for Big Lew climbing a girder himself, after he fires a worker for drinking beer on the job. There is an explosion and Big Lew falls from what was going to be the biggest building in the state (and since we're talking Kentucky here, thirty stories would just about do it).

The film goes down the elevator shaft from here. O'Neill is not convincing as Big Lew's daughter, who vows to get this building up. Nine floors have to be built in three weeks to stop the bank from transferring the building to Big Lew's loser of a brother, who runs a trucking business that specializes in substandard material that gets workers killed on the job.

The only way to top out Big Lew's building is to bring in Mike Catton, a legendary ironworker, as the site's "ramrod" (to push the job through) and his mystically powerful crew, made up of a Cherokee (although it was the Mohawks who did most of the high ironwork on skyscrapers for many years), Valentino (an Italian-American lover-boy), Harry (a comic former IRA terrorist who has been working as an explosives man at a strip mine), and so on. These guys get to break the rules: the (unnamed) ironworkers' union local lets them sign on immediately and suspends virtually all safety rules so that the building goes up on time.

Since this is Kentucky, we visit a bluegrass horse farm and Rupp Basketball Arena, where the bad guys, such as Big Lew's brother, get to play hardball. When the men are actually bolting girders high in the sky, we finally do pay attention. The finale, with helicopters bringing in the final top steel pieces, has a stirring moment or two, especially when we get a shot of men at the four corners of an unfinished tower waiting for their steel to come down from the sky.

This melodramatic film has the look of a bad TV cop show, although there are never any police officers in Lexington to prevent either the bad guys or the good guys from breaking as many laws as they wish. The spirit of the film harks back to the days of the heroic linemen of *Slim*, when real men took risks to get the job done. Lexington's need for additional office space may not be the moral equivalent of rural electrification, but the risks the workers take are clear enough. At one point the bad brother bribes a trucker's union official to set up a wildcat strike against the bad brother's company so he won't be able to deliver steel to the building he hopes eventually to take over. If that makes sense, then this film is worth seeing.

See also: *Bloodbrothers; Slim.*
Availability: Selected collections.

Further reading

Buckley, Tom. "Film: Hard Hats in 'Steel.'" *New York Times*, 13 December 1980, 55. A rare but mocking review.

Note: Also known as *Look Down and Die* and *Men of Steel*.

Street Scene

"Eees better to 'ave money"

1931, 78 mins., B&W
Director: King Vidor
Screenplay: Elmer Rice, from his play of the same title
CAST
Rose = Sylvia Sidney
Sam = William Collier Jr.
Mrs. Maurrant = Estelle Taylor
Mr. Maurrant = David Landau
Abe Kaplan = Max Montor
Sankey = Russell Hopton
Easter = Louis Natheaux

Elmer Rice's Pulitzer Prize stage play, quite successful in its Broadway run in 1929–30 (over 600 performances), had some of the same elements we identify with novels and films from the Depression but perhaps not with its plays: close attention to urban life in general, immigrant and poor people in particular, with a smattering of secretaries, clerks, and some professionals and Reds thrown in for good measure.

In both Rice's play and Vidor's film we see familiar jobs—mailmen and policemen—but also those that have long disappeared—street vendors and the iceman. This focus completes a kind of trilogy for Vidor, with rural cooperatives in *Our Daily Bread*, office life in *Our Crowd*, and street life in this film. It also brought in what would become an urban stereotype, the ethnic or immigrant character. Here the Italian-American character sets out a common theme, glibly but perhaps not too unfairly: "Een Eetaly, ees bewtiful, but ees no money. 'Ere ees not bewtiful, but ees plenty money. Eees better to 'ave money."

The motor of the plot is a bit of a cliché—married woman having an affair with the milkman, who is also married. The real interest is in Vidor's attempt to bring the "street scene" to life, both cinematically (with camerawork attributed to Gregg Toland, the master cinematographer of *Citizen Kane*, and George Barnes, Academy Award winner for *Rebecca*) and sociologically (with a broad range of working-class types).

See also: *One Third of a Nation; Our Daily Bread*.
Availability: Selected collections; DVD.

Further reading

Maxwell, Barri. "Street Scene." *DVD Verdict*, 26 October 2000, at ⟨www.dvdverdict.com/reviews/ streetscene.shtml⟩ More than just a review of the DVD version: "The film is a pre–Production Code piece that is quite gritty in its presentation of life in the tenements."

Rice, Elmer. *Three Plays*. New York: Hill & Wang, 1965. One of many collections with Rice's original play.

⤺
Strike

Or rebel or both

1924, 73 mins., B&W, Soviet Union
Director: Sergei Eisenstein
Screenplay: Sergei Eisenstein

CAST
Organizer = A. Antonov
Worker = Mikhail Gomarov
Spy = Maksim Shtraukh
Foreman = Grigory Aleksandrov
Lumpenproletariat = Judith Glizer, Boris Yurtzev, and other actors of the First Workers' Theater of the Proletkult Collective

This silent film portrays a strike in tsarist Russia in 1912. As the factory workers develop their strategy and tactics, they are constantly at the mercy of spies. The workers have no union, but they have an organization and a printing press: "Workers Unite!" is a typical leaflet and it reminds us that in this period, depicted by many Soviet filmmakers, shop-floor organizing and antigovernment rebellion were essentially one and the same.

The actual strike is touched off by the suicide of a worker who has been wrongly accused of stealing a tool. The workers walk out. Their demands for a reduction in hours and an increase in pay result in attacks by mounted policemen. The long strike forces families into hardship, as the management spies increase their ingenious tricks (at one point a camera disguised as a pocket watch photographs a worker removing a management sign). Management's desperation becomes obvious as they hire the King of the Underworld, whose gang hides out in disused underground wine vats, for an arson job. They are the ultimate in riffraff, portrayed almost literally as *lumpen* workers (the "lumpenproletariat," in Marxist terms). They plan to burn the factory and blame it on the workers. Although this plot fails, the fire brigades turn their hoses on the workers, not the burning building. Eventually the strike itself is forgotten in visually stunning shots of soldiers attacking the revolutionary masses.

The pessimistic ending of *Strike* was to have led, following Marxist analysis, to the eventual victory of the Bolshevik Revolution in a follow-up film. Sergei Eisenstein's experimental filmmaking had rejected stars, heroes, and plot. Instead we are confronted with Eisenstein's inventiveness: titles whirling and dissolving into parts of machines, point-of-view shots from the miniature spy camera, and the final close-up shot of staring eyes. The acting has an exaggerated clownlike quality throughout, but the montage—the clashing of images to build meaning, as in shots of the throat of a bull being cut as the soldiers attack the crowd—still has power to convey Eisenstein's revolutionary politics.

Strike has some other spectacular moments. The homeless riffraff emerging from their underground havens in response to the call of the King of the Underworld is the most remarkable image in a film filled with dramatic images. Although Eisenstein is certainly the greatest of Soviet filmmakers and a world-class film artist, his work eventually ran into trouble with a world-class censor, Stalin.

See also: *Mother.*
Availability: Selected collections; DVD.

Further reading

Eisenstein, Sergei. *The Complete Films of Eisenstein.* Trans. John Hetherington. New York: Dutton, 1974. Abbreviated film scenario with stills.

——. *Film Form and the Film Sense.* Trans. Jay Leyda. New York: Harcourt, Brace, 1957. Sometimes overcomplicated, sometimes helpful discussions of early Soviet film technique, with discussions of *Strike* and Eisenstein's other films throughout.

——. *Selected Works.* Vol. 1, *Writings, 1922–34.* Ed. and trans. Richard Taylor. London: British Film Institute, 1988. Eisenstein's essay "The Problem of the Dialectical Approach to Form" defends his experiment with "the 'manufactured' past of contemporary revolutionary reality."

Lawder, Standish. "Eisenstein and Constructivism." In *The Essential Cinema*, ed. P. Adams Sitney, 58–87. New York: Anthology Film Archives, 1975. A detailed (almost exclusively cinematic) analysis of the film.

Leyda, Jay. *Kino: A History of Russian and Soviet Film.* New York: Collier, 1971. An analysis of *Strike* in the context of the careers of Eisenstein and other Soviet filmmakers.

Nichols, Bill. *Blurred Boundaries: Questions of Meaning in Contemporary Culture.* Bloomington: Indiana University Press, 1994. Offers an

intriguing approach to the film as a variation of documentary filmmaking rather than as a feature film.

Swallow, Norman. *Eisenstein: A Documentary Portrait.* New York: Dutton, 1977. Recollections of Eisenstein by his contemporaries and collaborators.

∽

Struggles in Steel

Too little, too late

1996, 58 mins.
Directors: Ray Henderson and Tony Buba
Traditional documentary
PRINCIPAL FIGURES
Ray Henderson, interviewer and narrator
Black steelworkers: Lujana Deanda, Priscilla Burgess, Lattie King, Otis Bryant, William Graham, Nathan McLain, James Kidd, Donald Whittington, Francis Brown, James Langley
Dennis C. Dickerson, professor of history, Williams College
Leon Haley, Urban League, Pittsburgh

This is mainly an interview film, based in part on Dennis C. Dickerson's *Out of the Crucible,* with Ray Henderson interviewing and chatting with numerous black steelworkers, mainly in western Pennsylvania, although a few workers are from other areas such as Dundalk in the Baltimore area. The overall continuity is chronological, following Dennis Dickerson's book from the end of the nineteenth century through the collapse of many of the steel mills in the 1980s. Some of the visual interest lies in the shots of exploding and imploding mills as one after another falls victim to corporate economic collapse. In fact, the film argues that the final breakthroughs in black hiring in the steel mills—the result of key consent decrees won by black plaintiffs—came when the industry was literally disappearing from the industrial landscape.

Despite their criticisms of the union, many of the former steelworkers agree that "a bad union is better than no union" and that they could not and would not work in a steel mill without a union to protect them from management.

See also: *Voices from a Steeltown; Lightning over Braddock*.
Availability: Selected collections; California Newsreel.

Further reading

Dickerson, Dennis C. *Out of the Crucible: Black Steelworkers in Western Pennsylvania, 1875–1980*. Albany: SUNY Press, 1986. Comprehensive history, drawing on both interviews and the historical record, which attempts to demonstrate that "race, not class, has fixed the status of contemporary Black workers and has created the poverty and unemployment which perennially afflicts them."

Hoerr, John P. *And the Wolf Finally Came: The Decline of the American Steel Industry*. Pittsburgh: University of Pittsburgh Press, 1988. Its title comes from Joseph Odorcich, a VP of the USWA: "One of the problems in the mills is that no union man would trust any of the companies. To the average union man, they're always crying wolf."

Lynd, Staughton. "History, Race, and the Steel Industry." *Radical Historians Newsletter*, June 1997, 1, 13–16. Comprehensive review of the film and the related big issues of racism and unions.

Thomson, Patricia. "Images of Labor." *Independent Film Monthly*, June 1996, 33–38. Discussion of the film and the collaboration between steelworker Henderson and filmmaker Buba.

Web site:

⟨ww.braddockfilms.com⟩ Official site for Buba's films, including *Struggles in Steel*, with a history of the project, clips from the film, and a study guide.

↫

Sugar Cane Alley

A woman's angle on a boy's coming-of-age story

1983, 103 mins., French, with English subtitles, PG
Director: Euzhan Palcy

Screenplay: Euzhan Palcy, from Joseph Zobel's novel *Black Shack Alley*
CAST
Jose = Garry Cadenat
M'Man Tine = Darling Légitimus
Medouze = Douta Seck
Léopold = Laurent Saint-Cyr

The original French title, *Rue cases nègres* (translated as *Black Shack Alley*) captures the look of this unique film of life on sugarcane plantations on the Caribbean island of Martinique in the 1930s. Given that few films depict black labor, either slave or free, Euzhan Palcy's film makes a daring attempt to link African-Caribbean slavery and later virtual serfdom in the character of Medouze, an ancient working man who is a mentor to Jose, her young hero. *Sugar Cane Alley* concentrates on both the French education that his grandmother is working so hard to support and the folk stories of Medouze, wise in black history and the culture of the island.

Medouze explains their serfdom as a serious error after slavery was ended: "We were free but our bellies were empty. Our master had become our boss. . . . The whites owned all the land." He knows that he can "never go back to Africa" because "he has no one left there." He will return to Africa "when he's buried," but he "can't take the boy along."

In the meantime, M'Man Tine is working hard to keep the boy in school and, more to the point, out of the fields so that he can be trained in other ways: "Learning is the key that opens the second door to freedom," she says. Eventually, he performs well enough to get scholarships to the big school in Fort-de-France. Two related events bring the film and his early years to a close. M'Man Tine, like Medouze, has died and "gone back to Africa," and Léopold, Jose's biracial friend, is arrested for stealing a ledger to prove that the workers have been cheated in their cane quotas. Léopold is taken off by the police while the workers all sing a rebellious song.

Palcy's career as a Third World woman director making mainstream films is unique. Her original impulse was to film Alan Paton's

Cry, the Beloved Country, but she turned to Zobel's novel about the Martinique that she felt was her "daily reality": she was just 17 when she decided to make the film. Before directing *Sugar Cane Alley* she had been responsible for the first television drama from a French "overseas department"—that is, former colony. She then went on to adapt André Brink's novel *A Dry White Season*, about apartheid in South Africa.

Palcy has somewhat daringly mixed issues of class and race. Jose needs the white authority's system to escape the working-class drudgery of his family and friends. How much Palcy believes that escaping to the lower middle class is justified is not clear.

See also: *Life and Debt*.
Availability: Selected collections; DVD.

Further reading

Canby, Vincent. "Third World Truths." *New York Times,* 22 April 1984, II.17. A long appreciative review: "Euzhan Palcy is a new writer-director of exceptional abilities."

Cham, Mbye, ed. *Ex-iles: Essays on Caribbean Cinema*. Trenton, N.J.: Africa World Press, 1992. Includes a review of the film and an interview with the director.

Maslin, Janet. "Moving Up." *New York Times,* 6 April 1984, C24. A brief but positive review.

McKenna, Kristin. "Tough, Passionate, Persuasive." *American Film,* September 1989, 32–37. A profile of the filmmaker and her films.

Zobel, Joseph. *Black Shack Alley*. Trans. Keith Q. Warner. Boulder, Colo.: Lynne Rienner, 1997. Source novel, with a helpful forward.

🖎

Sullivan's Travels

Hollywood goes hobo

1941, 91 mins., B&W
Director: Preston Sturges
Screenplay: Preston Sturges
CAST
John L. Sullivan = Joel McCrea
The Girl = Veronica Lake
Sullivan's Butler = Robert Greig
Sullivan's Valet = Eric Blore

This wonderful satire begins with a political joke. The Sullivan of the title is a director who has just finished a film that is "an answer to the Communists." What we see of this film—two men duking it out on the roof of a boxcar until they knock each other into a river—becomes hilarious when we pull back from the screen-within-a-screen to hear Sullivan announce to his producers that it is about capital and labor destroying themselves. The director says that a film is a "sociological and artistic medium." Yes, his producers add, but always "with a little sex in it."

Eventually Sullivan decides that to make realistic films for the masses, he needs to join the riffraff, become a hobo, and cast aside his affluent Hollywood lifestyle. His butler and valet are suitably shocked and try to talk him out of it. "The poor," one of them says, "know all about poverty. Only the morbid or the rich would find it glamorous." But Sullivan goes off, exploring hobo jungles, Salvation Army kitchens, and life with the Depression homeless. Their camps resemble, in many ways, any homeless camp, even today's. His adventures are appropriately sociological, "with a little bit of sex in it"; for example, the Girl (Veronica Lake) strips as often as the plot (and the 1940s Motion Picture Code) will allow her to and has no illusions about poverty either.

Sullivan actually does become a hobo after he receives a knock on the head. Our Hollywood hero discovers at his lowest point—when he is held on a prison farm with a sadistic warden—that the poor want comedies, not Marxist newsreels.

Sturges's satire can be fairly obvious. A black rural church welcomes the integrated chain gang of prisoners for a film show of cartoons; the minister puts his congregation on notice: "We are all equal in the sight of the Lord." Sullivan has ended up on this chain gang, he thinks, because a railroad guard thought he was "just a bum." If Sullivan the director had smacked him, nothing would have come of it, but because Sullivan the bum did it, he got a seven-year sentence. If you are perhaps a little tired of Frank

Capra's sentimentality (*It's a Wonderful Life*), then it might be time to watch a Sturges film.

See also: *Gold Diggers of 1933*.
Availability: Easy; DVD.

Further reading

Bergman, Andrew. *We're in the Money: Depression America and Its Films*. New York: New York University Press, 1971. Excellent film history with a discussion of this film.

✍ Sunday Too Far Away

"Friday too tired, Saturday too drunk, Sunday too far away"—Ballad of a shearer's wife

1975, 94 mins., Australia
Director: Ken Hannam
Screenplay: John Dingwall
CAST
Jack Foley = Jack Thompson
Old Garth = Reg Lye
Ugly = John Ewart
Tim King = Max Cullen
Arthur Black = Peter Cummins
Tom = Robert Bruning
Frankie Davis = Ken Shorter
Sheila Dawson = Lisa Peers

If *Sunday Too far Away* weren't an Australian film, it would be an American western, at least in the initial scenes—a "gun" or top sheep shearer comes to an outback saloon in Gimal, he's been away so long that people are almost surprised to see him, a new man challenges his authority but he gets sent on his way, the remaining men gather up a posse of fellow workers and ride off to . . . do a union job of sheep shearing at still another remote location!

The sheep shearers have strict rules and rituals. They are hired by a contractor (usually an ex-shearer), they work both as a team (with set pay) and individually (for shearing the most sheep), and their work hours are long and strictly monitored (by the bell). This is a remarkably quiet film, despite a big punch-up with scabs toward the end when the government decides to cut the pay rate 15 percent, inevitably forcing the men out on strike. Foley, our lead, played by the popular actor Jack Thompson (also the leader of the "wharfies" in the Australian dock epic *Waterfront*), seems to take pleasure mainly from working hard and being the best, with only the relatively rare distraction of booze and a "sheila" (the daughter of the sheep owner, or "cockey"). Competition and camaraderie mark the film's many moments of labor. The interruptions in the routine—a bad cook or "poisoner" who needs to be disciplined, for example—are usually played for laughs. Foley and his mates, however, stop work when their old buddy dies; characteristically, they discipline the undertaker for not bringing the proper vehicle by making him ride up in front in the cab with the dead man.

When the government cuts the pay scale, the men all strike without hesitation. After an obligatory punch-up with scabs at the saloon, end titles tell us that the "strike lasted nine months" and that "the shearers won." We know it's an Australian film when we read these spirited final titles: "It wasn't the money so much. It was the bloody insult."

Neil Rattigan has argued that *Sunday Too Far Away* is "a strong contender for the most Australian film of the New Australian Cinema," taking pride of place among such outstanding films as *Picnic at Hanging Rock* and *Gallipoli*. Whether or not he is accurate, we have not seen many characters like Jack, whom Rattigan would describe as an "ocker" (a potentially uncouth but resourceful Aussie), in our Australian imports.

See also: *Waterfront*.
Availability: Selected collections.

Further reading

McFarlane, Brian, and Geoff Mayer. *New Australian Cinema*. Cambridge: Cambridge University Press, 1992. Studies the "sources and parallels in American and British film," arguing for *Sunday Too Far Away* as a leader in the new Australian film industry.

Murray, Scott, ed. *The New Australian Cinema.* London: Elm Tree Books, 1980. Part of an initiative "to evaluate critically the renaissance of the Australian film industry in the 1970s," it highlights the film as a comedy.

Rattigan, Neil. *Images of Australia: 100 Films of the New Australian Cinema.* Dallas: Southern Methodist University Press, 1991. A comprehensive and very helpful reference book, preceded by a helpful essay on the principles of "Australianness."

Sun Seekers

A radioactive dead end

1958 (1971), 116 mins., B&W, East Germany, in German, with English subtitles
Director: Konrad Wolf
Screenplay: Karl-Georg Egel and Paul Wiens

CAST
Lotte Lutz = Ulrike Germer
Franz Beier = Günther Simon
Jupp Koenig = Erwin Geschonneck
Emmi Jahnke = Manja Behrens
Sergei Melnikow = Viktor Avdyushko
Günter Holleck = Willi Schrade
Weinrauch = Erich Franz
Josef Stein = Norbort Christian

Despite a title that seems to promise a nudist camp, Wolf's film is actually another East German DEFA film banned after its production in 1958 because of a number of sensitive topics—hookers and an innocent runaway rusticated to work at the Wismut uranium mines, German–Soviet tensions at the site, and even some leftover Nazi–Soviet war wounds.

It is not hard to see why this project was originally green-lighted for production: it features East Germans and Soviet engineers and officers standing shoulder to shoulder mining uranium ore to build atomic weapons to "keep world peace" and "to break the U.S. nuclear monopoly" (as the opening titles tell us). It offers a vision of a country building socialism through hard (and dangerous) work. It tries to repair some of the wounds left by World War II between two former enemies, now allies.

What is a little hard to accept is that Lotte Lutz, sexy in a slatternly kind of way, would be the obsession of such different men—a young German miner, the pit boss (and former Nazi army man), and the Soviet engineer—given what seems to be a fair number of good-time women strewn about the workers' dormitories. Maybe she represents the soul of East Germany pursued by its demons and angels alike. She does end up with a baby (the future?) fathered by the young German miner, although a lot of hell, personal and occupational, has to be passed through to reach that point.

Coincidences and revelations abound. Jupp, played by Erwin Geshonneck, the extremely popular actor featured in *Carbide and Sorrel,* is one of the heroes (and a spokesman for socialism), but chooses his old flame—a hooker—for his wife. Pit boss Franz Beier, the former German officer, was present when the SS murdered the Soviet engineer's wife. An incompetent saboteur is caught red-handed belowground.

Labor struggles are nonetheless important in the film. Essential cables wear out and their replacements are delayed. Whether to shore up certain passageways to improve mining later or go for the quick removal of ore is a recurring problem.

This is a fascinating film. The amount of boozing is staggering, the quest for uranium is treated in labor terms as simply another mining job, and the vision of the mining city as an economic boom town is convincing. But all those jokes about radioactivity and all those Geiger counters ticking away without any indication that this is truly a dangerous activity will take one's breath away today.

The title is metaphorical in a number of ways. The most obvious connection between the power of nuclear bombs and the sun is made in a credit sequence when an image of sun flares and the sun's surface are replaced by the dial of a Geiger counter. But miners who toil underground need sun, too, one of the miners says, and by that he means excitement, life, a party or two.

Sun Seekers was banned almost immediately; Sean Allan argues (in an essay with the Icestorm videocassette) that the Soviet political line had shifted: the USSR had announced a unilateral end to their nuclear tests and didn't want a film to promote the frenzied mining of uranium to build more weapons. Wolf went on to direct *Professor Mamlock* in 1961, based on a famous anti-fascist play of the same title written by his father, Friedrich Wolf. Wolf's last film was *Solo Sonny,* dramatizing the difficult singing career and personal problems of a factory worker.

See also: *Carbide and Sorrel; Trace of Stones.*
Availability: Selected collections; Icestorm.

Further reading

Allan, Sean, and John Sandford, eds. *DEFA: East German Cinema, 1946–1992.* New York: Berghahn Books, 1999. Excellent collection of essays by diverse hands, including a discussion of Wolf's career by Anthony S. Coulson, "Paths of Discovery: The Films of Konrad Wolf."
Web sites:
⟨www.icestorm-video.com⟩ Official site of Icestorm, the international distributor of the DEFA films; includes numerous commentaries on the films.
⟨www.umass.edu/defa⟩ Sister educational site of the Icestorm DEFA film collection, with rental information, a bibliography, and other helpful information.

↜

Surviving the Good Times

. . . with longer hours, lower pay

2000, 50 mins.
Producers: Public Affairs Television—A Moyers Report
TV documentary
PRINCIPAL FIGURES
Bill Moyers, correspondent and executive editor

The Neumann Family: Terry and Tony Neumann and their children, Karissa, Adam, and Daniel
The Stanley Family: Jackie and Claude Stanley and their children, Nicole, Omega, Claude Jr., Keith, and Claudel

Using the general idea pioneered by Michael Apted's British "Up" series, Bill Moyers and filmmakers Tom Casciato and Kathleen Hughes have followed two working-class families from Milwaukee for almost ten years and created a very solid and moving TV documentary. Unlike Apted, the Moyers filmmakers use past footage only to evoke a sense of change or even loss: thus in this latest installment (the only one available in videocassette), black-and-white footage and stills from the earlier films (*Minimum Wages: The New Economy*, 1992, and *Living on the Edge*, 1995) are shown only at moments in the narrative when it seems that one of the speakers is at a critical or emotional juncture. The footage or stills serve as mainly visual or cinematic bridges to the past.

The Moyers Report is a mainstay of public television, often developing controversial or at least significant cultural issues. For this documentary Moyers concluded: "I believe we have produced a definitive account of how the changes in the American economy in the last part of the 20th century have affected working families" ("PBS Picks").

The males in the Neumann and Stanley families have had solid blue-collar, well-paying union jobs with two major Milwaukee employers, Briggs & Stratton and A. O. Smith. When they were both laid off, they were forced to turn to lower paying jobs, in some instances earning only half what they had been paid before. The African American couple, the Stanleys, tried two different routes: Claude waterproofed basements at only $7 an hour, while Jackie attempted to sell real estate, working out of a mainly white firm that serviced black neighborhoods. The Neumanns, living in what only appeared to be a safer and nicer white neighborhood, faced similar difficulties, with Tony working the night shift at a manufacturing company and Terry doing long and sometimes unpredictable shifts as an armored car driver.

Both families suffer not only economic dislocation but personal and family frustrations. The number of hours they need to work to try to stay even with their previous modest lifestyles, not to mention emergency medical bills and other unforeseen crises, obviously chip away at their mental and physical health. What comes through in this film, however, is their amazing drive and generally long-suffering good humor. In the end—after almost ten years of struggle—they begin to reach an economic sufficiency that seems safe. But there are some penalties—one of the Neumann children is dangerously close to dropping out of high school, Jackie still feels that African American real estate agents have to stay on their side of the fence, and in general family life and time with children are greatly compromised.

So much of this film takes place, in a sense, offscreen in its economic implications: Briggs & Stratton, for example, went south for cheaper labor when it laid off Claude; the Stanleys resort to paying their son's college tuition bill with a credit card (at high interest). It is a tribute to Moyers and the filmmakers that virtually every personal decision portrayed in the film represents a major issue of the 1990s.

See also: Children of Gozlow; 35 Up; 42 Up.
Availability: Selected collections; Facets.

Further reading

Alterman, Eric. "Still with Us." *Nation*, 24 April 2000, 12. Analyzes the lack of media attention to poor and working-class families, but notes that this Moyers Report as a major exception, especially since the documentary makes it clear that every time Alan Greenspan's Fed raises the interest rate, it puts families like these in greater debt.

Goodman, Walter. "Tracking the Toll after 2 Breadwinners Lose Jobs." *New York Times*, 28 March 2000, B5. Reports that the film is "a tribute to the resilience of their close-knit families and the efforts of all members to pull together."

～

Swing Shift

Goldie the Riveter

1984, 100 mins., PG
Director: Jonathan Demme
Screenplay: Rob Morton
CAST
Kay Walsh = Goldie Hawn
Lucky Lockhart = Kurt Russell
Hazel Zannini = Christine Lahti
Jack Walsh = Ed Harris
Biscuits = Fred Ward

For the real *Swing Shift* we may have to wait in vain for the director's cut—the version of the film the producers won't release because they don't think it will be commercial—since the director, Jonathan Demme, whose name is on the film but who wants it off, was apparently more or less secretly fired before the project was completed and no screenwriter would take credit onscreen for the film: hence the generic phony name of Rob Morton among the credits. (On director's cuts: it took Ridley Scott almost ten years to get his cut of *Blade Runner* released; more than thirty for Stanley Kubrick's *Spartacus*.) We know that Goldie Hawn chased Demme away. No one knows why for sure, but some commentators suggest that Demme's vision was too radical for her (see Vineberg).

Swing Shift is the story of a housewife turned Rosie the Riveter named Kay Walsh. Other than gender stereotypes, what could Demme and Hawn have been fighting about? Plenty, apparently. The level of the film is not always high. The sexy Hazel (played by Christine Lahti in her first big success) is told by a co-worker: "Isn't it amazing that someone with your looks is a riveter?!" Goldie's comeback when she fights with her new boyfriend: "If I can build a goddamn airplane, I can get myself home!"

The film should be seen with the documentary *The Life and Times of Rosie the Riveter*, which provides a reasonably complete image of the days when defense contractors and the government urged women to leave their homes and help their men win the war. At the end of the war, the propaganda machine went into reverse, and the women were supposed to say (prompted by newsreels), "I'm going to be busy—at home." *Swing Shift* dramatizes these dilemmas reasonably well, overlaying them with a triangle—Kay; her husband, Jack, now off in the Navy; and her workmate and new lover, Lucky (i.e., lucky enough to be 4-F).

A more interesting story of gender roles is lurking in this film—Kay at home with her husband is a frilly housewife, doing her duty, while with Lucky she seemingly lives at night clubs in sexy outfits, having fun—but the film stops far short of asking any big questions, such as "What do women want?" and maybe this is why Demme was sent packing. Demme has suggested he wanted to make a film about women's friendships during the war, not about the men in their lives.

Workplace life as portrayed here is more comic than real, although the teasing and sexual harassment of the women seem to be the genuine article. The workplace—an aircraft factory—is racially integrated, but so are some of the clubs the workers visit. Maybe.

See also: *Life and Times of Rosie the Riveter*. *Availability*: Easy.

Further reading

Canby, Vincent. "A Wartime Romance." *New York Times*, 13 April 1984, C13. The film "bends" but does not "break" the "clichés of a kind of romantic fiction not too far removed from World War II movies about the homefront."

Kael, Pauline. "Smaller than Life." *New Yorker*, 14 May 1984, 138–40. Argues that the film fails to convey "the sass and bounce of the women workers, earning good money for the first time," and does not "put across the feeling that's so rousing in documentaries about the period."

Kessler-Harris, Alice. "Rosie the Riveter Goes Hollywood." *Ms.*, July 1984, 46. Echoes Demme's belief that the film changed from an "exposé" to a "salute."

Maslin, Janet. "At the Movies." *New York Times*, 4 May 1984, C8. A brief survey of the production disputes.

Vineberg, Steve. "'Swing Shift': A Tale of Hollywood." *Sight and Sound*, Winter 1990/91, 8–13. A detailed comparison of Hawn's and Demme's versions, concluding that Hawn's version is a "political emasculation" of Demme's.

Take This Job and Shove It

Don't organize, use collateral

1981, 100 mins., PG
Director: Gus Trikonis
Screenplay: Barry Schneider, from a song written by David Allan Coe and sung by Johnny Paycheck
CAST
Frank Maclin = Robert Hays
Charlie Pickett = Art Carney
J. M. Halstead = Barbara Hershey
Harry Meade = David Keith
Ray Binkowski = Tim Thomerson
Dick Ebersol = Martin Mull
Samuel Ellison = Eddie Albert
Man with Hamburgers = Johnny Paycheck
Hooker = Charlie Rich
Beeber = Royal Dano

How low the low have fallen! Barbara Hersey was Boxcar Bertha (in an exploitation film with her nickname as title) just ten years before joining the cast of *Take This Job and Shove It* as a bank loan officer. As Boxcar Bertha she would rob the rich to help the poor; as J. M. Halstead she refuses loans to worried brewery workers because they have no collateral. (More on this technical term of capitalist analysis later.)

This film has a lot of important stuff in it. A big player on the national scene buys out one of his local competitors: Star Beer becomes Pickett Beer ("Pickett Beer for Men Who Picket" is one advertising slogan they consider). But Star Beer just wants to pump up the suds long enough to sell the brewery to a sucker with money. The line gets the speedup, some workers get the heave-ho, and others get reassigned to jobs they don't want. Welcome to Reagan Country.

An unlikely but acceptable plot twist brings Frank Maclin to his native Dubuque to engineer this corporate maneuver. He was a local boy who leaped out of his working-class roots to management via college: the men he worked under in summer jobs now take orders from him. His old buddies in the town figure their jobs will be safe, because Frank knows how "to take care of business"—that is, he won't let fiscal responsibility to his boss and his career interfere with being a good old boy.

The workers have grievances up the beer spout but their union man is onscreen for about ninety seconds. They opt for a fantasy solution, encouraged by Frank's seeming defection from corporate kowtowing and J. M. Halstead's expertise with the stuff that capitalism thrives on—collateral. If they put up their monster trucks and life savings as collateral, a bank will loan the workers enough capital for them to renovate still another brewery, forced out of business not very long ago. This worker-owned enterprise really never gets off the ground, for reasons that have to do mainly with the schlock content of this near-exploitation film: our hero Frank is too busy taking showers with one of his many girlfriends and her dog to attend to the business of workers' control of industry.

In the end the film opts for Animal House anarchism: having practiced their bottle-smashing and table-crunching behavior during a football game at the local bar (a scene that uses a roll of toilet paper as the football, a new low even for this genre), the workers and Frank proceed to destroy the production line at the brewery. How this would improve their economic lives is by now quite beside the point. The song that lent its name to this film supposedly symbolizes the only power that workers have—the refusal to work and the pleasure gained by saying it to the boss's face loud and clear.

See also: *Gung Ho*.
Availability: Selected collections.

Further reading

Maslin, Janet. "Take This Job and Shove It." *New York Times*, 29 August 1981, 17. Likes having country singer Charlie Rich play a capitalist and enjoys some of the silliness.

⤙

Tamango

Black queen, Hollywood rebel

1959, 98 mins., France/USA, released in both French and English versions
Director: John Berry
Screenplay: John Berry and George Neveux
CAST
Aiche = Dorothy Dandridge
Captain Ledoux = Curt Jürgens
Doctor Corot = Jean Servais
1st Mate Bebe = Roger Hanin

Tamango is an unusual film for many reasons, not the least of which is that it was a French-American co-production directed by a blacklisted (because of McCarthyism) American director, John Berry. Berry had been close to Orson Welles in the latter's Mercury Theatre in New York and followed Welles to Hollywood. When named as a Communist by fellow director Edward Dmytryk, Berry fled the House Un-American Activities Committee and settled in France, where he made *Tamango*.

Although the film is one of the few that emphasize the Middle Passage of the slave trade, it is not particularly realistic. Nonetheless, the viewer will witness the incredible hardship the constricted space created for the human cargo. Another daring aspect of the film was the depiction of an interracial relationship between the slave Aiche, played by Dorothy Dandridge, and Captain Ledoux, played by Curt Jürgens.

The film's politics tend to the sacrificial. Tamango would rather die than accommodate to the world of slavery the way Aiche has done in accepting her place as the white captain's mistress. Aiche, for her part, can defend her actions only so long before she feels the pull of solidarity and rebels.

Prosper Mérimée's remarkable story about the Middle Passage appeared in 1828. The Atlantic slave trade had been forbidden by various European congresses from 1815 through 1822. English ships seemed to enforce the ban more than other countries; Mérimée implies the French were lenient. Mérimée expected his story to strike a blow against abuses in the international slave trade and in its own way was part of the work of Victor Hugo and other French intellectuals and activists who protested violations of the Congress of Vienna's first prohibition of the slave trade in 1815. Mérimée's short story, a reflection of his "romantic penchant for exotic scenes of bloodshed and terror" (according to Maxwell Smith), was eventually included in standard school editions in France.

The film retains Mérimée's obvious irony in naming the captain Ledoux, which means "gentle," and his slave ship *L'Espérance*, or "hope." But Mérimée's Tamango has betrayed his own people and is in turn betrayed by the white slavers; the cinematic Tamango rebels against slavery from the first moment we meet him.

In Mérimée's story, Ledoux's liberalism extends to the cruel packaging of the slaves in only three feet, four inches of space between decks, so that they can be "comfortable" seated: "Once arrived in the colonies they will remain only too long on their feet." And the diagrams of slave packing we are now familiar with are geometrically embodied in Ledoux's plan. In the free space in the center of the ship he places ten (or more) slaves perpendicular to the others.

The film was produced in France but ignored the additional irony in the fact that the slaves were originally from the region of Africa that has become Senegal and was still controlled by the French. The natives' language in the 1950s, Wolof, was still not the national language. (See *Hyenas* for a discus-

Aiche (Dorothy Dandridge) reveals her slave brand in *Tamango*.

sion of Wolof in contemporary Senegalese films.) In an attempt to satisfy both an American and a French market, the latter's sexy scenes (such as they were) were even a little sexier. But to no avail. Racist distribution standards prevented even a light interracial clinch or two from being shown to any great extent in the United States in the 1950s. (See a similar discussion in the *Island in the Sun* entry.)

The producer, Sig Shore, went on to make the American blaxploitation cycle of *Superfly* films, while John Berry, the director and co-scriptwriter, directed plays (James Earl Jones in *Othello*, the Jean Genêt play *Les Blancs*, and a play by the South African writer Athol Fugard), but it wasn't until the black working-class drama *Claudine* (1974) that he resumed some of the Hollywood success so evident in the last film he made before he was blacklisted, the film noir *He Ran All the Way* (1951), with John Garfield as the lead.

See also: *Island in the Sun*.
Availability: Selected collections.

Further reading

Bogle, Donald. *Toms, Coons, Mulattoes, Mammies, and Bucks: An Interpretive History of Blacks in American Films*. 3d ed. New York: Continuum, 1994. Bogle devotes a section of his book to Dandridge, "the tragic mulatto."

Crowther, Bosley. "Tamango." *New York Times*, 17 September 1959, 48. Doesn't think much of the film, but hints that the interracial drama may entice some viewers into the theater (where they will probably be disappointed).

Johnson, Charles. *The Middle Passage*. New York: Atheneum, 1990. Winner of the 1990 National Book Award, this novel depicts similar events set in 1830.

McGilligan, Patrick, and Paul Buhle. *Tender Comrades*. New York: St. Martin's Press, 1997. Includes an interview with the blacklisted director.

Smith, Maxwell A. *Prosper Mérimée*. New York: Twain, 1972. A survey of Mérimée's career with a section on his short story.

↶

Taxi Dreams

New York realities

2001, 100 mins.
Director: Joanna Head
Traditional documentary
PRINCIPAL FIGURES
The cabbies: Om Dutta Sharma, India; Sumon (Mohammad Ahsan), Bangladesh; Rafik Bakayev, Tajikistan; Kwame Fosu, Ghana; Rizwan Raja, Pakistan
Robert Scott, Bolivia, poet-cabbie
Terry Gelber, Taxi Academy teacher

Yellow Cab drivers in New York are overwhelmingly recent immigrants to the United States. Most of them barely make ends meet after a twelve-hour shift. Although many of them go to such schools as The Taxi Academy and have to pass a city exam (not only on urban geography but also in English comprehension), quite a few of them encounter passengers who not only know the city much better than they do but in at least one instance recorded in this film volunteer to drive the cab.

With one exception (Sumon, who quits after one day to work in a relative's store), the cabbies portrayed in this documentary knock themselves out to work for a taxi fleet that rents them a cab. In this group there are no owner-operators, just small to medium businesses that desperately need drivers. Every shift averages 180 miles of driving, at the end of which the cabbie must pay his company rental and gas costs himself. (Sumon quit for two reasons: he barely knew how to drive and he lost money driving that first day.)

This film—a lively and perceptive look at Manhattanites—follows six cabbies from underdeveloped societies; one of them, Robert Scott, from Bolivia, recites his poems while he drives. These cabbies are a good antidote to the ones satirized in the black men and cabs episode of *TV Nation*.

See also: *Signal 7*; *TV Nation*.
Availability: Selected collections; PBS.

Web site:

⟨www.pbs.org/wnet/taxidreams⟩ Official site of the film, with interviews with some of its principal figures and other cabbies about the themes of the film, New York taxi history, "Taxi Tales" (passengers' whines and kudos), and other taxi lore.

~

Taylor Chain

Strong links, weak chain

A Story of a Union Local, 1980, 33 mins., B&W

A Story of Collective Bargaining, 1984, 30 mins.

Directors: Jerry Blumenthal and Gordon Quinn

Cinema verité documentaries

PRINCIPAL FIGURES IN *A STORY OF A UNION LOCAL*

Ted Pusty, electrician

Paul Martin, electrician and president, Local 4041, United Steelworkers of America (USWA)

John Bierman, USWA staff representative

Rose Davis, packer; secretary, Local 4041.

PRINCIPAL FIGURES IN *A STORY OF COLLECTIVE BARGAINING*

Bob Grantz, Carl Hildebrandt, Ted Pusty, and Henry Owczarzak, workers at Taylor Chain

Al Gonzalez, inspector, president, Local 4041, 1975–81

Howie Moore, president, Taylor Chain Company (TCC)

Winnie McCauley, shipper; president, Local 4041

Birdia Morris and Rose Davis, inspectors at Taylor Chain

Leon Rysicki, plant superintendent

John Sobolewski and Wally Moneta, union negotiation team

Steve Crist, TCC lawyer

Jerry Volkmann, TCC plant manager.

These two documentaries about the Taylor Chain Company of Hammond, Indiana, part of the sprawling industrial belt from Chicago east to Gary, Indiana, should be seen together: they chart two crucial stages in the life and death of a company established in 1873 by the Taylor family, who retained ownership and management through four generations. And, perhaps even more acutely, they chart the struggles of a union local to hold on to its contract in the face of the widespread devastation of their industry.

The first documentary focuses on a strike in 1972 by Local 4041 of the United Steelworkers for their third contract since winning recognition in 1967; the second film returns to the company, now virtually bankrupt and on the verge of going under despite a group of investors who try to save the plant and enter negotiations for the first time with Local 4041.

Both films take us inside the plant, for many years the leading Midwest supplier of chains for industry (shipping, logging, drilling, and steel mill operations) and home (tire chains and other hardware items). Although the actual making of the chains is featured in both films in quite fascinating detail—the filmmakers have a knack for seeing those interlocking links and their status as a flexible tool in the creation of industrial power—the real issue in the films is decision making, both at the local level, as the negotiating team walks a wavy line between the demands of the rank and file and the international, and at the bargaining table, as both union and management alternate between the hard and soft sell.

The first film concentrates almost exclusively on the leadership of the local and the rank and file. When the negotiations for the third contract stall, the men (98 percent of the work force) and women go on strike. The times were changing even then, for shots inside the strike headquarters trailer show not only a lot of *Playboy* posters but also a couple of nude men. Rose Davis, secretary and stalwart member of the union (she is still secretary nine years later in the second film) jokes about not knowing who would have put up the posters of the men.

With only five years of union membership at Taylor Chain, it wasn't clear even to the members how far they could go in insisting on strong health and safety language in the contract. Eventually the local meets to debate whether it can push the company on wages or on language. We see the negotiating process only from the vantage point of the interaction of the rank and file and their leadership. The latter is clearly split, with international rep Bierman favoring acceptance but other members of the committee urging the local to vote the contract proposal down, which they do.

There is some revealing interview footage when the issue of standing to indicate one's vote is discussed after the meeting. Some of the members agree with Bierman that such a procedure intimidates the membership. The second film shows a similar vote being taken nine years later by secret paper ballot. The film ends somewhat abruptly two weeks after this meeting with a ratified contract and the workers back at the plant.

The second film is more sophisticated in its presentation of the new situation with the company on the edge of bankruptcy. Not only is the film in color, but events are more carefully outlined and documented.

The heart of the second film, however, is the face-to-face meeting between the negotiating team and management after the collapse of the company—only twelve workers were on the floor—was temporarily staved off by new investors, who cut wages and workforce. The negotiating team tries to take a position of no concessions, even attempting to win back the 10 percent wage cut accepted just the year before. With an extended offer (1 percent wage increase restored each quarter), the contract is sent to the members, who ratify it. A year later, that contract is extended, but more layoffs cannot hold off what turns out to be the end: the company goes bankrupt.

The film's end titles summarize the sad tale of this Reagan-era disaster: of the 100 workers in 1980, a third had found other jobs, about half were unemployed, and a handful had retired. The film does not analyze these data politically or even economically: it is mainly a document of the running down of a local's livelihood. No Gekko-like investors from the world of *Wall Street* appear; in fact, the representatives of management, with rare exception, look as worried as the rank and file.

Kartemquin Educational Films has provided an excellent study guide for both films. Besides helpful general background on Chicago-area industrial issues, the guide emphasizes that the management of Taylor Chain represented two contradictory trends in the late 1970s and 1980s. On the one hand, atypically, Taylor Chain was in the end managed by an engineer, Howie Moore, the president of Taylor Chain; on the other hand, the company was barely keeping up with innovative and new machinery, part of the necessary profile to keep an American company competitive with Japan and Europe.

In the end, these films are testimonials to the human costs of plant closings, not to mention the erosion of collective bargaining traditions. They complement nicely John David Coles's *Rising Son*, in which a small starter-motor factory goes under. The filmmakers went on to make the successful *Hoop Dreams*.

See also: *American Dream; Rising Son; Wall Street.*
Availability: Selected collections.

Further reading

Lesage, Julia. "Filming for the City: An Interview with the Kartemquin Collective." *Cineaste* 7, no. 1 (1975). A profile of the filmmakers, who make "socially committed" documentaries.

Lynd, Staughton. *The Fight against Shutdowns: Youngstown's Steel Mill Closing.* San Pedro, Calif.: Singlejack Books, 1982. Recounts the same situation a state away and how community groups worked with the USWA to prevent the shutdowns.

Taylor Chain: A Study Guide for Workers and Corporations in the 1980s. Chicago: Kartemquin Educational Films, 1984. A guide to the regional and national issues of the changes in the industry.

Teague, Carol. "Easing the Pain of Plant Closure: The Brown and Williamson Experience." *Management Review*, April 1981, 23–27. The story of a three-year gradual shutdown, during which the company attempts to ease the pain for its employees and minimize production problems.

Zheutlin, Barbara, ed. "The Art and Politics of the Documentary: A Symposium." *Cineaste* 11, no. 3 (1981): 12–21. A number of filmmakers, including the Kartemquin group, which made the *Taylor Chain* films, discuss their films and their ideas about documentaries.

~~

Teamster Boss: The Jackie Presser Story

Another full-court press on Hoffa

1992, 111 mins., TVM
Director: Alastair Reid
Screenplay: Abby Mann, from James Neff's nonfiction book *Mobbed Up*
CAST
Jackie Presser = Brian Dennehy
Bill Presser = Eli Wallach
Carmen Presser = Maria Conchita Alonso
Tom Noonan = Jeff Daniels
Alan Dorfman = Tony Lo Bianco
Maisha Rockman = Robert Prosky
Tony Provenzano = Frank Pellegrino
Fat Tony Salerno = Val Avery

Teamster Boss is an intriguing film. An inept Jackie Presser, managing a bowling alley and lightly scamming a small Teamsters local, is catapulted into more prominent leadership roles by his father, Bill Presser, the second most powerful Teamster in the country. The elder Presser is dying and he wants someone to carry on the family business, which consists, in this case, of cheating Teamster members of their dues money. Dennehy plays young Presser as a foolish man who gradually realizes that there are worse things in life than being a union cheat and some dubious better things. He therefore becomes an informer for the FBI when he feels threatened by the same people who helped Hoffa disappear and hooks up with an FBI agent, Tom Noonan, whom he tells, "You use me; I use you."

The film credits Presser with an attack of conscience, especially after he finds a good woman (his fourth wife) and a terminal illness (lung cancer). Trying to maneuver against the likes of Fat Tony Salerno and Tony Provenzano, both formidably unpleasant guys with nasty reputations even inside the Mob, he thinks he can rely on his government contacts to help purify the Teamsters. Although Presser fails, the film credits him with causing enough of a hassle with the Mob so that the first "democratically" elected president, Ron Carey, has an even better chance of saving the Teamsters.

This was the first major post-Hoffa Teamsters movie that also attempted to interpret the Reaganite 1980s in the light of the Feds' secret relationships with organized labor. Ironically, very little of the Teamsters' daily life of working or even union organizing is shown. The emphasis is almost entirely on behind-the-scenes maneuvering among Teamster leaders, the Mob (both Jewish and Italian branches), the FBI, the Justice Department, and Reagan himself. The most obvious Teamster militancy is played out in a Cleveland local when the members try to keep their old leader and Hoffa's friend Bill Presser from imposing Jackie, his son, as president. Then baseball bats come out and the stereotypical violent Teamster is shown fighting—not cops or goons or scabs but his own leaders.

The film follows James Neff's interpretation of Presser in *Mobbed Up* as daddy's clown prince, who eventually tries to play the FBI and the Mob against each other to achieve some good ends for his membership. When he tries to outmaneuver the crown prince of Hollywood, Reagan himself, he fails miserably. Much is made of the difficulty of leading the nation's largest and most persecuted union: if its president cooperates with the Mob, the Feds throw him in jail; if he doesn't cooperate, he ends up like Jimmy Hoffa.

Should we accept this story as history? It's hard to say. On the surface, many details ring true. Presser was apparently an FBI informer, he did try to wheel and deal as if

Reagan's corrupt attorney general, Edwin Meese, would back him up (he didn't), and the Justice Department did force a major change in Teamster elections. The film is a better than average docudrama, in which real people (and sometimes actual footage) are edited into primarily a fiction film.

The film adds some bite to its tale when it includes shots of both Reagan and George Bush Sr. happily accepting the Teamsters' support for their presidential election campaigns. At one point a senator threatens Presser with a congressional investigation if the Teamsters do not help to bail out a savings and loan in trouble in his state. If only a third of this film is true, Presser and the Teamsters may yet wash a lot cleaner than most other Hollywood movies would indicate.

See also: *Blood Feud; F.I.S.T; Hoffa; Jimmy Hoffa; Power.*
Availability: Easy.

Further reading

La Botz, Dan. *Rank-and-File Rebellion: Teamsters for a Democratic Union*. London: Verso, 1990. An inside history by one of the founders of the TDU, with detailed narratives and analysis of the Presser years.

Neff, James. *Mobbed Up*. Boston: Atlantic Monthly Press, 1989. The reasonably well documented nonfiction source of the film.

O'Connor, John J. "Corruption, Love, and Murder, All from Real Life." *New York Times*, 11 September 1992, C34. Reviewer finds the film "packs the wallop of a political caricature by George Grosz," the great German antifascist artist.

Sloan, Arthur. *Hoffa*. Cambridge: MIT Press, 1992. The definitive academic biography of Hoffa, with important material about Presser as well.

✐

10,000 Black Men Named George

My name is not George!

2002, 112 mins., TVM
Director: Robert Townsend
Screenplay: Cyrus Nowrasteh

CAST
A. Philip Randolph = André Braugher
Milton Webster = Charles S. Dutton
Ashley Totten = Mario Van Peebles
Leon Frey = Brock Peters
Lucille Randolph = Carla Brothers
Barton Davis = Kenneth MacGregor

If any viewers have ever wondered why all the shipwrecked upper-class white passengers in Alfred Hitchcock's *Lifeboat* call Joe, their African American steward, "George," Robert Townsend's docudrama of the life of A. Philip Randolph and his Brotherhood of Sleeping Car Porters will provide the answer. Plus a stirring story of labor history oft neglected.

All the porters were black and all were called George, after George Pullman, the developer of the Pullman car, the moving bedroom of the American rail system from the 1920s through the 1960s. A. Philip Randolph, socialist editor of *The Messenger*, strove to form the first black union, organizing the Pullman porters from 1925 to 1937, when the Brotherhood of Sleeping Car Porters was finally recognized as their bargaining agent.

Randolph's task—also the subject of a documentary, *A. Philip Randolph*, in this volume—was to replace the company union, whose leader secretly supports his maneuvering, fight a racist management team led by Pullman president Barton Davis, and turn one of the best working-class jobs for black men into a source, if not of respect, at least of decent wages and hours.

Randolph also had to deal with turncoats in his own ranks, white unions that did not want him to organize, and a culture of subservience that was typified by a saying passed down through the years: "When Lincoln freed the slaves, George Pullman hired them" (Dyer). The Brotherhood of Sleeping Car Porters fought another civil war and won.

See also: *A. Philip Randolph.*
Availability: Easy.

Further reading

Dyer, Ervin. "Against All Odds, Pullman Porters Formed a Union." *Pittsburgh Post-Gazette*, 24

February 2002, at ⟨www.post-gazette.com/ lifestyle/2000220224pullman0224fnp2.asp⟩. History of the union and a few excerpts from interviews with porters still alive.

Wertheimer, Ron. "The Sleeping Car Porter Who Won the Last Round." *New York Times*, 23 February 2002, A28. Applauds this "compelling drama" and its historic lessons.

~

La terra trema

And so does the sea

1947, 160 mins., B&W, Italian, with English
  subtitles
Director: Luchino Visconti
Screenplay: Luchino Visconti, from
  Giovanni Verga's novel *The House by the
  Medlar Tree*
CAST
The villagers of Aci Trezza playing the
  following:

The Valastro Family: Antonio, Cola, Lucia,
  Mara
Nicola, laborer
Lorenzo, wharf supervisor
Don Salvatore, customs officer
Nedda, Antonio's sweetheart

La terra trema ("the earth shakes") is, on the surface, a simple tale of a Sicilian family's attempted rebellion against the system that has kept them hardworking but poor fishermen all their lives. Antonio, who has been on the mainland in the navy, "can't stand to see this injustice any more," in the words of one of his brothers.

Antonio mortgages the family house to buy a boat. His family will fish, salt the catch, and sell the barrels themselves. But they can't beat the system: the men who hire the fishing crews are also the ones who will bid—deliberately low—on Antonio's catch. When the brothers' boat is damaged in a storm, they lose their livelihood and their home.

The abortive rebellion of the fishermen in *La terra trema*. Courtesy British Film Institute Stills, Posters, and Designs.

Luchino Visconti filmed this very loose adaptation of Gionanni Verga's novel *The House by the Medlar Tree* in Aci Trezza, using local fishermen "acting as themselves" in a scripted drama. This classic of neorealism is a black-and-white odyssey of economic determinism. What little relief exists—three of the family have potential matches or marriages waiting—is also destroyed when the family's fortunes plunge. Antonio's rebellious gesture upsets more than just a single boat.

In the opening scene Antonio joyously throws the supervisor's scales into the sea. By the end of the film he is back at the wharf asking the same man for his old job back.

See also: *The Roof*.
Availability: Selected collections; DVD.

Further reading

Bazin, André. *What Is Cinema?* Trans. Hugh Gray. Vol. 2. Berkeley: University of California Press, 1971. Quirky but intriguing chapter on this film; Bazin finds it a "technical tour de force" but worries that it may bore the audience.

Hainsworth, Peter. "The Human Reality of the Despised South." *Times Literary Supplement*, 19 July 1996, 10. Brief but revealing overview of Verga's career.

Sitney, P. Adams. *Vital Crises in Italian Cinema*. Austin: University of Texas Press, 1995. Extensive discussion of the film and its source novel; essential companion for the film.

Verga, Giovanni. *The House by the Medlar Tree*. Trans. Raymond Rosenthal. Berkeley: University of California Press, 1964. The 1881 novel, with an excellent introduction by Giovanni Cecchetti.

Visconti, Luchino. *Two Screenplays*. Trans. Judith Green. New York: Orion Press, 1970. Includes *La terra trema*.

↩

These Hands

Labor intensive

1992, 45 mins., Tanzania, in Swahili and Kimakonde, with English subtitles

Director: Flora M'mbugu-Schelling
Cinema verité documentary
PRINCIPAL FIGURES
Women refugees from Mozambique

Director M'mbugu-Schelling explained why she used a pure form of cinema verité documentary filmmaking in *These Hands*, where film time and real time are virtually equal: "Certain things you can say with words and certain things you cannot find words for. . . . The time has passed when we can use the classic documentary style. I don't want to offend my audience by telling them what they should see or feel" (California Newsreel).

This is the ultimate cinema verité labor documentary: forty-five minutes of women cracking rocks with hammers with no commentary and with few establishing shots. We see mainly close-ups, two-shots, and group shots of the women; occasionally the camera will cut to a conveyor belt or the women eating. Are they in prison? No, we gradually realize that they are making gravel for what looks like a concrete business. Only from the film's distributor do we learn that these women are refugees from Mozambique working in a Tanzanian stone quarry.

This may be a film to visit for only selected sequences, because it is very hard to watch. But not as hard as what the women must do. Some of them balance children on their laps as they work. Occasionally they break into song. A few men shovel rocks nearby. Big rocks become small rocks. Over and over and over again.

See also: *The Girl Who Sold the Sun*.
Availability: Selected collections; California Newsreel.

Web sites:
⟨www.newsreel.org/topics/acine.htm⟩ California Newsreel's Library of African Cinema includes *These Hands* with numerous other films and essays about African cinema.

They Drive by Night

Riff-Raft

1940, 93 mins., B&W
Director: Raoul Walsh
Screenplay: Jerry Wald and Richard
    Macauley, from A. I. Bezzerides's novel
    The Long Haul
CAST
Joe Fabrini = George Raft
Paul Fabrini = Humphrey Bogart
Cassie Hartley = Ann Sheridan
Lana Carlsen = Ida Lupino

Warner Brothers' 1930s tradition of making films about tough guys and gals was continued in this saga of the Fabrini brothers, independent long-haul truckers who fight to remain owner-operators against all odds. When an accident causes one brother to lose an arm, they try to settle in to the easier job of working for a big trucking outfit. But it's not easy. The boss's wife has been trying to put the make on brother Joe for years and he has always resisted. She goes bonkers, see, and kills her husband (the boss) so Joe can take over and be hers too. When Joe resists yet again, she frames him for the killing, but later breaks down at the trial. The two brothers take over the business and turn it into a progressive driver-friendly line.

Fortunately for Warner Brothers, this trucker fantasy had two tough-guy icons—Humphrey Bogart and George Raft—and two tough-gal pinups—Ann Sheridan and Ida Lupino. Otherwise this film would have seemed even more unbelievable than it is. The *New York Times* reviewer was fair when he accepted some of the realism and some of the fantasy: the film was "sweaty with honest toil and very loose with suggestive repartee," as it starred "the cream of [Warner Brothers'] ungrammatical roughnecks, starting with George Raft and Humphrey Bogart, and their ace baggage, Ann Sheridan."

Although the film is often billed in video guides such as Leonard Maltin's as the story of tough "truck-driving brothers battling crooked bosses," there really are no "crooked bosses." The brothers are tough enough: "We're tougher than any truck that ever come off an assembly line." They drive by night to make it as independent owners, to be their own bosses. In short, it is a Depression story of working-class aspiration that never goes away: Ernest Borgnine continued the tradition in his working-class *Marty* in the 1950s and John Turturro updated it a little in *Mac*. In a strange way, this film also argues that although it may be a great idea to be an owner-independent, most working stiffs have a greater need for a benevolent boss.

See also: *Mac*; *Marty*.
Availability: Selected collections.

Further reading
Crowther, Bosley. "They Drive by Night." *New York Times*, 27 July 1940, 17. A brief but very positive review.
Sklar, Robert. *City Guys: Cagney, Bogart, and Garfield*. Princeton: Princeton University, 1992. A discussion of this film in the context of a relatively new working-class urban hero.

35 Up

"Give me a child until he is seven and I will show you the man."—Jesuit saying

1991, 128 mins., B&W and color, UK
Director: Michael Apted
Mixed cinema verité and traditional
    documentary
PRINCIPAL 35-YEAR-OLDS
Paul, Tony, Suzy, Bruce, John, Andrew,
    Charles, Nick, Jackie, Lynn, Sue, Symon,
    Neil, and Peter

35 Up focuses on all fourteen of the original children in Michael Apted's long-running documentary series of films on British class and character. (See *42 Up* for an overall introduction to the series.) Three who dropped out of the series earlier are treated more cursorily: Peter, a teacher who was very critical of British schools seven years earlier, is now preparing to enter law school; upper-class Charles, now a TV producer, knows better than to participate in a TV program; and Symon, the only black person in the group, does not participate for reasons of his own.

Those who have dropped out clearly have some negative feelings about the project; a number of reviewers have suggested that the recurring publicity may have unnerved them. Most poignant of all, however, is Neil, the happy son of two teachers at the age of 7, but quite depressed at 28 and a homeless drifter at 35. His only ties, to a rural village in the Shetland Islands, are marginal. His comeback in *42 Up* is quite a surprise.

Three working-class friends—Jackie, Lynn, and Sue—continue to be a spunky, good-humored, and very mature trio. One of the publicity shots characteristic of Apted's vision positions the three friends at age 35 holding a picture of the three friends at age 28 holding still another picture of the three friends at age 21. This cinematic mirroring seems especially appropriate for the three women, who—despite the difficulties they may have had over the years—accept themselves, their lives, and their friendships with continued good humor. Their portraits are also evidence of their enthusiastic acceptance of Apted's project.

Similarly, Apted films several of his subjects watching a video of themselves when they were younger. Even more characteristic of Apted's style is his continuous cutting from present to past and back again, as Tony at the age of 35, for example, talks about what has become of his life, giving way to Tony at ages 7 and 14 predicting what he will be when he grows up, and so forth. Sometimes Apted cuts back and forth among as many as fifteen clips at different ages.

If any sociological conclusions about class and labor can be drawn from Apted's series, it is simply that England's class system remains remarkably intact. Working-class Tony, who at the age of 7 wants to be a jockey, achieves this goal briefly but becomes a cab driver, and remains one despite a stint as a pub owner. The self-consciously upper-class boys—John, Andrew, and Charles—have gone on to become upper-class adults. At the age of 7, John defended the English public (we would say "private") school system: "I don't think it's a bad idea to pay for school, because if we didn't, schools would be so nasty and overcrowded." John at the age of 35 is seen with his wife, daughter of the ambassador to Bulgaria, fund-raising for Bulgarian charities.

The exceptions are still worth noting: Neil's homelessness is in a class by itself, but Nick, from a Yorkshire farming family, graduates from Oxford in physics and becomes a professor at the University of Wisconsin.

Although Apted makes it clear in interviews that the series has dominated his working life, he has also made feature films, including *Coal Miner's Daughter*, which, perhaps because of its subject matter, seems to be a remarkably *American* film for a British director to have undertaken.

See also: *Children of Golzow; Coal Miner's Daughter; 42 Up.*
Availability: Selected collections.

Further reading

Apted, Michael. "Filming Life, He Found His Own." *New York Times*, 12 January 1992, II.11, 17. Apted's own history of the project.

Canby, Vincent. "Onward, 'Up'-ward with Apted." *New York Times*, 16 February 1992), II.13–14. A detailed review of *35 Up*.

Ebert, Roger. "35 Up." *Chicago Sun-Times*, 14 February 1992. "The most engrossing long-distance documentary project in the history of film."

Hinson, Hal. "35 Up." *Washington Post*, 20 March 1992. The reviewer worries "that simply by their participation" in the series the participants have "somehow been blighted by self-consciousness, turned inward and maimed." (See *42 Up* for a reply to this idea.)

⤶

This Sporting Life

Even a night at the pub is safer

1963, 129 mins., B&W, UK
Director: Lindsay Anderson

Screenplay: David Storey, from his novel of the same title

CAST

Frank Machin = Richard Harris
Mrs. Margaret Hammond = Rachel Roberts
Weaver = Alan Badel
Johnson = William Hartnell
Maurice Braithwaite = Colin Blakely
Mrs. Weaver = Vanda Godsell
Judith = Anne Cunningham
Len Miller = Jack Watson
Stomer = Arthur Lowe
Wade = Harry Markham

David Storey's novel and this adaptation represented another entry in the British run of kitchen sink drama: angry young men— and at least in this film, one very angry young woman—express their rage at the British class system, which relegates workers like them to numerous pence-pinching experiences that leave them old before their time. Richard Harris and Rachel Roberts play the very angry lovers, she as a widow reluctant to take up with her boarder, he all rugby fury and macho posturing but attracted to a tender alternative.

Frank Machin and the widow's former husband both work in Weaver's local factory. Frank tortures Mrs. Hammond with the idea that her husband virtually committed suicide on the shop floor—that is, deliberately let himself in for a terrible accident in order to escape the workaday horrors of his life. Frank's escape is going to be rugby, although he curiously retains his factory job even after he signs for a considerable amount of money to play for Weaver's team.

This Sporting Life was Lindsay Anderson's first feature film after directing a number of documentaries as part of what became known as the Free Cinema movement of the 1950s. Later David Storey and Anderson collaborated on a pair of related theater pieces: *The Contractor*, in part about a work crew erecting a party marquee, and *In Celebration*, about the stresses in the lives of a miner's children. Neither play quite captures the potential violence in repressed working-class lives the way *This Sporting Life* does, proba-

bly because of the intense performances of the film's two leads.

See also: *Look Back in Anger; Saturday Night and Sunday Morning.*
Availability: Selected collections; DVD.

Further reading

Maschler, Tom, ed. *Declaration*. New York: Dutton, 1958. Anderson's essay about British culture in the 1950s, "Get Out and Push!" defends his cinematic interest (and daring) in taking "a camera and lights into a factory, or a coal mine, or a market."

Storey, David. *The Contractor; and, In Celebration*. Harmondsworth: Penguin, 1971. These provocative plays have never, as far as I know, been made into films.

Weiler, A. H. "This Sporting Life." *New York Times*, 17 July 1963, 19. The film gives "meaning and brilliance" to the genre of films in which "youth [are] wallowing in the lower depths of kitchen sink drama."

Tobacco Road

A dead end

1941, 84 mins., B&W
Director: John Ford
Screenplay: Nunnally Johnson, from Erskine Caldwell's novel of the same title

CAST

Jeeter = Charley Grapewin
Sister Bessie = Marjorie Rambeau
Ellie May = Gene Tierney
Dude Lester = William Tracy
Ada Lester = Elizabeth Patterson
Dr. Tim = Dana Andrews
Peabody = Slim Summerville
Lov = Ward Bond
Grandma = Zeffie Tilbury

When Lov at the end of this film gives Dude a knockout punch, the viewer's heart will soar, for in all the history of cinema there is probably no more exasperating character than William Tracy's Dude. One will also suspect, not far into this film, that John Ford (now in cinema heaven) must still have a controlling interest in this film, since it has never been released in videocassette. It shouldn't be.

This film is really a low point in the cycle of peckerwood or white trash films that began (not counting silent films) with *Cabin in the Cotton* in 1934, continued through the 1950s with another Erskine Caldwell adaptation, *God's Little Acre*, and could be said never to have ended, given the presence of Dogpatch and its various hillbilly representatives over the years. Certainly the stereotyping has not ceased, as we can see from Alicia Silverstone's character, Cher, in *Clueless* in 1995, when she denies her participation in a teenage marriage—"This isn't Kentucky, you know!"

The hillbilly stereotype is much broader than most of the southern rural and urban labor images we are surveying in this book (see the entry on *God's Little Acre*), but in considering Ford's adaptation of Caldwell's novel, in which he transforms a sharecropper into a hillbilly, it is helpful to remember J. W. Williamson's definition of the hillbilly as a "safely dismissible ... symbolic non-adult and willful renegade from capitalism." Ford's film in fact flees from the economic and social sordidness of Caldwell's original vision not only by making the characters hillbillies but by having their "rescue"—which they ignore by lazing on the porch—come in the form of another six months of free rent and some money to buy seed as a gift from the son of their old landlord. In the novel, their pathetic shack catches fire and kills both Jeeter and his wife in the midst of numerous other degradations.

See also: *Cabin in the Cotton; God's Little Acre.*
Availability: Not.

Further reading

Crowther, Bosley. "Tobacco Road." *New York Times*, 21 February 1941, 16. The reviewer notes that the rude original has been sanitized beyond belief; the result is "a leisurely picnic with a batch of moldy Georgia crackers."

"Tobacco Road." *Variety*, 26 February 1941. Argues that the sensationalism of the long-running play has "been deleted, altered, or attenuated to the point of dullness" and that the team responsible for the successful *Grapes of Wrath* just the year before—director John Ford and screenwriter Nunnally Johnson—misfires.

Williamson, J. W. *Hillbillyland*. Durham: University of North Carolina Press, 1995. A thorough survey of the hillbilly image in popular culture, but curiously quite light on Hollywood representations.

～

To Kill a Priest

... in Poland is a big (political) mistake

1988, 117 mins., R, France, in English
Director: Agnieszka Holland
Screenplay: Agnieszka Holland and Jean-Yvres Pitoun
CAST
Father Alek = Christopher Lambert
Stefan = Ed Harris
Josef = Peter Postlewaite
Helina = Cheri Lunghi
Anna = Joanne Whalley
Igor = Timothy Spall
Feliks = Tim Roth
The Colonel = Joss Ackland

Although *To Kill a Priest* was banned in Poland for many years, Holland's portrayal of the brutal murder of Jerzy Popieluszko, a pro-Solidarity priest, has not lost its ability to shock. Holland, an exiled Polish filmmaker (known for *Europa Europa*, the successful adaptation of the autobiography of a Jewish boy who passed for a Nazi) and a former assistant to Andrzej Wajda, has created a fictional context for the story of Popieluszko: she calls him Father Alek, adds a subplot about his relationship with a woman in the Solidarity movement, and dramatizes his doubts about his calling as a priest.

But the core of her story—a priest who openly defies the Communist government to preach about the virtues of Solidarity and is then murdered in 1984 in what seems to be an almost freelance operation by a Polish secret policeman—is here intact. Holland decided to dramatize the life of the secret policeman, played by Ed Harris, as well. The result is a film about a collision course between two fevered spirits, one religious and magnanimous, the other Stalinist and bigoted. Ed Harris's killer is both cold-blooded and ideological. In his practice speech for his show trial, he says that he is "a normal man" who would kill the priest again if it were necessary to "save" his country and his party: "The future is on our side," he concludes. His henchmen are played by Tim Roth and Timothy Spall, who, like so many in this excellent international cast, nonetheless seem to be having their lines spoken about three feet from their heads (most members of the cast are native English speakers, but the film still seems dubbed).

Her film was important, Holland has argued, in making the somewhat skeptical—and ultimately antireligious—film communities of the West understand the intensely devout following of the Catholic Church in Poland and the importance of the church in the fight for political freedom there. Indeed, in the end, in a tribute to Catholic Poland's devotion to this priest, whom Polish Catholics regard as a martyr to their faith, we see small wayside altars and pictures of the slain man in the traditional ways saints have been honored for centuries. Over the closing scene of a shrine to the priest, Joan Baez is singing "Crimes of Cain."

Such a tribute to the priest was inevitable, since his monthly Mass for the Motherland at St. Stanislaw Kostka Church in Warsaw drew thousands of worshipers in what became in effect a political rally. Recreated in the film, the mise-en-scène or look of the mass supports Lawrence Goodwyn's analysis that the Polish church is "so self-consciously the repository of a specific nationhood and . . . links its saints so intimately to the nation's struggle for independence."

See also: *Man of Marble*.
Availability: Selected collections.

Further reading

Goodwyn, Lawrence. *Breaking the Barrier: The Rise of Solidarity*. New York: Oxford University,
1991. A very thorough history of the Solidarity movement, with a section on Father Popieluszko's murder and its political implications.
Tagliabue, John. "One Dark Polish Undercurrent Stirs Another." *New York Times*, 15 December 1988, C15. A review and discussion of the film's private premiere in Poland.
Walsh, Brendan. *Poland's Priest Martyr: Jerzy Popieluszko*. London: Catholic Truth Society, 1989. A pamphlet from a London organization that publishes information on Catholic saints and other religious issues; has a clear and concise history of Solidarity and Popieluszko's life and murder.

To Save the Land and People

Not much choice there

1999, 57 mins.
Director: Anne Lewis
Traditional documentary

Viewers who do not know the concept of the broad-form deed or who need a crash course in the destruction visited on Appalachia by this diabolical tool used to make money for coal companies should watch this film. Concentrating on Knott County, whose resources are more or less solely owned by the Ford Motor Company, the filmmakers blend past and present, archival footage and contemporary interviews, to explain how even private property is not sacred when it comes to mineral rights.

Many residents of Eastern Kentucky signed deeds that gave coal companies the "broad right" to take all minerals by any means they saw fit. The surface rights—to live and to farm—belonged to the original owner. Unfortunately, when it came time to get the minerals out of the ground, strip or surface mining was often a lot cheaper and simpler than any traditional mining. The results were numerous personal wars between some landowners and the bulldozing team that came to clear land. Later—and this film documents this movement—Eastern

Kentuckians began to organize community groups to fight the broad-form deed.

See also: *Evelyn Williams*.
Availability: Selected collections; Appalshop.

Further reading

Caudill, Harry M. *My Land Is Dying*. New York: Dutton, 1971. Photographic documentation and essay on the history of strip mining by the late great chronicler of Appalachian culture.

Widener, Bill. "'To Save the Land and People' Documents Community against Strip Mining." Ace Magazine, at ⟨www.aceweekly.com/acemag/backissues/991027/fs991027.html⟩. Very positive review, ending with this quote from Gordon Singleton: "You're either on the side of money or the side of the people."

Web site:
⟨www.appalshop.org⟩ Full information about Appalshop's films and other activities.

.

To Sleep with Anger

... and wake up with the devil

1990, 102 mins., PG
Director: Charles Burnett
Screenplay: Charles Burnett
CAST
Harry Mention = Danny Glover
Gideon = Paul Butler
Sonny = DeVaughan Walter Nixon
Junior = Carl Lumley
Suzie = Mary Alice
Pat = Vonetta McGee
Babe Brother = Richard Brooks
Skip = Cory Curtis
Hattie = Ethel Ayler

Charles Burnett's story of a working-class family in Los Angeles literally bedeviled by an old country friend come to visit sets one of its leading characters on fire in the opening credit sequence. Gideon, dressed to the nines, is sitting stiffly by a table; first the bowl of fruit on the table, then his shoes, and finally his chest all burst into flame. We assume that this is only a dream, but after Gideon's fruitless search for his "Toby," or family good-luck charm, and the arrival of old friend Harry Mention, we realize that the Devil is literally up to his old tricks again. The credit sequence is therefore virtually a set piece of African American magic realism, as Burnett uses Harry as the trickster figure of African American folklore.

The film mixes the heartfelt drama of this extended family and its circle of friends and the mysterious ways of their visitor. When Gideon's grandson accidentally touches Harry with a broom, Gideon spits on it and throws salt over his shoulder; every time Gideon's pregnant daughter-in-law tries to shake Harry's hand, her baby kicks her violently.

Babe Brother resists the family's devotion to hard work. He sarcastically quotes his father's watchwords: "Idleness is sinfulness"; "Calluses and sweat are the mark of a man." In fact a work ethic is the essence of the difference between Gideon, who is compared to the legendary steel-drivin' man, John Henry, and Harry, who does no work to mention.

Gideon's son wants to get rich quick and is therefore an easy mark for Harry, whose smooth talk reveals a man who has not worked since he was on the railroad gang with Gideon. But Gideon's wife is also frustrated by her husband: "When are you going to fix the roof?!" Burnett seems to be telling a fable here of African American religion and work, two cornerstones of its working-class ethic.

There is even a nod to William Faulkner's novel *As I Lay Dying*, for in the end Harry lies dead in Suzie's kitchen for a day before the morgue sends a truck to pick him up. The family tiptoes around Harry as if he were a monument to a past they wish to forget, even at one point all leaving for a picnic their neighbors have been considerate enough to lay on while they are waiting. Harry's power is truly gone when one of Gideon's friends stops in, points to Harry's body with a piece of chicken, and says, "Who is that?"

The *New York Times* reviewer (Canby) was impatient with many of the voodoo interpretations of Harry's life and argued that Harry simply represents an "angry and unreconstructed" southern black sharecropper who has been overtaken by the kinds of things Los Angeles folks worry about, such as the midwifery classes Suzie teaches to white and black couples who want to get "in touch with themselves." Maybe. In any case, Harry has a history, and part of that history is lynching (in which he may have played an unpleasant part), work gangs, and sharecropping. To mention that these important subjects are mostly in the background is not to fault this unusual film, Burnett's first with a major budget, but to agree (at least symbolically) with Canby that there is a lot more story to be told about this family.

See also: *Nothing But a Man.*
Availability: Easy.

Further reading

Bates, Karen Grigsby. " 'They've Gotta Have Us': Hollywood's Black Directors." *New York Times Magazine,* 14 July 1991, 15–19, 38, 40, 44. Surveys the difficulties in marketing *To Sleep with Anger,* as well as films by Spike Lee, Bill Duke, and other black directors.

Canby, Vincent. "To Sleep with Anger." *New York Times,* 5 October 1990, C10. The reviewer finds it "a very entertaining, complex film."

☙

Tout va bien

Or not

1972, 95 mins., France, in English and French, with English subtitles
Directors: Jean-Luc Godard and Jean-Pierre Gorin
Screenplay: Jean-Luc Godard and Jean-Pierre Gorin
CAST
Her = Jane Fonda
Him = Yves Montand
Factory Manager = Vittorio Caprioli
Leftist Woman = Anne Wiazemsky

This project for the Dziga Vertov collective—mostly Godard and a collaborator, Jean-

Pierre Gorin—is an attempt at deconstructing the process of making a political film, the kind of project that Godard as a rule loved but that is not always easy for audiences to appreciate. This time I would say they were fairly successful. By taking Jane Fonda and Yves Montand, stars of American and French cinema, respectively, and placing them in a factory occupation that controls them rather than the other way around, we are treated to a very different narrative pace. The workers at the factory argue and rush about, sometimes dragging our hero and heroine around. Since as a director of film commercials (Him) and a radio broadcaster (Her), they were used to being dominant, their lack of control over the process and their interpretation of same unsettles them.

Some of the deconstruction is playful but ultimately quite trivial: for example, Godard opens the film by signing a bunch of checks to finance the production. But one sequence at the end, when the camera tracks laterally across the front of a hypermarket in a long take that includes cash registers jingling, a Communist Party group selling their blueprint for change, and a disruptive demonstration of radicals, is a comic and sharp revelation.

This assault on one of the temples of capitalism is actually typical of the recurring political themes of Godard and his collaborators, as well as the arguments of the radical workers in the film itself, usually more intent on attacking what were regarded as the "conservative" forces in the radical movements of 1968. While capitalism is the ostensible enemy, more energy is expended attacking the national trade union leadership and its dominant group, the Communist Party.

See also: *Blow for Blow.*
Availability: UK (PAL standard only).

Further reading

Dixon, Wheeler Winston. *The Films of Jean-Luc Godard.* Albany: SUNY Press, 1997. A helpful overview of Godard's career, with a filmography from 1954 to 1995 and a section, fairly negative, on *Tout va bien:* the film "dominates" the audience and also doesn't permit the participants to have much understanding of their situation.

Loshitzky, Yosefa. *The Radical Faces of Godard and Bertolucci.* Detroit: Wayne State University Press, 1995. An extensive analysis of the film, stressing Godard's reworking of the Hollywood Production Code.

MacCabe, Colin. "The Politics of Separation." *Screen* 16 (Winter 1975–76): 46–57. Compares the Godard film to Brecht's *Kuhle Wampe*, emphasizing that the latter looked for objective conditions to understand Germany while Godard—despite a winsome desire to question all premises of filmmaking—ends up too concerned with subjective states of people.

Porton, Richard. *Film and the Anarchist Imagination.* London: Verso, 1999. Offers an intriguing argument: the film represents the "workers' self-management" concept or syndicalism of classical anarchism.

~

Trace of Stones

"Nothing is lied about."—Wolf Biermann

1966 (1990), 133 mins., B&W, East Germany, in German, with English subtitles
Director: Frank Beyer
Screenplay: Frank Beyer, from Erik Neutsch's novel *Spur der Steine*
CAST
Hannes Balla = Manfred Krug
Kati Klee = Krystyna Stypulkowska
Werner Horrath = Eberhard Esche

It is not hard to see why East German authorities censored this film and drove its director out of DEFA, the state-sponsored film producing agency. *Trace of Stones* is an intricate, uncompromising, realistic look at a massive East German power plant construction site (Schkona) and its socioeconomic complexity of political intrigue and working-class consciousness. East German Communists in this film, despite some rhetorical flights of praise for the "higher morality" of Party members, do not inspire confidence. East Germans never saw the film while the Berlin Wall stood. It finally debuted at the Berlin International Film Festival in 1990, a year after the Wall came down, with other films banned at the same time (nicknamed the "rabbit films," after one satirical film by the DEFA co-founder Kurt Maetzig, *I'm the Rabbit,* also banned).

Originally lines from the poet Wolf Biermann (banned from performing and publishing in the GDR since 1965) were to open the film:

Nothing is lied about
Not even twisted
There is nothing sugar-coated
And polished up
This is life
Rude and clear
Crazy and true.

Apparently Biermann missed his lessons in East German dialectic: one doesn't lie, one explains how an action fits into the overall movement or progress of events. It's the only way, both sympathetic and unsympathetic characters agree, that a massive project can get done. At least this project is a power plant; three years before, in Beyer's earlier and successful (i.e., not banned) film *Carbide and Sorrel*, it was a cigarette factory.

Two major plot lines cross in the film. In one a love triangle forms among the Party secretary Horrath, the recently arrived engineer Kati, and a notorious bully of a site-gang leader, whom everybody simply calls, with curled lip, Balla. The other plot involves the construction of the power plant itself, with fouled-up and piss-poor design plans, a shortage of raw materials, and Balla's cock-of-the-walk attitude.

Balla's gang are featured in a brilliant opening sequence, dressed in the distinctive garb of their carpenter's craft, which resembles some kind of loopy Bavarian fantasy of an American cowboy outfit. They drink on the work site, obviously cut an important rally, grope women, and go skinny-dipping in front of everyone at the work site. Later they kidnap two loads of gravel headed for another site and bring it to their own. Most of the time they seem to get away with antics like this, and Horrath, at first incensed by such maneuvers, nevertheless believes that at heart they are great workers who need to be roped into some kind of discipline (although not, strictly speaking, *Party* discipline). Others, however, are tired of their excesses and are convinced they are simply angling for higher bonuses, not toiling selflessly for the socialist future.

The film is structured by a series of flashbacks to a hearing called to expel Horrath from the Party for gross immorality (he kept his relationship with Kati secret even after she became pregnant, among other things). As various witnesses come forward to testify, we go into the immediate past to discover who has been responsible for the successes—and occasional failures—in building the new power plant. The bully Balla turns out to be in love with Kati too, even though he knows he doesn't have a chance with her. In the meantime, Horrath is manipulating everyone in sight—generally taking the high road—to get the building schedule functioning.

This is an engrossing and convincing portrait of a culture too easily stereotyped in the past. Certain Communist bureaucrats behave badly and deserve more than the punch in the nose they almost get a number of times. An air of self-satisfaction among some of the Party leaders indicates that their peers in the film industry knew whom they were protecting—people like themselves—when they banned this film. Whether the film succeeds in convincing you that the real heroes are those—like Balla or Horrath—who know how to defy the Party's absurd sense of self-importance and actual power by being either bullies or successful infighters remains to be seen.

See also: *Carbide and Sorrel; Children of Gozlow; East Side Story*.
Availability: Selected collections; Icestorm.

Further reading

Allan, Sean, and John Sandford, eds. *DEFA: East German Cinema, 1946–1992*. New York: Berghahn Books, 1999. Excellent collection of essays by diverse hands, including a discussion of *Trace of Stones* in Karen Kramer's "Representations of Work in the Forbidden DEFA Films of 1965."
Murray, Bruce A., and Christopher J. Wickham, eds. *Framing the Past: The Historiography of German Cinema and Television*. Carbondale: Southern Illinois University Press, 1992. Barton Byg's essay, "Generational Conflict and Historical Continuity in GDR Film," outlines the "rabbit film" controversy.
Pflaum, Hans Günther, and Hans Helmut Prinzler. *Cinema in the Federal Republic of Germany*. Bonn: Inter Nationes, 1993. This very thorough reference work includes essays and production data on GDR films and filmmakers, including a section on Beyer and his films.
Web sites:
⟨www.icestorm-video.com⟩ Official site of Icestorm, the international distributor of the DEFA films; includes numerous commentaries on the films.
⟨www.umass.edu/defa⟩ Sister educational site of the Icestorm DEFA film collection, with rental information, a bibliography, and other helpful information.

The Triangle Factory Fire Scandal

Perjury and profit

1979, 100 mins., TVM
Director: Mel Stuart
Screenplay: Mel and Ethel Brez
CAST
Morris Feldman = Tom Bosley
Lou Rubin = David Dukes
Florence = Tovah Feldshuh
Sonya Levin = Lauren Frost
Rose = Janet Margolin
Gina = Stacey Nelkin
Vinnie = Ted Wass
Connie = Stephanie Zimbalist
Bessie = Charlotte Rae
Mrs. Levin = Erica Yohn
Mo Pincus = Larry Gelman

On 25 March 1911, one of the worst factory fires in history killed 146 employees, mostly young women, in just twenty minutes. The

Triangle factory fire was a disaster waiting to happen. It could have happened in any of the other buildings near Washington Square in Manhattan or on the Lower East Side, where immigrant women (and young girls) made the fashionable and useful shirtwaist, a blouse that became virtually the uniform of the "new women" of the early years of the twentieth century. But it happened in the Asch Building, which, as a voice-of-God narrator tells us at the beginning of the film, was "considered fire-safe."

This disaster and the subsequent scandalous trial certainly deserved better treatment than this underdeveloped fictionalization of the bare bones of the drama. The filmmakers chose to concentrate on three cute young ladies and their beaux (or lack of them). Jewish and Italian immigrants are featured, and it seems that—with the exception of the very religious Jews—most of the Lower East Side residents spent their time dancing in the street while their men pitched love at whatever shirtwaist walked by.

The real scandal of this film is that the scandal of the time is literally never mentioned. After the hideous fire, our heroines meet up again in their Easter Sunday finery and instruct the youngest, Gina, on how to smile at the dance they will attend that night. The Jewish factory supervisor, who miraculously escapes with his young daughter on his back on a ladder stretched over ten stories of air between two buildings, decides to visit the Easter parade. (Is this ecumenical visit likely?) Life must go on. But the trial of the Triangle factory owners occupied the attention and fervor of New Yorkers for months, as a parade of witnesses testified that doors were routinely locked and all safety precautions ignored.

The Triangle Shirtwaist factory fire became the tragic symbol of a decade of union organizing among immigrant garment workers. In 1909, the "Uprising of the 20,000," a movement of mostly Italian and Eastern European Jewish workers, had spread from New York City to Chicago and Cleveland, pursuing demands of the International Ladies' Garment Workers' Union (ILGWU). The movement culminated in a joint demonstration with women in the suffrage movement on 8 March 1909, with demands for better working conditions, an end to child labor, and the right to vote. (The anniversary of this date became International Women's Day.)

Just two years later, more than 300,000 marched in the funeral parade for the dead Triangle Shirtwaist factory women. During the memorial meeting sponsored by the Ladies' Waist and Dressmakers' Union (Local 29 of the ILGWU), speeches were delivered in Yiddish, Italian, and English (the latter by Morris Hillquit, the general counsel of the union and Socialist Party leader).

The only hint of this activity in the film comes from Lou Rubin, one of the shop engineers (a general fixit man), who speaks glowingly of "Dubinsky" (the ILGWU organizer) and the union. At one point he directs the only collective action of the film: when one woman's production of sleeves falls off, he solicits the women around her to donate some of their piecework to make up her quota. This is the kind of thing, he hints, that will come from unionism. His girlfriend, Rose, who is not so sure of this union business, gets more interested in Dubinsky when another overzealous suitor of hers calls the labor leader "Mr. Buttinsky Dubinsky."

What the film does best is to stage a convincing portrayal of the fire and the difficulty of evacuating the hundreds of women who worked in these sweatshops. As the actual cause of the fire the film offers a worn lighting connection that eventually caught fire and dropped a piece of burning debris on a bin of fabric. The camera follows the young women as they charge about the top three floors, desperately trying to find a way out. One woman slid down the elevator cable. Others tried to jump onto the life nets held by firemen below. (In real life no one succeeded in this maneuver because they were jumping from too great a height; in the film one Italian-American girl succeeds.) Other women threw themselves from open windows rather than face the fire. In one instance, we see a somewhat mysterious man holding a woman's hand as they jump together.

Viewers of this film should read Leon Stein's narrative of the fire and its aftermath, if only to understand the citizens' rage at the owners reflected in the editorial cartoons of the city's newspapers. Leon Stein reprints several of these cartoons: the *New York Call* pictured the "Real Triangle"—"Rent/Profit/ Interest"—while the *Evening Journal* captioned its drawing of a woman dead on the sidewalk "This Is One of a Hundred Murdered: Is Any One to Be Punished for This?"

The answer was no. The owners were acquitted of negligence, they collected insurance money, and only a union survived to carry the fight—often successfully—for better legislation to protect future shirtwaist workers and their peers in the industry.

See also: *Hester Street; The Inheritance.*
Availability: Selected collections.

Further reading

Crute, Sheree. "The Insurance Scandal behind the Triangle Shirtwaist Fire." *Ms*, April 1983, 81–83. After a computation of the insurance profits collected by the owners, we read a reminiscence by one of the few survivors (a child worker) alive in 1982.

Glenn, Susan A. *Daughter of the Shetl*. Ithaca: Cornell University Press, 1990. An excellent survey of immigrant women workers, with sections on the 1909–10 strike, which included the Triangle Shirtwaist Company.

Kaufman, Michael T. "Bessie Cohen, 107, Survivor of 1911 Shirtwaist Fire, Dies." *New York Times*, 24 February 1999. The obituary of the first of the two known survivors in the 1990s to die: she escaped by taking the stairs down (see McCracken below).

Malkiel, Theresa Serber. *The Diary of a Shirtwaist Worker*. Ithaca: ILR Press, 1990. A fictionalized diary of a 1909 New York striker.

McCracken, Elizabeth. "Out of the Fire." *New York Times Magazine*, 30 December 2001, 19–20. A memorial essay for the last survivor of the fire, Rose Rosenfeld Freedman, who died in 2001 at age 108; she escaped by taking the stairs

up and crossing over to the roof of an NYU building.

New York Times: "Many Now Tell of Fire Traps," 29 March 1911, 3; "Triangle Survivors Slide Down [Elevator] Cables," 12 October 1911, 4; "Triangle Witnesses Got Increased Pay," 22 December 1911, 7; "Triangle Owners Acquitted by Jury," 28 December 1911, 1: sample journalism about the investigation and the trial.

Stein, Leon. *The Triangle Fire*. 1962. Ithaca: ILR Press/Cornell Paperbacks, 2001. Thorough and readable, this is the only definitive narrative account.

Zandy, Janet. "Fire Poetry on the Triangle Shirtwaist Company Fire of March 25, 1911." *College English* 24 (October 1997): 33–54. A chronicler of "fire poetry" explains that the fire "becomes through memory and language and history a catalyst for breaking silence and recovering working-class identity."

Web site:
⟨www.ilr.cornell.edu/trianglefire⟩ A very rich and complete site of information, with bibliography, photos, and audio interviews.

Trouble on Fashion Avenue

Of all sizes

1982, 60 mins.
Directors: Stefan Moore and Claude Beller
Mixed traditional and agitprop documentary
PRINCIPAL FIGURES
Ed Koch, mayor, New York City
Ralph Cohen, manufacturer
Jerry Amato, independent contractor
Franz Leichter, representative, New York State Assembly
Doris Koo, leader, Asian-Americans for Equality
Jay Mazur, Henry Prastien, Louis Bertot, and Sol Chaiken, International Ladies' Garment Workers' Union (ILGWU).
Joe and Murray Berbasset and Shelly Silverstein, manufacturers
Eli Russo, owner, Russ Togs
Reuben Schwartz, attorney

Eli Elias, New York Skirt and Sportswear
  Association
Leon Stein, author, *The Triangle Fire*
Bill Blass, designer
Lt. Remo Francescini, New York City
  Police Department
Mr. Lee, garment worker
James Harmon, federal prosecutor,
  Organized Crime Strike Force
Morris Garfine, Rubin Budah, Shirley
  Novick, Celia Orlansky, retired ILGWU
  members and organizers
Matthew Eason, president, United
  Warehouse and Industrial Workers

The globalization of clothing manufacture has changed but not eliminated the world of garment and sweatshop workers depicted in this film. While Disney T-shirts and Gap sweaters are made thousands of miles from New York City's garment district (centered on Seventh or Fashion Avenue, but actually running from Broadway to Ninth Avenue between 42nd and 84th streets), hundreds of smaller manufacturers, operating through a complex system of independent contractors and sweatshop operators, union and nonunion facilitators, still turn out the goods. And still depend on hazardous working conditions, blocked fire exits, low and delayed pay, and job insecurity to control an almost exclusively immigrant workforce.

Leave it to Mayor Koch to say it loud and clear: 200,000 workers are involved in garment work in New York City, an industry valued at $16 billion in the 1980s. The trouble is, of course, that the history of the garment industry is the history of sweatshops, not only in the garment district so designated, but also in Chinatown, the second garment district, so to speak.

The conditions that led to the demonstrations and eventually the unionization of the mostly Jewish and Italian—and mostly women—garment workers in the second decade of the twentieth century have been revived since the middle of the century. Now the immigrants are from Latin America and China and the rest of Southeast Asia, and many of the sweatshops are still not union-ized, with dangerous firetraps, paying less than minimum wage and not always on time, and in many other ways illegal and marginal operations. The trucking industry associated with the delivery of the goods has been Mob infested, with some accusations (discussed in the film at times tentatively, at times res-olutely) of corruption in the upper levels of the ILGWU (now absorbed into UNITE! or the Union of Needle Trades, Industrial and Textile Employees).

The film is dominated by talking heads from every corner of the garment industry. It has a traditional documentary look in some ways, but in other ways the filmmakers clearly wanted to give their survey of the industry an agitprop twist. Two sequences can give the flavor of their approach. In one, Matthew Eason, an African American organizer of a union independent of the AFL-CIO, tries to have his members gain a foothold in the competitive—and scary—trucking side of the industry. He ends up needing a body-guard, in large part because he secretly records for a crime task force the promised bribes and threats of a Mob figure. In another sequence, a Chinese garment worker identi-fied only as Mr. Lee goes through harrowing experiences and eventual court battles just to get his back pay.

Trouble on Fashion Avenue was first broadcast as part of WNET Channel 13's *Nonfiction TV*, a public television series no longer playing. It needs updating (Andrew Ross's book *No Sweat* will help), but as a cin-ematic foray into a continuing and dangerous industry it is still worth a look.

See also: *The City; The Inheritance; Mickey Mouse Goes to Haiti; Nightsongs.*
Availability: Selected collections.

Further reading

Ross, Andrew, ed. *No Sweat: Fashion, Free Trade, and the Rights of Garment Workers*. London: Verso, 1997. Both a history of garment labor and an assessment of its contemporary global status.
Web sites:
⟨www.uniteunion.org⟩ Official site of UNITE! with extensive documentation of sweatshops and related issues.

Troublesome Creek: A Midwestern

"The midwestern reality is much more complicated than the western myth."— Steven Ascher

1997, 88 mins.
Directors: Jeanne Jordan and Steven Ascher
Cinema verité documentary
PRINCIPAL FIGURES
Russel and Mary Jane Jordan, farmers
Jeanne Jordan, their daughter and a filmmaker (also the narrator)
Steve Ascher, Jeanne's husband and a filmmaker
Jim Jordan, heir to the Jordan land
Gini Jordan, Jim's wife, and James, Jesse, and Grace, his children
Jon Jordan, another son and owner of a trophy business
Kim Jordan, Jon's wife
Tim Wolf, bank officer, Norwest Corporation
Dean Eilts, auctioneer

It's hard to follow in Michael Moore's footsteps. The director of *Roger & Me* set a new standard for documentary filmmaking that is not going to be easy to top. As a postmodernist with silly baseball caps (sometimes tractor caps) who stars in the very scenes he engineers to make his points about unfeeling capitalism, Moore has an unerring knack for puncturing the absurdities of a system that pays a CEO 430 times more than the average worker, while the CEO fires workers to save money.

Comes now a filmmaking team, Jeanne Jordan and Steven Ascher—producers, writers, directors—who want to make an arch if not comic film about the loss of the family farm in America. And not only family farms generically, but a farm that belongs to Jeanne Jordan's mom and dad, Russel and Mary Jane Jordan. The Jordans stand in somewhat convincingly for the Middle American Farm Family who got caught in the boom of the early 1980s and took out loans that eventually banks want to collect.

So far, so simple. And sad: this couple clearly work hard and have a dedicated set of offspring also involved in farming and a zillion relatives, all with J-names—Judy, Janet, Jim, Jon, Joe, Jan, Jigs, Jenny, Jenna, James, Jesse, and Justin. The names should have been played for laughs. The film could use some. (The *New York Times* reviewer was not amused.) The Jordans watch westerns on TV every free moment they get: hence the pun in the subtitle of this documentary. The filmmakers blow in from the Coast (Boston), where they have been busy not being farmers and can therefore be excused if they ask and record some pretty obvious farm facts. Most of us have never worked on a farm either, but we've seen a lot of documentaries about them, haven't we?

Maybe the problem is that the filmmakers are not particularly good or even silly actors. They're nice people, like their farming relatives, but they simply do not know how to milk the moment a farmer's fate has thrown in their faces. The western subplot almost works, too, and not because we don't sympathize with the way the Jordans wind down after a rough day at the barn. It's just that *High Noon,* especially the last minutes, is so good that we get lost in those dreamy looks between Gary Cooper and Grace Kelly and forget that the sheriff has just thrown his badge in the dirt in disgust at the townspeople's weakness. Have the Jordans been cheated of their justice—is that the point of the clip? Or is it simply enough that Coop and the Princess leave town? But the Jordans don't really have to *leave* town, they just have to *go* to town, while their son takes over the farm. To my unfarmerly eye, they lost a farm but secured an inheritance.

The critic Roger Ebert is more angry about this solution, because he thinks the family farms are worth saving: "Strange how for all the talk of individualism and resourcefulness from politicians, our country drifts every year closer to a totalitarianism of the corporation." The Jordans, perhaps to our amazement, generally think they won. The farm is out of debt, it's still in the hands of a Jordan, and Russel and Mary Jane seem reasonably content in their tiny new town house. PBS's Web site for the film (⟨www.pbs.org/wgbh/pages/amex/trouble⟩) makes it clear, however, that farmers, like cowboys and schoolmarms, don't always live happily ever after: Mary Jane died just after the film was completed and both Jim and Gini took full-time jobs while continuing to work the farm. Convinced that a medium-sized farm could not succeed in the face of government food policies, insurance companies, and corporate control of the livestock market, Jim became a civil engineer and Gini a teacher.

In case viewers do not know their westerns as well as the Jordans, here is a list of the films they watch (and a suggestion or two about their taste and how it reflects on their situation): *Dodge City,* a classic shoot-em-up to prepare us for the elder Jordans' various confrontations with bad bankers; *The Gunfighter,* Gregory Peck would rather farm than fight; *Red River,* round up the cattle and sell them; *Lonesome Dove,* more cattle drives; *High Noon,* a man has to stand up for his values and his wife sometimes has to give up hers.

Ebert was more taken with Gary Sinise's *Miles from Home* (1988), in which Richard Gere and Kevin Anderson starred as two brothers unable to make a go of their family's Iowa farm, which had been visited by Khrushchev as the "farm of the year" in 1959. The brothers drift into rural Bonnie and Clydism too easily for my taste. I prefer the "shootout" with a banker at Troublesome Creek.

See also: *Northern Lights.*
Availability: Easy.

Further reading

Goodman, Walter. "For an Iowa Family, No Happy Ending." *New York Times,* 14 April 1997, B2. The reviewer did not like the idea behind this film, its execution, its jokes, its J-names, its niceness to farmers: he found himself identifying with the banker putting the squeeze on the Jordans.

Johnson, Dirk. "Forget City Lights; Life on the Farm Suits Dan Berdo Fine." *New York Times,* 8

March 2000, D3. A view of another close Iowa farm family and how they handled passing the farm on to the next generation.

↩

Tucker: The Man and His Dream

The Big Three close ranks

1988, 111 mins., PG
Director: Francis Ford Coppola
Screenplay: Arnold Schulman and David Seidler
CAST
Preston Tucker = Jeff Bridges
Abe = Martin Landau
Vera Tucker = Joan Allen
Eddie = Frederick Forrest
Junior = Christian Slater
Jimmy = Mako
Howard Hughes = Dean Stockwell
The Michigan Senator = Lloyd Bridges

This film is a stirring exposé of a sordid chapter in American capitalism. Francis Ford Coppola's obsession with authenticity may make the film awkward at times, but how the Big Three automakers colluded with a Michigan senator to keep the safe Tucker cars off the market comes through loud and clear. Preston Tucker was an American innovator and a maverick soul: outside the mainstream, he fights the big guys and almost wins. He and a few of his mates (mostly engineers and white-collar types, not too many mechanics) manage to build fifty beauties bursting with extras.

The result is a fascinating excursion into entrepreneurial capitalism in the postwar period, when factories were retooled from war production to peacetime uses. A survey of returning GIs revealed that what they wanted most was a car. Tucker, whose fast (117 mph) tanklike "combat car" and a patented new "power-operated" gun turret were attempts to revolutionize military vehicles, was in an ideal position to satisfy the GIs and carry out his experimental ideas in auto

Preston Tucker (Jeff Bridges) inspects
his primitive assembly line.

design. He managed to rent the largest
demobilized factory in the United States,
the Dodge B-29 airplane plant in Chicago.
He sold dealerships, floated shares, raised
about $28 million, and was ready to turn out
the prototypes of his radical autos with rear
engines, seat belts, safety windshields, and
turning headlights.

Coppola follows fairly closely Tucker's
story as we know it from other accounts,
although occasionally there are lapses into
anachronistic foolishness. When Tucker
bemoans the lack of support for his innovations, he complains that in the future we may
be buying our radios from the very enemy
(the Japanese) we just defeated in the war.

Although articles by Lester Velie in
Collier's and *Reader's Digest* may not have
been the direct cause of Tucker's indictment
for fraud, his lawyers moved that Velie and
the editors of both magazines be held in
contempt for being "part of a conspiracy to
cause the whole Tucker venture to fail at
any cost." Tucker's motion was based on the
huge number of auto ads from the Big Three
that these two magazines ran routinely.
(Velie also wrote the articles on which *The
Garment Jungle* was based seven years later.
Hmmm.)

Tucker in both real life and Hollywood
won an acquittal but lost the war. Like his
innovative car, his motion to get even with
Velie failed. Most of the fifty Tuckers he built
are still roadworthy and his safety innovations are now routine. Even if Coppola's film
romanticizes the way cars could be put
together by a handful of idealistic misfits, it
is at least a tribute to a great inventor with
more than a touch of P. T. Barnum about him.

See also: *Gung Ho*.
Availability: Easy; DVD.

Further reading

Gross, John. "A Movie That Celebrates the
American Businessman as a Hero." *New York
Times*, 4 September 1988, II.33. Pokes fun at
Coppola's tendency to make a myth out of
Tucker.

Kearney, Jill. "The Road Warrior." *American Film,* June 1988, 21–27, 52–53. A detailed production history of the film.

Pearson, Charles T. *The Indomitable Tin Goose: The True Story of Preston Tucker and His Car.* New York: Abelard-Schuman, 1960. An extensive positive account of Tucker's career by an auto magazine writer who worked on Tucker's public relations campaign.

Velie, Lester. "The Fantastic Story of the Tucker Car." *Collier's,* 25 June 1949, 13–15, 68–72. The smear article that prepared the way for Tucker's indictment.

"Tucker Acquittal Asked by Counsel" and "Tucker and Aides Cleared of Fraud." *New York Times,* 20 January 1950, 40; 23 January 1950, 1. News articles that detail the film's hard-to-believe but (mostly) true courtroom ending.

Web site:

⟨www.tuckerclub.org⟩ Fans of the Tucker have created this site to celebrate the cars; bursting with information, photos, and many extras.

✎

Turumba

Woof

1984, 95 mins., Philippines, in Tagalog, with English subtitles
Director: Kidlat Tahimik
Screenplay: Kidlat Tahimik
CAST
Father (Kadid) = Herman Abiad
German Buyer = Katrin Luise

Given a commission by East German television for a 45-minute documentary, Kidlat Tahimik originally focused on the *turumba,* the Philippine religious festival that gives the film its title. Sometime later, however, he reworked the material into something quite different: a comic exploration of the ways capital transforms a cottage industry into an exploitative system. This premise is never allowed to make the film pretentiously political, mainly because of the papier-mâché dachshunds.

Papier-mâché dachshunds?! Sure. A German woman visits the village, spots some of the cute papier-mâché animals the locals use in their *turumba,* and decides to order 25,000 mascots for the Munich Olympics. At first the family works a little harder each day, figuring to add a few relatives as workers here and there in their quest to fill the order. Soon it is apparent that quite a few workers must be added, many of them children, and the hours of work must be extended, and the conditions of work are much less casual. The inexorable claims of the marketplace begin to ruin the animals as objects of affection and yes, even worship, not to mention the implied exploitation of the child workers.

After awhile, the children are tired of playing at work and just want to play: their dad or manager tells them to stay at work. The dachshunds are completed, but at what human cost? The head of the family is told by his grandmother to "stop this madness—for there is no end to it." Is this the craftsmanship, she demands to know, that she taught him?

See also: *Perfumed Nightmare.*
Availability: Selected collections.

Further reading

Maslin, Janet. "A Lot of Dachshunds." *New York Times,* 12 April 1984, C20. A short review celebrating the film's witty and "deceptively deadpan style."

"Turumba." *Variety,* 23 May 1984. Positive review of the film's "sly wit and . . . East-West insights."

✎

TV Nation

Mooreland

1994–95, Vol. 1, 120 mins.; Vol. 2, 116 mins.
Director: Michael Moore
Postmodern TV documentary series
Selected Episodes, Vol. 1 (1994)
Free Trade in Mexico
Taxi!
5 Million New Jobs
Selected Episodes, Vol. 2 (1995)
Beach Party
Crackers the Corporate Crime-Fighting Chicken

Michael Moore, Janeane Garofalo, Rusty
  Cundieff, and Louis Theroux

No one could easily replace Michael Moore
as the leading comic maker of documentaries
on labor and capital: it is as if Ernie Kovacs
has come back from the dead as Barbara
Kopple. Because of the tremendous success
with Moore's first film, *Roger & Me*, he
received corporate support for two projects—a feature film, *Canadian Bacon*, and a
TV series. While the feature was agreeable
fluff about treating Canada as a new Cold
War enemy, the TV series generated a fairly
outrageous string of satirical bits, a *Roger &
Me* to the *n*th power. Moore himself—or one
of his "correspondents" or reporters—would
go out in the world intending to do serious
harm to corporate America or some other
terminally prejudiced or deranged target.
Or, more likely, comic harm. These tapes
collect four shows, with five or six episodes
each. Plus a bonus: each tape "contains one
segment too controversial for network TV."
Any viewer of the TV show could easily have
added a few more favorites.

Michael Moore's credentials as a progressive revolutionary not unrelated to the mythical anarchist types (Yippies and Diggers) of
the 1960s is safe. Even when attacking the
most serious of targets, he cannot keep a
straight face. When interviewing the manager
of a maquiladora or American factory across
the Texas border with the ostensible intention of moving his entire TV production
team across the border to take advantage of
NAFTA and save money, he asks how to
say, "Where do you dump the PCVs?" in
Spanish.

In "The C.E.O. Challenge," an episode not
included in these volumes, Moore asks the
CEOs of major corporations to do whatever
is the essence of their company—the CEO of
IBM to format a disk, the CEO of Colgate-
Palmolive to put toothpaste in a tube, and the
CEO of Ford to change the oil in a car. Only
Alex Trotman, Ford's former CEO, accepted
the challenge and successfully changed the
oil on a pickup for Moore's camera.

(Trotman will become Moore's only pinup
CEO—see *The Big One*.)

He created "Crackers, the Corporate
Crime-Fighting Chicken," a political Big Bird
who terrorized corporations that believed
they were above the law (e.g., First Boston
Corporation, which got a tax break in New
York City when it promised it would not lay
off any workers and then began laying off
workers thirty days later). Crackers' motto
was "Don't Be Chicken, Report Corporate
Crime."

Because of the notorious difficulty black
men have in hailing cabs, Moore stationed
the Emmy-nominated black actor Yaphet
Kotto on a street corner in New York and a
white convicted felon and accused murderer,
Louis Bruno, nearby and had them both hail
cabs. Consistently—regardless of the race or
ethnicity of the drivers—cabs passed Kotto
by and picked up the felon. When Moore's
reporter questioned these cabbies, most of
them said they did not see the black man,
otherwise they certainly would have picked
him up. Imagine their surprise when the
reporter showed them a "Wanted" circular
for their white passenger.

In his triumphant book tour in 1997
extolling the virtues of his book *Downsize
This!* Moore would often entertain his fans
by playing the banned segments. This tour
soon turned into a Borders-baiting expedi-
tion, as Moore documents in *The Big One*,
because at the Borders store in Chicago he
supported the workers' efforts to unionize
and soon became persona non grata on his
own book tour. Crackers of course became
chicken non grata in corporate lobbies. (See
the second edition of *Downsize This!*)

We are not used to identifying labor issues
and postmodern documentary: *Koyan-
nisquatsi*, with its assembly lines of Twinkies
in an ultimate speedup, certainly conveyed a
sense of the absurdity of modern capitalism
and consumerism, but the impression was
imagistic (intentionally so) without any
analysis. Moore's strategy employs visual
cues that are self-consciously cultural as well
as political, arguing that we *are* a TV nation
because we cannot get certain images out of

our collective head. Thus the marvelous opening credit sequence includes Jackie Kennedy waving to the crowd, Lee Harvey Oswald grimacing in pain, Patty Hearst captured by a bank lobby camera, and Palestinian youths throwing rocks during the first *intifadeh*. These are already heavily mediated realities. And, not to be outdone, the *TV Nation* staff reinforces its program's own self-consciousness by wearing TV Nation gear and even flying a TV Nation flag during the *Apocalypse Now!* assault on the Greenwich beaches during the "Beach Party" episode, when the town's refusal to admit nonresidents to its beaches was contested. (In 2001 Greenwich had to comply with a state supreme court ruling against exclusion of nonresidents.)

We are in confrontation documentary territory here. No doubt the gun thug in *Harlan County, U.S.A.* was goaded into even greater thuggishness when he was confronted by Barbara Kopple's film crew the morning he was escorting scabs past the miners' picket line. But there is little doubt in our minds that he would do this kind of thing anyway. In Greenwich this is a political intervention of the affluent locals' space, not just a film crew sent out to hear their reactions to the idea of inviting street people from the Bronx to swim with them. Similarly the plant managers at the Texas-Mexico border are naive when they agree to permit Moore's crew to film their workers, all very young women: nothing necessarily evil is going on, but Moore's send-up of this economic miracle also involves a shot of Moore doing calisthenics with the young women in a factory owned by a Japanese company.

Every *TV Nation* episode was accompanied by a TV Nation Poll in which Moore's polling firm (Widgery & Associates) recorded such important results as that "29 percent of Americans believe that Elvis was right to shoot TV sets" and that "60 percent of Americans say that, if they could push a button that would make Larry King disappear, they would 'keep pushing it and not stop.'" Moore himself keeps pushing and apparently cannot stop.

See also: *The Big One; Roger & Me; The Awful Truth.*

Availability: Selected collections.

Further reading

Bullert, B. J. *Public Television: Politics and the Battle over Documentary Film.* New Brunswick: Rutgers University Press, 1997. Revealing review of the creation and aftermath of Moore's first film, *Roger & Me,* suggesting (at least to me) why Moore has had to move resolutely in a more and more postmodern documentary direction.

Fernández-Kelly, María Patricia. *For We Are Sold, I and My People.* Albany: SUNY Press, 1983. This study and participatory observer record of "women and industry in Mexico's frontier" is a clear and convincing document of great value.

Johnson, Steve. "Tongue in Beak." *Chicago Tribune,* 14 August 1955. This reviewer actually went to a Crackers rally in Chicago and came away impressed: "It's hard to imagine a television network like Fox having the courage to keep an apple-cart upending show like 'TV Nation' on its schedule." If it doesn't, then Crackers should bust Fox for a "corporate crime" as well. A chicken among the foxes has to worry, a lot!

Moore, Michael. *Downsize This!* 2d ed. New York: Crown, 1997. Political satire, with chapters subtly titled "Don't Vote—It Only Encourages Them," "Corporate Crooks Trading Cards," and "Why Are Union Leaders So F#!@ing Stupid?"

——— . "Media Matters." *Nation,* 4 and 18 November, 2 and 16 December 1996. Series of columns on the struggles to get *TV Nation* on the air and Moore's support of the Borders workers' union drive.

Ramirez, Anthony. "Actor Speaks and Listens to Cabbies at Bias Forum." *New York Times,* 6 December 1999, A31. The black actor Danny Glover lodges a complaint because "black men can't get cabs in New York."

Web site:

⟨www.dogeatdogfilms.com⟩ The official site of Moore's production company, with topical comments by Moore, reviews of his films, "People We Like" (list of "groups that are active in social change"), and occasional bonuses such as a cyberspatial duel with Nike using outtakes from *The Big One.*

Uncle Moses

Nephew Marx

1932, 87 mins., B&W, English and Yiddish,
 with English subtitles
Directors: Sidney Goldin and Aubrey
 Scotto
Screenplay: Maurice Schwartz, from
 Sholem Asch's novel of the same title
CAST
Masha = Judith Abarbanel
Uncle Moses = Maurice Schwartz
Moses' Father = Rubin Goldberg
Charlie = Zvee Scooler
Aaron Melnick = Mark Schweid
Masha's Mother = Rebecca Weintraub
Moses' Nephew = Sam Gertler

While *Hester Street* and a few documentaries
have brought the Jewish immigrant experience to life on film, there is probably no
substitute for this film, an example of the
Yiddish film industry that flourished between
the world wars. We know we are in a different world when—after a shot of the street
signs on Delancey Street and other locations
on the Lower East Side of Manhattan—
we see workers in a small garment factory
working and kvetching. The first subtitled
line—"Mr. Pedlar, give me a bagel!"—establishes the workers as generally at ease with
the labor and social conditions organized by
the rich patriarch known simply as Uncle
Moses.

This New world patriarch throws his
weight around in more ways than one, but
the woman he really falls for is Masha, the
daughter of one of his fired workmen. Her
fiery denunciation of Uncle Moses melts the
old lech's heart and he begins to woo her
with gifts and cash. The daughter must sacrifice herself for the good of her family.

The film makes Uncle Moses' nephew Sam
the heavy. In the novel he is simply greedy;
in the film he is a greedy and unpleasant
boss. After Uncle Moses falls in love and
eventually gets his heart broken (despite the
highly desired son Masha delivers him), he
couldn't care less about the terms of the settlement for the strike. The terms are revealing and perhaps utopian for 1932: an eight-
hour day, a 20 percent wage hike, new electric
sewing machines, Friday afternoon off for
the men to go to the washhouse for their
ritual cleansing, and the return of the peddler
to the open floor. The meeting itself has a
loopy humor but never conceals the seriousness of the issues; at one point, one of the
members chants the story of a different
Moses who led his people out of slavery, not
into it. When Charlie is eventually released
from prison and Uncle Moses accepts the
union's demands, the politico is sent away,
but his parting words to Charlie are: "If you
ever want to take care of the bosses, let me
know."

By 1932 Hollywood had already released
Taxi, a Warner Brothers film starring James
Cagney as a New York cabbie who speaks
Yiddish with a passenger. Although the film
version of *Uncle Moses* fits nicely in its early
Depression niche, it is actually based on an
adaptation of *Uncle Moses* by Maurice
Schwartz, the lead actor, which appeared in
the Yiddish Art Theatre's 1930–31 season. J.
Hoberman states that "for the first time,
a Yiddish talkie engaged directly the progressive currents of the day, political and
aesthetic."

As we look at this film all these many years
after it was made and almost as many since
the Nazis began to destroy European Jews,
we cannot help but be caught up in some
inadvertently horrifying moments—when
Uncle Moses' father, for example, talks
another old worker into accompanying him
back to their native town of Kuzmin, Poland,
so that they can be buried there in peace.

This is a film rich in contemporary speech,
not just the Yiddish but the rapidity with
which most of the characters go in and out of
Yiddish as they cope with new English words
and American folkways. Kevin Brownlow's
book documents the many silent films about
immigrant and work life we have lost from
the early days of filming. *Uncle Moses*, at
least, is available and comes like a traveler
on a time machine from a culture that has
virtually vanished.

See also: *Hester Street; The Inheritance.*
Availability: Selected collections.

Further reading

Asch, Sholem. *Three Novels.* New York: Putnam, 1938. Includes *Uncle Moses.*

Brown, Georgia. *Village Voice,* 26 November 1991, 61. Very positive review of the film upon its re-release by the National Center for Jewish Film.

Brownlow, Kevin. *Beyond the Mask of Innocence.* New York: Knopf, 1991. This treasure-trove of "films of social conscience in the silent era" about "sex, violence, prejudice, and crime" describes many films—alas, unavailable in videocassette with rare exceptions—about the immigrant experience.

Hoberman, J. *Bridge of Light: Yiddish Film between Two Worlds.* New York: Museum of Modern Art/Schocken, 1991. Exhaustive survey of Yiddish film in both Europe and America, with a section on *Uncle Moses.*

∽

Uncle Tom's Cabin

"Life among the lowly"—Harriet Beecher Stowe

1987, 120 mins., TVM
Director: Stan Lathan
Screenplay: John Gay, from Harriet Beecher Stowe's novel of the same title
CAST
Uncle Tom = Avery Brooks
Eliza = Phylicia Rashad
Simon Legree = Edward Woodward
Augustine St. Clare = Bruce Dern
Topsy = Endyia Kinney
Cassy = Paula Kelly
Emmeline = Troy Beyer
Little Eva = Jenny Lewis

Very few novels can be credited with changing public opinion on such a massive scale as Stowe's novel about the evils of slavery. The novel began as a serial publication in a small abolitionist magazine in 1851; within a year the demand for a book edition was so great that the printer had three presses going twenty-four hours a day, with three mills to supply the paper and 100 bookbinders to keep up the pace of production. Lincoln, ten years later, supposedly paid her this supreme compliment when at last they met: "So this is the little lady who made this big war."

Perhaps because of its incredible popularity then and the subsequent passage of so many of its characters into popular culture, the book has never been made into a first-class film. The characters most people know so well include Uncle Tom, the Christian slave who wants to turn the other cheek; Eliza, who makes a daring escape across the ice floes of the Ohio River to safety in free Ohio territory; Simon Legree, the vicious slave overseer; and Little Eva, the saintly young white girl who befriends Tom.

The TV miniseries *Roots* has become the standard for representations of slavery since it was first broadcast in 1979. It was also, above all, a historical drama of human endurance, and its success may explain why relatively few films on slavery as an institution of work have been filmed. While emphasizing the economic basis of slavery—especially the fact that slaves were freely exchangeable for cash—Stowe also wanted to tell a story with strong legal and religious implications. The Fugitive Slave Act of 1850, she believed, made the North complicit in the business of slavery, since it mandated the return of escaped slaves to their southern masters even if they had reached free soil in the North. Her novel ends with a warning of the Christian "day of judgment"—the moment of reckoning for a country that holds human souls as chattel.

Stowe was acutely aware of the economic implications of slavery, not only for African Americans but for southern whites. In the chapter "Poor White Trash" in her *Key to Uncle Tom's Cabin,* for example, she outlined, in remarkably modern language, one of the central premises of her novel: "The institution of slavery has accomplished the double feat, in America, not only of degrading and brutalizing her black working classes, but of producing, notwithstanding a fertile soil and abundant room, a poor white population as degraded and brutal as ever existed in any of the most crowded districts of Europe."

There have been several recent versions of Stowe's novel, two of which are currently available. The African American director Stan Lathan had adapted James Baldwin's *Go Tell It on the Mountain* in 1984, three years before he turned to *Uncle Tom's Cabin*. With Avery Brooks as a stronger, even more virile Uncle Tom than popular folklore has created from Stowe's saintly hero, Lathan did not have to apologize for promoting a despised stereotype as an admirable character. Lathan was helped in another way by casting Brooks, since he had received good notices for his portrayal of the kidnapped free man, Solomon Northup, in Gordon Parks Sr.'s *Half-Slave, Half-Free* three years before.

Lathan confronted the difficulties of this project, the adaptation of a novel that had not been checked out of the library of a black university such as Jackson State in Mississippi for twenty years: "I liked the challenge this production presented: a black man's interpretation of a white woman's interpretation of black reality—a reverse of 'The Color Purple.'"

Tom's progress and decline in the film follow Stowe's prescription for misery. After Eliza's escape to Ohio (not filmed on ice floes because Phylicia Rashad was pregnant during the production), Tom is sold to the good but weak St. Clare, whose saintly daughter, Eva, is the subject of one of the author's sentimental deathbed scenes. (Tom's is the other.) Tom is sold in the film to the vicious slaveholder Simon Legree, whose name, as a synonym for cruelty, has also entered our language, like Tom's and Topsy's ("I spect I growed. Don't think nobody never made me"). It is Legree's beating death of Tom, meek and forgiving to the end, that created (in part) the stereotype of an "Uncle Tom" as a black person who gives in too easily to whites.

The other version of *Uncle Tom's Cabin* that is currently available is best avoided. It was made in 1970 by what appears to be a German or Eastern European production company (the dubbing is awful) who believed that there were Franciscan monasteries in the South to which escaped slaves could go for sanctuary. A concluding voiceover no doubt reflected the filmmakers' frustrations: "Only God fully understands the United States." Amen.

Stowe's novel was not an economic treatise, but her analysis of slavery went beyond some of the sentimental characters she created. Lathan's film version, at least in some measure, faces that economic issue.

See also: *Half-Slave, Half-Free.*
Availability: Easy.

Further reading

Farber, Stephen. "Cable Service Dusts Off 'Uncle Tom's Cabin' for TV." *New York Times*, 13 June 1987, C50. Despite the incorrect remark that this is the first film of Stowe's novel "in 60 years," this is a favorable review of the production's attempt to retrieve the novel's original message.

Hedrick, Joan D. *Harriet Beecher Stowe: A Life*. New York: Oxford University Press, 1994. The definitive biography.

O'Connor, John J. "Uncle Tom's Cabin." *New York Times*, 12 June 1987, C30. Another favorable review of the film.

Stowe, Harriet Beecher. *Uncle Tom's Cabin*. 1851. Numerous editions available. The NAL Signet paperback has a dated but still helpful afterword about the novel.

——. *A Key to Uncle Tom's Cabin*. 1853. Port Washington, N.Y.: Kennikat, 1968. A collection of documents and arguments supporting Stowe's view of slavery as a vicious institution.

Note: Some video chain stores identify the version directed by Stan Lathan as "Uncle Tom's Cabin—1987—Phylicia Rashad." The other version, identified as "Uncle Tom's Cabin—1970—Hebert Lom," is the one to avoid, especially since the package promises Eartha Kitt, who is *not* in this film, as a member of the cast. (Herbert Lom plays Simon Legree.)

Union Maids

"For it's great to fight for freedom with a rebel girl"—Joe Hill

1976, 48 mins.
Directors: Julia Reichert, Jim Klein, and
  Miles Mogulesco
Traditional documentary
PRINCIPAL UNION MAIDS
Stella Nowicki, Kate Hyndman, and Sylvia
  Woods

The three "union maids" featured in this film had long and active careers as union organizers and proponents of radical change. From Alice and Staughton Lynd's source book, *Rank and File: Personal Histories by Working-Class Organizers*, we learn that two of the three (Stella and Kate) were openly Reds, but in the film only Kate's Communist affiliation is suggested ("Gary Woman Called Red" is one headline we see about her). Kate, for reasons never explained in book or film, goes by another name in the Lynds' book: Christine Ellis.

Most of the women's reminiscences are about the 1930s, when Reds and other radicals formed a solid contingent in the organizing committees of the CIO. Almost all of the women's activism was on the grass-roots level; Kate, for example, helped organize among the unemployed in Chicago, concentrating on resisting evictions.

The pace of the film is leisurely, gradually gaining in intensity as the filmmakers cut back and forth among the three women, interviewing them about their backgrounds, experiences, and opinions. Kate came to work in the Chicago stockyards from a farm in Michigan, where she said she knew that if she had remained, she would have been just a cook and servant to the men. Stella, whose father was a follower of Marcus Garvey, also worked in the Chicago stockyards. Sylvia, originally from New Orleans, helped organize black and white workers in a large commercial laundry in Chicago.

In almost every instance, the interviewers (who are, for the most part, disembodied voices off camera) lead their subjects to explain the sources of their radicalism. Kate, a veteran of numerous dangerous eviction protests in the 1930s, says, "I have no regrets. I feel there was a purpose in my life." Her brand of socialism tells her to "let the people decide." Stella believes that "we made a lot of changes." And Sylvia sees herself as continuing her radicalism in joining the women's movement, although she has some impatience with women in the movement who cannot relate to *working* women.

Union Maids is one of the pioneering efforts in documentaries on labor and women's history. It has a few creaky moments—a little too much historical footage unrelated to labor is used, for example—but it still packs an occasional visual punch, as in footage of black laundry workers fighting policemen in Chicago. The Lynds' book, in the interviewing style perfected by Studs Terkel in *Working* and other books, was very commendable; as a visual development of their book, the film rightly celebrates the special role and pluck of these union maids.

See also: *With Babies and Banners.*
Availability: Selected collections; Icarus
  Films.

Further reading

Lynd, Alice and Staughton, eds. *Rank and File: Personal Histories by Working-Class Organizers*. Boston: Beacon, 1973. Includes oral histories by other organizers and more details on the lives of the women featured in the film.
Rosenthal, Alan. *The Documentary Conscience*. Berkeley: University of California Press, 1980. Includes a detailed interview with the filmmakers.

The Uprising of '34

Unraveling the history of the textile
workers

1995, 90 mins.
Directors: George Stoney and Judith
  Helfand
Traditional documentary

Flora May Campbell, Sue Hill, Yvonne Hill, Opal McMichael, Jess Mitchell, Edna Neil, and Blanche Willis, mill workers

Dan Beacham and Joseph Lineberger, mill owners

Etta Mae Zimmerman, Local 1816, Hogansville, Georgia

Larry Blakeney, Charlie Wetzell, and Robert Ragan, sons of mill workers

The story of the massive movement of mostly white agricultural workers into the mills of the smaller developing cities of the South remains generally untold in film. The novelist Erskine Caldwell tried to explain this crucial fact of economic history in the 1930s and 1940s, but he was dismissed as a lefty the first time he tried and as a salacious hack the second. While this film does not tell the whole story, it does develop two crucial aspects of it—the failed efforts at widespread unionization and the erasure of the evidence of violence against the "lintheads." Such a cover-up helped to create a barely disguised vigilante atmosphere in some southern states, an atmosphere that continued to deny basic rights to African American citizens and all but prevented any further attempts at raising the depressed wage scales of both black and white.

The film traces organizing drives and strikes at factories in Georgia, Alabama, Tennessee, and North and South Carolina, which culminated in the great textile strike of 1934. Thousands of strikers were blacklisted because they would not accept the open violations of the New Deal's National Recovery Act (NRA) Cotton Textile Code, which set a minimum wage, a forty-hour week, no employment of children under age 16, and the right to organize.

One of the innovative tactics used was the "flying squadron" of male and female mobile picketers. When they were arrested by the National Guard, they were hauled off to prison camps established near Atlanta for Germans during World War II: "They don't treat us any better than the enemy," one of the interviewees stated. Although repression by government and employers succeeded in breaking the strike's momentum, it set the stage for the ultimate unpunished vigilante actions by men in the employ of one of the notorious strike targets, the Chiquola Mill in Honea Path, South Carolina: six strikers were shot in the back and killed by men firing from the factory's windows. No one was even arrested, although many of the townspeople knew who had done the deed. Although 10,000 strikers and other sympathetic folk attended the funerals for the slain men, the viciousness of the act—not to mention its intentional intimidating effects—helped to break the strike and bury the incident to create a long-festering boil. This film helped end that conspiracy of silence.

See also: *Our Land Too.*

Availability: Selected collections; Icarus Films.

Further reading

Byerly, Victoria. *Hard Times: Cotton Mill Girls*. Ithaca: ILR Press, 1987. A fine collection of personal histories of poor women in the South.

Hall, Jacquelyn Dowd, et al. *Like a Family: The Making of a Southern Mill World*. New York: Norton, 1987.

Rosenzweig, Roy. "The Uprising of '34." *Labor History*, Fall 1996, 535–36. Mostly positive review of the film's "admirable breadth" in covering so much of this unknown labor history, although he feels the film raises the issue of a cover-up of this story without resolving it.

Web site:

⟨www.itvs.org/external/Uprising/uprising.html⟩ Official site, with a statement from the directors and a list of resources.

Up to a Certain Point

On the machismo front

1983, 88 mins., Cuba, in Spanish, with English subtitles

Director: Tomás Gutiérrez Alea

Screenplay: Juan Carlos Tabio, Serafín Quiñones, and Tomás Gutiérrez Alea

CAST

Oscar = Oscar Álvarez

Lina = Mirta Ibarra

Flora = Ana Vina
Arturo = Omar Valdés
Marian = Coralia Veloz
Diego = Rogelio Blain
Claudio = Claudio A. Tamajo
Quiñones = Luis Celeiro

Tomás Gutiérrez Alea's film is a Cuban post-modern or self-reflexive film, modest in its scope, a film with characters watching films, and is about the process of writing a film. Oscar, a middle-class playwright, is supervising filmed interviews with dockworkers to gather material for a fiction film he is writing about machismo on the docks. We are therefore in a film-dense scenario. But since it is Cuba, Alea's film still needs to be about a real subject as well, in this case the tendency of Cuban men to want to have their sweet and eat it too.

Gender equality is the law in Cuba; as the first "real" interview in this film demonstrates, the reality is that the majority of Cuban men accept liberated women only "up to a certain point." That point, the first interviewee says, varies: he thinks he can accept women as equals "80 percent, maybe even 87 percent," but beyond that point he could not go.

The film dramatizes what happens when a women, Lina, a dockworker, begins to expect (just a little) men to go beyond 87 percent. Both her boyfriends, the new and the old, know that they have a very special woman. She is a dedicated dockworker, a job-site reformer, and of course beautiful. That neither of them can even get close to 80 percent is one of the not-so-hidden jokes of the film.

The film does not idealize the situation on the Havana docks. The workers know why their work is difficult, that conditions cry out for change—more repairs to the infrastructure, better management, improvement in workers' attitudes—and for the most part the men realize that they do not always treat the women fairly. Alea's touch is light, and it makes the film a pleasant alternative to the socialist realism of any Communist country. At one point one of the guys says he knows

it is better to "let" women have jobs; his friend's wife, made to stay at home, fell in love with another man!

This film is perhaps less well known among fans of foreign films than Alea's other films (*Memories of Underdevelopment* and *Strawberry and Chocolate*), but it would be unfortunate if this film continued to be ignored.

See also: *The Last Supper*.
Availability: Selected collections; Facets.

Further reading

Canby, Vincent. "Macho Man." *New York Times,* 13 March 1985, C19. Finds the interviews "the best things in a movie that otherwise seems to be as contrived as the screenplay" that the lead character, Oscar, is writing. (*I* thought that was the self-reflexive point of the film.)

Crowdus, Gary. "Up to a Certain Point." *Cineaste* 14, no. 2 (1985): 26–29. Rave review, emphasizing the film's ability to deal with important issues not only in Cuban society but in film-making as well.

Downing, John D. H., ed. *Film and Politics in the Third World*. New York: Autonomedia, 1987. Detailed analysis of the film's issues in the editor's essay, "Four Films of Tomás Gutiérrez Alea."

Pick, Zuzanna M. *The New Latin American Cinema*. Austin: University of Texas Press, 1993. A good survey of both Cuban film in general and this one in particular.

Note: Also known as *Hasta cierto punto* and *Up to a Point*.

The Valley of Decision

To invest or not to invest

1945, 111 mins., B&W
Director: Tay Garnett
Screenplay: John Meehan and Sonya Levien, from Marcia Davenport's novel of the same title
CAST
Mary Rafferty = Greer Garson
Paul Scott = Gregory Peck
William Scott = Donald Crisp

Pat Rafferty = Lionel Barrymore
Jim Brennan = Preston Foster
Constance Scott = Marsha Hunt
Clarissa Scott = Gladys Cooper
McCready = Reginald Owen
William Scott Jr. = Dan Duryea
Louise Kane = Jessica Tandy
Delia = Barbara Everest
Ted Scott = Marshall Thompson

If ever there was going to be a *Gone with the Wind* of Pittsburgh steel, *The Valley of Decision* was it. Instead of antebellum plantations, we have the post–Civil War industrializing North. Perhaps thankfully, however, only the first section (approximately one-third) of Marcia Davenport's best-seller, tracing seventy years of an iron-and-steel family dynasty, was filmed. Whether this was a practical or a political decision is unclear: the strike at the mill in 1877, the year of labor unrest throughout the United States and an oblique reference to the most famous strike of the year at the Homestead works in Pittsburgh specifically, is one of the few major labor events developed. Since the film never leaves the 1870s, we are deprived of the filmmakers' version of the CIO's Steel Organizing Committee, which Davenport somewhat lightly but positively develops at the end of her 800-page novel.

By focusing on only one major labor–management conflict, the film conveniently finesses most of the novel's description of the class conflicts and the tremendous disparity in wealth between mill owner and workers (not to mention servants), and we end up not too many flights above a Cinderella story (a fact that the *New York Times* reviewer noted with some disdain). In this instance, Cinderella is Mary Rafferty, played by Greer Garson as a remarkable Irish-American servant girl, whose good sense and moral stamina help to protect the English mill-owning family she serves.

Cinderella does, however, have a family of her own—a widowed sister with a baby and an angry father in a wheelchair, who holds Mary's master responsible for his crippled and useless legs. Although Lionel Barrymore plays Mary's father as a sputtering fountain of venom, there is at least some truth in what he says: it was inevitable that workers, exhausted by twelve-hour shifts, would be maimed in accidents. Davenport's novel provides a rationale for twelve-hour shifts both in the process of nineteenth-century ironmaking and in the wage structure that the men favored. Since we are very rarely even near any workers or furnaces in the film, the viewer is never provided such information.

At least the film is true to the melodrama that was Davenport's conception. Mary and Paul Scott, the owner's son, fall in love and try to broker a truce between the workers and the company. Jim Brennan, another of Mary's beaux, is an innovative worker, Paul's friend, and the union's spokesman. Both sides agree to meet on the bridge that connects the public path and company property. But tragedy strikes, and Mary's father, believing that the company has broken its word about importing scabs and thugs, shoots Mary's potential father-in-law, the family patriarch.

Contemporary viewers will see these characters on both sides of the class struggle as pitching more woo than iron. The film would have driven most sensitive people back to the novel, although Davenport would hardly have satisfied most of them. Davenport's William Scott is a mill owner of the old school: "Strike! . . . They'd never dare."

The film ends with an impossible scenario that Davenport pursues for the last two-thirds of the novel: Mary and Paul cannot marry—because of their class differences and the inconvenient fact that *her* father (brother in the novel) killed *his*—but are obviously eternally in love. Paul throws his wife of convenience (played scathingly by Jessica Tandy in one of her earliest roles) out of his house and trots off with Mary into the remarkably unsmoky Pittsburgh sunset in a carriage for two. The End. We are never told what could possibly happen next. And we certainly never find out whether the union comes to stay in the old man's mill.

Once the decision was made to cast Greer Garson as Mary Rafferty, it was inevitable that Garson would straighten out the twists and turns of the difficult life of Davenport's original heroine. Garson had already charmed her way through such triumphs as *Mrs. Miniver* (coping with World War II) and *Madame Curie* (coping with pesky radioactivity).

Davenport revealed in her autobiography that much of her research for her novel was accomplished through her first husband's association with *Fortune* magazine as managing editor and by "constantly meeting industrialists and men of business big and small, whom he brought to our house." Despite her husband's contact with Philip Murray and other "labor statesmen of Big Steel," her interest—as the film captures—was usually focused on Big Investors.

See also: *The Molly Maguires*.
Availability: Selected collections.

Further reading

Crowther, Bosley. "The Valley of Decision." *New York Times*, 4 May 1945, 23. "Miss Davenport's fine American saga is barely perceived in this film, produced most extravagantly by Metro. But there is here a full romantic show."

Davenport, Marcia. *Too Strong for Fantasy*. New York: Scribner, 1967. Although she declares herself content with the "faithful and gripping representation of the third of the book which had been used," she does not discuss the significant changes in the film adaptation.

↪
Voices from a Steeltown

. . . were once loud and clear

1985, 29 mins.
Director: Tony Buba
Traditional documentary

The industrial city with the dubious motto "What Braddock makes the world takes" barely survived a hundred years of steeltown history. As the site of Andrew Carnegie's first Pittsburgh-area steel mill, Braddock entered the twentieth century as a boom town. By the 1980s it was dying, and Tony Buba designated himself as the comic guide to its demise. Buba's numerous film awards and continuing success as a documentary filmmaker have justified the fickle finger of fate that set him down in Braddock, his hometown, as unemployment soared.

See also: *Lightning over Braddock; Struggles in Steel*.
Availability: Selected collections; New Day Films.

Further reading

"Artists Record the Death of the Mill's Way of Life." *New York Times*, 1 July 1985: D12. Discussion of documentaries on working-class Chicago and Pittsburgh.

↪
Wall Street

"If you're not inside, you're outside."— Gordon Gekko

1987, 124 mins., R
Director: Oliver Stone
Screenplay: Oliver Stone and Stanley Weiser
CAST
Bud Fox = Charlie Sheen
Carl Fox = Martin Sheen
Gordon Gekko = Michael Douglas
Darian Taylor = Daryl Hannah
Lou Mannheim = Hal Holbrook
Sir Harry Wildman = Terence Stamp
Kate Gekko = Sean Young

Although the Ivan Boesky insider-trading scandals of Wall Street and Eastern Airlines' battle between Frank Lorenzo and the International Association of Machinists (IAM) in the 1980s would be two good reasons to watch Oliver Stone's version of the Reagan years, the real reason most people watch the film is to see the greedy antics of the leading trader, Gordon Gekko, played to perfection by Michael Douglas and appropriately named after a lizard (although the gecko is not as scary as it looks). Gekko, as one character says, received an "ethical bypass at birth." He clearly loves money, but the ruthless pursuit of money excites him even more. That Gekko is like an unstoppable male beast in rut is clearly Stone's metaphorical intention. Thus the first time we see and hear Gekko, he is on the phone making a deal and announces, "Raise the sperm count of the deal!" When he is asked to meet for a meal, he replies: "Lunch? You got to be kidding! Lunch is for women."

Douglas's performance as Gekko reaches a high point at the stockholders' meeting of the Geldar Paper Corporation, which Gekko is trying to raid. He makes his now-legendary "greed is good" speech at this meeting and attacks the thirty-three vice presidents on the dais as do-nothings with dubious job descriptions. Management, not Wall Street, he tells the stockholders, is the real enemy: "I am not a destroyer of companies. I am a liberator of them." That his lies seem to work for such a long time—he basically wants to hold on to a company only long enough to loot its cash assets and sell off anything that is left—is part of his attraction to other Wall Street hustlers.

The film takes its plot line from two key events of the 1980s: the struggle between Eastern Airlines and the Machinists and, more resolutely, the insider-trading scandals, typified by Ivan Boesky. In the film, Gekko apprentice Bud uses insider information on Blue Star Airlines that he receives from his father, the head of the airline's maintenance union. Gekko deceives Bud into thinking that the airline will be allowed to survive. Bud ends up in a secret war against Gekko in order to save the company by forming an alliance of the pilots' and flight attendants' organizations, his father's union, and one of Gekko's chief rivals. Instead of a "garage sale at Blue Star," the company survives. Unlike Eastern Airlines, we might add.

Wall Street is a fable primarily because a potentially good guy realizes the error of his ways and uses a stock war between Wall Street velociraptors for a noble end. (Bud's parallel in real life, Boesky's apprentice crook, Martin Siegel, was also wired to trap others, but he had no altruistic goals.) Clearly Stone has a point here: the deals at the top can make or break the people on the bottom. Boesky did get caught; Gekko is captured on tape incriminating himself. But Eastern Airlines is long gone, and so are millions of dollars past accounting.

See also: *Collision Course; Working Girl.*
Availability: Easy; DVD.

Further reading

Canby, Vincent. "Greed." *New York Times*, 11 December 1987, C3. A mixed review that you have to love because he writes that Darryl Hannah "has the screen presence of a giant throw pillow."

Robinson, Jack E. *Free Fall: The Needless Destruction of Eastern Air Lines and the Valiant Struggle to Save It*. New York: Harper & Row, 1992. Discusses Lorenzo and the unions that squared off against him (ALPA, the pilots; TWU, the flight attendants; and IAM, the machinists).

Stewart, James B. *Den of Thieves*. New York: Simon & Schuster, 1991. A detailed narrative of Boesky and his fellow inside traders.

Waterfront

Struggles on the docks down under

1983, 294 mins., Australia
Director: Chris Thomson
Screenplay: Mac Gudgeon
CAST
Anna Chieri = Greta Scacchi
Maxey Woodbury = Jack Thompson
Laughing Les = Warren Mitchell
Maggie = Noni Hazelhurst
Sam Elliot = Ray Barrett
Ernie Donaldson = Chris Haywood
Davo = Jay Mannering
Vera Donaldson = Elin Jenkins
Paddy Ryan = Frank Gallacher
Sheila Ryan = Jan Friedl

Viewers seeking an Australian equivalent to *On the Waterfront* will probably be disappointed by this epic evocation of waterfront life in the port city of Melbourne in the 1930s. *Waterfront* tries to do much more than the American film, although it doesn't always rise above some operatic *Gone with the Wind* histrionics. The centerpiece of the film is a long strike, led for the most part by the "wharfies," white union men who must walk a thin line between the sufferings of the strike and the rising collusion of management and the fascists. Complicating matters are a partly corrupt leadership with ties to gangsters, Italian immigrants who scab, and the occasional Communist activist. Mix these with the story of a stunning Italian immigrant (Greta Scacchi) and a reluctant rank-and-file leader (Jack Thompson, who played the lawyer for soldiers being railroaded in the Australian film *Breaker Morant*) and you have an Australian miniseries.

While the love affair between the "Eyetalian" immigrant Anna and the wharfie Maxey is inevitably soap-operaish, a significant subplot is the relation of the Italian antifascist immigrants to their new home. Anna, whose husband and brother were murdered by Mussolini's thugs, keeps up the revolutionary spirit as best she can by singing the "Internationale" at a Matteotti Club meeting. (The Socialist Party leader Giacomo Matteotti was kidnapped and murdered by the Fascists in 1924, when all opposition parties were banned.) It's all the more pressing, then, for Maxey to persuade the Italians not to join management's scab labor scheme.

A rising national fascist movement, the White Guards, creates havoc on the wharves, making it virtually impossible for the union to survive. Even the left-wingers in the union can't convince Maxey: "Revolution in this country? You'd have to advertise in the sports pages!" But Maxey does learn some ancient wisdom of political organizing when Anna's father lends him Machiavelli's *The Prince* for some serious study. Unfortunately, Maxey's union mentor has had some criminal ties, and all of these political and social forces prove too much for Maxey in the end and he is murdered. His new girlfriend has to leave as well, for the union's power has been effectively broken. Its allies in the Labour government, its own muscle, and its leadership are not enough to defeat the reactionary forces.

See also: *On the Waterfront*.
Availability: Selected collections; Facets.

Further reading

Murray, Scott. *Australian Film, 1978–1992*. New York: Oxford University Press, 1993. Reviews other films by the director but not *Waterfront*.

∾

We Dig Coal: A Portrait of Three Women

Mining can "seep in your soul."—Merle Travis

1982, 58 mins.
Directors: Thomas C. Goodwin, Dorothy McGee, and Geraldine Wurzburg
Traditional documentary
PRINCIPAL FIGURES
Bernice Dombroski and Mary Louise Carson, coal miners
Marilyn McCusker and Alan McCusker, coal miner and her husband
Harry and Jane Koptchik, coal miner and his wife
Dorothy McGhee, interviewer

This film about three miners who are women focuses mainly on Marilyn McCusker, whose two-year effort and sex discrimination suit in a federal court finally brought her employment as a deep miner. The three women were hired by the Rushton Mining Company of Pennsylvania in 1977. McCusker worked just two years before she became the first (known) woman to die inside a deep mine: while she was installing roof bolts, a 20' × 16' × 3' piece of shale fell on her.

McCusker's life and death highlighted safety issues in the mines as well as the hidden history of women workers underground. Research has revealed that women worked in coal mines during World War II and in family-owned mines at other times. When women were finally hired as a result of McCusker's suit, they often found themselves in a new kind of bind: foremen assigned them to unpleasant and dangerous jobs hoping they would quit or, failing that, would "prove" themselves—as women— prone to injuries.

This may in fact have been McCusker's fate, as some comments (not included in the film) from the Rushton Company's safety director suggest: "She would have been ten steps away" from the roof slate that killed her if she had been a man; that is, an experienced miner (quoted in Serrin). In fact, the man she was working with did successfully run to safety.

Since Marilyn McCusker was not alive when the film was made, her husband tells a good deal of her story. Bernice Dombrowski and Mary Louise Carson tell their own stories. When Carson's husband was diagnosed with emphysema and had to leave the mines, she left her relatively low paying job in a sewing factory to "take his place." Both women report much harassment—such as having rocks thrown at them underground— but both agree with Carson's remark that "the only way to get me out is to carry me out."

By the time this film was made, 3,000 women had joined the 150,000 male miners. The two other subjects of this documentary, Dombrowski and Carson, were still working in the mines when the film was released. In 1977, 144 miners died underground; Marilyn McCusker was the only woman.

The film doesn't cover the subsequent legal problems of McCusker's survivors. After her death, McCusker's husband and son received survivors' benefits, despite a Pennsylvania state law that guaranteed benefits for widows but not for widowers. Rushton Mining agreed to pay the benefits on the eve of a scheduled workers' compensation hearing two months after she died.

See also: *Coalmining Women; Moving Mountains; Wildrose.*

Availability: Selected collections; Cinema Guild.

Further reading

Franklin, Ben A. "Women Who Work in Mines Assail Harassment and Unsafe Conditions." *New York Times*, 11 November 1979, 30. A report on the first UMWA conference on women miners.

Moore, Marat. *Women in the Mines*. New York: Twain, 1996. A comprehensive collection of interviews with women who are miners or active in union organizing and support movements.

O'Connor, John J. "TV Weekend." *New York Times*, 2 July 1982, C21. A brief but positive review of the film.

Serrin, William. "One Fight for Women's Rights: A Coal Miner's Life and Death." *New York Times*, 8 November 1979, A1, 16. An extended profile of Marilyn McCusker.

The Whistle at Eaton Falls

It blows for us

1951, 96 mins.
Director: Robert Siodmak
Screenplay: Lemist Elder and Virginia Shaler
CAST
Brad Adams = Lloyd Bridges
Mrs. Doubleday = Dorothy Gish
Eddie Talbot = Charleton Carpenter
Al Webster = Murray Hamilton
Joe London = James Westerfield
Abby = Lenore Loergan

The pitch of this film may seem somewhat off since it combined the talents of Robert Siodmak, a director known for his dark gangster films (such as the 1949 film noir classic *Criss Cross*), and Louis de Rochemont, a producer known for his newsreel documentaries (the famous *March of Time* series, which accompanied double features throughout the 1930s and 1940s). We end up with a feature using documentary footage, shot on location in a New England mill town with real mill workers as extras and the unlikely elevation of a union leader from the rank and file to the presidency of the old mill upon the death of its owner, played by one of the grand matriarchs of Hollywood, Dorothy Gish.

Brad Adams is the former union leader who is forced to lay off his old co-workers and friends. Both labor and management become too cranky to reconcile. When it seems that unending unemployment is the only option for the future, a miracle happens: a new gadget, to be manufactured on labor-saving machines, brings all the workers back on three round-the-clock shifts.

Rochemont's choice of topic was not unusual, for his *March of Time* newsreels never backed away from controversy. He had more recently taken on another American "problem" film, *Lost Boundaries*, in which a light-skinned black doctor (played by José Ferrer) and his family are challenged in numerous ways as they try to "pass" in a small New Hampshire town. Robert Siodmak was an odder choice, perhaps, for the film noir director knew more about how to frame an innocent man (*Phantom Lady* in 1944) than how to portray the unemployed. The *New York Times* reviewer was fair: "It is no reflection upon [Rochemont's] good intentions or his social integrity to observe that this overheated discourse on the relations of labor and management leaves much to be desired."

In another (perhaps more speculative) sense, Rochemont's production of *The Whistle at Eaton Falls* was a harbinger of the cinematic link that would be made between documentary realism and gangster-associated unionism. Rochemont had already produced two successful spy films at the end of the 1940s (*The House on 92nd Street* and *13 Rue Madeleine*), both "based on the files of the FBI." Hollywood did not have to reach very far to make *The Garment Jungle* and *On the Waterfront*, both part of its union-gangster cycle of the 1950s.

See also: *Other People's Money*.
Availability: Not.

Further reading

Crowther, Bosley. "'Whistle at Eaton Falls' Depicts Management-Labor Problems." *New York Times*, 11 October 1951, 49. A contemporary review.

Elson, Robert T. *Time, Inc.: The Intimate History of a Publishing Empire, 1923–1941*. New York: Atheneum, 1968. Includes a survey of Rochemont's *March of Time* series for the Luce news empire.

~

The White Rose

Expropriation or death

1961, 100 mins., Mexico, in English and Spanish, with English subtitles
Director: Roberto Gavaldón
Screenplay: Roberto Gavaldón, Phil Stevenson, and Emilio Carballido, from B. Traven's novel of the same title
CAST
Don Jacinto Yáñez = Ignacio López Torres
Collins = Reinhold Olszewski

B. Traven's novel and Gavaldón's film trace a remarkable and disturbing pattern of exploitation in U.S.–Mexican economic relationships. The *padrón* of an extensive landholding in Vera Cruz in 1937 runs his hacienda in a benevolent and compassionate way. He is as much a product of Indian peasant stock as his many workers. Unfortunately he is sitting on a rich reserve of oil. When Condor Oil, an American company, tries to buy him out, he refuses, citing his many dependent workers as his primary reason. He is eventually murdered by the oil interests, led by the CEO of Condor Oil, who steal his land. He is literally disappeared, while everything he has created is bulldozed. The peasants can choose: work for the new owners or disappear too. Most of them stay and work, although his son leads (eventually) a successful demonstration against Condor.

This radical critique of American imperialism was banned from Mexican screens for many years. Too many Mexican officials would have been embarrassed and too many sensitive issues raised if this cinematic critique of Mexican-American partnerships became well known, although the film ends with a celebration of the union's campaign against the oil company because it refuses to pay death benefits for workers killed in an oil derrick accident. Even the Mexican supreme court and the president are moved to support the workers. Soon the political situation gets out of hand, and the Mexican government moves to nationalize the oil industry. Collins, the evil head of Condor Oil, isn't worried: he spins the globe in his office and announces that there are many more "white roses" in the world, specifically in Arabia.

Moments like this are chilling. Roberto Gavaldón, the director, and Gabriel Figueroa, Mexico's most famous cinematographer, are just as obvious in their other symbolic shots: a bush of white roses is splashed by oil when a well is sunk and Collins's mistress is given a diamond brooch in the shape of a sprig of roses. Some hope, however small, is held out by Don Jacinto's son, who leads a demonstration against Condor Oil: "The time for justice is now."

See also: *The Burning Season*.
Availability: Selected collections.

Further reading

Paranaguá, Paulo Antonio, ed. *Mexican Cinema*. Trans. Ana M. López. London: British Film Institute, 1995. Excellent survey of Mexican cinema, with a chapter on Gavaldón's career by Ariel Zúñiga, who argues that "in a country where film production was fundamentally linked to the state," to be opposed to the state was to commit suicide as an active director.

Traven, B. *The White Rose*. 1929. Trans. Donald J. Davidson. Westport, Conn.: Lawrence Hill, 1979. The source novel, still another Traven exposé of American greed and a celebration of Mexican Indian ways.

Note: Also known as *La rosa blanca*.

Who Killed Vincent Chin?

The killing of the American dream

1989, 82 mins.
Directors: Christine Choy and Renée Tajima
Traditional documentary
PRINCIPAL FIGURES
Vincent Chin, Chinese-American engineer
Lily Chin, his mother
Helen Zia, leader of American Citizens for Justice
Ron Ebens, unemployed Chrysler Motors superintendent
Nita Ebens, former auto worker; Ron Ebens's wife
Michael Nitz, unemployed Chrysler Motors worker; the Ebenses's stepson
Racine Colwell, Fancy Pants Club waitress
Starlene, Fancy Pants Club dancer

Vincent Chin, a 27-year-old Chinese-American man, was celebrating his bachelor party on June 19, 1982, at a Detroit bar when Ron Ebens, a foreman from Chrysler Motors, and his stepson, Michael Nitz, apparently mistook Chin for a Japanese or Japanese-American and an argument—in part based on Ebens's ethnic slurs—broke out. The fight continued outside the bar, but Chin and his friends escaped. When Ebens and Nitz spotted Chin at a nearby McDonald's, they beat him to death with a baseball bat. A series of trials followed as Detroit Asian-Americans, led by Chin's mother, fought for a vindication of her son's death.

Ebens and Nitz plea-bargained: for their plea of guilty to the reduced charge of manslaughter, they were sentenced to fifteen years, but the sentence was suspended to three years' probation and a fine of $3,780, certainly a lenient sentence by any standards. So lenient, in fact, that for their brutal crime the men spent only one night in jail (the night of their arrest), and Ebens complains bitterly even about that.

The indignation of the Asian-American community led to the creation of a community organization, American Citizens for

Justice, which pressured the Justice Department to indict the two men for federal civil rights violations. In June 1984 a jury of the U.S. District Court in Detroit acquitted Nitz but sentenced Ebens to twenty-five years in prison. Ebens appealed, and at a new trial in Cincinnati, Ohio, in 1987 he was acquitted. The film offers a regional interpretation of this acquittal: Cincinnati jurors, living in a conservative city, knew nothing of the auto industry in Detroit and had no experience with hostility to Asian-Americans.

The filmmakers (in the PBS *Point of View* interviews that are part of the Indiana University videocassette release) suggest that their intention was to gather numerous points of view in an imitation of the Japanese classic fiction film *Rashomon*, in which the principal characters and an eyewitness narrate conflicting versions of a crime. Most viewers will find, however, that the filmmakers believe some of their witnesses more than others. Ebens, who admits to beating Chin to death but believes that it "could happen to anyone," denies that he ever said these fighting words to Chin as they sat opposite each other at the topless dance club: "It's because of you little mother__s that we're out of work!" Racine Colwell, waitress at the club, testified he did.

Vincent Chin's tragedy is therefore seen as part of the gradual collapse of some elements of the Michigan auto industry, under heavy competition from Japanese car companies. The filmmakers portray a city under siege—a hunger emergency declared in 1982 by the mayor—and a region looking for scapegoats. Shots of foreign-car sledgehammer bashes at malls suggest a rising surge of anger and violence in the community. The filmmakers also suggest that the clash of white blue-collar workers and those they perceive to be "stealing" their jobs is compounded by the difficulty of some Americans to distinguish one hyphenated Asian-American from another.

Before the first civil rights trial in March 1984, Jesse Jackson spoke to the committee: "Perhaps it would have been a fairer trial if all the politicians, all the corporate executives, the union leaders, and the journalists who have told the American people to 'blame it on the Japanese' had stood trial with those two auto workers." Jackson often mentioned the Chin case in his presidential campaign speeches that year, but perhaps unfortunately the film includes only a clip of Jackson comparing Chin's death with the martyrdom of Martin Luther King and Jesus Christ.

The film contains a few awkward moments. It is never clear how two armed police officers could have been eyewitnesses to Chin's extended beating and killing without intervening. We hear from—very briefly and then never again—an unidentified African American man who says he was hired by Ebens and Nitz (for $20) to help them find Chin after the fights at the club were over. How these incidents affected the jurors' decisions in the various trials is never documented. Further, some footage of Chol Soo Lee, a Korean-American convicted of a crime he did not commit (and the subject of the film *True Believer*), is shown but never explained.

Ultimately, this is a film less about trials than about changes in political and social consciousness (or, in the case of Ebens and Nitz, a refusal to admit any consciousness). The final words of the film are reserved for Lily Chin, the distraught mother who gave up her self-effacing role as a traditional Chinese woman to help American Citizens for Justice: "I want justice for my son." Some measure of justice came in a cash settlement of her wrongful-death suit against Ebens, but this development is not covered in the film.

The film has won numerous awards, including Best Documentary at the Hawaii International Film Festival in 1988, and received an Academy Award nomination in the same category the next year.

See also: *Alamo Bay*.
Availability: Selected collections; Filmakers Library; Indiana University.

Further reading

Clemetson, Lynette. "20 Years Later, Michigan Killing Still Galvanizes Asian-Americans." *New York Times*, 18 June 2002, A1, 17. The continuing story of American Citizens for Justice.

"Ex-Auto Worker Guilty in Slaying." *New York Times*, 29 June 1984, A10. A survey of the case after the civil rights conviction.

Leong, Russell, ed. *Moving the Image: Independent Asian Pacific American Media Arts*. Los Angeles: UCLA Asian American Studies Center, 1991. An overview of Asian-American films, including *Who Killed Vincent Chin?*

Nichols, Bill. *Blurred Boundaries: Questions of Meaning in Contemporary Culture*. Bloomington: Indiana University Press, 1994. Argues that the film is "the most important political documentary of the 1980s."

"$1.5 Million in Wrongful Death." *New York Times*, 1 August 1987, 32. Ebens agrees to lifetime monthly payments to Chin's estate.

Wei, William. *The Asian American Movement*. Philadelphia: Temple University Press, 1993. Sets the Chin case in the context of Asian-American political movements.

Wilkerson, Isabel. "For Asian-Americans, Acquittal in Rights Case Arouses Outrage and Fear." *New York Times*, 6 May 1987, A20. A survey of the case after the final trial.

↵

Who's Getting Rich and Why Aren't You?

"Making money's a good deal."—T. J. Rodgers

1996, 60 mins.
TV documentary
PRINCIPAL FIGURES
Harry Smith, narrator
T. J. Rodgers, CEO, Cypress Semiconductors
Bruce Klatsky, CEO, Van Heusen
Andy Rusnack, former employee, Traveler's Insurance
Terry Howley, mayor, Decatur, Illinois
Martin Mangan, priest, Decatur, Illinois

The extremes of wealth and success in America meet in Harry Smith's CBS report.

In 1995 the CEOs we meet in this TV documentary earned 141 times as much as the average worker in their companies; in 1980, the ratio was 42 to 1. Of course that is the ratio when the workers have jobs: Smith traces a number of workers who have lost their jobs to downsizing and to overseas manufacturing.

The CEO of Cypress Semiconductors, an essential company in the early years of Silicon Valley successes, is the American dream poster boy for free-market competition. T. J. Rodgers says, with no irony and as if *Wall Street*'s Gordon Gekko had never appeared in a theater near him: "Making money's a good deal. It's moral, it's proper, it's correct. You don't have to be embarrassed about it."

Decatur, Illinois, with its Caterpillar and Staley lockouts, is an unfortunate example of another process whereby corporations maximize their profits: union-busting. The mayor of Decatur would have us believe his constituents work for the sheer pleasure of it: "This is middle America. This is blue-collar. People here love to work. They like to work hard." Father Martin Mangan, also featured in the agitprop documentary *Struggle in the Heartland* (in the entry with *Deadly Corn*), sees the struggle in moral terms: "In Nazi Germany there was a systematic destruction of a certain group of people. And the church did not stand up to that. And so I just sort of made an analogy that there's a systematic destruction of a group of people: working people."

Smith's documentary argues that the middle class is also being destroyed by corporate greed: "Here on Wall Street and in other financial capitals around the world the spirit of Charles Darwin is alive and well. The fittest survive: the rest get pink slips. If you perceive yourself to be part of the middle class and feel threatened by some of what you have seen in the last hour, that fear may be justified." No longer are blue-collar workers necessarily the first to be shown the gate: "Without an exceptional ability or special skill that helps your boss make lots of money," Smith concludes, "everyone is replaceable."

See also: *Deadly Corn; Struggle in the Heartland.*
Availability: Not.

Further reading

Rodgers, T. J. "What's Good for Microsoft . . ." *New York Times*, 20 October 1998. Supports Microsoft during its antitrust case: "Using the courts to regulate the marketplace [is] a hypocrisy Ayn Rand called 'a free market, enforced by law.'"

——. "Yes, Even the Rich Deserve a Tax Cut." *New York Times*, 4 November 2000: "If the federal government cuts my taxes, I won't drink an extra bottle of Laffite-Rothschild per day; I'll invest my tax break in 130 Silicon Valley companies rather than the 110 I currently invest in. I'll spend my company's share of the tax break on research and development. That's the right thing to do for the rich, the poor and everyone in between."

Who's Getting Rich and Why Aren't You? CBS Reports, 8 August 1996. Transcript for sale at ⟨www.burrelles.com⟩.

Web site:

⟨www.cypress.com⟩ Official site of Cypress Semiconductors, with press releases, statements by CEO T. J. Rodgers, and detailed information that explains this company profile: "Over 4,400 employees worldwide; manufacturing excellence, world-class fabrication, assembly, and test plants; 2000 revenues of $1.288 billion."

↪

Wild Boys of the Road

And girls too

1933, 77 mins., B&W
Director: William Wellman
Screenplay: Earl Baldwin, from Daniel Ahern's story "Desperate Youth"
CAST
Edward "Eddie" Smith = Frankie Darro
Tommy Gordon = Edwin Phillips
Grace = Rochelle Hudson
Sally = Dorothy Coonan
Judge White = Robert Barrat
Red = Ward Bond

The "wild boys" of the title are the same Depression youth documented in *Riding the Rails*—part of an army of teenagers who for economic or personal reasons became temporary hoboes. The lead characters, Eddie and Tommy, take off because their fathers have lost their jobs; they exchange their pleasant high school life of dances and jalopies for dangerous freight rides and police harassment. One of the two girls they hook up with is raped by a train worker and another boy loses a leg rushing a freight.

The film encourages rebellion. When a large group of the teens are thrown off a train by seven or eight railroad dicks, a hobo observing the scene tells them that there are a hundred teens but only a handful of cops: "You're an army, aintcha?" The boys turn around and attack the cops with fruit they've lifted from the boxcars. And in a glorious sequence, they climb on the train again and leave the yard pelting the cops into submission.

Their high spirits carry them over to the much more sober moment when they realize that one of their girls has been raped by the train brakeman. When he shows up, they beat him mercilessly and push him out of the car as the train happens to be going over a bridge. He obviously falls to his death.

At this point the youths, now quite bonded, create a virtually utopian Hooverville in a jungle of sewer pipes. But the encampment is short-lived when the community mobilizes a formidable police force against them.

Their story comes to an end with Eddie's innocent participation in a holdup. He and his pals are hauled before a judge who resembles President Roosevelt, according to some critics. (Not to my eye, especially when you think of the FDR look-alike at the "good" migrant labor camp in *The Grapes of Wrath*.) In any case, under the watchful eye of the New Deal's National Recovery Act (NRA) eagle displayed on the wall, the judge resolves their plight in what could only be called a celebration of the New Deal: he offers them all jobs because "things are going to be better now" all over America, not only for them, but for their fathers too.

See also: *Riding the Rails*.
Availability: Selected collections.

Further reading

Roddick, Nick. *A New Deal in Entertainment: Warner Brothers in the 1930s*. London: British Film Institute, 1983. This fine study highlights *Wild Boys of the Road* as an example of "rehabilitation" cinema.

Rottman, Peter, and Jim Purdy. *The Hollywood Social Problem Film*. Bloomington: Indiana University Press, 1981. Includes a very helpful section on this film.

Note: Also known as *Dangerous Days*.

⤸
Wild River

Mud on the stars, indeed

1960, 110 mins.
Director: Elia Kazan
Screenplay: Paul Osborn, from both Borden Deal's novel *Dunbar's Cove* and William Bradford Huie's novel *Mud on the Stars*
CAST
Chuck Glover = Montgomery Clift
Carol Baldwin = Lee Remick
Ella Garth = Jo Van Fleet
Hank Bailey = Albert Salmi
Hamilton Garth = Jay C. Flippen
Cal Garth = James Westerfield
Joe John Garth = Big Jeff Bess
Ben = Robert Earl Jones

On the surface, TVA country does not seem to be Elia Kazan territory: the director of *On the Waterfront* and *A Streetcar Named Desire* demands an urban scene to develop, some proletarian played by Brando to prowl around, and a frustrated middle-class dame or two. Instead Kazan took on a TVA suit who falls in love with a country lassie, while all hell breaks loose around them, in the form of a family uprooted from a home in the path of a TVA dam and blacks who get the same pay as whites.

Montgomery Clift plays the TVA advance man, whose job is to get the local landowners to sell out to the government; he also has to hire local folk to clear the purchased lands to allow the course of the new river to develop smoothly. What looks like still another routine deal turns difficult when he confronts a matriarch who refuses to sell. Furthermore, he falls in love with her granddaughter, thereby making his name mud among the local good old boys, one of whose number takes it upon himself to teach the outsider some redneck lessons he won't forget.

Thus we have two-thirds peckerwood soap opera and one-third New Deal history lesson: not bad fractions if the film looked like a 1930s melodrama, but the pretty Technicolor makes it look like a 1950s M-G-M musical, replete with a chorus of aged black retainers who at first choose the matriarch's benevolence over the TVA's high wages. A similar situation results when we compare the colorful Cagney playing a Huey Long type in *A Lion Is in the Streets* with the black-and-white Broderick Crawford in the same role in *All the King's Men*: the latter film *looks* as though it's about real peckerwood politics.

Nonetheless, a few moments of this film are worth another look: the performances of the leads (Remick at least was sober) are compelling, the river and its quaint hand-rope ferry looks authentic, and visiting *the* key economic issue of the peckerwood South—equal wages for blacks—is very important. Whether these moments will suffice while the soapy waters churn is an open question.

See also: *The River* in *New Deal Documentaries*.
Availability: Not.

Further reading

Chase, Donald. "Wild River." *Film Comment*, November–December 1996, 10–15. An enthusiastic appreciation of the film's power.

The TVA suit (Montgomery Clift) lands in forbidden territory with a new friend (Lee Remick) in *Wild River*.

Davidson, Donald. *The Tennessee*. 2 vols. New York: Rinehart, 1948. Part of the immensely popular Rivers of America series, Davidson's second volume reviews (perhaps too benignly) the TVA's acquisition of lands and the displacement of families, the latter statistically negligible.

Huie, William Bradford. *Mud on the Stars*. New York: L. B. Fischer, 1942. The original title was changed to *Wild River* (and the novel slightly edited) when it was released as a movie tie-in edition in 1960. The novel is filled with sanctimonious unreconstructed southern gibberish (the Scottsboro boys were guilty of rape, northern ideas ruined sharecroppers, etc.) and not really much about the TVA.

Weiler, A. H. "Wild River." *New York Times*, 27 May 1960, 22. A balanced review, concluding that it is "an interesting but strangely disturbing drama rather than a smashing study of a historic aspect of the changing American scene."

⤳

Wildrose

Untamed

1984, 95 mins.
Director: John Hanson
Screenplay: John Hanson and Eugene Corr
CAST
June Lorich = Lisa Eichhorn
Rick Ogaard = Tom Bower
Pavich = Jim Cada
Karen = Cinda Jackson
Ricotti = Dan Nemaniack
Katri Sippola = Lydia Olsen
Nolan = Ernest Tomatz

One of the few reviewers of this film about a strip mine worker in the Mesabi Range in

Minnesota complained that the film is "tongue-tied" in its attempts to tell the dramatic story of June, who is the "wildrose" of the title. But it is the character June herself who is tongue-tied: she speaks so little we are sometimes afraid she has not been given the same script as the rest of the actors. She is virtually screen center for the entire film, so this is a serious problem. It has to be one of the most underwritten roles in the history of feature films.

Her story is dramatic enough: she drives one of those mammoth open-pit dump trucks (also seen being driven by women in *Moving Mountains*) until she gets bumped down to pit laborer because of layoffs and matters of seniority. Trying to do a "man's" job gets her taunted by men in her pit-rat crew. In the meantime, she has to put up with a drunken lout of an ex-husband.

Although her union is never identified, we see the local debating issues such as seniority, cost-of-living allowances (COLAs), and Occupational, Safety, and Health Administration (OSHA) regulations. One of her union brothers recites a speech she has heard too often, even from her mother, to the effect that the local unemployment problem would go away if women were no longer hired.

Into this life of quiet desperation comes a complication: a fellow pit rat falls for her and she (less enthusiastically) for him. His dream is to be the owner-operator of his own commercial fishing boat on Lake Superior. Part of the drama of the film is anticipating her decision regarding what we know will be his eventual offer: give up this dirty mining business and join him in commercial fishing. This offer, surprisingly, finally gets her verbal motor going. Don't attack my job, she insists.

John Hanson's direction of *Wildrose* has a lot in common with his direction of his earlier black-and-white feature *Northern Lights*. He has a genuine feel for rural working-class people, their rituals (a big family fish fry), their behavior (June finds it difficult to stand up to her ex-husband), and their opinions (when June does speak). But some of these scenes, shot with a mixture of professional and nonprofessional actors, have the look of overcompetent home movies and often lack a point other than that they show "real people."

Perhaps characteristic of this film, which seems so promising, is the log cabin June is building. It is a spare-time project: she's hewing, notching, and setting the logs single-handed. She seems to be making good progress, and the task shows her independent spirit, enables her to spend a lot more time on screen without talking, and helps us to measure and appreciate her physical strength as well. But we never see her finish the cabin.

See also: *Moving Mountains; Northern Lights; We Dig Coal.*
Availability: Selected collections.

Further reading

Maslin, Janet. "Breaking Ground." *New York Times*, 5 April 1985, C4. A brief but positive review.

The Willmar 8

Eight women against one bank

1981, 55 mins.
Director: Lee Grant
Traditional documentary
PRINCIPAL FIGURES
Sandi Treml, cashier
Shirley Solyntjes and Terri Novotny, bookkeepers
Glennis Andresen and Sylvia Erickson, tellers
Doris Boshart, head bookkeeper
Jane Harguth, head operator
Irene Wallin, head teller
Leo Pirsch, president, Citizens National Bank

On 16 December 1977 eight women, employees of the Citizens National Bank of Willmar, Minnesota, began the first bank strike in the history of the state. The members of the self-styled Willmar Bank Employees Association,

Local 1, struck because they were asked to train still another man to be a manager over their heads. When they refused, the bank president told them, "We're not all equal, you know." For one and a half years, through two Minnesota winters, the women (and occasionally a few labor and National Organization for Women allies) walked a picket line in front of the bank. They brought their case to the National Labor Relations Board (NLRB) and asked for back pay and reinstatement (since other women had been given their jobs).

Lee Grant, an actor and director, came to the Minnesota town (population: 14,000) midway through the strike. Previously, Willmar had been known as the American city with the highest rate of coffee consumption and one of the largest turkey-processing plants in the region. With a few exceptions, she was met by a wall of silence: the Willmar 8 had apparently committed the unpardonable sin. No one in Willmar would speak openly to Grant and her camera crew except the members of one poker club, mostly upper-middle-class women with friends among the bank's executives and families. The card players ranged from noncommittal and defensive to near-hostile: their overriding message was that the bank women should just leave well enough alone. Only the Unitarian church would invite the Willmar 8 to a service to explain their situation. Oddly enough, the bank president's son was a Minnesota AFL-CIO official who supported their strike.

The Willmar 8 became close friends despite their differences in age, religious beliefs, and interests. One of the women admitted that she didn't want to strike and would not do it again, but she remained a faithful picketer throughout the strike. The head bookkeeper, Doris Boshart, was hired back but demoted. The other women accepted her decision to go back, and Doris picketed with them every day during her lunch break.

Toward the end of the strike, with their strike fund exhausted, the women learned that their agitation had stunted the bank sufficiently that it had to be sold. The NLRB ruling on 23 March 1979, however, was unfavorable. The board ruled that the bank had committed unfair labor practices, but that they were not the reason for the strike. The women ended their strike, but first they posed for a final portrait for Grant on the sidewalk where they had spent so many cold days: each close-up shows loss but not defeat. Six months after the strike, only Boshart remained a bank employee; of the others, one became a student, two were unemployed, and the rest were working in jobs ranging from bookkeeper for K-Mart to nurse's aide.

A Rochester, Minnesota, local of the United Auto Workers (pre–AFL-CIO merger) sends money and support in the form of marchers, but there are more than a few hints that the state AFL-CIO may not have given the women as much support as it could have. It may be a weakness of the film that it does not explore some of these important issues. Perhaps because the women did not win, Grant seems to put more of her faith in legal and government action: her end titles emphasize the legal battles women in banking have won since the Willmar 8 went down to defeat, and she ends with the announcement that in 1978 the Department of Labor targeted the banking industry for enforcement of equal employment.

Four years later Grant made a (perhaps unfortunately titled) TV movie for NBC, *A Matter of Sex*, also about the Willmar 8, but it is not available on videocassette.

See also: 9 to 5; Working Girl.
Availability: Selected collections.

Further reading

James, Judith. "The Long March of 'The Willmar 8.'" *Ms*, 1978, 19. A sample of the publicity in the feminist press that actively supported the strikers.

Kellett, Suzy. "In Trouble." *People*, 27 November 1978, 107. A sample of the fairly positive national publicity for the strikers.

With Babies and Banners: The Story of the Women's Emergency Brigade

Union maids and rebel girls in Big Auto

1978, 45 mins.
Directors: Lorraine Gray, Anne Bohlen, and Lyn Goldfarb
Traditional documentary

PRINCIPAL FIGURES

Nellie Bessen, Genora Johnson Dollinger, and Ruth Pitts, Emergency Women's Brigade

The subtitle of this film refers to the brave and militant organization of working women and auto workers' wives, mothers, sisters, and girlfriends who led the outside strike while their men occupied the General Motors plant in the great Flint sit-down strike of 1936–37. The documentary argues convincingly that the women's strike kitchens, daycare centers, picket lines, family aid, and community propaganda helped to win the strike.

The women had double trouble, of course, since they were squeezed economically by company policy and confronted traditional sexist attitudes from their men and from society, too. The women who worked at buildings targeted for sit-downs, for example, were sent home so no one could accuse the remaining men of sexual improprieties. When some of the women volunteered at union headquarters, they were considered at first too "feminine" (i.e., they were on the make) or too "queer" or too intellectual. But over and over again the women demonstrated their courage and resourcefulness. When tear gas was shot into a building, the women smashed the windows to let the gas out; they fought on the propaganda front, too, with the "children's picket line" ("My daddy strikes for us little tykes. On to victory!").

This Academy Award nominee for best documentary combines archival footage, still photos, and contemporary interviews into a lively documentary that tells women's history from the bottom up. Hazel Dickens sings her memorable version of the old Joe Hill IWW song, "The Rebel Girl," as the coda to the film.

One of the participants (Genora Johnson Dollinger) professes to be much happier with the British documentary *The Great Sitdown Strike* (filmed for the BBC series *Yesterday's Witness* in 1976). To my eye, that is a much less vibrant film, often failing to identify the participants interviewed. It is not generally available in any case.

See also: *The Life and Times of Rosie the Riveter; Union Maids.*
Availability: Selected collections; New Day Films.

Further reading

Dollinger, Sol, and Genora Johnson Dollinger. *Not Automatic: Women and the Left in the Forging of the Auto Workers' Union.* New York: Monthly Review Press, 2000. A revisionist examination and oral history of the birth of the UAW, emphasizing the role of the left in strategic planning; includes a critique of the film by one of the participants (Genora Johnson).

Wittstock, Wittstock

East Germany, East Germany

1997, 119 mins., East Germany, in German, with English subtitles
Director: Volker Koepp
Cinema verité documentary

PRINCIPAL FIGURES

Edith Dahlke, Elsbeth Fischer, and Renate Lust

In a sense this project is parallel to the Junges' *Children of Gozlow* series, the longest-running documentary exploration of working-class lives. Like Gozlow, Wittstock is a provincial place, but the factory provided consistent and good employment opportunities. Unlike the makers of the Gozlow project and the British *Up* series, however, Koepp began with adults and assumed that the project would be short-lived, since he was not tracking children growing up. Koepp began by following just three women who began working at the new factory and remained there more than ten years. With the fall of the Wall and the repositioning of East German industry in a competitive (capitalist) system, the textile factory did not survive, and the three women were forced to go in new directions.

Wittstock, Wittstock recapitulates the entire career of the three women through 1996, using footage from the earlier films (none of which are available in subtitled versions):

1975: *Girls in Wittstock* (*Mädchen in Wittstock*)
1976: *Back to Wittstock* (*Wieder in Wittstock*)
1978: *Wittstock III*
1981: *Living and Weaving* (*Leben und Weben*)
1984: *Life in Wittstock* (*Leben in Wittstock*)
1991: *What's Up in Wittstock* (*Neues in Wittstock*)

When the fourth (long) film was completed in 1984, Koepp felt that the project was probably over: the women had married, had continued to work at the factory, and had all moved into new flats. But the fall of the Wall in 1989 made their experience typical of many East Germans, and Koepp filmed "how the Soviet soldiers had gone away, how businesses had changed, how the big textile factory had contracted, and the first redundancies had begun" (interview with Koepp in the 41st London Film Festival program). Elsbeth tried numerous training courses for new positions (without much luck), Renate took a job as a hotel chambermaid, and Edith (formerly a bit of a rebel) has settled down in a new community.

Koepp believed that documentaries are "always subversive to a degree," since they represent a reality that cannot be denied. Perhaps his experience has been overly

determined by years in the GDR, but with the Wall down, his images of the effects on ordinary workers of an economic and political system now defunct retain their importance.

See also: *Children of Golzow*.
Availability: Not.

Further reading

Allan, Sean, and John Sandford, eds. *DEFA: East German Cinema, 1946–1992*. New York: Berghahn Books, 1999. Excellent resource book on DEFA generally, with two essays on documentary, discussing Koepp's work in passing.

Pflaum, Hans Günther, and Hans Helmut Prinzler. *Cinema in the Federal Republic of Germany*. Bonn: Inter Nationes, 1993. This very thorough reference work includes essays and production data on GDR films and filmmakers, including Koepp.

Richter, Erika. "The Creation of Documents." *Forum*, Film Festival Berlin, January 1997, at ⟨www.fdk-berlin.de/forum97/f086e.html⟩. Interview with Koepp, who argues for "documentaries as documents": "Sometimes a film was approved [in the GDR], but only one copy would be made. . . . There was no mass audience. We consoled ourselves by saying that at least we are filming, the images are preserved."

Web site:

⟨www.german-cinema.de/archive⟩ "A database offering information on the German films presented in previous issues of KINO-Magazine," with brief reviews, directors' bios, and production data.

⟿

The Wobblies

"Hold the fort, for we are coming . . ."

1979, 90 mins.
Directors: Stewart Bird and Deborah Shaffer
Traditional documentary
PRINCIPAL FIGURES
Roger Baldwin, founder, American Civil Liberties Union
Violet and Jack Miller, Joe Murphy, Nels Peterson, Nicolas Steelink, and Sam Krieger, migratory workers

Tom Scribner, Irv Hanson, and Vaino Onga, lumberjacks
James Fair, longshoreman
Irma Lombardi, Dominic Mignone, and Sophie Cohen, silk weavers
Angelo Rocco, textile worker
Katie Pintek, miner's wife
Art Shields, reporter
Fred Thompson, newspaper editor, *The Industrial Worker*
Utah Phillips, folk singer.

Like many documentaries about labor history, this film intercuts archival footage, old photographs, and contemporary interviews with surviving members (then in their 80s and 90s) of the Industrial Workers of the World, a.k.a. the Wobblies, a.k.a. the One Big Union, into a satisfying survey of an important and (arguably) unique unity. The Wobblies wanted all workers in one union, but had to be satisfied with some of the most exploited and tough members of the American proletariat (which included many recent immigrants). Their occupations were in part represented by the list of "witnesses" or interviewees for this film—especially migratory workers, lumberjacks, mill workers, and miners.

Most of these workers were unskilled or semiskilled: they felt excluded from Samuel Gompers's AFL—which one of the Wobblies said they always called the "A.F. of Hell"— in part because of his pro-war stance but mainly because of his skilled-trades orientation. (Gompers called the IWW the "fungus on the labor movement.") Indeed, at the Wobbly founding convention in 1905, Big Bill Haywood said that he didn't even care if any skilled workers came into the One Big Union. The preamble to the IWW constitution proclaimed its revolutionary aims: "Instead of the conservative motto, 'A fair day's wage for a fair day's work,' we must inscribe on our banner the revolutionary watchword, 'Abolition of the wage system.'"

The heart of this documentary is the cadre of old Wobblies who still stand steadfast for their ideals. They form a narrative chorus on the highlights of Wobbly history—the strike of women mill workers of Lawrence, Massachusetts, in 1912; the strike of silk workers in Paterson, New Jersey, in 1913; and the tragic massacre of Wobbly free-speech advocates in Everett, Washington, in 1916—as well as their tidbits of personal history. One rail-riding working stiff recalls their battles against "hijackers," men who tried to prey on the workers, often holding up a hundred men until they found the Wobbly organizer with a stash of cash from headquarters. The Wobblies had to send out a "flying squadron" to deal with one of these crooks: they cut the letter I in his forehead and two W's in his cheeks, one man recalled, and then poured potassium permanganate in the wounds to signify what would happen if hijackers came around again.

Another witness recalled how Elizabeth Gurley Flynn, the Rebel Girl of Wobbly fame, asked the young women of the Lawrence strike if they wanted to have dresses "like their bosses' daughters." When they shouted yes, she told them, "Well, you can't!" and urged them to fight on nonetheless. Still another witness told of infiltrating the scab crews that were sent out from the city to work in fields struck by the Wobblies: as the supposed scabs approached the picket line, they burst into one of the Wobbly hymns, "Hold the Fort, for We Are Coming," and had a good laugh at the employers' expense. (Steinbeck used a similar scene when a punch-drunk character infiltrates the scab crew in *In Dubious Battle*.)

One minor difficulty with the witnesses is that they are introduced by still photos with name and occupation in the first minute of the film and never identified again. It would be hard to recall on first or even subsequent viewing a single name or two from a list of almost twenty.

Directors Bird and Shaffer were fortunate in being able to use some animated propaganda from the anti-union Disney folks: we see "Little Red Henski," a cartoon featuring Alice's Egg Plant, which is disrupted by the arrival of the Little Red Henski (who looks like Lenin), who organizes the egg layers into demanding "smaller eggs" and "shorter hours." This short film is almost worth the price of admission in itself: Alice is played by a real actress, while a Felix the Cat look-alike is the foreman, in an early example of mixing animated and live-action modes. When Alice yells at the striking hens, "Get to work. I need those eggs," a hen replies, "You'll get your egg," as she lays one on the spot and hits Alice in the kisser with it.

As intrinsically entertaining as this cartoon is, the filmmakers use it to illustrate a tricky point in Wobbly symbols. Their propaganda cartoons almost always used both the black cat and wooden shoe (the "sabot" of "sabotage"), but one of the Wobblies interviewed said that for them sabotaging their own workplace by burning it down, for example, would be foolish; instead, he said, they defined "sabotage" as the "conscious withdrawal of efficiency"—shorter hours and smaller eggs.

Another animated short demonstrates how the war for public opinion against the Wobblies was won. A farmer is proudly displaying his prosperous-looking sacks of "American Institutions" as a giant rat gnaws its way closer through the wall. "Bolsheviks are the rats of civilization," the farmer shouts as he smashes the Bolshevik/IWW rat with his shovel. This would be funnier if it didn't turn out to have a real-life parallel in the ferocity with which established forces attacked the Wobblies' pacifist "free-speech fights" and other organizing drives.

The numerous historical battles—many well known, others not—waged by the Wobblies may convince some viewers that they were more than the songbirds of the working class. Nevertheless, Wobbly Ralph Chaplin's "Solidarity Forever" (1915) is sung virtually everywhere as the anthem of the American labor movement.

Wobbly characters in film have popped up in some unlikely places (probably one or two of the band of prospectors in *The Treasure of the Sierra Madre*) and in some likely places (the mine workers' organizer in *Matewan*). But like the One Big Union itself, they come too often to a righteous but tragic death.

See also: *Joe Hill; Matewan.*
Availability: Selected collections.

Further reading

Dubofsky, Melvin. "Film as History: History as Drama." *Labor History* 22 (1981): 136–39. A balanced review of the film.

Georgakas, Dan. "The Wobblies—The Making of a Historical Documentary." *Cineaste* 10 (Spring 1980): 14–19, 58. An in-depth interview with the film's co-directors.

Georgakas, Dan, Stewart Bird, and Deborah Schaffer, eds. *Solidarity Forever: An Oral History of the IWW*. Chicago: Lake View Press, 1985. A collection of interviews with many of the film's participants.

Goldberg, David J. *A Tale of Three Cities: Labor Organization and Protest in Paterson, Passaic, and Lawrence, 1916–1921*. New Brunswick: Rutgers University Press, 1989. Reviews the competition with the A. J. Muste–founded Amalgamated Textile Workers of America and supports the claim that the IWW did not sustain poststrike organizing efforts (see Golin for a counterview).

Golin, Steve. *The Fragile Bridge: Paterson Silk Strike, 1913*. Philadelphia: Temple University Press, 1988. Argues for the success of the IWW and its Greenwich Village intellectual allies.

Gomez, Joseph A. "History, Documentary, and Audience Manipulation: A View of 'The Wobblies.'" *Labor History* 22 (1981): 141–45. A hostile review, objecting to almost everything about the film, including the projection speed of the silent archival footage.

Kornbluh, Joyce, ed. *Rebel Voices: An IWW Anthology*. Ann Arbor: University of Michigan Press, 1964. An admirably edited, thorough, and very rich collection of Wobbly writings and graphic art.

Maslin, Janet. "The Wobblies." *New York Times*, 11 October 1979, C15. A brief review that considers the film a gentle, almost too gentle, depiction of the rowdy Wobbly days.

O'Connor, Harvey. *Revolution in Seattle*. New York: Monthly Review Press, 1964. A very readable memoir of Northwest Coast Wobblies by a former member and newspaper reporter.

Porton, Richard. *Film and the Anarchist Imagination*. London: Verso, 1999. Although "it is considerably more radical than anything imagined by Hollywood," the film is soft, Porton argues, on the anarchist and anarchistic-syndicalist roots of the IWW.

Women of Steel

Women in and out of steel

1985, 30 mins.
Directors: Steffi Domike and Randy
Strothman
Traditional documentary
PRINCIPAL FIGURES
Beth Destler, Sheryl Johnson, Pat Turnell,
Linda Cable, and Carolyn Demeler,
former steelworkers
Sherry Oratlono, current steelworker

This documentary is somewhat rare in that
the principal figures, with one exception, are
laid-off steelworkers. (The exception, Sherry
Oratlono, was a millwright helper when the
film was made.) The film, which the women
helped to make themselves, focuses on their
lives after they broke the gender barrier at
U.S. Steel's mill in Homestead, Pennsylvania,
only to be laid off as the industry collapsed
in the early 1980s. They were hired as the
direct result of an agreement signed by
U.S. Steel with the United Steelworkers of
America in April 1974 to begin a five-year
plan to hire more women and minorities in
the relatively high-paying jobs offered in the
mills.

The film offers the testimony of women
whose working and family lives took a hard
fall almost immediately. A daring opening
scene—for a documentary on women
workers, in any case—sets the downward
spiral of this select group of women workers:
we see a woman strip off her dirty work
clothes down to her bra and then transform
herself into a waitress. In concrete terms the
women went from $12 an hour to $2 an hour;
they went from repairing tracks and laying
electric cables to serving tables at Pizza Hut.
(And even their waitress jobs got worse as a
result of the turndown in steel: Pat Turnell
complains that she has to wash dishes and
clean windows because her table volume has
gone down.)

When the big blow in steel came in 1983—
the demolition of the blast furnaces—unemployment figures climbed for both men and
women, but, as the film makes clear, it was
always harder for the women to get rehired
whenever a company did call back some
workers.

As a document on the effects of an industry's collapse on women, the film is like one
continuous bad headline—an almost unre-
lieved tale of broken hopes and broken families. There are a few bright spots: Cheryl
Johnson shows her unemployment committee organizing and demonstrating and
lobbying for relief; Beth Destler emphasizes
how the women were able to stick together
as friends and, of course, eventually work on
this documentary.

The sound track includes feisty songs ("I
Got Trouble," "Fight Back") by Holly Near,
who performs here as a labor film trouba-
dour, and what seems like a song commissioned for the film, "Women of Steel," by
Maria Hurt and CoCo Coleman.

See also: *Moving Mountains; Wildrose.*
Availability: Selected collection; University
of Pittsburgh Press.

Further reading

Lynd, Staughton. *The Fight against Shutdowns:
Youngstown's Steel Mill Closings*. San Pedro,
Calif.: Singlejack Books, 1982. Community and
church groups work with organized labor to save
jobs.

The Women of Summer

"The program was built out of their
lives."—Esther Peterson

1986, 55 mins.
Directors: Suzanne Bauman and Rita
Heller
Traditional documentary
PRINCIPAL FIGURES
Esther Peterson, union organizer and
teacher
Hilda Smith ("Jane"), dean, Bryn Mawr
Summer School for Women Workers in
Industry

Marjorie Lynch Logan and Jennie Silverman, students
Holly Near and Ronnie Gilbert, singers

The Bryn Mawr Summer School for Women Workers in Industry was established in 1921 by the president of Bryn Mawr College (M. Carey Thomas) and John D. Rockefeller Jr. and was supported by the recruiting efforts of such organizations as the YWCA Industrial Department, the National Consumers' League, and unions dominated by women workers: the Amalgamated Clothing Workers of America, the International Ladies' Garment Workers' Union, and the Textile Workers Union of America. Hilda W. Smith, founder and first dean of the school, wrote in the original statement of purpose in 1921 that the school would "offer young women of character and ability a fuller education in order that they may widen their influence in the industrial world, help in the coming social reconstruction, and increase the happiness and usefulness of their own lives" (quoted in Schneider). In its eighteen-year history (it was replaced by the Hudson Shore Labor School in 1938), 1,610 women workers went to the school.

Esther Peterson, the recreation director of the school for several years, recalled in a memoir (see Kornbluh and O'Farrell) the practical and democratic nature of study sessions: "We didn't have textbooks. We'd just ask, 'What was it like when the boss said those things?' We acted out the whole thing. . . . The program was built out of their lives and it began with who they are and where they are."

This documentary history of the Bryn Mawr Summer School for Women Workers is framed by a class reunion fifty years after most of these workers left their unusual experimental school in worker's education. Some of the alumnae from the late 1920s recalled the days when support rallies were held in Philadelphia for Sacco and Vanzetti and one of the regular Bryn Mawr faculty members was arrested. Holly Near commemorates those days in a moving song, in part about Judge George Webster Thayer,

who, in sentencing the men to death, spoke "to the living/In the language of the dead."

Some of the other alumnae recall the difficulties of attending the school during the Depression. They were dealing with the hungry and homeless, sometimes within their own families. Occasionally little sisters would be openly smuggled in to live in the dormitory.

This film chronicles an early and important moment in labor education. It demonstrates how removing women workers from their busy homes and working lives even for a brief time strengthened their participation in the labor movement once they were back in the real world.

See also: *The Inheritance*.
Availability: Selected collections.

Further reading

Kornbluh, Joyce L., and Brigid O'Farrell. "You Can't Giddyup by Saying Whoa: Esther Peterson Remembers Her Organized Labor Years." *Labor's Heritage*, Spring 1994, 38–59. An oral history of an organizer and activist who worked at the Bryn Mawr Summer School.

Schneider, Florence Hemley. *Patterns of Workers' Education: The Story of the Bryn Mawr Summer School*. Washington, D.C.: American Council on Public Affairs, 1941. An early history and analysis of the eighteen years in which the school was in existence.

The Worker and the Hairdresser

Blow-drying the proletariat

1996, 101 mins., Italy, Italian, with English subtitles
Director: Lina Wertmüller
Screenplay: Leo Benvenuti, Piero de Bernardi, and Lina Wertmüller
CAST
Tunin = Tullio Solenghi
Zvanin = Gene Gnocchi
Rossella = Veronica Pivetti
Anitina = Cyrielle Claire
Palmina = Piera degli Espositi

Mariolina = Cinzia Leone
Tazio = Giacomo Centola
Volga = Alexandra La Capria
Natascia = Maria Zulima Job

For viewers who do not have a passion for Italian politics or who have not seen *Sacco and Vanzetti* with its outlandish vision of an American courtroom, it may come as a surprise that a popular delegate to the Italian parliament from 1987 to 1992 was Ilona Staller, a.k.a. Cicciolina, a self-styled "pornostar." Any society that has had Cicciolina as a member of Parliament helps to explain (if not justify) *The Worker and the Hairdresser*, a "sex comedy" about Italian politics and class identification.

Lina Wertmüller has been a successful director of two related kinds of political comedies. In one type, politics dominate, as in *Love and Anarchy*, in which an anarchist hides in a brothel while waiting to kill Mussolini, and *Seven Beauties*, in which a ne'er-do-well tries to survive in a Nazi concentration camp by seducing the female commandant. In the other, sex dominates, as in *Swept Away by an Unusual Destiny in the Sea of August*, in which an upper-class woman takes up with a working-class deckhand when they are shipwrecked. The Italian title of this film translates as *The Worker and the Hairdresser in a Whirl of Sex and Politics*, thus combining her two favorite themes.

In all of her films, issues of sexuality, fascism (or political dominance of any kind), and class interest are never far apart, and sexual farce usually prevails. This is certainly the case in *The Worker and the Hairdresser*, for the worker is a Communist union man and the hairdresser is a supporter of the right-wing Northern League, which wants Northern Italy to secede from the country, leaving it to consist of the low-class region known as Southern Italy. Of course, for them, anything south of Milan is low class; Rome is not only low class but politically corrupt. The Northern League, which calls its new country Padania, issues its own stamps, and flies its own flag, is not usually considered a laughing matter. Which is probably why Wertmüller was attracted to this story.

A Fiat metalworker, Tunin, has always been a strong union man, but once he spots Zvanin, he naturally begins to do his thinking with a part other than his head, and—since this is a Wertmüller film—he also has conversations with this part warning it not to bother him. But of course it does, and despite family and class allegiances, he pursues Zvanin recklessly, alternating fits of love-making and knock-down fights. She is a fascist, after all, he reasons, when he does his thinking with his head . . . or his heart.

Most Italian films never enter the English-speaking market, so why this one? Primarily Wertmüller's reputation. This film does not come close to the horrifying beauties of her earlier successes, even though they too mixed sexual farce and political tragedy. Perhaps this film is too pared to the bone, too unrelentingly about—and only about—this sexy Northern Leaguer and her Red jack-in-the-box. The hairdresser doesn't betray her class, after all, since he's the one doing the crawling, and that makes for an unequal duel, unlike Wertmüller's other mock-epic confrontations.

This is a class-conscious slap-and-giggle film, Italian style. Cicciolina could have been invented by Wertmüller for this film. She wasn't. Cicciolina wants women to go on strike (no sex) when the ruling men screw up. Now that's an idea for a Wertmüller film (or a play by Aristophanes called *Lysistrata*).

See also: *Bread and Chocolate; The Organizer*.
Availability: Selected collections.

Further reading

Carroll, Rory. "Northern League's New Threat to Italian Unity." *Guardian*, 18 September 2000, at ⟨www.guardianunlimited.co.uk/Print/0,3858,406 4836,00.html⟩. The Northern League continued to win elections in 2000, as this article documents, building toward secession from "the South."

Iuliano, Alfonso. "Metalmeccanico e parrucchiera in un turbine di sesso e di politica." At ⟨www.tempimoderni.com⟩. The reviewer (in

Italian) emphasizes Wertmüller's satire on the nature of televised politics in Italy.

Note: Also known as, in Italian, *Metalmeccanico e parrucchiera in un turbine di sesso e di politica*, and in English, *The Blue Collar Worker and the Hairdresser in a Whirl of Sex and Politics*.

The Working Class Goes to Heaven

Or?

1971, 125 mins., Italy
Director: Elio Petri
Screenplay: Elio Petri and Ugo Pirro
CAST
Lulu Massa = Gian Maria Volonté
Lidia = Mariangela Melato
The Syndicalist = Gino Pernice
Adalgisa = Mietta Albertini
Militina = Salvo Randone

Like too many significant or unusual labor films, especially those from outside the United States, this fascinating mix of Freud and Wilhelm Reich, the inventor of the "orgone box" for accumulating sexual energy, has never been released on videocassette and only rarely appears at film festivals. When Reich and working-class politics combine, we usually think of the zany films of the Yugoslav director Dusan Makavejev, whose *W. R.: Mysteries of the Organism*—which actually appeared in 1971 as well—argues, with some conviction, that Stalinism and sexual repression go, well, hand in hand.

Elio Petri's hero, Ludovico Massa, works so hard that he loses part of a finger to the machines he tends. He becomes like a Soviet stakhanovite of the 1930s, a worker who produces record-breaking results, like another fanatic in the Polish *Man of Marble*. After his accident, Lulu the Tool, as he is nicknamed, becomes victim to both his anger and his sexual frustration. His alienation from the factory floor and from his wife's and mistress's beds literally drives him crazy.

Actually Massa's breakdown is not quite as resolute as that of his aptly named friend Militina, who is incarcerated in a mental hospital. Militina is not so easily swayed by the siren song of militancy, since he rejects Massa's gift of *The Sayings of Chairman Mao*. In the view of Richard Porton (who should be credited with reestablishing the importance of this film), Militina has become an anarchist, suspicious of both capitalist and communist. Massa himself, after his newfound political energy gets him fired, is rehired in what his union thinks of as a telling concession of the bosses. Yet the final images of the film—an inexorable assembly line and Massa's view of a paradise lost—indicate more impotent rage against the world.

The only film by Petri that has received wide circulation is *An Investigation of a Citizen above Suspicion* (1970), in which an official kills his mistress and tracks the investigation to find out how far above suspicion he really is. Closer to Petri's comic anarchism, however, is *The Worker and the Hairdresser*.

See also: *The Worker and the Hairdresser*.
Availability: Not.

Further reading

Porton, Richard. *Film and the Anarchist Imagination*. London: Verso, 1999. An extended and convincing analysis of the film, which stresses the Reichian elements and finds that the film attempts to resolve important theoretical questions raised by the Italian Marxist Antonio Gramsci.

Note: Also known as *La classe operaia va in paradiso* and *Lulu the Tool*.

Working Girl

But not a union maid

1988, 113 mins., R
Director: Mike Nichols
Screenplay: Kevin Wade

CAST
Katherine Parker = Sigourney Weaver
Tess = Melanie Griffith
Mick Dugan = Alec Baldwin
Jack = Harrison Ford
Cyn = Joan Cusack

Although the only place sophisticated New Yorkers think is a funnier place to live than Staten Island is New Jersey, *Working Girl* begins with a shot of the Staten Island ferry as a prelude to a class-conscious comedy. And sure enough, we see immediately two nine-to-five working girls with Really Big Hair: our heroine, Tess, and her best friend, Cyn.

And as in many comedies and dramas about class consciousness, our heroine wants out of the working class and into one of the jobs held by sophisticated people like her new boss, played by Sigourney Weaver, or the two Wall Street louts who work near her and keep setting her up with losers who only want sex.

What Griffith's Tess wants is a way into the class of people who *have* secretaries. Her boss is, alas, the approximate equivalent of Gordon Gekko in *Wall Street;* she is an acquisitions and mergers ace whose hold on her top position includes using—while pretending to mentor—Tess. Since this is a Mike Nichols film, we are not quite at the level of viciousness Oliver Stone is capable of with Gordon Gekko. In fact, Katherine's speeches of advice to Tess are a curious mixture of Wall Street savvy and *Cosmo* Woman snap: when Katherine is confronted by a jerk at an office party, Tess compliments her on how deftly she handled him. "Today's senior prick, tomorrow's senior partner," Katherine quips.

Katherine the Great provides other pertinent advice as well, since Tess has not realized how much her appearance is a class marker (her hair-do, her excessive use of jewelry, and those clothes!) because she has been too busy getting herself through night school. Katherine's equivalent of the great Gekko on greed is to quote Coco Chanel: "Dress shabbily and they notice the dress. Dress impeccably and they notice the woman." When she discusses the likelihood of a marriage proposal, her mind is stuck in a groove of deals: "I've indicated that I'm receptive to an offer. I've cleared the month of June. And I am, after all, me."

As Tess studies the system, she comes up with a good merger idea, which she tries out on Katherine. Katherine, of course, will steal it, but it takes Tess a while to figure that out. The resulting comedy of money and manners involves a shared boyfriend and eventually Katherine's comeuppance.

The potential comic investigation into social class is compromised somewhat by the classic comedy feature of one couple forming—Tess and Jack—while others break up—Jack and Katherine, Tess and Mick. We see some of Tess's Staten Island roots at Cyn's engagement party and in Tess's boyfriend, but because Griffith's acting range is so narrow, we're not convinced Tess is giving up a really bad thing to get such a good thing (an administrative position on Wall Street). In the end, office workers cheer when she gets her new man and her Wall Street job, but the scene is too reminiscent of the scene in *An Officer and a Gentlemen* in which the working-class girl captures her officer. If this world of top guns is so attractive, why has it been so easy to satirize it?

The critic Ben DeMott (among others) has isolated one scene that epitomizes Tess's difficulties in bridging the class gap. She is on the floor helping Katherine put on ski boots. Tess has failed to get Katherine the best room at a European ski chalet. Katherine calls the resort herself, speaking in perfect German. The world of difference between Katherine's fluent German and Tess's Staten Islandese could not be more apparent.

See also: *9 to 5; Wall Street.*
Availability: Easy

Further reading

DeMott, Benjamin. "In Hollywood, Class Doesn't Put Up Much of a Struggle." *New York Times*, 20 January 1991, II.1, 22. Examines the unreality of *Working Girl* and other films about working-class characters that "are driven by near-total dedication to a scam—the maddening, dangerous deceit that there are no classes in America."

Harrington, Mona. "'Working Girl' in Reagan Country." *New York Times*, 15 January 1989, IV.27. A feminist defense of Tess's boss, Katherine, and an anti-Reaganite attack on Tess!

Maslin, Janet. "Cinderella in a Business Suit." *New York Times*, 21 December 1988, C22. Admires the film but acknowledges its fairy-tale aspects.

Note: A similarly titled film, *Working Girls*, is about prostitutes.

∽

The Wrath of Grapes

¡Viva la huelga!

1986, 15 mins.
Directors: Leona Parlee and Lenny Bourin
Agitprop documentary
PRINCIPAL FIGURES
Mike Farrell, narrator
Dolores López and Felipe Franco, children of farm workers
George Deukmejian, governor of California
Dr. Marion Moses, United Farm Workers (UFW) physician
Cesar Chavez, UFW leader

The dangerous effect of pesticides on the farm workers was always an important issue for Cesar Chavez, who once said: "In the old days, miners would carry birds with them to warn against poison gas. Hopefully, the birds would die before the miners. Farm workers are society's canaries." In this agitprop documentary, Marion Moses, a doctor who works for the farm workers, phrased it a little differently: "Workers are . . . the canaries of consumers out there." Carrying this analogy a step further and attempting to build support for their new grape boycott in 1987, the United Farm Workers (UFW) decided to make pesticides and chemical poisoning the cornerstone of their campaign.

Fifty thousand copies of this film were distributed, probably the most extensive agitprop film campaign ever. And, strangely enough, a court ordered its circulation halted nonetheless.

A number of mid-1980s incidents had fueled this campaign: a hundred citrus workers in a San Joaquin Valley orchard had been burned by chemicals in 1986, while cancer clusters (a statistically unusual incidence of cancers occurring in one locale) in Delano and McFarland in Southern California's Imperial Valley were panicking mothers (we see children damaged at birth in the film). Consumers were also shocked to discover that hundreds of people had become ill after eating watermelons illegally sprayed with a pesticide.

The Wrath of Grapes (punning on John Steinbeck's title, *The Grapes of Wrath*) is a deliberately urgent cry for help: farm workers' children, some of them with shocking deformities, are exhibited as examples of the farm owners' greed and deliberate disregard of their workers' health by using dangerous pesticides. It looks as though even DDT, banned by the California Agricultural Labor Relations Act, is going to make a comeback, as the pro-farm-owner governor (George Deukmejian) subverts the letter and spirit of the law.

The growers, for their part, went to court to stop distribution of the film. They managed to talk some of the mothers shown in the film into objecting to their presence in the film on the grounds that they signed an agreement to appear in a boycott film, not a fund-raising one. Since the two functions were virtually inseparable, the union lost its day in court and had to stop sending the films out (see Ferris below).

So many copies had already been released, however, that the union's demands—fair elections, good-faith bargaining, and testing for pesticide residues in supermarkets—once more became part of the public discourse. The film is a convincing pamphlet: we learn why grapes are particularly vulnerable to pesticide poisoning and that millions of pounds of pesticides had been spread on the fields, inevitably contaminating the underground water supply.

By the end of the film a bowl of green seedless grapes looks like a time bomb, and no canaries can detect that. Officially the

UFW did not call off this boycott until November 2000, sixteen years after it was first announced. It was at least the third in a series, starting with the one in the 1960s, which helped build the union; the second, in the 1970s, campaigned for the passage of California's Agricultural Labor Relations Act.

See also: *The Fight in the Fields*.
Availability: Not (although some union locals may still have copies).

Further reading

Ferris, Susan, and Ricardo Sandoval. *The Fight in the Fields: Cesar Chavez and the Farmworkers Movement*. New York: Harcourt Brace, 1997. Companion volume to the film *The Fight in the Fields* (q.v.), with sections on *The Wrath of Grapes* and related pesticide issues (as well as examples of other graphic arts used by the farm workers, including the most famous, a skeletal "Sun Mad" figure, parodying the cheery white farm-working lass who appears on the Sun Maid Raisins boxes).

Mandelbaum, Robb. "Sour Grapes." *New York Times Magazine*, 10 December 2000, 62. This aptly named article outlines the history of the successes and failures of the grape boycott.

Viramontes, Helena Maria. *Under the Feet of Jesus*. New York: Dutton, 1995. A novel about young farm workers (who are dusted with pesticide in one terrifying scene) by a Mexican-American woman who worked in Southern California fields as a child.

Web site: ⟨www.ufw.org⟩ The official site of the UFW, with current campaigns, white papers (such as "Five Cents for Fairness: The Case for Change in the Strawberry Fields"), links to reports (such as "Fields of Poison: California Farmworkers and Pesticides," released jointly by the Pesticide Action Network of North America, United Farm Workers, California Rural Legal Assistance Foundation, and Californians for Pesticide Reform), and historical documents and speeches; a very rich and complete site.

Xala

Ouch

1975, 123 mins., Senegal, in Wolof and French, with English subtitles

Director: Ousmane Sembene
Screenplay: Ousmane Sembene, from his novel of the same title
CAST
Hadji Aboucader Beye = Thierno Leye
Adja Assatu (Beye's first wife) = Seune Samb
Minister Kebe = Makhouredia Gueye

In Ousmane Sembene's satirical look at emerging African nations, impotence becomes the metaphorical condition of the new black bourgeoisie. As Hadji Abdoucader Beye established his leadership in Senegal's Businessman's Group, whose "ambition [was] to gain control of their country's economy" by replacing the white neocolonial elite, the only thing he ends up trying to control is his sex life. As a rich Muslim (the title Hadji announces that he has made the hajj, or pilgrimage to Mecca prescribed for all Muslims), he decides to take a third (young) wife, but he becomes impotent under a curse, or *xala* (pronounced *hala*). His influence, his business success, his . . . well, everything turns to nothing.

As the Hadji tries to discover the source of his curse, his control of his family, his business, and his standing in the elite all begin to fall apart. And while the new black elite has an unidentified white adviser, the cause of the country's catastrophes are based clearly on the elite's self-absorption and corruption. The only way the Hadji can presumably be released from his curse is to have the poor and the cripple spit on him. And so they do.

In the 1970s Sembene became Senegal's world-class filmmaker and novelist. Some of his books were autobiographical. Born in colonial French West Africa (later divided into Senegal, Mali, Benin, Guinea, French Sudan, Niger, and Burkina Faso), he participated in the Allied invasion of Italy as a French soldier and became a longshoreman in Marseilles (in part the subject of his novel *Black Docker*). His novel *God's Bits of Wood* chronicles the railwaymen's strike in 1948 across French West Africa and the women's march of support. He was an apprentice to the Russian director Mark Donskoi, whose most famous films were the trilogy based on Maxim Gorky's autobiographical novels. *Xala* was a success at the 1975 New York Film Festival, one of the first African films to break through a long history of neglect of Third World films.

Unfortunately, neither of Sembene's fascinating later films is currently available. *The Camp at Thiaroye* (1990) dramatizes (and justifies) the mutiny of French West African soldiers who fought for the Free French Army but were treated horribly when the war was over. *Guelwaar* (1993), also based on an actual incident, more closely combines Sembene's anticolonial economic argument and Senegalese history: the murdered Guelwaar ("noble one" in Wolof) was a leader who criticized other members of the Senegalese elite who depended on foreign aid to prop up their regime (and fill their pockets with graft). The latter film shares its critique of the native bourgeoisie with Amadou Saalum Seck's *Saaraba* (1988), also from Senegal.

See also: *Hyenas*.
Availability: Selected collections.

Further reading

Gadjigo, Samba, et al., eds. *Ousmane Sembene: Dialogues with Critics and Writers*. Amherst: University of Massachusetts Press, 1993. Helpful collection of essays surveying Sembene's career.

Gonzalez, Ed. "Xala." *Slant Magazine*, at ⟨www.slantmagazine.com/film/archive/xala.html⟩. The reviewer argues that the film "blames the dilapidation of Senegal's sociopolitical environment on both Eurocentricity and African auto-destruction."

Pfaff, Francoise. *The Cinema of Ousmane Sembene*. Westport: Greenwood, 1984. An early appreciation and analysis of Sembene's films, including discussion of *Xala*.

Sembene, Ousmane. *Xala*. Trans. Clive Wake. Westport, Conn.: L. Hill, 1974. Lawrence Hill, 1976. The short but brilliant source novel.

~

Xica

Diamonds are a slave's best friend

1976, 109 mins., Brazil, in Portuguese, with English subtitles
Director: Carlos Diegues
Screenplay: Carlos Diegues and João Felicio Dos Santos
CAST
Xica = Zeze Motta
João Fernandes = Walmor Chagas
Conde = José Wilker
Intendente = Altair Lima
Hortensia = Elke Maravilha
José = Stepan Nercessian
Teodoro = Marcus Vicinius
Sargento-Mori = Rodolfo Arena

Xica (pronounced *Shee*-ka) was the nickname of Francisca da Silva, an eighteenth-century slave who gained her freedom by becoming the mistress of a Portuguese contractor, João Fernandes de Oliveira, whom the king had given the diamond monopoly in the Brazilian province of Minas Gerais. João Fernandes was therefore free to become immensely wealthy as long as he paid a percentage to the crown. He discovered new beds of diamonds, developed new methods for their extraction, and established himself as one of the wealthiest New World colonists. He fell in love with Xica, freed her, and allowed her to dominate the culture of a society that was not used to taking orders from a black woman.

Xica is therefore a fictional and symbolic story of racism, colonialism, and economic power, based on a story probably more folkloric than real.

Both *Xica* and Diegues's related *Quilombo* are carnivalesque interpretations of Brazilian slave history (see *Brazilian Cinema*): metaphorically the films celebrate lower-caste heroes, especially their funkiness and laughter (in contrast to the upper class's rigidity). They eat, dance, drink, and have sex as if freedom meant carnival all the time. Their stories are also literally of carnival season, as Diegues develops his films from Rio's "samba school" pageants, literally cadres or schools who rehearse for months for performances in parades, using songs, dances, and costumes to recreate actual and sometimes fanciful moments of Brazilian history. (Diegues's *Orfeu*, a re-visioning of the classic *Black Orpheus*, explores the carnivalesque literally.)

Rio's carnival, like so many in the Catholic orbit, is a part of a long tradition of folk festivals in which (as Randal Johnson argues in *Cinema Nova X 5*) "existing social hierarchies were abolished." Because Xica's master now worships her body, he allows her to do whatever she wants: in one of the most Felliniesque moments in the film, he builds her a lake with a sailing ship because she has never seen the sea. She permits only blacks free use of this vessel, and—to complete this deconstruction of racism—lets whites come aboard only as musicians or servants.

Everything Xica does deconstructs the racism of her former masters: she suggests that the church be painted black; when an investigator comes from the crown to "clear" (*claro*, a pun on light-colored) things up, she wears extravagant white makeup and warns the inspector away from the "chicken in brown sauce"—that is, herself.

Of course the carnival cannot go on forever. With her protector, João Fernandes, recalled to Lisbon as a result of the investigator's report, Xica is the target of the town's wrath. She escapes to a monastery where a former lover is hiding and they resolve "to piss on the king and his followers" (by having sex). With this carnivalesque but impossible wish the film ends.

The labor of the diamond extraction is not central to this film, although we do see some crudely mechanized but successful mining operations. (The diamonds harvested look as though they came from a giant disco mirrored ball.) We also learn—and this begins his undoing—that one of João Fernandes's dams designed to aid in diamond extraction has collapsed, causing numerous deaths. The film contains the seeds of revolt against this colonial and capitalist exploitation. Joaś defects from his class to join the rebellion, but the hiding place of another rebel group (led by still another of Xica's lovers) was unfortunately revealed by Xica herself. Portugal will not be easily defeated, but the *idea* of freedom—both bourgeois and slave—is present.

Not all viewers will be happy with a comic treatment of slavery, nor will all approve of Xica's sexy body as a weapon for liberation. (Some nudity is presented in the film.) But within those terms, Diegues has created a fascinating parable of political oppression to a Brazilian dance beat.

See also: *Quilombo*.
Availability: Selected collections.

Further reading

Canby, Vincent. *New York Times*, 10 September 1982, C6. "A live-action social-political cartoon."

Johnson, Randal. *Cinema Nova X 5: Masters of Contemporary Brazilian Film*. Austin: University of Texas Press, 1984. Surveys Diegues's career through *Bye Bye Brasil*.

Johnson, Randal, and Robert Stam, eds. *Brazilian Cinema*. 2d ed. New York: Columbia University Press, 1995. Excellent survey with sections on Diegues and his films.

Rohter, Larry. "Brazil Builds Bigger and Better Telenovelas." *New York Times*, 27 August 2000, II.21, 24. The myth of Xica endures; she returns as the star of her own Brazilian TV soap opera.

Thomas, Kevin. "Xica." *Los Angeles Times Calendar*, 4 October 1982, 4. The reviewer calls it a "Vincente Minnelli movie with a social conscience," in large part because Xica's "amusingly garish gowns and wigs look like Carmen Miranda's notion of what Marie Antoinette would wear."

"Xica." *Variety*, 1 December 1976. "Technically sumptuous with good playing," concludes the reviewer, but he suspects there is more than meets his eye in the film's portrayal of its racial situations.

∽

Yellow Earth

The Sound of Maoism

1984, 89 mins., China, in Chinese, with
  English subtitles
Director: Chen Kaige
Screenplay: Zhang Ziliang, from Ke Lan's
  essay "Echo in the Valley"
CAST
Cuiqiao = Xue Bai
Gu Qing = Wang Xueqi
Father = Tan Tuo
Hanhan = Liu Qiang
Dancers = The Peasant Waist-Drum Troop
  of Ansai County

The filmmakers of this austere but beautiful
film have combined three remarkable stories
into one seamless narrative. Red Army
soldier Gu visits Shaanxi Province to collect
folksongs as part of the Communist Party's
aesthetic ideal of transforming popular
culture into political culture. As he collects
songs from the peasants (actually he tends
to exchange songs), he witnesses feudal
marriage customs and folk rituals of vibrant
energy (especially the waist-drum performances). Finally he becomes the object of a
very young girl's admiration. She daydreams
of slipping away with him to the Red Army,
where she can cut off her hair and join the
fight against the Japanese.

So far, so good. Or bad, since the hopes of
Cuiqiao (looking older than her supposed 12
years) are not likely to be realized. She is
nonetheless a champion singer, specializing
in the "bitter songs" the region features—
songs about the frustrations of seasonal
labor, for example—and that everyone in her
small family can sing: her father's song is a
pointed ballad about a 14-year-old widow
who commits suicide. Her brother fares a
little better, because the seemingly retarded
and mute boy is actually a fantastic singer as
well, making this region ring with the sound
of Mao.

Since this is a contemporary Chinese film,
however, there is always more than meets the
eye. As a Fifth Generation filmmaker, Chen
has constructed an elaborate interpretation
of Chinese Communist history as well, in
particular as it pertains to the region of the
film, Mao's original base area, home to the
revered caves of Yenan, where the Communists gathered in the 1930s to form the
policies and strategy that led them to the successful leadership of virtually the entire
country by 1949. (Their rivals, Chiang
Kai-shek's Nationalists, once allies against
the Japanese, were driven out of the mainland and occupied Taiwan, where they
remain to this day.) Chen's film seems to
suggest that the ideal of the "Red fish in the
warm sea of the peasants" was often hard to
find: the peasants in this film still have to pray
to the rain god to save their crops, one of
their daughters commits suicide rather than
accept a feudal marriage, and our Red
soldier-hero cannot reconnect with the
family he has lived with.

The colors of the film also parallel some of
the political interpretations. The glorious
reds throughout the film are not only
Communist red but also the color of wedding
ceremonies, which—on the surface—are
feasts. Guests are served, however, wooden
fish to remind them of what they would like
to have and the marriage ceremonies are
really feudal economic deals. The yellow of
the hills and mighty river represent the symbolic home of the Chinese people themselves: supposedly the grave of the legendary
first emperor of China is located here. The
Yellow River both gives life and takes it
away, washing the topsoil to the south. The
Communist Party does not appear to be the
savior.

See also: *Red Sorghum*.
Availability: Selected collections.

Further reading

Chow, Rey. *Primitive Passions: Visuality, Sexuality,
  Ethnography, and Contemporary Chinese
  Cinema.* New York: Columbia University Press,
  1995. A jargony but intriguing study, with a long
  section on *Yellow Earth*, emphasizing (among
  many other things) how the identity of its tragic
  heroine is linked to her music.

Goodman, Walter. "Yellow Earth." *New York Times*, 11 April 1986, C19. Positive review.

McDougall, Bonnie S. *The Yellow Earth: A Film by Chen Kaige*. Hong Kong: Chinese University Press, 1991. Includes the screenplay and an authoritative account of the genesis of the film and its reception in China and elsewhere.

Rayns, Tony. "Yellow Earth." *Monthly Film Bulletin* (London), October 1986, 295. Detailed analysis of the film, its political subplot, and its aesthetic achievement as "one of the very first [Chinese] features of the 1980s that has broken new ground."

Robin, Diana, and Ira Jaffe, eds. *Redirecting the Gaze: Gender, Theory, and Cinema in the Third World*. Albany: SUNY Press, 1999. Among the essays in this collection is Hu Ying's "Beyond the Glow of the Red Lantern; or, What Does It Mean to Talk about Women's Cinema in China?" (257–82), which is critical of such films as *Yellow Earth* for representing a "Western" view of Chinese culture and ritual.

Silbergeld, Jerome. *China into Film*. London: Reaktion Books, 1999. An excellent survey of contemporary Chinese cinema, emphasizing that the production of *Yellow Earth* "meant that an independent-minded cultural critique of the entire socialist experiment in China could be read through the framework of China's own government-controlled film industry."

Thematic Index

Belfast, Maine
Fast Food Women
Harlan County, U.S.A.
Salesman
Startup.com
Trouble on Fashion Avenue
Troublesome Creek

Films mainly about COLLECTIVE
   BARGAINING
American Dream
The Devil and Miss Jones
Hoffa
Sit Down and Fight
Taylor Chain I and II

COMPUTER INDUSTRY films
Automation
Computers in Context
Office Space
Secrets of Silicon Valley
Startup.com

Films about CONSTRUCTION
Bloodbrothers
Mac
Steel
Trace of Stones

CONTROVERSIAL films
American Dream
The Angry Silence
Blue Collar
Hoffa
The Molly Maguires
On the Waterfront
Roger & Me

Films about CORRUPTION in unions
Act of Vengeance
Blood Feud
Blue Collar
F.I.S.T.
Hoffa
Inside Detroit
Jimmy Hoffa
Teamster Boss
On the Waterfront
Power

CUBAN films
I Am Cuba

The Last Supper
Portrait of Teresa
Up to a Certain Point

Films about the DEPRESSION
America and Lewis Hine
The Electric Valley
Female
Fury
Gold Diggers of 1933
The Grapes of Wrath
The Great Depression
Heroes for Sale
I Am a Fugitive from a Chain Gang
Love on the Dole
Modern Times
New Deal Documentaries
Of Mice and Men
One Third of a Nation
Our Daily Bread
The Plow That Broke the Plains (see New
   Deal Documentaries)
Power and the Land (see New Deal
   Documentaries)
Riding the Rails
Riffraff
The River (see New Deal Documentaries)
Sit Down and Fight
Slim
Sounder
Street Scene
Sullivan's Travels
The Uprising of '34
Wild Boys of the Road
With Babies and Banners

DOCUMENTARIES
A. Philip Randolph
America and Lewis Hine
American Dream
American Standoff
Año Nuevo
At the River I Stand
Automation
The Awful Truth
The Big One
Brass Valley
The Buffalo Creek Flood
Buffalo Creek Revisited
The Business of America
Chaos
Chemical Valley

Eastern EUROPEAN Films
The Camera Buff
The Land of Promise
Man of Iron
Man of Marble
To Kill a Priest

Films about EUROPEAN ethnics
Bloodbrothers
Hester Street
The Inheritance
Mac
Marty
The Molly Maguires

Western EUROPEAN films (other than
    UK)
Aclà's Descent into Floristella
Ådalen '31
The Bicycle Thief
Bitter Rice
Blow for Blow
Bread and Chocolate
Burn!
Camera Buff
Daens
Human Resources
Joe Hill
Kameradschaft
Kuhle Wampe
Land without Bread
Man of Marble
Metropolis
1900
The Organizer
La Promesse
Ramparts of Clay
Rocco and His Brothers
The Roof
Sacco and Vanzetti
La terra trema
To Kill a Priest

EXPLOITATION films
Boxcar Bertha
Last Exit to Brooklyn

FACTORY dramas
Chance of a Lifetime
Female
The $5.20 an Hour Dream
Gung Ho

Human Resources
Keeping On
Millions Like Us
Rising Son
Sons of Steel
Stanley and Iris
Take This Job and Shove It

Films about FARM WORKERS
And the Earth Did Not Swallow Him
Bitter Rice
Bound for Glory
Cabin in the Cotton
Captain Boycott
The Churning
Comrades
A Corner in Wheat
Earth
The Fight in the Fields
Freedom Road
God's Little Acre
The Golden Cage
The Grapes of Wrath
Half-Slave, Half-Free
Harvest of Shame
Land without Bread
Legacy of Shame
The Migrants
1900
Northern Lights
Of Mice and Men I, II, III
Our Land Too
Sounder
Sugar Cane Alley
Sunday Too Far Away
Tobacco Road
Troublesome Creek
Uncle Tom's Cabin
The White Rose
Wild River
The Wrath of Grapes

Films by cinematographer Gabriel
    FIGUEROA
Los olvidados
The White Rose

Films about the GARMENT
    INDUSTRY
The Garment Jungle
Hester Street
I Can Get It for You Wholesale

The Inheritance
Land of Promise
Nightsongs
The Pajama Game
The Triangle Factory Fire Scandal
Trouble on Fashion Avenue
The Uprising of '34

Films about GAYS and work
Aclà's Descent into Floristella
Last Exit to Brooklyn
Out at Work

Films about GLOBALIZATION
Le Franc
Life and Debt
The Little Girl Who Sold the Sun
Mickey Mouse Goes to Haiti
The New Rulers of the World

Films about Jimmy HOFFA
American Standoff
Bloodfeud
F.I.S.T.
Hoffa
JFK, Hoffa, and the Mob
Jimmy Hoffa
Power

Films about HOMELESSNESS
Cathy Come Home
Down and Out in America
Riff-Raff

Films about IMMIGRANT labor
Alamo Bay
America and Lewis Hine
Bread and Chocolate
The City
Hester Street
Nightsongs
Picture Bride
La Promesse
Sacco and Vanzetti
These Hands
Uncle Moses

Films directed by Barbara KOPPLE
American Dream
Harlan County, U.S.A.
Keeping On
Out of Darkness

LATIN AMERICAN films (other than
    Cuban and Mexican)
Quilombo
Xica

Films about LATINOS, CHICANOS, and
    MEXICAN-AMERICANS
The Burning Season
The City
The Golden Cage
El norte

Films by Anne LEWIS
Chemical Valley
Evelyn Williams
Fast Food Women
Justice in the Coalfields
Roving Pickets
Rough Side of the Mountain
To Save the Land and People

Films by Ken LOACH
Bread and Roses
Cathy Come Home
Days of Hope
The Flickering Flame
Looks and Smiles
The Navigators
The Price of Coal
Riffraff

MEXICAN films
Illusion Travels by Streetcar
Los olvidados
The White Rose

Films about MIGRANT workers
Angel City
And the Earth Did Not Swallow Him
Año Nuevo
Children of the Harvest
The Fight in the Fields
Harvest of Shame
Long Road Home
Legacy of Shame
Migrants
New Harvest, Old Shame
The Wrath of Grapes

Films about MINERS and MINING
Act of Vengeance
Black Fury

Brassed Off
The Buffalo Creek Flood
Buffalo Creek Revisited
Burning Rage
The Citadel
Coal Miner's Daughter
Coalmining Women
Coal Wars
The Corn Is Green
Days of Hope
Evelyn Williams
Fury Below
Germinal
Harlan County, U.S.A.
Harlan County War
How Green Was My Valley
Justice in the Coalfields
Kameradschaft
Margaret's Museum
Matewan
The Molly Maguires
Moving Mountains
October Sky
Our Land Too
Out of Darkness
The Price of Coal
Proud Valley
Rough Side of the Mountain
Roving Pickets
Salt of the Earth
The Stars Look Down
Sun Seekers
We Dig Coal
Wildrose
Xica

MOCK-DOCS
Blow for Blow
Cathy Come Home
Dadetown
I Am Cuba
Native Land

Michael MOORE's films
The Awful Truth
The Big One
Roger & Me
TV Nation

MUSICALS
Never Steal Anything Small

Newsies
The Pajama Game

MUST-SEE films
American Dream
Bread and Roses
The Grapes of Wrath
Harlan County, U.S.A.
Harvest of Shame
The Killing Floor
Matewan
The Molly Maguires
On the Waterfront
The Organizer
A Raisin in the Sun
Roger & Me
Salt of the Earth

Italian NEOREALIST films
The Bicycle Thief
Bitter Rice
Rocco and His Brothers
The Roof
La terra trema

Films definitely NOT FOR CHILDREN
Blue Collar
Last Exit to Brooklyn
1900

Films about OFFICE WORKERS
Clockwatchers
Computers in Context
Desk Set
The Devil and Miss Jones
9 to 5
Office Space
Working Girl

Films about union ORGANIZING
The Big One
Bread and Roses
The Fight in the Fields
Harry Bridges
The Killing Floor
Matewan
Norma Rae
The Organizer
Northern Lights
The Raid
Sit Down and Fight
Strike

Struggles in Steel
10,000 Black Men Named George
The Wobblies

Films about PECKERWOODS, crackers,
    and poor white trash
Cabin in the Cotton
God's Little Acre
Keeping On
A Lion Is in the Streets
Tobacco Road
The Uprising of '34
Wild River

Films about PITTSBURGH
Lightning over Braddock
The River Ran Red
Struggles in Steel
The Valley of Decision
Voices from a Steeltown

Films with POSITIVE images of unions
At the River I Stand
Business as Usual
Final Offer
Harlan County, U.S.A.
Harry Bridges
The Inheritance
Matewan
Moving Mountains
Newsies
Norma Rae
Out of Darkness
Sit Down and Fight
Taylor Chain
10,000 Black Men Named George
With Babies and Banners

POSTMODERN Documentaries
The Awful Truth
The Big One
British Sounds
The Gleaners and I
Lightning over Braddock
TV Nation

Films about RACISM
Alamo Bay
A. Philip Randolph
At the River I Stand
Black Legion
Brother John
Edge of the City

Freedom Road
Goin' to Chicago
The Killing Floor
Learning Tree
El norte
Nothing But a Man
A Raisin in the Sun
Struggles in Steel
10,000 Black Men Named George
Who Killed Vincent Chin?
Xica

Films about RAILROADS and
    RAILROAD workers
A. Philip Randolph
The Navigators
Riding the Rails
10,000 Black Men Named George
Wild Boys of the Road

Films about working-class RESENTMENT
Black Legion
Joe
Look Back in Anger
A Raisin in the Sun
Saturday Night and Sunday Morning
This Sporting Life

Films about REVOLUTION
Mother
Strike
To Kill a Priest

Films directed by Martin RITT
Edge of the City
Norma Rae
Sounder

Films about SAILORS, fishermen, and the
    sea
The Long Voyage Home
Tamango
La terra trema

SILENT films
A Corner in Wheat
Earth
The End of St. Petersburg
The General Line
Mother
Metropolis
Strike

Films about SLAVERY
Burn!
Freedom Road
Half-Slave, Half-Free
The Last Supper
Quilombo
Tamango
Uncle Tom's Cabin
Xica

SLEEPERS
The Blue Eyes of Yonta
Boys from the Blackstuff
The City
Daens
Heroes for Sale
Illusion Travels by Streetcar
Land of Promise
Quilombo
Spices
To Sleep with Anger
Turumba

SOVIET films
Earth
The End of St. Petersburg
Enthusiasm
The General Line
Mother
¡Que viva México!
Strike

Films about STEEL and related industries
An American Romance
The Business of America
Lightning over Braddock
Making Steel
Shout Youngstown
Steel
Struggles in Steel
Taylor Chain I and II
The Valley of Decision
Voices from a Steeltown
Women of Steel

Films made from works by STEINBECK
The Grapes of Wrath
Of Mice and Men
The Raid

Films set in STREET MARKETS
The Blue Eyes of Yonta

Le Franc
The Little Girl Who Sold the Sun
Los olvidados

Films mainly about STRIKES or lockouts
Ådalen '31
American Dream
American Standoff
The Angry Silence
At the River I Stand
Blow for Blow
The End of St. Petersburg
F.I.S.T.
Germinal
Harlan County, U.S.A.
Harlan County War
Hoffa
Last Exit to Brooklyn
Matewan
Newsies
One Day Longer
The Stars Look Down
Salt of the Earth
Strike
10,000 Black Men Named George
Tout va bien
Waterfront
The Whistle at Eaton Falls
The Willmar 8

American TELEVISION FEATURE
    FILMS
Act of Vengeance
And the Earth Did Not Swallow Him
Blood Feud
The Burning Season
Half-Slave, Half-Free
Harlan County War
The Killing Floor
Long Road Home
The Migrants
A Raisin in the Sun [II]
Rising Son
Teamster Boss
10,000 Black Men Named George
The Triangle Factory Fire Scandal
Uncle Tom's Cabin

TELEVISION DOCUMENTARIES
Children of the Harvest
Harvest of Shame
Legacy of Shame

Life and Debt
New Harvest, Old Shame
The New Rulers of the World
Surviving the Good Times
Who's Getting Rich and Why Aren't You?

Films about the THIRD WORLD (other
than African and Caribbean)
The Burning Season
El norte
Perfumed Nightmare
Sugar Cane Alley
Turumba

Films from the TOP DOWN
Barbarians at the Gate
Chance of a Lifetime
Desk Set
The Electric Valley
Gung Ho
I'm All Right, Jack
I Can Get It for You Wholesale
Ladies Who Do
Land of Promise
Other People's Money
The Richest Man in the World
Roger & Me
The Solid Gold Cadillac
Sons of Steel
Startup.com
Take This Job and Shove It
Tucker
Turumba
TV Nation
Wall Street
Who's Getting Rich and Why Aren't You?
Working Girl

Films about TRUCKERS (other than
Hoffa)
Convoy
Mother Trucker
They Drive by Night

Films from the U.K. (mostly British)
The Angry Silence
Boys from the Blackstuff
Brassed Off
British Sounds
Business as Usual
Captain Boycott
Cathy Come Home

Chance of a Lifetime
Comrades
Days of Hope
Educating Rita
Fame Is the Spur
Flame in the Streets
The Flickering Flame
The Full Monty
High Hopes
Hungry Hill
I'm All Right, Jack
The Kitchen
Ladies Who Do
Look Back in Anger
Looks and Smiles
Love on the Dole
The Man in the White Suit
Millions Like Us
The Navigators
The New Rulers of the World
The Price of Coal
Proud Valley
Ratcatcher
Riff-Raff
Saturday Night and Sunday Morning
The Scar
Seacoal
42 Up
35 Up
This Sporting Life

Films about UNEMPLOYMENT
American Job
The Bicycle Thief
Boys from the Blackstuff
Brassed Off
Cathy Come Home
Down and Out in America
The Full Monty
Looks and Smiles
Margaret's Museum
On to Ottawa
Surviving the Good Times
Wild Boys of the Road

Films about URBAN workers
The Bicycle Thief
Bread and Roses
Clockwatchers
Eight Hours Are Not a Day
Free Voice of Labor
The Killing Floor